K
564
.C6
L45
2005

Legal issues in the
global information
society.

BAT

$150.00

Legal Issues in the Global Information Society

Editors:
Dennis Campbell
Center for International Legal Studies

and

Chrysta Bán
Bán, S. Szabó & Partners

OCEANA PUBLICATIONS, INC. / DOBBS FERRY, NY

Library of Congress Control Number: 2004104341

ISBN 0-379-21516-0

Manufactured in the United States of America on acid-free paper.

DEDICATION

This book is dedicated to the memory
of Pommel Lynn Campbell.

TABLE OF CONTENTS

PREFACE

Dennis Campbell
Center for International Legal Studies
Salzburg, Austria

The International Telecommunication Union (ITU), following a proposal by the Government of Tunisia, resolved at its Plenipotentiary Conference in Minneapolis in 1998 (Resolution 73) to hold a World Summit on the Information Society (WSIS) and place it on the agenda of the United Nations.

In 2001, the ITU Council decided to hold the Summit in two phases, the first 10–12 December 2003, in Geneva, and the second 16–18 November 2005, in Tunis. This was endorsed by the United Nations General Assembly (Resolution 56/183), according the lead role to the ITU in cooperation with other interested organizations and partners.

United Nations General Assembly Resolution 56/183 further recommended that preparations for the Summit take place through an open-ended, intergovernmental Preparatory Committee that would define the agenda of the Summit, decide on the modalities of the participation of other stakeholders in the Summit, and finalize both the draft Declaration of Principles and the draft Plan of Action. It invited the ITU to assume the leading managerial role in the Executive Secretariat of the Summit and invited governments to participate actively in the preparatory process of the Summit and to be represented in the Summit at the highest possible level.

In Resolution 56/183, the General Assembly also encouraged contributions from all relevant United Nations bodies and other intergovernmental organizations, including international and regional institutions, non-governmental organizations, civil society and the private sector to actively participate in the intergovernmental preparatory process of the Summit and the Summit itself.

It is in this respect that the Center for International Legal Studies, as a non-governmental organization, assumed its role at the WSIS sessions in Geneva and Tunis.

The Center for International Legal Studies is a non-profit research, training, and law publications institute, established and operating under Austrian law since 1976, with its international headquarters based in Salzburg, Austria. The Center has a close cooperation with the Salzburg Seminar, Suffolk

University Law School of Boston, Massachusetts, the Faculty of Law of the University of Salzburg, the Faculty of Law of the University of Amsterdam, the Faculty of Law of the University of Durham, England, the Faculty of Law of Universidad Adolfo Ibañez of Santiago, Chile, and the Faculty of Law of Eötvös Loránd University of Budapest, Hungary.

The essential purpose of the Center for International Legal Studies is the dissemination of information among members of the international legal community, this being achieved through the Center's various research and law publication projects, the administration of post-graduate and professional training programs, and the operation of several continuing legal education conferences each year. More than 4,500 lawyers worldwide have been designated as Fellows of the Center for International Legal Studies in recognition of their contributions to the Center's publications and conferences. Nearly 500 Honorary Fellows have taken membership in the Congress of Fellows. In addition to its role in the United Nations WSIS, the Center provides accredited observers at meetings of the United Nations International Trade Law Commission and its Working Groups in Vienna and New York.

The Center proposal for WSIS was to assemble an international team of lawyers to consider certain of the legal issues confronting the expanding information society. That effort has included the making of research materials available to all WSIS delegates and organizations on the WSIS web site, conducting briefings in Geneva and Tunis and, finally, this publication.

AUTHORS AND EDITORS

SAKARI AALTO

Roschier Holmberg, Attorneys Ltd.
Keskuskatu 7 A
00100 Helsinki
Finland
Tel: (358) 205 066 030
Fax: (358) 205 066 031
Email: sakari.aalto@roschier.com

Sakari Aalto is a partner with Roschier Holmberg Attorneys Ltd., Finland, heading its information technology and communications practice tream and maintaining a high specialization in matters relating to software and intellectual property rights licensing, communications, copyright, and electronic commerce. Prior to joining Roschier Holmberg, Mr. Aalto was an associate in the Brussels office of Morrison & Foerster LLP and, prior to that, a legal counsel with Sonera Limited.

STEWART A. BAKER

Steptoe & Johnson LLP
1330 Connecticut Avenue, N.W.
Washington, D.C.
United States 20036-1795
Tel: (1202) 429 3000
Fax: (1202) 4293 902
Email: sbaker@steptoe.com

Stewart A. Baker is a partner in the Washington, D.C., office of Steptoe & Johnson LLP. His private practice involves a variety of high-tech, mass media, and telecommunications issues, with an emphasis on international and appellate matters. He serves on the President's Export Council Subcommittee on Export Administration, the Industry Functional Advisory Committee on Electronic Commerce for Trade Policy Matters of the Department of Commerce, and the Markle Foundation's Task Force on National Security in the Information Age. From 1992 to 1994, Mr. Baker served as General Counsel of the National

Security Agency. He has been named to numerous United States government and international bodies dealing with electronic commerce and related topics and has been retained as a consultant on computer security issues by a variety of international bodies, including the International Telecommunication Union, the Organization for Economic Cooperation and Development, and the Government of Japan.

CHRYSTA BÁN

Bán, S. Szabó & Partners
József Nádor Tér 5–6
H-1051 Budapest
Hungary
Tel: (361) 266 3522
Fax: (361) 266 3523
Email: cban@bansszabo.hu

Dr. Chrysta Bán, Managing Partner of Bán, S. Szabó & Partners, Budapest, Hungary, is a Hungarian and United States attorney with wide experience in civil and commercial law, mergers and acquisitions, securities regulations, and competition law. She received a Juris Doctor degree from Eötvös Loránd University Law School, Budapest, and an advanced degree in international commercial law from the Institute of Advanced Legal Studies at Eötvös Loránd University. She is qualified to practice law in Hungary and is a member of the California Bar. Dr. Bán served as an associate law professor at Eötvös Loránd University and at McGeorge School of Law, University of the Pacific, Sacramento, California, before joining Shearman & Sterling in Budapest as senior Hungarian attorney. In 1997, she was one of the founding partners of Bán, S. Szabó & Partners.

DANA BELDIMAN

Carroll, Burdick & McDonough, LLP
44 Montgomery Street, Suite 400
San Francisco, California
United States 94104
Tel: (1415) 989 5900
Fax: (1415) 989 0932
Email: dbeldiman@cbmlaw.com

Dana Beldiman is a partner with the San Francisco law firm Carroll, Burdick & McDonough LLP, where she has been in practice since

1985, and is an adjunct professor at Santa Clara University School of Law. Her experience includes both litigation and transactions, and she counsels United States and foreign clients on matters of intellectual property protection, technology law, and cross-border transactions. Ms. Beldiman teaches courses in international intellectual property and business transactions in the United States and abroad and is the author of numerous articles on these topics. She chairs the International Section of the San Francisco Bar Association and has served on the E-Commerce Task Force of the International Section of the American Bar Association and chair of its Telecommunications Committees.

DENNIS CAMPBELL

Center for International Legal Studies
P.O. Box 19
A-5033, Salzburg
Austria
Tel: (43 662) 835 399
Fax: (43 662) 835 399 22
Email: cils@cils.org

Professor Dennis Campbell is the director of the Center for International Legal Studies, Salzburg, Austria. He is an Adjunct Professor at Suffolk University Law School in Boston, Massachusetts, where he teaches a course on International Legal Practice. He has served as Adjunct Professor at the Franklin Pierce Law Center and Director of International Programs, University of the Pacific, McGeorge School of Law, and has lectured at Stockholm University and Warsaw University. Professor Campbell is a member of the Iowa State Bar, New York State Bar, and the International Bar Association.

WINNIE CHANG

Steptoe & Johnson LLP
Clements House, 14-18 Gresham Street
London EC2V 7JE
England
Tel: (44207) 367 8000
Fax: (44207) 367 8001
Email: wchang@steptoe.com

Winnie Chang is an associate in the London office of Steptoe & Johnson and a member of the technology group. Ms. Chang is qualified in the United Kingdom and Malaysia. Her experience includes electronic commerce, intellectual property, and data protection matters. Ms. Chang is experienced in export licensing proceedings involving the United States Department of Commerce and National Security Agency, as well as encryption use, export, and import in the United Kingdom, Canada, Japan, China, and other jurisdictions.

PROBIR ROY CHOWDHURY

J. Sagar Associates
4121/B, 19th A Main
6th Cross, Hal II Stage Extension
560 038 Bangalore
India
Tel: (9180) 2520 0045
Fax: (9180) 2520 0044
Email: probir@jsalaw.com

Probir Roy Chowdhury is an associate with J. Sagar Associates, Bangalore, India, and is part of the firm's technology practice. His practice areas are corporate commercial and information technology. He has been involved in advising on diverse issues pertaining to the Foreign Exchange Management Act, export and import policy, corporate laws, the Securities & Exchange Board of India Regulations, the Maharashtra IT Policy 2003, the Information Technology Act, the Transfer of Property Act, and the Securitization Act. Mr. Chowdhury also has written articles on several topics, including the Competition Act, the Securitization Act, cyber-terrorism, and the transfer of urban land.

JULIAN DING

First Pinciples Sdn Bhd
Level 36, Menara Maxis
Kuala Lumpur City Centre
50088 Kuala Lumpur
Malaysia
Tel: (603) 2615 0010
Fax: (603) 2615 0088
Email: julian.ding@firstprinciples.com.my

Julian Ding is the founding member of the First Principles law firm and is a partner in the firm's technology practice. Formerly, Mr. Ding was a senior partner and one of the founders of Zaid Ibrahim & Co., the largest law firm in Malaysia. He has been a commercial lawyer for more than 17 years, is a Fellow of the Center for International Legal Studies, a member of the Malaysian Bar, and a member of Who's Who International. Mr. Ding advises clients on a broad range of Internet-related issues, including disputes relating to domain names and cyber squatting, and he was the principle architect for two frameworks affecting e-transactions and e-government tentatively called the Electronic Transactions Act and the Electronic Government Activities Act, respectively. Mr. Ding completed his law studies at the University of London, BA (Law Hons. 1984) and completed his Masters in Public Policy and Management at Monash University in 2004.

ROXANNE A. ESCH

Arent Fox, PLLC
1050 Connecticut Avenue, N.W.
Washington, D.C.
United States 20036-5339
Tel: (1202) 857 6000
Fax: (1202) 857 6395
Email: esch.roxanne@arentfox.com

Roxanne A. Esch is an associate in the Trade Mark Practice Group at Arent Fox, PLLC. Her practice includes all areas of intellectual property law, with a focus on trade mark litigation, trade mark policing, counseling clients on Internet policies, and conducting legal research on novel intellectual property issues. Ms. Esch earned her Masters in Business Administration in Finance and International Business from the University of Connecticut.

JON DAVID GROSSMAN

Dickstein Shapiro Morin & Oshinsky LLP
2101 L Street N.W.
Washington, D.C.
United States 20037-1526
Tel: (1202) 785 9700
Fax: (1202) 8870 689
Email: grossmanj@dsmo.com

Jon Grossman is a partner with Dickstein Shapiro Morin & Oshinsky LLP. He practices in the area of computer law, with a focus on intellectual property issues, including the licensing and acquisition of software rights, with a background in patents, copyrights, and trade secrets. Mr. Grossman assists clients with patenting business methods, Internet applications, banking and insurance industry software, multimedia communications, human resources patents, and a host of office applications programs. Additionally, Mr. Grossman has significant commercial licensing experience that includes all aspects of licensing and contracting of computer software, databases, and hardware. He also has provided a full range of counseling to clients in the areas of strategic acquisitions, outsourcing, and joint ventures, and he has worked closely with clients in obtaining financing from venture capitalists.

DAVID C. GRYCE

Arent Fox, PLLC
1050 Connecticut Avenue, N.W.
Washington, D.C.
United States 20036-5339
Tel: (1202) 857 6000
Fax: (1202) 857 6395
Email: Gryce.David@arentfox.com

David Gryce chairs the Technology Practice Group of the Washington, D.C., law firm of Arent Fox, PLLC. He has practiced in the fields of intellectual property for 20 years, and his practice covers all phases of copyright, trade mark, and unfair competition law, both domestically and internationally. Mr. Gryce is a proponent of alternative dispute resolution and is a member of the International Trademark Association's Panel of Neutrals. He has lectured before the American Intellectual Property Law Association, the International Trademark Association, and the American Bar Association Forum on Franchising and is the author of numerous articles and publications. Mr. Gryce currently holds or has held leadership positions with the American Bar Association's Intellectual Property Section and the International Trademark Association's Alternative Dispute Resolution Committee.

STEPHEN C. HICKS

Suffolk University Law School
120 Tremont Street
Boston, Massachusetts
United States 02108-4977
Tel: (1617) 573 8381
Fax: (1617) 305 3089
Email: stephen.hicks@suffolk.edu

Stephen C. Hicks, M.A., LL.B., LL.M., is the Director of the Graduate Law Program in Global Technology and Professor of Law at Suffolk University Law School, Boston. He has law degrees from Cambridge University, England, and the University of Virginia. He is the author of a book on modern legal theory and has co-authored two books on feminism, gender bias, and the law. He was an editor of Black's Law Dictionary. In addition, Professor Hicks has published more than 30 articles and papers in the areas of legal theory, the history of ideas, and comparative law. He is an experienced mediator and arbitrator, specializing in personal injury cases. He has been a visiting scholar at Harvard University, a guest lecturer at Helsinki University and Lund University and has spoken at conferences and meetings around the world through his activities in the American Society of Comparative Law and the International Association of Legal and Social Philosophy.

AMRUT JOSHI

J. Sagar Associates
4121/B, 19th A Main
6th Cross, Hal II Stage Extension
560 038 Bangalore
India
Tel: (9180) 2520 0045
Fax: (9180) 2520 0044
Email: amrut@jsalaw.com

Amrut Joshi is an associate with J. Sagar Associates, Bangalore, India, and his practice areas are corporate and commercial laws with emphasis on company law, regulatory reforms, and infrastructure projects. Mr. Joshi has worked on framing regulations under the Electricity Act, 2003, for the State Electricity Regulatory Commission. He is supporting the firm's initiatives in several infrastructure projects, including the New Bangalore International Airport Project and two

NHAI annuity-based projects involving construction and maintenance of National Highways in the States of Tamil Nadu Andhra Pradesh. Additionally, Mr. Joshi advises clients on real estate law and corporate law.

LEENA KERPPILÄ

Roschier Holmberg, Attorneys Ltd.
Hämeenkatu 26 A 4. Krs
33200 Tampere
Finland
Tel: (358) 205 066 547
Fax: (358) 205 066 031
Email: Leena.Kerppila@roschier.com

Leena Kerppilä is an associate with Roschier Holmberg Attorneys Ltd., Finland, working at the firm's Tampere office which focuses on technology, media, and communications. Her practice areas are intellectual property and contract law, with emphasis on information technology transactions.

LAURI MERTALA

Roschier Holmberg, Attorneys Ltd.
Hämeenkatu 26 A 4. Krs
33200 Tampere
Finland
Tel: (358) 205 066 547
Fax: (358) 205 066 031
Email: lauri.mertala@roschier.com

Lauri Mertala is an associate with Roschier Holmberg Attorneys Ltd., Finland, working at the firm's Tampere office, which focuses on technology, media and communications. Mr. Mertala provides advice in information technology specializing in software and copyright licensing and open source software. During 2004, Mr. Mertala worked as a visiting lawyer with Nokia Corporation, Espoo, Finland, in its Technology Platforms unit.

KAREN MILLS

KarimSyah Law Firm
Level 11, Sudirman Square Office Tower B
Jl. Jenderal Sudirman Kav. 45–46
12930 Jakarta
Indonesia
Tel: (6221) 577 1177
Fax: (6221) 577 1947
Email: kmills@cbn.net.id

Karen Mills has practiced in Indonesia for more than 20 years and is one of the founders of the KarimSyah (formerly Karim Sani) law firm in Jakarta. She is a chartered arbitrator and fellow of the Chartered Institute of Arbitrators and of the Singapore and Hong Kong Institutes, acts as special advisor to the board of Indonesia's arbitral institution, BANI, for which she prepared its new procedural rules, and is on the panel of arbitrators of a number of other institutions, including the domain name institutions in Hong Kong and China. Ms. Mills founded and has chaired the Professional Services Committee and co-chaired the Tax Committee of the American Chamber of Commerce in Indonesia for many years, and she served as Vice Chair of the Indonesian branch of the International Fiscal Association for seven years. She is a member of several committees of the International Bar Association, the New York State Bar Association, and the Inter-Pacific Bar Association, for which she is currently chairing the program committee for the 2005 Annual conference to be held in Bali. Ms. Mills is a graduate of New York University School of Law and a member of the New York Bar. She teaches and writes extensively on arbitration and other Indonesian legal matters, and her papers are published in many books and international professional journals.

MARK A. NADEAU

Squire, Sanders & Dempsey LLP
Two Renaissance Square
40 North Central Avenue, Suite 2700
Phoenix, Arizona
United States 85004
Tel: (1602) 528 4001
Fax: (1602) 253 8129
Email: mnadeau@ssd.com

Mark A. Nadeau is a partner with Squire, Sanders & Dempsey in Phoenix, Arizona, and he leads the firm's international arbitration activities, focusing his practice on complex commercial litigation with an emphasis on contract, corporate, lender-liability finance litigation, unfair competition, product liability, and securities cases. Mr. Nadeau has an extensive background in all types of real estate disputes, has acted as lead counsel on several multi-party construction and hospitality cases, and has defended many class action suits in the financial sector. Currently, he is lead counsel in several high-profile satellite communications industry multibillion-dollar disputes throughout the United States that involve retransmission and antitrust issues. Mr. Nadeau is a member of the London Court of International Arbitration, has attended the World Congress of the International Chamber of Commerce, and is named in Who's Who in American Law and Who's Who in International Law.

GOVIND NAIDU

J. Sagar Associates
4121/B, 19th A Main
6th Cross, Hal II Stage Extension
560 038 Bangalore
India
Tel: (9180) 2520 0045
Fax: (9180) 2520 0044
Email: bangalore@jsalaw.com

Govind Naidu is an associate with J. Sagar Associates, Bangalore, India, and his practice areas are corporate commercial, mergers and acquisitions, and securities laws. He has trained in the areas of company law, securities law, and industrial law, and he has a keen interest in merger and acquisition activities and crossborder transactions in connection with which he has undertaken international legal due diligence projects. Mr. Naidu also has worked on transactions involving structuring of investment into companies dealing with insurance, power, telecommunications, and business-process outsourcing.

ELIZABETH PARSONS

Dickstein Shapiro Morin & Oshinsky LLP
2101 L Street N.W.
Washington, D.C.
United States 20037-1526
Tel: (1202) 785 9700
Fax: (1202) 887 0689
Email: parsonse@dsmo.com

Elizabeth Parsons is an associate with Dickstein Shapiro Morin & Oshinsky LLP in the Intellectual Property Group. Her practice includes counseling clients regarding intellectual property issues in connection with corporate transactions, including sales and acquisitions of multinational corporations. Ms. Parsons also is experienced in patenting technologies in the fields of biotechnology and semiconductors.

FREDRIK ROOS

Setterwalls
Kungstorget 2, Box 112 35
404 25 Göteborg
Sweden
Tel: (4631) 701 1700
Fax: (4631) 701 1701
Email: fredrik.roos@setterwalls.se

Fredrik Roos is an associate at Setterwalls Law Firm in Sweden and specializes in information technology law and intellectual property law. He has a background as a researcher at the Department of Informatics at Gothenburg University where his area of research was "Control of Information in an Online Environment".

MICHAEL L. RUSTAD

Suffolk University Law School
120 Tremont Street
Boston, Massachusetts
United States 02108-4977
Tel: (1617) 573 8171
Fax: (1617) 395 6276
Email: mrustad@suffolk.edu

Michael L. Rustad, Ph.D., J.D., LL.M., is the Thomas F. Lambert Jr. Professor of Law and Co-Director of the Intellectual Property Program at Suffolk University Law School in Boston, Massachusetts. He is a core faculty member in Suffolk's LL.M program in global technology, where he teaches courses in international sales law, e-commerce law, and Internet law. He is the co-editor of the E-Business Legal Handbook (4th ed.) and co-editor of the Bi-Monthly Review of Law Books. His most recent book is In Defense of Tort Law (2003). His numerous law review articles and book chapters have been cited by the United States Supreme Court, federal district and appellate courts, and state supreme courts. He has testified before both Houses of Congress and has been interviewed by NBC Dateline, The New York Times, The Economist, and The Wall Street Journal, and other international publications. He has been elected to the American Law Institute and has been appointed as a task leader of the American Bar Association Business Section on Software Contracting.

DAVID J. SIMONELLI

Clark Hill PLC
500 Woodward Avenue, Suite 3500
Detroit, Michigan
United States 48226-3435
Tel: (1313) 965 8266
Fax: (1313) 965 8252
Email: dsimonelli@clarkhill.com

David J. Simonelli is a member of Clark Hill PLC's Business Practice Group, practicing in the area of intellectual property, and focusing on patent, trade mark, copyright, and technology transfer matters, as well as intellectual property litigation. In addition to more than a dozen years of experience in intellectual property matters, Mr. Simonelli held the position of Electronics Engineer with the National Security Agency from 1986–1987. He has made presentations on patent and copyright laws and has participated in panel discussions with European patent attorneys on the harmonization of the intellectual property laws between the United States and other countries worldwide. Mr. Simonelli is admitted to practice in the state courts of Michigan, the United States District Courts for the Eastern and Western Districts of Michigan, the United States Court of Appeals for the Federal Circuit, and the United States Patent and Trade Mark Office. He is a member of the State Bar of Michigan, the American Bar Association, and the United States Patent Bar. He also is a member of the American Intellectual Property Law Association, the Michigan Intellectual Property Law Association, the Licensing Executives Society, and the Institute of Electrical and Electronics Engineers.

MAURY D. SHENK

Steptoe & Johnson LLP
Clements House, 14-18 Gresham Street
London EC2V 7JE
England
Tel: (44207) 367 8000
Fax: (44207) 367 8001
Email: mshenk@steptoe.com

Maury Shenk is managing partner of the London office of Steptoe & Johnson and is a dual-qualified United States and United Kingdom lawyer. His practice focuses on the international aspects of electronic commerce and telecommunications. Mr. Shenk provides advice on regulatory, commercial, and policy matters involving electronic commerce, supervising the firm's leading encryption export/import practice. He is experienced in export licensing proceedings involving the United States Department of Commerce and National Security Agency, as well as encryption exports and imports in the United Kingdom, France, Russia, China, and other jurisdictions.

SAJAI SINGH

J. Sagar Associates
4121/B, 19th A Main
6th Cross, Hal II Stage Extension
560 038 Bangalore
India
Tel: (9180) 2520 0045
Fax: (9180) 2520 0044
Email: sajai@jsalaw.com

Sajai Singh is a resident partner with J. Sagar Associates, Bangalore, India. Mr. Singh's areas of expertise are biotechnology, information technology, business-process outsourcing, and strategic alliances. He undertakes transactional work in the areas of foreign inbound investments, joint ventures, strategic alliances, and technology transfers, and he represents clients in a cross section of industries, including knowledge- based and high technology industries, media, communication and entertainment, private equity funds, and BPOs. Mr. Singh has represented many international businesses and funds including established and emerging technology companies, Internet startups, connectivity specialists, e-commerce ventures, conversion technology, and technology based entertainment industries. Mr. Singh is a member of the American Bar Association and the International Bar Association.

CHAPTER 1

TOWARDS THE FURTHER LEGALIZATION OF GLOBAL INFORMATION LAW

Stephen C. Hicks and Michael L. Rustad
Suffolk University Law School
Boston, Massachusetts, United States

Such is the unity of all history that any one who endeavors to tell a piece of it must feel that his first sentence tears a seamless web.

Frederic William Maitland[1]

1.01   Introduction

The reader should be aware that the first few sentences in this chapter may well do just that to Maitland's observation. The Internet signifies a wholesale transformation in the way people and communities are formed and interact. The network of networks is a global medium that connects the home pages of every person and every nation in the world into a different kind of "seamless web". The Internet's "virtual" world not only changes one's primary medium of communication, and thus any model we may be using of human communication, but it allows an online business to sell goods and render services in any country connected to the web that comprises the Internet.

This changes the perception of the world as a place we inhabit, and it creates new worlds that need ordering through law. While the Internet is still a two-dimensional space, as seen externally as a platform for users in real space and time, it "shrinks distances" so that "the provider and consumer need not share the same geographic space".[2] It also "flattens time" so that communication may be

---

1   Maitland, "A Prologue to a History of English Law", 14 *Law Quarterly Review* 13 (1898).
2   Jenson and de Sousa Santos, *Globalizing Institutions: Case Studies in Regulation and Innovations* (2000), at p. 10.

instantaneous and across many different avenues, as if everyone were in the same place at the same time. The discontinuity of our normal experience of time in which we may live in the moment of excitement or endure days of boredom in an hour or two is leveled into a virtual and global instantaneity.[3]

Finally, one may say that it also renders everything uniform, in that the same website information appears for everything, regardless of its magnitude or importance, and hugely complex devices of bionic, computing, transmitting, and creative power utilize the same technologies and are, therefore, vulnerable to the same problems which may previously have only arisen in one dimension of time and space, but which now exist in virtual reality and which, therefore, the law must solve.

It follows from this uniformity, instantaneity, and placelessness that the "seamless web" of history must be torn asunder to grasp the importance of the changes that the seamless web of the Internet and cyberspace make in our lives. It marks a new stage in human history, one that may, as time unfolds, come to be seen as great a change in our way of living as was industrialization, the printing press, the emergence of the organized state, and even the appearance of a codified system of law itself, as one looks back over two thousand years of history.[4]

At all of these times in history, the law has lagged behind changes in technology, and so it is now. Still, there have been a number of myths constructed about Internet time and how it has transformed society. The unsupported mantra through the 1990s that Internet traffic was doubling every 100 days fuelled much of the excitement about what the technological revolution — that famous "paradigm shift" — would mean for telecoms, dot-coms, and other technology companies.[5] What is different, however, is that Internet commerce takes place in a virtual world, not that of live interaction or voice to voice distant communication. Legal solutions, as a result, must be accommodated to the new problems of this new reality of the Internet and cyberspace.

For example, the growth of electronic commerce raises a great potential for litigation over the validity of:

1.   Contracts by electronic agents;[6]

---

3   Hillis, *Digital Sensations* (1999), at pp. 79 and 80.

4   Hewitt de Alacantara, "The Development Divide in a Global Age", 5 *Technology, Business, and Society,* United Nations Research Institute for Social Development Program, Paper Number 4 (August 2001).

5   Wahl, "The Superhighway to Hell", *Canadian Business* (28 March/10 April 2005), at p. 19.

6   The electronic contracting provisions of article 2 of the United States Uniform Commercial Code (UCC) include definitions of "electronic", "electronic agent", "record", "electronic record", and "information processing system", and certain electronic aspects of "receive" closely parallel those of the Uniform Electronic Transactions Act and the federal Electronic Signatures in Global and National Commerce Act. Sales contracts may be made by the interaction of electronic agents. Proposed Comment to Uniform Commercial Code, revised section 2-103(g) (Proposed 2002 Amendments to article 2 of the Uniform Commercial Code).

2. Mass-market license agreements;[7]

3. Digital signatures;[8]

4. Validity of e-contracts;[9]

5. Choice of law, and forum clauses;[10] and

6. Use of disabling devices in software.[11]

These are new problems for the law. The purpose of this chapter is to provide a context for understanding the subsequent chapters concerning the progress the law has made towards solving these problems.

The chapters in this volume reflect the problems of adapting diverse substantive fields of law to the new technologies and point towards the need for a global legal order. The World Summit on the Information Society (WSIS) is a step in the direction of coming to grips with the problems of a global legal

---

7   The first case in which a shrink-wrap software license agreement was enforced even though the terms were not disclosed prior to purchase. *ProCD, Inc. v. Zeidenberg*, 86 F3d 1447 (7th Cir., 1996). The *ProCD* court held that the licensee was bound to the terms of the license agreement for a software package called SelectPhone because he had an opportunity to review the restrictive license term prior to being bound. In that case, the licensee was found to be infringing the copyright in disseminating the licensed software on the Internet.

8   Internet Law and Policy Forum, *Survey of State Electronic and Digital Signature Legislative Initiatives* (compiled by Perkins, Coie LLP) (visited 22 February 2005), at http://www.ilpf.org/groups/update.htm (surveying state digital laws).

9   Uniform Commercial Code, revised section 2-103(h) (Proposed 2002 Amendments) (defining "electronic agent" to mean "a computer program or an electronic or other automated means used independently to initiate an action or respond to electronic records or performances in whole or in part, without review or action by an individual"). See also Uniform Commercial Code, revised section 2-105(o) (defining "record" to mean "information that is inscribed on a tangible medium or that is stored in an electronic or other medium and is retrievable in perceivable form"). National Conference of Commissioners on Uniform State Laws, Revision of Uniform Commercial Code, article 2 — Sales (2002 Annual Meeting, 26 July/2 August 2002).

10 *In re America Online Version 5.0 Software Litig.*, 168 F. Supp. 2d 1359 S.D. Fla., 2001); *Williams v. America Online, Inc.*, 2001 Mass. Super. Lexis 11 (Mass. Super. Ct., 8 February 2001) (refusing to dismiss claim and enforce AOL's choice-of-forum clause in cause of action arising out of claim that personal computers were damaged by America Online Version 5.0 software).

11 The 2002 Amendments to UCITA prohibit the use of disabling devices or remote shut-offs by licensors. Section 816(b) prohibits electronic repossession in all mass-market transactions. If the parties agree to permit electronic self-help in non-mass market licenses, the licensee must separately manifest assent to a term authorizing use of electronic self-help. See section 816(c). Detailed procedures for executing electronic self-help are found in section 816(c) and (d), National Conference of Commissioners on Uniform State Laws, Amendments to Uniform Computer Information Transactions Act, Meeting in its One-Hundred-and-Eleventh Year, Tucson Arizona, 26 July/2 August 2002 (2002 UCITA Amendments).

order in the information age and an emerging knowledge economy. In Geneva, in 2003, certain themes emerged from the Roundtable Discussions which will be followed up in Tunis in 2005. The themes were "access", "diversity", and "development".

The primary concern voiced by all at the Geneva Summit was the appearance of a "digital divide" between the "haves" and the "have-nots". This obviously speaks equally loudly of an "economic development divide" which transcends digital access, diversity, and development as such.[12]

To the extent that nations can create their own "e-strategies" and initiatives for entrepreneurship, investment, and subsequent regulation, which simultaneously preserve local culture and heritages within the trend towards globalization, the barriers of education and skills and of the cost and availability of the hardware to connect with the "seamless web" of global networking might be overcome. In the first phase of the World Summit on the Information Society, the conferees declared that the first principle was the:

> . . . development-oriented Information Society, where everyone can create, access, utilize and share information and knowledge, enabling individuals, communities and peoples to achieve their full potential in promoting their sustainable development and improving their quality of life, premised on the purposes and principles of the Charter of the United Nations and respecting fully and upholding the Universal Declaration of Human Rights.[13]

An abyss exists between the principle of equal access to information and the empirical reality of a world system trifurcated into "core",[14] "semi-periphery",[15]

---

12   Hewitt de Alacantara, "The Development Divide in a Global Age", 5 *Technology, Business, and Society*, United Nations Research Institute for Social Development Program, Paper Number 4 (August 2001).

13   World Summit on the Information Society: Geneva 2003, Tunis 2005, Declaration of Principles, Building the Information Society: A Global Challenge in the New Millennium (visited 1 May 2005), at http://www.itu.int/wsis/docs/geneva/official/dop.html.

14   The first core nations to develop were England, France, and Holland in northwestern Europe, between 1300–1450. *Modern History Sourcebook: Summary of Wallerstein on World System* Theory (visited 13 February 2005), at http://www.fordham.edu/halsall/mod/wallerstein.html.

15   The semi-periphery regions were in the borderland between core and periphery countries in terms of stages of developments. The semi-periphery consists of countries in decline or peripheral countries "attempting to improve their relative position in the world economic systems", *Modern History Sourcebook*: *Summary of Wallerstein on World System Theory* (visited 13 February 2005), at http://www.fordham.edu/halsall/mod/wallerstein.html.

and "periphery"[16] nations. The worldwide trade framework of the World Trade Organization, including China, Russia, the former Soviet Republics, Taiwan, and Saudi Arabia, has spearheaded the development of a world system.[17]

The "Action Plan" for the Tunis Summit aims at 2015 as the target date for reducing measurable income disparities in economic growth, which have hitherto been exacerbated by technology. An obstacle to this is that one of the themes found in many of the chapters in this book is the degree to which major powers, such as the United States, are attempting to impose their legal norms on less-developed countries.[18] In this respect, one may consider the "open source" movement, or the distribution of "free software", as mechanisms that may offer ways around the direct confrontation between investment/profit and access/innovation to the benefit of developing nations entering the Information Age.

The creation of civil society for the digital age depends on an engineered consensus based on participation in the constitution of norms rather than the command and control of rules and regulation.[19] Radically different cultures and legal systems are placed into conflict with the rise of the Internet. The

---

16   The countries of the periphery were at the opposite end of the economic development continuum. During early capitalism, the less-developed regions were Eastern Europe and Latin America. *Modern History Sourcebook: Summary of Wallerstein on World System Theory* (visited 13 February 2005), at http://www.fordham.edu/halsall/mod/wallerstein.html. Wallerstein argued that the core countries "expropriated much of the capital surplus generated by the periphery through unequal trade relations". *Modern History Sourcebook: Summary of Wallerstein on World System Theory* (visited 13 February 2005), at http://www.fordham.edu/halsall/mod/wallerstein.html. Today, there is a new global system applicable to the Internet. In the new knowledge-based economy, the United States is the core hegemonic power seeking to impose its sovereignty on less-developed countries (semi-periphery and periphery). The problem for periphery and semi-periphery countries is that the core powers make the rules and control the markets. The United States has spearheaded a new system of global intellectual property rights. To date, much of the controversy over "global intellectual property rules" stems from the ability of the United States and other core powers to "ratchet up intellectual property standards". Drahos and Mayne (eds.), *Global Intellectual Property Rights: Knowledge, Access, and Development* (2002) (arguing that the Agreement on Trade-Related Aspects of Intellectual Property Rights (TRIPS) is an "extension of monopoly by these rules allow[ing] powerful Northern-based companies to extend control over markets and raise the price of vital technology goods").

17   King, "The WTO: What It Does and Doesn't Do, How it Affects U.S. Business", 22 *Middle East Exec. Rep.* 8 (October 1999). The World Trade Organization that developed TRIPS now has 145 members as of 5 February 2005. World Trade Organization, Documents on Line (visited 28 February 2005), "WTO Membership Rises to 145", (visited 1 April 2005), at http://www.wto.org/english/news_e/news_e.htm#armenia145.

18   Müller, "Who Owns the Internet? Ownership as a Legal Basis for American Control of the Internet" (21 March 2004) (visited 11 May 2005), at http://ssrn.com/abstract=520682.

19   Crawford, "Cyberspace: Defining a Right to Internet Access through Public Accommodation Law", 76 *Temple L. Rev.* 225 (2003); Benoliel, "Technological Standards Inc: Rethinking Cyberspace Regulative Epistemology", 92 *Cal. L. Rev.* 176 (2004)).

forces dictating convergence represent those of the economically powerful, while the forces resisting are those of the groups and institutions and interests of civil society which know from history the important difference between a top-down system of authority, such as the *ecclesia*, or body of the church, and a bottom-up system, such as that of a *mund*, the quasi-representative body of a pre-feudal Germanic village.[20] Medieval history is instructive regarding the analogy between the divine right of a king, representing the "aristocratic" wealth of major corporations, and the sacred power of an emperor or a pope, representing the natural order of the "given world" and the real world of the people, who need representation, as they did before modern times.

The United Nations Project on the Information Society recognizes the need for greater legalization to achieve the promise of the interconnected digital world.

Nevertheless, a premise of the Geneva Summit, one that has since been affirmed, is that one cannot challenge the private/corporate leadership and/or domination of the information technology revolution. The role of governments is to educate their populations about this reality, and the role of civil society is to work within this from the bottom up. Therefore, a global world of Internet users is not going to resemble a homogenous group like the followers of a charismatic leader, members of a nation state, or believers in a true faith. Rather, they will look and act like members of a corporation who also are consumers of its products.

Even so, this does not mean that the United States controls the Internet. The Internet is no longer the exclusive province of the United States Department of Defense. The Internet is gaining a foothold on every continent. Internet usage is growing rapidly in China, which was expected to surpass Japan in late 2003.[21]

By December of 2002, the number of mobile phone subscribers in China was more than 200-million.[22] Asia alone (with the exceptions of Japan and the Republic of Korea) added 21-million new users to the Internet in a single year.[23] The globalization of the information society is occurring at a rapid rate. Asian and Pacific countries are harnessing the power of e-commerce to

---

20   Ullman, "Juristic Obstacles to the Emergence of the State in the Middle Ages", *The Church and State in the Earlier Middle Ages* (1975), at p. 264.

21   PTI, "Asia-Pacific Nations Pledge to Promote E-Commerce", *Economic Times* (visited 22 February 2005), at http://economictimes.indiatimes.com/cms.dll/xml/comp/articleshow?artid=29089893.

22   NUA Internet Survey, December 2002 (visited 2 February 2005), at http://www.nua.com/surveys/?f=VSandart_id=905358668andrel=true (citing *ZD Net Report*; released by The Ministry of Information Industries).

23   Greenspan, "The Web Continues to Spread" (visited 20 January 2005), at http://cyberatlas.internet.com/big_picture/geographics/article/0,5911_1556641,00.html.

accelerate development.[24] In China, Malaysia, Indonesia, and East Asia, where software piracy is rampant, authorities are responding to outside pressure to restrain the online trading of software, music, and movies.[25] Broadband technology poses the greatest threat to copyright, as it shortens the download time for pirated media.[26]

However, the point is that formation technology resists state control, whether it be taxation, censorship, or channeling through legalization. Civil society pushes back to be open, free, voluntary and, above all, uncoerced.

However, there still remains the reality of the digital divide and the economics of overcoming it, as the following chart demonstrates.

Chart I: The Internet as a Modern World System[27]

Ideal Type	Core	Semi-Periphery	Periphery
Characteristics	Large numbers of Internet users, hosts; high proportion of personal computer ownership.[28]	Distribution networks not as seamless as core countries (lack of local warehouses, unable to compute price, delivery, taxes, or tariffs accurately).[29]	Low level of Internet users (10 per cent or less of population), low percentages of personal computer owners, low number of host servers, relatively few servers.

24 TI, "Asia-Pacific Nations Pledge to Promote E-Commerce" (visited 12 March 2005), at http://economictimes.indiatimes.com/cms.dll/xml/comp/articleshow?artid=29089893.

25 McCullagh, "Mexico Summit Urges Anti-Piracy Action" (visited 12 March 2005), at http://news.com.com/2100-1023-963538.html.

26 NA's *Internet Law News* (ILN) (8 October 2002) (visited 1 March 2005), at http:www.online.wsj.com/article/0,SB1034042124444014600,00.html (reporting an article in *Wall Street Journal*).

27 The authors wish to acknowledge the research assistance of Tracey Tom, who constructed this chart and assisted with the reconceptualization of the world system analogy for the World Wide Web.

28 The rise of the World Wide Web may be signaling a paradigm shift but, today, only approximately 14 per cent of the world's population is connected (888,681,131 out of 6,412,067,185 (13.9 per cent). Africa, for example, has achieved an Internet penetration of only 1.5 per cent (13,468,600 out of 900,465,411). Only 7.5 per cent of the population of the Middle Eastern countries is connected to the Internet (19,370,700 out of 259,499,772). In the Asian countries, Internet users total 302,257,003 out of 3,612,363,165. Latin America fares only slightly better with 10.3 per cent of the population connected to the Internet (56,224,957 out of 546,917,192). Australia/Oceana has 48.6 per cent of its population connected to the Internet (16,269,080 out of 33,443,448). Slightly greater than one-third of Europeans (35.5 per cent) are connected to the Internet (259,653,144 out of 730,991,138). North America leads the world with 220,437,647 out of 328,387,059 connected to the Internet. "Internet Usage Statistics — The Big Picture", *World Internet Users and Population Stats 2005* (visited 28 April 2005).

29 Forrester Report, "Mastering Commerce Logistics" (August 1999), reprinted as Tariff Product Fact Sheet (visited 22 February 2005), at http://tariffic.com/Docs/Newsroom/mediakit1.htm.

Country Policies	Focus on facilitating e-commerce, such as the United States moratorium on Internet taxes and new, multiple, and discriminatory taxes on e-commerce.	Primary focus on protecting intellectual property rights and enacting telecommunications laws: greater likelihood of government censorship or regulation.	Internet is often very strictly monitored in these countries.
Implication for Exporters	Large, sophisticated markets for all types of e-commerce activities. Likely targets for most e-business activities.	Lower percentage of Internet users and relatively low level of e-commerce in contrast to core countries.	Very low percentage of Internet users and very low level of e-commerce, particularly because of strict monitoring.
Exemplars	Australia, Canada, England, France, Japan, The Netherlands, New Zealand, United States.[30]	Argentina, Brazil, Chile, China,[31] India, Indonesia, Malaysia, Mexico, Philippines, Portugal, South Korea, Spain.	Cambodia, Cameroon, Central African Republic, Chad, Myanmar, Nepal, Rwanda, South Africa, Tunisia, Vietnam.

The contributors to this volume shed light on the barriers to an achievable information-based society. Each of the chapters in this volume confirms the rapid internationalization of information law that stems from a rapidly evolving global information society.[32] While each contributor to this volume

---

30   The United States also is core of the top domains in the new economy. For example, the most popular websites visited by UK Internet users were predominately American sites: (1) Yahoo; (2) Freeserve; (3) MSN; (4) Microsoft; (5) AOL; (6) GeoCities; (7) Demon; (8) Amazon; (9) Excite; and (10) BBC. Cyberatlas, "Geographics: European Internet Audience Data" (visited 3 March 2005), at http://cyberatlas.internet.com.

31   By September 2002, China had more than 54-million Internet users among its population of 1.3-billion, the third largest Internet user-base after the United States and Japan. However, due to its monitoring of Internet use and still-developing distribution networks, the country remains for now in the semi-periphery category. PTI, "China Has World's Third Largest Internet User Base" (visited 12 February 2005), at http://economictimes. indiatimes.com/cms.dll/xml/comp/articleshow?artid=29435857. UNCTAD, *Annual Report*, AFP, "Internet Users to Reach 655 Million by Year-End" (visited 14 February 2005), at http://www.smh.com.au/articles/2002/11/19/1037599406943.html), which states that China's Internet user base is 56.6-million, the second largest Internet population in the world.

32   Goldstein, "Introduction: Legalization and World Politics", in Goldstein, *et. al., Legalization and World Politics* 3 (2001) (defining key qualities of legalization as "[i]nternational institutions-enduring sets of rules, norms, and decision-making procedures that shape the expectations, interests, and behavior of actors but which vary on many dimensions").

has a slightly different perspective on global information law, each raises serious legal and policy issues necessary for further legalization of the information society. Each chapter raises a panoply of legal issues that need to be addressed by international treaties or conventions.

Legalization, the process of developing international legal constraints on nation-states, can be seen in many of the legal developments discussed in this volume as responses to changing information technologies, such as:

1. The Cybercrime Convention;

2. The World Intellectual Property Organization (WIPO) Uniform Dispute Resolution Proceedings for Resolving Domain Name Conflicts; and

3. European Union (EU) Directives Governing jurisdiction, electronic commerce, privacy, and the regulation of the information society.[33]

The United Nations Project on Information Technology is a first step to achieving a transborder legal order where there is democratic participation. At present, there is disagreement among the participants at the open consultations on the form of Internet governance arrangements.[34] The principal fissure at the open consultations has been between those who seek Internet governance based on a United Nations framework versus those seeking a market-based private sector approach.[35]

In an interesting way, this mirrors two different metaphors for conceiving of the Internet, namely, as the mythic open frontier for unfettered exploration or as a feudal society of mutually indebted and integrated levels of different stakeholders.[36]

At present, the patchwork of disparate attempts to regulate the Internet signals the failure of civil society to govern the virtual world. Further harmonization is

---

33 Directive 95/46/EC of the European Parliament and of the Council of 24 October 1995 on the Protection of Individuals with Regard to the Processing of Personal Data and on the Free Movement of Such Data, 1995 *Official Journal* (L281) 31 (visited 1 March 2005), at http:europa.eu.int/eur-lex/en/lif/date/1995/en395L0046.html.

34 "UN E-Governance Panel Focuses on Spam, Web Governance", *DMEurope* (21 April 2005).

35 "UN E-Governance Panel Focuses on Spam, Web Governance", *DMEurope* (21 April 2005).

36 Yen, "Western Frontier or Feudal Society: Metaphors and Perceptions of Cyberspace", 17 *Berkeley Tech. L.J.* 1207 (2002).

needed to solve the growing substantive and procedural problems[37] of crossborder Internet-related litigation.[38]

Just as the leading Western nations cooperated to create a unified law of the sea, advances in cyberspace technology are creating international problems that need to be addressed through a consistent cross-national legal regime. It is the form that this will take that remains uncertain at present. This provides the big picture context for considering both the problems and legal solutions of the global information society.

1.02   Electronic Contracting Issues

(a) The Law of E-Contracting in the World System

In a *New Yorker* cartoon, two dogs are seated in front of a computer. The caption reads:

> On the Internet, nobody knows you're a dog.

Buying online is one important step removed from buying from a catalogue. Computer-to-computer contracts require a reworking of traditional contract law. A Clinton White House Report on Electronic Commerce contends that we "are on the verge of a revolution that is just as profound as the change in the economy that came with the Industrial Revolution".[39] Since society is at every point changing, global commercial law also must change. The law lags behind social and technological change, and it must be continually updated. The Clinton Administration's concept of the Global Information Infrastructure included wired and wireless networks, information appliances, and a global matrix of interconnected computer networks.[40]

---

37   For example, the Anti-Cybersquatting Consumer Protection Act recognizes an *in rem* remedy useful in obtaining jurisdiction over foreign defendants. The United States Court of Appeal for the Fourth Circuit affirmed the lower court's dismissal of the automobile manufacturer's *in rem* action in *Porsche Cars N. Am, Inc. v. Porsche.net* 302 F.3d 248 (4th Cir., 2002).

38   In *Int'l Bancorp, LLC v. Société Des Bains De Mer Et Du Cercle Des Etrangers a Monaco*, 192 F. Supp. 2d 467 (E.D, Va., 2002), a trade mark infringement action involved the plaintiff Casino de Monte Carlo against off-shore defendants who had registered 53 ".com" and ".net" domain names that incorporated, in various ways, the name "Casino de Monte Carlo". The plaintiff claimed that the companies' use in United States commerce of the term "Casino de Monte Carlo" in the disputed domain names and on various websites constituted trade mark infringement in violation of the Lanham Act. The court concluded that the companies' use of 43 domain names created a likelihood of confusion because the plaintiff's mark had secondary meaning.

39   White House, "A Framework for Global Electronic Commerce", 1 July 1997, at p. 1 (quoting Vice-President Albert Gore, Jr.).

40   White House, "A Framework for Global Electronic Commerce", 1 July 1997, at p. 6.

Since article 2 of the Uniform Commercial Code was drafted more than a half century before the emergence of Internet contracts, it is not surprising that sales law is out of step with electronic commerce.[41] The article 2 now in effect was a product of the 1940s and 1950s, long before the rise of the Internet. The revised article 2 will permit parties to sign sales contracts by executing a digital signature.[42] The exchange of paper forms by humans is increasingly being replaced by contracts conducted by electronic means.

The licensing of Internet-related software, for example, requires licensors to comply with United States law as well as the law of every foreign nation where software is licensed.[43] The economics of the advanced industrial states are being broadly impacted by e-commerce, an entirely new mode of delivering goods and services in a networked world. The past decade witnessed the formation of "thousands of new ventures based largely on new business models".[44]

"The Internet is turning the process of contracting on its head. More and more, ordinary people enter into contracts electronically, over the Internet, through electronic mail, and by installing software".[45] In 2003, the business-to-business Internet commerce "market will increase to US $3.6-trillion, and at the end of 2004, worldwide business-to-business Internet sales transactions are forecast to reach US $6-trillion".[46] Direct marketers spent US $217-billion in 2004 — half of all advertising — and the business to-business market segment accounted for US $114.7-billion.[47] Global electronic commerce creates an array of legal questions on what contract regime will facilitate business while at the same time honor the law of contract.

---

41 The revision of article 2 is a joint project of the American Law Institute (ALI) and the National Conference of Commissioners on Uniform State Law (NCCUSL).

42 Section 2-102(1) of the proposed draft will permit parties "to sign, or to execute or adopt a symbol or sound, or encrypt a record in whole or in part" as a functional equivalent to the paper-based signature; revised article 2 (Proposed Draft, 1 March 1998).

43 One of the greatest difficulties is that "some foreign jurisdiction may apply its laws . . . in an inconsistent or unpredictable way". Twiddy, "United States: International Licensing: A Guide to Entering the Foreign Marketplace", Mondaq's Article Service: Kilpatrick, Stockton LLP, 26 February 2005 (visited 2 March 2005), at http://www.mondaq.com/article.asp?articleid=2045.

44 Baghy, "Cyberlaw: A Forward", 39 *Am. Bus. L.J.* 521 (2002).

45 Hillman and Rachlinski, "Standard-Form Contracting in the Electronic Age", 77 *N.Y.U.L. Rev.* 429 (2002).

46 Gartner Group, "Worldwide Business-to-Business Internet Commerce to Reach US $8.5 trillion in 2005" (visited 3 February 2005), at http://www4.gartner.com/5_about/press_room/pr20010313a.html.

47 "U.S. Direct Industry Boosts Revenues to US $2.3 Trillion", *Precision Marketing* (1 April 2005), at p. 9.

(b) E-Contract Rules: Substantive and Procedural Issues

E-contract law makes it possible to make agreements to order goods or render services by any reasonable method, including the exchange of electronic records. Every web-based business must enter into a large number of online contracts to be competitive. Karen Mills addresses the question of the formation of contracts transacted through electronic means in a crossborder legal environment. The validity of electronic contracts will be determined on not only the facts and intentions of the parties, but how the contract will be interpreted, governed, and enforced. Her thesis is that an innovative contract law paradigm must evolve to accommodate to the "new e-conomy".

The critical question is whether the parties in an electronic transaction have reached an agreement and how the terms of the agreement will be interpreted. Mills reminds us that the substantive provisions of commercial law as well as the transactions have not fundamentally changed. What has changed is the means of purchasing goods and services, the financing of assets and projects, the issuance and transfer of stocks and bonds, the perfection of security interests, and cross-border transfers of commercial paper. In the Internet environment, contracts may be entered into through "click-wrap" or "browse-wrap" contracts or by simply downloading software with universal terms of service. However, she notes that negotiated contracts also may be entered into through electronic means where the language is dickered over in e-mail.

In her chapter, she compares contract formation rules in Common Law and Civil Law systems. Under the Common Law of contracts, formation occurs when the parties manifest a desire to be bound. She notes how normally this process is memorialized by an offer and acceptance. Common law contract, according to Mills, is based on a mutual declaration of an intention to be bound. The Civil Law paradigm of contracting rests on a bedrock of formal requirements. Once the formal requirements are met, the inquiry shifts to whether parties voluntarily intended to adhere to specific terms. She notes that individual Civil Law jurisdictions have their own formal requirements that address the question of when the parties are bound. Civil law countries do not require consideration, which is a requirement of the Common Law contract.

Given the significant differences in Civil Law and Common Law jurisdictions on the basic issue of contract formation, there will be prickly issues when parties are from entirely different legal traditions.

She next examines the different types of e-contracting practices that have evolved over the past decade. The simplest form of sales contract is the "click-wrap" agreement where the buyer clicks a box signifying that they agree with the terms set by the seller. While millions of click-wrap agreements are entered into each day, it is unsettled as to what constitutes an offer or acceptance.

Mills notes how questions arise as to exactly when contract formation has occurred. She notes that the so-called "browse-wrap" contracts used by websites are even more problematic. United States courts will be more inclined to enforce mass-market license agreements so long as the licensee has notice of terms and an opportunity to manifest assent. However, she questions whether courts outside the United States will find electronic formation for many of these mass-market agreements. European consumers, unlike American consumers, have an absolute right to file suit against sellers or suppliers if they pursue commercial or professional activities in the member state of the consumer's domicile.[48]

In the United States, consumers may waive their right to rights and remedies including the choice of law and forum.[49]

This means that a United States business that directs its consumer transactions to Europe can be sued in the consumer's home court.[50] It is quite likely that a website with different languages and accepting the Euro as a currency is directing its activities to member states.[51]

An American website that does not wish to be subject to the home court rule for jurisdiction over consumer contracts needs to employ blocking software or implement other techniques for "red flagging" European consumer

---

48   Brussels Regulation, article 15.1(c).

49   Compulsory arbitration clauses in mass-market license agreements have been enforced by a number of United States courts. *Westendorft v. Gateway 2000, Inc.*, 2000 Del. Ch. LEXIS 54 (Del. Ch. Ct., 16 March 2000); *Brower v. Gateway 2000, Inc.*, 676 N.Y.S. 2d 569 (1998); *Lieschke v. RealNetworks, Inc.*, 2000 U.S. Dist. LEXIS 1683 (N.D., 2000) (enforcing arbitration clauses in mass market licenses); *America Online, Inc. v. Booker*, 781 So. 2d 423, at p. 425 (Fla. Dist. Ct. App., 2001) (upholding forum selection clause in "freely negotiated agreement" and holding that the unavailability of a class action procedure in Virginia was not a sufficient basis for striking down a forum selection clause; *Caspi v. Microsoft Network, LLC*, 323 N.J. Super. 118, 732 A2d 528, at pp. 530, 532, and 533 (N.J. Super. Ct. App. Div., 1999) (upholding forum selection clause where subscribers to online software were required to review license terms in a scrollable window and to click "I Agree" or "I Don't Agree"); *Burnett v. Network Solutions, Inc.*, 38 S.W. 3d 200, at pp. 203 and 204 (Tex. App., 2001) (upholding forum selection clause in online contract for registering Internet domain names that required users to scroll through terms before accepting or rejecting them); *Specht v. Netscape Commun. Corp.*, 306 F3d 17 (2d Cir., 2002) (holding that user's downloading software where the terms were submerged did not manifest assent to arbitration clause); *Klocek v. Gateway, Inc.*, 104 F. Supp.2d 1332 (D. Kan., 2000) (declining to enforce arbitration clause on grounds that user did not agree to standard terms mailed inside computer box).

50   Article 15(1)(c) extends the consumer home forum rule to entities that direct activities to member states. Brussels Regulation, article 15(1)(c).

51   Article 6.1 of the Brussels Regulation provides that a company may be subject to jurisdiction if a co-defendant is domiciled in one of the member states. Brussels Regulation, article 6.

transactions. The European Court of Justice ruled that the Brussels Convention[52] applied to a Canadian company in a contract action brought in a French court.[53]

She notes how it is easy to electronically construct letterhead and difficult to determine the originator of documents. Cybercriminals, for example, use pseudonyms, false identities, and forged e-mail addresses to swindle consumers.[54] Internet fraudsters seamlessly transmit Internet fraud artists, for example, use auto-dialer programs to commit financial crimes. "The auto-dialer programs change Internet users' dial-up settings to call an international number without their knowledge."

To paraphrase Gertrude Stein, as far as the Internet is concerned, not only is there perhaps "no there there", the "there" is everywhere there is Internet access.[55] There is no physical object for the subject to control in space; nor is it the subject which controls through time. Interaction is dispersed and not experienced as such. Contracting parties may fraudulently transmit electronic messages using any letterhead they wish. Documents may be copied, morphed, or transformed at a click of the mouse. Just as people invent identities in chat-rooms, so too are parties to contracts created in cyberspace, as well as their contracts. The immateriality of the Internet is a challenge for law.[56]

Mills argues that the key question is to determine whose rules and what terms dictate contract law in this seamless and borderless contracting environment. She notes how the fundamentals of contract formation are so unsettled in the borderless electronic environment. The primary issue of open advertisements as an "offer to treat" or an "invitation to make an offer" is decided differently in Common Law than in Civil Law jurisdictions. She points to the language of article 14 of the Convention for the International Sales of Goods as a possible uniform view.

Legalization must begin with a clear cut methodology for entering into a legal, binding, and enforceable contract. The author practices in Indonesia and the contracting rules evolved out of Dutch law, which has norms which

---

52   The 1968 Brussels Convention was replaced by the Brussels Regulation in March 2002.

53   Gulland, "All the World's a Forum: Businesses That Benefit from the Increased Globalization of Commerce Also Face Increased Risks of Liability Abroad", *New Jersey Law Journal* (29 April 2002) (discussing *Group Josi Reinsurance Co. SA v. Universal General Insurance Co.*, 2000 E.C.R. I-5925).

54   *Zixit Corp. v. VISA USA. Inc.*, 2002 W.L. 3219734 (Tex. Dist., 31 July 2002) (reporting defamation lawsuit against VISA based on more than 400 anonymous messages on an Internet message board).

55   *Digital Equip. Corp. v. Altavista Technology, Inc.*, 960 F. Supp. 456, at p. 462 (D. Mass., 1997) (J. Gertner).

56   Poster, *What Is the Matter with the Internet?* (2001), at p. 17.

vary substantially from the Anglo-American law of contracts. All systems of contract law must answer as to who can be parties to contracts, as well as when, where, what, and why. Despite these differences, the Indonesian concepts of legal capacity, certainty of obligations, contractual purpose, and consent share much common ground with the Common Law.

One of the critical questions is whether an international regime of contract law will be the legal recognition of electronic signatures. Mills begins her survey of electronic signatures with a discussion of the United Nations International Trade Law Commission (UNCITRAL) Model Law on Electronic Signatures (2001). UNCITRAL's Model Law provides the basic concepts and methods for cross-border electronic contracting rules. She documents how electronic signatures are gaining acceptance in the United States (with the enactment of the E-Sign Act of 2000) and around the globe. She notes how software firms are offering sophisticated encryption products that permit authentication of signatures. The cross-border practitioner needs a globalized paradigm of electronic commerce law to facilitate commercial transactions in cyberspace.

(c) Cryptography and E-Signatures

The use of encryption as a means of protecting the global communications infrastructure raises difficult legal and political questions. Cryptography or the science of secret writing is a "science that has roots stretching back hundreds and perhaps thousands of years".[57] Encryption runs readable messages called plaintext through a computer which in turn translates the message according to an algorithm into unreadable cipher text. Decryption then translates cipher text back to plaintext. Encryption methods are either conventional or symmetric and public-key or asymmetric cryptography.[58] Public-key cryptography is based on algorithms such as RSA and DSA, which are well-explained by Maury Shenk, Stewart Baker, and Winnie Chang in their chapter, "Cryptography and Electronic Signatures".

The authors explain that AES, DES, and Blowfish are symmetric algorithms that permit the exchange of confidential communications through the use of a shared key. Symmetrical cryptography employs a single key to encrypt and decrypt messages, whereas public-key cryptography employs a pair of complimentary keys: a private and public key. Asymmetrical algorithms, in contrast, such as RSA, employ a two-key system, one of which is usually public.

---

57   *Bernstein v. United States Department of Justice*, 176 F3d 1132 (9th Cir., 1999).

58   Oei, "Primer on Cryptography", in Smedinghoff, ed., *Online Law: The Software Publishing Association's Legal Guide to Doing Business on the Internet* (1996), at p. 497 (describing the two generic types of cryptography).

The chapter by Shenk and his colleagues discusses the regulation of the export, import, and use of products and technology involving use of cryptography. In the United States, government control over encrypted communications has been the subject of great controversy. The Federal Bureau of Investigation implemented the Carnivore system to intercept electronic mail and instant messaging information pertaining to suspects from Internet Service Providers (ISPs).[59] The USA Patriot Act gives law enforcement the authority "to collect addressing information of electronic communications (e.g., e-mail) without a warrant".[60] Encryption makes it possible to conduct electronic commerce safely. However, the seamy side of encryption is that it can be used by terrorists to conceal their communications.

Shenk, Baker, and Chang describe the types of encryption regulations, as well as the Wassenaar Arrangement (adopted by 33 countries) that sets the floor-boards but not the ceiling tiles for export regulations, including mass market software. The Wassennar Agreement is a transnational regime that seeks to increase the transparency of global transfer of conventional arms and dual-use goods, such as encrypted software products.) They note how the United States approach to encryption controls is functionally equivalent to the Wassennar rules. Australia, Canada, the European Union (EU), and Japan have implemented export controls closely tracking Wassenaar controls. While Hong Kong and Singapore are not signatories to the Wassennar Arrangement, they have policies that also track Wassenaar guidelines. However, not all countries follow this model, with China, Israel, and Kazakhstan applying various *ad hoc* controls.

In general, the United States reserves the most rigorous restrictions on encryption technology, proprietary source code, and open cryptographic interfaces (OCIs) exported to countries which do not qualify as favored countries. The authors note that the favored countries include the member states of EU, Australia, Japan, New Zealand, Norway, and Switzerland. However, the overall picture suggests the eventual deregulation of encryption products.

The authors' global survey of export rules reveals a lack of harmony between Europe and the rest of the world. Throughout Europe, there are no meaningful controls on mass-market encryption products, regardless of key length. These products may be freely exported outside the EU. There also is no restriction on encryption used for scientific research. In addition to European Community-wide regulations, individual countries such as France may their own controls which are quite restrictive.

---

59   Lemley, *Software and Internet Law* (2003), at p. 911.
60   Lemley, *Software and Internet Law* (2003), at pp. 911 and 912.

Prior to 11 September 2001, the path of encryption controls was to gradually deregulate these products. In the post-911 period, this trend has been reversed. The authors note that there is little agreement as to the best approach to encryption regulation. In general, the core countries or those with advanced encryption industries have a stronger basis for implementing export controls. However, the authors doubt whether there is any realistic way of enforcing controls on the exporting of strong encryption products.

A digital signature is defined as an electronic signature "created and verified by means of cryptography, the branch of applied mathematics that concerns itself with transforming messages into seemingly unintelligible forms and back again".[61] The purpose of a digital signature is to protect the integrity and authenticity of electronic messages The first wave of electronic signature statutes enacted in several states of the United States adopted a prescriptive approach marked by inflexibility. More recently, an enabling approach is becoming popular, exemplified by the Uniform Electronic Transaction Act (UETA). However, most counties still adopt a hybrid solution, such as the EU's Electronic Signature Directive. The final section of the Shenk, Baker, and Chang chapter explores the thorny issue of regulating digital signatures that employ public key cryptography. The authors call for a globalized regime for encryption controls in a crossborder environment.

1.03   Torts, Delicts, and Contractually-Based Remedies for Defective Software

Sakari Aalto, Lauri Mertala, and Leena Kerppilä examine the "Vendor's Liability for Defective Software". They conclude that the law of software has yet to develop an internationally accepted regime outside the field of intellectual property protection. Software law has been slow to develop because the courts tend to enforce one-sided software industry contracts that disclaim responsibility for defects in the United States, as well as in France, Germany, and Finland.

Legal remedies for software failure must be addressed in an international legal regime. Increasingly, the global infrastructure, from the "electronic power grid to air traffic control, is migrating to the Internet".[62] Hospitals and other health care providers are increasingly using the Internet to transmit

---

61   This definition was devised by the Information Security Committee, American Bar Association, Committee on Science and Technology, Digital Signature Guidelines with Model Legislation (1995).

62   Landau, "Sun Microsystems Inc., The Internet, Security, and Politics" (visited 16 November 2004), at https://your.trash.net/pipermail/siug-discuss/2001-October/001829.html.

medical images or provide medical consultations,[63] a process that has the potential of producing a large amount of tort litigation.

Aalto, Mertala, and Kerppilä describe a software industry too willing to race to market before adequately testing products and services. They argue that the industry releases products with serious defects or bugs relying on its customers to discover problems long after the release of software. The practice of testing products in the marketplace rather than the laboratory may make software more affordable, but not more secure. The authors argue that the allocations of liability in the delivery chain are inadequate from their multi-national survey of applicable regimes of substantive law. It may be cheaper not to fix known software defects where there is, in effect, a liability-free zone.

The authors' survey of software contracting law in the United States, Germany, France, and Finland reveals that freedom of contract is moderated by provisions in the law that protect software licensees. Under French law, the vendor is accountable for the consequences of software defects despite exculpatory language. The Finnish Sale of Goods Act also places the burden of proof on the vendor as under German law. Throughout Europe, unlike the United States, there are meaningful consumer protections and other mandated terms in business-to-consumer software contracts.

Under French law, even business licensees may be entitled to mandatory terms, such as non-disclaimable warranties and limits on the ability of the seller to disclaim liability. The French recognize the concept of a minimum adequate remedy that limits the power of the vendor to reallocate all of the costs of defective software. The authors note how the concept of "professional of the same specialty" (*professionnel de la même spécialité*) applies to French business-to-business software transactions.

In the United States, Maryland and Virginia have enacted the pro-licensor Uniform Computer Information Transactions Act (UCITA). UCITA permits software vendors to disclaim all warranties and limit vendors' remedies to a refund. UNCITRAL's Convention for the International Sale of Goods (CISG) is more user friendly, but it does not explicitly govern software. The authors note that the applicability of CISG continues to be an unsettled issue.

The information-based world system needs a harmonized software law that balances the interests of licensors and licensees. Aalto and his colleagues have documented the need for a new cross-border law governing vendors' liability for bad software. We have entered a new information-based

---

63   Telemedicine may involve a physician answering a question on a website, or it may take a more complex form, such as having an emergency room physician in Milwaukee consult with a colleague in New York. The Internet makes it possible for a cardiologist in Miami to assess sounds of the heart and lung of a patient located in a small hospital in the Red River Valley of Northwest Minnesota.

economy based on software and other transfers of information. There is an urgent need for harmonizing the rights and remedies for the victims of defective software.

Next, the authors examine the problem of defining defects in performance or the quality of software. Apart from security problems, software may have design defects that cause problems with formatting, processing speeds, the amount of data that could be handled, and problems of system integration with other software components or users.[64] However, the authors note that software failure may be a problem of compatibility with hardware or other software. Products liability has yet to be extended to the worldwide software industry that has evolved in less than a quarter century.

The authors contend that product liability cannot develop until there is widespread agreement on what constitutes a defect. The law of software warranties has evolved faster than the theory of strict products liability. A defect is a predicate to a products liability action. Products liability is a branch of tort law concerned with "the bases for, defenses to, and scope of liability of manufacturers and others who are in the business of selling or supplying goods for harms caused by defective tangible products".[65]

The authors document that the law of software in France, Germany, and Finland is primarily based on contract rather than tort, as in the United States. The principal obligation of a software vendor is to deliver products that perform in conformity with product specifications. The authors argue that meaningful remedies are needed for the licensees of software as liability serves the reparative function of compensating the victim of defective software. In addition, software liability also serves a preventative function in leading to more careful software design and testing. If licensors are permitted to disclaim any of the consequences of failed software, they will have an insufficient incentive to take remedial steps to improve their products and services.

Cybercriminals routinely exploit software holes or defects to launch denial of service attacks, to crash servers, disable anti-virus protection, conduct script insertion attacks, execute arbitrary code, bypass firewalls, alter e-mail headers, and obtain elevated privileges on computer networks. Security holes on Internet Explorer, for example, permit junk to be "installed on a user's PC by merely visiting a single site".[66] The number of malicious code reports skyrocketed from "just eight in 1988 to almost 53,000 in 2001", and

---

64   Rustad, "Making UCITA More Consumer-Friendly", 18 *J. Marshall J. Computer and Info. L.* 547, at p. 574 (1999) (citing survey of Computer Law Association members conducted by Michael Rustad and Cynthia Anthony).

65   Dobbs, *The Law of Torts* (2000), at p. 970.

66   Edelman, "Who Profits from Security Holes?" (visited 26 November 2004), at http: www.benedelman.org/news/111804_1.html.

the spread of viruses is not trending downward.[67] At present, software licensees are left without a meaningful remedy for the consequences of defective software that enables cybercrime. The authors note that the purchaser's contributory actions may exacerbate software failure.

One of the difficulties in developing software law with teeth is that this intangible is neither a product nor goods. Software is licensed, not sold like other products. "Software licenses do not transfer title and only the right to use information. Software contracts, access contracts, multimedia contracts, anti-viral products and services, and a multitude of other products are licensed."[68] The installation of network security may involve the sale of goods, the licensing of software, and the expert services of computer engineers.

The present legal environment does not make vendors accountable for the consequences of marketing defective software. In business-to-business transactions freedom of contract is the prevailing ideology. However, apart from the United States, many countries place limits on the vendor's power to limit or exclude warranties or remedies. The authors discuss possible warranty remedies for off-the-shelf (mass-market) software as well as products for the business-to-business marketplace. The Finnish attorneys draw on developments from Finland, France, Germany, and the United States in concluding that vendors' liability for software is undeveloped, outside of the law of warranties.

At present, vendors have no tort liability for marketing products with known vulnerabilities. Each system surveyed provides contractually based remedies for defective software. However, the content of the protection offered licensees is not uniform. The authors call for an international treaty to harmonize remedies for defective software.

1.04   Harmonized Intellectual Property

(a)   Protecting Digital Content in the Global Information Economy

Dana Beldiman raises the difficult policy issue of how to protect digital property rights on the Internet. The threat of the uncontrolled dissemination of copyrighted material led the information industries to lobby Congress for stronger intellectual property protection. Congress has enacted several

---

67   Gelbstein and Kamal (United Nations ICT Task Force), "Information Insecurity: A Survival Guide to the Uncharted Territories of Cyber-Threats and Cyber-Security" (2002) (visited 24 November 2004), at http://www.itu.int/wsis/docs/background/themes/security/information_insecurity_2ed.pdf.

68   A license is permission to use information under restricted conditions, such as the software, in only one single-user computer. A sale, in contrast, involves the passage of title to goods for a price. Software does not require a fixed inventory or even raw materials. There is an infinite supply of "1s" and "0s", and they may be delivered without passing title. Licenses are based on the number of copies licensed, the method of distribution, the type of end user, and the form of the license agreement.

statutes increasing the power of the "haves" in cyberspace.[69] *America Online,*[70] *Playboy Enterprises,*[71] *Verizon,*[72] *Universal Studios,*[73] and Microsoft[74] are typical of large Internet stakeholders that have litigated aggressively to solidify their market position in cyberspace.[75] Beldiman's chapter surveys the legal and technological measures developed to protect copyrighted content on the Internet and how this affects the interests of powerful media.

She examines three means of protection of digital information, namely:

1. Copyright law;

2. The technology itself; and

3. Other legal responses.

---

69 The only significant consumer victories have been cases where the government was the prevailing plaintiff, not individuals. *Time Warner Entertainment Co. v. FCC,* 2001 U.S. App. LEXIS 3102 (D.C. Cir., 2001) (ruling in favor of the FCC imposing limits on cable system and channel capacity). *Ford Motor Co. v. Texas DOT,* 106 F. Supp. 2d 905 (W.D. Tex., 2000) (ruling in favor of Texas state governmental unity in cases involving the sale of used automobiles on the Internet); *State of Missouri ex rel. Nixon v. Beer Nuts Ltd.,* 29 SW3d 828 (Mo. Ct. App., 2000) (upholding Missouri ban on the online sale of beer to Missouri residents); *FTC v. Dell Computer and Micron Electronics,* FTC File Number 982 3563; FTC File Number 982 3565 (1999) (entering consent order against computer companies).

70 *America Online, Inc. v. Huang,* 106 F. Supp.2d 848 (E.D. Va., 2000); *America Online, Inc. v. IMS,* 24 FSupp.2d 548 (E.D. Va., 1998); *America Online, Inc. v. LCGM, Inc.,* 46 F. Supp.2d 444 (E.D. Va., 1998); *America Online, Inc. v. National Health Care Discount, Inc.,* 174 F. Supp.2d 890 (N.D. Iowa, 2001); *America Online, Inc. v. Prime Data Systems, Inc.* 1998 W.L. 334016692 (E.D. Va., 1998); *America Online, Inc. v. Superior Court,* 108 Cal. Rptr. 2d 699 (Cal. App., 1 Dist., 2001).

71 *Playboy Enterprises, Inc. v. Asiafocus Intern., Inc.,* 1998 W.L. 724000 (E.D. Va., 1998); *Playboy Enterprises, Inc. v. Frena,* 839 F. Supp. 1552 (M.D. Fla., 1993); *Playboy Enterprises v. Netscape Communications Corp.,* 55 F. Supp.2d 1070 (C.D. Cal., 1999); *Playboy Enterprises v. Russ Hardenburgh, Inc.,* 982 F. Supp. 503 (N.D. Ohio, 1997); *Playboy Enterprises v. Terri Welles Inc.,* 78 F. Supp. 2d 1066 (S.D. Tex., 1997); *Playboy Enterprises, Inc. v. Webbworld, Inc.,* 991 F. Supp. 543 (N.D. Tex., 1997).

72 *RIAA v. Verizon Internet Services,* 2003 U.S. App., Lexis 25735; C.A. 2-MS-0323 (D.D.C., 2002).

73 *Universal City Studios, Inc. v. Reimerdes,* 82 F. Supp. 2d 211 (S.D.N.Y., 2000); *RIAA v. MP3.com,* 2000 US. Dist. LEXIS 5761 (S.D.N.Y., 2000).

74 Microsoft is a frequent defendant as well as plaintiff in Internet-related cases. *United States v. Microsoft Corp.,* 253 F3d 34 (D.C. Cir., 2001); "Microsoft Sues Online Pirates", *Wired News* (8 December 1999), with "Priceline.com Files Suit against Microsoft", *CNETcom* (visited 11 October 2004), at http://news.com.com/2100-1001-231384.html? legacy=cnet.

75 Fortune 500 bricks-and-mortar companies also have been active in cyberspace litigation. *Ford Motor Co. v. Lane,* 67 F. Supp. 2d 745 (E.D. Mich., 1999); *Sony Computer Entertainment v. Connectix Corp.,* 48 F. Supp. 2d 1212 (N.D., 1999); *Sega Entertainment, Ltd. v. Maphia,* 857 F. Supp. 679 (N.D. Cal., 1994), modified, 948 F. Supp. 923 (N.D. Cal., 1996); *Mattel, Inc. v. Adventure Apparel,* 2001 U.S. Dist. LEXIS 13885 (S.D.N.Y., 2001); *Mattel, Inc. v. barbie-club.com,* 2001 US. Dist. LEXIS 5262 (S.D.N.Y., 2001); *Cable News Network LP, LLLP v. cnnnews.com,* 162 F. Supp. 2d 484 (E.D. Va., 2001); *Lockheed Martin v. Network Solutions,* 141 F. Supp. 2d 648 (N.D. Tex., 2001); *E and J Gallo Winery v. Spider Webs LTD, et al.,* 129 F. Supp. 2d 1033 (S.D. Tex., 2001); *Fleet Boston Financial Corp. v. fleetbostonfinancial.com,* 138 F. Supp. 2d 121 (D. Mass., 2001); *Harrods Limited v. Sixty Internet Domain Names,* 110 F. Supp. 2d 420 (E.D. Va., 2000); *Caesars World, Inc. v. Caesars-Palace.com et al,* 2000 U.S. Dist. LEXIS 2671 (E.D. Va., 3 March 2000).

The Digital Millennium Copyright Act (DMCA) is an example of a third tier response. It provides Hollywood with new weapons to battle the downloading of copyrighted music and images by college students.[76]

So too, the Anti-Cybersquatting Consumer Protection Act of 1999 (ACPA) was enacted to deter the unauthorized registration or use of trade marks as Internet domain names.[77] The ACPA addressed the problem of dot.com startups and cyberpirates who registered domain names that were confusingly similar or identical to well-known marks. In addition to domestic statutes, stakeholders are protected by World Intellectual Property Organization (WIPO) treaties.

Civil code countries such as France, Germany, and The Netherlands are pursuing a different legal path forging a different balance between intellectual property stakeholders and the public interest, the trend of United States copyright law. The Dutch, for example, generally regard online music swapping as non-infringing. The networked world is causing a clash between litigants from radically different legal traditions. A French court ruled that radio stations may not stream musical extracts on their websites without the express permission of music producers. This producers' right to control communications to the public was decided under the French Intellectual Property Code.[78] On the other hand, a United Kingdom court held that a British Internet café chain infringed United Kingdom copyright law by providing a commercial service for downloading music onto recordable CDs for customers.[79]

The Internet will increasingly involve crossborder contractual disputes, such as in *Profile Publ'g and Mgmt. Corp. APS v. Musicmaker.com,*[80] which pitted the Danish owner of musical recordings by the musical group The Who against a website providing consumers with custom disc compilation services. Musicmaker, which owned and operated an Internet website, had no permission to copy digital musical recordings on compact discs. When threatened with a lawsuit, Musicmaker.com entered into an agreement to

---

76 The DMCA arms the entertainment industry with new remedies against using circumvention devices designed to decrypt the contents of DVDS that are cosseted by a Content Scramble System (CSS). The peer-to-peer file sharing movement on the Internet pits the movie, record, and film industry against Internet users. In *A and M Records, Inc. v. Napster, Inc.,* 239 F3d 1005 (9th Cir. 2001), the Ninth Circuit upheld a federal court order enjoining Napster for facilitating the wholesale copying of music on its service. *Universal City Studios, Inc. v. Reimerdes,* 82 F. Supp.2d 211 (S.D.N.Y., 2000) (enjoining websites from posting the Decks software which circumvents software controls on DVDs).

77 15 United States Code, section 1125(d) (2004).

78 *Société des Producteures de Phonogrammes en France Union des Producteurs Ponographiques Francais Independants, Tribunal de Grande Instance de Partis* (15 May 2002), reported in 2002 ILRWeb PandF 1713 (2002).

79 *Sony Music Entertainment (UK) Ltd. v. Easyinternetcafe Ltd.,* H.C. 2 C01798 (High Court of Justice, Chancery Division, 30 January 2005), reprinted at 2005 ILRWeb (PandF) 1055 (2005).

80 *Profile Publ'g and Mgmt. Corp. APS v. Musicmaker.comProfile,* 2005 U.S. Dist. LEXIS 991 (S.D.N.Y., 24 January 2005).

pay royalties. After Musicmaker.com shut down its website, it failed to pay the full amount of royalties due. The court ordered them to honor their installment contract and assessed sanctions against the company and its attorneys for frivolous counterclaims and defenses.

Courts outside the United States may not be as receptive by attempts by large corporations to "push the envelope" by asserting an ever-expanding array of intellectual property rights. Beldiman's chapter begins with a lucid discussion of the United States approach to digital rights protection. Powerful United States copyright owners seek to "keep the cat in the bag" and yet participate in the new networked economy where information is transferred seamlessly at the click of a mouse. Beldiman argues that it is difficult to protect digital content while permitting the unfettered distribution of content. She argues that copyright law provides a strong, but not an absolute protection in the digital world. The critics of the United States approach argue that the copyright moguls such as Hollywood and the recording industry are "pushing the envelope" on protecting content, which critics describe as "simple overrereaching". Beldiman explains the opposing views in copyright law as part of the growing pains of a new emergent copyright paradigm.

Beldiman's chapter clearly explains content protection technologies, privacy enhancing technologies, payment mechanisms, and other rights management that depends on legal norms against anti-circumvention. The entertainment industry has pressed for increasing civil and criminal penalties for those seeking to circumvent digital rights management software. She reviews the Digital Millennium Copyright Act or the DMCA, which was a byproduct of the 1996 WIPO Copyright Treaties. Movie producers, for example, lobbied for the passage of the Digital Millennium Copyright Act,[81] providing remedies against circumventing copyright protection software used in distributing Digital Versatile Discs (DVDs).[82] Next follows a discussion of the logic and the limits of the DMCA comparing United States law to the EU Copyright Directive.

The Beldiman chapter concludes with a synoptic survey of other law governing digital content as well as a discussion of emergent business models which will likely reshape global copyright law. The global rules for streaming media broadcast and entertainment transmitted digitally over the Internet are presently being negotiated between stakeholders and the government. He hypothesizes that the DMCA and other copyright law will become less important as new technologies evolve, such as the globalized "pay per use" system of commercializing and protecting digital content.

---

81 Pub. L. Number 105-305, 112 Stat. 2860 (1998).

82 "On 12 October 1998, Congress passed the Digital Millennium Copyright Act (DMCA), a complex piece of legislation which makes major changes in United States copyright law to address the digitally networked environment". Band, "The Digital Millennium Copyright Act" (visited 11 May 2005), at http://www.arl.org/info/frn/copy/band.html.

(b) Towards a Globalized Fair Use Standard

Jon Grossman and Elizabeth Parsons examine the problem of developing an international fair use standard. Their chapter pays particular attention to the path of United States copyright law focusing on the difficult topic of fair use. The chapter surveys governmental as well as industry approaches to fair use for digital information. Finally, the chapter suggests the need for a new international standard for copyright protection and identifies factors that should comprise the cross-border fair use rules.

In December 2002, WIPO released a report, "Intellectual Property on the Internet: A Survey of Issues", that examines the impact of the globalization of the Internet on intellectual property rights. WIPO argues for expanded protection for digital technologies in rights to "copyrights, trade marks and patents, as well as domain names. The WIPO report explores the particular concerns that face developing countries in e-development, and outlines the ways in which WIPO is addressing these various issues".[83]

The advanced industrial nations control many of the digital technologies, and WIPO's proposed treaty process is a tool for extending intellectual property rights of the cyberspace core[84] into the semi-periphery and periphery.[85]

---

83 World Intellectual Property Organization, Intellectual Property on the Internet: A Survey of Issues (December 2002) (visited 28 January 2005), at http://ecommerce.wipo.int/survey.

84 Sociologist Immanuel Wallerstein conceptualized the "world system" to explain why European countries arose to world dominance in the period 1300–1450. Wallerstein, *The Modern World System I: Capitalist Agriculture and the Origins of The European World Economy in the Sixteenth Century* (1974). Wallerstein's model defined the first core nations as England, France, and Holland in northwestern Europe. Core countries have a lasting advantage because they develop the new technologies first and use their expertise to dominate periphery and semi-periphery countries economically, militarily, and culturally. In the 16th Century, the core states "developed strong central governments, extensive bureaucracies, and large mercenary armies". *Modern History Sourcebook: Summary of Wallerstein on World System Theory* (13 June 2001) (visited 2 February 2005), at http://www.fordham.edu/halsall/mod/wallerstein.html. The core countries used their technological superiority to expropriate the resources of the less-developed countries. Nations with sufficient expertise and other resources to partially resist appropriation are defined as satellite or semi-periphery countries. By the 16th Century, the semi-periphery included declining core nations, such as Spain and Portugal as well as Italy, southern Germany, and southern France, which had yet to attain core status. Finally, the 16th century periphery consisted of nations in Eastern Europe, Africa, and Latin Africa, which had little or no ability to resist the demands of the core states. Today, the core nations of the networked world are the United States, Canada, the countries of Western Europe, Japan, South Korea, Australia, and New Zealand. This core of Internet-user nations have a significant advantage over less-developed countries with low numbers of Internet users and hosts, low percentage of personal computers, and poorly developed cyber-infrastructure.

85 The United States sought to negotiate a 20-year copyright term extension with Taiwan which would bring the total copyright term to 70 years, but Taiwan has yet to accede to this request. Reuters, "Taiwan Rejects U.S. Copyright Demands" (visited 17 February 2005), at http://www.siliconvalley.com/mld/siliconvalley/news/editorial/4260499.htm.

The policy concern is that too much control would stifle the creative commons. Grossman and Parsons compare the United States doctrine of fair use to approaches found in European countries. The creation of an international "fair use" standard is needed in an age of seamless access to digital copies. The challenge in developing this new standard is to appropriately balance the rights of digital intellectual property owners with the rights of other stakeholders.

(c) Towards a Globalized Regime for Domain Names

Frederick Roos proposes the further legalization of domain names. Roos begins his chapter with a discussion of how domain names clash with the trade marks of powerful corporations. In the early 1990s, cyberspace was referred to as the Wild West because predatory entrepreneurs staked out the domain names containing trade marks of distinctive or internationally known companies and held them for ransom. Roos discusses the unsavory practices of cybersquatting, warehousing, and misspellings, as well as the misuse and abuse of "expired" domain names.

According to Roos, cyberpirates warehoused thousands of domain names with no intention of ever launching a website. The business of warehousing domain names was to place the domain name on the market for the highest bidder or to extort a multi-million dollar settlement from a national company. In addition, the author discusses the difficult problem of "gripe-sites", which is an issue that places trade mark rights in conflict with the right of expression.

In the United States, information age moguls convinced the United States Congress to fortify the rights and remedies of famous and distinctive trade mark owners. Domain name defendants have responded by becoming more creative in misusing and abusing domain names. In a recent case, an adult entertainment company modified a domain address to "surreptitiously . . . re-direct traffic" for www.sexnet.com to its address — a practice known as "domain name hijacking",[86] Internet predators make profits from their callous calculation that many Internet surfers will mistype domain name addresses. These "entrepreneurs" register the most common misspellings of well-known trade marks to divert unwary users to their nefarious sites.

Roos discusses how "mouse trapping" involves capturing the careless typist to the website of a competitor or to a pornography haven with no exit. Like

---

86 *Telemedia Network v. Sunshine Films Inc.*, 2002 Cal. App. unpub. LEXIS 10369 (Ct. of App. Ca., 13 November 2002) (describing hijacking "as the defendant surreptitiously . . . re-directing traffic" for www.sexnet.com to Sunshine's address — in effect "hijacking" the sexnet.com domain name using the Sexnet mark. As a result, any customer attempting to access Sexnet would be sent automatically to a website operated by Sunshine but with no content).

the Roach Motel, entrance into these unsavory sites is easy, but escaping them is made all but impossible by resourceful programmers. Attempts to leave are thwarted by software commands that control the computer's back browser and enmesh the victim ever more deeply into a web of pop-up advertising.

He describes how European courts, as well as those in China, are devising different solutions to the problem of domain names. He surveys alternative dispute resolution systems, such as the ICANN system as well as new legislation and rules for resolving domain name disputes. Sweden, for example, has recently abandoned its domain name registration system based on entitlements to a more modern system.

Roos critiques the Swedish domain name registration system that was based on "prior assessment". The author next turns to the domain name registration systems of individual countries that have led to a balkanization of country-wide registrations. A strong convergence between the United States and European law of domain names has resulted from the internationalization of dispute resolution.

The author next critiques the role of the ICANN and UDRP dispute resolution system that has evolved since the late 1990s. The Internet Corporation for Assigned Names and numbers (ICANN), created in 1998, has responsibility for technical functions of the Internet. ICANN coordinates the assignment of IP address numbers, protocol parameter and port numbers, and the stable operation of the Internet's root server systems.[87] ICANN states that it:

> . . . is the global forum for developing policies for coordination of some of the Internet's core technical elements, including the domain-name system (DNS). ICANN operates on the basis of consensus, with affected stakeholders coming together to formulate coordination policies for the Internet's core technical elements in the public interest.[88]

The Internet Assigned Numbers Authority (IANA) delegates or redelegates top-level domains and manages the domain-name system root.[89] The registration of domain names within two-letter country code top-level domains (CCTLDS), such as ".uk" (United Kingdom), ".se" (Sweden), or ".au" (Australia), are administered by country-code managers.[90]

---

87 Internet Corporation for Assigned Names and Numbers, "Introduction to ICANN" (visited 2 February 2005), at http://www.icann.org/.

88 Internet Corporation for Assigned Names and Numbers, "ccTLD Resource Materials" (2 February 2005), at http://www.icann.org/cctlds/.

89 Internet Assigned Names Authority, "IANA Report on Redelegation of the la Top-Level Domain" (visited 2 February 2005), at http://www.iana.org/reports/la-report-11dec02.htm.

90 Internet Corporation for Assigned Names and Numbers, "ccTLD Resource Materials" (2 February 2005), at http://www.icann.org/cctlds/.

The Internet domain name system consists of a directory, organized hierarchically, of all the domain names and their corresponding computers registered to a particular com. All accredited domain-name registrars for domain names ending in ". com", ".net", and ".org" are required to adhere to the Uniform Dispute Resolution Policy (UDRP). The UDRP is a good example of legalization. The UDRP's crossborder dispute resolution system offers a cost-effective solution for resolving cybersquatting or cyberpiracy claims. When a United States company applies for a domain name (or renews it), they are asked to represent that the registration of the domain name will not infringe the intellectual property rights of others.[91] All domain name registrants, wherever they are located, submit to the virtual UDRP dispute resolution system.

The Max-Planck Institute completed a content analysis of the first generation of cases decided under the UDRP procedure between 1999 and 2001.[92] The researchers found that UDRP panels ordered transfers of domain names in 76.7 per cent of the cases and cancellations in 1.4 per cent of the cases. Complaints were dismissed in only approximately 21 per cent of the cases. Results varied significantly by provider. Complainants prevailed 82 per cent in decisions rendered by WIPO panels in contrast to only 59 per cent before the now defunct eResolutions. Eighty-four percent of the complaints were filed by registered trade mark owners.

The Max Planck study confirms the Swedish author's thesis that further legalization is required. A globalized solution to domain names must successfully balance intellectual property rights against the right of expression. The lack of predictability, legitimacy, freedom of speech, and conflicting norms in different countries remain obstacles in arriving at a global solution. The author surveys ways that domain name governance is being deployed in the battle against crossborder spam.

---

91   "By applying to register a domain name, or by asking us to maintain or renew a domain name registration, you hereby represent and warrant to us that (a) the statements that you made in your Registration Agreement are complete and accurate; (b) to your knowledge, the registration of the domain name will not infringe on or otherwise violate the rights of any third party; (c) you are not registering the domain name for an unlawful purpose; and (d) you will not knowingly use the domain name in violation of any applicable laws or regulations. It is your responsibility to determine whether your domain name registration infringes or violates someone else's rights." ICANN, Uniform Dispute Resolution Policy (visited 17 December 2004), at http://www.icann.org/dndr/udrp/policy.htm.

92   Kur, Max Planck-Institute, Munich, "UDRP: A Study by the Max-Planck-Institute for Foreign and International Patent, Copyright, and Competition Law" (in cooperation with the Institute for Intellectual Property Law and Market Law, University of Stockholm and Institute for Information Law and Technical University of Karlsruhe (Germany) (visited 18 December 2005), at http://www.intellecprop.mpg.de/Online-Publikationen/2002/UDRP-study-final-02.pdf.

The author's magisterial survey confirms that we are a long way to developing an effective global regime for domain names. Any solution to the domain name problem will need to consider radically different cultures and norms as well as the semantic meaning of trade marks in different languages. Participants in the WSIS consultation process "agreed that spam unsolicited or 'junk' e-mail while not yet officially on the international agenda, must be discussed as a matter of priority".[93] The battle to restrain spam and online pornography is leading to greater international cooperation in the field of domain names.

(d) Patent Law for a Global Information Age

David Simonelli examines the difficult problem of internationalizing patent law. He begins by comparing patent protection to that of copyright and trade mark law. Every introductory patent textbook begins with the aphorism that a patent is a monopoly granted for a limited period. The United States law of patents began in 1790 when the United States Secretary of State Thomas Jefferson granted the first United States patent for a method of making potash, which is an ingredient for soap. Simonelli questions whether Jefferson had a monopoly in mind in his concept of patent law.

In fact, Simonelli quotes Jefferson who hoped that the United States' capitalist system would soon rid the economy of all forms of monopolies. Simonelli also dismantles the conventional wisdom that patents should give patent holders a monopoly. He notes how patent law's "monopoly" is subject to doctrines such as the compulsory licenses. Patent law, like every other branch of intellectual property, balances the public's rights against the owner of the intellectual property right.

With copyright law, the exclusive rights of the owner are moderated by the doctrine of fair use. Trade mark owner's rights are subject to the doctrine of parody and fair use, among other limitations. Each branch of intellectual property in the information-based world system must balance the need to protect proprietary rights against the public interest in access to information.

Simonelli suggests that the United States-style patent monopoly places less developed countries at a disadvantage. He suggests ways to protect patent rights while permitting pharmaceuticals and other patents to be used in Third World countries. He proposes a new institution that balances patent owners' rights with the rights of the periphery and semi-periphery countries to have access to medical products and processes, and suggests that an international entity be formulated that would certify Third World entity status.

---

93   "UN E-Governance Panel Focuses on Spam, Web Governance", *D.M. Europe* (21 April 2005).

Another possibility would be to mandate compulsory licenses for Third World entities. He uses the concept of "permissive infringement" to recognize the need for Third World countries to innovate and grow. Simonelli's proposal recognizes the responsibility of core countries to periphery and semi-periphery countries. Nevertheless, his proposal is only the first step in developing a global regime.

United States patent law conflicts with many of the basic features of the law of patents found in the rest of the world. The United States Patent and Trade Mark Office grants patents to the first person to invent, whereas the rest of the world awards patents to the "first to file" the patent application.[94] To date, WIPO has been unable to negotiate a treaty to harmonize these divergent patent laws.[95] The United States has recently become a member of the Patent Cooperation Treaty (PCT) that permits the filing of a single international patent application. The PCT permits individuals and companies within member countries or regional patent systems to file a single patent application in one member country and then file a second patent application in a second country, within the first year of filing, and have the benefit of priority.[96]

The European system of patents not only recognized national patents, but a relatively new European patent granted by the European Patent Office in Munich. The European patent system was created by article 237 of the EC Treaty.[97] The European Patent Convention provides protection to patent holders in member states for a term of 20 years.

The Europeans have lagged behind the United States in developing patents for e-commerce. In contrast, e-commerce patents have skyrocketed since the United States federal court decision in *State Street Bank and Trust Co. v. Signature Financial Group, Inc.*[98] The United States was the first country to recognize e-commerce or business methods patents which are not yet recognized in Europe. No European country has yet to issue patents for Internet-related business methods.

---

94 International Chamber of Commerce, "Current and Emerging Issues Relating to Specific Intellectual Property Rights" (visited 3 March 2005), at http://www.iccwbodot.org/hom/intellectual_property/current-emerging/roadmap.asp.

95 International Chamber of Commerce, "Current and Emerging Issues Relating to Specific Intellectual Property Rights" (visited 3 March 2005), at http://www.iccwbodot.org/hom/intellectual_property/current-emerging/roadmap.asp.

96 Kirsch, "Strategies for the Use of Patents by Start-Up Internet Companies", *Gigalaw.com* (visited 3 March 2005), at http://www.gigalaw.com/articles/kirsch-2000-07-p5.html.

97 The European Commission, Internal Market, Patents-Commission Approves Green Paper (25 June 1997 (visited 3 March 2005), at http://europa.eu.int/comm/internal_marekt/en/introp/indprop/558.ht.

98 *State Street Bank and Trust Co. v. Signature Financial Group, Inc* 149 F3d 1368 (Fed. Cir., 1998) (ruling that a mathematical algorithm used in a mutual fund hub and spoke business method for computing interest in mutual funds produced "a useful, concrete and tangible result").

Software patents are not well-established in some countries. The United Kingdom's Patent Office issued a report rejecting patent protection for computer software as well as for methods of doing business.[99]

A proposed European Directive would "harmonize the conditions for the patentability of inventions related to computer programs".[100] Recently, the European Commission has suspended further development of the new Directive on software patents. Although European patent protection for software or methods of doing business is not well-established, enforcement of patent rights is robust.

In a United Kingdom case, the High Court rejected an argument that British bookmakers were not infringing a gaming system patent simply because their host computers were in the Netherlands Antilles.[101] Patent litigation rules vary significant across European countries. In Germany, there is no discovery but, in France and Italy, the court can order the inspection of the premises in a patent case.[102]

The underlying jurisprudence behind patent law varies. In France and England, the theory is that a patent represents a contract between society and the inventor.[103] The German view, in contrast, is paternalistic and "[p]atents are granted because the state has decided, in its wisdom and part of the exercise of its power as *parens patriae*".[104] Simonelli's chapter signals the need for a harmonized patent law for the global information society.

(e) Resolving Disputes over Information Transfers

Mark Nadeau's survey of the law of technology transfers suggests the need for further legalization of the information-based world system. Increasingly, information and communication technologies (ICTs) are becoming the

---

99   The United Kingdom Patent Office, "Should Patents Be Granted for Computer Software or Ways of Doing Business: The Government's Conclusions" (visited 3 March 2005), at http://www.patent.gov.uk/about/consultations/conclusions.htm.

100 World Intellectual Property Organization, "What Is the PCT" (visited 3 March 2005), at http://www.wipodot.org/pct/guide/en/gdvo11-01.htm.

101 "British High Court Rules in Jurisdictional Dispute over Game System Patent", 4 *Mealey's Litigation Report*: *Cyber Tech and E-Commerce* (April 2002).

102 Ladas and Perry, "Ladas and Perry Guide to European Patent Office Practice, Post-Grant Issues" (visited 3 March 2005), at http://www.ladas.com/GUIDES/PATEN/EPOPractice/EOPractGuide-8.html.

103 Ladas and Perry, "Ladas and Perry Guide to European Patent Office Practice, Post-Grant Issues" (visited 3 March 2005), at http://www.ladas.com/GUIDES/PATEN/EPOPractice/EOPractGuide-8.html.

104 Ladas and Perry, "Ladas and Perry Guide to European Patent Office Practice, Post-Grant Issues" (visited 3 March 2005), at http://www.ladas.com/GUIDES/PATEN/EPOPractice/EOPractGuide-8.html.

subject of crossborder disputes in the information age. This is because of the proliferation of online contracts, software licenses and other virtual practices over the Internet, which have a global reach. Without a reliable means to enforce rights and seek remedies, intellectual property rights will disappear with a click of the mouse.

Nadeau lays out the fundamental concepts underlying the resolution of intellectual property disputes and considers the various methods available for parties. He argues in favor of a less adversarial process than is found in most legal systems at present. As a result, he calls for a new international forum, created by international treaty, as many of the contributors also do for their respective areas of interest. This treaty would encompass a consistent set of rules for choice of law, enforcement of foreign judgments, and alternative modes of settlement for the parties to choose from prior to suit. Nevertheless, there are dimensions to this project that involve very real differences, in addition to those imposed by cyberspace.[105]

(f) Data Base Protection and Privacy Regulation in a Global Economy

David Gryce and Roxanne A. Esche make it plain that any transborder legal regime governing databases also must protect privacy. Gryce and Esche review the concepts and methods of the Database Directive expertly describing key questions such as what protected data is and who can claim rights. They argue that intellectual property right holders need protection since they have invested significant resources in collecting information that they then store in electronic databases. Information must be protected to return value to the intellectual property right holder.

Gryce and Esche next review the legislative regimes that apply to protecting databases or proprietary data. Civil Law jurisdictions generally accord greater protection of personal data than the Common Law countries.[106] Finally, the authors propose specific database protection that will harmonize the law of databases. They endorse further international efforts to protect databases and privacy and see this balance as the key to seamless transborder data flows.

The balance between database protection and the free exchange of scientific or other data has yet to be achieved in many countries. In the United States, there is no copyright protection for databases that are mere compilations

---

105 Renteln, "Cross-Cultural Dispute Resolution: the Consequences of Conflicting Cultural Norms", 10 *Willamette. J. Int'l and Dispute Res.* 103 (2002).

106 Whitman, "The Two Western Cultures of Privacy: Dignity v. Liberty", *Yale Law School Public Law and Legal Theory Research Paper Series Number 64* (2004).

because they lack originality.[107] The information industry proposed database protection in the Conference Report for the Digital Millennium Copyright Act of 1998.[108]

In contrast, the EU's 1996 Database Directive provides copyright protection for databases meeting the originality standard as well as a *sui generis* protection for non-original databases.[109] Copyright protection applies if the selection and arrangement of the data or contents' qualities as an original intellectual creation. In contrast, a *sui generis* term of protection for 15 years is granted to databases where there has been a substantial investment in obtaining, verifying, or presenting contents.

Europeans endorse the "sweat of the brow" theory, which is an approach not followed in the United States. In *British Horseracing Board Ltd., v. William Hill Organization Ltd.*,[110] the court held that racing information compiled by a governing body of horseracing violated a horseracing body's *sui generis* database rights under EU law. The plaintiff maintained an extensive database of information on races, jockeys, owners, and other information that it supplied to the defendant. The defendant then began to use the horseracing body's database rights on its website. Absent a license agreement, there would be no cause of action in the United States for a similar usage. The radically different concepts of data protection found in the United States and Europe are a case in point for greater harmonization. It is instructive to note that the different approaches do not merely mirror the Common Law and Civil Law divide.

Another major difference between the United States and Europe is in data collection of personally identifiable information. The Europeans treat privacy as a fundamental human right versus the weak tradition of privacy protection in the United States. The United States approach to privacy has

---

107 Under United States copyright law, a work needs some minimum modicum of originality to qualify for copyright protection and a work is original if it was independently created by the author and possesses a minimum level of creativity. The United States Supreme Court ruled, in *Feist Publications, Inc. v. Rural Telephone Service Co.*, 499 United States 340 (1991), that a telephone directory consisting of white and yellow pages lacked the minimum originality to receive copyright protection. The Court rejected a "sweat of the brow" theory that the time and effort in compiling and organizing a database satisfied the originality requirement.

108 Band, "Digital Millennium Copyright Act" (visited 3 March 2002), at http://www.drfcdot.org/issues/graphic/2281/JB-Index?JB-Memo/jb-memo.html.

109 Directive 96/9/EC of the European Parliament and of the Council of March 1996 on the legal protection of databases: *Official Journal* L j077 of 27 March 1996 (396L009 (Database Directive).

110 *British Horseracing Board Ltd., v. William Hill Organization Ltd.*, H.C. 2000 1335 (High Court of Justice, Chancery Division, 9 February 2001), reported in 8 *I.L.R.* (P and F 629 (2001).

focused on a self-regulatory or market-driven approach[111] supplemented by statutory protection in sectors such as health care[112] and financial service.[113]

Since October 1998, the European member states have been implementing the Directive by enacting national legislation. The European approach to Internet privacy is a command and control model with precise rules governing the handling of personal information, in contrast to the United States which relies largely on a market-based solution to privacy.

In contrast, the purpose of the European Data Protective Directive is to create uniformity in the processing of personal information across member states.[114] The Data Protection Directive gives data subjects control over the collection, transmission, or use of personal information. The data subject has the right to be notified of all uses and disclosures about data collection and processing.

Gryce and Esche examine the role of the Organization for Economic Cooperation and Development (OECD) in formulating guidelines for the protection of privacy in the context of transborder flows of personal data. Under the OECD principles, a company, for example, is required to obtain explicit consent as to the collection of data on race and ethnicity, political opinions, union membership, physical and mental health, sex life, and criminal records.

The EU's Data Protection Directive requires that personal information be protected by adequate security. Data subjects have the right to obtain copies of information collected as well as the right to correct or delete personal data. It is important that consent be obtained from the data subject prior to entering in to the contract.[115] Data may not be transferred to other countries without an "adequate level of protection".[116] EU member states are required

---

111 The authors' analysis of Federal Trade Commission cases shows that the Commission is stepping up its enforcement of online privacy. If a website has a privacy policy, but its information collection and use practices are inconsistent with that policy, the Commission has authority to investigate and restrain the mispresentations in the privacy policy as unfair or deceptive trade practices. Nahra, "What Every Insurer Needs to Know About Privacy", *5 Mealey's Litigation Report: Emerging Insurance Disputes* 1 (8 November 2000).

112 The requirements of the Health Insurance Portability and Accounting Act (HIPPA) apply equally well to the Internet.

113 The requirements of the Gramm-Leach-Bliley Act focus on privacy protection for the individual customers of financial institutions. Nahra, "What Every Insurer Needs to Know About Privacy", *5 Mealey's Litigation Report: Emerging Insurance Disputes* 1 (8 November 2000).

114 The data protection traditions varied significantly across member states. Germany, France, and United Kingdom had a tradition of strong protection of privacy versus non-existent regulation in Greece. Mann and Winn, *Electronic Commerce* (2002), at p. 7.

115 Data Protection Directive, article 7.

116 Data Protection Directive, article 25.

to provide that a transfer of personal data to a third party takes places only if there is assurance of an adequate level of data protection. A company is civilly liable for the unlawful processing of personal data. Damages may be assessed for collection or transmitting information without data subject consent.[117]

The fundamental principles of United States privacy law are less developed outside the medical, financial services, and a few other sectors. Unlike Europe, there is no real codification of privacy rights in United States law. The Founders of the United States Constitution did not explicitly address privacy as a fundamental right.[118] The American law of privacy has evolved in a crazy quilt of piecemeal statutes at the federal and state levels. The path of United States privacy law has been to limit governmental intrusion into a sphere of personal conduct and relations by defining the boundaries between the individual and the government.[119]

In contrast, the United States prefers that the business community develop industry standards, such as the Better Business Bureau's Online Privacy Seals or other certification programs. The United States seeks to develop a transnational online privacy seal that can be earned by adherence to industry norms.[120] The EU Data Protection Directive sought to establish a regulatory framework that would guarantee free movement of personal data. However, each individual is guaranteed a basic level of privacy by requiring each provider or transmitter to adhere to a set of guidelines.[121]

The Directive stated that organizations were forbidden to transfer personal information of Europeans unless the transferee complied with the notice and choice principles.[122] Organizations were required to ascertain whether third parties subscribed to the principles of the Directive before transferring information to them. The authors note that, in the interconnected

---

117 Data Protection Directive, article 23.

118 "Constitutional privacy law has evolved largely from textual and inferential construction of the Bill of Rights; in particular, the First, Fourth, Fifth, and Ninth Amendments, as well as the Fourteenth Amendment." Schacter, *Informational and Decisional Privacy* (2005), at p. 8.

119 Schacter, *Informational and Decisional Privacy* (2005), at p. 25.

120 Rustad and Daftary, *E-Business Legal Handbook: 2003 Edition* (2005), section 8.02[D].

121 The legal grounds defined in the Directive are "consent, contract, legal obligation, vital interest of the data subject, or the balance between the legitimate interests of the people controlling the data and the people on whom data is held (i.e., data subjects)". European Commission Press Release: IP/95/822, Council Definitively Adopts Directive on Protection of Personal Data, 25 July 1995 (visited 3 March 2005), at http://www.privacy.org/pi/intl_orgs/ec/dp_EC_press_release.txt.

122 United States Department of Commerce, "Safe Harbor Privacy Principles" (visited 2 March 2005), at http://www.export.gov/safeharbor/shprinciplesfinal.htm.

information-based world economy, there is an increased danger that personal information will be misused or abused. Increasingly, the digital economy poses a risk that personally identifiable information is inaccurate or is intentionally misused by third-party cybercriminals. They note how the private/public split has become a false dichotomy with the distinction between commercial and government uses of personal information becoming blurred, increasing the possibility of the invasion of privacy and the loss of individual rights.

Few sectors of the American economy adhered to the minimum data protection principles which threatened to shut down large portions of the global information economy.[123] The United States Commerce Department negotiated a "safe harbor" with the EU by agreeing to adhere to reasonable precautions protecting data integrity.[124] Europeans generally find American industry offers insufficient protection for personal data.

The authors call for a transborder legal regime of intellectual property that strikes the correct balance between ensuring sufficient private returns on investment in innovations in exchange for the disclosure and diffusion of those new inventions. Without such a balance, there will be interruptions in data flow that will harm the world system.

1.05   Regulating the Global Internet

(a) Technology-Assisted Surveillance

Sajai Singh, Probier Roy Chowdhury, Armut Joshi, and Govind Naidu begin their chapter by introducing the concept of communications surveillance and its close cousin, physical surveillance. To understand the law of surveillance, one must understand cultural as well as technological developments. In the United States, as in Europe, greater surveillance has been justified on the grounds of crime control.

Their chapter examines the various arguments in favor of surveillance and reviews statutes governing surveillance from the United States, the United Kingdom, the EU, Canada, and India. The chapter also examines the objections to surveillance advanced by privacy advocates. Finally, the chapter

---

123 The Europeans were generally satisfied with privacy protection for the personal information of medical patients.

124 The United States is lobbying international organizations to convince them to adopt America's self-regulatory approach to privacy. The United States is participating in the Platform for Privacy Protection (P3P), which is an industry standard developed by the World Wide Web Consortium that will enable visitors to express privacy preferences through their browsers; Third Annual Report, United States Government Working Group on Electronic Commerce (2000), at p. 40.

calls for greater balance between the right to conduct surveillance weighed against the individual right to privacy.

(b) Internet Regulation

Julian Ding attempts a global model of Internet regulation to reconcile the difficult problem of clashing regulatory regimes. He begins with the basic question of who should be the sovereign in cyberspace, the reasons for regulation, and the meaning of regulation. Governments race to regulate the Internet because of market failure, political pressure, and national self-interest. It is a consequence of the system of nation-states that individual regulation is often conflicting, overlapping, or leaves gaps. The decision in *Yahoo!, Inc. v. La Ligue Contre Le Racisme et L'Antisemitisme*[125] highlights the problem of asserting sovereignty in cyberspace.

In that case, Yahoo!, an Internet Service Provider (ISP), convinced a California federal court to declare another Internet-related judgment unenforceable in the United States. Originally, a Paris tribunal directed Yahoo! not to post any items of Nazi memorabilia for sale through its online auction network accessible in France. The United States federal court ruled that the action was not enforceable because it violated public policy protected by the First Amendment. The *Yahoo!* case is perhaps the best-known examples of how the Internet creates the potential for clashing legal norms.

Further international legalization is necessary to facilitate cross-border cooperation, to permit enforceable global jurisdiction, to collect monetary judgments, to enjoin defendants in off-shore havens, to pierce corporate veils designed to frustrate accountability, to harmonize dispute settlement systems, and to generally construct a supranational cyberspace law. The advanced-core industrial nations have entered an information age in which the entertainment and software industries are displacing the durable goods economy as a primary source of wealth and power. Information is the chief commodity of the new economy.

"Digital information can be perfectly copied and instantaneously transmitted around the world, leading many content producers to view the Internet as one giant, out-of-control copy machine."[126] The information revolution has helped propel the field of intellectual property from a sleepy backwater of esoteric specialization into the center of public policy debates. The shape of intellectual property law will determine the ultimate winners and losers in

---

125 *Yahoo!, Inc. v. La Ligue Contre Le Racisme et L'Antisemitisme*, 169 FSupp. 2d 1181 (N.D. Cal., 2001).
126 Shapiro and Varian, *Information Rules, A Strategic Guide to the Networked Economy* (1998), at p. 4.

the world Internet economy. Global stakeholders are engaged in a protracted conflict over who shall determine the rules, norms, and decision-making processes for extracting value from consumers.

1.06   Conclusion

Internet law does not descend from the cyber heavens in the form of stone tablets.[127] It is a field more accountable to Darwin than to Newton, in that it is responsive to the felt needs of the networked world and continues to be in the process of becoming, rather than appearing against, a fixed horizon.

This volume confirms that the Internet is in the process of rapid legalization. The choices courts and legislatures make and the future they are forging will determine the path of global Internet law. The external view of the Internet as a network of users, and the internal view of cyberspace as a virtual reality, are competing models that offer insights for legal solutions to new problems. By considering both perspectives, it will be possible to forge new material and metaphoric tools to define the meaning of harm, property, premises, and persons in the information based world system.[128]

All of the core countries are facing functionally equivalent legal dilemmas: the protection of databases, illegal copying of computer games, software, the deep linking of websites, and the regulation of Internet lotteries, the privacy rights of ordinary citizens, the publicity rights of celebrities on the Internet. Courts throughout the core nations are grappling with the issue of whether mass-market licenses, such as click-wrap or shrink-wrap licenses, should be enforced and under what conditions.

What we know from the chapters in this volume is that no one core country can regulate the Internet or impose its norms on the semi-periphery and the periphery. The unilateral imposition of law will have a short and unhappy life, much like hatching sea turtles are devoured by everything from birds to mammals on shore and fish in the oceans.

The Internet, by its very nature, is multi- and trans- and inter-national, and it will require new global approaches to solutions, like those suggested in many of the chapters in this volume. One-billion Internet users worldwide will be online by the end of 2005, and the value of e-commerce was estimated to reach as high as US $2.3-billion in 2002 and US $3.9-billion by the

---

127 The authors are updating the famous Legal Realist aphorism of Felix Cohen. Cohen, "Transcendental Nonsense and the Functional Approach", 35 *Colum. L. Rev.* 809, at p. 834 (1935).

128 Frischmann, "The Prospect of Reconciling Internet and Cyberspace", 35 *Loyola U. Chicago L.J.* 205 (2003).

end of 2003.[129] The future path of Internet law will require greater convergence between the law of the core countries and a concerted effort to include the less-developed countries in law formation.

One possibility drawn from history, which would validate Maitland's original insight that we began with, might be to turn to the idea of the informal "law merchant" tradition, as a model of an original source of Internet law from which to analogize solutions on an *ad hoc* basis to particular problems. The law-merchant tradition, or *lex mercatoria*, refers to the customary rules and standards that apply universally to international trade.[130] The medieval fair was a precursor to the marketplace of towns, which is a precursor to the cross-border and virtual Internet marketplace.

A historical continuity between the medieval piepowder courts and Internet law can be drawn. Just as the law merchant was the source of law for negotiable instruments, bills of lading, warehouse receipts, and other commercial law devices, a new global law merchant must search for solutions for e-commerce, and do so quickly and satisfactorily to all. The advantage of the *lex mercatoria* of the medieval period was its speed, flexibility, and ability to decide disputes that crossed territorial borders. The new *lex mercatoria* of cyberspace must serve the same function for a future model for legalization.

Forging a transnational commercial law for cyberspace is necessary because of the great changes wrought by technology today, and is possible because of the same changes, that is, "practitioners and academics have at their disposal, by means of the internet, a highly accessible online working tool".[131] Indeed, online dispute resolution already exists to meet the needs of parties who cannot have access to the same court.[132]

The law of cyberspace requires a body of law with instant and easy access to its contents at any time and everywhere over the world.[133] The law of the global information economy must not be a treasure trove crammed full of useless legal artifacts preserving the past like a fly in amber.[134] Global information law must be a living law that takes into account radically different cultures and legal systems, and the radically different medium of the Internet, and the radically different experience offered us by cyberspace.

---

129 Reuters, "Internet, E-Commerce Boom Despite Slump" (visited 13 February 2005), at http://economictimes.indiatimes.com/cms.dll/xml/comp/articleshow?artid=28739383.

130 Trakman, *The Law Merchant: The Evolution of Commercial Law* (1983).

131 Berger, "Lex Mercatoria Online: The Central Transnational Law Database", at http://www.tldb.de.

132 Katsch and Rifkin, *Online Dispute Resolution: Resolving Disputes in Cyberspace* (2001); Rule, *Online Dispute Resolution for Business* (2002).

133 Berger, "Lex Mercatoria Online: The Central Transnational Law Database", at http://www.tldb.de.

134 Gilmore, "On the Difficulties of Codifying Commercial Law", 57 *Yale L.J.* 1341, at p. 1342 (1948).

CHAPTER 2

DATA PROTECTION AND TRANSBORDER DATA FLOWS: BALANCING PROPRIETARY AND PRIVACY RIGHTS

David C. Gryce and Roxanne A. Esch
Arent Fox, PLLC
Washington, D.C., United States

2.01   Introduction

(a) In General

The tremendous increase in transborder data flows and the existence of international data banks which are used in everything from the processing of the most mundane daily tasks to the creation of the most advanced information products reflects the increasing dependence on digital information resources. They also highlight the need for harmonization of national policies seeking to encourage the unencumbered flow of information and the need to balanced proprietary rights in the data against the right to restrict the collection, processing, and dissemination of data that is of a personal nature.[1]

The free flow of information is important because it diffuses, throughout the world, innovative ideas and technology — two critical ingredients of economic growth.[2] Through human endeavor, these two ingredients are

---

1   Organization for Economic Cooperation and Development, Council Recommendation Concerning Guidelines Governing the Protection of Privacy and Transborder Flows of Personal Data, 20 *I.L.M.* 422, at p. 430.

2   "The New Economy: Beyond Hype — The OECD Growth Project", 2001 *Gen. Econ. & Future Stud.* 9, at p. 41 (July 2001).

transformed into new innovations and technological developments, forming the primary fuel for future development.[3]

National policies must encourage and support the development and diffusion of new innovations throughout the world economy, and one of the primary ways policy makers can ensure the generation and gain of new knowledge is by establishing proper incentives for innovation, such as those created through intellectual property rights regimes.[4]

While the Organization for Economic Cooperation and Development (OECD) recognized early on that national policies should establish standards along with incentives for innovation, it also recognized the value of and began establishing guidelines for the protection of privacy in the context of transborder flows of personal data. The OECD is made up of:

> 30 member countries [who share] a commitment to democratic government and the market economy . . . . With active relationships with some 70 other countries, NGOs, and civil society, it has a global reach . . . . The OECD produces internationally agreed instruments, decisions and recommendations to promote rules of the game in areas where multilateral agreement is necessary for individual countries to make progress in a globalize economy . . . . For more than 40 years, the OECD has been one of the world's largest and most reliable sources of comparable statistical, economic and social data. OECD databases span areas as diverse as national accounts, economic indicators, the labor force, trade, employment, migration, education, energy, health, industry, taxation, tourism and the environment . . . . Non-members are invited to subscribe to OECD agreements and tre aties, and the Organization shares expertise and exchanges views on topics of mutual concern with more than 100 countries worldwide, from Brazil, China and Russia to least developed countries in Africa . . . . The OECD grew out of the Organization for European Economic Cooperation (OEEC), which was set up in 1947 with support from the United States and Canada to coordinate the Marshall Plan for the reconstruction of Europe after World War II. Created as an economic counterpart to NATO, the OECD took over from the OEEC in 1961 and, since then, its mission has been to help governments achieve sustainable economic growth and employment and rising standards of living in member countries while maintaining financial stability, so contributing to the development of the world economy.

The Organization for Economic Cooperation and Development (2005), at www.oecd.org/about.

---

3   "Information and Communications Technologies, OECD Information Technology Outlook 2004: Highlights", 2004 *Sci. & Info. Tech.* 15 (December 2004).

4   "The New Economy: Beyond Hype — The OECD Growth Project", 2001 *Gen. Econ. & Future Stud.* 9, at pp. 41 and 42 (July 2001).

These guidelines establish minimum standards for the protection of privacy and individual liberties with respect to personal data and aim to reduce the differences among domestic rules and practices of countries. These standards also promote the economic interests of countries by encouraging data flows while preventing undue interference with such flows from personal data protection schemes.[5]

Figure 1. Balancing Proprietary and Privacy Rights: Who Can Claim a Right?

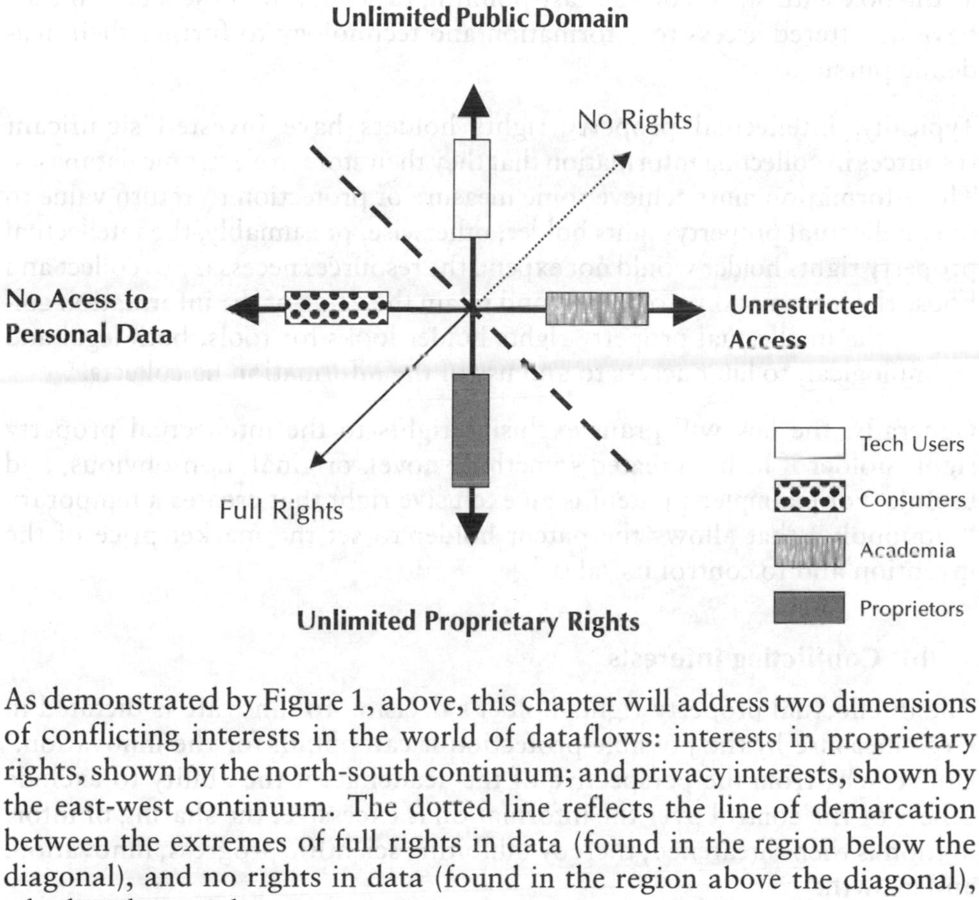

Unlimited Public Domain

No Rights

No Acess to
Personal Data

Unrestricted
Access

Tech Users

Consumers

Academia

Proprietors

Full Rights

Unlimited Proprietary Rights

As demonstrated by Figure 1, above, this chapter will address two dimensions of conflicting interests in the world of dataflows: interests in proprietary rights, shown by the north-south continuum; and privacy interests, shown by the east-west continuum. The dotted line reflects the line of demarcation between the extremes of full rights in data (found in the region below the diagonal), and no rights in data (found in the region above the diagonal), whether those rights are proprietary in nature or pertain to privacy.

For purposes of this illustration, four basic constituencies can be identified, although no group reflects a simple, pure interest. The easiest constituency to identify is the proprietors of technology, as intellectual property rights holders, who are shown as the fully shaded box on the south-pointing ray. Their

5   Organization for Economic Cooperation and Development, Council Recommendation Concerning Guidelines Governing the Protection of Privacy and Transborder Flows of Personal Data, 20 *I.L.M.* 422, at p. 435.

interest is in having unlimited proprietary rights. Another easy group to identify is consumers, who are shown as the dotted white box on the west-pointing ray. Their interest is in having maximum protection for their personal data.

The third group consists of users (and not proprietors) of technology, shown as the white box on the north-pointing ray. They flourish in an unlimited public domain, as they have no claim to or desire to encounter vested interests in rights in the technology they use. The final group, academia, is shown as the box with stripes on the east-pointing ray. They are best served if they have unfettered access to information and technology to further their academic pursuits.

Typically, intellectual property rights holders have invested significant resources in collecting information that they then store in electronic databases. The information must achieve some measure of protection to return value to the intellectual property rights holder; otherwise, presumably, the intellectual property rights holder would not expend the resources necessary to collect and house the information. To protect and retain the value of the information collected, the intellectual property rights holder looks for tools, both legal and technological, to limit access to and use of the information he collects.

Generally, the law will grant exclusive rights to the intellectual property rights holder if he has created something novel, original, non-obvious, and useful.[6] For example, a patent is an exclusive right that creates a temporary "monopoly" that allows the patent holder to set the market price of the invention and to control its sales.[7]

(b) Conflicting Interests

The intellectual property rights holder's decision to innovate is dictated in large measure by the possible protection it can obtain for the innovation.[8] Conversely, from the perspective of the academic, if the ability to exclude others or the control over the information is excessive, the sharing of information is then threatened, thereby inhibiting scientific progress, innovation, and growth.[9]

---

6   Report of the Department of Justice's Task Force on Intellectual Property, United States Department of Justice, Office of the Attorney General, at p. 1 (October 2004).

7   "Patents and Innovation: Trends and Policy Challenges", 2004 *Sci. & Info.* Tech. 4, at p. 9 (2004).

8   "The New Economy: Beyond Hype — The OECD Growth Project", 2001 *Gen. Econ. & Future Stud.* 9, at p. 43 (July 2001).

9   "The New Economy: Beyond Hype — The OECD Growth Project", 2001 *Gen. Econ. & Future Stud.* 9, at p. 44 (July 2001).

With respect to the consumer, or the individual, the Privacy Commissioner for British Columbia, Canada, has identified four tensions created by trends in data flows, namely:

1. Partly because there is no international consensus on the fundamental principles on which the protection of the individual should be based,[10] technology's impact on data management has driven public policy on privacy when, arguably, public policy should drive the data management methods employed.

2. Without consistent privacy regimes, regulating the use of personal information once it crosses borders is virtually impossible.

3. As the world's reliance on digitally stored, analyzed, and accessed personal information increases, so does the risk that the information is inaccurate, that the information will be used out of context, or that the information will simply be misused, whether intentionally or not.

4. The distinction between commercial and government uses of personal information is becoming blurred and will increase the risks to privacy and to other individual rights and interests.[11]

However, when information is viewed at a macro or collective level, and not as individual records, concerns for personal privacy may give way to other concerns about affording collectors of information a reward for the sweat of their brow and encouraging the free flow of information for the betterment of society. These social forces are the underpinnings of intellectual property rights — the *quid pro quo*. Rights in intellectual property should strike a balance between ensuring sufficient private returns on investment in innovations in exchange for the disclosure and diffusion of those new inventions.[12]

Through this exchange, human endeavor flourishes. Innovators are inspired by new ideas or artistic visions, and those inspirations lead to the creation of new works, such as books and music, or inventions for the nation's benefit.[13]

Yet, if there is unequal access to new technology or the tools to learn how to use technology effectively, this exchange is no longer what society has

---

10 Organization for Economic Cooperation and Development, Council Recommendation Concerning Guidelines Governing the Protection of Privacy and Transborder Flows of Personal Data, 20 *I.L.M.* 422, at p. 430 (1981).

11 Report on the Privacy and the USA Patriot Act; Implications for the British Columbia Public Sector Outsourcing, Information and Privacy Commissioner for British Columbia, at p. 14, (October 2004).

12 "The New Economy: Beyond Hype — The OECD Growth Project", 2001 *Gen. Econ. & Future Stud.* 9, at p. 43 (July 2001).

13 Report of the Department of Justice's Task Force on Intellectual Property, United States Department of Justice, Office of the Attorney General, at p. 1 (October 2004).

bargained for. Such inequality has become a matter of major policy concern because a knowledge and technology divide could lead to whole segments of society becoming less and less capable of participating in the economy.[14]

Additionally, disparities in national legislation could hamper the flow of personal data across borders. Restrictions on these information flows could cause serious disruption in important sectors of the economy, such as banking and insurance. Data flows in these industries have greatly increased in recent years, and further increase is anticipated due to the widespread introduction of new computer and communications technologies.[15] At the governmental level, countries have a common interest in policy harmonization to prevent the creation of locations where national regulations on data processing can be circumvented easily.[16] Without harmonization, transborder data flows will confront inconsistent barriers, creating technological vacuums.

When societies and cultures are open and subject to the free flow of data, the markets available to innovators and consumers increase, as does diffusion of knowledge, technologies, and new business practices. Furthermore, the international mobility of people and goods in commerce reinforces the need for consistent practices with regard to the processing of personal data.[17]

This is especially true in light of the advent of the Internet. Globally, the Internet supports critical infrastructures such as energy, transportation, and finance and causes the world to be interconnected by allowing information to flow easily across national borders.[18] Harmonization of the opposing interests of intellectual property rights and the public domain, personal privacy, and the free flow of data requires a balance of the elements shown in Figure 1 and described above, whereby harmonization becomes greatest at the center point.

---

14   "The New Economy: Beyond Hype — The OECD Growth Project", 2001 *Gen. Econ. & Future Stud.* 9, at p. 67 (July 2001).

15   Organization for Economic Cooperation and Development, Council Recommendation Concerning Guidelines Governing the Protection of Privacy and Transborder Flows of Personal Data, 20 *I.L.M.* 422, at p. 427 (1981).

16   Organization for Economic Cooperation and Development, Council Recommendation Concerning Guidelines Governing the Protection of Privacy and Transborder Flows of Personal Data, 20 *I.L.M.* 422, at p. 431 (1981).

17   Organization for Economic Cooperation and Development, Council Recommendation Concerning Guidelines Governing the Protection of Privacy and Transborder Flows of Personal Data, 20 *I.L.M.* 422, at p. 431 (1981).

18   "Organization for Economic Cooperation and Development, Guidelines for the Security of Information Systems and Networks", 2002 *Sci. & Info. Tech.* 9 at p. 7 (2002).

2.02   Framework for Discussion

(a) In General

Data is generally defined as representations of information or concepts in any form.[19] A subset of data is personal data, which refers to any information relating to an identified or identifiable individual.[20]

The transmission or movement of personal data across national borders is referred to as transborder flows of personal data.[21] Laws that regulate transborder flows of personal data are known as data protection, or privacy protection, laws.[22]

The flow of data and the subsequent analysis of that data are critical to the information and communication technology sector, which plays a pivotal role in the world economy.[23] The information and communication technology sector comprises manufacturing and services industries that capture, transmit, and display data and information electronically and is the portion of the global economy that best measures the use of data and transborder data flows.[24]

(b) Data Mining

One type of analysis that is performed on data is called "data mining". Data mining is:

> . . . the application of database technology and techniques to uncover patterns and relationships in data and to undertake the prediction of future results or behaviour.[25]

---

19 Personal Information Protection and Electronic Documents Act, ch. 5, S.C. 31 (1) (2000) (Can.).

20 Organization for Economic Cooperation and Development, Council Recommendation Concerning Guidelines Governing the Protection of Privacy and Transborder Flows of Personal Data, 20 *I.L.M.* 422, at p. 423 (1981).

21 Organization for Economic Cooperation and Development, Council Recommendation Concerning Guidelines Governing the Protection of Privacy and Transborder Flows of Personal Data, 20 *I.L.M.* 422, at p. 423 (1981).

22 Organization for Economic Cooperation and Development, Council Recommendation Concerning Guidelines Governing the Protection of Privacy and Transborder Flows of Personal Data, 20 *I.L.M.* 422, at pp. 422 and 424 (1981).

23 "The New Economy: Beyond Hype — The OECD Growth Project", 2001 *Gen. Econ. & Future Stud.* 9, at p. 3 (July 2001).

24 "Measuring the Information Economy 2002: The ICT Sector", 2002 *Sci. & Info. Tech.* 14, at p. 81 (2002). Gray *et. al.*, "Memorandum on the Legal Need for H.R. 3261, the Database and Collections of Information Misappropriation Act", 21 No. 5 *Comp. & Internet L.* 2 (2004).

25 Report on the Privacy and the USA Patriot Act; Implications for the British Columbia Public Sector Outsourcing, Information and Privacy Commissioner for British Columbia, at p. 14 (October 2004).

The "raw" data that is collected and any subsequent data generated through processing techniques, such as data mining, are then stored in data banks.

Indeed, data mining can be used to:

> . . . discover previously unknown facts and phenomena about a database, answering questions users did not know to ask. They carry out the analysis without receiving a hypothesis from the human analyst, instead searching for hidden patterns on their own . . . mak[ing] predictions about future data.[26]

Data banks are collections of data intended for retrieval and other purposes.[27] In non-technical terms, a database connotes any electronic compilation of data that is organized and indexed in a way that allows users to access, retrieve, and query data efficiently.[28] While the compilation and production of information contained in databases is expensive, the electronic form of the data coupled with digital technology make it cheap to copy.[29] Furthermore, despite the expense associated with compiling data, data alone does not qualify for legal protection through intellectual property rights regimes.

(c) Proprietary and Privacy Rights

The recognition of data in intellectual property rights schemes fuels debates on the essence of proprietary rights. The achievement of intellectual property rights status requires that certain conditions be met or bargains struck — the *quid pro quo*. Of all intellectual property rights, the ones considered most potent are those granted to holders of patents. Patents are granted for an invention that is novel, non-obvious, and industrially applicable and are awarded to:

> . . . [w]hoever invents or discovers any new and useful process, machine, manufacture, or composition of matter, or any new and useful improvement thereof . . . .[30]

Patents promote the useful art and, as such, cannot be granted for some types of newly discovered substances, theories, abstract ideas, or laws of nature because doing so takes away from the public body of knowledge and would

---

26 Zarsky, "Mine Your Own Business!: Making the Case for the Implications of the Data Mining of Personal Information in the Forum of Public Opinion", 5 *Yale L.J.* 4 (2002).

27 Organization for Economic Cooperation and Development, Council Recommendation Concerning Guidelines Governing the Protection of Privacy and Transborder Flows of Personal Data, 20 *I.L.M.* 422, at p. 430 (1981).

28 Greenbaum, "The Database Debate: In Support of an Inequitable Solution", 13 *Alb. L.J. S.C.I & Tech.* 431, at p. 441 (2003).

29 Gibson, "Re-Reifying Data", 80 *Notre Dame L. Rev.* 163, at p. 164 (2004).

30 35 United States Code, section 101.

unnecessarily grant a patent holder the right to constrict the flow of information. Once granted, the patent holder has the legal authority to exclude others from commercially exploiting the invention for the limited period of time of the grant, generally 20 years.[31]

In return for the legal authority to exclude others, the patent holder must disclose information relating to the invention for which protection is granted. The patent holder's disclosure of the invention's details in exchange for a grant of legal authority is thus an important aspect of the patenting system *quid pro quo*.[32]

This exchange both encourages the development of inventions and the practical application of those inventions by making the invention available to the rest of the industry and the general public from which to learn. The diffusion of inventions under this type legal framework leads to greater innovation that ultimately impacts and increases economic performance on a national scale.[33]

A similar framework exists for copyrights, another form of intellectual property rights. As with patents, copyrights make an author's work exclusive, which provides an incentive to incur the costs of producing or creating the work, so long as these costs are less than or equal to the value that consumers, or the marketplace, put on the work.[34]

However, data and facts are the building blocks for subsequent inventions or works and are too useful to restrict access to them through property rights.[35] From the perspective of the public domain, facts are valuable components of future works and should be available and free for all to use.[36] As summarized by the United States Supreme Court:

> . . . [t]he economic philosophy behind the clause empowering Congress to grant patents and copyrights is the conviction that encouragement of individual effort by personal gain is the best way to advance public welfare through the talents of authors and inventors in science and useful art.[37]

Under this philosophy, databases are copyrightable in the United States as compilations of information that consist of data that have been processed

---

31   Schwartz, *Patent Law and Practice* (4th ed., 2003), at p. 65.

32   *Organization for Economic Cooperation and Development, Compendium of Patent Statistics* (2004), at http://www.oecd.org/dataoecd/60/ 24/8208325.pdf, at p. 7 (2004).

33   *Organization for Economic Cooperationd and Development, Compendium of Patent Statistics* (2004), at http://www.oecd.org/dataoecd/60/24/ 8208325.pdf, at p. 7 (2004).

34   Green, "Copyrighting Facts", 78 *Ind. L.J.* 919, at p. 925 (2003).

35   Green, "Copyrighting Facts", 78 *Ind. L.J.* 919, at p. 921 (2003).

36   Green, "Copyrighting Facts", 78 *Ind. L.J.* 919, at p. 922 (2003).

37   *Mazer v. Stein*, 347 U.S. 201, at p. 219 (1954).

along with the original data elements, or pre-existing information that was collected.[38] To qualify for copyright protection, the work must demonstrate originality and creative authorship as prerequisites to copyright protection, as opposed to depending on the industrious effort, i.e., sweat of the brow, or commercial value standards.[39] Therefore, copyright protection does not extend to facts or ideas, regardless of the effort or expense incurred in obtaining them.[40] Derived from this concept is "one of the most pervasive and oft-cited principles in copyright law" — copyright protects the expression of an idea, but not the idea itself.[41] The level of proprietary rights in data, therefore, is dependent on the amount and type of processing that is done to the data after it is collected.

A slightly different philosophy has been implemented in Europe. There, European Union (EU) Directives have established a database right that is measured in terms "of its own kind", or *sui generis*, and not by the creative additions made by the author. This database right is determined by the level of investment in the database and is designed to protect the investment from those who wish to take advantage of its value, whether the information itself, its accuracy, or its completeness, without compensating the database owner.[42]

An effective adjunct to these rights is the notion of trade secrecy, whereby the maintenance of the secret nature of information affords the holder a real or potential economic advantage. Rights of trade secret holders against misappropriation is a fundamental intellectual property right in the world of data collectors and databases and an alternative to the *quid pro quo* of patent and copyright rights, so long as the confidentiality of the information remains intact.

Although the assumption from an intellectual property rights perspective is that data, without more, does not satisfy the requirements necessary for a patent, copyright, *sui generis* right, or trade secret protection and is freely

---

38 Leaffer, *Understanding Copyright Law* (3d ed., 1999), at pp. 68 and 73. 17 United States Code, section 101 ("A compilation is a work formed by the collection and assembling of pre-existing materials or of data that are selected, coordinated, or arranged in such a way that the resulting work as a whole constitutes an original work of authorship").

39 Leaffer, *Understanding Copyright Law* (3d ed., 1999), at pp. 56 and 64, citing *Feist Publications, Inc. v. Rural Telephone Service Co.*, 499 U.S. 340 (1991). 17 United States Code, section 102 ("[c]opyright protection subsists . . . in original works of authorship").

40 17 United States Code, section 102(b) ("In no case does copyright protection for an original work of authorship extend to any idea . . .").

41 Leaffer, *Understanding Copyright Law* (3d ed., 1999), at p. 77.

42 Stephens, "Database Rights: A Surprise Judgment by the European Court of Justice", 18 *World Intell. Prop. Rep.* 12 (1 December 2004).

available to all; however, from a privacy rights perspective, those about whom the data pertain may nonetheless prohibit the free distribution and access to data containing personal information. Indeed, the amount of processing done to data raises concerns about the impact of information technology on privacy.[43] One such concern is that:

> The hidden patterns and subtle relationships that data mining detects are recorded and become personal information about the individual whose characteristics or habits are being searched and analyzed.[44]

While the right to privacy is not absolute, the increased international flow of personal information from both the private and the public sectors has triggered nations to reevaluate privacy protections. As early as the 1970s, European countries began enacting the first privacy laws in response to the increased collection, processing, and subsequent transborder flow of data.[45] These laws have now seen their maturation in the EU Data Protection Directive and similar laws, such as the Personal Information Protection and Electronic Documents Act of Canada.

(d) The Expanding Market for Information

Concurrently, advances in technology and trade liberalization have increased the market for information products and services.[46] For example, data-management companies compete to offer technology and services for storing, organizing, and accessing information.

Governments are following the lead of corporations and are contracting out data processing and other data services formerly done in-house.[47] This leads inexorably back to the axes of Figure 1 — the goal of harmonization is to tame the tensions of antipodal interests through the intellectual property rights *quid pro quo* and to balanc the personal right to privacy with the gains to be derived from data compilations and analysis.

---

43 Report on Privacy and the USA Patriot Act; Implications for the British Columbia Public Sector Outsourcing, Information and Privacy Commissioner for British Columbia, at p. 12 (October 2004).

44 Report on Privacy and the USA Patriot Act; Implications for the British Columbia Public Sector Outsourcing, Information and Privacy Commissioner for British Columbia, at p. 14 (October 2004).

45 Report on Privacy and the USA Patriot Act; Implications for the British Columbia Public Sector Outsourcing, Information and Privacy Commissioner for British Columbia, at p. 13 (October 2004).

46 Lipton, "Balancing Private Rights and Public Policies: Reconceptualizing Property in Databases", 18 *Berkeley Tech. L.J.* 773, at pp. 779–783 (2003).

47 Report on Privacy and the USA Patriot Act; Implications for the British Columbia Public Sector Outsourcing, Information and Privacy Commissioner for British Columbia at pp. 12 and 13 (October 2004).

2.03   The Value of Data

(a) In General

Data has tremendous value, as reflected in the wide range of information products it has spawned. Examples of information products based on personal data include statistics on consumer spending habits and health, insurance, or financial status. Other products are based on factual data, such as scientific, technological, or educational information. Often databases derive their value directly from the commercial value of the business, such as when they form the core of a company's business operations, as they do in travel planning, stock brokering, and online shopping.[48]

Additionally, if the database qualifies for legal protection under intellectual property rights regimes, the database is transformed from an intangible electronic asset into an exclusive property right with independent market value because it can be licensed, mortgaged, or leveraged to obtain financing for other business ventures.[49]

Physical assets no longer necessarily represent the bulk of the value of a company. "Increasingly, and largely as a result of the information technologies revolution and the growth of the service economy, companies are realizing that intangible assets are often becoming more valuable than their physical assets."[50] Now, the development and application of intellectual property rights are "the keys to greater competitiveness in fiercely competitive markets."[51]

With respect to markets for information products, there are other competitive forces at play. The data contained within the information products and in databases are a mixture of public and private interests, as demonstrated by Figure 1. Those who seek to exploit the databases commercially value the private property rights in databases. Those whose consumer spending habits are contained in the database value their individual privacy above the intellectual property rights holder's right to exploit the database, while those in academia who seek answers and explanations to life's mysteries value the data for its research and teaching potential.[52]

---

48 Lipton, "Balancing Private Rights and Public Policies: Reconceptualizing Property in Databases", 18 *Berkeley Tech. L.J.* 773, at p. 775 (2003).

49 *Intellectual Property for Business*, World Intellectual Property Organization, Small and Medium-Sized Enterprises Division, at pp. 6 and 15 (2005).

50 *Intellectual Property for Business*, World Intellectual Property Organization, Small and Medium-Sized Enterprises Division, at p. 5 (2005).

51 *Intellectual Property for Business*, World Intellectual Property Organization, Small and Medium-Sized Enterprises Division, at p. 5 (2005).

52 Lipton, "Balancing Private Rights and Public Policies: Reconceptualizing Property in Databases", 18 *Berkeley Tech. L.J.* 773, at pp. 779 and 780 (2003).

(b) Impact of the Internet on Value

The World Intellectual Property Organization (WIPO) predicted that, since most literary and artistic works can be digitized or are created digitally, the Internet would be the logical way to access them.[53]

The WIPO further predicted that the Internet would become an immense library of all existing works where creators worldwide would have available, at their discretion, the building blocks to create new works. In building new works, authors then simply revise and combine existing works in new ways.[54] This is the "big bang" theory of cyberspace, where masses of digital works swirling over electronic networks become the breeding ground for explosions in global intellect.

(c) Sales of Intellectual Property Rights

Another way to value data is by sales of intellectual property rights. In 2002, United States copyright industries accounted for an estimated six per cent of the nation's Gross Domestic Product, or US $626.6-billion), and sold and exported US $89.3-billion to foreign nations.[55]

Additionally, in the fourth quarter of 2002 alone, the United States had more than US $14-billion in retail e-commerce[56] sales, which was more than 1.6 per cent of retail sales.[57] E-commerce and the sale of intellectual property rights are considered part of the information and communication technology sector.[58]

In general, firms have benefited from increased productivity resulting from the use of information and communication technology. Recent surveys show that 24 per cent of businesses in Japan use information and communication technology, followed by 20 per cent in Canada, 17 per cent in the United

---

53 Electronic Commerce and Copyright: A Key Role for WIPO, World Intellectual Property Organization, Advisory Committee on Management of Copyright and Related Rights in Global Information Networks, at section II(1) (1999).

54 Electronic Commerce and Copyright: A Key Role for WIPO, World Intellectual Property Organization, Advisory Committee on Management of Copyright and Related Rights in Global Information Networks, at section II(1) (1999).

55 Report of the Department of Justice's Task Force on Intellectual Property, United States Department of Justice, Office of the Attorney General, at p. 7 (October 2004).

56 "Measuring the Information Economy 2002: The ICT Sector", 2002 *Sci. & Info. Tech.* 14, at p. 89 (2002) (e-commerce is narrowly defined as an Internet transaction that consists of the sale or purchase of goods or services between any two entities conducted over the Internet, though the payment and ultimate delivery of the good or service may be conducted off-line).

57 Seizing the Benefits of ICT in a Digital Economy, Meeting of the OECD Council at Ministerial Level, at p. 6, fig. 1 (2003).

58 "Measuring the Information Economy 2002: The ICT Sector", 2002 *Sci. & Info. Tech.* 14, at pp. 81 and 82 (2002).

States and Korea, and 14 per cent in Germany and Ireland.[59] In this sector, scientific and technological advances have resulted from waves of innovation that are centered less on individual firms and more on global networks of information products and databanks.[60]

(d) Value through Grants of Intellectual Property Rights

Another means to value data from the perspective of the government is by measuring the number of intellectual property rights grants made. A primary measure of innovation and technology output are patents, because they presumably reflect inventive performance. Since part of the intellectual property rights grant includes disclosure of information about the patent, patents also indicate the level of diffusion of knowledge across technology areas and countries.[61] Worldwide, the total number of patents has grown by more than four per cent per year since 1985, with 44,000 patents with a priority date in 2000.[62]

The number of patents takes into account filings in different countries for substantially the same claims.[63] The priority date is the date closest to the date of invention.[64] Using the priority date removes the bias that the application or grant dates introduce, which are associated with administrative delay and a prosecution strategy, neither of which reflect technology output.[65]

In addition, there is a time lag between the priority date and the availability of the application or grant information.[66] In 2002, more than 850,000 patent applications were filed in Europe, Japan, and the United States, up from approximately 600,000 in 1992. Between 1992 and 2002, the number of patent applications filed in Europe, Japan, and the United States increased by more than 40 per cent.[67]

---

59   ICT Access Now, Widespread but Laggard Users Risk New Digital Divide, Warns OECD, Seizing the Benefits of Information and Communication Technology in a Digital Economy, Meeting of the OECD Council at Ministerial Level, at p. 6, fig.1 (14 December 2004).

60   "Patents and Innovation: Trends and Policy Challenges", 2004 *Sci. & Info. Tech.* 4, at p. 5 (2004).

61   *Organization for Economic Cooperation and Development, Compendium of Patent Statistics* (2004), at http://www.oecd.org/dataoecd/60/24/ 8208325.pdf, at p. 7 (2004).

62   *Organization for Economic Cooperation and Development, Compendium of Patent Statistics* (2004), at http://www.oecd.org/dataoecd/60/24/ 8208325.pdf, at p. 14 (2004).

63   *Organization for Economic Cooperation and Development, Compendium of Patent Statistics* (2004), at http://www.oecd.org/dataoecd/60/24/ 8208325.pdf, p. 11 (2004).

64   *Organization for Economic Cooperation and Development, Compendium of Patent Statistics* (2004), at http://www.oecd.org/dataoecd/60/24/ 8208325.pdf, p. 40 (2004).

65   *Organization for Economic Cooperation and Development, Compendium of Patent Statistics* (2004), at http://www.oecd.org/dataoecd/60/24/ 8208325.pdf, p. 10 (2004).

66   *Organization for Economic Cooperation and Development, Compendium of Patent Statistics* (2004), at http://www.oecd.org/dataoecd/60/24/ 8208325.pdf, p. 40 (2004).

67   *Organization for Economic Cooperation and Development, Compendium of Patent Statistics* (2004), at http://www.oecd.org/dataoecd/60/24/ 8208325.pdf, p. 5 (2004).

(e) Commercial Value of Collection and Use of Data

"The collection and sale of information is an industry worth many billions of dollars a year to American companies and is a primary engine of economic growth."[68] Economic growth in the information and communication technology sector on correlates with increased collection of and uses of personal data. Innovation has become increasingly a collaborative, global process involving a larger number of more diverse actors, primarily involving multinational enterprises.[69] Furthermore, the expansion of information and communication technology and the Internet has accelerated the availability of information and facilitated the globalization of innovation. Businesses, governments, consumers, and key infrastructures increasingly rely on the use of information and communication technology, which are often interconnected at the global level.[70]

The commercial value of personal data, therefore, tracks the value of data in general. Indeed, it may be more valuable, because the data information and communication technology users encounter are guaranteed to contain and rely on personal data. Not surprisingly, as e-commerce transactions have increased, so have consumer complaints regarding security and privacy protection.[71]

Databases and databanks that house all of the data collected and created from transactions and data mining are prone to full-scale misappropriation because the information contained within them is highly vulnerable, in its electronic form, as "[i]nformation, by its very nature, is ubiquitous, inexhaustible, and indivisible".[72]

The digital format of data adds value to the data because computers can then process data on a massive scale, thereby vastly expanding the possibilities of storing, comparing, linking, selecting, and accessing personal data through the combination of computers and telecommunications technologies while facilitating misappropriation. Not surprisingly, then, unauthorized copying of databases has already reached significant levels.[73]

---

68 Green, "Copyrighting Facts", 78 *Ind. L.J.* 919, at p. 923 (2003).

69 *Organization for Economic Cooperation and Development, Compendium of Patent Statistics* (2004), at http://www.oecd.org/dataoecd/60/24/ 8208325.pdf, p. 15 (2004).

70 Seizing the Benefits of ICT in a Digital Economy, Meeting of the OECD Council at Ministerial Level, at p. 18 (2003).

71 Seizing the Benefits of ICT in a Digital Economy, Meeting of the OECD Council at Ministerial Level, at p. 20 (2003).

72 Grosheide, "Database Protection — The European Way", 8 *Wash. U. J.L. & Pol'y* 39, at p. 40 (2002).

73 Green, "Copyrighting Facts", 78 *Ind. L.J.* 919, at p. 923 (2003).

In addition to potentially violating any number of laws, misappropriation leads to public disclosure of the information, after which the information can potentially be used without any obligation to the original intellectual property rights' holder.[74]

Misappropriation of intellectual property rights impacts society in two ways. First, intellectual property theft alters the economic equilibrium of markets and undermines competition. Second, intellectual property theft can impact the health, safety and financial well-being of individuals, for example, through counterfeit products and identify theft.[75]

(f) Counterfeiting

It is estimated that counterfeiting accounts for five per cent to seven per cent of global merchandise trade, equivalent to US $512-billion in lost sales.[76] Worldwide, intellectual property theft is estimated to cost American companies alone US $250-billion a year.[77]

As a direct result of counterfeit products and Internet theft of intellectual property, governments and the economy suffer, for example, from the loss of hundreds of millions of dollars in tax revenues, wages, and investment dollars, not to mention hundreds of thousands of jobs.[78]

(g) Identity Theft

Another risk of the dissemination of personal data in a digital format over the Internet is identity theft. In the United States, identity fraud costs consumers more than US $50-billion.

It is estimated that there are more than 9-million new identity theft victims per year at a cost of more than US $5,500 per victim, who spend on average 28 hours resolving the problems caused by the fraud.[79]

---

74 Grosheide, "Database Protection -—The European Way", 8 *Wash. U. J.L. & Pol'y* 39, at p. 40 (2002).

75 Report of the Department of Justice's Task Force on Intellectual Property, United States Department of Justice, Office of the Attorney General, at p. 7 (October 2004). The report also explains that intellectual property theft has been linked to organized crime and possibly funds terrorism.

76 Balfour, "FAKES! The Global Counterfeit Business is Out of Control, Targeting Everything from Computer Chips to Life-saving Medicines. It's so Bad That Even China May Need to Crack Down", *Business Week*, at p. 56 (2005).

77 Report of the Department of Justice's Task Force on Intellectual Property, United States Department of Justice, Office of the Attorney General, at p. 8 (October 2004).

78 Report of the Department of Justice's Task Force on Intellectual Property, United States Department of Justice, Office of the Attorney General, at p. 8 (October 2004).

79 *Identity Fraud Survey Report* 2005, Better Business Bureau, at p. 3 (2005).

(h) Enforcement

There is a general concern that, because intellectual property crime is lucrative and has immense profit margins, current enforcement methods are inadequate to combat it.[80]

In the face of a dearth of statutory or judicially created property rights in raw data and inconsistent regimes to enforce what rights there are, the value of data has led data collectors to use contracts and technological protections to control information for commercial exploitation.[81]

Risk of theft and misuse is mitigated when there are fair and clear standards for enforcement of laws that protect the various rights and when enforcement efforts are effective and not arbitrary. On a global scale, this requires harmonization. The EU has recognized that "to remove the obstacles to flows of personal data, the level of protection of the rights and freedoms of individuals with regard to the processing of such data must be equivalent" wherever the data goes.[82]

Furthermore, harmonization is vital to the market economy, "especially in view of the scale of the divergences which currently exist between the relevant laws".[83] As such, there needs to be global coordination of the laws "to ensure that the cross-border flow of personal data is regulated in a consistent manner".[84]

2.04 Legal Factors in Protecting Intellectual Property

(a) In General

Intellectual property rights, including patents, copyrights, trade secrets, and trade marks, provide a panoply of tools to protect intellectual property, in general, each variety with its own unique qualities, characteristics, and limitations.

---

80 Report of the Department of Justice's Task Force on Intellectual Property, United States Department of Justice, Office of the Attorney General, at p. 9 (October 2004).

81 Lipton, "Balancing Private Rights and Public Policies: Reconceptualizing Property in Databases", 18 *Berkeley Tech. L.J.* 773, at p. 781 (2003).

82 Directive 95/46/EC of the European Parliament and of the Council on the Protection of Individuals with Regard to the Processing of Personal Data and on the Free Movement of Such Data, 24 October 1995, *O.J.* (L 281/31) 8.

83 Directive 95/46/EC of the European Parliament and of the Council on the Protection of Individuals with Regard to the Processing of Personal Data and on the Free Movement of Such Data, 24 October 1995, *O.J.* (L 281/31) 8.

84 Directive 95/46/EC of the European Parliament and of the Council on the Protection of Individuals with Regard to the Processing of Personal Data and on the Free Movement of Such Data, 24 October 1995, *O.J.* (L 281/31) 8.

The world has seen substantial efforts to harmonize the national treatment of intellectual property rights. In fact, harmonization efforts, in the form of treaties and international agreements, reflect an integral part of the intellectual property rights landscape. Some of the more renowned treaties are discussed below.

(b) Berne Convention

The Berne Convention is the oldest international treaty in the field of copyright, boasting 159 signatories.[85] It aims "to protect, in as effective and uniform a manner as possible the rights of authors in their literary and artistic works",[86] and provides for national treatment, such that works originating in one of the member states are to be given the same protection in each of the member states as those granted to works of their own nationals.[87]

The Berne Convention protects authors of works,[88] which include any original production in the literary, scientific and artistic domain, or derivative

---

85   The Contracting Parties are: Albania, Algeria, Andorra, Antigua and Barbuda, Argentina, Armenia, Australia, Austria, Azerbaijan, Bahamas, Bahrain, Bangladesh, Barbados, Belarus, Belgium, Belize, Benin, Bhutan, Bolivia, Bosnia and Herzegovina, Botswana, Brazil, Bulgaria, Burkina Faso, Cameroon, Canada, Cape Verde, Central African Republic, Chad, Chile, China, Colombia, Comoros, Congo, Costa Rica, Croatia, Cuba, Cyprus, Czech Republic, Côte d'Ivoire, Democratic People's Republic of Korea, Democratic Republic of the Congo, Denmark, Djibouti, Dominica, Dominican Republic, Ecuador, Egypt, El Salvador, Equatorial Guinea, Estonia, Fiji, Finland, France, Gabon, Gambia, Georgia, Germany, Ghana, Greece, Grenada, Guatemala, Guinea, Guinea-Bissau, Guyana, Haiti, Holy See, Honduras, Hungary, Iceland, India, Indonesia, Ireland, Israel, Italy, Jamaica, Japan, Jordan, Kazakhstan, Kenya, Kyrgyzstan, Latvia, Lebanon, Lesotho, Liberia, Libyan Arab Jamahiriya, Liechtenstein, Lithuania, Luxembourg, Madagascar, Malawi, Malaysia, Mali, Malta, Mauritania, Mauritius, Mexico, Micronesia (Federated States of), Monaco, Mongolia, Morocco, Namibia, The Netherlands, New Zealand, Nicaragua, Niger, Nigeria, Norway, Oman, Pakistan, Panama, Paraguay, Peru, Philippines, Poland, Portugal, Qatar, Republic of Korea, Republic of Moldova, Romania, Russian Federation, Rwanda, Saint Kitts and Nevis, Saint Lucia, Saint Vincent and the Grenadines, Saudi Arabia, Senegal, Serbia and Montenegro, Singapore, Slovakia, Slovenia, South Africa, Spain, Sri Lanka, Sudan, Suriname, Swaziland, Sweden, Switzerland, Syrian Arab Republic, Tajikistan, Thailand, The Former Yugoslav Republic of Macedonia, Togo, Tonga, Trinidad and Tobago, Tunisia, Turkey, Ukraine, United Arab Emirates, United Kingdom, United Republic of Tanzania, United States, Uruguay, Uzbekistan, Venezuela, Viet Nam, Zambia, and Zimbabwe. The World Intellectual Property Organization (2005), at http://www.wipo.int/treaties/en/ShowResults.jsp?lang=en&treaty_id=15.

86   "International Treaties and Conventions on Intellectual Property", *World Intellectual Property Organization Intellectual Property Handbook: Policy, Law, and Use*, at p. 262 (quoting Berne Convention preamble).

87   "International Treaties and Conventions on Intellectual Property", *World Intellectual Property Organization Intellectual Property Handbook: Policy, Law, and Use*, at p. 262.

88   Berne Convention, article 3.

works, which are based on other, pre-existing works, such as translations, adaptations, arrangements, or alterations of a literary or artistic work.[89] The Berne Convention establishes minimum standards of protection for the works of authors and the minimum duration of such protection.[90] For example, authors are granted the exclusive right of reproduction in any manner or form and the exclusive right to make adaptations, arrangements, or other alterations of the author's work.[91]

In keeping with its philosophical underpinnings of *quid pro quo*, the Berne Convention also provides limitations on the author's exclusive rights. These exceptions allow for the use of a work, without the owner's authorization and without obligation to pay the owner for the use.[92] Examples of such uses are called "free use" of protected works and include use by way of illustration or teaching purposes and use for the purpose of reporting current events.[93] Examples from the United States are:

1. Necessary copies that are required for operation of a program or a back-up copy;[94]

2. The "first sale doctrine;"[95] and

3. The "fair use" doctrine.[96]

These statutory exceptions are designed to keep the balance between the intellectual property rights holder's exclusive rights and the furtherance of the art.

While the Berne Convention was revised regularly to respond to new technological developments, new treaties were needed as the international norms of the Berne Convention failed to provide adequate guidance for the challenges of new technologies.[97] Under article 20 of the Berne Convention, the countries of the Union may "enter into special agreements among themselves, in so far as such agreements grant to authors more extensive rights than those granted by the

---

89 Berne Convention, article 2.

90 "International Treaties and Conventions on Intellectual Property", *World Intellectual Property Organization Intellectual Property Handbook: Policy, Law, and Use*, at p. 263.

91 Berne Convention, articles 9 and 12.

92 "International Treaties and Conventions on Intellectual Property", *World Intellectual Property Organization Intellectual Property Handbook: Policy, Law, and Use*, at p. 264.

93 Berne Convention, articles 10 and 10 *bis*.

94 17 United States Code, section 117(a).

95 17 United States Code, section 109.

96 17 United States Code, section 107.

97 "International Treaties and Conventions on Intellectual Property", *World Intellectual Property Organization Intellectual Property Handbook: Policy, Law, and Use*, at p. 269.

Convention, or contain other provisions not contrary to th[e] Convention".[98] Through this provision, the WIPO Copyright Treaty of 1996 was created.[99]

(c) World Intellectual Property Organization Copyright Treaty

The WIPO Copyright Treaty applies to computer programs and compilations of data or other material, such as databases, in any form, for which by reason of the selection or arrangement of their contents constitute intellectual creations.[100] In fact, the WIPO Copyright Treaty has "established the new international legal norms for [the] protection of technological measures".[101] Entering into force on 6 March 2002, the WIPO Copyright Treaty is now in force in 51 countries, with more than 20 more signatories.[102] The Director General of WIPO is the depositary of the WIPO Copyright Treaty.[103]

The Treaty addresses:

> . . . the need to introduce new international rules and clarify the interpretation of certain existing rules to provide adequate solutions to the questions raised by new economic, social, cultural and technological developments . . . .[104]

It also recognizes:

> . . . the profound impact of the development and convergence of information and communication technologies on the creation and use of literary and artistic works . . . .[105]

---

98 Berne Convention, article 20.

99 "International Treaties and Conventions on Intellectual Property", *World Intellectual Property Organization Intellectual Property Handbook: Policy, Law, and Use*, at p. 269.

100 World Intellectual Property Organization Copyright Treaty, articles 4 and 5.

101 Current Developments in the Field of Digital Rights Management, World Intellectual Property Organization Standing Committee on Copyright and Related Rights, 1 August 2003, S.C.C.R./10/2, at p. 41.

102 The Contracting Parties are Argentina, Armenia, Austria, Belarus, Belgium, Bolivia, Botswana, Bulgaria, Burkina Faso, Canada, Chile, Colombia, Costa Rica, Croatia, Cyprus, Czech Republic, Denmark, Ecuador, El Salvador, Estonia, European Communities, Finland, France, Gabon, Georgia, Germany, Ghana, Greece, Guatemala, Guinea, Honduras, Hungary, Indonesia, Ireland, Israel, Italy, Jamaica, Japan, Jordan, Kazakhstan, Kenya, Kyrgyzstan, Latvia, Lithuania, Luxembourg, Mali, Mexico, Monaco, Mongolia, Namibia, The Netherlands, Nicaragua, Nigeria, Panama, Paraguay, Peru, Philippines, Poland, Portugal, Republic of Korea, Republic of Moldova, Romania, Saint Lucia, Senegal, Serbia and Montenegro, Singapore, Slovakia, Slovenia, South Africa, Spain, Sweden, Switzerland, The former Yugoslav Republic of Macedonia, Togo, Ukraine, United Arab Emirates, United Kingdom, United States, and Uruguay. WIPO Copyright Treaty, article 20. World Intellectual Property Organization (2005), at http://www.wipo.int/treaties/en/ShowResults.jsp?lang=en&treaty_id=16.

103 World Intellectual Property Organization Copyright Treaty, article 25.

104 World Intellectual Property Organization Copyright Treaty, Preamble.

105 World Intellectual Property Organization Copyright Treaty, Preamble.

Furthermore, the WIPO Copyright Treaty aims to:

> ... maintain a balance between the rights of authors and the larger public interest, particularly education, research and access to information, as reflected in the Berne Convention.[106]

Article 11 of the WIPO Copyright Treaty obliges its signatories, or "contracting parties", to provide legal remedies against the circumvention of technological measures used by authors in connection with the exercise of their rights and against the removal or altering of information, such as certain data that identify works or their authors, which are necessary for the management and distribution of their intellectual property rights.[107] The WIPO Copyright Treaty obliges each contracting party to adopt, in accordance with its legal system, the measures necessary to ensure the application of the WIPO Copyright Treaty.

In particular, the contracting party must ensure that enforcement procedures are available under its law so as to permit effective action against any act of infringement of rights covered by the WIPO Copyright Treaty.[108] Such action must include expeditious remedies to prevent infringement and remedies, which will constitute an effective deterrent to further infringements.[109]

Despite these enhanced enforcement provisions, the WIPO Copyright Treaty remains true to the *quid pro quo* concept. Although it recognizes the "outstanding significance of copyright protection as an incentive for literary and artistic creation",[110] it reaffirms the limits of copyright protection "to expressions and not to ideas, procedures, methods of operation, or mathematical concepts", or raw data.[111]

Furthermore, the WIPO Copyright Treaty allows contracting parties to provide for limitation of or exceptions to the rights granted to authors of literary and artistic works under the treaty in certain special cases that do not conflict with the normal exploitation of the work.[112] These limitations, in conjunction with the limiting language of article 11 of the Treaty, enable the Contracting Parties to allow for exceptions such as fair use by not allowing an author to exercise rights that are beyond those granted by the Berne Convention.[113]

---

106 World Intellectual Property Organization Copyright Treaty, Preamble.
107 World Intellectual Property Organization Copyright Treaty, article 11.
108 World Intellectual Property Organization Copyright Treaty, article 12.
109 World Intellectual Property Organization Copyright Treaty, article 14.
110 World Intellectual Property Organization Copyright Treaty, Preamble.
111 World Intellectual Property Organization Copyright Treaty, article 2.
112 World Intellectual Property Organization Copyright Treaty, article 10.
113 "International Treaties and Conventions on Intellectual Property", *World Intellectual Property Organization Intellectual Property Handbook: Policy, Law, and Use*, at p. 42.

(d)　Trade Related Aspects of Intellectual Property Rights Agreement

Another substantial step in intellectual property rights harmonization occurred when the Trade Related Aspects of Intellectual Property Rights Agreement (TRIPS) came into effect on 1 January 1995. To date, it is the most comprehensive multilateral agreement on intellectual property.[114] The areas of intellectual property that it covers are:

1.　Copyright and related rights (i.e., the rights of performers, producers of sound recordings, and broadcasting organizations);

2.　Trade marks, including service marks;

3.　Geographical indications, including appellations of origin;

4.　Industrial designs;

5.　Patents, including the protection of new varieties of plants;

6.　Layout-designs of integrated circuits; and

7.　Undisclosed information, including trade secrets and test data.[115]

Like the international treaties before it, TRIPS provides for national treatment.[116] TRIPS sets out the minimum standards of protection and the duration of protection to be provided by each member state for the above areas of intellectual property. Furthermore, TRIPS establishes general principles that are applicable to all intellectual property rights enforcement procedures. As a minimum standards agreement, TRIPS allows member states to provide more extensive protection of intellectual property and to determine the appropriate method of implementation of the TRIPS' provisions within national law.[117]

Article 10 of TRIPS addresses computer programs and compilations of data. It "clarifies that databases and other compilations of data or other material shall be protected as such under copyright even where the databases include data that as such are not protected under copyright".[118] Specifically, article 10 states:

> Compilations of data or other material, whether in machine readable or other form, which by reason of the selection or arrangement of their

---

114　There are 148 members of the World Trade Organization.

115　World Trade Organization, at http://www.wto.org/english/tratop_e/trips_e/intel2_e.htm (2005).

116　Trade Related Aspects of Intellectual Property Rights Agreement, article 3. ("Each member shall accord to the nationals of other members treatment no less favorable than that it accords to its own national with regard to the protection of intellectual property").

117　World Trade Organization, at http://www.wto.org/english/tratop_e/trips_e/intel2_e.htm (2005).

118　World Trade Organization, at http://www.wto.org/english/tratop_e/trips_e/intel2_e.htm (2005).

contents constitute intellectual creations shall be protected as such. Such protection, which shall not extend to the data itself, shall be without prejudice to any copyright subsisting in the data or material itself.[119]

TRIPS also provides enhanced protection against unfair competition by protecting undisclosed information, such as trade secrets and know-how, so long as that information is secret, has commercial value because it is secret, and has been subject to reasonable steps to keep it secret.[120]

(e) Paris Convention

Another intellectual property treaty is the Paris Convention, which provides international protection of industrial property within the Union.[121] Industrial property is one category of intellectual property "which includes inventions (patents), trademarks, industrial designs, and geographic indications of source"; the other category of intellectual property is copyright, "which includes literary and artistic works such as novels, poems and plays, films, musical works, artistic works such as drawings, paintings, photographs and sculptures, and architectural designs".[122]

The Paris Convention guarantees the right to national treatment, the right of priority, establishes a number of common rules in the field of substantive law, and establishes the administrative framework to implement the Convention.[123] The industrial property covered by the Paris Convention includes:

1. Patents;

2. Utility models;

3. Industrial designs;

4. Trade marks;

5. Service marks;

6. Trade names; and

7. Indications of source or appellations of origin.[124]

Moreover, the Paris Convention applies not only to industrial property used in commerce and industry, but also to agricultural and extractive industries

---

119 Trade Related Aspects of Intellectual Property Rights Agreement, article 10.

120 Trade Related Aspects of Intellectual Property Rights Agreement, article 39.

121 Paris Convention, article 1(1). ("The countries to which this Convention applies constitute a Union").

122 World Intellectual Property Organization, at http://www.wipo.int/about-ip/en/ (2005).

123 "International Treaties and Conventions on Intellectual Property", *World Intellectual Property Organization Intellectual Property Handbook: Policy, Law, and Use*, at p. 242.

124 Paris Convention, article 1(2).

and to all manufactured or natural products.[125] It establishes protection against direct or indirect use of a false indication of source of the goods or the identity of the producer, manufacturer, or merchant[126] and against any act of competition contrary to honest practices in industrial or commercial matters, or unfair competition.[127]

Under the Paris Convention:

> ... [n]ationals of any country of the Union shall, as regards the protection of industrial property, enjoy in all the other countries of the Union the advantages that their respective laws now grant ... to nationals; all without prejudice to the rights especially provided for by this Convention ... .[128]

This concept of national treatment means that each country that is a party to the Paris Convention must grant the same protection it grants to its own nationals to nationals of other member countries.[129]

This means that there is no requirement of reciprocity.[130] This national treatment rule protects foreigners and guarantees that they will not be discriminated against in any way.[131] In the world of data protection, this means the Paris Convention is at least one antidote for bias based on residence.

(f) European Database Directive

As noted above, in contrast to the United States, the EU provides a *sui generis* right in databases. This right was created by the Database Directive 96/9/EC.[132] The Database Directive protects unoriginal databases in which there has been substantial investment and is distinguished from copyright protection, which grants protection in databases based on the author's own

---

125 Paris Convention, article 1(3).

126 Paris Convention, article 10(1).

127 Paris Convention, article 10 *bis*.

128 Paris Convention, article 2(1).

129 "International Treaties and Conventions on Intellectual Property", *World Intellectual Property Organization Intellectual Property Handbook: Policy, Law, and Use*, at p. 242.

130 "International Treaties and Conventions on Intellectual Property", *World Intellectual Property Organization Intellectual Property Handbook: Policy, Law, and Use*, at p. 243 ("Supposing that a given member country has a longer term of patent protection than another member country: the former country will not have the right to provide that nationals of the latter country will enjoy a term of protection of the same length as the term of protection is in the law of their own country").

131 Paris Convention, article 242.

132 Directive 96/9 EC of the European Parliament and of the Council on the Legal Protection of Databases, 11 March 1996, *O.J.* (L 77/20).

intellectual creation through original selection or arrangement of its contents, i.e.,[133] copyright protects the structure of the database and the *sui generis* right protects the data in the database, irrespective of the copyrightability of the data.[134]

The European Court of Justice has qualified the notion of substantial investment by holding that investment in the creation of the data in the database cannot be considered. Rather, the term "substantial investment in either the obtaining, verification or presentation of the contents" refers to seeking out independent materials and collecting them, ensuring the reliability of the information, monitoring the database for its accuracy, and arranging the data.[135] It is important to note that, unlike copyright, *sui generis* is not an exclusive right; others are not prohibited from independently gathering the same data from other original sources.[136]

The Database Directive defines a database "as a collection of independent works, data, or other materials arranged in a systematic or methodical way and individually accessible by electronic or other means".[137] The European Parliament and the Council of the European Union recognize that databases are a "vital tool in the development of an information market"[138] and that the creation of "databases requires the investment of considerable human, technical, and financial resources while such databases can be copied or accessed at a fraction of the cost needed to design them independently".[139]

Furthermore, as databases are "not sufficiently protected"[140] and there is an "absence of a harmonized system of unfair-competition legislation" to protect database owners from "unauthorized extraction and/or re-utilization of the contents of a database",[141] the Directive is a "means to secure the remuneration of the maker of the database".[142] While the Database Directive "afford[s] an appropriate and uniform level of protection [to] databases", its

---

133 Stephens, "Database Rights: A Surprise Judgment by the European Court of Justice", 18 *World Intell. Prop. Rep.* 12 (1 December 2004).

134 Grosheide, "Database Protection — The European Way", 8 *Wash. U. J.L. & Pol'y* 39, at p. 40 (2002).

135 Stephens, "Database Rights: A Surprise Judgment by the European Court of Justice", 18 *World Intell. Prop. Rep.* 12 (1 December 2004).

136 Stephens, "Database Rights: A Surprise Judgment by the European Court of Justice", 18 *World Intell. Prop. Rep.* 12, at p. 45 (1 December 2004).

137 Directive 96/9 EC, article 1(2).

138 Directive 96/9 EC, Recital 9.

139 Directive 96/9 EC, article 7.

140 Directive 96/9 EC, article 1.

141 Directive 96/9 EC, article 6.

142 Directive 96/9 EC, article 48.

provisions "are without prejudice to data protection legislation", specifically Directive 95/46/EC "on the protection of individuals with regard to the processing of personal data and on the free movement of such data".[143]

The Database Directive prohibits the "temporary or permanent reproduction by any means and in any form, in whole or in part" of the database, in addition to "translation, adaptation, arrangement and any other alteration", and "any form of distribution to the public of the database or of copies thereof".[144] However, after the first sale of a copy of the database, the right to control the resale of that copy is exhausted.[145]

Exceptions to the *sui generis* right exist for non-commercial use as an illustration for teaching or scientific research, and for use for the purposes of public security or administrative or judicial procedure.[146] Additionally, the term of protection granted under *sui generis* is limited to 15 years from the date of completion or from the date of substantial change resulting from substantial new investment.[147]

(g) Criminal Law

Criminal laws also weigh in on the side of intellectual property rights holders, but they are far less harmonized. For example, the United States Federal Communications Act protects intellectual property rights holders in radio or satellite cable programming from unauthorized interception and publication.[148] Willful violators of the Act are subject to a fine of up to US $2,000 and/or six months' imprisonment;[149] however, if the violation is for private or commercial financial gain, the penalties increase to up to US $50,000 and/or two years' imprisonment for the first violation.[150]

Another United States law is the Federal Communications Act. It also contains a special provision for violations that involve a "device or equipment [that] is primarily of assistance in the unauthorized decryption of satellite cable programming" which, for each violation, calls for fines of up to US $500,000 and/or up to five years in prison.[151]

---

143 Directive 96/9 EC, article 48.
144 Directive 96/9 EC, article 5.
145 Directive 96/9 EC, article 5(c).
146 Directive 96/9 EC, article 6.
147 Directive 96/9 EC, article 10.
148 47 United States Code, section 605(a).
149 47 United States Code, section 605(e)(1).
150 47 United States Code, section at 605(e)(2). The penalty for subsequent convictions increases to up to US $100,000 and/or five years' imprisonment.
151 47 United States Code, section 605(e)(4).

Lastly, the United States Anti-Counterfeiting Amendments Act of 2004 is part of a larger regime aimed at preventing the counterfeiting of copyrighted works and phonorecords.[152] The penalty for affixing illicit or counterfeit labels to, among others, a copy of a computer program, motion picture, literary work, or documentation or packaging is a fine and/or imprisonment for up to five years.[153]

(h) Contract Law

One cannot discuss protection of data unless one addresses self-help measures available to intellectual property rights owners. In the United States and elsewhere, contract law is often used by intellectual property rights holders to protect their digital works. The contracts take the form of licenses, with "shrink wrap" and "click on" licenses being the most common because they require the end user to accept the conditions of the license as a condition of installing and using the program.[154]

While the "freedom to contract" is a powerful rights enforcement tool, a contract does not create exclusive rights and, as such, it only affects the parties to the contract and not others.[155] Furthermore, contracts run the risk of being preempted by national law or international treaty.[156] Such preemption may occur when the contract, for example, exceeds the limitations of copyright law by prohibiting fair use or violating the first-sale doctrine.[157]

Another method of self-help is maintaining information in secret and not disclosing it as a means of protecting against misappropriation. If the information has value, it may be a trade secret.[158] So long as the information has value, is maintained as a secret, and is not generally known to the industry, trade secrets serve as the primary alternative form of intellectual property rights protection to patents.[159]

Trade secrets legislation protects the intellectual property rights owner against misappropriation of trade secrets through improper means.[160] In the

---

152 Intellectual Property Protection and Courts Amendments Act of 2004, Pub. L. Number 108-482 2004 H.R. 3632 (2004).

153 Intellectual Property Protection and Courts Amendments Act of 2004, Pub. L. Number 108-482 2004 H.R. 3632 (2004). An illicit label is a genuine document or certificate that is used to verify the authenticity of a copy that has been altered or misused.

154 Leaffer, *Understanding Copyright Law* (3d ed., 1999), at p. 25.

155 Leaffer, *Understanding Copyright Law* (3d ed., 1999), at p. 493.

156 Leaffer, *Understanding Copyright Law* (3d ed., 1999), at p. 489.

157 Leaffer, *Understanding Copyright Law* (3d ed., 1999), at p. 493.

158 United States Uniform Trade Secrets Act, section 1(4) (amended 1985).

159 Adelman *et al.*, *Cases and Materials on Patent Law* (1998), at p. 51.

160 United States Uniform Trade Secrets Act, sections 1(2) and 3.

United States, damages for misappropriation include both actual losses and the unjust enrichment caused by the misappropriation, or the cost of a reasonable royalty, plus, in the case of willful and malicious misappropriation, exemplary damages and reasonable attorney's fees.[161]

In Civil Law jurisdictions, unfair competition protects against the misconduct of the one who appropriates the contents from a database under a form of tortious liability for the value of the data or information. In Common Law jurisdictions, misappropriation law applies to prevent one business from "passing off" its goods or services as those of another.[162] In either type of jurisdiction, the intellectual property rights holder must prove the tortious act, which typically requires more than just evidence of direct copying.[163]

Thus, while the intellectual property rights regimes of the world are more and more becoming a single fabric, the fabric is more like a quilt of national variations on a theme imposed through international treaties. So long as each national variation is enforced fairly and consistently, the promise of innovation's reward and the societal benefits from the free flow of innovation can co-exist and flourish.

2.05   Legal Factors in Protecting Privacy

(a) Criminal Laws

Personal data protection laws have taken on various shapes and hues. At its most fundamental is the right of a person to be protected against the theft of his identity. For example, the Identity Theft Penalty Enhancement Act in the United States establishes the crime of aggravated identity theft for the unauthorized transfer, possession, or use of another person's means of identification during the course of certain enumerated felonies, which generally relate to fraud, nationality, and citizenship.[164]

However, identity theft is just one form of harm that can flourish unless limits are placed on what one may do with the private information concerning another. Not surprisingly, beyond the restrictions on identity theft are a host of laws that apply to protection afforded to the privacy of personal information. Those protections fall into two categories, these being restrictions on government and restrictions on private parties. Both categories are evolving.

---

161 United States Uniform Trade Secrets Act, sections 3 and 4.

162 rosheide, "Database Protection —The European Way", 8 *Wash. U. J.L. & Pol'y* 39, at p. 45; Leaffer, *Understanding Copyright Law* (3d ed., 1999) at p. 38.

163 Grosheide, "Database Protection —The European Way", 8 *Wash. U. J.L. & Pol'y* 39, at p. 45.

164 Identity Theft Penalty Enhancement Act of 2004, Pub. L. Number 108-275, section 2, H.R. 1731 (2004).

(b) Privacy Act of Canada

An example of restrictions on the government's handling of personal data is the Privacy Act of Canada, which regulates personal information about individuals held by a government institution and provides individuals with a right of access to that information.[165] Personal information under the Canada Privacy Act includes information about an identifiable individual that is recorded in any form, including race, national or ethnic origin, color, religion, age, marital status, information relating to education, medical, financial, criminal, or employment history, and any identifying numbers, symbols, or marks assigned or ascribed to the individual, such as address, fingerprints, or blood type.[166] The regulations place limits on the collection, use, and disclosure of this information by specifying that:

1. Any information collected must relate directly to a program or activity of the government institution,[167]

2. The individual must be informed of the collection and the use of the information;[168]

3. The information must be used for the purpose for which the information was obtained;[169] and

4. The individual must consent to any other use or disclosure, except as provided by the Act.[170]

The Privacy Act of Canada allows Canadians to:

1. Access any relevant personal information which is under the control of the government;

2. Request that omissions or errors be corrected;

3. Have the request for correction, if not granted, noted on the information; and

4. Require that the correction, or the denied request for correction, be given to anyone to whom the personal information was disclosed within the two years prior to the request for correction.[171]

---

165 Privacy Act of Canada (1980–1983), c. 111, sched. II.
166 Privacy Act of Canada, section 3.
167 Privacy Act of Canada, section 5(1).
168 Privacy Act of Canada, section 5(2).
169 Privacy Act of Canada, section 7(a).
170 Privacy Act of Canada, sections 7 and 8(1).
171 Privacy Act of Canada, section 12.

The Governor in Council has the authority to extend the right of access to non-citizens and to set conditions on the right of access as the Governor in Council deems appropriate.[172]

(c) United States Privacy Act

In a similar fashion, the United States Privacy Act of 1974[173] requires government agencies to publish notices in the Federal Register on the establishment or revision of systems of records, to account for disclosures of certain records, and to agree in writing with another agency before entering into a computer matching program, and to provide individuals access to records maintained about them.[174]

Privacy-related concerns impact national security laws and programs. For example, funding legislation for the United States Department of Homeland Security requires that technology used to screen aviation passengers and identify those who may pose a security threat must, prior to deployment:

1. Contain safeguards to prevent abuse and unauthorized access;

2. Address any privacy concerns posed by its system architecture; and

3. Provide a system of due process whereby targeted passengers can appeal the determination and correct any erroneous information that facilitated the false determination.[175]

In addition to privacy controls implemented as a condition of funding, the United States Department of Homeland Security has a statutorily required Privacy Officer.[176] This Privacy Officer's primary responsibility is over the United States Department of Homeland Security privacy policy, which includes assuring that the use, collection, and disclosure of personal information by the United States Department of Homeland Security complies with the Privacy Act and ultimately sustains, and does not erode, established privacy protections.[177]

However, national security and law enforcement must, to some extent, erode privacy protections. Two exceptions to the Privacy Act of Canada illustrate

---

172 Privacy Act of Canada, section 12(3).

173 5 United States Code, section 552(a).

174 Homeland Security Privacy Office Report on Privacy and Protecting Our Homeland, Report to Congress, at p. 11 (April 2003–June 2004).

175 Department of Homeland Security Appropriations Act, Pub. L. Number 108-3342, section 522(a), 2004 H.R. 4567 (18 October 2004).

176 Homeland Security Privacy Office Report on Privacy and Protecting Our Homeland, Report to Congress, at p. 1 (April 2003–June 2004).

177 Homeland Security Act of 2002, Pub. L. Number 107-296, section 222, 116 Stat. 2155 (2002).

this point. First, government institutions are not obligated to inform the individual of the purpose of the information collection if the notice of such collection may jeopardize the accuracy of the information collected or defeat the purpose or prejudice the use for which the information is collected.[178] Second, government institutions may deny the right of access to personal information contained in an "exempt bank".[179] Exempt banks are designated as such by the Governor in Council and are repositories of personal information that, in general, relates to national security or law enforcement.[180]

(d) European Data Protection Directive

Shifting to restrictions on private entities, one must begin with the seminal archetype of privacy legislation, Directive 95/46/EC, the EU Data Protection Directive. The Data Protection Directive guarantees the protection of individuals with regard to the processing of personal data and its free movement across borders. It states as its objective "protect[ing] the fundamental rights and freedoms of natural persons, and in particular their right to privacy with respect to the processing of personal data"; however, the enforcement of such rights "shall neither restrict nor prohibit the free flow of personal data between Member States for reasons connected with the protection afforded" to natural persons.[181]

The Data Protection Directive establishes the conditions under which the processing of personal data is lawful.[182] Under the Directive, "personal data" means any information relating to an identified or identifiable natural person and which data can directly or indirectly identify the person, whether by an identification number or physical attributes. The "processing of personal data" includes any:

> ... operation or set of operations which is performed on personal data, whether or not by automatic means, such as collection, recording, organization, storage, adaptation or alteration, retrieval, consultation, use, disclosure by transmission, dissemination or otherwise making available, alignment or combination, blocking, erasure or destruction . . . .[183]

Additionally, the Directive applies to both electronic information and manual records that are part of a structured filing system.[184]

---

178 Privacy Act of Canada, section 5(3).

179 Privacy Act Canada, section 18(2).

180 Privacy Act of Canada, sections 21 and 22.

181 Directive 95/46/EC, article 1.

182 Directive 95/46/EC, article 5.

183 Directive 95/46/EC, article 2(6).

184 Privacy Office at www.dataprivacy.i.e./4aii.htm (2005) (Ireland).

Under the Directive, "personal data must be collected for specified, explicit and legitimate purposes and not further processed in a way incompatible with those purposes".[185] Prior to processing personal data, the data subject must "unambiguously give . . . his consent",[186] unless certain narrow exceptions are met, such as the "processing is necessary for the performance of a contract to which the data subject is party".[187] Processing of data in special categories, such as racial or ethnic origin, political opinions, religious or philosophical beliefs, trade union membership, health, or sex life is strictly prohibited, unless the data subject has given his explicit consent or the processing is absolutely necessary.[188]

One notable point of distinction of the Data Protection Directive is that individuals have the right to deny consent to be:

> . . . subject to a decision which produces legal effects concerning him or significantly affects him and which is based solely on automated processing of data intended to evaluate certain personal aspects relating to him, such as his performance at work, creditworthiness, reliability, and conduct.[189]

Data subjects also can object to the processing of their data for direct marketing activities.[190]

The Directive lays out additional fundamental principles. The data subject must be provided with the information necessary to guarantee the fair processing of the data collected, including the identity and contact information of the entity controlling the information ("data controller") and the purposes of the processing for which the data are intended.[191] Furthermore, the data controller must provide the data subject access to the data in order, generally, to confirm that the data is accurate and is being processed as disclosed and in conformance with the Directive.[192]

Personal data must be kept confidential and secure during processing as to prevent "accidental or unlawful destruction or accidental loss, alteration, unauthorized disclosure or access . . . and all other unlawful forms of processing".[193] The data controller is obligated to make its processing operations transparent and to make them public by registering the operations with the proper national authority.[194]

---

185 Directive 95/46/EC, article 61(b).
186 Directive 95/46/EC, article 7(a).
187 Directive 95/46/EC, article 7(b).
188 Directive 95/46/EC, article 8.
189 Directive 95/46/EC, article 15.
190 Directive 95/46/EC, article 14(b).
191 Directive 95/46/EC, articles 10, 11, and 19.
192 Directive 95/46/EC, article 15.
193 Directive 95/46/EC, articles 16 and 17.
194 Directive 95/46/EC, article 21.

The national authority is then responsible for determining if any risks to the rights and freedoms of the data subjects are present.[195] Finally, the Directive mandates that the member states provide remedies to data subjects for any breach of the rights guaranteed to the data subjects by the applicable national law, including the entitlement to receive compensation for actual damages and sanctions for infringement of the provisions of the Directive.[196]

Article 25 of the Directive prohibits the transfer of personal data to a third country unless the third country ensures an adequate level of protection, as compared to the Directive and as determined by the Commission. The Commission has published standard contractual clauses to facilitate data flows from the Community where the third country has unequal data protection standards.[197] As expected, the contract clauses mirror the Principles of the Directive; however, they specifically exclude punitive damages[198] and give an opportunity to cure allegations of breach of duty.[199]

The clauses also give the data subject the right "to proceed directly against a data exporter that has failed to use reasonable efforts to determine that the data importer is able to satisfy its legal obligations under these clauses",[200] which would seem to imply that the data exporter has an obligation to audit the data importer's practices.

(e) Personal Information Protection and Electronic Documents Act of Canada

The Directive served as the model for Canada's legislative protections with respect to regulation of private entities and, as such, the Canadian legislation contains the same basic privacy principles:[201]

> For the purposes of article 25(2) of Directive 95/46/EC, Canada is considered as providing an adequate level of protection for personal data

---

195 Directive 95/46/EC, article 20.

196 Directive 95/46/EC, articles 22, 23, and 24.

197 Commission Decision Amending Decision 2001/497/EC as Regards the Introduction of an Alternative Set of Contractual Clauses for the Transfer of Personal Data to Third Countries, 27 December 2004.

198 Commission Decision Amending Decision 2001/497/EC as Regards the Introduction of an Alternative Set of Contractual Clauses for the Transfer of Personal Data to Third Countries, clause III(a).

199 Commission Decision Amending Decision 2001/497/EC as Regards the Introduction of an Alternative Set of Contractual Clauses for the Transfer of Personal Data to Third Countries, clause III(b).

200 Commission Decision Amending Decision 2001/497/EC as Regards the Introduction of an Alternative Set of Contractual Clauses for the Transfer of Personal Data to Third Countries, clauses II(g) and III(b).

201 Singh, "Lack of Minimum Global Privacy Standard Said to Impair Outsourcing, Online Business", 10 *Elec. Commerce & L.* 7 (16 February 2005).

transferred from the Community to recipients subject to the Personal Information Protection and Electronic Documents Act.[202]

The Personal Information Protection and Electronic Documents Act of Canada applies to all personal information collected, used, or disclosed by private sector organizations in the course of commercial activity.[203]

The Act sets out a series of obligations, found in Schedule I to the Act, which are based on the 10 Privacy Principles of the Code, as set out in the national standard of Canada, the Model Code for the Protection of Personal Information.[204] The Privacy Principles are:

> . . . accountability, identifying the purposes for the collection of personal information, obtaining consent, limiting collection, limiting use, disclosure and retention, ensuring accuracy, providing adequate security, making information management policies readily available, providing individuals with access to information about themselves, and giving individuals a right to challenge an organization's compliance with these principles.

The Personal Information Protection and Electronic Documents Act of Canada holds private organizations accountable for the personal information under their control.[205] The accountability extends to information that has been transferred to a third party, even if that party is located outside the borders of Canada. Additionally, the accountability applies to information that will not be "used", but merely "processed" under a business outsourcing agreement.[206]

As a result, organizations transferring personal information are required to "use contractual or other means to provide a comparable level of protection while the information is being processed by a third party".[207] This means that the private organization in Canada must ensure, prior to any transborder transfer, that the

---

202 Commission Decision Pursuant to Directive 95/46 EC of the European Parliament and of the Council on the Adequate Protection of Personal Data Provided by the Canadian Personal Information Protection and Electronic Documents Act, 20 December 2001.

203 Personal Information Protection and Electronic Documents Act, section 4. The Personal Information Protection and Electronic Documents Act also applies to employment records collected, used, or disclosed in connection with a federally regulated industry, such as banking and railroad, ship, or air transportation.

204 Personal Information Protection and Electronic Documents Act, Summary and Schedule 1.

205 Personal Information Protection and Electronic Documents Act of Canada, Schedule 1, section 4.1.

206 Personal Information Protection and Electronic Documents Act of Canada, Schedule 1, section 4.1.3.

207 Personal Information Protection and Electronic Documents Act of Canada, Schedule 1, section 4.1.3.

third party in another country will provide a level of protection comparable to that which the personal information would receive in Canada.[208]

Of course, the general rule in Canada is that any collection, use, or disclosure of personal information by a private commercial entity can only occur if all the requirements of the Personal Information Protection and Electronic Documents Act have been met.[209] A primary concern with cross-border transfers of personal information is security and the prevention of unauthorized access or disclosure.[210]

For example, a problem is presented when the transferee is located in a country where the laws permit certain disclosures to that country's government or law enforcement agencies in a manner not authorized by the Personal Information Protection and Electronic Documents Act. The foreign third party transferee will not be able to contract against the local law; therefore, because the transferor in Canada has a duty to protect personal information under its control from unauthorized disclosure, it may find that the transfer is not permissible.[211]

(f) Other Regimes

However, not all privacy regimes follow the same path. Indeed, for example, a wholly different regime exists in Argentina. Argentina requires Argentine and foreign companies doing business in Argentina to register all databases, whether in electronic or hard-copy format, that contain personal data that is shared with third parties and is subject to treatment or processing.[212] This registry was implemented as part of the Habeas Data Law and applies to for-profit and not-for-profit transfers of personal data.

Under the law, all individuals and legal entities must provide detailed information on, for example, the kind of data their databases contain, what their purpose is, the means and place of storage, how the information was obtained, as well as safekeeping measures.[213]

---

208 Report on Privacy and the USA Patriot Act; Implications for the British Columbia Public Sector Outsourcing, Information and Privacy Commissioner for British Columbia, section 4 (October 2004).

209 Personal Information Protection and Electronic Documents Act, section 4(1)(a).

210 Personal Information Protection and Electronic Documents Act, section 4.7.1.

211 Other laws, treaties, or agreements or memorandums of understanding between the originating country and the specific governments and law enforcement agencies may exist that would otherwise authorize the transfer. Generally, these overriding exceptions are specific to the industry involved, such as commercial airlines.

212 Haskel, "Argentina Implements Mandatory Registration Requirement for Databases", 4 *Privacy & Sec. L.* 9 (28 February 2005).

213 Haskel, "Argentina Implements Mandatory Registration Requirement for Databases", 4 *Privacy & Sec. L.* 9 (28 February 2005).

The legislation bans transferring database contents to third parties without written consent from the individuals involved. The request must indicate the reasons why the handover is necessary. This applies even if the transfer is between different locations of the same company. However, when transfer of the data is necessary to render adequate services, a contact pledging to honor the data privacy may suffice.[214]

Habeas Data is a constitutional right granted in several countries in Latin America, which translated means "you should have the data". In general, the right "is designed to protect, by means of an individual complaint presented to a constitutional court, the image, privacy, honor, information self-determination and freedom of information of a person".[215]

Despite its differences as compared to the EU regime:

> . . . [f]or the purposes of article 25(2) of Directive 95/46/EC, Argentina is regarded as providing an adequate level of protection for personal data transferred from the Community.[216]

(g) National Inconsistencies

Despite the fact that many nations offer an "adequate level of protection for personal data", yet, inconsistencies abound. For example, the Privacy Act of Canada, which regulates the collection, use, and disclosure by governmental institutions of personal information, does not require the same safeguards to prevent the unauthorized disclosure of personal information about Canadians as a result of a cross-border transfer.[217]

The potential impact of the transborder flow of information was raised when the British Columbia Government and Services Employees' Union challenged the British Columbia Ministry of Health Services when it sought to outsource the administration of British Columbia's public health insurance program to a US-linked private service provider.[218]

---

214 Haskel, "Argentina Implements Mandatory Registration Requirement for Databases", 4 *Privacy & Sec. L.* 9 (28 February 2005).

215 Guadamuz, "Habeas Data: The Latin-American Response to Data Protection", 2000 *J. Info, L. & Tech.*, at http://elj.warwick.ac.uk/jilt/00-2/guadamuz.html.

216 Commission Decision Pursuant to Directive 95/46/EC of the European Parliament and of the Council on the Adequate Protection of Personal Data in Argentina, article 1, 30 June 2003.

217 Report on Privacy and the USA Patriot Act; Implications for the British Columbia Public Sector Outsourcing, Information and Privacy Commissioner for British Columbia, at p. 10 (October 2004) (other legislation or contractual agreements may provide limited protection).

218 Report on Privacy and the USA Patriot Act; Implications for the British Columbia Public Sector Outsourcing, Information and Privacy Commissioner for British Columbia, at p. 23 (October 2004). The challenge has been presented to the British Columbia Supreme Court and was scheduled to be heard in March 2005. The petition and associated affidavits can be found at http://www.bcgeu.ca/index.php4?id=2093.

The provincial government is also seeking to privatize its revenue and tax services, and the union is concerned that a wide range of detailed financial records will be exposed to potential scrutiny by the United States Federal Bureau of Investigation (FBI) and other United States government agencies.[219]

This case points up "a nearly universal misconception that the United States has no privacy framework that might be viewed as consonant with those of other countries".[220] Additionally, there is a:

> ... perception that the US interest in privacy protection and privacy rights may be parochial, isolated to Americans only, fueling the misperception of United States non-comparability with basic information privacy protections afforded in many other regions of the world to any individual, regardless of status.[221]

In an effort to address this concern, the United States Department of Homeland Security has entered into more stringent privacy agreements with other entities and incorporated enhanced privacy procedures. For example, a recent posting in the Federal Register stated that "[w]hile non-United States persons are not covered by the Privacy Act, such persons will still be afforded the same access and redress remedies" as United States persons by contesting and seeking amendment of records kept through the United States Department of Homeland Security Privacy Office.[222]

While the United States and the European Union share the goal of enhancing privacy protection for their citizens, the United States takes a different approach to privacy from that taken by the European Union. The United States uses a sectoral approach that relies on a mix of legislation, regulation, and self-regulation. Given those differences, many United States organizations have expressed uncertainty about the impact of the EU-required "adequacy standard" on personal data transfers from the European Union to the United States.[223] For now, these differences are resolved through a safe

---

219 "British Columbia Government and Service Employee's Union, Latest Government Records Privatization Deal a Further 'Betrayal' Charges BCGEU", paragraph 2 (26 November 2004), at www.bcgeu.ca/2583. British Columbia Government and Service Employee's Union, Quick Facts, Powers of the USA Patriot Act (6 August 2004) at www.bcgeu.ca/index4?id=2440.

220 Homeland Security Privacy Office Report on Privacy and Protecting our Homeland, Report to Congress, at p. 11 (April 2003–June 2004).

221 Homeland Security Privacy Office Report on Privacy and Protecting our Homeland, Report to Congress, at p. 11 (April 2003–June 2004).

222 68 Fed. Reg. 148, at p. 45269 (1 August 2003) (regarding contesting records for Computer Assisted Passenger Prescreening System, CAPPS II).

223 Commission Decision Pursuant to Directive 95/46/EC of the European Parliament and of the Council on the Adequacy of the Protection Provided by the Safe Harbor Privacy Principles and Related Frequently Asked Questions Issued by the United States Department of Commerce at Annex 1 (26 July 2000).

harbor program where United States companies can voluntarily agree to abide by the principles by certifying adherence to the United States Department of Commerce and publishing their privacy policies.

> For the purposes of article 25(2) of Directive 95/46/EC, for all the activities falling within the scope of that Directive, the "Safe Harbor Privacy Principles" (hereinafter "the Principles"), as set out in Annex I to this Decision, implemented in accordance with the guidance provided by the Frequently Asked Questions issued by the United States Department of Commerce on 21 July 2000, as set out in Annex II to this Decision, are considered to ensure an adequate level of protection for personal data transferred from the Community to organizations established in the United States.[224]

In short, the safe harbor requires that a United States company provide conspicuous notice to individuals about the purposes for which it collects and uses personal data. Included in that notice should be information on how to contact the company with inquiries and complaints, the types of third parties to which it discloses the information, and choices available to the individual for limited disclosure.[225]

Additionally, the company must offer individuals an opportunity to opt out from third-party disclosure and from having the information used for a purpose that is incompatible with the original purpose of collecting the data. The company can then transfer the information to a third party only if that party either subscribes to the Principles itself or if the company enters into a written agreement with the third party where the third party is bound to provide at least the same level of privacy protection as is required by the Principles.[226]

The company also must take reasonable precautions to protect the data's security and integrity, i.e., that the data is reliable for its intended use, accurate, complete, and current. Finally, the company must provide individuals

---

224 Commission Decision Pursuant to Directive 95/46/EC of the European Parliament and of the Council on the Adequacy of the Protection Provided by the Safe Harbor Privacy Principles and Related Frequently Asked Questions Issued by the United States Department of Commerce at Annex 1 (26 July 2000).

225 Commission Decision Pursuant to Directive 95/46/EC of the European Parliament and of the Council on the Adequacy of the Protection Provided by the Safe Harbor Privacy Principles and Related Frequently Asked Questions Issued by the United States Department of Commerce at Annex 1 (26 July 2000).

226 Commission Decision Pursuant to Directive 95/46/EC of the European Parliament and of the Council on the Adequacy of the Protection Provided by the Safe Harbor Privacy Principles and Related Frequently Asked Questions Issued by the United States Department of Commerce at Annex 1 (26 July 2000).

access to their information and must provide recourse to individuals' complaints regarding the company's adherence to the Principles.[227]

The United States is likely to undergo a waive of legislation regarding the collection, sale, and disclosure of personally identifiable information due to the recent incident where the data broker ChoicePoint, Inc., sold information to criminals posing as legitimate business customers of ChoicePoint.[228]

ChoicePoint gathers information on millions of people and is the largest data broker in the United States. As a result of this incident, ChoicePoint sent notice to 145,000 individuals in the United States telling them that their personal information had been improperly accessed.[229] Within the United States, the State of California is the only state that requires such notice.[230]

(h) Exceptions

Exceptions to privacy laws abound. The Privacy Act of Canada allows government institutions to disclose personal information for a purpose other than the original use for which the information was obtained, without the consent of the individual to whom it relates, when other laws or regulations permit the disclosure,[231] in response to a court order[232] or, in general, for the purpose of enforcing any law of Canada[233] or when the public interest in disclosure clearly outweighs any invasion of privacy that could result from the discolsure.[234]

The Personal Information Protection and Electronic Documents Act of Canada provides that organizations may disclose personally identifiable information without the knowledge or consent of the individual only if the disclosure qualifies as one of the specifically enumerated statutory exceptions.[235] These exceptions allow disclosure, for example, to comply with a

---

227 Commission Decision Pursuant to Directive 95/46/EC of the European Parliament and of the Council on the Adequacy of the Protection Provided by the Safe Harbor Privacy Principles and Related Frequently Asked Questions Issued by the United States Department of Commerce at Annex 1 (26 July 2000).

228 Tumey, et. al., "State, Federal Response Triggered By ChoicePoint Data Breach Incident", 10 Elec. Commerce & L. 9 (2 March 2005).

229 Mahoney, "Data Broker Warns 145,000 Consumers Of Security Breach, Potential Identity Theft", 10 Elec. Commerce & L. 8 (23 February 2005).

230 "Leahy Calls for Senate Judiciary Probe On Government, Industry Data Collection", 10 Elec. Commerce & L. 9 (2 March 2005).

231 Privacy Act of Canada, section 8(2)(b).

232 Privacy Act of Canada, section 8(2)(c).

233 Privacy Act of Canada, section 8(e).

234 Privacy Act of Canada, section 8(m)(i).

235 Personal Information Protection and Electronic Documents Act of Canada, section 7(5).

court order,[236] for research when obtaining consent is impracticable and the purposes of the research cannot be achieved without disclosure,[237] in cases of emergency that threaten the life, health, or security of an individual,[238] and when a government authority requests disclosure of the information as part of enforcing any law of Canada[239] or ensuring national security.[240]

Article 13 of the EU Data Protection Directive provides exemptions, for example, for national security, defense, public security, criminal investigations, and important economic or financial interest of a member state or of the European Union, including monetary, budgetary, and taxation matters.[241]

2.06   New Tools, New Enforcement Questions

(a)   In General

Intellectual property rights and privacy rights are only as viable as they are enforceable. Data protection is relatively new and least consistently applied globally, while intellectual property rights have a rich history of enforcement buttressed by a wealth of international treaties.

Generally, the first step in enforcing data protection laws is for the data subject to file a complaint with his national Privacy or Data Protection Commissioner.[242] This is a primary purpose for the public registries.[243] Although premised on a private right to complain, personal data protection laws are increasingly enforced by government agencies.

(b)   Other Statutory Monitoring, Privacy Impact Assessments

(i)   United States Privacy Impact Assessment

In other instances, the government agency is proactive. The United States E-Government Act of 2002, section 208, mandates a Privacy Impact Assessment

---

236 Personal Information Protection and Electronic Documents Act of Canada, section 7(3)(c).

237 Personal Information Protection and Electronic Documents Act of Canada, section 7(3)(f).

238 Personal Information Protection and Electronic Documents Act of Canada, section 7(3)(e).

239 Personal Information Protection and Electronic Documents Act of Canada, section 7(3)(c.1)(i) and 7(3)(d)(ii).

240 Personal Information Protection and Electronic Documents Act of Canada, section 7(3)(c.1)(ii) and 7(3)(d)(i).

241 Directive 95/46 EC, article 13.

242 Privacy Office, at www.dataprivacy.i.e./2.htm (Data Protection: Your Rights 2005) (Ireland).

243 Privacy Office, at www.dataprivacy.i.e./2.htm (Data Protection: Your Rights 2005) (Ireland).

(PIA) for all federal agencies when there are new collections of, or new technologies applied to, personally identifiable information. The purpose of a PIA is to ensure that information technology systems of the federal government are maintained in conformity with fair information principles concerning notice, consent, access, redress, data integrity, and security.[244]

For example, the United States Department of Homeland Security Privacy Office is statutorily required to evaluate all new technologies used in the furtherance of its security mission for their impact on personal privacy and to provide an annual report to Congress on the Department's activities that affect privacy.[245] This report includes complaints of privacy violations and an evaluation of the Department's internal controls.[246] Additionally, the United States Department of Homeland Security Privacy Office investigates data sharing and data mining practices and reports its conclusions to Congress.[247]

Separately, the Homeland Security Act provides that the United States Department of Homeland Security Privacy Officer conduct PIAs that address the type of personal information collected and the number of people affected for proposed rules of the Department of Homeland Security[248] because:

> . . . [e]ven when actual Privacy Act violations are not found, it is nevertheless important that clear rules be in place to ensure that information sharing is done in a legitimate, respectful, and limited way.[249]

(ii) Canada Privacy Commissioner Audit

The Personal Information Protection and Electronic Documents Act of Canada gives the Privacy Commissioner the authority to audit the personal information management practices of a private organization if it reasonably believes that the organization is not following the Act.[250] Following the audit, the Commissioner must report the findings to the organization and

---

244 United States E-Government Act of 2002, section 24.

245 Homeland Security Act of 2002, Pub. L. Number 107-296, section 222(1), H.R. 5005 (2002). Homeland Security Privacy Office Report on Privacy and Protecting Our Homeland, Report to Congress, at p. 1 (April 2003–June 2004).

246 Homeland Security Act of 2002, Pub. L. Number 107-296, section 222(5), H.R. 5005 (2002).

247 Homeland Security Privacy Office Report on Privacy and Protecting Our Homeland, Report to Congress, at p. 11 (April 2003–June 2004)).

248 Homeland Security Act of 2002, Pub. L. Number 107-296, section 222(4), H.R. 5005 (2002).

249 Homeland Security Privacy Office Report on Privacy and Protecting Our Homeland, Report to Congress, at p. 10 (April 2003–June 2004).

250 Personal Information Protection and Electronic Documents Act, section 18(1).

may make recommendations.[251] While it is unlawful to knowingly obstruct the audit,[252] the enforcement authority of the Commissioner is limited.[253]

The Commissioner may then make public any information relating to the personal information management practices of the organization if the Commissioner deems it in the public interest to do so.[254] The Commissioner may also include this information in the annual report to Parliament.[255]

(c) Digital Rights Management

(i) In General

In contrast to an aggrieved data subject, intellectual property rights owners have had a traditional array of enforcement tools available through the civil justice systems of the intellectual property rights regimes under which they enjoy rights. Yet, that array is increasingly viewed as too slow, cumbersome, and expensive to be effective. Intellectual property rights holders, therefore, are increasingly turning to digital rights management as the primary method of battling online infringement.[256]

Electronic copyright management systems, or digital rights management, generally identify technologies, or technical protection measures, that allow an intellectual property rights holder to control and restrict the use of his or her work when it is in an electronic form. Digital rights management opponents chidingly call this term "digital restrictions management" because they claim the protection measures often exceed the owner's rights in the underlying work.[257]

Digital rights management includes not only software, but hardware as well. Through "Trusted Computing" or "Secure Engineering", intellectual property rights holders are developing microprocessor-based devices that use

---

251 Personal Information Protection and Electronic Documents Act, section 19(1).

252 Personal Information Protection and Electronic Documents Act, section 28.

253 The court has authority to order, in addition to other remedies, an organization to correct its practices; however, under the Act, it appears that investigations initiated by the Commissioner are not eligible for court hearings. Personal Information Protection and Electronic Documents Act, articles 11 and 14.

254 Personal Information Protection and Electronic Documents Act, section 20(2).

255 Personal Information Protection and Electronic Documents Act, section 25.

256 "EC Privacy Advisors Warn That IP Enforcers Could Be Skirting Data Protection Directive", 10 *Elec. Commerce & L.* 6 (9 February 2005).

257 For example, the *bona fide* purchaser of a *bona fide* copy of the work may be prevented from selling the copy purchased, as would otherwise be allowed under the "first sale doctrine" which, in the United States, is codified at 17 United States Code, section 109. The statute states, in part that "the owner of a particular copy . . . lawfully made . . . is entitled, without the authority of the copyright owner, to sell or otherwise dispose of the possession of that copy . . .". Additionally, there have been claims that digital rights managements have been used to place restrictions on works in the public domain.

both hardware and software to protect digital intellectual property.[258] Other methods of digital rights management include technologies for identification, metadata, rights expression language, encryption, persistent association, privacy, and payment, all of which create a secure environment for the delivery of intellectual property rights-based content.[259] These technologies closely track the digital content and the user to ensure that the content is used according to the intellectual property rights holder's pre-determined conditions.

(ii) United States, the Digital Millennium Copyright Act

In the United States, the Digital Millennium Copyright Act supports the use of digital rights management and provides that "no person shall circumvent a technological measure that effectively controls access to a work protected" under the copyright law.[260]

Two exceptions are for reverse engineering, "for the sole purpose of achieving interoperability of an independently created computer program", and to prevent the collection of personally identifiable information that is collected "without providing conspicuous notice of such collection" and "without providing such person with the capability to prevent or restrict" the collection.[261]

(iii) European Union Copyright Directive

The EU Copyright Directive 2001/29/EC provides similar support for digital rights management by mandating that Member States "shall provide adequate legal protection against the circumvention of any effective technological measures".[262] "The Copyright Directive is broader than the Digital Millennium Copyright Act because it also prohibits acts of circumventing copyright control measures and other acts not authorized by the rights holder", not just those used to control access to the work.[263]

Additionally, the Copyright Directive differs in that it provides greater leeway to private contractual agreements as opposed to enumerating specific exceptions or defenses to infringement.[264]

---

258 "International Treaties and Conventions on Intellectual Property", *World Intellectual Property Organization Intellectual Property Handbook: Policy, Law, and Use*, at p. 13.

259 "International Treaties and Conventions on Intellectual Property", *World Intellectual Property Organization Intellectual Property Handbook: Policy, Law, and Use*, at p. 14.

260 17 United States Code, section 1201(a).

261 17 United States Code, section 1201(f) and (i).

262 Directive 2001/29 EC, article 6.

263 "International Treaties and Conventions on Intellectual Property", *World Intellectual Property Organization Intellectual Property Handbook: Policy, Law, and Use*, at p. 74.

264 "International Treaties and Conventions on Intellectual Property", *World Intellectual Property Organization Intellectual Property Handbook: Policy, Law, and Use*, at p. 75.

(iv) European Union Data Protection Directive

Article 29 of the EU Data Protection Directive establishes the authority for a "Working Party" to examine the application of the Directive and to advise the Commission on any matters regarding divergences likely to affect the equivalence of protection for data subjects and the protection of persons with regard to the processing of personal data in the Community.[265] The Working Party has issued a document with regard to data protection and intellectual property rights.[266]

It "notes that the increasing exchange of information linked to the development of the Internet touches more and more the delicate question of control over copyright protected information".[267] The Working Party expresses concerns over the copyright holder's use of digital rights managements to protect his intellectual property rights "insofar as digital rights managements provide for the identification and tracing of individuals accessing legally protected information (e.g., songs, software) on the Internet" and "the possibilities available to copyright holders to enforce their rights against individuals suspected of copyright violation".[268]

With respect to the copyright management systems, digital rights managements potentially:

> . . . monitor . . . every single act of reading, listening and viewing on the Internet by individual users thereby collecting highly sensitive information about the data subject concerned.[269]

With respect to enforcement, the Working Party notes a potential conflict between digital rights managements and legislation supporting digital rights managements, which allow intellectual property rights holders to conduct their own investigations, and privacy laws, in addition to other laws that protect fundamental rights:[270]

> The Working Party calls for a development of technical tools offering privacy compliant properties, and more generally for a transparent and limited use of unique identifiers, with a choice option for the user.[271]

---

265 Directive 95/46/EC, articles 29 and 30.

266 Article 29 Data Protection Working Party Report (18 January 2005).

267 Article 29 Data Protection Working Party Report (18 January 2005), at p. 2.

268 Article 29 Data Protection Working Party Report (18 January 2005), at p. 2.

269 Article 29 Data Protection Working Party Report (18 January 2005), at p. 3 (citing the International Working Group on Data Protection in Telecommunications, "Common Position on Privacy and Copyright Management").

270 Article 29 Data Protection Working Party Report (18 January 2005), at p. 4.

271 Article 29 Data Protection Working Party Report (18 January 2005), at p. 8.

2.07 Impact

The tensions are very real — protection of intellectual property rights versus the public domain and the protection of privacy versus the free use of personal data (the regions above and below the diagonal in Figure 1) — requiring utmost attention to balance if transborder flow of data is to remain unobstructed. Where there is a lack of harmonization of the laws pertaining to proprietary and privacy rights, there is likely restricted transborder dataflows.

Previously, it was thought that the restrictions on these dataflows would widen the "digital divide". However, "information and communication technologies are now in daily household use in OECD countries", and the digital divide appears to be narrowing. Now, the OECD is concerned with the socio-economic differences that determine how people interact with information and communication technologies.

These differences are increasingly linked to unequal use, which seems to be shifting the digital divide from an "access" divide to a more complex "use divide". The Internet amplifies social differences as new uses emerge. This suggests that attention should increasingly be paid to "how-to-use" issues.[272]

However, perhaps a more appropriate concern should be the "ability to use" the data. Self-help digital rights management technologies and hardware will have a profound economic impact, restricting the ability to use information products worldwide. Without harmonization of intellectual property rights and privacy regimes, intellectual property rights holders will continue to turn to protection of their digital works through digital rights management to offset failures seen elsewhere in intellectual property rights systems. This self-help measure is legally sanctioned, but some claim there are insufficient governmental regulations to temper the effects of digital rights management, as there are with intellectual property rights regimes.

Digital rights managements promote the use of non-standard equipment that is specialized to protect the data. The non-standard equipment carries with it an additional cost to potential users. Furthermore, the non-standard equipment restricts the transfer of subsequent works, if any. Thus, through a digital rights management regime, the intellectual property rights holder can obtain rights greater than that offered by traditional intellectual property rights regimes. This is because the intellectual property rights holder is establishing its own *quid pro quo*. For a price, the intellectual property rights holder will grant certain enumerated rights. The exchange, therefore, is

---

272 "Information and Communications Technologies, OECD Information Technology Outlook 2004: Highlights", 2004 *Sci. & Info. Tech.* 15 (December 2004), at p. 10.

limited to the intellectual property rights holder and the user and there is no contemplation of the public domain.

Digital rights management systems also expose the user to potential privacy risks. An extreme digital rights management measure may enforce control over the work through trusted computing that allows the purchaser's computer to be remotely manipulated without warning to the purchaser.[273]

Therefore, a side-effect of digital rights management technology is that it can collect personal data in connection with a user's purchase of a digital file in violation of international data protection directives:[274]

> The legitimate purpose followed by right holders to prevent misuse of protected information often results in the tracing of users and the monitoring of their preferences. In particular, the use of unique identifiers linked with the personal information collected leads to the processing of detailed personal data.[275]

While digital rights management may create new content industries and improve on the traditional models of access to intellectual property,[276] the varied standards and delivery mechanisms may actually hinder access. There is apprehension "that the emerging digital rights management regime is stacked against users" and that the lack of interoperability is intentional.[277] This is not to say that all digital rights management is bad. To the contrary, it is a legally sanctioned method of preserving intellectual property rights in the whirl of our Information Age. However, like anything else, if left without proper guidance, it can be abused.

2.08   Conclusion

Harmonization of privacy and intellectual property rights laws that balance the elements shown in Figure 1 is the key to freer transborder flows of data, which in turn fuels innovation and human endeavor. Many believe "[t]he global adoption of a robust, Canadian-style privacy standard is needed to foster consumer confidence in the online medium" and "minimum

---

273 "International Treaties and Conventions on Intellectual Property", *World Intellectual Property Organization Intellectual Property Handbook: Policy, Law, and Use*, at p. 13.

274 "EC Privacy Advisors Warn That IP Enforcers Could Be Skirting Data Protection Directive", 10 *Elec. Commerce & L.* 6.

275 Article 29 Data Protection Working Party Report, at p. 4 (18 January 2005).

276 "International Treaties and Conventions on Intellectual Property", *World Intellectual Property Organization Intellectual Property Handbook: Policy, Law, and Use*, p. 11.

277 "EC Privacy Advisors Warn That IP Enforcers Could Be Skirting Data Protection Directive", 10 *Elec. Commerce & L.* 6.

but meaningful" standards are now necessary to support cross-border outsourcing of information-based work.[278]

Any void left by privacy legislation and intellectual property laws will be filled by sanctioned self-help, which may result in data collectors and intellectual property rights owners locking up content using private tools under anti-circumvention provisions, such as those of the Digital Millennium Copyright Act, to preserve and even expand their rights without sufficient *quid pro quo.*

In summary, proprietary rights and privacy rights do not operate in a vacuum. For instance, as discussed earlier, government and private industry alike are increasing the outsourcing of their data processing. Further, an increasing percentage of "data processing" involves both personal data and other business data that ultimately in combines to forms some type of information product. These information products, as discussed earlier, give the data tremendous commercial value. This commercial value dictates that both personal data and proprietary data are in need of protection from misappropriation.

Using outsourcing as the concluding example, for harmonization to exist, the country where the outsourcing is to take place must first recognize the proprietary rights in the commercial data. Otherwise, the outsourcing company would not voluntarily risk misappropriation of the valuable data. The type of proprietary right, or specific form of intellectual property right granted, so long as it is comparable to any of the modern regimes, is not as important as the ability to enforce the right.

Second, the country where the outsourcing is to take place must then recognize the Privacy Principles in its own supporting legislation as to provide an adequate level of privacy protection. Alternatively, the entity conducting the outsourced activity may seek to be bound by contractual clauses that effectively provide an adequate level of protection. Presumably, however, the contract must be enforceable in the country where the entity conducting the outsourcing is located. Without both protection of proprietary rights in the data and protection of the privacy rights in the data, there will be a barrier preventing the transborder flow of the data to the country where the outsourcing would take place.

---

278 "EC Privacy Advisors Warn That IP Enforcers Could Be Skirting Data Protection Directive", 10 *Elec. Commerce & L.* 7.

CHAPTER 3

TECHNOLOGY SURVEILLANCE

Sajai Singh, Probir Roy Chowdhury, Amrut Joshi, and Govind Naidu
J. Sagar Associates
Bangalore, India

3.01 Introduction

To make a case for the regulation, and not abolition, of surveillance of individuals requires that surveillance in some form first be justified and then that safeguards be devised to limit its misuse.

The voluntaristic concepts of state formation, which most people know as the theories of social contract popularized by Hobbes, Locke, and Rousseau, conceive of the state as coming into existence by means of a contract among individuals to bring about regulation of their lives and order in society. The structural approach advocated by Marx and Engels theorized that the state emerged when better industrial techniques made possible the presence of different classes and that the states' function was to mediate the conflict between these classes by means of setting out laws and rules.

Other approaches to state formation, such as the ecological approach, believe that demographic expansion and the resultant pressures on resources provide the impetus for the formation of the state as a means of regulating access to and use of resources. More basic coercive models of state formation attribute the formation of the state to the need to expand and manage territories, although the examples used here are mostly ancient civilizations, like the Mayan and Aztec civilizations.

The common thread that runs through all of these approaches to state formation is the role of the state in governance and regulation by means of rules that people are required to follow. Having such a structure therefore requires that the population adhere to these rules for the system to work.

One way to achieve this is to rely on voluntary compliance by the population, and the other is to put in place a system of surveillance and retribution in order to punish violators of the rules laid down. Most, if not all, systems of governance have adopted the latter means of compliance and, therefore, states have a surveillance mechanism in place.

The limits of surveillance and the degree of intrusion into the private lives of individuals has been a topic of debate for years and has also featured prominently in literature for years, with authors like Aldous Huxley and, after him, George Orwell, conjuring up worlds regulated and monitored to an extreme. Most mythologies view the Gods as looking over humankind and intervening periodically to aid and protect it, a role many governments claim to be fulfilling today.

Anecdotal evidence from various texts and records illustrates the historicity of surveillance, and these cut across time and civilizations. The *Arthashastra*, by Kautilya, an Indian dating from approximately 300 B.C., places great emphasis on the role of knowledge gleaned from spies, both internally in a nation and outside it in maintaining a grip on power, echoes of which can be seen in Machiavelli's Prince written hundreds of years later. As long as surveillance has been a part of human life so probably has opposition to its excesses.

This chapter explores the ways by which laws of various jurisdictions seek to achieve the "correlation between adequate intelligence to guarantee our nation's security on the one hand, and the preservation of basic human rights on the other" that President Carter referred to. The next section looks at the technologies available to entities for undertaking surveillance.

This is followed by a section that looks at the rights of an entity conducting surveillance and the situations under which surveillance may be undertaken. The chapter then looks at the protections a subject of surveillance can invoke and then the procedure to be followed when surveillance is carried out. It must be kept in mind that the statutes and case law analyzed in this chapter are indicative in nature and are not exhaustive. They have been chosen to illustrate the principles states apply while dealing with the issue of surveillance.

3.02   Modes of Surveillance

(a) In General

In the 1960s, there were two identifiable forms of surveillance, i.e., physical and data,[1] the most basic form of surveillance is physical surveillance, which

---

1   Westin, *Privacy and Freedom* (1967).

comprises of watching and listening (visual and aural surveillance). However, with the constant evolution in technology, monitoring today may be undertaken remotely in space, with the aid of image amplification devices such as field glasses, infrared binoculars, light amplifiers, and satellite cameras, and sound-amplification devices, such as directional microphones.

Today, the boundaries have been blurred with the application of information technology linking surveillance techniques into a near seamless web of surveillance. Thus, it may be appropriate to categorize surveillance that is carried out with the assistance of technological devices as "technology-assisted surveillance". Some of the common tools of "technology-assisted surveillance" are described below.

(b) Dataveillance

(i) In General

Apart from physical surveillance and technologically assisted surveillance, the other major form of surveillance is referred to as dataveillance. Dataveillance is the systematic use of personal data systems in the investigation or monitoring of the actions of communications of one or more persons. dataveillance could be further categorized into two major categories, i.e., personal dataveillance and mass dataveillance.

The distinction between personal and mass dataveillance is that the former is concerned with analyzing the information held on a particular individual or group (i.e., one which has already been singled out), while mass dataveillance is concerned with the examination of a wide range of subjects in an attempt to identify those who "fit" the search criteria (in other words, personal dataveillance is the end result of mass dataveillance).[2]

(ii) Credit Bureaus

Some of the major players in the information collection industry are the so-called "credit bureaus". The largest three in the United States are Experian (formerly TRW Information Systems and Services), Equifax, and Trans Union.

In the United States, legal recourse for matters concerning credit bureaus can be sought through the Fair Credit Reporting Act of 1970, which requires that bureaus provide correct and complete information in credit reports. However, the legislation has been criticized on the grounds that anyone with a "legitimate business need" can obtain a credit report. The word legitimate is not defined in the Act.

---

2   Clarke, *Information Technology and Dataveillance*, at http://www.anu.edu.au/people/ Roger.Clarke/DV/CACM88.html, visited on 2 September 2004.

(iii) Computer Matching and Profiling

While data matching and profiling are particular kinds of dataveillance techniques, they are not synonymous terms. Data matching refers to:

> . . . exercises designed to assist in the detection of fraud are widely in operation in both the public and private sectors. The term "data matching" essentially means the comparison of data collected by different data users (or by the same data user in different contexts).

The aim of the comparison is not primarily the creation of a larger file of information about the data subject, but the identification of anomalies and inconsistencies within a single set of data or between two or more different sets.

Profiling, on the other hand, is a technique whereby a set of characteristics of a particular class of person is inferred from past experience, and data-holdings are searched for individuals with a close fit to that set of characteristics. An example of profiling is that of airline passenger profiling. Some mass dataveillance systems available in the United States are discussed below to illustrate the extent to which dataveillance can be conducted.

(iv) ECHELON

The United States National Security Agency has created a global spy system, code-named ECHELON, which captures and analyzes virtually every telephone call, telefax, email, and telex message sent anywhere in the world. ECHELON is controlled by the National Security Agency and is operated in conjunction with the Government Communications Headquarters (GCHQ) of England, the Communications Security Establishment (CSE) of Canada, the Australian Defense Security Directorate (DSD), and the General Communications Security Bureau (GCSB) of New Zealand. These organizations are bound together under a 1948 agreement, UKUSA.

ECHELON is designed primarily for non-military targets: governments, organizations, businesses, and individuals in virtually every country. It potentially affects every person communicating between (and sometimes within) countries anywhere in the world.

The backbone of the ECHELON network is the massive listening and reception stations directed at the Intelsat and Inmarsat satellites that are responsible for the vast majority of phone and fax communications traffic within and between countries and continents. The 20 Intelsat satellites follow a geo-stationery orbit locked onto a particular point on the Equator. These satellites carry primarily civilian traffic, but they do additionally carry diplomatic and governmental communications that are of particular interest to the UKUSA parties.

The extraordinary ability of ECHELON to intercept most of the communications traffic in the world is breathtaking in its scope. However, the power of ECHELON resides in its ability to decrypt, filter, examine, and codify messages into selective categories for further analysis by intelligence agents from the various UKUSA agencies. As the electronic signals are brought into the station, they are fed through the massive computer systems, where voice recognition, optical character recognition (OCR), and data information engines work on the messages.

(v)   Total Informational Awareness

Total Informational Awareness is a project of the United States Department of Defense. Total Informational Awareness (TIA) is designed to gather personal data on a grand scale, including emails, telephone calls, financial records, transportation habits, and medical information.

Its proponents believe that, by scanning and analyzing this massive amount of data, government agents will be able to predict and prevent crime.

(vi) Carnivore

Carnivore is an Internet surveillance program, which is currently used by the United States government. It is somewhat similar to ECHELON. Contrary to prior assertions, a subsequent government-commissioned review panel found that Carnivore is indeed capable of collecting all communications over the segment of the network being watched.

Carnivore is being replaced by an even more powerful system, known as DCS 1000, or Enhanced Carnivore, which reportedly has higher capacity to deal with speedier broadband networks. The United States government also has issued a controversial field guidance memorandum regarding the installation and operation for this family of surveillance tools.

(vii) Oasis and Fluent

Oasis and Fluent are two programs which experts believe may be used to enhance ECHELON's capabilities. One of these, Oasis, automatically creates machine-readable transcripts from television and audio broadcasts. Reports indicate that Oasis can distinguish individual speakers and detect personal characteristics (such as gender) and denote these characteristics in the transcripts it creates.

The other program, FLUENT, allows English-language keyword searches of non-English materials. This data-mining tool not only finds pertinent documents, but also translates them, although the number of languages that can currently be translated is apparently limited (Russian, Chinese, Portuguese, Serbo-Croatian, Korean, and Ukrainian). In addition, FLUENT displays the frequency with which a given word is used in a document and can handle alternate search term spellings.

(viii) CALEA

The United States Communications Assistance for Law Enforcement Act (CALEA) generally requires telecommunications carriers to modify their existing networks and to design and deploy new generations of equipment (including software), all to ensure that carriers can meet certain specified "capability" and "capacity" requirements related to the ability of authorized government agencies to engage in wiretapping.

3.03   Conditions for Surveillance

(a) United States

In the United States, the Foreign Intelligence Surveillance Act, 1978, was enacted for the purpose of regulating national security. The Foreign Intelligence and Surveillance Court that was constituted under the Foreign Intelligence Surveillance Act was set up primarily for dealing with cases relating to national security that have a foreign nexus and where the role of the surveyor is assumed by the state.

Under the Foreign Intelligence Surveillance Act, for an application for surveillance to be upheld, the state is required to show that the target of the investigation is a foreign power or agent of a foreign power and that the place to be monitored or searched is or will be used by the target.[3] However, when the subject is a United States person, a higher probable cause standard is imposed and the application must show that "the acquisition of such information is necessary to national defense or security or the conduct of foreign affairs".[4]

Therefore, as long as the application relates to a foreign power or agent of a foreign power, the test to be satisfied relates to the identity of the subject. In contrast, probable cause in a criminal investigation:

> . . . exists where the facts and circumstances within their [the officers] knowledge . . . [are] sufficient in themselves to warrant a man of reasonable caution in the belief that an offence has been or is being committed.[5]

---

3   50 United States Code, section 1805(a).

4   National Security Agency Report to Congress: "Legal Standards for the Intelligence Community in Conducting Electronic Surveillance" (2001), available at http://www.fas.org/irp/nsa/standards.html (last visited 17 December 2002).

5   *Brinegar v. United States*, (338 U.S. 160, at pp. 175–76) (1949) (first and third alterations in original) (quoting *Carroll v. United States*, (267 U.S. 132, at p. 162) (1925)).

This test, which is the kind of standard most jurisdictions use for investigations, relates to a state of fact or events.

Courts have permitted evidence gathered in the Foreign Intelligence Surveillance Act investigations to be used in criminal convictions with the stipulation that foreign intelligence gathering be the "primary purpose" of the surveillance.[6] The courts have found that evidence resulting from surveillance conducted under the Foreign Intelligence Surveillance Act warrant is not prohibited even if the government foresees that the results of such surveillance will later be used as evidence in a criminal trial.[7]

There is an exception to the warrant requirement in the Foreign Intelligence Surveillance Act process. If something illegal is in plain view, there is no need for a warrant because law enforcement officials did not need to search to find it. Originally, the exception required that police discover the evidence inadvertently.[8] In *Horton v. California*,[9] however, the Supreme Court eliminated the inadvertence requirement for a plain view seizure.

Another exception to the warrant requirement is the open fields' doctrine. The doctrine suggests that if an item cannot be classified as a person, house, paper, or effect, the item is not entitled to Fourth Amendment protection against search or seizure.[10] This is particularly true where the owner has not taken reasonable precautions to ensure privacy.

(b) United Kingdom

(i) In General

The United Kingdom has enacted several laws that lay down the grounds on which surveillance can be conducted. The following discussion deals with the various legislation and the requisites.

(ii) Data Protection Act, 1998

The Data Protection Act mostly covers workplace surveillance where the employer assumes the role of the surveyor. The Data Protection Act provides

---

6   *United States v. Megahey*, 553 F. Supp. 1180, at pp. 1189–1190 (E.D.N.Y., 1982).

7   *United States v. Pelton*, 835 F2d 1067, at p. 1076 (4th Cir., 1987) (holding that "the Foreign Intelligence Surveillance Act surveillance is not tainted simply because the government can anticipate that the fruits of the surveillance may later be used . . . in a criminal trial").

8   *Coolidge v. New Hampshire*, 403 U.S. 443, at pp. 469–471.

9   *Horton v. California*, 496 U.S. 128 (1990).

10   The Fourth, Amendment specifically discusses "the right of the people to be secure in their persons, houses, papers, and effects . . .". United States Constitution, Amendment IV. However reasonable a landowner's expectations of privacy may be, those expectations cannot convert a field into a "house" or an "effect". *Oliver v. United States*, 466 U.S. 170, at p. 184 (1984) (White, J., *concurring*).

says that personal data that is processed for the purpose of preventing or detecting crime is exempt from the fair processing code and from the general obligation that the personal data be processed fairly. If an employer uses workplace surveillance for the purpose of detecting fraud, no notice is required to be given to workers about the data processing involved.

It provides that personal data may be obtained only for one or more specified and lawful purposes and may not be further processed in any manner incompatible with that purpose or those purposes. The principles of the Data Protection Act do not apply to the disclosure by a data controller of personal data processed for the purpose of preventing or detecting crime, to the extent that compliance with the principle would be likely to prejudice that purpose. Exemptions also are provided in the case of personal data whose disclosure is necessary for:

1. The purpose of, or in connection with, any legal proceedings (including prospective legal proceedings); or

2. The purpose of obtaining legal advice, or is otherwise necessary for the purposes of establishing, exercising, or defending legal rights, to the extent that the principle is inconsistent with the disclosure in question.

Thus, an employer may disclose to the police information gained through workplace surveillance that discloses criminal behavior, even where the possibility of such disclosure has not been previously notified to the worker.

Surveillance-related data whose processing was otherwise permitted by the Act would breach that provision if the data subject or other person who supplied it to the data controller was misled as to the purposes for which it was to be processed, save where the processing was in connection with the detection or prevention of a criminal offence or the apprehension or prosecution of an offender.

Furthermore, data processing will comply with the principles only where workers are provided with information as to the purpose or purposes for which the data is being processed. The only surveillance-related cases in which the obligation to process personal data fairly is likely not to apply is where the processing is "for the purpose of preventing or detecting crime" (as in a case in which surveillance is conducted to detect fraud).

The draft of the Code of Practice on Employment issued by the Information Commissioner (which deals with monitoring and surveillance) says that monitoring should occur only:

1. Where there is an identified business need;

2. Where its aims are not outweighed by its impact on staff;

3. To the extent that it is necessary; and

4. Save in exceptional cases, only with the full knowledge of staff concerned.

The Commissioner states that monitoring and surveillance should not go beyond that necessary to the aim pursued and that employers should strive to find alternative methods to achieve the ends pursued and suggests that covert monitoring can only be used where criminal behavior is suspected (and then only as narrowly as possible). The Data Protection Act, therefore, has the potential to curtail the ability of employers to lawfully engage in workplace-related surveillance.

(iii) Regulation of Investigatory Powers Act, 2000

The Regulation of Investigatory Powers Act was enacted to ensure that surveillance conducted by public authorities complies with the provisions of the Human Rights Act, 1998. To impose effective regulation on the interception of communications, section 1 makes it an offense:

> . . . for a person intentionally and without lawful authority to intercept, at any place in the United Kingdom, any communication in the course of its transmission . . . .[11]

The new regime applies to both public postal and telecommunications systems and also to private telecommunications systems that are linked to a public network (such as business switchboards).[12] This interception offence is subject to two limitations.

Under section 1(3), if the interception is carried out without lawful authority under the Regulation of Investigatory Powers Act, then it will be actionable in civil law. However, by section 1(6), conduct is excluded from criminal liability if perpetrated or permitted by a person lawfully entitled to control the operation or the use of the system. Second, by section 1(5) the interception has lawful authority under the Regulation of Investigatory Powers Act if it falls within section 3, 4, or 5 (see text, below) or where an existing statutory power is used to obtain stored communications (such as a search under warrant or on arrest under powers in the Police and Criminal Evidence Act, 1984.

Section 3 authorizes certain kinds of interception where all parties to a communication have consented to the interception, or where the recipient consents and the communication is subject to surveillance under Part II of the

---

11   "Interception" and "transmission" of communications (but not postal items) are defined in section 2. "Communications" for these purposes do not include "traffic data", since they are regulated by Part 1, Chapter 2. The territorial limitation of the Regulation of Investigatory Powers Act is explained by sections 2(4) and 20.

12   This responds to *Halford v. United Kingdom* (1997) 24 *E.H.R.R.* 523; *A v. France*, Ser A 277/B. It replaces a Home Office Circular 15/1999, Interception of Non-Public Telecommunications Networks (1999).

Regulation of Investigatory Powers Act. Section 4 provides for situations like complying with international agreements for mutual assistance[13] and for certain cases where interception and recording is necessary for the carrying on of any business of monitoring or keeping a record.

More explicit lawful authority is provided for in the shape of interception warrants issued by the Home Secretary under section 5. The warrant issued must be "proportionate" to the purpose for which it is sought and it must be "necessary".

> (3) . . . a warrant is necessary on grounds falling within this subsection if it is necessary:
>
> (a) In the interests of national security;
>
> (b) For the purpose of preventing or detecting serious crime;
>
> (c) For the purpose of safeguarding the economic well-being of the United Kingdom; or
>
> (d) For the purpose, in circumstances appearing to the Secretary of State to be equivalent to those in which he would issue a warrant by virtue of paragraph (b), of giving effect to the provisions of any international mutual assistance agreement.
>
> (5) A warrant shall not be considered necessary on the ground falling within subsection (3)(c) unless the information which it is thought necessary to obtain is information relating to the acts or intentions of persons outside the British Islands.

(c) European Union

In the European Union (EU), there are no specific statutes stating the grounds for surveillance. The European courts have laid down standard safeguards, which the surveying authority would have to keep in mind before conducting surveillance. The European Court of Justice adopts the approach that procedural standards should be complied with and, in a recent report,[14] summarizes those as comprising:

1. Legality — The possibility of such interference must be clearly laid out in law, readily accessible, and precise so that citizens are aware of the circumstances under which surveillance may be undertaken or communications intercepted. It should go without saying that legality requires that the grounds for surveillance should be subject to prior judicial scrutiny.

---

13   For example, articles 12 and 13 of the Convention on Mutual Assistance in Criminal Matters between Member States of the European Union.

14   European Court of Justice, *Justice: Under Surveillance: Covert Policing and Human Rights Standards* (1998).

2. Necessity — The interference should be necessary because less intrusive means have been tried and failed or are inappropriate and the operation is likely to produce valuable material that would aid the investigation.

3. Proportionality — The intrusive measures should be proportional to the seriousness of the offence, bearing in mind the rights not only of the individual, but also those of others likely to be affected.

4. Accountability — There must be proper controls and adequate and effective remedies against abuse.

3.04 Protection Offered to a Subject of Surveillance

(a) United States

American scholars as far back as the 1800s have debated the existence of the right to privacy.[15] The United States Supreme Court has found a limited "right to privacy" stemming from a combination of the First, Third, Fourth, Fifth, Ninth, and Fourteenth Amendments.

The United States Constitution does not provide an explicit right to privacy, but it is implied in the Fourth Amendment. The Fourth Amendment protects people, not places. What a person knowingly exposes to the public, even in his own home or office, is not a subject of Fourth Amendment protection. However, what he seeks to preserve as private, even in an area accessible to the public, may be constitutionally protected.

The Supreme Court, in *Keith*,[16] noted that:

> . . . there is, understandably, a deep-seated uneasiness and apprehension that electronic surveillance capability will be used to intrude on cherished privacy of law-abiding citizens.

The challenge for the court involved balancing the necessity of ensuring national security against the threat to individual liberties posed by unchecked executive surveillance authority.[17]

In weighing these competing interests, Justice Powell's opinion expanded the principles that would guide all three branches of the federal government in the application of the Fourth Amendment to national security electronic surveillance.[18] Powell noted that national security cases present a particularly

---

15 Warren and Brandeis, "The Right to Privacy", 4 *Harv. L. Rev.* 193 (1890).

16 *United States v. United States District Court (Keith)*, 407 U.S. 297 (1972).

17 18 United States Code, section 2511(3).

18 *United States v. Duggan*, 743 F2d 59, at p. 72 (2d Cir., 1984) (noting that decision in Keith "made clear that the requirements of the Fourth Amendment may change" depending on governmental interests and that interests in national security context are "substantially different" from those in criminal investigations).

prickly situation because of the tremendous governmental interest and the likelihood of both unreasonable invasions of privacy and jeopardy to free speech rights.[19]

Although he recognized the vital importance of protecting the national security, Justice Powell's primary concern was ensuring the sanctity of political dissent — both public and private — in determining the application of the Fourth Amendment to national security surveillance.[20]

For Powell, the Fourth Amendment had to serve as:

> . . . an important working part of our machinery of government, operating . . . to check the "well-intentioned" but mistakenly over-zealous executive officers.

This constitutional function could not be guaranteed when domestic security surveillance was left entirely to the discretion of the executive:

> Unreviewed executive discretion may yield too readily to pressures to obtain incriminating evidence and overlook potential invasions of privacy and protected speech.

Thus, the court reiterated its assertion in *Katz* that some interposition of the judiciary between citizens and law enforcement must exist.[21]

It is clear that the United States provides to its citizens an implied right to privacy through the Constitution. The concept of the rational test basis would imply that a balance would have to be struck between the rights of the individual, on one hand, and societal needs, on the other.

---

19 *United States v. United States District Court (Keith)*, 407 U.S. 297 (1972), at p. 312 (noting that without national security, all constitutional liberties are at risk). See also at p. 313 ("National security cases, moreover, often reflect a convergence of First and Fourth Amendment values not present in cases of "ordinary" crime. Though the investigative duty of the executive may be stronger in such cases, so also is there a greater jeopardy to constitutionally protected speech").

20 *United States v. United States District Court (Keith)*, 407 U.S. 297 (1972), at p. 314 (discussing political dissent). Justice Powell noted: "The price of lawful public dissent must not be a dread of subjection to an unchecked surveillance power. Nor must the fear of unauthorized official eavesdropping deter vigorous citizen dissent and discussion of Government action in private conversation. For private dissent, no less than open public discourse is essential to our free society".

21 *United States v. United States District Court (Keith)*, 407 U.S. 297 (1972), at p. 317 (noting that, while surveillance at issue may have been entirely reasonable, the court had never let this fact excuse lack of judicial involvement prior to surveillance); *id. United States v. United States District Court (Keith)*, 407 U.S. 297 (1972), at p. 318 (noting that judicially created exceptions to warrant requirement did not dilute principle of obtaining warrant prior to surveillance whenever practicable).

(b) Europe and the United Kingdom

The European Convention on Human Rights, 1950, addresses the issue of privacy as follows:

> 8(1). Everyone has the right to respect for his private and family life, his home, and his correspondence.

> 8(2). There shall be no interference by a public authority with the exercise of this right except such as is in accordance with the law and is necessary in a democratic society in the interests of national security, public safety or the economic well being of the country, for the prevention of disorder or crime, for the protection of health or morals, or for the protection of the rights and freedoms of others.

Article 8 of the European Convention on Human Rights provides a right to respect for private and family life, subject to the qualification in Article 8(2) that interference may occur where it is "in accordance with the law and is necessary in a democratic society in the interests of" the prevention of disorder or crime. The interrelationship between article 8(1) and (2) is not one of balancing the legitimate interference against the right;[22] the article 8(2) qualifications clearly represent exceptions to article 8(1). The court determines whether surveillance interfered with privacy rights as broadly interpreted in article 8(1)[23] before assessing the article 8(2) elements in turn.

Article 13 provides that:

> . . . everyone whose rights and freedoms as set forth in this Convention are violated shall have an effective remedy before a national authority notwithstanding that the violation has been committed by persons acting in an official capacity.

In the face of considerable opposition, this provision was not incorporated in the Human Rights Act.[24]

In Convention terms, article 13 requires an "effective remedy" when there is a breach of article 8.[25] Logically, the effectiveness of the available remedy must lie in its ability to secure the protection offered by article 8 — in this context, a respect for privacy. The fact that the Human Rights Act does not incorporate article 13 does not negate domestic obligations to provide an

---

22   McHarg, "Reconciling Human Rights and the Public Interest: Conceptual Problems and Doctrinal Uncertainty in the Jurisprudence of the European Convention on Human Rights" (1999) 62 *M.L.R.* 671; Ashworth, "Serious Crime and Criminal Procedure", *Human Rights* (2002).

23   *Kopp v. Switzerland* (1998) 27 E.H.R.R. 91; *Klass v. Germany* (1978) 2 E.H.R.R. 214.

24   Emmerson and Ashworth, *Human Rights and Criminal Justice* (2001), chapter 3.

25   Harris, O'Boyle, and Warbrick, *The Law of the European Convention on Human Rights* (1995), chapter 14.

effective remedy because the Convention must always be read as a whole,[26] and section 8 of the Human Rights Act provides a right to just and appropriate remedy.

In the United Kingdom, until the passage of the Human Rights Act, 1998, the concept of privacy was one that neither Parliament nor the courts had taken the initiative to develop.[27]

In 1996, in *R v. Brown*,[28] Lord Hoffman stated that, "English common law does not know a general right of privacy and Parliament has been reluctant to enact one". The House of Lords, later that year in a case concerning covert police surveillance, commented on the "continuing widespread concern at this apparent failure of the law".[29] Such a reluctance to develop the law has partly been a result of the inherent difficulties in defining such a nebulous concept.

However, although "privacy" as a domestic legal term in England might be lacking clear parameters, the right to respect for private life under article 8 of the Convention brings with it decades of developing jurisprudence. The European Court's jurisprudence lays down a minimum set of values that must be respected in signatory states, and, even prior to the Human Rights Act, this had impacted United Kingdom law and practice indirectly.[30]

The Human Rights Act has brought about the development of a coherent and comprehensive system to ensure that all police action that might interfere with article 8 is convention compliant. It has also ensured that the courts must address directly the question of when a particular action interferes with the right to respect for private life.

A number of general principles have derived from the interpretation of the exceptions to the general right. First, if the primary right is engaged in a particular case, the restriction on that right must be "in accordance with the law". European Convention jurisprudence has interpreted article 8(2) to mean that, regardless of the end to be achieved, no right guaranteed by the Convention should be interfered with unless a citizen knows the basis for the interference through an ascertainable national law.[31] That law should be sufficiently clear

---

26   *Abdulaziz, Cabales, and Balkandali v. United Kingdom* (1985) 7 E.H.R.R. 471, at paragraph 60.

27   Feldman "Secrecy, Dignity, or Autonomy? Views of Privacy as a Civil Liberty" [1994] C.L.P. 41. Although, in recent years, the law of confidence had been developing: Fenwick and Phillipson, "The doctrine of confidence as a privacy remedy in the human rights era" [2000] 63 M.L.R. 660.

28   *R v. Brown* (1996) 1 All E.R. 545, at p. 556.

29   *R v. Khan* (1997) A.C. 558, at p. 582.

30   *R v. Secretary of State for the Home Department Ex p. Brind* [1991] 1 A.C. 696.

31   *Malone v. United Kingdom.* (1985) 7 E.H.R.R. 14; *Leander v. Sweden* (1987) 9 E.H.R.R. 433.

and accessible to ensure that people can adequately determine with some degree of certainty when and how their rights might be affected.

Second, any interference with the primary right must be directed towards a legitimate aim. In terms of the right to private life, restrictions that may be justified are found in article 8(2). The restrictions on the primary right are numerous and widely drawn, and it could be argued that it is not overly burdensome to require state conduct to remain within such boundaries. However, the list is intended to be exhaustive, and there should be no capacity for the state to add to those grounds.

In addition to being lawful, and for one of the prescribed purposes, the restriction also must be "necessary in a democratic society". "Necessity", although not defined in the Convention itself, has been interpreted by the European Court as not synonymous with "indispensable", but not as flexible as "ordinary, useful, reasonable", or "desirable".[32] Instead, what is required is that the interference with the primary right should be in response to "a pressing social need".

The Human Rights Act has brought the concept of proportionality directly into play in the United Kingdom. In the context of qualified rights, such as article 8, proportionality has a special relevance. In *Brown v. Stott*,[33] Lord Steyn commented:

> . . . a single-minded concentration on the pursuit of fundamental rights of individuals to the exclusion of the interests of the wider public might be subversive of the ideal of tolerant European liberal democracies. The fundamental rights of individuals are of supreme importance but those rights are not unlimited: we live in communities of individuals who also have rights.

Proportionality is a vital factor that attempts to find a balance between the interests of the individual and the interest of the wider community. Despite not explicitly appearing within the text of the Convention itself, it is said to be a defining characteristic of the way in which the courts seeks to protect human rights. It is, according to the Court, "inherent in the whole of the Convention".[34]

The jurisprudence of the European Court identifies numerous factors to be taken into account when considering the issue of proportionality.[35] For example, at the extreme, if a measure which restricts a right does so in such a way as to impair the very essence of the right, it will almost certainly be

---

32 *Silver v. United Kingdom* (1983) 5 E.H.R.R. 347, at paragraph 97.

33 *Brown v. Stott* [2001] 2 W.L.R. 817.

34 *Soering v. United Kingdom* (1989) 11 E.H.R.R. 439, at paragraph 89.

35 Starmer, *European Human Rights Law: The Human Rights Act 1998 and the European Convention on Human Rights* (1999), chapter 4.

disproportionate.[36] Furthermore, the need to have relevant and sufficient reasons provided in support of the particular measure has been emphasized:

> The Court will look at the interference complained of in light of the case as a whole and determine whether the reasons adduced by the national authorities to justify it are relevant and sufficient and whether the means employed were proportionate to the legitimate aim pursued.

It also should be considered whether there is a less-restrictive alternative. It is unlikely that a measure could be considered to be proportionate where a less restrictive or intrusive alternative was available.

A balancing exercise takes place that requires a consideration of whether the interference with the right is greater than is necessary to achieve the aim.

This is not an exercise in balancing the right against the interference, but instead balances the nature and extent of the interference against the reasons for interfering.[37]

A further factor in the proportionality equation is to assess the adequacy of procedural fairness in the decision-making process. Where a public body has exercised a discretion that restricts an individual's Convention rights, the rights of the affected individual should have been taken into account. For example, the policy should not be arbitrary but should be based on relevant considerations.[38] The guarantee against arbitrariness is one at the heart of the European Convention on Human Rights provisions. Proportionality can be more easily established where it could be shown that there are sufficient safeguards against abuse in place. This was expressed clearly in *Klass v. Germany*:

> One of the fundamental principles of a democratic society is the rule of law . . . [which] implies, *inter alia*, that an interference by the executive authorities with an individual's rights should be subject to an effective control . . . .

Given that most policing actions will have a basis in law and will invariably satisfy the requirement of being in pursuit of a legitimate objective (principally, the prevention and detection of crime), the crux of a case will often be the proportionality of the action under scrutiny. In *Ex p. Kebilene*, Lord Hope commented:

> . . . the Convention should be seen as an expression of fundamental principles rather than a set of mere rules. The questions which the

---

36   *Rees v. United Kingdom* (1987) 9 E.H.R.R. 56.
37   Feldman, *Civil Liberties and Human Rights in England and Wales* (2nd ed., 2002), at p. 57.
38   *W v. United Kingdom* (1988) 10 E.H.R.R. 29.

courts will have to decide in the application of these principles will involve questions of balance between competing interests and issues of proportionality.

The European Court has never sought to give a conclusive definition of privacy, considering it neither necessary nor desirable. However, in *Niemietz v. Germany*, the Court stated:

> It would be too restrictive to limit the notion to an "inner circle" in which the individual may live his own personal life as he chooses and to exclude therefrom entirely the outside world not encompassed within that circle. Respect for private life also must comprise to a certain degree the right to establish and develop relationships with other human beings. There appears, furthermore, to be no reason of principle why this understanding of the notion of "private life" should be taken to exclude activities of a professional or business nature since it is, after all, in the course of their working lives that the majority of people have a significant, if not the greatest opportunity of developing relationships with the outside world.

(c) India

In India, two main articles of the Constitution address privacy. These are the fundamental rights guaranteed by the Constitution to its citizens.

Article 21[39] gives protection of life and personal liberty. The Supreme Court has held that several un-enumerated rights fall within article 21, since the expression "personal liberty" is of the widest amplitude. This covers the right to privacy.[40] Wire-tapping of voluntary conversations, for the purpose of investigation of crime, has been upheld,[41] assuming that privacy of conversation would be derived from "personal liberty".

The judicial stand in India is that privacy is an inherent right guaranteed by the Constitution. There are certain safeguards that are provided in article 19(1)(d), read with article 21, to ensure that privacy rights are not violated and, until specific legislation is enacted in this regard, the judicial pronouncements will govern the field of the right to privacy.

---

39 Article 21 reads: "Protection of life and personal liberty. No person shall be deprived of his life or personal liberty except according to procedure established by law".

40 *Gobind v. State of MP*, A.I.R. 1975 S.C. 1378 (paragraph 28); (1975) 2 S.C.C. 148. In this case, the petitioner was subjected to domiciliary visits by the police and was put under surveillance on the basis of criminal history.

41 *Malakani, RM v. State of Maharashtra*, A.I.R. 1973 S.C. 157, paragraph 30); (1973) 1 S.C.C. 471.

3.05   Procedures to Be Followed for Surveillance

(a) United States

In the mid-1970s, reports appeared in the American press alleging that the Central Intelligence Agency (CIA) had compiled files on thousands of American citizens. The reports led Congress to form investigative committees to consider the extent of executive surveillance abuses. The committees found that during the 1960s and 1970s, the CIA compiled a computerized database containing thousands of records chronicling the involvement of individual participants in the domestic antiwar movement. From these databases, the CIA:

> . . . produced a steady stream of reports to the FBI and other agencies detailing the results of its various intelligence activities with respect to the antiwar movement.[42]

The conclusion reached was that existing legal and policy constraints on intelligence activities were inadequate and that proper supervision and accountability within the Executive branch and to the Congress were sorely lacking. Although Title III provided a framework for criminal surveillance, the foreign intelligence exception was the creation of muddled judicial doctrine. Congress recognized that under the then-current system, action by the judiciary was purely remedial, and the courts essentially were powerless to prevent executive abuses before they occurred. Thus, Congress reacted to the executive's abuse of the foreign intelligence exception by creating a system in which "the judiciary would . . . be involved from the onset", effectively curbing the executive's ability to conduct warrantless national security surveillance that arguably contravened constitutional requirements.

The Foreign Intelligence Surveillance Act, 1978, was thus enacted. United States courts have permitted evidence gathered in the Foreign Intelligence Surveillance Act investigations to be used in criminal convictions with the stipulation that foreign intelligence gathering be the "primary

---

42   Reimers, notes: "Congressional involvement . . . remained minimal until the mid-1970s, [when] a series of especially troubling revelations appeared in the press concerning United States. Intelligence activities. Covert action programs involving assassination attempts against foreign leaders and covert efforts to effect changes in other governments were reported for the first time. The efforts of intelligence agencies to collect information concerning the political activities of United States citizens during the late 1960s and early 1970s were also documented extensively by the press". (quoting Select Committee on Intelligence, United States Senate, 103d Cong., 2nd Sess., Report on Legislative Oversight of Intelligence Activities: The United States Experience 3, at p. 4 (Comm. Print, 1994)).

purpose" of the surveillance.[43] The courts have found that evidence resulting from surveillance conducted under the Foreign Intelligence Surveillance Act warrant is not prohibited even if the government foresees that the results of such surveillance will later be used as evidence in a criminal trial.[44]

In *Duggan*, the court acknowledged that surveillance in the interest of national security and criminal prosecution will often overlap, but that this intersection is mitigated by the requirement that foreign intelligence information gathering be the primary objective of the surveillance.[45] Courts have pointed out that the language of the Act itself, as well as the legislative history, indicates that evidence obtained through the Foreign Intelligence Surveillance Act surveillance was expected to be admissible in criminal proceedings.

The Foreign Intelligence Surveillance Act requires a showing of probable cause that an individual is linked to a foreign power or terrorist organization. It requires the preparation and presentation of a complete Foreign Intelligence Surveillance Act application to the Foreign Intelligence and Surveillance Court within 24 hours after the Attorney General's authorization.[46]

Neglecting to meet these time limit results is suppression of the information obtained during the surveillance or search. the Foreign Intelligence Surveillance Act is a complex statute outlining specific procedural requirements for conducting electronic surveillance. The Foreign Intelligence Surveillance Act restricts the use of electronic surveillance to monitoring "foreign powers" or their "agents" including "United States persons" to obtain "foreign intelligence information".[47] After first obtaining the approval of the Attorney General, a federal official may apply for Foreign Intelligence Surveillance Act electronic surveillance warrant. The official must submit an application that includes:

1. The identity of the surveillance target;

---

43   *United States v. Megahey*, 533 F. Supp. 1180, at pp. 1189 and 1190 (E.D.N.Y., 1982).

44   *United States v. Pelton*, 835 F2d 1067, at p. 1076 (4th Cir., 1987) (holding that "the Foreign Intelligence Surveillance Act surveillance is not tainted simply because the government can anticipate that the fruits of the surveillance may later be used . . . in a criminal trial").

45   *United States v. Duggan*, 743 F2d 59, at pp. 75–78 (2d Cir., 1984).

46   50 United States Code, sections 1805(e) and 1824(d) (1994).

47   Chiarella, "So Judge, How Do I Get That Foreign Intelligence Surveillance Act Warrant?: The Policy and Procedure for Conducting Electronic Surveillance", *Army Law* (October 1997).

2. The information indicating that the target is a "foreign power"[48] or an "agent of a foreign power";[49]

3. Evidence that the location indicated for surveillance is being used or is about to be used by the foreign power or its agent; and

4. The type of surveillance, proposed minimization procedures, and certification that the information sought is "foreign intelligence information".[50]

---

48   50 United States Code, section 1801(a). "Foreign power" is defined as: (1) a foreign government or any component thereof, whether or not recognized by the United States; (2) a faction of a foreign nation or nations, not substantially composed of United States persons; (3) an entity that is openly acknowledged by a foreign government or governments to be directed and controlled by such foreign government or governments; (4) a group engaged in international terrorism or activities in preparation therefor; (5) a foreign-based political organization, not substantially composed of United States persons; or (6) an entity that is directed and controlled by a foreign government or governments.

49   50 United States Code, section 1801(b). "Agent of a foreign power" is defined as: (1) any person other than a United States person, who - (A) acts in the United States as an officer or employee of a foreign power, or as a member of a foreign power as defined in subsection (a)(4) of this section; (B) acts for or on behalf of a foreign power which engages in clandestine intelligence activities in the United States contrary to the interests of the United States, when the circumstances of such person's presence in the United States indicate that such person may engage in such activities in the United States, or when such person knowingly aids or abets any person in the conduct of such activities or knowingly conspires with any person to engage in such activities; or (2) any person who — (A) knowingly engages in clandestine intelligence gathering activities for or on behalf of a foreign power, which activities involve or may involve a violation of the criminal statutes of the United States; (B) pursuant to the direction of an intelligence service or network of a foreign power, knowingly engages in any other clandestine intelligence activities for or on behalf of such foreign power, which activities involve or are about to involve a violation of the criminal statutes of the United States; (C) knowingly engages in sabotage or international terrorism, or activities that are in preparation therefor, or on behalf of a foreign power; or (D) knowingly enters the United States under a false or fraudulent identity for or on behalf of a foreign power or, while in the United States, knowingly assumes a false or fraudulent identity for or on behalf of a foreign power; or (E) knowingly aids or abets any person in the conduct of activities described in subparagraph (A), (B), or (C) or knowingly conspires with any person to engage in activities described in subparagraph (A), (B), or (C).

50   50 United States Code, section 1801(e). "Foreign intelligence information" is defined as: (1) information that relates to, and if concerning a United States person is necessary to, the ability of the United States to protect against — (A) actual or potential attack or other grave hostile acts of a foreign power or an agent of a foreign power; (B) sabotage or international terrorism by a foreign power or an agent of a foreign power; or (C) clandestine intelligence activities by an intelligence service or network of a foreign power or by an agent of a foreign power; or (2) information with respect to a foreign power or foreign territory that relates to, and if concerning a United States person is necessary to — (A) the national defense or the security of the United States; or (B) the conduct of the foreign affairs of the United States.

After the Foreign Intelligence Surveillance Act application has been approved by the appropriate federal agency, it is forwarded to the Office of Intelligence Policy Review at the Department of Justice.

The Office of Intelligence Policy Review assists the Attorney General and other senior Justice Department officials in fulfilling national security-related responsibilities. It provides legal advice and guidance to various elements of the United States Government that are engaged in national security-related activities. It oversees the implementation of the Foreign Intelligence Surveillance Act and other statutory, Executive Order, or Attorney General-based operational authorities for national security-related activities.[51] The Office of Intelligence Policy Review conducts an independent review of the application to confirm that it contains all the required information. If the application is approved by the Office of Intelligence Policy Review, it is forwarded to the Foreign Intelligence and Surveillance Court.

The Foreign Intelligence and Surveillance Court performs an independent review of the Foreign Intelligence Surveillance Act application. Before issuing the order, the Foreign Intelligence and Surveillance Court determines whether there is "probable cause to believe that the target of the [electronic] surveillance is a foreign power or an agent of a foreign power".[52] In the case of a United States person, the determination must be that the target of the surveillance is not being considered "an agent of a foreign power solely on the basis of activities protected by the first amendment to the Constitution of the United States".[53] The Foreign Intelligence and Surveillance Court also ascertains that the application includes requisite certification from the Department of Justice, indicating that the information sought is "foreign intelligence information" which cannot be obtained by other means.

The Foreign Intelligence and Surveillance Court consists of seven United States District Court judges drawn from different circuits, serving staggered, non-renewable, seven-year terms.[54] The Chief Justice of the United States chooses the Foreign Intelligence and Surveillance Court judges, who rotate their

---

51 United States Department of Justice, Office of Intelligence and Policy Review Organization, Mission and Functions Manual; see http:// www.usdoj.gov/jmd/mps/mission.htm (last visited 26 November 2002).

52 *United States v. Pelton*, 835 F2d 1067, 1075 (4th Cir., 1987).

53 50 United States Code, section 1805(a)(3)(A).

54 Poole, "Inside America's Secret Court: The Foreign Intelligence Surveillance Act"; see http://fly.hiwaay.net/~pspoole/fiscshort.html (last visited 8 September 2002) (describing the nature of the Foreign Intelligence and Surveillance Court proceedings).

duties in Washington, D.C. The judges carry out their duties in a "cipher-locked, windowless, secure room on the top floor of the Department of Justice".[55]

The Foreign Intelligence and Surveillance Court meets two days out of every month, with two of the judges routinely available on other days. The consideration of the Foreign Intelligence Surveillance Act applications is non adversarial and based solely on the presentation of the application through an Office of Intelligence Policy Review representative.[56]

If an application is denied, it is immediately transmitted to a three-judge court of appeal, also composed of selected federal judges. If the appellate court affirms the Foreign Intelligence and Surveillance Court denial of a warrant, the government may apply for a writ of *certiorari* to the Supreme Court.[57]

The Foreign Intelligence Surveillance Act's secrecy also presents a unique problem for a criminal defendant seeking to suppress the Foreign Intelligence Surveillance Act's surveillance evidence or challenge a conviction based on such evidence. Section 1806(f) of the Act requires that the district court judge entertaining a defendant's challenge to a Foreign Intelligence Surveillance Act application "review *in camera* and *ex parte* the application, order, and such other [necessary] materials relating to the surveillance" whenever "the Attorney General files an affidavit under oath that disclosure or an adversary hearing would harm the national security of the United States".

Thus, the Foreign Intelligence Surveillance Act often will not allow a defendant the opportunity to contest adequately the validity of surveillance or the admissibility of crucial evidence obtained thereby. Although courts have affirmed the constitutionality of this reality, the provision nevertheless augments the possibility that governmental abuse of the Foreign Intelligence Surveillance Act will go undiscovered.[58]

The definition of "foreign intelligence information" contained in the Foreign Intelligence Surveillance Act includes "sabotage or international terrorism

---

55 Foreign Intelligence Surveillance Act: Oversight Hearings Before the Subcommittee on Courts, Civil Liberties, and the Administration of Justice of the House Committee on the Judiciary, 98th Cong. 2, at p. 5 (1983) (statement of Mary C. Lawton, Counsel for Intelligence Policy).

56 Robinson, "We're Listening! Electronic Eavesdropping, the Foreign Intelligence Surveillance Act, and the Secret Court", 36 *Willamette L. Rev.* 51, at p. 65 (2000).

57 Birkenstock, "The Foreign Intelligence Surveillance Act and Standards of Probable Cause: An Alternative Analysis", 80 *Geo. L.J.* 843, at p. 848 (1992).

58 *United States v. Belfield*, 692 F2d 141, at pp. 148 and 149 (D.C. Cir., 1982) (finding that 50 United States Code, section 1806(f), does not violate the Fifth and Sixth Amendments).

by a foreign power or an agent of a foreign power". The definition of an "agent of a foreign power" includes any person who "knowingly engages in clandestine intelligence gathering activities . . . which involve or may involve a violation of the criminal statutes of the United States", or "knowingly engages in sabotage or international terrorism".

"International terrorism" means activities that involve violent acts or acts dangerous to human life and that are a violation of the criminal laws of the United States or of any State. The first thing that should be apparent is the breadth of these definitions. "Agent of a foreign power" is defined in behavioral terms, as one engaged in activities which "involve or may involve a violation of the criminal statutes of the United States", or as one who engages in international terrorism. The definition of "international terrorism" has now been expanded to encompass any violent act that would violate the criminal laws of the United States or of any state.

The Foreign Intelligence and Surveillance Court carefully detailed these definitions in showing how the Foreign Intelligence Surveillance Act permits the investigation of criminal behavior. The terms used above include definitions of criminal behavior so broad as to encompass any violation of the criminal statutes of the United States, and any violent act which would violate the criminal law of the United States or any state. It is this broad definition of criminal behavior which the Foreign Intelligence and Surveillance Court says can now provide the purpose behind the Foreign Intelligence Surveillance Act surveillance.

In effect, the exception permitting investigation of some criminal activity swallows the rule that foreign intelligence information should be the primary purpose behind the surveillance. This reasoning permits surveillance not governed by the dictates of the Fourth Amendment to be used to conduct investigations which are primarily criminal so long as the Attorney General informs the Foreign Intelligence and Surveillance Court that "a significant purpose" behind the surveillance also is foreign intelligence. The court's ruling not only offends the Fourth Amendment, but it is a tragically bad policy.[59]

The Uniting and Strengthening of America by Providing Appropriate Tools Required to Intercept and Obstruct Terrorism Act (United States Patriot Act) was enacted on 26 October 2001, less than two months after the terrorist attacks. In a press release, a member of the United States Congress commended the passage of the Act, indicating:

> The Patriot Act modernizes wiretapping laws to keep up with changing technologies such as cell phones, voice mail and e-mail. Current wiretapping laws are outdated. In today's technologically advanced society,

---

59   50 United States Code, section 1801(e)(1)(B) and 1801(b)(2)(A) and (C).

people communicate through a variety of means . . . . By allowing "roving surveillance" of suspected terrorists, law enforcement officials will be able to more effectively monitor their communications and intercept terrorist activity.[60]

The United States Patriot Act expands the Foreign Intelligence Surveillance Act to allow "roving" surveillance, enabling government investigators to intercept all of a suspect's wire or electronic communications relating to the conduct under investigation, regardless of the suspect's location when communicating. This modification was necessary to address the evolution of modern technology. Such roving wiretaps enable surveillance of a person's conversations on a cellular phone or of a target that moves from phone to phone.

The United States Patriot Act extends the roving wiretap authority to intelligence wiretaps.[61] This authorization has the potential to extend nationwide.

The United States Patriot Act expands the government's ability to obtain a court order under the Foreign Intelligence Surveillance Act for pen register or trap and trace surveillance. This eliminates the requirement that the government certify that it has reason to believe that the surveillance is being conducted on a line or device that is or was used in "communications with" someone involved in international terrorism or intelligence activities that may violate United States criminal law or a foreign power or its agent whose communication is believed to concern terrorism or intelligence activities that violate United States law.[62]

This requirement is replaced with the requirement that the government certify that the information sought is "relevant to an ongoing criminal investigation". If the government makes such a showing, a judge "must" grant the order. There is a limitation placed on this expanded provision, stating that a Foreign Intelligence Surveillance Act court order should not authorize the gathering of foreign intelligence information for an investigation concerning surveillance of a United States person when the person has been singled out for investigation "solely on the basis of" First Amendment activities.[63]

These changes are a significant alteration to the mechanics of the Foreign Intelligence Surveillance Act because the language of the United States Patriot Act appears to obviate judicial discretion. The judge "must" grant the order, a

---

60　Uniting and Strengthening America by Providing Appropriate Tools Required to Intercept and Obstruct Terrorism (United States Patriot Act) Act of 2001, Pub. L. Number 107-56, 115 Stat. 272 (2001).

61　United States Patriot Act, section 206.

62　United States Patriot Act, section 214(a)(4) (amending 50 United States Code, section 1842(c)(3)).

63　United States Patriot Act, section 214 (amending 50 United States Code, section 1842(d)(2)(A)).

phrase that seems to mandate judicial issuance of a Foreign Intelligence Surveillance Act warrant.[64] Changes to the provisions for trap and trace would also permit a much broader collection of information than previously permitted under the Foreign Intelligence Surveillance Act. The Federal Bureau of Investigation (FBI) could collect not only the e-mail address of a communication, but also the subject header and information about URLs accessed, revealing information such as search queries, Web sites viewed, and online purchases.

(b) United Kingdom

(i) In General

Legislation was passed permitting a broad range of surveillance activity in the United Kingdom, promising to protect human rights and act as a check on the government's surveillance powers, i.e., the Regulation of Investigatory Powers Act, 2000. The Regulation of Investigatory Powers Act and the Terrorism Act, 2000, are permanent pieces of legislation, granting broad investigatory powers to the government, whose existence is not contingent on a state of emergency.

The United Kingdom government responded to the September 11 attacks by aggressively using these powers and justifying their expansion and solidification.[65]

(ii) Regulation of Investigatory Powers Act, 2000

The Regulation of Investigatory Powers Act was enacted to ensure that certain surveillance activities, conducted by public authorities, complied with the Human Rights Act 1998. The Act signals both the importance of forms of surveillance as techniques of policing and the human rights apprehensions which those strategies engender.

The Regulation of Investigatory Powers Act regulates various privacy invasive activities through a system of authorizations and warrants. The authorizations or warrants can only be granted when the investigatory activity is necessary for one of the statutorily prescribed purposes and is a proportionate means of achieving that purpose. This system is designed to ensure that any interference with article 8(1) of the European Convention on Human Right right can be justified as necessary limitations on the right.

---

64 Strickland, "Information and the War against Terrorism, Part III: New Information-Related Laws and the Impact on Civil Liberties", *Bull. Am. Soc'y for Info. Sci.*, (February–March, 2002), at p. 23.

65 Amnesty International, United Kingdom: "Rights Denied: the UK's Response to 11 September 2001"; see http://www.statewatch.org.

Interception of communications may be authorized by an interception warrant, issued by the Secretary of State. Such a warrant can only be issued if the Secretary of State believes that the interception is necessary in the interests of national security, for the purpose of detecting or preventing serious crime or for the purpose of safeguarding the economic well-being of the United Kingdom.[66] In addition, the Secretary of State must believe that the conduct authorized by the warrant is proportionate to the objective of the interception, which includes consideration of alternative means of achieving the objective.[67]

At a theoretical level, these limits on the issuance of warrants comply fully with article 8(2) of the European Convention on Human Rights' necessity requirements. However, as discussed below, theoretical compliance is no guarantee of practical compliance in the absence of an effective supervisory system.

Authorization for access to communications data follows the necessity and proportionality approach taken in relation to interception warrants. However, there are two significant points of difference. First, authorization may be an internal process and does not require the approval of the Secretary of State.[68] Second, access may be authorized on substantially wider grounds than those applicable to interceptions. The permissible grounds include:

1. The interests of national security and the prevention or detection of crime or disorder;

2. The economic well-being of the United Kingdom;

3. The interests of public safety;

4. The protection of public health;

5. The assessment or collection of tax, duty, levy, or other governmental charge;

6. In an emergency, entailing threat of death or injury, or damage to a person's health; or

7. Any other purpose specified by the Secretary of State by order.[69]

It is doubtful whether the assessment or collection of governmental charges falls within the legitimate aims. Furthermore, the provision for "any other

---

66   Regulation of Investigatory Powers Act, section 5(2) and (3).

67   Regulation of Investigatory Powers Act, section 5(2)(b) and (4).

68   Regulation of Investigatory Powers Act, section 22. The European Court of Human Rights criticized internal authorization in *Kopp v. Switzerland* (1998) 27 *E.H.R.R.* 91, indicating that such a practice is inconsistent with the rule of law.

69   Regulation of Investigatory Powers Act, section 22(2).

purpose" to be specified by the Secretary of State is inconsistent with the tightly prescriptive nature of article 8.

Directed surveillance and the use of covert human intelligence sources may be authorized on a similar basis as access to communications data. While the list of permissible purposes is slightly narrower, the problematic purposes, identified above, are both present. By contrast, the bases of authorization for intrusive surveillance are significantly more limited. Authorization can only be granted in the interests of national security, for the prevention or detection of serious crime or in the interests of the economic well-being of the United Kingdom.

Authorization also can be granted where the authorized activity is proportionate to what it seeks to achieve. Only the Secretary of State has the authority to prohibit certain conduct or impose additional requirements for authorization on certain types of directed surveillance.

The Regulation of Investigatory Powers Act provides for independent scrutiny of the investigatory powers through the appointment of various Commissioners. The Interception of Communications Commissioner has responsibility for reviewing the granting and exercise of interception warrants, as well as monitoring access to communications data and investigations involving encrypted data.[70] Covert surveillance is, in the main part, the responsibility of the Chief and Assistant Surveillance Commissioners.[71]

Finally, the Intelligence Services Commissioner reviews the authorization and exercise of covert surveillance activities and investigations into encrypted data undertaken by the intelligence services, Ministry of Defense, and armed forces, in places other than Northern Ireland.[72]

The supervision and monitoring provided by the Commissioners is the central privacy safeguard in the Regulation of Investigatory Powers Act system. In practical terms, it is of more importance than the Investigatory Powers Tribunal since the value of a complaints-based system of scrutiny is undermined by the inherent secrecy of covert investigatory activities. Unfortunately, this key supervisory and accountability mechanism has serious deficiencies.

Its major failing is the absence of independent judicial authorization of activities. The role of the Commissioners is limited to retrospective review of the exercise of the Regulation of Investigatory Powers Act powers. The only exception to this position involves intrusive surveillance authorizations, which are subject to approval by a Surveillance Commissioner, except in

---

70 Regulation of Investigatory Powers Act, section 57.

71 Regulation of Investigatory Powers Act, sections 62 and 63.

72 Regulation of Investigatory Powers Act, section 59. The Investigatory Powers Commissioner for Northern Ireland, provided for in section 61, has monitoring responsibility for Northern Ireland.

cases of urgency.[73] Retrospective review is likely to be less rigorous than prior scrutiny, and it may well be easier to satisfy the requirements of necessity and proportionality when armed with the incriminating results of the surveillance. This creates the risk that although the statutory authorization regime may comply with article 8, individual exercises of the investigatory powers could be unnecessary or disproportionate.

A further concern is that not all authorizations are subject to scrutiny; only those selected at random by the Commissioner will be reviewed. Accordingly, a substantial number of authorizations may never be subject to any form of independent scrutiny. This prospect is particularly alarming when regard is had to the significant number of errors reported by the Commissioners. For example, in his 2001 Report, the Interception Commissioner stated that there had been 43 errors and that he remained "concerned about the number of errors reported during the year".[74]

In addition to functional deficiencies, it is questionable whether the Commissioners have the time and resources necessary to provide effective oversight. Both the Chief Surveillance and Interception Commissioners in their annual reports have identified staffing shortages as major problems.[75] Although the situation has improved as a result of staff increases, shortages are likely to reoccur with the substantial increase in duties that will occur when further provisions of the Regulation of Investigatory Powers Act enter into force. The limits on the ability of the Commissioners to provide rigorous review is reflected in the comment of the Chief Surveillance Commissioner that:

> I am hopeful that . . . I shall be able to keep under review, as amply as Parliament must be taken to expect of me, the exercise and performance of the surveillance powers and duties.[76]

Complementing the appointment of Commissioners, Part IV of the Regulation of Investigatory Powers Act establishes the Investigatory Powers Tribunal as a means of receiving complaints and providing redress. The Tribunal's key functions are to address complaints, under section 7(1)(a) of the Human Rights Act, against the intelligence services and in relation to the exercise of powers under the Regulation of Investigatory Powers Act.[77]

While its jurisdiction may be comprehensive, its efficacy as a check and balance on those exercising investigatory powers is limited by a number of

---

73   Regulation of Investigatory Powers Act, section 36.

74   Report of the Interception of Communications Commissioner for 2001 (2002 H.C. 1243), at paragraphs 11 and 67.

75   Report of the Interception of Communications Commissioner for 2000, Cm. 5296 (2001), at paragraph 20.

76   Home Office Briefing (January 2002).

77   Regulation of Investigatory Powers Act, section 65.

factors. First, the absence of any disclosure obligation means that the majority of interference with privacy will be undetected.[78] In most cases, an individual will only discover that he or she has been the subject of interception or surveillance if criminal proceedings ensue. Secondly, the secrecy surrounding Tribunal proceedings impedes the ability of complainants to present an effective case. Finally, the lack of any appeal process denies an opportunity for potential deficiencies in the initial hearing to be remedied at a later stage.[79]

Applicants have challenged the secretive nature of Tribunal proceedings. In a recent decision on that challenge, the Tribunal quashed a rule made by the Home Secretary which obliged the Tribunal to conduct all proceedings in private, irrespective of the circumstances.[80]

It creates the possibility that, in the future, the Tribunal will hear certain elements of proceedings in public and that complainants, as well as their legal representatives, will be able to attend parts of the hearing. However, it is likely that this transparency will extend only to the procedural aspects of proceedings and that the substantive content will remain secret. Indeed, the decision does not alter the position that complainants cannot be informed of arguments made or see evidence adduced by a public authority where to do so would entail a risk to national security, even when that information is critical to the case.

Under section 71 of the Regulation of Investigatory Powers Act, the Secretary of State is required to issue one or more Codes of Practice relating to the exercise of the investigatory powers and duties. These Codes are designed to provide guidance to the public authorities affected by the Act and may serve as a guide to good practice. A number of Codes of Practice have been the subject of public consultation, and three have entered into force.[81]

The Codes currently in force contain additional safeguards which may assist in limiting arbitrary interference with privacy. All three Codes stipulate that particular care should be taken in cases where the affected individual might reasonably expect a high degree of privacy or where confidential information is involved.[82]

---

78 The Tribunal received only 102 new applications between 2 October 2000 and 31 December 2001.

79 Regulation of Investigatory Powers Act, section 67(8).

80 This decision was described by the Tribunal itself as "the most significant case ever to come before the Tribunal".

81 The Covert Surveillance Code of Practice, Interception of Communications Code of Practice, and Covert Human Intelligence Sources Code of Practice have entered into force. There has also been consultation on the Draft Access to Communications Data Code of Practice.

82 Part 3 of both the Covert Surveillance Code of Practice and the Covert Human Intelligence Sources Code of Practice and paragraph 3.2 of the Interception of Communications Code of Practice.

In addition, a number of safeguards are set out in relation to communications subject to legal privilege.[83] However, as the Codes have no binding force and there are no consequences for their disregard, the value of these safeguards is limited.

(iii) Police Act

Part III of the Police Act, 1997, establishes a system to authorize various methods of covert surveillance. Its great weakness is that the scheme does not require mandatory judicial supervision.[84] There are, however, many constraints:

1. Authorization will normally be given by the chief officer of the force and not by lower ranks;

2. The criteria for interference with property are reasonably specific;

3. All authorizations will be scrutinized by the commissioners; and

4. There are channels for complaint.

The key criteria for authorizations are laid down in section 93(2) of the Police Act. The authorization should only be given where the authorizing officer believes that:

1. The action is necessary as it will be of "substantial value" in the prevention or detection of "serious crime";[85]

2. The objectives of the action cannot reasonably be achieved by other means; and

3. The action should be proportional, i.e., the extent of the intrusion should be commensurate with the seriousness of the offence.

(c) European Union

As discussed above, European courts have adopted the approach that procedural standards should be complied, which include:

1. Legality;

2. Necessity;

3. Proportionality; and

4. Accountability.

---

83 Paragraphs 3.3–3.9 of both the Covert Surveillance Code of Practice and the Covert Human Intelligence Sources Code of Practice and paragraphs 3.3-3.8 of the Interception of Communications Code of Practice.

84 Prior judicial authorization is the norm in Australia, New Zealand, the United States, Canada, France, and The Netherlands before there can be lawful interception of communications.

85 Police Act, section 93(4).

In *Klass v. Germany*, the court provided the following general guidance as to the legislation authorizing surveillance:

1. The legislation must be designed to ensure that surveillance is not ordered haphazardly, irregularly, or without due and proper care;

2. Surveillance must be reviewed and must be accompanied by procedures which guarantee individual rights;

3. It is, in principle, desirable to entrust the supervisory control to a judge in accordance with the rule of law, but other safeguards might suffice if they are independent and vested with sufficient powers to exercise an effective and continuous control; and

4. If the surveillance is justified under article 8(2) of the European Convention on Human Rights, the failure to inform the individual under surveillance of this fact afterwards is, in principle, justified.

(d) Canada

In Canada, there are certain prescribed guidelines for surveillance conducted by employers. To minimize the negative effects of searching and monitoring employees while effectively protecting legitimate employer interests, all employers (unionized or not) are well-advised to adhere to the legal principles established by Canadian labor arbitrators. Employers must balance their needs against employees' privacy interests and ensure that the search and surveillance methods they use are commensurate with their legitimate business interests.

For example, limiting surveillance to determining the time, origin, destination, and length of an e-mail transmission will allow an employer to determine if the communication was for business or personal purposes. By restricting monitoring in this way, employers can protect their interests without accessing the content of personal communications. With respect to the Internet, the types of websites visited by an employee will indicate whether an employee is using the Internet for personal or business use and whether the employee is accessing illegal or inappropriate material.

Furthermore, employers should establish policies regarding proper monitoring procedures for e-mail, Internet, and telephone usage. The policies should make clear to employees the scope and intent of the monitoring, including:

1. The purpose of the monitoring;

2. The extent to which monitoring will be conducted;

3. The fact that telephones, voice mail, e-mail, and the Internet are to be used for business purposes only;

4. The basis on business use will be distinguished from personal use;

5. The means for accomplishing monitoring and its proposed frequency; and

6. A clear demarcation between what is considered to be a public versus a private communication.[86]

Monitoring policies also should emphasize that employees have a reduced expectation of privacy in the workplace. If possible, such policies should be made part of the terms and conditions of employment at the time of hire. Employers should also consider seeking signed acknowledgements from employees indicating that they understand the policy and consent to monitoring consistent with the policy.

Monitoring employees' use of e-mail, the Internet can be done from a technical point of view. It may be done legally in many circumstances. Employers certainly have a legitimate interest in ensuring that their resources are used in an appropriate manner and that their workplaces are secure.

Nonetheless, it is not self-evident that employers should monitor employees to the full extent of their ability to do so since the corresponding erosion of employee privacy also may have negative effects on the workplace to the employer's ultimate detriment.

In the final analysis, employers must keep in mind that positive employee relations are fundamental to maintaining a productive workplace, and that this interest should be at the heart of any decision to conduct searches or surveillance of employees.

(e) India

The Indian Constitution guarantees to all its citizens, under article 21, the right to life and personal liberty.

The legal framework in India does provide for protection for privacy of individuals. If such fundamentals are already imbedded into the basic framework, it would not be difficult to frame rules or regulations that could govern surveillance procedures and at the same time afford protection to the citizens from indiscriminate intrusions.

In *People's Union of Civil Liberties v. Union of India and Another*,[87] the Supreme Court of India laid down the following guidelines for interception

---

86　Sherrard, "Workplace Searches and Surveillance versus the Employee's Right to Privacy", 48 *U.N.B. L.J.* 283.

87　*People's Union of Civil Liberties v. Union of India and Another*, W.P. (C). Number 256/1991.

of telephonic conversations; it does not address the issue of surveillance *per se*, but is a forerunner for regulations to be framed. The Supreme Court held:

1. An order for telephone-tapping in terms of section 5(2) of the Act may not be issued except by the Home Secretary, Government of India (Central Government) and Home Secretaries of the State Governments. In an urgent case, the power may be delegated to an officer of the Home Department of the Government of India and the State Government not below the rank of Joint Secretary. A copy of the order must be sent to the Review Committee concerned within one week of the passing of the order.

2. The order must require the person to whom it is addressed to intercept in the course of his transmission, by means of the public telecommunication system, such communications as are described in the order. The order also may require the person to whom it is addressed to disclose the intercepted material to such person and in such manner as is described in the order.

3. The matters to be taken into account in considering whether an order is necessary under section 5(2) of the Act must include whether the information that is considered necessary to acquire could reasonably be acquired by other means.

4. The interception required under section 5(2) of the Act must be the interception of such communications as are sent to or from one or more addresses, specified in the order, being an address or addresses likely to be used for the transmission of communications to or from, one particular person specified or described in the order or one particular set of premises specified or described in the order.

5. The order under section 5(2) of the Act must, unless renewed, cease to have effect at the end of the period of two months from the date of issue. The authority which issued the order may, at any time before the end of the two months' period, renew the order if it considers that it is necessary to continue the order in terms of section 5(2) of the Act. The total period for the operation of the order may not exceed six months.

6. The authority that issued the order must maintain the following records: (a) the intercepted communications, (b) the extent to which the material is disclosed, (c) the number of persons and their identity to whom any of the material is disclosed, (d) the extent to which the material is copied, and (e) the number of copies made of any of the material.

7. The use of the intercepted material must be limited to the minimum that is necessary in terms of section 5(2) of the Act.

8. Each copy made of any of the intercepted material must be destroyed as soon as its retention is no longer necessary in terms of section 5(2) of the Act.

9. There must be a Review Committee consisting of the Cabinet Secretary, the Law Secretary and the Secretary, Telecommunication, at the level of the Central Government, The Review Committee at the State level shall consist of the Chief Secretary, Law Secretary, and another member other than the Home Secretary, appointed by the State Government.

The Committee must, on its own and within two months of the passing of the order by the authority concerned, investigate whether there is or has been a relevant order under section 5(2) of the Act. Where there is or has been an order, it must be determined whether there has been any contravention of the provisions of section 5(2) of the Act.

If, on an investigation, the Committee concludes that there has been a contravention of the provisions of section 5(2) of the Act, it must set aside the order under scrutiny of the Committee. It must further direct the destruction of the copies of the intercepted material.

If, on investigation, the Committee comes to the conclusion that there has been no contravention of the provisions of section 5(2) of the Act, it must record the finding to that effect.

The provisions in India relating to technology-assisted surveillance have not yet been framed, and the above provides the only safeguards in India against interception of telephonic conversations. There may not be a concrete system in place, but there are insights as to what could be a proposed regulatory authority.

Although there is an Information Technology Act 2000 ("Act") in India, the Act does not cover provisions of surveillance and only covers the unauthorized use of information technology for hacking purposes and viewing unauthorized websites.

3.06   Conclusion

As indicated above, technology is making it increasingly possible to develop physically non-intrusive techniques of surveillance. The use of satellites and other remote monitoring tools have lessened the need to physically intrude on a person's privacy.

This kind of technology has been both praised and pilloried — praised for enabling states to monitor data more effectively and so provide better security to their citizens and pilloried for enabling the state to intrude into what used to be private spaces and conversations. Therefore, technology cuts both ways, and jurisprudence needs to keep up with these changes to ensure that the use of technology does not spread unchecked.

This is especially necessary in the light of the spread of global terrorism and the increased activity on the part of states to limit and control it. Moving to an extreme position in the name of national security could be a fallout, and legislatures and courts need to be wary of this possibility. Having looked at the statutes that govern the use of surveillance for the purposes of national security, one can see that they do not impose a very high threshold for surveillance. This is probably due to the nature of the subject they deal with, where governments would rather err on the side of caution and indulge in more, rather than less, surveillance so that the security of the country is not compromised. In contrast, statutes and case law that deal with surveillance of employees by their employers have higher thresholds since the concern being addressed there is not as critical as national security.

Given the nature of national security requirements, it may not be possible to put in place a detailed pre-surveillance approval procedure since speed is of the essence in such cases, but the surveillance authority should at least be able to make out a *prima facie* case for surveillance to some approving authority. An example of this process is the process in place under the Foreign Intelligence Surveillance Act in the United States where judges, who are not part of the same administrative set-up as the investigators, decide the validity of the applications made to them.

This system seems preferable to that under the Regulation of Investigatory Powers Act in the United Kingdom, where the approval for interception of and access to information is internal to the department and therefore possibly much more likely to be granted. The Foreign Intelligence Surveillance Act thus has a clearer system of checks and balances in place at the stage of starting surveillance.

In areas other than national security, for example, cases of other criminal laws, such a system also must be put in place so that the authority that wants to undertake surveillance does not become the authority that takes a decision on whether the surveillance is permissible or not. What needs to be ensured is that decisions on validity or otherwise are taken expeditiously so that the nothing gets delayed.

Cases such as employee surveillance, where the urgency of the matter is less, or the investigation of business-related offences, like those under the Enterprise Act of the United Kingdom, can undergo a slightly more rigorous process of pre-surveillance scrutiny because time need not be of the essence in these cases.

Once the decision to undertake surveillance is taken and the investigative authorities have begun the process, one must ensure that the process of surveillance does not overstep the limits set out for it. If the investigation yields results and reaches the stage of prosecution in any case, the judge will examine the means by which the evidence was obtained, but even cases where no prosecution results need to be examined to prevent misuse of the surveillance procedures.

Periodic reporting requirements to the authority that sanctioned the surveillance could be put in place so that the sanctioning authority is aware of whether the original premise under which the sanction was granted was correct or not. Again, since this is prior to the subject of surveillance being informed, this also would be non-adversarial and would rely on a *prima facie* case being made out rather than clear-cut evidence being unearthed.

This kind of a procedure of periodic checks may actually be helpful for the rate of conviction in some countries because if the investigators need to report periodically, their method of investigation will be such as to satisfy the tests laid down in law and may run a much lower risk in court later of being rejected as having been done in violation of law.

In the event a person finds out he is the subject of surveillance, he needs to have recourse to the courts of law if the surveillance is intruding on his privacy. To this end, concepts of privacy have been developed in most jurisdictions which lay down the boundaries within which the state, or any other entity, cannot enter without the consent of the individual but which recognize that sometimes access to private information is necessitated by reasons of public safety and crime prevention. In cases where the intrusion is deemed necessary by the investigator, the court process forces the investigator to make the case for intrusion and assure that it satisfies the tests laid down in law for the intrusion.

If the case is made out, the subject will be obliged to go along with the investigation and, if not, the investigation must cease. The problem a subject of surveillance faces is that, other than physical surveillance, for example, where a person is being shadowed or a house is searched, it is very hard to establish covert and remote surveillance because the surveillance is not physically intrusive and because all the records of such surveillance are normally secret and inaccessible and, even in a court proceeding, the subject of surveillance may not be able to get full access to the surveillance documents and methodology.

This problem of granting access to surveillance documents is not one that can be solved easily, and there will always be proponents of granting no access in the name of security and of granting full access in the name of greater liberty and openness. A possible compromise between these two ends is the strengthening of the scrutinizing process that the investigators are subject to.

In the event the investigation is subject to a meaningful and independent scrutiny and periodic evaluation, the credibility of the investigation is enhanced and concerns of individuals will be addressed to some extent. While there may not be any means to completely eliminate the possibility of misuse of surveillance, it is possible thus to minimize it to some extent. It must be kept in mind that this process of scrutiny must be in addition to, and not a replacement for, the present procedural safeguards that have been built into surveillance procedures, as they exist today.

CHAPTER 4

COPYRIGHT AND THE CHALLENGES OF THE DIGITAL-AGE — CAN ALL INTERESTS BE RECONCILED?

Dana Beldiman
Carroll, Burdick & McDonough, LLP
San Francisco, California, United States

4.01 Introduction

(a) In General

Digital technology and the Internet have profoundly changed the manner in which copyrighted content can be distributed. Copyright owners, who in the pre-digital-age controlled the market, were faced with the spectrum of uncontrolled dissemination of copyrighted content on the Internet.

This threat prompted them to introduce massive legal and technological protection measures to secure their position in the digital environment. These measures, in turn, disturbed the balance of interests built into copyright law and impacted other stakeholders, in particular, the computer technology industry and the public at large.

This chapter examines the main legal and technological measures devised to contain unauthorized dissemination of copyrighted content on the Internet, and the impact of these measures on each of the stakeholders in the digital copyright debate. It concludes by discussing possible future scenarios for distribution and consumption of digital content.

Part I of this chapter describes the legal and technological measures currently available for protection of digital content. These measures are conceptualized in the form of a three-tier structure, in which traditional copyright law forms the first tier, technological protection measures the second, and digital-age legislation to reinforce the technological protections, the third.

The first tier grants creators limited exclusive rights to their works. Its broader objective is to ensure future contributions to the collective store of knowledge by virtue of such creations. Traditional copyright law works well in a controlled market and territorial setting. It is not equipped to protect content in a global digital environment.

Digital technology and the Internet brought with them the ability to make unlimited copies and, as a result, rightsholders were unable to control the unauthorized dissemination of content via the Internet.

In response to this new environment, rightsholders developed a second tier of protection — technological measures designed to control access to and use of copyrighted content (also referred to as digital rights management). It soon became apparent, however, that these new protection methods were easily circumventable.

A third protection tier followed, in the form of legal reinforcement of the technological protection layer. The international community agreed to address the problems of the digital-age, specifically circumvention of technological measures in the World Intellectual Property Organization (WIPO) Treaties. The expectation underlying these treaties was that unlawful distribution of digital works on the Internet would be contained once all member countries had enacted anti-circumvention laws into their national legislations.

Part II of this chapter examines the impact of the three-tier structure and its impact on each of the stakeholders in the digital content debate.

(b) The Rightsholders

The availability of digital rights management operates a fundamental change of paradigm for rightsholders, marked by new ways of presenting content, new tools for distribution and consumption, and new markets.

However, the new technology also makes unauthorized dissemination of content hard to contain. The content industry suffers huge losses as a result of piracy. Intensive enforcement actions under digital-age legislation and other laws have met with mixed results: although the rightsholders have in general prevailed, the unauthorized dissemination has migrated to forms less easy to enforce.

(c) The Public

The public is one of the prime beneficiaries of the vast amounts of information and cultural products digital technology and a networked society have made available.

However, the three-tier protection measures jeopardize the structure of limitations and exceptions built into traditional copyright law for the benefit of the public. The result is that consumption options such as browsing, re-using, quoting, sharing, time shifting, and space shifting are disappearing, and fundamental rights, such as the rights to information and expression, risk being invaded.

(d) The Technology Providers

The information technology industry provides both the channels for distribution of digital content and the means for controlling them. To maintain the market for copyrighted digital products, the content industry needs to acquire control over both.

The content industry has sought to gain control over newly developed technologies, by various legal means, including enactment of the Digital Millennium Copyright Act's anti-trafficking provisions, litigation against technology providers utilizing theories of secondary liability for infringement, and legislative proposals.

(e) Future Scenarios

This chapter concludes by discussing two categories of future scenarios of the digital content debate. The first category builds on existing building blocks and is based on the assumption that developments will occur naturally without passage of additional legislation.

These scenarios include digital rights management-based models, which favor rightsholders, and the collaborative model, which favors the public. Some of the scenarios which require the passage of legislation are the Levy Model, Increased Deterrent by Stronger Copyright Laws, and the Public Utility Model.

4.02   An Overview

In the pre-digital-age, creative works were protected by traditional copyright law. In response to the "digital threat" and virtually uncontrollable proliferation of copyrighted content on the Internet, the content industries[1] introduced technological protection measures (digital rights management). These measures were easy prey to the hacker community, and digital rights management technologies were being circumvented on a regular basis.

---

1   The industries affected by unlawful dissemination of copyrighted content on the Internet are mainly the music, video entertainment, movie, and publishing and software industries, collectively referred to as the content industries.

This prompted international action in the form of the WIPO Treaties in 1996. The 51 member states agreed to pass digital rights legislation and implement anti-circumvention provisions into their national laws. In the following years, legislation consistent with the WIPO Treaties was passed in the United States, Japan, and Australia. The European Union (EU) Copyright Directive incorporating the requirements of the WIPO Treaties was passed in 2002. EU member states are thereby obligated to enact laws implementing the Directive. Several EU member states have done so, and others are in the process of passing legislation.

In those countries which have adopted digital rights legislation consistent with the Copyright Treaty, the structure of legal and technological protection available for digital content can best be conceptualized in the form of three superimposed tiers:

Tier	Type of Protection	Nature of Protection	Implementation
First Tier	Pre-digital copyright law	Legal	National pre-digital copyright laws
Second Tier	Technological protection measures	Technological	Digital Rights Management protection optionally applied by rightsholders
Third Tier	Laws reinforcing technological protection ("digital-age laws")	Legal	National implementations, such as United States (Digital Millennium Copyright Act), Germany (*Urheberrechtsgesetz*, articles 95 and 96); Australia (Digital-Agenda Act of 2001)

Following this structure, this chapter proposes to outline the main legal developments and their interaction with technological developments, and to assess their impact on the stakeholders involved.

4.03   First Tier — Copyright in the Pre-Digital-Age

(a) Copyright and Authors' Rights

The rights of creators are protected by "copyright" in the Anglo-American Common Law tradition and by "authors' rights" in the continental European system. These two systems have evolved out of two fundamentally different philosophical underpinnings.

The Anglo-American Common Law doctrine of copyright evolved out of printing privileges and was first codified in England as the Statute of Anne in

1710.[2] The Statute was intended to serve "for the encouragement of learned men to compose and write useful books".[3] The rationale underlying this statute[4] blended with 18th century utilitarianism[5] and was adopted by the copyright clause of the United States Constitution.[6]

It remains the cornerstone of copyright law in the United States today. Copyright has been adopted in most of the English-speaking countries, including Canada, Australia, New Zealand, and the United States. While copyright law grants exclusive rights to creators as an incentive to further creation, many consider its broader goal to be to ensure contributions to the store of collective knowledge.[7]

Author's rights, prevalent in Civil Law jurisdictions, are based on the confluence of two philosophical lines of thought, namely:

1. John Locke's natural rights philosophy, which justifies the existence of a property right as the right to the fruit of one's labor;[8] and

2. The personalist view, which perceives an author's work as an extension of his personality, and entitles the author to substantial control over his work.[9]

---

2   Cornish, *Intellectual Property, Patents, Copyrights, Trademarks, and Allied Rights* (4th ed., 2000), at p. 340.

3   The law was entitled "An Act for the Encouragement of Learning, by Vesting the Copies of Printed Books in the Authors or Purchasers of Such Copies". Ginsburg, "A Tale of Two Copyrights: Literary Property in Revolutionary France and America", 64 *Tul. L. Rev.* 991, at p. 998 (1990).

4   Ginsburg, "A Tale of Two Copyrights: Literary Property in Revolutionary France and America", 64 *Tul. L. Rev.* 991, at p. 998 (1990). Professor Ginsburg points out that the framers of the United States Constitution adopted terms reminiscent of the Statute of Anne's policy of incentivizing creation and expanding learning.

5   The philosophical justification of copyright law lies in the utilitarianism of Jeremy Bentham, which "commands a state to maximize the utility of the community". The utility and benefit to society of intellectual products justify legal norms, which grant adequate incentives for creation of such property for the public good. The Copyright Clause of the United States Constitution reflects this thought in that it rewards authors by granting them exclusive rights to their writings. Chisum, *Principles of Patent Law*, at p. 54 (2001), citing Hampton, *Political Philosophy*, at p. 124 (1997).

6   United States Constitution, article I, section 8, clause 8, grants Congress the power "to promote the Progress of Science and useful Arts, by securing for limited Times to Authors . . . the exclusive Right to their respective Writings".

7   *Harper & Row v. Nation Enterprises*, 471 U.S. 539, at p. 546 (1985). The two objectives of copyright law are to "secure a fair return for an 'author's' creative labor" and to "stimulate artistic creativity for the general public good".

8   Geiger, *Droit D'auteur et Droit du Public a L'information*, at pp. 23–25 (2004).

9   Geiger, *Droit D'auteur et Droit du Public a L'information*, at p. 25, n. 4, citing Cabrillac, "La Protection de la Personalite de L'ecrivain et De L'artiste", *Essai Sur Le Droit Moral*, at p. 5 (1926).

The first efforts to legislate authors' rights in 19th century resulted in the French *droit d'auteur*,[10] which holds a dualist view of rights, i.e., authors' rights, are viewed as consisting of two separable components, property rights and personal rights.[11]

The other main trend in continental European authors' rights is the German monistic *Urheberrecht* (creators' rights), which views the property and personal interests as intertwined, forming an inseparable unit.[12] The Civil Law authors' rights doctrine was initially adopted in the jurisdictions of continental Europe and, from there, spread to other countries, such as Japan and China.[13]

Despite the fundamental differences between copyright and authors' rights,[14] in modern times, there has been increasing convergence between the systems.[15]

The need for international exchange of cultural goods forced harmonization in the form of bilateral, and later, multilateral international agreements. The main such instrument, which even today is the primary governing copyright treaty, is the Berne Convention.[16] The Berne Convention has, from the

---

10 Ginsburg, "A Tale of Two Copyrights: Literary Property in Revolutionary France and America", 64 *Tul. L. Rev.* 991, at p. 1006. Different countries adopted different legal philosophies, with the result that, e.g., United States and United Kingdom copyright is quite different from the French *droit d'auteur* (author's right) and German *Urheberrecht* (creator's right).

11 Rehbinder, *Urheberrecht*, at p. 19 (2004).

12 Rehbinder, *Urheberrecht*, at p. 20 (2004).

13 "Copyright law of Japan", at http://www.cric.or.jp/cric_e/csj/csj_main.html.

14 There is support for the view is that, even at the outset, copyright and *droit d'auteur* were not fundamentally different. Historically, a certain amount of congruity can be found between the systems in that they both seek to advance the progress of knowledge and public learning while, at the same time, grapple with the amount of recognition and compensation to give the creator. Ginsburg, "A Tale of Two Copyrights: Literary Property in Revolutionary France and America", 64 *Tul. L. Rev.* 991 (1990).

15 Davies, "The Convergence of Copyright and Authors' Rights — Reality or Chimera?", 26 *IIC* 964 (1995). Examples of convergence: the United States having adopted the Visual Artists' Rights Act, 17 United States Code, section 106A, which provides limited moral rights to visual artists; authors' rights jurisdictions yielding to modern day economic realities, by limiting the moral rights for software, *Code de la Propiete Intellectuelle*, article L121-7.

16 The Berne Convention has been adhered to by 159 countries. The United States felt the need for greater international harmonization and protection as exports of intellectual property increased. Antezana, "The European Union Internet Copyright Directive as Even More Than It Envisions: Toward a Supra-EU Harmonization of Copyright Policy and Theory", 26 *B.C. Int'l & Comp. L. Rev.* 415, at p. 429 (2003)., "The European Union Internet Copyright Directive as Even More Than It Envisions: toward a Supra-EU Harmonization of Copyright Policy and Theory", 26 *B.C. Int'l & Comp. L. Rev.* 415, at p. 429 (2003). Its adherence to Berne came into effect in 1989. See http://www.wipo.int/treaties/en/.

outset, been a bridge between the Common Law copyright systems and the Civil Law *droit d'auteur* systems.[17]

(b) Scope of Rights

(i) Economic Rights

The underlying concern of both copyright and *droit d'auteur* systems is to prohibit illegal use by third parties and to preserve the economic benefits of the creation to the author.

Copyright law recognizes mainly an author's economic rights, expressed in United States law as the rights to reproduce, prepare derivative works, distribute, perform, and display publicly.[18] In United Kingdom law, rights are divided into rights of reproduction and adaptation, and performance-related rights, consisting of performance in public, broadcasting and cable casting.[19]

Droit d'auteur systems divide the exclusive rights granted to authors into economic rights and personal (moral) rights.[20] Economic rights generally include the rights of reproduction, exploitation through communication to the public, and adaptation.

The German Copyright Act, for instance, provides the exclusive right to exploit tangibles, including rights to copy/reproduce, distribute, and display.[21] The exclusive right to exploit intangibles covers the rights to perform, broadcast, reproduce on visual or audio media, and reproduce via broadcasts.[22] "Other" economic rights include the rights to modify/adapt, *droit de suite* (resale right), and compensation for rental and loans.[23]

(ii) Moral Rights

Separate from the author's economic rights, Civil Law jurisdictions also recognize the personal rights of the creator, in the form of moral rights. Grounded in personal rights philosophy, moral rights are based on the concept that the work is an extension of the author.[24] By publishing a work the author projects his or her personality into the world, thus subjecting it and

---

17   Dinwoodie, "The Development and Incorporation of International Norms in the Formation of Copyright Law", 62 *Ohio L. J.* 733, at p. 765 (2001).

18   17 United States Code, section 106.

19   Cornish, *Intellectual Property, Patents, Copyrights, Trademarks, and Allied Rights* (4th ed., 2000), at pp. 426–433.

20   German Copyright Act, sections 12–18; French Copyright Law (*Code de la propriete intellectuelle*), articles L121-1 *et seq.* and L122-1 *et seq.*

21   German Copyright Act, section 15–18.

22   German Copyright Act, sections 15–18.

23   German Copyright Act, sections 25–27.

24   Geiger, *Droit D'auteur et Droit du Public a L'information*, at p. 25.

the author to potential criticism and ridicule or loss of reputation.[25] This view justifies a significant degree of control in the author. France, the paradigmatic moral rights country, recognizes the moral rights to paternity (attribution),[26] publication (divulgence),[27] integrity,[28] and withdrawal.[29]

Under French law, most moral rights are perpetual and inalienable, i.e., they cannot be transferred to third parties.[30] German law recognizes the moral rights of publication, attribution, and prevention of distortion.[31]

(c)　Limitations and Exceptions

(i)　In General

Copyright assures authors only a limited exclusivity in exploitation of their work.[32] This fact is expressed in doctrines limiting the exclusive right (such as the idea/expression dichotomy, fair use, private use, and the quotation right), often viewed as safety valves to ensure that the benefit to individual authors does not outweigh the benefit to the public.[33]

These limiting doctrines grant the author substantial but not complete rights over the work, and the public some, but not complete, use of the work.[34] Their role is to help build an intellectual and cultural commons.[35]

Two systems of limitations and exceptions have evolved. The United States practices mostly the open system, such as the "fair use" doctrine, which leaves the determination of permissibility to the courts, based on a number of criteria, initially set forth by statute,[36] but evolving with case law.[37]

25　Halpern, *Copyright Law Protection of Original Expression* (2002).

26　French Copyright Law, article L 121-1.

27　French Copyright Law, article L 121-2.

28　French Copyright Law, article L 121-1.

29　French Copyright Law, article L 121-4. This right is subject to indemnity rights by third parties.

30　French Copyright Law, article L 121-1-4.

31　German Copyright Act, section 12-14.

32　Ginsburg, "Copyright and Control of New Technologies of Dissemination", 101 *Colum. L. Rev.* 1613, at p. 1616 (2001).

33　Frey, "Unfairly Applying the Fair Use Doctrine: Princeton University Press v. Michigan Document Services", 99 F3d 1381 (6th Cir., 1996), 66 *U. Cin. L. Rev.* 959, at p. 1001 (1998). Examples of limiting doctrines are the idea/expression dichotomy and fair use.

34　Lessig, *Code and Other Laws of Cyberspace*, at p. 135 (1999).

35　Lessig, *Code and Other Laws of Cyberspace*, at p. 135 (1999). "The law strikes that balance. It is not a balance that would exist in nature. Without the law, and before cyberspace, authors would have very little protection; with the law, they have significant, but not perfect protection. The law gives authors something they otherwise would not have in exchange for limits on their rights, secured to benefit the intellectual commons as a whole."

36　17 United States Code, section 107.

37　*Harper & Row Publishers Inc. v. Nation Enterprises*, 471 U.S. 539 (1985); *Campbell v. Acuff-Rose Music, Inc.*, 510 U.S. 569 (1994).

The other system is the "closed catalog" of exceptions, prevalent mostly in Civil Law countries, under which criteria for the applicability of each individual exception is set forth in detail by statute.

(ii)   The Idea/Expression Dichotomy

It is commonly accepted that copyright protection extends only to the expression of ideas and not to ideas themselves[38] or, as formulated in Civil Law jurisdictions, the authors' rights only cover the form and not the substance (or content).[39]

The Berne Convention does not expressly contain this limitation. The closest is article 2(8), which denies copyright protection to "news of the day or to miscellaneous facts having the character of mere items of press information".[40]

In the United States, the idea/expression dichotomy is statutorily captured in the Copyright Act, and it precludes copyright protection for ideas, procedures, processes, systems, concepts, and principles.[41] The policy goal underlying this rule is to encourage third parties to build freely on ideas and information conveyed by an author's work.[42]

However, when it comes to trying to separate protected "expression" from "unprotected" ideas, the difference between idea and expression is one of degree.[43]

---

38   *International News Service v. Associated Press*, 248 U.S. 215, at p. 250 (1918).

39   Rehbinder, *Urheberrecht*, at p. 18 (2004); Geiger, *Droit D'auteur et Droit du Public a L'information*, at p. 210.

40   Berne Convention, article 2(8).

41   17 United States Code, section 102 b. "In no case does copyright protection for a work of authorship extend to any idea, process, procedure, system, method of operation, principle, concept of discovery, regardless of how it is embodied in the work". In addition, the Copyright Office Regulations, in 37 Code of Federal Regulations, section 202.1, also list a categorization of "material not subject to copyright".

42   *Feist Publications, Inc. v. Rural Telephone Service Co., Inc.*, 499 U.S. 340, at pp. 349 and 350 (1991).

43   *Nichols v. Universal Pictures Corp.*, 45 F2d 119, at p. 121 (2d Cir., 1930). "The analysis involves examining a series of increasing abstractions of the fact pattern presented, with the goal of finding the point where they are no longer protected. This 'point', however, varies from one case to another. On any work, and especially on a play, a great number of patterns of increasing generality will fit equally well, as more and more of the incident is left out. The last may perhaps be no more than the most general statement of what the play is about, and at times might consist only of its title; but there is a point in this series of abstractions where they are no longer protected, since otherwise the playwright could prevent the use of his ideas."

A case-by-case analysis is required in each instance to separate idea from expression.[44] The determination is made entirely based on the subjective judgment of the examining party.[45]

The analysis is quite difficult even in the traditional context of literary works, but it becomes virtually impossible in the context of multimedia. Some dismiss the idea/expression distinction as a "formalism from another era" because of the practical inability to apply it to music, video, pictures, cartoons, and movies.[46] It may be that this is simply a line that cannot be drawn.[47]

In Civil Law jurisdictions, this rule is expressed as the dichotomy of form and content.[48] Under French law, the authors' rights only extend to the form, and not to the content or substance, of the work because ideas, data, facts, and information, all categorized as "content" of a work, are part of common ownership, such as the air or the sea, properly described as *res communis*.[49]

This norm expresses the cultural and scientific policy mandate of promoting popular education.[50] While this doctrine is not statutorily captured, it is regularly applied by the courts.

(iii) Fair Use

The main exception to the exclusive rights provided by the United States Copyright Act is the fair use doctrine, a test that examines permissibility of borrowing

---

44 Halpern, *Copyright Law, Protection of Original Expression*, at p. 51 (2002).

45 The absence of any clear rules prompted one aggravated court to note: "The first axiom of copyright is that copyright protection covers only the expression of ideas and not ideas themselves. The second axiom of copyright is that the first axiom is more of an amorphous characterization than it is a principled guidepost". *Chuck Blore & Don Richman Inc. v. 20/20 Advertising Inc.*, 674 F. Supp 671, at p. 676 (D. Minn., 1987).

46 Lessig, Interview with *Intellectual Property LawCast* (3 March 2002) (on file with author).

47 Lessig, Interview with *Intellectual Property LawCast* (3 March 2002) (on file with author).

48 The German Copyright Act, sections 1 and 2, protects *persönliche geistige Schöpfung* (individual creation), which underlies the distinction between *Form* (form) and *Inhalt* (content). The former, akin to the concept of protected expression, is protected in all instances, while the latter is protected only as expression of individuality and is not part of common cultural property. Ideas are not protected. Ilzhoefer, *Patent-, Markent und Urheberrecht*, at p. 165 (2002).

49 Geiger, *Droit D'auteur et Droit du Public a L'information*, at p. 211.

50 Geiger, *Droit D'auteur et Droit du Public a L'information*, at p. 210, quoting Strubel, *La protection des oeuvres scientifiques en droit d'auteur francaisé* (1997) ("l'éxpression juridique d'impéatifs de politiques culturelles ou scientifiques, qui s'imposent a tout état désireux de favoriser l'édification de sa population").

of copyrighted material in light of four factors.[51] Fair use is discussed in detail elsewhere in this book. For purposes of the present chapter, suffice it to point out that the four factors allow courts considerable latitude in interpretation. This has caused the fair use doctrine to be criticized for its high degree of subjectivity and vagueness[52] and its resulting low-outcome predictability.[53]

(iv) Fair Dealing

Unlike United States fair use, the United Kingdom fair dealing doctrine relies almost entirely on specified statutory limitations, including research or private study, reporting current events, criticism, or review.[54]

The fair dealing doctrine is discussed elsewhere in this publication.

(v) Limitations to Authors' Rights

Germany   Germany provides an example of a closed, fairly narrowly defined catalogue of limitations.[55] The stated policy objective is to promote culture and education by benefiting individual users, cultural life, and the public.[56] Excepted uses include:

1. Quotation;[57]

2. Personal use for specified purposes;[58]

3. Works in exhibition or auction catalogues;[59]

---

51   17 United States Code, section 107; *Campbell v. Acuff Rose Music. Inc.*, 510 U.S. 569 (1994).

52   Statement of Marybeth Peters, Register of Copyrights, before the Subcommittee on Courts, the Internet, and Intellectual Property, Committee on Judiciary Piracy, Prevention and the Broadcast Flag, at http://www.copyright.gov/docs/regstat030603.html.

53   Nimmer, "The Public Domain, Fairest of Them All, and Other Fairy Tales of Fair Use", 66 *Law & Contemp. Prob.* 263, at p. 280 (2003). Professor Nimmer prepared a chart examining 60 cases dealing with the four fair use factors. The chart examines the frequency each of the four factors supported the basis of the court's holding. The conclusion was a range was between 42 per cent and 57 per cent, for an average of 51 per cent. This means that, in 51 per cent of the instances examined, an individual factor supported the holding of the court. Based on this fact, the article concludes that "the four factors fail to drive the analysis, but rather serve as convenient pegs on which to hang antecedent conclusions". Nimmer, "The Public Domain, Fairest of Them All, and Other Fairy Tales of Fair Use", 66 *Law & Contemp. Prob.* 263, at pp. 282 and 283 (2003).

54   Cornish, *Intellectual Property, Patents, Copyrights, Trademarks, and Allied Rights* (4th ed., 2000), at pp. 434–436; United Kingdom Copyright, Designs and Patents Act 1988, sections 30 *et seq.*

55   German Copyright Act, sections 45–61.

56   Rehbinder, *Urheberrecht*, at pp. 213 *et seq.* (2004).

57   German Copyright Act, section 51.

58   German Copyright Act, section 53.

59   German Copyright Act, section 58.

4. Non-profit activities;

5. Use for public safety;[60]

6. Use of public speeches;[61] and

7. Use of press articles and broadcast reports.[62]

Private use under section 53 of the German Copyright Act[63] is an exception in the nature of a compulsory license in that levies are imposed on the sale of audio and video recording equipment, copying equipment, and certain operators of such equipment, including universities, libraries, and copy shops.[64] Permitted uses are subdivided into the following sub-categories:

1. Private use;

2. Personal use; and

3. Educational use.

The first sub-category is limited to use in the private sphere, while the latter two sub-categories also allow copies for professional use. "Personal" use extends to scientific uses, personal archives, personal information on current events in case of a broadcast work, and even to personal use within a business setting, as long as the use does not become business use. "Educational" use is limited to printed matter, and it envisions use in teaching, classroom use, and examinations. University teaching does not benefit from this exception.[65] A separate exception provides for use of audiovisual works for educational purposes.[66]

The right to quote from work protected by copyright under section 51 of the German Copyright law is one of the more significant exceptions to copyright under German law. It is grounded in the right to receive information guaranteed by the German Constitution.[67] It is viewed as one of the cornerstones of the fundamental right and freedom to exchange opinions and ideas, and is meant to encourage the development of cultural and scientific life in the interest of the public.[68]

---

60   German Copyright Act, section 45.

61   German Copyright Act, section 48.

62   German Copyright Act, section 49.

63   This occurs in the form of a levy imposed on copying devices. The amounts thus collected are then distributed to the creators.

64   Netanel, "Impose a Noncommercial Use Levy to Allow Free Peer-to-Peer File Sharing", 17 *Harv. J. Law & Tech.* 1, n. 107 (2003); German Copyright Act, section 54.

65   Rehbinder, *Urheberrecht*, at p. 259 (2004), at 259; Geiger, *Droit D'auteur et Droit du Public a L'information*, at p. 244 (2004).

66   German Copyright Act, section 47.

67   German Constitution (*Grundgesetz*), article 1.

68   Geiger, *Droit D'auteur et Droit du Public a L'information*, at p. 237.

The extent of the quotation is limited to the amount "appropriate under the circumstances",[69] but it does not exclude quotation of a work in its entirety, if in a new and independent creation. The source must be indicated in all instances,[70] as well as any changes made to the original work. The quotation right applies to many types of works, including literary, graphic, scientific, or musical.[71]

France   French law provides a much shorter list of exceptions than German law. These exceptions reflect policies of freedom of expression and the public right to information. Thus, the author of a published work may not prohibit use of the work for analysis and brief quotations for purposes of criticism, education, science, or information.[72]

The quotation right is, as in Germany, particularly strong, as it guarantees free circulation of ideas for the general societal benefit.[73] Nonetheless, quotations are subject to a number of conditions: that the work be previously published, the source be named, and the quotation be brief and incorporated into another work.[74] Press reviews and certain public speeches are similarly subject to exceptions meant to satisfy the right to information.[75]

The private copy exception under the French Code of Intellectual Property allows copies strictly for personal, not including collective, use.[76] This very significant doctrine is one of the main instruments by which copyright law achieves its societal justification of disseminating knowledge.[77] It constitutes the primary manner in which an individual can obtain information on topics of interest, whether they relate to scientific endeavors, education, current events, or politics.[78] This exception is particularly important because French law does not contain specific exceptions for educational purposes.[79]

At the same time, the limited conditions in which it is applicable avoid abuse of the doctrine, e.g., a teacher sharing material copied under this exception with her students would constitute prohibited "collective use".[80]

---

69   German Copyright Act, section 51.

70   German Copyright Act, section 63.

71   German Copyright Act, section 63.

72   French Copyright Law, article L 122-5-3. Other exceptions include reproduction of art works in catalogues, and representation or reproduction of works located in public places.

73   Geiger, *Droit D'auteur et Droit du Public a L'information*, at p. 225.

74   French Copyright Law, article L 122-5-3.

75   French Copyright Law, article L 122-5-3.

76   French Copyright Law, article L 122-5-2.

77   Geiger, *Droit D'auteur et Droit du Public a L'information*, at p. 233.

78   Geiger, *Droit D'auteur et Droit du Public a L'information*, at p. 233.

79   Geiger, *Droit D'auteur et Droit du Public a L'information*, at p. 233.

80   Geiger, *Droit D'auteur et Droit du Public a L'information*, at p. 234, n. 2.

4.04   Technological Developments and Their Impact on Copyright

Traditional copyright law served well for several hundred years in the pre-digital world. However, the advent of digital technology and the Internet changed the existing distribution model[81] and disturbed the balance built into traditional copyright.

The pre-digital model of distribution and consumption of copyrighted material was based on scarcity of supply, a precondition for the existence of a market.[82] Scarcity was the natural result of high costs of reproduction and distribution. High equipment costs, technological complexity requiring a high-level skill set, physical distribution costs, and intermediaries all operated to limit high-volume production and copying to relatively substantial businesses.[83]

These physical limitations made pirating and counterfeiting economically relatively unattractive.[84] A counterfeiter had to print books, copy CD's, and then create channels for distribution. The difference in cost between pirating and legitimate distribution was simply not big enough to justify pirating on such a large-scale basis.[85]

The cost of copying operated as an inherent barrier against widespread piracy and enabled rightsholders to maintain control of the market. The exclusive distribution rights granted to authors by copyright law reinforced the authors' control over the market. Given the limited and tightly controlled market, copyright violations could be dealt with at the source with relative ease.[86]

---

81 *MGM v. Grokster*, 380 F3d 1154, at p. 1167 (9th Cir., 2004). The introduction of new technology is always disruptive to existing markets, and "particularly to those copyright owners whose works are sold through well-established distribution mechanisms".

82 Cohen, "Lochner in Cyberspace: The New Economic Orthodoxy of 'Rights Management'", 97 *Mich. L. Rev.* 462, at p. 511 (1998). "Property rights in patents and copyrights make possible the creation of a scarcity of the products appropriated which could not otherwise be maintained."

83 *Universal City Studios, Inc. v. Reimerdes*, 111 F. Supp. 2d 294, at p. 318 (S.D.N.Y., 2000), *aff'd sub nom Universal City Studios, Inc. v. Corley*, 273 F3d 429, at p. 451 (2d Cir., 2001). "There was a time when copyright infringement could be dealt with quite adequately by focusing on the infringing act. If someone wished to make and sell high quality but unauthorized copies of a copyrighted book, for example, the infringer needed a printing press. The copyright holder, once aware of the appearance of infringing copies, usually was able to trace the copies up the chain of distribution, find and prosecute the infringer, and shut off the infringement at the source". Dratler, *Cyberlaw: Intellectual Property in the Digital Millennium*, section 1.02[2] (2004).

84 Lemley and Reese, "Reducing Digital Copyright Infringement without Restricting Innovation", 56 *Stan. L. Rev.* 1345 (2004).

85 Lemley and Reese, "Reducing Digital Copyright Infringement without Restricting Innovation", 56 *Stan. L. Rev.* 1345, at p. 1373 (2004). Mark Lemley points out that the difference in the cost between pirating and legitimate distribution is that some are sold on the street and others in legitimate retail establishments.

86 Dratler, *Cyberlaw: Intellectual Property in the Digital Millennium*, section 1.02[2] (2004).

Over time, reproduction and storage technology improved in quality and capabilities.[87] Early analog devices. such as copiers and VCRs, foreshadowed the issues that would be raised by digital technology.[88]

Then came devices[89] capable of producing identical digital copies, such as CDs, DVDs, and PCs (as both a productivity tool and an entertainment platform). The Internet, increased bandwidth, and file sharing P2P technology gave rise to new methods for distributing digital content. Collectively, these technologies enabled users to create unlimited numbers of copies which are identical and virtually perfect, at a negligible cost, and capable of instantaneous dissemination worldwide, beyond the capabilities of national enforcement.[90]

These capabilities moved the locus of copying, and of potential piracy, away from substantial businesses, to the home of consumers, who now have direct access to virtually unlimited digital content.[91] This put an end to scarcity and, with it, to the traditional distribution model for copyrighted content. Several additional factors play into this scenario.

First, end-user copying gains in significance. In an analog environment, piracy by end-users could be safely ignored, because an illegal copy made by an end-user deprived the rightsholder of a single sale.[92] In an Internet environment, a single copy made by an end-user has the capacity of depriving the rightsholder of tens or hundreds of thousands of sales and replacing the product in the market.

Second, consumption patterns accelerate downloading and sharing of content. Tangible copies come at a cost and rapidly become obsolete. The convenient availability of digital content through downloading and sharing

---

87 *Universal City Studios, Inc. v. Corley,* 273 F3d 429, at p. 436 (2d Cir., 2001). "[D]igital format brings with it the risk that a virtually perfect copy, i.e., one that will not lose perceptible quality in the copying process, can be readily made at the click of a computer control and instantly distributed to countless recipients throughout the world over the Internet."

88 *MGM v. Grokster,* 380 F3d 1154, at p. 1158 (9th Cir., 2004). "From the advent of the player piano, every new means of reproducing sound has struck a dissonant chord with musical copyright owners, often resulting in federal litigation."

89 Many other devices have over the course of history having an impact on traditional distribution mechanisms of copyrighted material include the player piano, a copier, a tape recorder, a video recorder, a personal computer, a karaoke machine, or an MP3 player. *MGM v. Grokster,* at 1167.

90 GartnerG2 and the Berkman Center for Internet & Society at Harvard Law School, "Copyright and Digital Media in a Post-Napster World" (2003), at p. 11.

91 Dratler, *Cyberlaw: Intellectual Property in the Digital Millennium,* section 1.02[2] (2004).

92 Lemley and Reese, "Reducing Digital Copyright Infringement without Restricting Innovation", 56 *Stan. L. Rev.* 1345, at pp. 1375 and 1376 (2004).

allows users to keep up with "the latest" product. A taste for the latest product is developed in this way which, in turn, spurs further downloading and sharing.[93]

Finally, illegal copying is increasingly hard to enforce. Because large-scale copying is no longer limited to substantial businesses,[94] individual infringers operate out of homes and are geographically dispersed.[95] Even if identified, their conduct may not be prohibited under the legal regime of their place of residence. As a result, "most individual infringers remain anonymous and free from prosecution".

The consequence of these developments is that digital content is virtually impossible to contain. Traditional copyright law mechanisms are not effective in the digital environment and are of little help to rightsholders in controlling illegal copying.[96]

Faced with this reality, rightsholders began to seek solutions for regaining control over the circulation of copyrighted content and reinforcing their threatened market.

4.05   Second Tier — Technological Measures Used to Protect Content

(a) What Is Digital Rights Management?

In response to these technological developments, content owners devised technological measures to protect digital content from unauthorized distribution. They also are referred to as "DRM".

Described in very simple terms, a rightsholder uses digital rights management to package the digital content into an "envelope". The envelope additionally contains a unique identifier, a description of the content, and rules governing the use of the content. This envelope can then be distributed to the user in any form desired, including via the Internet.

---

93   Dratler, *Cyberlaw: Intellectual Property in the Digital Millennium*, section 1.02[2] (2004).

94   Dratler, *Cyberlaw: Intellectual Property in the Digital Millennium*, section 1.02[2] (2004).

95   Dratler, *Cyberlaw: Intellectual Property in the Digital Millennium*, section 1.02[2] (2004).

96   GartnerG2 and the Berkman Center for Internet & Society at Harvard Law School, "Copyright and Digital Media in a Post-Napster World" (2003), at p. 11. *In re Aimster Copyright Litigation*, 334 F3d 643, at p. 645 (7th Cir., 2003). "Recognizing the impracticability or futility of a copyright owner's suing a multitude of individual infringers [. . .] the law allows a copyright holder to sue a contributor to the infringement instead, in effect as an aider and abettor", citing Picker, "Copyright as Entry Policy: The Case of Digital Distribution", 47 *Antitrust Bull.* 423, at p. 442 (2002). "[C]hasing individual consumers is time consuming and is a teaspoon solution to an ocean problem".

At the user end, the envelope is identified as having reached the intended user and the user's permissions are verified. The user can then access the content in accordance with the rules, e.g., the rules could allow the user to copy the content, replay it a number of times, and transfer it a number of times. The rules also record the various uses and ensure that the rightsholder is compensated accordingly.[97]

(b) Digital Rights Management Functionalities

(i) In General

The conceptual building blocks of technological protection consist of three functions, namely:

1. Identification of content;

2. Description of content; and

3. Establishment of the desired rules of distribution.[98]

Each of these functions is implemented by means of an architecture of software components.

(ii) Identification of Content

Identification is effected essentially by a system of labels by which content is associated with certain information that facilitates its retrieval, such as the author's identity, rightsholder's identity, and user information.[99] In this manner, systems understand they are talking about the "same thing" and are able to unambiguously identify certain content.

Standard content identifiers have been developed under the oversight of the International Organization for Standardization (ISO),[100] such as International Standard Musical Work (ISWC),[101] International Standard Recording (ISRC),[102] International Standard Book Number (ISBN) in the analog library

---

97　World Intellectual Property Organization, Standing Committee on Copyright and Related Rights, "Current Developments in the Field of Digital Rights Management" (2003), at pp. 13 *et seq.*

98　World Intellectual Property Organization, Standing Committee on Copyright and Related Rights, "Current Developments in the Field of Digital Rights Management" (2003), at p. 20.

99　World Intellectual Property Organization, Standing Committee on Copyright and Related Rights, "Current Developments in the Field of Digital Rights Management" (2003), at p. 19.

100　See http://www.iso.org.

101　The International Standard Musical Work provides a unique, permanent, and internationally recognized reference number for the music industry. See http://www.iswc.org.

102　The International Standard Recording provides an international identification system for sound recordings and music video recordings via a permanent indentifier encoded into a product as its digital fingerprint. See http://www.ifpi.org.

world, but now International Standard Text Work Code (ISTC),[103] and International Standard Audiovisual Number (ISAN) for audiovisual works.[104]

Description is accomplished by metadata, i.e., information which describes the content and includes information about ownership, the rightsholder's identity, date of creation, and country of creation.[105] Its function is disambiguation, i.e., to determine the difference between two superficially similar items.

Finally, the rights expression function allows rights holders to set the parameters within which the content can be used, and thereby define the individual business model. Rights and interests in content, whether under copyright or contractual agreements, are expressed via a digital rights expression language (REL).

The rights express the conditions under which content, otherwise inaccessible to the user, can be consumed and appear in the form of a rights data dictionary, which contains instructions to a microprocessor-based device. Rights expression can range from the very simple "you can print but not copy" to very complex ones, such as XrMl, specifically designed for expressing rights and conditions associated with digital content in a custom tailored manner.[106]

Digital rights management is mostly used by rightsholders to prevent uncontrolled distribution of digital content. However, digital rights management also can be configured to ensure that the consumers' interests and expectations are met.

(c) Types of Technological Measures Used for Protecting Content

(i) In General

An effective digital rights management system consists of several interacting components, each designed to accomplish the functions described above.

The components can be software programs operating independently or embedded in a platform infrastructure, such as the Microsoft Palladium Initiative[107] or the Trusted Computing Platform Alliance (TCPA).[108]

---

103 The International Standard Text Work Code provides an internationally recognized permanent reference numbering system that uniquely distinguishes one textual work from another. The International Standard Text Code is identified as ISO Project 21047. See http://www.iso.org.

104 See http://www.isan.org.

105 World Intellectual Property Organization, Standing Committee on Copyright and Related Rights, "Current Developments in the Field of Digital Rights Management" (2003), at p. 19.

106 See http://www.contentguard.com and http://www.xml.org.

107 See http://www.microsoft.com. Based on a combination of hardware and software components, Palladium is integrated as a set of features of Microsoft Windows.

108 See http://www.trustedcomputinggroup.org. The Trusted Computing Group was founded in 1999 by several major platform manufacturers, including Microsoft, Intel, HP, IBM, and Compaq.

(ii) Encryption

Encryption operates as a "content packaging" system, by means of which the package of content can be "locked" and "unlocked" by digital keys. The system is based on private public mathematical (digital) key technology that generates key-pairs, which work in a complementary manner: information encrypted by one key can be decrypted by using the other.

A merchant would thus encrypt ("lock") the content package by using the public key and send it over the Internet to the user. When the user receives the encrypted content, he can use his private key to decrypt ("unlock") the package and use the content. As long as the private key remains secure, the merchant can be sure that only the intended user has access to the content.[109]

Encryption is one of the most well-developed technologies in the digital rights management arena.[110]

(iii) Persistent Association Technologies

In General   Persistent association technologies are the digital equivalent of printing an identifier on a book. Their function is to ensure that the identifier and metadata are consistently associated with the proper content. These technologies include:

1. Fingerprinting;

2. Watermarking; and

3. Digital signatures.

Their individual characteristics make each of these technologies, particularly well suited for protection of certain types of content.[111]

Fingerprinting   Fingerprinting is a technology which identifies content by extracting characteristics of a content file and storing them on a database.

It is used widely in audio and video, such as monitoring of audio stations, compiling radio and video charts, and distribution of royalties to rights owners by collecting societies.[112]

---

109 World Intellectual Property Organization, Standing Committee on Copyright and Related Rights, "Current Developments in the Field of Digital Rights Management" (2003), at pp. 23–25.

110 World Intellectual Property Organization, Standing Committee on Copyright and Related Rights, "Current Developments in the Field of Digital Rights Management" (2003), at p. 24.

111 World Intellectual Property Organization, Standing Committee on Copyright and Related Rights, "Current Developments in the Field of Digital Rights Management" (2003), at p. 27.

112 World Intellectual Property Organization, Standing Committee on Copyright and Related Rights, "Current Developments in the Field of Digital Rights Management" (2003), at pp. 28 and 29.

Watermarking   Watermarking consists of information ("IP identifier") embedded into a digital file that is imperceptible to the normal consumer and can only be extracted by means of special software.

A "transaction watermark", stores information about particular transactions (uses) of content and is used primarily with audio and video.[113]

Digital Signatures   Digital signatures provide a certificate by a certification agency that uniquely identifies the signatory and ensure that identification and rights expression can be trusted. Based on encryption technology, a digital signature performs the same function as its physical counterpart — the sender "marks" a piece of information so that recipients can verify that the message really came from the sender and whether its content (metadata) has been altered.

Countries are increasingly affording digital signatures the same status as physical/manual signatures.[114]

(iv) Privacy Enhancing Technologies

Privacy enhancing technologies (PETs) protect the identity of a user, thereby ensuring anonymous consumption of content.

(v) Payment Mechanisms

Payment mechanisms currently rely mostly on credit cards, however, technologies, such as electronic wallets, are being developed.

(d) Digital Rights Management at Work

As these technologies mature, increasingly sophisticated uses become possible. Fine nuances in rights expression languages can satisfy the needs of both rightsholders and users with respect to controlling distribution and consumption of digital content.

For instance, assume "Teenage User" desires to identify music products to impress her group of friends. The following would be a likely scenario:

1. User samples songs on a retail website and selects five songs. Sampling is free with ultimate purchase.

2. User can purchase the following at different price levels (a) permission to listen for a specified period of time, e.g., four hours or two months,

---

113 World Intellectual Property Organization, Standing Committee on Copyright and Related Rights, "Current Developments in the Field of Digital Rights Management" (2003), at pp. 30–32.

114 World Intellectual Property Organization, Standing Committee on Copyright and Related Rights, "Current Developments in the Field of Digital Rights Management" (2003), at pp. 32 and 33.

(b) permission to listen a specified number of times, (c) permission to transfer a copy to a specified number of third persons, e.g., three friends, and (d) permission to port the songs to other platforms.

3. User purchases a two-month license to the five songs, with permission to port the songs to her MP3 player, and she purchases a license to transfer the five songs to her three friends individually, each having permission to listen to the song once.

4. If one of the three friends actually purchases the song, User receives an incentive: free-of-charge extension of her license for another month or permission to listen to a new song for, e.g., one month free of charge.

This scenario meets the user's needs in identifying and sharing products. The content provider's distribution and future marketing needs also are met: the product has been sold and the prospect of future sales has been created by incentivizing the user to disseminate the product. Virtually unlimited business models can be structured in this manner for all types of digital content.[115]

(e) Remaining Challenges

Advocates of the public interest are concerned that digital rights management imposes an additional layer of protection, inconsistent with traditional copyright law. Limitations and exceptions are built into copyright law to ensure the proper balance of interests between rightsholders and the public domain. These limiting doctrines confer a certain "permeability" to traditional copyright law.

Whether individual limitations and exceptions are applicable in any given case is determined by subjective judgment based on the individual circumstances of the case. Technological protection operates mechanically and is therefore incapable of making the subjective differentiation between protectable and unprotectable content.

At this time, digital rights management is therefore not equipped to honor the system of limitations and exceptions built into copyright law. Although, in theory, rights expression language could be developed to include semantics to express user rights,[116] thus far, there as been little initiative in this direction. The concern is that, absent effective limiting doctrines, copyright law becomes an absolute monopoly, which it was never intended to be.

The content industry, on the other hand, has great hopes for the future of digital rights management. Digital rights management allows the content

---

115 See http://www.ezdrm.com.

116 Even if such capabilities were developed, it is unlikely that the rightsholder would elect to use them in this manner (absent being compelled by law).

industry to take full advantage of the opportunities distribution on the Internet must offer. Services, such as filtration of information, formatting, pay per view, online subscriptions, and paid downloads will become available. Distribution and payment mechanisms will be refined so as to offer appropriate levels of access at an appropriate price,[117] i.e., that users can select the exact type and amount of product for the exact price they are willing to pay.

These plans are not without challenges. The digital rights management industry is still in its infancy. Apart from a few established technologies, applications are fragmented and interoperability among technologies and platforms limited. This prevents digital rights management applications from gaining broad-based acceptance in the industry. However, without adequate protection, distribution of typically valuable content over the Internet is very risky.

Furthermore, the introduction of digital rights management, even if fully functional, is not a complete solution for the content industry's problems. Protection of digital content based solely on technological measures is illusory, and considerable incentive to invent around these measures is inherent in the very value of the digital content.[118]

Newly launched protection technologies are being circumvented with predictable regularity, and the circumvention tools posted on the Internet.[119] In an Internet environment, it is enough for a single hacker to obtain a single copy of a protected file, and for that file to be replicated in an uncontrolled manner on the "darknet", beyond the lawful owners' ability to contain it.[120]

It became increasingly obvious that neither copyright law alone, nor copyright law combined with technological protection measures, was strong

---

117 Testimony by Shira Perlmutter to the Advisory Committee of the Congressional Internet Caucus 2003; H.R. 107, at http://www.netcaucus.org/events/2003/drm/video.shtml. Bullesbach and Dreier, *Wem Gehört zu Information im 21. Jahruhundert?*, at p. 62 (2004).

118 Hoeren, "Lex, Lügen, und Video", *KUR* 3/2003, p. 58, at http://www.uni-muenster.de/ Jura.itm/inhalte/publikationen/. A study on digital rights management systems published by the European Commission in March 2002 concluded that no existing digital rights management system was secure.

119 "Five Scenarios for Digital Media in a Post-Napster World", the Berkman Center for the Internet & Society at Harvard Law School, at http://cyber.law.harvard.edu/ publications.

120 Indeed, cracking digital rights management has become somewhat of a sport in the hacker community. The Norwegian hacker Jon Johansen, famous for cracking DVD encryption, announced in August 2004 that he revealed the public key used by Apple Airport Express, a wireless networking protocol, to encrypt music sent between iTunes and a wireless base station. See http://www.nanocrew.net/blog/.

enough to effectively control the distribution of digital content[121] and to provide a secure environment for the rapidly growing field of electronic commerce.[122]

Legislative options at this point included:

1. Following the traditional approach of focusing on the conduct of copying and directing enforcement to substantial businesses;

2. Tracing individual transactions in copyrighted content; and

3. Shifting focus from copying to copy-control technology.

The latter option was the only one deemed to be realistic and consistent with democratic values.[123] Possible alternatives to the legislative focus adopted were to:

1. Follow the traditional approach of directing enforcement to substantial businesses;

2. Tracing individual transactions in copyrighted matter; and

3. Shifting focus from copying to copy-control technology, only the last one being realistic and consistent with democratic values.

In this spirit, the international legal community[124] set out to consider new legislation, which shifts its focus away from the act of infringement, to protection of the technology surrounding distribution of copyrighted content.

Prohibitions under this approach are not the infringement itself, but the circumvention of technological protection measures. This new legislation operates as a third tier of protection of digital content, whose function it is to reinforce the underlying technological protection layer. Its first appearance came in the form of the WIPO Treaties discussed in detail below.

---

121 Bullesbach and Dreier, *Wem Gehört zu Information im 21. Jahruhundert?*, at pp. 29 and 30 (2004).

122 Antezana, "The European Union Internet Copyright Directive as Even More Than It Envisions: toward a Supra-EU Harmonization of Copyright Policy and Theory", 26 *B.C. Int'l & Comp. L. Rev.* 415, at p. 429 (2003). "The European Union Internet Copyright Directive as Even More Than It Envisions: Toward a Supra-EU Harmonization of Copyright Policy and Theory", 26 *B.C. Int'l & Comp. L. Rev.* 415, at p. 429 (2003), at p. 11.

123 Dratler, *Cyberlaw: Intellectual Property in the Digital Millennium*, section 1.02[2] (2004).

124 Antezana, "The European Union Internet Copyright Directive as Even More Than It Envisions: Toward a Supra-EU Harmonization of Copyright Policy and Theory", 26 *B.C. Int'l & Comp. L. Rev.* 415 (2003). A further legislative goal was to harmonize the laws of different nations in light of the advances of digital technology.

4.06　Third Tier — Legal Responses to the Digital Environment

(a)　World Intellectual Property Organization Copyright Treaty

(i)　In General

In the early 1990s, it became evident in the course of WIPO negotiations that the development of information and communication technologies and their impact on copyrighted content mandated a specially tailored legal regime.[125] The WIPO Copyright Treaty[126] is the first multilateral treaty[127] to address the impact of digital technology on copyrights.[128]

In addition to addressing the issues raised by technological development,[129] its stated purpose is to expand and harmonize the role of copyright and neighboring rights in the international arena and to maintain a balance between the rights of authors and the larger public interest, such as education, research, and access to information.[130]

(ii)　Provisions of the WIPO Treaty

In General　The Treaty requires member states[131] to provide two distinct layers of legal protection. The first layer consists of traditional copyright provisions extending the provisions of the Berne Convention to digital-age issues.

125　World Intellectual Property Organization Copyright Treaty, Preamble; Antezana, "The European Union Internet Copyright Directive as Even More Than It Envisions: Toward a Supra-EU Harmonization of Copyright Policy and Theory", 26 *B.C. Int'l & Comp. L. Rev.* 415 (2003).

126　The World Intellectual Property Organization Copyright Treaty and its companion treaty, the Performances and Phonograms Treaty (which protects broadcasters, performers, and producers) (WPPT), both adopted in Geneva on 20 December 1996, adopted at the WIPO Diplomatic Conference in Geneva on 20 December 1996, came into force on 6 March 2002; see http://www.wipo.int/treaties/en/general/. Reinbothe and von Lewinski, *The WIPO Treaties* 1996, at p. 200 (2002).

127　Because the TRIPS Agreement was largely negotiated in 1991 and came into effect before WIPO treaties, it does not in depth take into account the intellectual property issues resulting from Internet and digital media distribution as well as digital rights management.

128　The World Intellectual Property Organization Copyright Treaty is a "special arrangement" within article 20 of the Berne Convention, which means that interpretation of any provision of the WIPO Treaty may not result in less protection than that granted under the Berne Convention. World Intellectual Property Organization Copyright Treaty, article 1. Reinbothe and von Lewinski, *The WIPO Treaties* 1996, at pp. 136, 137, 146, and 147 (2002).

129　Dinwoodie, "The Development and Incorporation of International Norms in the Formation of Copyright Law", 62 *Ohio L. J.* 733, at p. 765 (2001). The treaties also clarify certain rights that had proved problematic prior to 1996. For example, article 4 of the WIPO Treaty now states that computer programs are to be protected as literary works within the meaning of standard copyright law. Article 5 acknowledges that databases require some form of protection independent of copyright.

130　World Intellectual Property Organization Copyright Treaty, Preamble. Ginsburg, "Achieving Balance in International Copyright Law: The WIPO Treaties 1996", 26 *Colum. J.L. & Arts* 201 (2003).

131　Member states are described as "Contracting Parties" in the Treaty.

The second layer is based on the assumption that rightsholders utilize technological measures to protect digital content. It directs member states to enact legislation prohibiting circumvention of such technological protection, by an additional legal reinforcement layer.

Traditional Copyright Layer   The first layer's main substantive provisions address the rights of distribution and communication to the public.[132] The right of distribution under article 6 vests in rightsholders the "exclusive right of authorizing the making available to the public" of their works.[133]

The right of communication to the public under article 8 grants rightsholders the exclusive right of "authorizing any communication to the public of their works by wire or wireless means."[134] This right also includes the "making available to the public of works in such a way that members of the public may access these works from a place and at a time individually chosen by them".[135]

Early drafts of the treaty included provisions relating to the exclusive right of reproduction of literary and artistic works. These provisions were dropped from the final version because of the Berne Convention's broad formulation of the reproduction right.[136] Reproduction in "any manner or form"[137] was deemed to be broad enough to include reproduction in forms unknown at the time of drafting and, therefore, cover copies in RAM, electronic storage and communications.[138]

For purposes of the present chapter, the traditional copyright rights of distribution and communication set forth in the WIPO Treaty, together with the rights under the Berne Convention,[139] are referred to as the first tier of protection.

Technological Protection Enforcement Layer   In article 11, the WIPO Treaty requires member states to implement "adequate legal protection" and "effective legal remedies" against the circumvention of technological measures used

---

132 World Intellectual Property Organization Copyright Treaty, articles 6 and 8.

133 World Intellectual Property Organization Copyright Treaty, article 6.

134 World Intellectual Property Organization Copyright Treaty, article 8.

135 World Intellectual Property Organization Copyright Treaty, article 8.

136 Ginsburg, "Achieving Balance in International Copyright Law: The WIPO Treaties 1996", 26 *Colum. J.L. & Arts* 201, at p. 206 (2003).

137 Berne Convention, article 9.

138 Ginsburg, "Achieving Balance in International Copyright Law: The WIPO Treaties 1996", 26 *Colum. J.L. & Arts* 201, at p. 206 (2003).

139 World Intellectual Property Organization Copyright Treaty, article 1. "Nothing in this Treaty shall derogate from existing obligations that Contracting Parties must have toward each other under the Berne Convention for the Protection of Literary and Artistic Works."

by authors in the exercise of their rights under copyright law.[140] The technological measures must restrict acts "which are not authorized by the authors concerned or permitted by law".[141] This wording indicates that rightsholders' anti-circumvention measures are deemed to be coextensive with the rights available to rightsholders under traditional copyright law. Uses permitted by copyright law, such as fair use or private copies, would not be subject to the anti-circumvention provisions.

Finally, the WIPO Treaty establishes benchmarks for protection of rights management information (RMI) to identify the work, author, owner, terms of use, numbers, and codes that represent this information.[142] The Treaty prohibits knowing removal or alteration of rights management information and distribution, import for distribution, broadcast, or communication to the public of works knowing that RMI has been removed or altered.[143]

These mandates, which reinforce the technological protections utilized by rightsholders, constitute the third layer of digital content protection.

(iii) Limitations

Member states may, in their discretion, enact limitations and exceptions, appropriate for the digital environment, to the authors' copyright rights.[144]

All limitations, however, are required to conform to the three-step test, which restricts limitations and exceptions to "special cases that do not conflict with a normal exploitation of the work and do not unreasonably prejudice the legitimate interests of the author".[145]

(iv) Interpretation and Implementation

The World Intellectual Property Organization Copyright Treaty's very general provisions are intended to establish minimum standards, granting members considerable latitude in implementation. In fact, the WIPO Treaty does not specifically require passage of new anti circumvention legislation; member states may determine, in their discretion that existing measures are "adequate" and "effective".

---

140 World Intellectual Property Organization Copyright Treaty, article 11. "Contracting parties shall provide adequate legal protection and effective legal remedies against the circumvention of effective technological measures that are used by authors in connection with the exercise of their rights in this Treaty or the Berne Convention and that restrict acts in respect of their works, which are not authorized by the authors concerned or permitted by law."

141 World Intellectual Property Organization Copyright Treaty, article 12.

142 World Intellectual Property Organization Copyright Treaty, article 12.

143 World Intellectual Property Organization Copyright Treaty, article 12.

144 World Intellectual Property Organization Copyright Treaty, article 10.

145 World Intellectual Property Organization Copyright Treaty, article 10.

Some questions regarding the interpretation of the WIPO Treaty remain open. Technological measures can be of two kinds, i.e., use controls (which prevent a user from copying, distributing, performing, or displaying a work) and access controls (which prevent a user from accessing the copyrighted work at all).[146]

On its face, the WIPO Treaty does not affect access to works, since it applies to technological measures "used by authors in connection with the exercise of their rights" under the WIPO Treaty and the Berne Convention.[147] If access is not a right granted by the Berne Convention, and the WIPO Treaty does not explicitly require access control, this leaves member states the freedom to protect access controls or not.

On the other hand, it must be considered that, in the digital age, access is a prerequisite to making reproductions of or communicating the work. A user cannot experience the work without making at least one temporary copy in a computer's RAM. If this copy is a reproduction within the meaning of the Berne Convention, it could be inferred that access is protected under the WIPO Treaty as directed by Berne.[148]

The term "effective" technological measures further raises the question what level of effectiveness is required. Obviously, if the measures are fully effective, no further legal protection is required to reinforce the technological layer.[149]

Finally, the WIPO Treaty only requires protection against the act of circumvention, not against preparatory or related activities, such as manufacturing and import of circumventing devices. This raises the question of whether preparatory acts, i.e., distribution (or trafficking) of circumventing technology should be read into the text, to satisfy the requirement of "effective" measures.[150]

---

146 Literature distinguishes between technological measures that control access to a work, such as encryption, and those which control use, i.e., copying, distribution, performance, and display, such as SCMS or Macrovision. Marks and Turnbull, "Technical Protection Measures: The Intersection of Technology, Law and Commercial Licenses", 22 *Eur. Intell. Prop. Rev.* 198, at p. 201 (2000).

147 World Intellectual Property Organization Copyright Treaty, article 11. Reinbothe and von Lewinski, *The WIPO Treaties* 1996, at pp. 143 and 144 (2002).

148 Ginsburg, "Achieving Balance in International Copyright Law: The WIPO Treaties 1996", 26 *Colum. J.L. & Arts* 201, at p. 213 (2003).

149 World Intellectual Property Organization, Standing Committee on Copyright and Related Rights, "Current Developments in the Field of Digital Rights Management" (2003), at p. 42. *Quaere*, if a protection measure that has been circumvented and the circumventing tool is freely available, such as DeCSS, is still "effective" for purposes of the WIPO Treaty and its progeny?.

150 Quaere, whether this affords "adequate" and "effective" protection if the act of circumvention takes place in homes and is therefore beyond enforcement.

Overall, perhaps because of this inherent ambiguity, the WIPO Treaty is perceived as creating a fair balance between enhanced protection in the digital environment and promotion of lawful unauthorized uses.[151]

The World Intellectual Property Organization Copyright Treaty has been ratified by 51 countries, including the United States and the European Community.[152] Its terms have been implemented in legislation in the United States and Japan and have been incorporated into the EU Copyright Directive.

(b) United States Digital Millennium Copyright Act

(i) In General

The United States took the lead in enacting the anti-circumvention provisions of the WIPO Treaties into national legislation.[153]

Congress was interested in fostering the rightsholders' participation in digital distribution via the Internet, and concluded that reinforcement of copyright would increase their confidence in distributing copyrighted assets of value via the Internet.[154] Congress deemed that the benefit of such participation would outweigh any potential detriment to the public that could result from the prohibition of circumvention devices.[155] Thus, in 1998, the United States passed the Digital Millennium Copyright Act, enacted as an amendment to the United States Copyright Act.[156]

(ii) Provisions of the Digital Millennium Copyright Act

In General   The Digital Millennium Copyright Act's two distinct prohibitions are:

1. A ban on acts of circumvention of technological measures; and

2. A ban on trafficking tools to circumvent technological measures.

Anti-Circumvention   Section 1201(a)(1) of the Digital Millennium Copyright Act prohibits the act of circumvention of technological measures that

---

151 Ginsburg, "Achieving Balance in International Copyright Law: The WIPO Treaties 1996", 26 *Colum. J.L. & Arts* 201, at p. 215 (2003).

152 See http://www.wipo.int/treaties/en/general/.

153 H.R. Rep. Number 551 (Part 2), 105th Cong., 2d Sess. 20 (22 July 1998) ."The purpose of . . . the Digital Millennium Copyright Act . . . is to implement two international treaties (i.e., the 'Copyright Treaty', and the 'Performances and Phonograms Treaty') signed by the United States and more than 125 other countries before the World Intellectual Property Organization (WIPO)".

154 Ginsburg, "Copyright and Control of New Technologies of Dissemination", 101 *Colum. L. Rev.* 1613, at p. 1618 (2001).

155 Ginsburg, "Copyright and Control of New Technologies of Dissemination", 101 *Colum. L. Rev.* 1613, at p. 1618 (2001).

156 17 United States Code, sections 1201 *et seq.*

effectively control access to a copyrighted work (access controls).[157] By way of analogy, the act of circumvention can be likened to "breaking into a locked room to obtain a copy of a book".[158]

Circumventing the encryption of a digital work would, for instance, be a prohibited act. This type of violation is separate and distinct from copyright infringement. If a user were to circumvent encryption of a non-copyrighted work (or portion of a work, which the user would otherwise be authorized to access under the United Copyright Act), she would still incur liability under section 1201(a)(1).

Anti-Trafficking Two provisions of the Digital Millennium Copyright Act prohibit trafficking of tools which can be used to circumvent protective technology, to wit:

1. Section 1201(a)(2) applies to technology which relates to access controls; and

2. Section 1201(b)(2) applies to technology which relates to use controls.[159]

"Trafficking" means for purposes of both sections the act of "manufacture, import, offer to the public, provide, or otherwise traffic".[160] The tools prohibited are defined broadly as "any technology, product, service, device, component, or part thereof"[161] which:

1. Are "primarily designed or produced" for the respective purposes of (a) circumventing access control measures or (b) circumventing copyright control measures;

---

157 17 United States Code, section 1201(a)(1)(A), provides that "No person shall circumvent a technological measure that effectively controls access to a work protected under this title".

158 Dratler, *Cyberlaw: Intellectual Property in the Digital Millennium*, section 2.04[1] (2004). "The act of circumventing a technological protection measure put in place by a copyright owner to control access to a copyrighted work is the electronic equivalent of breaking into a locked room to obtain a copy of a book."

159 17 United States Code, section 1201(a)(2). "No person shall manufacture, import, offer to the public, provide, or otherwise traffic in any technology, product, service, device, component, or part thereof, that — (A) is primarily designed or produced for the purpose of circumventing a technological measure that effectively controls access to a work protected under this title; (B) has only limited commercially significant purpose or use other than to circumvent a technological measure that effectively controls access to a work protected under this title; or (C) is marketed by that person or another acting in concert with that person with that person's knowledge for use in circumventing a technological measure that effectively controls access to a work protected under this title".

160 17 United States Code, section 1201(a)(2) and (b)(1).

161 17 United States Code, section 1201(a)(2) (preamble), (b)(1) (preamble).

2. Have only limited commercially significant purpose other than engaging in the prohibited conduct; or

3. Are marketed with knowledge of use in circumventing.[162]

Summarized in simple terms, a person is subject to liability under the Digital Millennium Copyright Act's trafficking section if that person traffics in a tool for circumventing a technological measure for access control or copyright control, respectively, that is effective in the case of access controls, in controlling access to, or in the case of copyright controls, in protecting a right of a copyright holder, in a work protected under Title 17 (in the case of access controls) or more narrowly, by copyright (in the case of copyright controls).[163]

For offenses related to access controls under subsection (a)(2), there are two additional elements, namely:

1. The access control must have been imposed with the copyright holder's authority; and

2. The circumvention must be accomplished without the copyright holder's express or implied consent.[164]

As with liability for the act of circumvention, liability for trafficking is separate and distinct from possible liability for copyright infringement. The Digital Millennium Copyright Act does not prohibit the act of circumventing technological measures that protect an owner's exclusive right to authorize use of work, i.e., the act of circumvention of use controls. According to Congress' reasoning, in most instances the ultimate act — unauthorized copying — would infringe copyright.

Limitations and Exceptions   The provisions of the Digital Millennium Copyright Act are subject to seven explicit exceptions.[165] The exceptions foster both socially useful activities, in general, and socially valuable activities related to copyright, in particular.[166] The exceptions cover:

1. Non-profit libraries, archives, and educational institutions, if for good faith determination whether to purchase;[167]

2. Law enforcement, intelligence, or other governmental agencies;[168]

---

162 17 United States Code, section 1201(a)(2)(A)–(C) and section 1201(b)(1)(A)–(C).

163 Dratler, *Cyberlaw: Intellectual Property in the Digital Millennium*, section 2.05[1] (2004).

164 Dratler, *Cyberlaw: Intellectual Property in the Digital Millennium*, section 2.05[1] (2004).

165 17 United States Code, section 1201(d)–(j).

166 Dratler, *Cyberlaw: Intellectual Property in the Digital Millennium*, section 3.01 (2004).

167 17 United States Code, section 1201(d).

168 17 United States Code, section 1201(e).

3. Reverse engineering of computer programs, if using a lawfully obtained copy and, if to achieve interoperability with independently created program elements that are otherwise not readily available, for activities are not infringing;[169]

4. Encryption research, subject to several conditions;[170]

5. Protection of minors;[171]

6. Protection of personally identifying information;[172] and

7. Security testing.[173]

Impact on Fair Use   By its express terms, the Digital Millennium Copyright Act purports not to affect the pre-existing structure of limitations and defenses available under traditional copyright law, including fair use.[174] The reality is, however, that access control rules preclude access to works for purposes which would otherwise be lawful and authorized under the Copyright Act. This risks disturbing the balance built into the Copyright Act in favor of rightsholders.

Recognizing this danger, Congress authorized the Library of Congress to determine the potential adverse impact of these provisions on users, in particular classes of works[175] and to grant certain limitations through informal rulemaking.[176] The Library of Congress has issued two rulemakings, both of which have been moderate in scope.[177]

---

169 17 United States Code, section 1201(f).

170 17 United States Code, section 1201(g). Activities necessary to identify and analyze flaws and vulnerabilities of encryption technologies, to advance the state of knowledge, or to assist in the development of encryption products are permitted subject to four conditions: (a) the copy has been lawfully obtained, (b) the act is necessary for research, (c) good faith effort to obtain authorization, and (d) the act does not infringe other laws.

171 17 United States Code, section 1201(h).

172 17 United States Code, section 1201(i), permits circumvention where technological measures collect or disseminate personally identifying information and where collection or dissemination is done without conspicuous notice and the sole effect is to disable the collection and dissemination capability.

173 17 United States Code, section 1201(j).

174 17 United States Code, section 1201(c)(1).

175 17 United States Code, section 1201(a)(1)(B)–(D), sets forth the scope Library of Congress rulemaking proceedings in detail.

176 17 United States Code, section 1201(a)(1)(B), (C), and (D) — the limitations are (1) that the exemption apply only to anti-circumvention under section 1201(a)(1); (2) that exemptions must cover a particular class of works; (3) a need for the exemption exists because of substantial adverse effect; and (4) the exemption is limited to a three-year period.

177 Dratler, *Cyberlaw: Intellectual Property in the Digital Millennium*, section 2:03 (2004). "The action taken by the Library of Congress under these powers has been criticized as not being sufficiently 'daring and aggressive' [. . .] in its rulemaking and not giving sufficient consideration to the fact that the almost 300-year-old doctrine of 'fair use' had all been obliterated from the Digital Millennium Copyright Act". Consequently, the proposals for change made by the Library of Congress were minimal and failed to restore the underlying balance of the Copyright Act.

The first, in October 2000, authorizes circumvention of technological measures in two types of works, these being:

1. Compilations of websites blocked by filtering software; and

2. Literary works that deny access due to malfunction, damage, or obsoleteness.[178]

The second rulemaking, in October 2003, announced the exemption from anti-circumvention prohibitions of certain compilations, computer programs in obsolete formats, and ebooks.[179]

Copyright Management Information　　The Digital Millennium Copyright Act also contains provisions prohibiting interference with copyright management information (CMI). The offenses are:

1. Providing, distributing, or importing for distribution copyright management information that is false, knowingly and with the intent to induce, enable, facilitate, or conceal infringement;[180] and

2. Intentionally removing or altering copyright management information, distributing or importing for distribution copyright management information removed or altered, and distributing or importing for distribution or performing works where copyright management information has been removed or altered without authorization.[181]

The latter two prohibitions are in the nature of "trafficking" offenses under section 1201. These acts listed in this section are subject to a knowledge requirement.[182]

As used in the Digital Millennium Copyright Act, copyright management information is information that describes the work including title, names of author, copyright owner, performer (if the performances are fixed in the work) writers, performers, and directors (for an audiovisual work), terms and conditions of use, identifying numbers or symbols, and additional information specified by the Register of Copyright.[183]

---

178 37 Code of Federal Regulations, section 201, 65 Fed. Reg. 64556 (27 October 2000). Exemptions to Prohibition on Circumvention of Copyright Protection Systems for Access Control Technologies.

179 See http://www.copyright.gov/1201/.

180 17 United States Code, section 1202(a). No person shall knowingly and with the intent to induce, enable, facilitate, or conceal infringement: (1) provide copyright management information that is false, or (2) distribute or import for distribution copyright management information that is false.

181 17 United States Code, section 1202(b).

182 17 United States Code, section 1202(b).

183 17 United States Code, section 1202(c).

Online Providers' Safe Harbor   The United States Online Copyright Infringe- ment Liability Limitation Act[184] provides for safe harbors from copyright liability for activities such as transmission, systems caching, storage of material owned by third parties, and providing information location tools.

The Act sets forth a set of procedures which, if followed by the online provider, can insulate the online provider from liability.[185]

Criticism of the Digital Millennium Copyright Act   Unlike the WIPO Treaty, the Digital Millennium Copyright Act does not contain provisions relating to traditional copyright law because of already existing legislation in this regard in the United States.[186] By its express terms, nothing in the Digital Millennium Copyright Act affects existing copyright law.[187]

However, the Digital Millennium Copyright Act goes much farther in its anti-circumvention rules than the mandates of the WIPO Treaty require. The WIPO Copyright Treaty requires protection against acts of circumvention of use control measures. It could arguably be read to extend to preparatory acts, i.e., trafficking of technologies that circumvent use controls, to satisfy the "effective" measures requirement.[188]

By prohibiting access control, both the act of circumvention itself[189] and trafficking of tools that circumvent access controls,[190] the Digital Millennium Copyright Act exceeds the mandates of the WIPO Treaty.

Concerns have been raised that, by doing so, the Digital Millennium Copyright Act has given rightsholders a new right — the right to grant access — separate and independent from the rights of traditional copyright law.[191]

---

184 17 United States Code, section 512. The Act was enacted as part of the Digital Millennium Copyright Act.

185 17 United States Code, section 512.

186 Samuelson, "Intellectual Property and the Digital Economy: Why the Anti-Circumvention Regulations Need to Be Revised", 14 *Berkeley Tech. L. J.* 519, at p. 530 (1999).

187 17 United States Code, section 1201(c)(1).

188 Quaere, whether this affords "adequate" and "effective" protection if the act of circumvention takes place in homes and is, therefore, beyond enforcement.

189 17 United States Code, section 1201.

190 17 United States Code, section 1201(a)(2).

191 Basler, "Technological Protection Measures in the United States, the European Union and Germany: How Much Fair Use Do We Need in the 'Digital World?'", 8 *Va. J.L. & Tech.* 3 (2003). The article raises the question whether the new right to access could replace the pre-digital physical limitations to copying. If there is a new right to access, it is in effect a right to control access granted to distributors.

Such a new right could exclude users from access to a copyrighted work for uses which are otherwise permitted by copyright law.[192]

Regarding copyright limitations, the express terms of the Digital Millennium Copyright Act purport not to impact limitations or defenses of copyright law. However, access controls are not subject to the limitations and exceptions of traditional copyright law. Thus, if for instance a work were protected by an access-control technology, such as encryption, and a use-control measure, a user would escape liability for circumventing use-control technology if for purposes authorized by copyright law.

As a result of access control, uses such as quoting, re-reading, time shifting, and porting to different platforms, which were possible in analog format, are precluded. Every time a user would want to obtain access to the work for such purposes, a fee would be charged.[193]

The impact of these provisions has given rise to substantial criticism of the Digital Millennium Copyright Act among consumers, in academic circles,[194] educational institutions, and librarian associations. This criticism has resulted in several unsuccessful efforts to amend the Digital Millennium Copyright Act.[195]

(c) European Union Copyright Directive

(i)   In General

The Directive on the Harmonization of Certain Aspects of Copyright and Related Rights in the Information Society[196] was passed by the European Union and became effective in 2001, implementing the provisions of the WIPO treaties. The text of the Directive constitutes a compromise of positions, after years of lengthy negotiations and debate.[197]

---

192 The Digital Millennium Copyright Act has been criticized for not limiting circumvention of tech measures to a particular purpose or effect of infringing copyright; instead, it prohibits circumvention *per se*. Lipton, "Copyright in the Digital Age: A Comparative Survey", 27 *Rutgers Computer & Tech. L.J.* 333, at p. 358 (2001).

193 Samuelson, "Intellectual Property and the Digital Economy: Why the Anti-Circumvention Regulations Need to be Revised", 14 *Berkeley Tech. L. J* 519 (1999).

194 Dratler, *Cyberlaw: Intellectual Property in the Digital Millennium*, section 1.02[3] (2004). "In a 16 September 1997 letter to Congress, 62 copyright law professors expressed their concern about the implications of regulating devices in the name of copyright law."

195 Digital Choice and Freedom Act, H.R. 5522, 107th Cong. 2d Sess. (2002); Digital Media Consumers' Rights Act, H.R. 5544 107th Cong. 2d Sess. (2002) reintroduced as H.R. 107, 108th Cong. 2d. Sess. (2003).

196 European Union Copyright Directive 2001/29/CE. The Directive also is referred to as the "Copyright Directive" or "InfoSoc Directive".

197 Hugenholtz, "Why the Copyright Directive Is Unimportant and Possibly Invalid", 2000 *E.I.P.R.* 11, at pp. 501 and 502, at http://www.ivir.nl /publications/hugenholtz/opinion-EIPRhtml.

The two-fold objective of the Directive was to bring EU member state legislation in line with the needs of the information society and to achieve harmonization among member states to ensure a smooth functioning of the internal market.[198]

(ii) Provisions of the European Union Copyright Directive

In General The first part of the Directive covers three main substantive rights pertaining to traditional copyright, namely:

1. The reproduction right;[199]

2. The right of communication to the public, including the right to make available to the public;[200] and

3. The distribution right.[201]

Reproduction Rights The reproduction right grants authors, performers, phonogram and film producers, and broadcasting organizations the "exclusive right to authorize or prohibit direct or indirect, temporary or permanent reproduction by any means in any form, in whole or in part".[202] This right also covers temporary reproduction, such as copies into RAM.

Communication Rights The rights of communication to the public of works and of making these available to the public grant performers, phonogram and film producers, and broadcasting organizations the exclusive right to authorize or prohibit communications to the public by wire or wireless means.

This right includes the making available to the public in a way that the public may access the works from a place and at a time of their choice.[203]

Authorization Rights Finally, authors are granted the exclusive right to authorize or prohibit distribution to the public.[204] The distribution right covers works incorporated in tangible goods.

Because distribution is contemplated to occur across EU borders, the Directive contains a provision on exhaustion. Rights to tangible goods are exhausted by the first sale of the original by the right holder or with his consent within the European Community.[205]

---

198 European Union Copyright Directive 2001/29/CE, Preamble.
199 European Union Copyright Directive 2001/29/CE, article 2.
200 European Union Copyright Directive 2001/29/CE, article 3.
201 European Union Copyright Directive 2001/29/CE, article 4.
202 European Union Copyright Directive 2001/29/CE, article 2.
203 European Union Copyright Directive 2001/29/CE, article 3.
204 European Union Copyright Directive 2001/29/CE, article 4.
205 European Union Copyright Directive 2001/29/CE, article 4.2.

Anti-Circumvention   Article 6 contains the EU Copyright Directive's digital- age anti-circumvention provisions.

Protection of technological measures provides for "adequate legal protection against the circumvention of effective technological measures", if carried out with knowledge or reason to know that the objective of circumvention is prohibited.[206] Because the article applies to "any type of technological measures", no distinction is made between access control and copy control measures.

The EU Copyright Directive's anti-trafficking provisions are very similar to those of the Digital Millennium Copyright Act in that they prohibit trafficking and possession of tools that:

1. Are promoted, advertised, or marketed for the purpose of circumvention;

2. Have only limited commercially significant purpose other than circumstances; or

3. Are primarily designed for enabling or facilitating circumvention.[207]

Technological measures include any technology that:

> . . . in the normal course of its operation, is designed to prevent or restrict acts, in respect of works or other subject matter, which are not authorized by law [. . .] .

An "effective" technological measure is an "access control or protection process which achieves the protection objective".[208] Such a measure could be a transformation of the work via encryption or scrambling or a copy control mechanism.[209]

(iii) Limitations and Exceptions

The EU Copyright Directive's regime of exceptions and limitations, set forth in article 5, displays a strong preference for private sector arrangements in lieu of statutorily mandated provisions.

At a first level, article 6(4) contemplates that rightsholders make available to users, by voluntary arrangement with a third party,[210] the benefits of the

---

206 European Union Copyright Directive 2001/29/CE, article 6.1.

207 European Union Copyright Directive 2001/29/CE, article 6.2.

208 European Union Copyright Directive 2001/29/CE, article 6.3.

209 European Union Copyright Directive 2001/29/CE, article 6.3.

210 The identity of the third party is not specified by the European Union Copyright Directive. It could apply to users, as well as to technology providers.

exceptions and limitations set forth in article 5.[211] Only if rightsholders fail to do so may member states take appropriate measures to make available these same the benefits to users.[212]

Article 5.1, the only mandatory exception, provides an exemption for transient and incidental copies, essential to a technological process, and which have no economic significance of their own.[213] The remaining exceptions and limitations may be implemented in the discretion of member states.[214]

The more significant limitations include paper copies (provided the rightsholder receives compensation), reproduction, communication, and distribution for private use, libraries, educational establishments' or museums' archival copies, quotation, press use, non-commercial teaching, and scientific research.[215]

Finally, the application of all limitations listed above is tempered by the requirement that limitations be applied only in certain special cases which do not conflict with a normal exploitation of the work and do not unreasonably prejudice the legitimate interests of the right holder,[216] commonly called the "three-step test".

(iv) Rights Management Provisions

The rights management section of the EU Copyright Directive prohibits knowing unauthorized removal or alteration of electronic rights management information and "trafficking"[217] in works whose rights management information has been removed or altered, with knowledge of a rights violation.[218]

---

211 European Union Copyright Directive, article 6.4: ". . . in the absence of voluntary measures taken by rightsholders, including by agreement" rightsholders must make available to the beneficiaries "the means of benefiting from that exception or limitation to the extent necessary and where the beneficiary has legal access to the protected work or subject matter concerned".

212 European Union Copyright Directive, article 6.4.

213 European Union Copyright Directive, article 5.1.

214 European Union Copyright Directive, article 5(2) and (3).

215 European Union Copyright Directive, article 5(2) and (3). The discretionary exceptions and limitations further include photocopying, non-commercial reproduction by libraries, educational establishments, museums or archives, ephemeral recordings by broadcasting organizations, non-commercial reproductions by social institutions, illustration of teaching or scientific research, uses for the benefit of people with a disability, and use for the purposes of public security or performance of administration, parliamentary, or judicial proceedings.

216 European Union Copyright Directive, article 5.5.

217 European Union Copyright Directive, article 7.1 ("distribution, importation for distribution, broadcasting, communication, or making available to the public").

218 European Union Copyright Directive, article 7.1.

(v) Criticism of the European Union Copyright Directive

Comparing the scope of its anti-circumvention provisions to those of the WIPO Treaty and the Digital Millennium Copyright Act, the EU Copyright Directive clearly covers the broadest ground. By its express terms, the WIPO Treaty prohibits acts circumventing only use controls, and not access controls. The Digital Millennium Copyright Act prohibits the act of circumventing only access controls, but not use controls (as well as trafficking in both access and use control circumvention tools).

The European Union Copyright Directive goes beyond all of these prohibitions in that it covers the acts of circumventing both access and use controls (in addition to the prohibition of trafficking both access-control and use-control circumvention tools).

Following in the footsteps of the WIPO Treaty and the Digital Millennium Copyright Act, the EU Copyright Directive has arguably created a new "right to grant access" in the rightsholder.[219]

If a user received permission from a rightsholder to access a work but subsequently circumvented a use-control measure that act would be a violation of the European Union Copyright Directive. Because the Digital Millennium Copyright Act does not prohibit circumvention of use-control measures, the same conduct could be legal under the Digital Millennium Copyright Act, if in pursuit of a purpose permissible under copyright law.

Critics view the Directive as having failed its main objective, i.e., harmonization of copyright law among EU member states.[220] Because the EU Copyright Directive itself is the product of heavily negotiated compromise, its language serves a diversity of different interests.

As a result, it has become "an ambiguous piece of legislation",[221] an instrument that does not increase the "legal certainty" of the EU's copyright law, but instead raises additional questions as to how it should be interpreted.[222]

---

219 Basler, "Technological Protection Measures in the United States, the European Union and Germany: How Much Fair Use Do We Need in the 'Digital World?", 8 *Va. J.L. & Tech.* 3 (2003).

220 Hugenholtz, "Why the Copyright Directive Is Unimportant and Possibly Invalid", 2000 *E.I.P.R.* 11, at pp. 501 and 502, at http://www.ivir.nl /publications/hugenholtz/opinion-EIPRhtml; Antezana, "The European Union Internet Copyright Directive as Even More Than It Envisions: Toward a Supra-EU Harmonization of Copyright Policy and Theory", 26 *B.C. Int'l & Comp. L. Rev.* 415 (2003).

221 Hugenholtz, "Why the Copyright Directive Is Unimportant and Possibly Invalid", 2000 *E.I.P.R.* 11, at pp. 501 and 502, at http://www.ivir.nl/publications/hugenholtz/opinion-EIPRhtml. In addition, given the ambiguities and discretion granted to national legislators in several regards, most notably implementation of article 6(4) of the EU Copyright Directive, there is concern about potential discrepancies in the respective national implementations.

222 Hugenholtz, "Why the Copyright Directive Is Unimportant and Possibly Invalid", 2000 *E.I.P.R.* 11, at pp. 501 and 502, at http://www.ivir.nl/publications/hugenholtz/ opinion-EIPRhtml.

Within the EU's regulatory scheme with relevance to copyright law, the EU Copyright Directive is but the most recent instrument.[223]

It is viewed as being part of the "second generation" of Directives, and the intent is to harmonize inconsistent terms of the "first generation" Directives with the EU Copyright Directive.[224]

(d) National Implementation of Digital-Age Legislation

(i) In General

The deadline for implementation of the EU Copyright Directive in member states was the end of 2002. Yet, implementation has been slow.[225] Only a few countries have implemented the Copyright Directive into their national legislation.[226]

Outside the implementations in the United States and EU member states, national digital-age legislation consistent with the terms of the WIPO Treaty has been enacted in Japan[227] and Australia.[228]

(ii) Germany

In Germany, the EU Copyright Directive has been implemented in articles 95a and 95b of the German Copyright Act. The anti-circumvention portion

---

223 The European Union has passed several Directives touching on copyright over 10 years. These include the Software Directive (91/250/EC); the Rental Right Directive (92/100/EEC); the Term of Protection Directive (93/98/EEC); the Database Directive (96/9/EC); the Directive on Electronic Commerce (2000/31/EC); and the Directive on Access Control Services (98/84/EC).

224 Commission Staff Working Paper on the Review of the EC Legal Framework in the Field of Copyright and Related Rights, Brussels, 19 July 2004, at http://www.europa.eu.int/comm/internal_market/copyright/docs/review/sec-2004-995_en.pdf. Walter, "The Future of European Copyright", Speech at the Copyright Conference, Santiago de Compostela, June 2002, at http://www.europa.eu.int/comm/internal_market/copyright/docs/conference/2002-06-santiago-speech-walter_en.pdf.

225 The Finnish parliament rejected the proposed law implementing the European Union Copyright Directive. Press Release, Electronic Frontier Finland, "EFFI: Finland kills European Union Copyright Directive — for Now" (31 January 2003).

226 European Union Copyright Directive, article 13.1. As of the date of this writing, only Germany, Austria, Greece, Denmark, Italy, and Luxemburg have implemented the Copyright Directive. In the other member states, the Directive is in various states of legislative proposals.

227 In 1999, Japan amended its Copyright Act to comply with the WIPO Treaties and established new provisions on "Technological Measures" and "Rights Management Information". Japan Copyright Office, Agency for Cultural Affairs, Government of Japan, December 2004, Copyright Research and Information Center (CRIC), at http://www.cric.or.jp/cric_e/csj/csj_main.html.

228 Digital-Agenda Act of 2001, an amendment of the Australian Copyright Act of 1968.

of article 95 a(1) prohibit acts circumventing "effective[229] technological"[230] measures which protect exclusive rights under German copyright law if done without consent of the rightsholder, and the actor knows or has reason to know that the goal of circumvention is to access a protected work.[231]

The anti-trafficking portion under article 95 b(3) prohibits manufacture, importation, distribution, sale, rental, advertisement for purposes of sale or rental, and possession for commercial purposes of devices, products, or components, as well as the rendering of services which meet three conditions which generally correspond to the ones set forth by article 6.2 of the EU Copyright Directive and sections 1202(a)(2) and (b)(1) of the United States Digital Millennium Copyright Act.[232]

The structure of exceptions and limitations differs markedly from that of the Digital Millennium Copyright Act. Article 95b obligates right holders to make available to users the means necessary to take advantage of certain exceptions and limitations of the copyright law. Several provisions are listed, notably the right to reproduce for "private or other personal use".[233]

Reproduction for private use is limited to paper copies or reproduction by photomechanical or equivalent means (i.e., the right does not extend to digital copies). Significantly, agreements to waive the obligations under article 95b are void.[234] Thus, a rightsholder would not be able to take advantage of enhanced bargaining power over a user to contract out from these obligations.

However, these obligations are not effective in case a work is made available based on a contractual arrangement in a manner that would allow access at a time and place of the user's choice.[235]

---

229 "Effective" means essentially controlled by access control, measures such as encryption, distortion or other transformation, or copy control. German Copyright Act, section 95a(2). Effective controls include both access and use control.

230 German Copyright Act, section 95a(2). The term "technological measures" refers to technologies, devices, and components meant to prevent acts not authorized by the rightsholder. "Effective" means essentially controlled by access control, measures such as encryption, distortion or other transformation, or copy control.

231 German Copyright Act, section 95 a(1).

232 German Copyright Act, section 95b(3). The conditions are that the tools (1) are marketed for purposes of circumvention, (2) have limited commercial use other than circumvention, and (3) are primarily designed to allow circumvention.

233 German Copyright Act, section 95b 2–6. The exceptions and limitations include provisions for the benefit of disabled persons, collection for church, school and educational use, school radio broadcasts, and private copying.

234 German Copyright Act, section 95b(7). Agreements to exclude the obligations under paragraph 1 of section 95b(7) are void.

235 German Copyright Act, section 95b(3).

4.07   Impact on Rightsholders

(a) Who Are the Rightsholders?

The original copyright incentive scheme grants "authors" exclusive rights to their works in exchange for further creation.[236] The economics of production and distribution of copyrighted works require substantial resources.

Because such resources are usually unavailable to the individual creator, copyright rights are generally transferred to and held by intermediaries, producers, and distributors, such as publishing houses, record labels, and movie studios. These entities, collectively referred to as the content industry, are organized in effective industry organizations,[237] which represent the industry in litigation, lobbying, and other public *fora*. Because the content industry, rather than the creator, is at the forefront of developments relating to digital rights, the following will primarily discuss the impact on rightsholders as represented by the content industry.

(b) Opportunities for Digital Technology

For rightsholders, the availability of digital rights management has operated a fundamental change of paradigm in various ways. First, digital technology is capable of producing more sophisticated tools for distribution and consumption of digital content. Second, with the advent of the Internet, distribution alternatives have been vastly expanded. This in turn gives access to new market opportunities and a worldwide audience.[238] Rights holders have taken full advantage of these opportunities. Whole new industries have arisen around creation of content, creation of distribution technology, and technology protecting digital content.

Digital technology has enabled rightsholders to develop new product features and business models. The area of video products allows instant access to movies via digital cable, digital video on demand, movie services, and online video offerings. These services have all the conveniences of analog

---

236 This theory is put forward as justification for copyright exclusivity in the Common Law utilitarian system. It is recognized that the term "authors" in the Berne Convention derives from a Civil Law natural rights legal philosophy. However, the relevance for present purposes is that both systems recognized the author as creator as the beneficiary of the exclusive rights to a work.

237 Recording Industry Association of America (RIAA, at http://www.riaa.com); Motion Picture Association of America (MPAA, at http://www.mpaa.org); IFPI, worldwide representative of the recording industry (at http://www.ifpi.com); International Intellectual Property Alliance (IIPA, at http://www.iipa.com); and *Gesellschaft für Verfolgung von Urheberrechtverletzungen* (GUV, at http://www.guv.de).

238 Policy Statement of the MPAA to Internet Caucus Advisory Committee, at http://www.netcaucus.org/events/2003/drm/video.shtml.

technology such as pausing, rewind, fast forward, and replay, with the added benefit of portability and rapidly decreasing prices.[239] In the music area, paid MP3 file-downloading services offer features such as sharing, platform portability, e-mailing, wireless streaming to home speakers, and CD burning while, at the same time, allowing rightsholders to build marketing incentives into their products.[240]

The book-publishing field makes available sophisticated navigation capabilities for highlighting, searching, copying, excerpting, and annotating text with automated speed and precision.[241] As a result of all of these new developments, copyright-based industries provide significant numbers of jobs and play an increasingly important role in the economy.[242]

The content industry anticipates that, as digital rights management technologies[243] mature and gain in sophistication, they will give rise to even more diversified business models, closely tailored to consumers' needs and expectations. Services, such as filtration of information, formatting, and multimedia applications, will render traditional analog uses uninteresting and obsolete.

Distribution, protection, and pricing mechanisms will be refined to a point that they can provide the consumer with the exact amount of content for the exact price the consumer is willing to pay.[244]

---

239 Such services include Cinemanow (at http://www.cinemanow.com), Soap City Downloads (at http://www.soapcity.com), Netflix (at http://www.netflix.com), Yahoo (at http://www.yahoo.com), and Realnetworks (at http://www.realnetworks.com), which provide online video services.

240 As an example, see Apple's iTunes service using the iPod MP3 player, at http://www.apple.com/itunes/store/. Apple reports that more than 200-million songs have been sold online through the iTunes music store.

241 See, for example, eBook by Adobe, at http://www.swlearning.com/ebooks/walkthru/walkthru.html. Policy Statement of the Association of American Publishers to Internet Caucus Advisory Committee, at http://www.netcaucus.org/events/2003/drm/video.shtml.

242 In 2002, the United States "total" copyright industries accounted for an estimated 12 per cent of the United States gross domestic product (US $1.25-trillion). The "total" copyright industries employed 8.41 per cent of United States workers in 2002 (11.47-million workers). Siwek, "Copyright Industries in the United States Economy", 2004 Report, Prepared for the International Intellectual Property Alliance, at http://www.iipa.com.

243 Ginsburg, "Achieving Balance in International Copyright Law: The WIPO Treaties 1996", 26 *Colum. J.L. & Arts* 201, at p. 215 (2003), citing Perlmutter, "Convergence and the Future of Copyright", 24 *Colum. J.L. & Arts* 163, at p. 171 (2001).

244 Sobel, "DRM as an Enabler of Business Models: ISPs as Digital Retailers", 18 *Berkeley Tech. L.J.* 667 (2003). Sobel proceeds based on two premises: (1) digital rights management, although technologically in its infancy, is legally mature and here to stay, having been validated in the form of "technological measures" and copyright management information by the WIPO Treaty and its progeny, i.e., the United States Digital Millennium Copyright Act and the European Union Copyright Directive and national implementations thereof; and (2) digital-rights management in one form or another will be at the foundation of whatever business model will ultimately evolve relating to digital content.

(c) Challenges of Digital Technology

The very technology that makes possible these increasingly sophisticated digital rights management applications also presents a threat. Despite the combined use of legal and technological protection measures, the rate of piracy remains high.

The software industry, the first industry to suffer from piracy, estimates its losses in the United States at approximately US $6.5-billion in revenues per year.[245] The recording industry reports losses due to piracy of several million dollars a day, or approximately US $4.2-billion a year.[246]

The Motion Picture Association of America and its international counterpart estimate that the United States motion picture industry loses in excess of US $3-billion annually in potential worldwide revenue.[247] Not surprisingly, the content industry has approached the "copyright wars" as a war for survival. Extraordinary resources in terms of personnel, finances, lawyers, lobbyists, and campaign contributions are being committed to enforcement.[248]

(d) Enforcement under the United States Digital Millennium Copyright Act

Early enforcement began in the United States,[249] and it was directed against circumvention or "cracking" of technological protection measures. Once cracked, these technologies were published on the Internet and, as a result, virtually impossible to contain.

Among the most prominent enforcement actions is the one relating to the DVD protection code. In 1999, Jon Johansen, a Norwegian teenager, reverse engineered the encryption of the CSS (Content Scramble System), the main encryption technology used to protect the content of DVDs. Johansen's stated purpose for decoding the encryption was to create a mechanism for playing DVDs on Linux operating systems, which lacked that capability.

Johansen created the DeCSS, a tool allowing decryption of DVDs and copying them to disc drives.[250] The DeCSS tool was widely circulated on the

---

245 Weiss, "One Third of Software Pirated — Industry Group Estimates 2003 losses at US $29-billion Worldwide", *PC World* (7 July 2004).

246 See http://www.riaa.com.

247 See http://www.mpaa.org.

248 Litman, "Copyright Law as Communications Policy: Convergence of Paradigms and Cultures: War Stories", 20 *Cardozo Arts & Ent. L.J.* 337, at p. 365 (2002).

249 However, digital-age enforcement actions also have been undertaken in the United Kingdom (*Sony Computer Entertainment v. Owen*, E.W.H.C. 45 (C.H.) (2002)) and in Australia (*Kabushiki Kaisha Sony Computer Entertainment v. Stevens* [2003] F.C.A.F.C. 157. In both cases, liability was found against the circumventing party.

250 See http://www.dvdcca.org.

Internet. The owners of CSS[251] and several major film studios responded by having criminal charges filed against Johansen in Norway under Norwegian criminal law.

However, in early 2003, the Norwegian court dismissed the action, holding that Johansen's actions in bypassing CSS to play DVDs on his Linux PC were not illegal under Norwegian criminal law.[252]

In the meantime, the DeCSS code, and the story behind it, had been published by a number of mainstream publications, including the *New York Times*, the *San Jose Mercury News*, and the *Village Voice*.[253] Numerous websites posted the code on their sites and provided links to it.

The owners of CSS and the motion picture industry responded aggressively and filed several lawsuits against publishers of the code.[254]

One of the cases, *Corley/Reimerdes*,[255] arose out of the posting of the DeCSS decryption program on the website of 2600 Enterprises Inc. The site also provided links to other sources of the code. Corley was charged with violating section 1201(a)(2) of the Digital Millennium Copyright Act, which prohibits trafficking of tools that are primarily designed to circumvent access control or which have only limited commercially significant purpose other than circumvention of access control.[256]

The court held that the material posted infringed section 1201(a)(2). The defendants' challenge of the Digital Millennium Copyright Act's constitutionality on freedom of expression grounds was unsuccessful. The court held that the program had both a non-speech and a speech component, and the posting prohibition targeted only the non-speech component. The site was enjoined from posting DeCSS and from linking to any website on which DeCSS was posted.[257]

---

251 The DVD Copy Control Association licenses CSS to DVD manufacturers and others. See http://www.dvdcca.org.

252 *The Register*, "DVD Jon is free — Official (7 January 2003), at http://www.theregister.co.uk/ 2003/01/07/dvd_jon_is_free_official.

253 Eaton-Salners, "DVD Copy Control Association v. Bunner: Freedom of Speech and Trade Secrets", 19 *Berkeley Tech. L.J.* 269 (2004).

254 *DVD Copy Control Ass'n v. Bunner*, 75 P3d 1, at p. 20 (Cal., 2003); *Universal City Studios v. Reimerdes*, 111 F. Supp. 2d 294 (S.D.N.Y., 2000) *aff'd sub nom Universal City Studios, Inc. v. Corley*, 273 F3d 429 (2d Cir., 2001); *321 Studios v. MGM Studios, Inc.*, 307 F. Supp. 2d 1085, (N.D. Cal., 2004); *Paramount Pictures Corp. v. 321 Studios*, 2004 U.S. Dist. LEXIS 3306 (S.D.N.Y., 3 March 2004). EFF, Press Release, "2600 Magazine Won't Seek Supreme Court Review in DVD Case" (3 July 2002), at http://www.eff.org.

255 *Universal City Studios v. Reimerdes*, 111 F. Supp. 2d 294(S.D.N.Y., 2000) *aff'd sub nom Universal City Studios, Inc. v. Corley*, 273 F3d 429 (2d Cir., 2001).

256 17 United States Code, section 1201(a)(2).

257 *Universal City Studios v. Reimerdes*, 111 F. Supp. 2d 294 (S.D.N.Y., 2000) *aff'd sub nom Universal City Studios, Inc. v. Corley*, 273 F3d 429, at pp. 434 and 435 (2d Cir., 2001).

In a different incident, Dmitry Sklyarov, a Russian programmer employed by Elcomsoft in Moscow, Russia, developed a program that allows users to convert the Adobe eBook format into PDF files, thus circumventing the eBook's access and copy controls. The software was made available on the company's website, hosted in Chicago, Illinois.

Both Sklyarov and Elcomsoft were charged with criminal violation of the Digital Millennium Copyright Act.[258] Sklyarov was arrested while attending a conference in Las Vegas, at which he presented details about the program. In a jury trial, both Sklyarov and Elcomsoft were acquitted.[259]

The *Felten* matter[260] involved a watermarking technology called Secure Digital Music Initiative (SDMI), designed to prevent copying of music files. SDMI issued a public challenge inviting individuals to attempt to break the software code. Several academic encryption researchers from prominent universities, including Professor Felten of Princeton University, cracked the technology.

Their attempts to publish these findings were met by a letter from the RIAA, threatening liability under the Digital Millennium Copyright Act. The researchers withdrew their paper and sued for declaratory relief that their activities are not in violation of the Digital Millennium Copyright Act. The action was eventually dismissed.

The Digital Millennium Copyright Act also served as the basis for lawsuits by industries other than the entertainment industry. One action involved the alleged circumvention of a printer engine program that limited the printer to the original manufacturer's cartridge.[261]

Another suit involved reverse engineering of software controlling a garage door system.[262] Because the Digital Millennium Copyright Act prohibits only "forms of access that bear a reasonable relationship to the protections that the Copyright Act . . . affords copyright owners",[263] these actions were found to be beyond the scope of the Digital Millennium Copyright Act.

(e) Effectiveness of Digital Millennium Copyright Act Enforcement

As the above cases indicate, efforts to contain digital content and circumvention tools by means of the Digital Millennium Copyright Act have had mixed

---

258 17 United States Code, section 1204; *United States v. Elcom Ltd.*, Number CR-01-20138 (N.D. Cal., 17 January 2002).

259 Carby, "Russian company acquitted in Adobe EBook copyright case", *San Francisco Chronicle* (18 December 2002).

260 Compl. Declaratory J. and Injunctive Relief, *Felten* (Number CV-01-2669), available at http://www.eff.org/Legal/Cases/Felten_v_RIAA/20010606_eff_felten_complaint.html.

261 *Lexmark Int'l, Inc. v. Static Control Components, Inc.*, 387 F3d 522 (6th Cir., 2004).

262 *Chamberlain Group, Inc. v. Skylink Technologies Inc.*, 381 F3d 1178 (Fed. Cir., 2004).

263 *Chamberlain Group, Inc. v. Skylink Technologies Inc.*, 381 F3d 1178 (Fed. Cir., 2004).

results. The effectiveness of digital-age legislation is limited in part due to the lack of international harmonization. Because content circulates on the Internet globally, circumventors can easily place themselves beyond the reach of national enforcement.

While some countries have strong anti-circumvention laws, such as the United States, others have no digital-age legislation at all[264] or, if they do, the terms of their national implementations may be less stringent.[265] The Sklyarov incident points out the serendipitous nature of international enforcement. Had Elcomsoft made its software available from a server located in Moscow, rather than in Chicago, and had Sklyarov not participated in the Las Vegas conference, the owners of eBook would have had no recourse against the creator of the circumventing code.

Even where stringent digital-age laws exist, national legal systems may offer different remedies and sanctions. Jon Johansen was acquitted by the Norwegian court for an act for which he would have likely been convicted under the provisions of the United States Digital Millennium Copyright Act. Following his acquittal, Jon Johansen continues to reverse engineer digital rights management tools while communicating the results via a blog entitled "So sue me" from Norway.[266]

As a result, DeCSS and similar programs proliferate, not only on hackers' websites, but in mainstream publications and their archives.[267] A brief search of the Internet reveals countless sites which offer the DeCSS code as well as advice on its use.[268]

While the various lawsuits under the Digital Millennium Copyright Act were in progress, a new challenge arose. The mainstay of illegal copying activity

---

264　Fifty-one countries have ratified the WIPO Treaty. See http://www.wipo.int/treaties/en. Relatively few of these have actually enacted national laws under the WIPO Treaty. At the time of this writing, only Austria, Denmark, Germany, Greece, Italy, and Luxemburg had implemented the European Union Copyright Directive. In the remainder of the European Union, the Copyright Directive still is in various stages of legislative proposals. Countries such as Australia and Japan also have digital-age laws.

265　Australian Copyright Act, section 116A(1). Australian law is more favorable to users than the European Union Copyright Directive and the United States Digital Millennium Copyright Act in that it does not prohibit the act of circumvention of access or use controls.

266　For example, the Johansen of DVD fame decoded a portion of the iTunes software and announced this fact on his blog, at http://www.nanocrew.net/blog/.

267　Eaton-Salners, "DVD Copy Control Association v. Bunner: Freedom of Speech and Trade Secrets", 19 *Berkeley Tech. L.J.* 269 (2004).

268　See http://www.pzcommunications.com/decss/main.htm, which provides the "Ultimate DeCSS Resources"; "DeCSS Central" at http://www.lemuria.org/DeCSS/main.html, which advertises that "This site contains links and local copies of all relevant information about DVD, CSS, DeCSS, LiVid, the DVD CCA and MPAA, and the various lawsuits surrounding DeCSS".

migrated to peer-to-peer (P2P) file sharing, a technology which allows large numbers of individuals to download copyrighted content from their homes. The three-tier protection structure offered no adequate remedy against such massive copying in dispersed locations. At the time the WIPO Treaty and the Digital Millennium Copyright Act were negotiated, peer-to-peer file sharing was not within the contemplated realm.[269]

Rightsholders were forced into a new approach: rather than proceed against the infringers themselves, they sued the provider of the technology which made the infringement possible (see text, below).

(f) Rightsholders' Legislative Efforts

In parallel to the legal enforcement actions, rightsholders are continually seeking to amend the legislative and regulatory framework governing unauthorized dissemination of copyrighted content. One such effort is the INDUCE Act, which proposes criminal sanctions against a party who induces, i.e., "intentionally aids, abets, induces, or procures" copyright infringement.[270] The Act, in effect, bans technology that can be used for infringing purposes.[271]

A further legislative proposal is the Consumer and Computer Owner Protection and Security (ACCOPS) Act of 2003, introduced at the behest of the content industry. The Act makes the release of a copyrighted work on Internet subject to felony prosecution.[272] Neither of these bills was adopted.

An endeavor that proved more successful for the content industry was the United States Federal Communication Commission's adoption of the "broadcast flag", a technology to control distribution of video content. The broadcast flag technology embeds into television programs a digital file that signals that the program must be protected from unauthorized redistribution. The broadcast flag will be implemented on all digital television broadcasts in the United States.[273]

In conclusion, rightsholders have gained from digital technology and stand to lose from it, as well. As the race with technology continues, the introduction of

---

269 In the early 1990s, when the WIPO Treaty discussions began, the impact of the Internet as a distribution mechanism was not appreciated; similarly, in 1998, when the Digital Millennium Copyright Act was passed, file-sharing technology in its present form was not anticipated. In 2004, the content industry sought to pass the INDUCE Act, designed specifically to address the P2P file sharing issue that had begun plaguing the industry in 2001.

270 See http://thomas.loc.gov/home/thomas.html.

271 Intent is determined based on the particular circumstances of the case. See http://thomas.loc.gov/home/thomas.html. Therefore, there is low predictability of outcome for a technology provider.

272 See http://thomas.loc.gov/home/thomas.html, Bill H.R. 2752, Release of a copyrighted work in the Internet shall be deemed distribution of at least 10 copies of that work, with a retail value of more than US $2,500, which places it above the threshold for felony prosecution.

273 See http://www.mpaa.org; adopted by the Federal Communications Commission in late 2004.

new distribution technologies is followed by new legal remedies, which in turn are followed by new distribution technologies. As the tension among stakeholders mounts, an imminent satisfactory solution seems unlikely.

4.08　　Impact on the Public

(a)　In General

The other main interest protected by copyright law is the interest of society at large and its increasing need for new cultural and knowledge-related values. The direct beneficiaries of this policy are users (consumers)[274] of information, whether individual or institutionalized, such as libraries, educational institutions, and research institutions.

(b)　Benefits of the Digital-Age

The public is the beneficiary of the vast amount of free content that becomes available as the Internet grows into a truly global communications and distribution mechanism. Massive projects for digitizing content and placing it on publicly accessible servers are under way. Major libraries, such as Harvard University, Stanford University, the University of Michigan, Oxford University, and the New York Public Library, have made arrangements to digitally scan books from their collections and include them in databases publicly searchable by users worldwide.[275] The Open Course Ware initiative of the Massachusetts Institute of Technology (MIT) is designed to place the entirety of MIT courses on the Internet.[276]

Governments routinely place large amounts of information on publicly accessible servers.[277] Numerous international organizations[278] and non-profit groups make works widely available on the Internet.

Copyright-protected paid content also is available in abundance. Digital rights management technologies provide the individual user with an ever-increasing

---

274　For purposes of the present discussion, consumer and user, used interchangeably, denote the category of people intended to benefit from the limitations and exceptions of copyright laws. The use follows the traditional rightsholder-user dichotomy, regardless whether the use is primarily for personal use, for research, for commercial use. It is recognized that, in the digital-age, with increased productive use of content, the roles of user and rightsholder may become interchangeable.

275　"Google Checks Out Library Books", Google Press Release (14 December 2004), at http://www.google.com/press/pressrel/print_library.html.

276　Under this initiative, the Massachusetts Institute of Technology is placing all educational materials online free of charge and available to the public. MIT retains the copyright to the materials. See http://ocw.mit.edu/index.html.

277　For example, European Union sites are publicly available at http://www.europa.eu.int. The United States government sites include http://www.doc.gov, http://www.fcc.gov, and many others.

278　See http://www.wipo.int.

variety of features and services, designed to facilitate and enhance consumption of digital content products. As the content industry seeks to increase the public acceptance of its digital rights management controlled products, decisions on how digital content is offered are made increasingly with the consumer in mind. Thus, because the "consumer is king", users are likely to have some say in shaping future offers of digital content.[279]

(c) Expansion of Rights

Despite these developments, scholars and public interest advocacy groups express concern about the fact that digital technology and the ensuing legislation work to the benefit of rightsholders and to the detriment of the public. The three-tier protection structure has caused exclusive rights to expand, while limitations and exceptions have shrunk. The result is an ongoing "doctrinal creep".[280] Although used in the context of trade mark law, this term is equally applicable to copyright that disturbs the balance inherent in traditional copyright law and has potentially detrimental effects on the overall society.[281]

The expansion of the scope of copyright rights has accelerated with technological development as legislators and rightsholders responded to the new reality of digital technology. Thus, protection for "literary and artistic works" has expanded to cover computer programs,[282] computer chips,[283] and useful articles.[284]

Copyright laws went from prohibiting literal copying to covering work with the same "concept and feel".[285] Under the guise of copyright protection, laws were passed which control content distribution technologies, such as the Audio Home Recording Act of 1992[286] and the Digital Millennium Copyright Act.[287]

---

279 Some commentators believe that sheer market power and consumer demand will determine less draconian measure. Ginsburg, "Achieving Balance in International Copyright Law: The WIPO Treaties 1996", 26 *Colum. J.L. & Arts* 201, at p. 215 (2003), citing Perlmutter, "Convergence and the Future of Copyright, 24 *Colum. J.L. & Arts* 163, at p. 171 (2001).

280 Lemley, "The Modern Lanham Act and the Death of Common Sense", 108 *Yale L. J.* 1687, at p. 1698 (1999).

281 Lessig, *Code and Other Laws of Cyberspace* (1999); Lessig, *Free Culture: How Big Media Uses Technology and the Law to Lock Down Culture and Control Creativity* (2004); Litman, *Digital Copyright* (2001).

282 17 United States Code Annotated, section 117.

283 17 United States Code Annotated, section 902.

284 17 United States Code Annotated, section 101.

285 *Cavalier v. Random House*, 297 F2d 815 (9th Cir., 2002).

286 17 United States Code Annotated, sections 1001 *et seq*. The Audio Home Recording Act prohibits the importation, manufacture, and distribution of digital audio recording devices unless the devices are equipped to prevent "serial copying".

287 17 United States Code Annotated, sections 1201 *et seq*. The law makes actionable circumvention of technological measures that effectively control access to copyright protected work and trafficking in such technology, as well as interfering with copyright management information.

The term of copyright law has been extended, in Europe from 50 to 70 years *post mortem auctoris*;[288] in the United States, from an original 14-year renewable term to its current duration of 70 years *post mortem auctoris*.[289] The national implementations of the WIPO Treaties raised further questions regarding the appropriate scope of copyright law.[290]

Scholars are critical of digital-age legislation, because it has created a new right "to grant access" to a protected work, a right which previously did not exist under traditional copyright law.[291]

(d) Erosion of Limitations and Exceptions

Limitations and exceptions are equally impacted by the three-tier protection structure. Public interest advocates and scholars are concerned that these doctrines are being eroded to a point where basic freedoms are at stake.[292] These freedoms include the freedom of expression, the freedom to exchange ideas and information, and rights to privacy and are well anchored in the legislation of democratic society.[293]

Limiting doctrines have been built into traditional copyright law to preserve the proper balance of interest among stakeholders by acting as prevention against copyright law interfering with these fundamental freedoms.[294]

---

288 Council Directive 93/98/EEC of 29 October 1993, harmonizing the term of protection of copyright and certain related rights.

289 In the United States, in the course of implementation of the Berne Convention, a number of Civil Law concepts were imported into the United States legislative scheme, including a copyright term measured by the life of the author. In an effort toward international harmonization, the copyright term was successively increased.

290 Ginsburg, "Achieving Balance in International Copyright Law: The WIPO Treaties 1996", 26 *Colum. J.L. & Arts* 201, at p. 214 (2003).

291 Ginsburg, "Achieving Balance in International Copyright Law: The WIPO Treaties 1996", 26 *Colum. J.L. & Arts* 201, at p. 214 (2003).

292 Litman, *Digital Copyright*, at p. 289 (2001).

293 For example, the rights under the United States Constitution, including the First Amendment and the right to information and free expression in the legislation of Civil Law countries.

294 Frey, "Unfairly Applying the Fair Use Doctrine, Princeton University Press v. Michigan Document Services", 66 *Univ. of Cincinnati L. Rev.* 959, at p. 1001 (1998). Lipton, "Copyright in the Digital-Age: A Comparative Survey", 27 *Rutgers Computer & Tech. L.J.* 333, at p. 358 (2001). ". . . the privilege to use ideas gives access to almost all the benefits of free speech and dissemination of thoughts, while constraining only the form of their communication. The exclusive rights over the form of expression, on the other hand, seem to provide sufficient incentives to serve the purposes of copyright". *Harper & Row Publishers Inc. v. Nation Enterprises*, 471 U.S. 539, at pp. 558 and 559 (1985). "In view of the First Amendment protections already embodied in the Copyright Act's distinction between copyrightable expression and uncopyrightable facts and ideas, and the latitude for scholarship and comment traditionally afforded by fair use, we see no warrant for expanding the doctrine of fair use to create what amounts to a public figure exception to copyright".

The limiting doctrines operate by excluding certain material from copyright[295] protection and thus giving copyright law a "permeable" character. However, the permeability is not carried through into the technological protection tier.

For instance, it is well established that copyright law protects expression, but excludes from protection ideas, concepts, and systems because they are reserved for common use.[296]

The distinction between such unprotectable ideas and protected expression is highly subjective, and the mechanical operation of technological measures is incapable of making it. As a result, the technological layer indiscriminately covers both protectable and unprotectable material, and the permeability is lost at the level of technological protection measures. The "impermeable" technological protection is then reinforced by digital rights legislation.

Because the technological protection mechanism is incapable of recognizing the "permeability", users are subject to liability under digital rights legislation even if their conduct is permissible under traditional copyright law. Thus, a user's circumvention of technological protection in an effort to reach unprotectable ideas in a work is a violation of the Digital Millennium Copyright Act, as well as of other digital-age laws, even though the user engaged in an act authorized by copyright law.[297] The United States fair use doctrine is a particular challenge to digital rights management because of the particular subjectivity of its four-factor balancing test.[298]

---

295 Boyle, "The Second Enclosure Movement and the Construction of the Public Domain." 66 *Law and Contemporary Problems* 33, at p. 60 (2003), summarizing the view expressed in Patterson and Lindberg, *The Nature of Copyright, a Law of User's Rights* (1991). "The United States copyright law system is designed to feed the public domain [by] providing temporary and narrowly limited rights [to authors, the rights] themselves subject to considerable restrictions even during their existence."

296 Article 2 of the WIPO Treaty provides that "copyright protection extends to expression and not to ideas, procedures, methods of operation or mathematical concepts as such". *International News Service v. Associated Press*, 248 U.S.215, at p. 250 (1918). "In no case does copyright protection for a work of authorship extend to any idea, process, procedure, system, method of operation, principle, concept of discovery, regardless of how it is embodied in the work." 17 United States Code, section 102 b. See also categorization of "material not subject to copyright". 37 Code of Federal Regulations, section 202.1. Article 2 of the WIPO Treaty provides that "copyright protection extends to expression and not to ideas, procedures, methods of operation or mathematical concepts as such".

297 Samuelson, "Digital Rights Management (and, or, vs) the Law", *Communications of the ACM*, volume 46, Issue 4 (April 2003).

298 Nimmer, "The Public Domain, Fairest of Them All and Other Fairy Tales of Fair Use", 66 *Law & Contemp. Prob.* 263, at p. 280 (2003).

Digital rights management technology is incapable of such refined evaluation[299] and, consequently, as a practical matter, no fair use can be made of a work protected by digital rights management. The private use[300] and quotation[301] right of Civil Law jurisdictions also are at risk,[302] unless the particular national implementation of digital-age legislation allows for specific exemptions from liability for exercise of these rights.[303]

Content users are concerned that the erosion of copyright exclusions and limitations will result in the disappearance of uses taken for granted in an analog environment, such as the ability to browse, re-use, quote, share, time shift, and space shift. The fear is that consumption of digital content gradually moves towards an all-comprising pay-per-use model.

The content industry acknowledges the need to accommodate users' fair-use interests into digital rights management technologies.[304] However, as a practical matter, the content industry has little incentive to do so. First, development of new capabilities involves certain costs. Furthermore, if unrestricted fair use/private use copies of a work become freely available on the Internet, they threaten to replace the entire work in the market. For this reason, the fair use debate is an "all or nothing" situation for the content industry. Unless seriously pressured by legislature or the market, the content industry will seek to maintain the "all" status quo, rather than risk the "nothing" by enabling fair use.

(e) Does the Public Have a Voice?

Historically, users of copyrighted material have not acted in concert to protect their rights in legislative bodies, courts, and other public *fora*.[305]

---

299 The technology and content industries assert that they have made it a priority to develop technology capable of discerning fair from infringing use. See Internet caucus policy statements, at http://www.netcaucus.org/events/2003/drm/video.shtml.

300 For example, the German Copyright Act, section 53(1), allows private copying to the extent that the original has been lawfully obtained.

301 For example, the German Copyright Act, section 53(1), allows private copying to the extent that the original has been lawfully obtained.

302 Public interest groups are actively seeking to exempt the private copy, quotation right, and other exceptions from the operation of digital-age legislation. See http://www.privatkopie.net.

303 Germany Copyright Act, section 53(1).

304 See http://www.netcaucus.org/events/2003/drm/video.shtml.

305 Some attribute the fact that present-day copyright laws are unfavorable to consumers to the lack of representation of the public interest. Commentators attribute copyright's expanding doctrinal creep to the absence of the public interest at the legislative negotiation table. For example, in the United States, for more than 100 years Congress has essentially delegated the legislative drafting to the industry affected, with the result that legislation is both industry-negotiated and industry-drafted. Litman, *Digital Copyright* (2001), at p. 62.

As consumption of content is playing an increasing role in today's knowledge-based society, advocacy groups have begun to represent the public interest in the debate surrounding digital content.[306] Digital copyright law issues are coming into the forefront of public attention as a result of incidents such as the criminal prosecution of Sklyarov, the demise of Napster, and RIAA lawsuits against individual P2P downloaders.[307]

Both in the United States and the European Union,[308] efforts are being made to pass legislation to restore some of the traditional copyright limitations, which are being eroded by the combined effect of digital rights management and digital-age legislation. Public interest groups represent copyright users in litigation,[309] and numerous groups speak out in court actions to avoid decisions adverse to the public interest.[310]

However, the ultimate success of such efforts depends on whether the public interest's cause can gain support sufficiently widespread to affect legislation.[311]

4.09 Impact on Technology Providers

(a) Tension between Rightsholders and Technology Providers

Digital technology allows distribution of content through increasingly complex technological channels. This fact has brought a third stakeholder into the balancing process — the information technology industry. Its role is significant because it makes available the channels for distribution of digital content and the means of controlling them. These elements are critical to the rightsholders' ability to control the digital content market.

---

306 Public advocacy groups include the Electronic Frontier Foundation, Privatkopie, and various academic institutions, such as the Stanford Center for Internet and Society.

307 The recording industry is filing approximately 700 individual lawsuits a month against individual infringers. "New Round of Lawsuits Against 717 Illegal File Sharers Includes Continued Focus On University Network Users Who Illegally Download Music", RIAA Press Release (24 January 2005), at http://www.riaa.com.

308 See Privatkopie, at http://www.privatkopie.net; Electronic Frontier Foundation, at http://www.eff.org.

309 For example, the Stanford Center for the Internet and Society represented Eric Eldred in his action to challenge the Sonny Bono Copyright Term Extension Act; *Eldred v. Ashcroft*, 534 U.S. 1126 (2002).

310 Forty-six law professors signed an *amicus* brief in *MGM v. Grokster*, 380 F3d 1154, at p. 1160 (9th Cir., 2004), advocating that the standard for contributory copyright infringement set forth in *Sony v. Universal Studios* not be altered.

311 For example, California Congresswoman Zoe Lofgren, who supports the interests of the digital consumer, introduced H.R. 1066, the Benefit Authors without Limiting Advancement or Net Consumer Expectations (Balance) Act of 2003 and proposes that digital transmissions be treated as fair use, storing, adapting, and archiving copies be permitted, and circumvention for non-infringing uses be legalized. The bill did not pass.

The existence of a digital content market is based on scarcity of supply of digital content.[312] New distribution technologies create unlimited supply of content and thus threaten to disrupt the market.[313]

As one court pointed out, the introduction of new technology, whether a "player piano, a copier, a tape recorder, a video recorder, a personal computer, a karaoke machine, or an MP3 player",[314] is always disruptive to existing markets, particularly to those copyright owners using well-established distribution mechanisms.[315]

To limit supply and restore the market, copyright owners seek to gain control over newly developed technologies. Such efforts include standard-setting legislation for devices capable of reproducing digital content,[316] legislation criminalizing manufacture and distribution of such devices,[317] and litigation against technology manufacturers.

Technology providers are increasingly concerned that such efforts to control new technologies can operate as a deterrent to innovate.[318]

(b) Liability of Technology Providers under Secondary Infringement Theories

Efforts to impose liability on technologies are not new. The doctrines of contributory and vicarious copyright infringement have been asserted against technology providers in the past.[319]

---

312 "Property rights in patents and copyrights make possible the creation of a scarcity of the products appropriated which could not otherwise be maintained". Cohen, "Lochner in Cyberspace: The New Economic Orthodoxy of 'Rights Management'", 97 Mich. L. Rev. 462, at p. 511 (1998).

313 A tension has always existed between rightsholders' exercise of control under copyright law, on the one hand, and the availability of new technology, on the other. Ginsburg, "Copyright and Control over New Technologies of Dissemination", 101 *Colum. L. Rev.* 1613, at p. 1616 (2001).

314 *MGM v. Grokster*, 380 F3d 1154 (9th Cir., 2004).

315 *MGM v. Grokster*, 380 F3d 1154 (9th Cir., 2004).

316 The American Home Recording Act (AHRA), 17 United States Code, sections 1001 *et seq.*, requires installation of serial copy management system chips in all consumer-grade digital audio tape technologies. The Digital Millennium Copyright Act requires Macrovision's copy-control technology to be installed in all post-1998 video cassette recording devices. 17 United States Code, section 1201(k).

317 Inducing Infringement of Copyrights Act of 2004 (INDUCE Act), section 2560, at http://thomas.loc.gov.

318 One commentator points out that technologies over which rightsholders have had control, such as digital audio tape decks, dual-deck VCRs, laserdiscs, and Divx machines have not been successful. Lemley, "The Modern Lanham Act and the Death of Common Sense", 108 *Yale L. J.* 1687, at p. 1698 (1999).

319 The doctrine derives from the tort of *respondeat superior. Fonovisa Inc. v. Cherry Auction*, 76 F3d 259 (9th Cir., 1996). The elements of contributory infringement are: (1) direct infringement by a primary infringer, (2) the defendant's knowledge (actual or constructive) of the infringement, and (3) material contribution to the infringement. Vicarious liability is present if there is: (1) direct infringement by a primary infringer, (2) a direct financial benefit to the defendant, and (3) the right and ability to supervise the infringers. *A&M Records v. Napster*, 239 F3d 1004, at p. 1022 (9th Cir. 2001).

As early as 1984, Universal Studios claimed, in *Sony Corp. of America, Inc. v. Universal City Studios (Sony/Betamax)*,[320] that Sony was contributorily liable for the infringing use of Sony's video recording device, the Betamax.[321]

Fair and non-infringing use is a defense to contributory liability. Based on this defense, a manufacturer of devices capable of substantial fair and non-infringing uses can escape liability.[322] Because the Betamax was capable of the fair use of time shifting, i.e., recording copyrighted programs for later, personal non-commercial viewing, the Supreme Court found the device capable of substantial non-infringing use, sufficient to exempt Sony from contributory liability (despite the fact that other infringing uses of Betamax were shown).

In exonerating the technology provider, the *Sony* court fully appreciated the risk that, if found, such liability:

> . . . would enlarge the scope of respondents' [film studio] statutory monopolies to encompass control over an article of commerce [the Betamax] that is not the subject of copyright protection . . . [and] . . . block the wheels of commerce.

Several cases decided under the Sony doctrine reached similar results.[323]

Nonetheless, these doctrines remain attractive to copyright owners, because a single lawsuit against the provider of infringing technology can eliminate the infringement of large numbers of users.[324] These doctrines are particularly advantageous in situations such as file sharing where, because of the

---

320 *Sony Corp. of America, Inc. v. Universal City Studios, Inc.*, 464 U.S. 417 (1984).

321 Sony does not differentiate between contributory and vicarious liability, indicating that the doctrines are too close given the particular facts. *Sony Corp. of America, Inc. v. Universal City Studios*, Inc., 464 U.S. 417, at p. 435 (1984).

322 *Sony Corp. of America, Inc. v. Universal City Studios*, Inc., 464 U.S. 417, at p. 433 (1984); *A&M Records v. Napster*, 239 F3d 1004, at p. 1012 (9th Cir., 2001); and *A&M Records v. Napster*, 114 F. Supp. 2d 896, at pp. 905–908 (N.D. Cal., 2000).

323 *Vault Corp. v. Quaid Software, Ltd.*, 847 F2d 255, at p. 262 (5th Cir., 1988), a software program that defeated anti-copying software did not give rise to liability; *Recording Indus. Ass'n of Am. v. Diamond Multimedia Sys., Inc.*, 180 F3d 1072, at p. 1079 (9th Cir., 1999), MP3 players do not infringe because they are used for space shifting; *Lewis Galoob Toys, Inc. v. Nintendo of Am., Inc.*, 964 F2d 965, at pp. 970 and 971 (9th Cir., 1992), alteration of a copyrighted video game did not entail liability.

324 Lemley and Reese, "Reducing Digital Copyright Infringement without Restricting Innovation", *56 Stan. L. Rev.* 1345, at p. 1376 (2004). Suing facilitators is more cost effective because one lawsuit can eliminate the dissemination mechanism for a large number of end-user copies.

vast number of dispersed file sharers operating from their homes,[325] individual prosecution is unduly cumbersome and expensive, if practicable at all.[326]

In 1999, members of the recording industry sued Napster, a popular song file sharing service that enabled users to download music, including copyrighted music files, free of charge.[327] Napster was estimated to facilitate the download of more than 1-billion songs a month.[328] The recording industry asserted theories of contributory and vicarious liability.

The court held that Napster had knowledge of infringing activity and the right and ability to control it. For this reason, the *Sony* exemption from liability of devices with substantial non-infringing uses was not applicable.[329] The Napster service was forced to close down.[330]

The *Napster* decision was followed shortly by a similar decision in the consolidated cases of *In re Aimster Litigation*.[331] Aimster conducted a service which used AOL's instant messaging system to transfer files among members of the services, including copyrighted music files. Following the *Napster* precedent, Aimster was found liable and forced to close down.[332]

---

325   *In re Aimster Copyright Litigation*, 334 F3d 643, at p. 645, (7th Cir., 2003). "Recognizing the impracticability or futility of a copyright owner's suing a multitude of individual infringers . . . the law allows a copyright holder to sue a contributor to the infringement instead, in effect as an aider and abettor" . . . "chasing individual consumers is time consuming and is a teaspoon solution to an ocean problem".

326   Nonetheless, the recording industry is pursuing infringers on an individual basis as well, filing approximately 700 individual lawsuits a months. "New Round of Lawsuits Against 717 Illegal File Sharers Includes Continued Focus on University Network Users Who Illegally Download Music", RIAA Press Release (24 January 2005), at http://www.riaa.com.

327   Napster provided a collection of centralized servers for the file sharing purposes, as well as indexing services to facilitate file location.

328   Smith, "Napster enabled 1.4bn song swaps in September", *The Register* (14 October 2000).

329   *A&M Records v. Napster*, Inc., 239 F3d 1004, at pp. 1020 and 1022 (9th Cir., 2001).

330   Bertelsman AG, a Germany media conglomerate, attempted to acquire Napster's assets. Wingfield, "Napster Files for Chapter 11, May Sell Assets to Bertelsmann", *The Wall Street Journal Online* (4 June 2002). This effort was blocked by United States Bankruptcy Court in September 2002. Ahrens, "Judge Blocks Napster's Sale to Bertelsmann", *WashingtonPost.com* (4 September 2002). Subsequently, all of Napster's assets were acquired by Roxio, an Internet media company. See http://www.roxio.com/ en/company/news/archive/prelease021115.jhtml.

331   *In re Aimster Copyright Litigation*, 177 F. Supp. 2d 1380 (Judicial Panel on Multidistrict Litigation 2001).

332   *In re Aimster Copyright Litigation*, 177 F. Supp. 2d 1380 (Judicial Panel on Multidistrict Litigation 2001). The *Aimster* court found that Aimster had actual knowledge, because its services included indexing, ranking, and commenting on the MP3 music for the benefit of its users.

As a result of successful legal action by the recording industry against Napster, Aimster, and others, the music downloading activity migrated to a different file sharing system, generally known as peer-to-peer (P2P). The P2P method of file sharing is not contingent on the existence of a centralized server and therefore not subject to the Napster precedent.

The most prominent file sharing services, Grokster, Morpheus, and Kazaa, were sued by the movie and recording industries in 2002 for contributory and vicarious copyright infringement. Grokster, Morpheus, and Kazaa are distributors of software that, once installed on a user's computer, automatically connects to a network and allows users to copy digital files, containing text, video, and music from each other. The entertainment industry plaintiffs argued that these services are similar in nature to Napster and should, therefore, be shut down. The court of appeal accepted the defense that the defendants' software was capable of substantial non-infringing uses, because they lacked knowledge[333] of infringement and the ability to control the file sharing.[334]

(c) Liability of Technology Providers under the Digital Millennium Copyright Act

The Digital Millennium Copyright Act's anti-trafficking provisions are an alternate source of liability to technology providers, because their prohibitions extend to developers and distributors of tools, capable of circumventing access or use control measures.[335] A technology provider is prohibited from creating or trafficking devices "primarily designed or produced" for the respective prohibited purposes that have "only limited commercially significant purpose or use" other than engaging in the prohibited conduct and that are marketed with knowledge of use in circumventing.[336]

Although the Digital Millennium Copyright Act purports not to "enlarge or diminish vicarious or contributory liability for any technology manufacturers",[337] it subtly changes the pre-existing standard of secondary liability set forth in *Sony* and its progeny.

---

333 *MGM v. Grokster*, 380 F3d 1154, 1160 (9th Cir., 2004). If a product is capable of "substantial or commercially significant non-infringing uses", then the right holder must show that the defendant had knowledge of specific infringing files and failed to act on such knowledge; if it is not capable of substantial uses, then the rightholder must only show constructive knowledge.

334 The court found that the defendant's software distributors did not provide file storage and index maintenance, infringing messages or file indices did not reside on their computers, and they did not have the ability to suspend user accounts. Rather, it is the users of the software who, by connecting to each other over the internet, create the network and provide the access.

335 17 United States Code, section 1201(a)(2) and (b)(1).

336 17 United States Code, section 1201(a)(2) and (b)(1).

337 17 United States Code, section 1201(c)(2).

First, the Digital Millennium Copyright Act refers specifically to a "commercially significant" purpose or use and, thus, focuses solely on the circumventing technology's commercial impact. The Sony standard, on the other hand, is broader, leaving room for non-commercial considerations.[338]

Second, the focus under the Digital Millennium Copyright Act is on circumvention and not on copyright infringement. Whether the uses made were otherwise authorized under copyright law and whether copyright is infringed in the course of circumvention are irrelevant.[339]

Third, under the Digital Millennium Copyright Act, liability is based on the manufacturer's intent, not on the use of the device at issue. Thus, a technology developer who merely contemplated a technology defeating use could be held liable even though the device was never used or was used solely for non-infringing purposes.[340]

The result of these changes is that the scope of defenses available to technology providers under *Sony* have been reduced by the Digital Millennium Copyright Act.

(d) Potential to Deter Innovation

The potential exposure of technology providers under the secondary liability doctrines or the Digital Millennium Copyright Act can operate as a powerful deterrent to the freedom to innovate.[341] A provider of technology that is capable of both infringing and non-infringing uses (dual-use technology) accused of a Digital Millennium Copyright Act violation must be prepared to demonstrate that its technology is "primarily" or "substantially" used for non-infringing purposes.[342]

---

338 Dratler, *Cyberlaw: Intellectual Property in the Digital Millennium*, section 2.04[2] (2004).

339 17 United States Code, section 1201(a)(1), prohibits the act of circumvention of technological measures; section 1201(a)(2) and (b)(1) prohibits trafficking of devices. The act of copyright infringement remains prohibited under traditional copyright law; the Digital Millennium Copyright Act is simply not concerned with it.

340 The argument can be made that circumvention technology that intended to allow users the benefits of authorized uses is not "primarily designed" to circumvent protection measures or that it has a commercially significant purpose other than circumvention.

341 "The anecdotal evidence of such deterrence is quite strong. When programmers started being prosecuted criminally for writing code that violated the Digital Millennium Copyright Act's anti-circumvention provisions and online magazines were sued for writing stories that linked the reader to allegedly unlawful sites, the result was to chill programming, deterring some from working on encryption at all and steering others away from work in certain areas perceived as sensitive". Lemley and Reese, "Reducing Digital Copyright Infringement without Restricting Innovation", 56 Stan. L. Rev. 1345, at p. 1388 (2004).

342 Lemley and Reese, "Reducing Digital Copyright Infringement without Restricting Innovation", *56 Stan. L. Rev.* 1345, at p. 1388 (2004); Dratler, *Cyberlaw: Intellectual Property in the Digital Millennium*, section 2.05, n. 256 (2004).

In making design decisions, technology providers may be forced to consider alternate designs, which reduce or eliminate the possibility of infringing uses.[343] These concerns can easily stifle inventiveness.[344] Even if a technology provider is ultimately successful in defending against such claims, this type of litigation is so costly that it can easily put a small company out of business.

Courts dealing with actions against technology companies are forced to make a choice between the interests of the rightsholder and those of the technology provider. If the rightholder prevails, the court must ban the service or device, declare it contraband, and prohibit its sale.[345] This result effectively eliminates the particular technology.[346]

A ban is most likely an excessive penalty against the company that has invested resources into the creation of a technology. The loss to the company is compounded by the loss to overall social welfare, as a result of the technology being eliminated altogether.[347] Along with the technology itself, its "spillover" effects, those unanticipated future benefits which the banned technology could have brought also are eliminated.

Often, the value of the "spillover" exceeds the immediate value of the banned technology.[348] An obvious example is the VCR. A technology that the copyright industry tried to ban, later developed in unanticipated ways and created new markets that have provided tremendous benefit to the very copyright owners who would have outlawed it.[349]

---

343 Lemley and Reese, "Reducing Digital Copyright Infringement without Restricting Innovation", 56 *Stan. L. Rev.* 1345, at p. 1362 (2004).

344 Lemley and Reese, "Reducing Digital Copyright Infringement without Restricting Innovation", 56 *Stan. L. Rev.* 1345, at p. 1388 (2004).

345 Lemley and Reese, "Reducing Digital Copyright Infringement without Restricting Innovation", 56 *Stan. L. Rev.* 1345, at p. 1386 (2004).

346 For example, the *321 Studios* cases arose out of distribution, but 321 Studios distributed software and instructions for copying DVDs. The court found in favor of the content owners, and the company was enjoined from manufacturing, distributing, or otherwise trafficking in any type of DVD circumvention software. *321 Studios v. MGM Studios, Inc.*, 307 F. Supp. 2d 1085 (N.D. Cal. 2004); *Paramount Pictures Corp. v. 321 Studios*, 2004 U.S. Dist. LEXIS 3306 (S.D.N.Y., 3 March 2004).

347 Lemley and Reese, "Reducing Digital Copyright Infringement without Restricting Innovation", 56 *Stan. L. Rev.* 1345, at p. 1386 (2004). It is reduced by the net social value of the particular innovation.

348 Lemley and Reese, "Reducing Digital Copyright Infringement without Restricting Innovation", 56 *Stan. L. Rev.* 1345, at p. 1387 (2004).

349 Lemley and Reese, "Reducing Digital Copyright Infringement without Restricting Innovation", 56 *Stan. L. Rev.* 1345, at p. 1387 (2004). The early history of radio offers a similar lesson.

Finally, while courts may be reluctant to ban well-established technologies with proven non-infringing uses, newer technologies whose advantages and social value can be easily perceived, remain particularly vulnerable to such challenges.[350]

Despite the potential of stifling innovation of dual-use devices, the technology industry has generally benefited from the content industry's continuing technological needs in the digital rights management field and the consumers' needs for new and diversified means of content consumption. Possibly because of this benefit, the technology industry in the past not advocated its concerns very vigorously.[351] It remains to be seen whether these benefits continue to outweigh the threat to innovation posed by the continued efforts to impose liability on technology providers, such as the INDUCE Act.

4.10   Future Scenarios

(e) In General

If one were to sum up the needs of each of the stakeholders in a few words, it would read something like this:

1. Rightsholders need payment;

2. The public needs some free access; and

3. The technology industry needs freedom to innovate.

Can these interests be reconciled in a single solution? This is a difficult task for policymakers, complicated by the fact that an acceptable solution must be internationally sanctioned. The following will discuss some views discussed in recent literature as to how future scenarios could play out.

(f) Models Based on Existing Building Blocks

(i)   In General

Because one of the challenges in this debate is passing legislation acceptable to all stakeholders involved, the first category of scenarios is based on already existing building blocks, and the assumption of no new legislation in the copyright field.[352]

---

350 Lemley and Reese, "Reducing Digital Copyright Infringement without Restricting Innovation", 56 *Stan. L. Rev.* 1345, at p. 1389 (2004).

351 It should be noted here nonetheless that the technology industry's lobby resulted in the addition of section 512 to the Digital Millennium Copyright Act, a section that exonerates online service providers from liability for copyright infringement if certain procedures are complied with. 17 United States Code, section 512.

352 Legislation for the purpose of these scenarios is understood as a major restructuring of the system, rather than minor adjustments to the present situation.

(ii) Digital Rights Management-Based Models (Pay-Per-Use)

Digital rights management is likely to be the basis of most future business models and, despite the criticism brought against it, digital rights management is likely here to stay.[353] A likely scenario, based on digital rights management and already in use to a limited extent, is the pay-per-use model.

In a pay-per-use system, users would be able to buy access to a particular work in the exact amount they wish to consume, rather than obliging them to invest in a larger quantum of works that they do not need.[354] In its simplest version, if a user wished to look up a certain definition in an encyclopedia which costs US $500, a pay-per-use model could allow the user to read the necessary definition at a cost of, for example, US $1, or download it at a cost of, for example, US $2, or any other means of access that the content provider's creative marketing could devise.

This would result in the most efficient allocation of resources in the market; a transaction between two willing parties. For the content provider it is a way to monetize its product and, for the user, it is a way of fulfilling the need for information by purchasing a product.[355]

Full functionality of this model is simply a matter of time. The main hurdles to overcome are the immaturity of digital rights management[356] and the lack of consumer acceptance.[357] No particular legislative intervention is required to enable this model.

The model favors rightsholders in that it unqualifiedly meets their needs for a market in which product is exchanged for payment. It only meets the user's needs to a limited extent, i.e., the free limited access to works to which users are entitled under traditional copyright law will be curtailed, if not eliminated. Whether the flexibility and convenience of the offer can compensate for this remains to be determined.

---

353 Sobel, "DRM as an Enabler of Business Models: ISPs as Digital Retailers", 18 *Berkeley Tech. L.J.* 667 (2003). The article lists several different models and, including the Internet Service Providers as digital retailers, would place the distribution task with ISPs. It would give the rightsholder control over the content, but delegate the technological aspect to the ISP.

354 Ginsburg, "Copyright and Control over New Technologies of Dissemination", 101 *Colum. L. Rev.* 1613, at p. 1645 (2001).

355 For the user, it is simply an economic decision which option to purchase. If engaged in major research that would require consulting the encyclopedia several hundreds of times, US $500 might be an appropriate investment.

356 Digital rights management must be capable of performing the dual function of controlling access and use and offering differentiated products. These requirements are based on improved interoperability of individual digital rights management technologies.

357 Consumer acceptance would necessitate attractive selection of products and competitive prices.

(iii) The Collaborative Model

Another model whose building blocks already exist is the collaborative model.[358] The model envisions the collaborative commons-based creation of cultural products. Traditional concepts of copyright ownership remain in place; however, content is distributed by free sharing with a wide audience.

The audience can consist either of content consumers or, alternatively, of producers of new creations, based on the work shared. The distribution of such content is based on a license agreement which, in most instances, grants a royalty-free perpetual license to reproduce, modify, distribute, display, and perform in public. It also is often subject to certain limitations, such as the requirement that the work be attributed to the original author.[359]

Theorists supportive of this model explain that, in a digitally networked environment, cultural goods and information are increasingly produced by collaborative production of numerous individuals.[360] Production occurs in the form of joint contribution by individuals who are organized in diverse productive enterprises, operating in a decentralized but coordinated manner.[361]

The participation of numerous and diverse contributors would provide a wider range of cultural goods with greater accessibility and at lower cost.[362]

---

358 This model also is referred to as the "commons" or "peer production" model.

359 See http://www.opensource.org. The source code is made available royalty-free, with no restrictions on it redistribution. See also the "creative commons" license, at http://creativecommons.org/licenses/by/2.0/legalcode.

360 Ginsburg, "Copyright and Control over New Technologies of Dissemination", 101 *Colum. L. Rev.* 1613, at p. 1619 (2001). Creators also could benefit from technological developments. Digital media may give creators the ability to distribute without help of intermediaries. The public may obtain greater variety. It has been suggested that "digital media by making the means of production and dissemination available to any computer-equipped author, give authors a realistic opportunity to bring their works to the public without having to put themselves in thrall to traditional intermediaries. The technological measures that reinforce legal control may enable and encourage authorial entrepreneurship, because authors may be able to rely on these measures to secure distribution of and payment for their works. Greater author control not only enhance the moral appeal of the exercise of copyright, but also may offer the public an increased quantity and variety of works of authorship, as authors whom the traditional intermediary-controlled distribution system may have excluded may now directly propose to the public (and be compensated for) their creations".

361 Benkler, "Freedom in the Commons: Towards a Political Economy of Information", 52 *Duke L.J.* 1245, at p. 1257 (2003). Benkler also refers to this process as "peer production".

362 Benkler, "Freedom in the Commons: towards a Political Economy of Information", 52 *Duke L.J.* 1245, at p. 1261 (2003).

The significance of proprietary market-based cultural production, on the other hand, would decrease.[363]

The most prominent example is that of open source software. The Open Source Initiative is based on the philosophy of an "open license", i.e., allowing software to evolve by freely allowing programmers to read, redistribute, and modify any piece of software.[364] Similarly, the GNU/Linux initiative which licenses software under the GNU license, is dedicated to "promoting computer user's right to use study, copy, modify, and redistribute computer programs".[365] Open-source software has seen rapid development and has gained support and acceptance worldwide.

In addition to software development, projects based on collaborative use of "open content"[366] are under way in a number of areas, such as:

1. Education, the MIT OpenCourseWare imitative;[367]

2. Music distribution, LOCA Records;[368]

3. General cultural creation, Creative Commons;[369]

4. Software documentation, the Linux documentation project,[370] and

5. The Wikipedia, an online encyclopedia.[371]

This model favors consumers in that works would be freely accessible. It will likely constitute a threat to the content industry as it risks disrupting

---

363 Benkler, "Freedom in the Commons: towards a Political Economy of Information", 52 *Duke L.J.* 1245, at p. 1254 (2003).

364 See http://www.opensource.org. The source code is made available royalty-free, with no restrictions on it redistribution. See also GNU/Linux Project of the Free Software Foundation, at http://www.gnu.org.

365 See http://www.gnu.org/fsf/fsf.html.

366 "Open content" refers to creative work that is in the public domain or is subject to a free license.

367 Under this initiative, the Massachusetts Institute of Technology (MIT) is placing all educational materials free online available to the public, whereby MIT retains copyright to the materials. See http://ocw.mit.edu/index.html.

368 An independent United Kingdom record label which releases music under GNU type licenses. See http://www.locarecords.com.

369 See http://www.creativecommons.org.

370 The Linux documentation project is a volunteer project that maintains and develops documentation for Linux. It contains more than 475 documents contributed by a large number of authors. See http://www.tldp.org.

371 The materials are produced collaboratively by more than 2,000 distributed volunteers; Benkler, "Freedom in the Commons: Towards a Political Economy of Information", 52 *Duke L.J.* 1245, at p. 1258 (2003). See http.//www.wikipedia.com. Works include articles, pictures, audio, and video published in a format that explicitly allows the copying and modification of the information by third parties. See http://en.wikipedia.org/wiki/Open_content.

established distribution channels. However, in an increasingly networked society and given the growing technological sophistication of the average consumer, migration of part of the cultural production of our society to this model cannot be ruled out.

(g) Models Enabled by Future Legislation

(i) Non-Commercial Use Levy

A non-commercial use levy, limited to digital use, would be imposed on the sale of consumer products or services whose value is substantially enhanced by P2P file sharing,[372] including any devices involved in the reproduction, storage, or distribution of P2P files, such as Internet access, P2P software and services, computer hardware, CDs, MP3 players, and video recorders. Non-commercial downloading, copying, and distribution, as well as adaptations and modifications of the underlying work would be granted immunity in exchange for the levy.[373]

The collection mechanism would be based on creators and would be identified by a unique file name registered with a copyright office or equivalent, which tracks transmissions of the work on the Internet. The collected levies would be allocated among copyright holders in proportion to the popularity of the work.

The concept underlying this system is similar to the levy system underlying the private use exceptions in, e.g., German copyright[374] and the Audio Home Recording Act in the United States.[375]

---

372 Netanel, "Impose a Noncommercial Use Levy to Allow Free Peer-to-Peer File Sharing", 17 *Harv. J. Law & Tech*. 1 (2003).

373 Netanel, "Impose a Noncommercial Use Levy to Allow Free Peer-to-Peer File Sharing", 17 *Harv. J. Law & Tech*. 1, at p. 29 (2003). A variation of this model, the Tax and Royalty System, would tax ISP access and technologies used to perform music, but it would not allow creation of derivative works by the user. Fisher, *Digital Music: Problems and Possibilities* (2000), at http://www.law.harvard.edu/faculty/tfisher/Music.html.

374 However, it should be noted that levies in conjunction with digital rights management lead to a double payment by users/compensation to rightsholders. This was pointed out in Recital 39 of the European Union Copyright Directive, which provides for modification or phase-out of levies where digital rights management is used.

375 Audio Home Recording Act, 17 United States Code, sections 1001–1010. Netanel, "Impose a Noncommercial Use Levy to Allow Free Peer-to-Peer File Sharing", 17 *Harv. J. Law & Tech*. 1, at p. 33 (2003). "The AHRA imposes a levy on consumer devices primarily designed to make digital recordings of music for private use and on blank media on which such recordings are stored. In return for the levy (and for requiring manufacturers of digital audio tape recorders to incorporate technology preventing serial digital copying), the Act prohibits suits against consumers for non-commercial copying of music using digital or analog equipment designed for that purpose."

This model is based on the recognition that P2P sharing is fundamentally speech, not theft.[376] Rather than attempting to prohibit an advance of technology that has the capability of disseminating information to an unprecedented extent, it seeks to take advantage of it and allow users to freely engage in copying and modification of copyright-protected content on a non-commercial basis.[377]

From a copyright standpoint, the impact would be to grant a statutory compulsory license to certain currently prohibited uses. Furthermore, the incentive model remains in effect, in that creators are compensated based on the commercial success of their work.[378]

Because the basic incentive model inherent in copyright law remains in place, the economic impact on stakeholders would be limited.[379] The model is advantageous to the content industry in that it would eliminate the current losses resulting from P2P file sharing.[380] Users willing to pay for use of content are equally favored, as the cost is likely to be lower than they would pay under a proprietary copyright regime.[381]

Finally, the increased distribution over the Internet and the need for tracking content are likely to open up a new market and increase revenues of ISPs and technology providers.

The criticism that could be brought against this model is that the increased prices are ultimately passed on to the consumer. The consumer is likely to pay for non-protectable content that is rendered inaccessible by the action of digital rights management. This fact is removed from the consumers' focus due to the indirect nature of the payment. Furthermore, the model introduces an additional administrative layer, which reduces the net compensation to the creators.[382]

(ii) More Effective Remedies against Users

Increasing the deterrent effect of copyright laws may be achieved by creating more effective remedies against users, e.g., by means of severe criminal

---

376 Netanel, "Impose a Noncommercial Use Levy to Allow Free Peer-to-Peer File Sharing", 17 *Harv. J. Law & Tech*. 1, at p. 83 (2003).

377 Netanel, "Impose a Noncommercial Use Levy to Allow Free Peer-to-Peer File Sharing", 17 *Harv. J. Law & Tech*. 1, at pp. 83 and 84 (2003).

378 This is a mechanism used in, for example, the German private copy/levy system.

379 Berkman Center for Internet and Society at Harvard Law School, Five Scenarios for Digital Media in a Post-Napster World, at http://www.cyber.law.harvard.edu/publications.

380 Berkman Center for Internet and Society at Harvard Law School, Five Scenarios for Digital Media in a Post-Napster World, at http://www.cyber.law.harvard.edu/publications.

381 Netanel, "Impose a Noncommercial Use Levy to Allow Free Peer-to-Peer File Sharing", 17 *Harv. J. Law & Tech*. 1, at pp. 83 and 84 (2003).

382 Netanel, "Impose a Noncommercial Use Levy to Allow Free Peer-to-Peer File Sharing", 17 *Harv. J. Law & Tech*. 1, at pp. 83 and 84 (2003).

penalties against high-volume uploaders combined with active government prosecution, quick and inexpensive dispute resolution systems. and imposition of severe criminal penalties.[383]

(iii) Treatment of Content as a Public Utility

Treatment of copyrighted content as a public utility is a scenario suggested by the similarity in structure of the vertically integrated and concentrated media industry to other highly regulated industries, such as telephone and power companies.[384]

4.11 Conclusion

The digital environment has caused changes in the distribution mechanism of digital content. Faced with the threat of uncontrolled dissemination of content on the Internet, rightsholders have devised a massive protection structure which, in turn, threatens the other stakeholders. The balance of copyright interests is disrupted, and the polarization of positions among stakeholders is growing. Because of this, a legislative compromise solution acceptable to everyone involved seems unlikely.

If regulatory intervention of any magnitude is not a likely option, what will the future bring? The scenarios based on existing building blocks are still in very incipient stages. However, given time, they could separately or jointly develop into structures which could help restore the lost balance of copyright.

---

383 Lemley and Reese, "Reducing Digital Copyright Infringement without Restricting Innovation", 56 *Stan. L. Rev.* 1345, at pp. 1396 *et seq.* (2004).

384 Berkman Center for Internet and Society at Harvard Law School, Five Scenarios for Digital Media in a Post-Napster World, at http://www.cyber.law.harvard.edu/publications.

CHAPTER 5

LIMITING COPYRIGHTS: CONSIDERATIONS FOR AN INTERNATIONAL FAIR USE STANDARD

Jon David Grossman and Elizabeth Parsons
Dickstein Shapiro Morin & Oshinsky LLP
Washington, D.C., United States

5.01   Introduction

Copyright laws granting copyright owners limited monopolies over creative works among countries are based on differing principles. Regardless of the particular principles to which a country subscribes, all countries recognize the need to balance the interests of copyright owners with those of the public by limiting certain rights granted to copyright owners. New and emerging technologies threaten the balance. To date, much attention has been given to the threat of new technologies to the interests of copyright owners.

Recognition of the effects of new technologies to interests of the public, and the balance between the interests of the public and copyright owners, is essential to effectively foster the underlying principles of copyright laws and maintain adequate access to information. This chapter considers different countries' approaches to limiting copyright protections. Particular attention is paid to the United States' doctrine of fair use as compared to limitations provided by other countries.

Furthermore, this chapter considers industry and governmental responses to digital technologies on behalf of copyright owners, and the effect of the responses on the balance between the interests of copyright owners and the public. Finally, this chapter identifies the need for an international standard for limitations on copyright protection and identifies considerations for developing such a standard in light of new and developing technologies.

5.02   Principles of Copyright Law

Since its inception, copyright principles have been largely a European phenomenon. In many cases, the modern idea of copyright was brought to other parts of the world either through colonization or as a price of participation in world trade.[1]

Western copyright laws are based on two basic principles: a utilitarian, economic theory of incentives and a natural rights, personality-driven theory of authorship.[2] The differences in focus between the copyright system in the United States and those in most European countries stem from the differences between these two principles. In practice, however, the resulting copyright systems function similarly.

Anglo-American-based copyright systems, such as those in the United States, are based on the utilitarian theory of copyright.[3] The focus in such a system is to encourage the creation of works and public access to the works.[4] The utilitarian viewpoint holds that "society as a whole benefits from an author's creative effort".[5]

The incentives-based system gives the author control over the work only to the extent that this control provides the necessary incentive for the author to create the work in the first place.[6] Rights not allocated to the author are available to the public. Balancing these incentives with public access to the works is a focus of copyright legislation in countries that subscribe to this utilitarian theory.

Countries that follow the natural rights, personality-driven theory of copyright, such as France and Germany, focus on the "moral rights" of authors, based on the premise that authors should have the right to control their creative outputs.[7] Under the natural rights theory, the creator of the work has inherent ownership in the work, and copyright is recognition of this

---

1   Jackson, "Harmony or Discord? The Pressure toward Conformity in International Copyright", 43 *Idea* 607, at p. 612 (2003).

2   Jackson, "Harmony or Discord? The Pressure toward Conformity in International Copyright", 43 *Idea* 607, at p. 613 (2003).

3   Jackson, "Harmony or Discord? The Pressure toward Conformity in International Copyright", 43 *Idea* 607, at p. 608 (2003).

4   Dallon, "The Problem with Congress and Copyright Law: Forgetting the Past and Ignoring the Public Interest", 44 *Santa Clara L. Rev.* 365, at p. 367 (2004).

5   Jackson, "Harmony or Discord? The Pressure toward Conformity in International Copyright", 43 *Idea* 607, at p. 614 (2003).

6   Jackson, "Harmony or Discord? The Pressure toward Conformity in International Copyright", 43 *Idea* 607, at p. 614 (2003).

7   Jackson, "Harmony or Discord? The Pressure toward Conformity in International Copyright", 43 *Idea* 607, at p. 616 (2003).

ownership.[8] These countries, when developing copyright legislation, focus on the integrity of the authors, allowing them much more control over their works.

Both theories of copyright balance the interests of the public with those of copyright owners, but do so in different ways. Differences between the utilitarian and personality-driven theories have been summarized as follows:

> "In Common Law countries that follow the utilitarian model, copyright laws are passed to stimulate production of the widest variety at the lowest price, and lawmakers will expand copyright protection only if 'necessary to stimulate the creation of new works'. In Civil Law countries that follow the natural rights model, copyright is a matter of right and justice and lawmakers will extend rights and reject new legislation 'only if the extended protection would materially hamper socially valuable uses of protected works'.[9]

Many Eastern nations, such as Japan and China, did not historically recognize a right in intellectual property,[10] but they have adopted copyright laws more recently and after external pressures.[11] The historical lack of copyright protection in Eastern countries stems from social attitudes toward the roles of individuals in society.[12] Western cultures focus on what is best for the individual, whereas Eastern cultures tend to focus on what is best for society as a whole.[13]

For example, unlike in the United States, where copyright creates a financial incentive for the individual author, copyright law in Japan balances the interests of individuals and society.[14] The law does not secure exclusive rights but "prescribes the rights of authors" and speaks of "promoting the protection of the rights of authors, etc., giving consideration to a fair exploitation of

---

8   Dallon, "The Problem with Congress and Copyright Law: Forgetting the Past and Ignoring the Public Interest", 44 *Santa Clara L. Rev.* 365, at p. 368 (2004).

9   Jackson, "Harmony or Discord? The Pressure toward Conformity in International Copyright", 43 *Idea* 607, at pp. 617 and 618 (2003) (quoting Goldstein, *International Copyright* 4 (2001).

10   Feder, "Note, Enforcement of Intellectual Property Rights in China: You Can Lead a Horse to Water, but You Can't Make It Drink", 37 *Va. J. Int'l L.* 223, at pp. 230 and 231 (1996).

11   Feder, "Note, Enforcement of Intellectual Property Rights in China: You Can Lead a Horse to Water, but You Can't Make It Drink", 37 *Va. J. Int'l L.* 223, at pp. 230 and 231 (1996).

12   Rosen and Usui, "Japan: The Social Structure of Japanese Intellectual Property Law", 13 *UCLA Pac. Basin L.J.* 32, at p. 34 (1994).

13   Rosen and Usui, "Japan: The Social Structure of Japanese Intellectual Property Law", 13 *UCLA Pac. Basin L.J.* 32, at pp. 34 and 35 (1994).

14   Rosen and Usui, "Japan: The Social Structure of Japanese Intellectual Property Law", 13 *UCLA Pac. Basin L.J.* 32, at pp. 34 and 35 (1994).

these cultural products, and thereby . . . contributing to the development of culture".[15] Modern copyright law in China was enacted in 1990, due mostly to outside pressure from other developed nations.[16] The stated purposes of China's copyright laws are:

> . . . protecting the copyright of authors in their literary, artistic and scientific works and rights and interests related to copyright . . . encouraging the creation and dissemination of works which would contribute to the construction of socialist culture and ethics and material civilization, and . . . promoting the development and flourishing of the socialist culture and sciences.[17]

Copyright systems universally recognize the need to balance the interests of copyright owners with those of the pubic. The foundations for such a balance are the principles underlying a particular copyright system. Accordingly, the various ideas on which countries base their copyright laws cause countries to balance the interests of copyright owners and the public differently.

5.03   Limitations on Copyrights

(a)   United States Fair Use Doctrine

The United States provides balance between the interests of copyright holders and the public under its fair use doctrine. Fair use recognizes a need to limit the exclusive rights of the copyright holder to allow some socially beneficial activities.[18] It allows a copyrighted work to be used "for purposes such as criticism, comment, news reporting, teaching (including multiple copies for classroom use), scholarship, or research" without liability for infringement.[19]

---

15   Rosen and Usui, "Japan: The Social Structure of Japanese Intellectual Property Law", 13 *UCLA Pac. Basin L.J.* 32, at pp. 34 and 35 (1994) quoting *Chosaku-ken Ho* (Copyright Law), Law Number 48 of 1970, article 1.

16   Feder, "Note, Enforcement of Intellectual Property Rights in China: You Can Lead a Horse to Water, but You Can't Make It Drink", 37 *Va. J. Int'l L.* 223, at p. 238. Although China now has copyright laws on the books, there is still a major problem of enforcement of these laws. Reid, "Enforcement of Intellectual Property Rights in Developing Countries: China as a Case Study", 13 *Depaul-LCA Art & Ent. L.* 63, at p. 3.

17   Feder, "Note, Enforcement of Intellectual Property Rights in China: You Can Lead a Horse to Water, but You Can't Make It Drink", 37 *Va. J. Int'l L.* 223, at p. 238 (1996) (quoting the Copyright Law of the People's Republic of China, 7 September 1990, article 1 (effective 1 June 1991).

18   Copyright Act of 1976, 17 United States Code, section 107 (2004).

19   Copyright Act of 1976, 17 United States Code, section 107 (2004).

Fair use is a standard that:

> . . . permits (and requires) courts to avoid rigid application of the copyright statute when, on occasion, it would stifle the very creativity which that law is designed to foster.[20]

(b) Other National Approaches to Limitations on Authors' Rights

Most European countries do not have a fair use doctrine by name. The closest concept in Europe is the United Kingdom's concept of "fair dealing", which is written into the copyright law. Instead, many countries have specific laws that define the balance between the interests of copyright owners and the public.[21] Civil law countries such as France and Germany have "free utilization" doctrines, which allow copying without liability in certain specific enumerated cases; however, they are not as broad as the exceptions allowed under fair use.[22]

Japan takes a different approach to limiting copyrights. In Japan, the public's interest is taken into account in the allocation of rights.[23] Accordingly, while the public receives a positive grant of rights, the effect is a limit on the rights of copyright owners. For example, a copyrighted work "may be reproduced by a user for the purpose of his personal use, family use, or other use similar thereto within a limited area . . .".[24]

While other countries incorporate exceptions to copyright protection into their copyright systems, none are as flexible as that of the United States doctrine of fair use.[25] The flexibility of fair use comes from the fact that it is a standard by which courts balance the interests of copyright owners and the public by applying a four-factor balancing test. The flexibility springs from the universality of the test to any work, or any use.

---

20 *Stewart v. Abend*, 495 U.S. 207, at p. 236 (1990) (quoting *Iowa State Univ. Research Found., Inc. v. Am. Broad. Cos.*, 621 F2d 57, at p. 60 (2d Cir., 1980)); accord *Campbell v. Acuff-Rose Music, Inc.*, 510 U.S. 569, at p. 577 (1994).

21 Leaffer, "The Uncertain Future of Fair Use in a Global Information Marketplace", 62 *Ohio St. L.J.* 849, at p. 863 (2001).

22 Leaffer, "The Uncertain Future of Fair Use in a Global Information Marketplace", 62 *Ohio St. L.J.* 849, at pp. 863 and 864 (2001).

23 Rosen and Usui, "Japan: The Social Structure of Japanese Intellectual Property Law", 13 *UCLA Pac. Basin L.J.* 32, at p. 36 (1994).

24 Rosen and Usui, "Japan: The Social Structure of Japanese Intellectual Property Law", 13 *UCLA Pac. Basin L.J.* 32, at p. 36 (1994) (quoting *Chosaku-ken Ho* (Copyright Law), Law Number 48 of 1970, article 30.

25 Jackson, "Harmony or Discord? The Pressure toward Conformity in International Copyright", 43 *Idea* 607, at p. 626 (2003).

Typically, laws of other countries specify particular limits and/or exceptions to copyrights for particular types of activities or works. While courts of those countries must still interpret and apply those specific limits and/or exceptions, leaving some room for flexibility, fair use by its nature is meant to be flexible to allow courts to balance the interests of copyright owners and the public on a case-by-case basis for every activity. This flexibility is essential as society's uses of protected works change. Accordingly, section IV below discusses fair use as applied by United States courts. In addition, particular attention is paid to those cases addressing fair use in the context of new technologies.

5.04   Governmental Treatment of Exceptions to Copyright Protections

(a) United States Fair Use

(i)   In General

Fair use is an affirmative defense to copyright infringement. The defense is equitable in nature and difficult to distill to any simple formula as its application depends on the circumstances of each case.[26] In other words, the defense is "an equitable rule of reason, no generally applicable definition is possible, and each case raising the question must be decided on its own facts".[27]

Although fair use is an old concept in Anglo-American law, its origins dating back to 1803, it took until 1976 for the United States Congress to codify the doctrine as part of an overhaul of the Copyright Act.[28] Section 107 of 17 United States Code embodies the fair use standard as codified, and it lists four non-exclusive factors for evaluating whether an otherwise infringing use will be excused as a fair use. The statute provides:

> Notwithstanding the provisions of section 106 and 106A, the fair use of a copyrighted work, including such use by reproduction in copies or phonorecords or by any other means specified by that section, for purposes such as criticism, comment, news reporting, teaching (including multiple copies for classroom use), scholarship, or research, is not an infringement of copyright. In determining whether the use made of a work in any particular case is a fair use the factors to be considered shall include:
>
> (1) the purpose and character of the use, including whether such use is of commercial nature or is for nonprofit education purposes;

---

26   M. Nimmer and D. Nimmer, *Nimmer on Copyright*, at section 13.05(A) (1994).

27   H.R. Rep. Number 94-1476, at p. 65 (1976), reprinted in 1976 *USCCAN 5659*, at p. 5679.

28   *Campbell v. Acuff-Rose Music, Inc.*, 510 U.S. 569, at pp. 575 and 576 (1994); Copyright Act of 1976, Pub. L. Number 94-553, section 107, 90 Stat. 2546.

(2) the nature of the copyrighted work;

(3) the amount and substantiality of the portion used in relation to the copyrighted work as a whole; and

(4) the effect of the use on the potential market for or value of the copyrighted work.

The fact that a work is unpublished shall not itself bar a finding of fair use if such finding is made on consideration of all the above factors.[29]

(ii) Legislative History of the Fair Use Defense

The text of the statute does not instruct courts how to apply the four factors. The legislative history, however, provides valuable insight into its intended purposes. The codification of fair use did not abrogate the Common Law history of the defense. Rather, Congress intended section 107 "to restate the present judicial doctrine of fair use, not to change, narrow, or enlarge it in any way".[30] In other words, Congress believed the four factors of section 107 were the essence albeit non-exclusive essence, of existing judicial criteria.[31]

Given the equitable nature of the defense, Congress recognized that over time, courts must be free to shape the doctrine to new situations. In particular, the revised Copyright Act:

> Endorses the purpose and general scope of the judicial doctrine of fair use, but there is no disposition to freeze the doctrine in the statute, especially during a period of rapid technological change. Beyond a very broad statutory explanation of what fair use is and some of the criteria applicable to it, the courts must be free to adapt the doctrine to particular situations on a case-by-case basis.[32]

Finally, Congress provided examples of fair use:

> Quotation of excerpts in a review or criticism for purposes of illustration or comment; quotation of short passages in scholarly or technical work, for illustration or clarification of the author's observations; use in a parody of some of the content of the work parodied; summary of an address or article, with brief quotations, in a news report, reproduction by a library of a portion of a work to replace part of a damaged copy; reproduction by a teacher or student of a small part of a work to illustrate a lesson; reproduction of a work in legislative or judicial proceedings or

---

29 17 United States Code, section 107.

30 H.R. Rep. Number 94-1476, at p. 66 (1976), reprinted in 1976 *USCCAN 5659*, at p. 5680.

31 H.R. Rep. Number 94-1476, at p. 65 (1976), reprinted in 1976 *USCCAN 5659*, at p. 5680.

32 H.R. Rep. Number 94-1476, at p. 66 (1976), reprinted in 1976 *USCCAN 5659*, at p. 5680.

reports; incidental and fortuitous reproduction, in a newsreel broadcast, of a work located in the scene of an event being reported.[33]

(iii) Purpose of Copyright Protections and the Fair Use Defense

The exclusive rights afforded to copyright holders by 17 United States Code, sections 106 and 106A, and the protections of fair use work together in furtherance of the principles underlying United States copyright law: to promote creativity and the dissemination of knowledge as intended by the Constitution.[34] In discussing the relationship of copyright protections and fair use, the Supreme Court has stated:

> The monopoly privileges that Congress may authorize are neither unlimited nor primarily designed to provide a special private benefit. Rather, the limited grant is a means by which an important public purpose may be achieved. It is intended to motivate the creative activity of authors and inventors by the provision of a special reward, and to allow the public access to the products of their genius after the limited period of exclusive control has expired.[35]

In other words, "[t]he copyright law, like the patent statutes, makes reward to the owner a secondary consideration".[36]

The purpose of copyright is undermined without fair use.

Thus, fair use "permits courts to avoid the rigid application of the copyright statute when, on occasion, it would stifle the very creativity which that law is designed to foster".[37]

(iv) Application of the Fair Use Defense in the United States Supreme Court

In General   To understand the scope of fair use, it is necessary to examine its application by the courts. Since 1984, the United States Supreme Court has decided several cases which provide insight into the doctrine of fair use, to wit:

1. *Sony Corporation of America v. Universal City Studios, Inc;*[38]

---

33 H.R. Rep. Number 94-1476, at p. 65 (1976), reprinted in 1976 *USCCAN 5659*, at p. 5680.

34 The United States Constitution provides that Congress shall have the power: "To promote the Progress of Science and Useful Arts, by securing for limited Times to Authors ... the exclusive Right to their respective Writings". United States Constitution, article I, section 8, clause 8.

35 *Sony Corp. of Am. v. Universal City Studios, Inc.*, 464 U.S. 417, at p. 429 (1984).

36 *Sony Corp. of Am. v. Universal City Studios, Inc.*, 464 U.S. 417, at p. 429 (1984) (quoting *United States v. Paramount Pictures, Inc.*, 334 U.S. 131, at p. 158 (1948).

37 M. Nimmer and D. Nimmer, *Nimmer on Copyright*, at section 13.05 (1994) (quoting *Iowa State Univ. Research Found., Inc. v. Am. Broad. Cos.*, 621 F2d 57 (2d Cir., 1980)).

38 *Sony Corp. of Am. v. Universal City Studios, Inc.*, 464 U.S. 417 (1984).

2. *Harper and Row, Publishers, Inc. v. Nation Enterprises;*[39] and

3. *Campbell v. Acuff-Rose Music, Inc.*[40]

Sony   In *Sony*, the Supreme Court determined that the non-commercial home taping of television programs for later viewing at home constituted fair use.[41] At the time this case began, video recording was a new technology. Accordingly, *Sony* is an illustration of how the Supreme Court applies fair use to a new technology.

Universal City Studios claimed its copyrights were being violated by owners of Sony's Betamax VTRs (video tape recorders). Universal sought money damages, an equitable accounting of profits, and an injunction prohibiting Sony from manufacturing and marketing VTRs.[42] Universal claimed Sony was liable under a theory of contributory infringement. The Supreme Court determined that, under the staple article of commerce doctrine, because VTRs were capable of substantial non-infringing use, Sony was not liable for contributory infringement.[43] Because that question is unrelated to fair use, it will not be addressed further.

In preparation for trial, the parties studied the use of the VTR, finding the primary use of VTRs was time-shifting. According to the Supreme Court:

> Time-shifting enables viewers to see programs they otherwise would miss because they are not at home, are occupied with other tasks, or are viewing a program on another station at the time of a broadcast that they desire to watch.[44]

While both surveys found a substantial number of users were accumulating libraries of tapes, Sony found that about 80 percent of VTR owners were watching as much TV as they had before acquiring the machine. Sony was

---

39   *Harper and Row, Publishers, Inc. v. Nation Enterprises*, 471 U.S. 539 (1985).

40   *Campbell v. Acuff-Rose Music, Inc.*, 510 U.S. 569 (1994). The Supreme Court also decided *Stewart v. Abend*, 495 U.S. 207 (1990). *Stewart* was the third case decided by the Supreme Court since the codification of fair use, but it is largely unhelpful in understanding the defense. The main issue addressed by the Supreme Court in Stewart was the assignability of a copyright holder's exclusive rights in its work before the expiration of the term of protection. *Stewart v. Abend*, 495 U.S. 207, at pp. 216–236 (1990). As for fair use, the Supreme Court's discussion and decision is unremarkable. Relying in part on *Sony* and *Harper and Row*, the Supreme Court concluded that the movie *Rear Window* was not a fair use of the book it was based on. *Stewart v. Abend*, 495 U.S. 207, at pp. 236–238 (1990).

41   *Sony Corp. of Am. v. Universal City Studios, Inc.*, 464 U.S. 417, at pp. 454 and 455 (1984).

42   *Sony Corp. of Am. v. Universal City Studios, Inc.*, 464 U.S. 417, at p. 420 (1984).

43   *Sony Corp. of Am. v. Universal City Studios, Inc.*, 464 U.S. 417, at p. 456 (1984).

44   *Sony Corp. of Am. v. Universal City Studios, Inc.*, 464 U.S. 417, at p. 423 (1984).

also able to introduce evidence that some copyright holders, such as professional sports leagues, did not object to taping for home use.

Reversing the Ninth Circuit,[45] the Supreme Court held unauthorized time-shifting constituted fair use.[46]

The Supreme Court found the first factor of section 107, the "purpose and character of the use", weighed in Sony's favor because time-shifting was a "non-commercial, non-profit activity".[47] With little discussion, the Supreme Court also found the second and third factors of section 107 supported Sony:

> When one considers the nature of a televised copyrighted audiovisual work and that time-shifting merely enables a viewer to see such a work which he had been invited to witness in its entirety free of charge, the fact that the entire work is reproduced does not have its ordinary effect of militating against a finding of fair use.[48]

The bulk of the Supreme Court's analysis focused on the fourth factor, "the effect of the use on the potential market for or value of the copyrighted work".[49]

The Supreme Court established two presumptions. First, "every commercial use of copyrighted material is presumptively an unfair exploitation of the monopoly privilege that belongs to the owner of the copyright".[50] Second, a non-commercial use that does not affect the market for the original work is fair use.[51] The presumption that a non-commercial use is fair may be rebutted if the plaintiff offers:

> . . . proof either that the particular use is harmful, or that if it should become widespread, it would adversely affect the potential market for

---

45 The district court ruled in Sony's favor, holding that "non-commercial home use recording of material broadcast over the public airwaves was a fair use" and that Sony was not liable for infringement. *Sony Corp. of Am. v. Universal City Studios, Inc.*, 464 U.S. 417, at p. 425 (1984). The Ninth Circuit, however, held that unauthorized time-shifting did not constitute fair use. It concluded "as a matter of law that the home use of a VTR was not a fair use because it was not a 'productive use'". *Sony Corp. of Am. v. Universal City Studios, Inc.*, 464 U.S. 417, at p. 427 (1984). According to the Ninth Circuit, because time-shifting is not a productive use, "it was unnecessary for [Universal] to prove any harm to the potential market for the copyrighted works . . . [and] that it seemed clear that the cumulative effect of mass reproduction made possible by VTRs would tend to diminish the potential market for respondents' works". *Sony Corp. of Am. v. Universal City Studios, Inc.*, 464 U.S. 417, at p. 427 (1984).

46 *Sony Corp. of Am. v. Universal City Studios, Inc.*, 464 U.S. 417, at p. 456 (1984).

47 *Sony Corp. of Am. v. Universal City Studios, Inc.*, 464 U.S. 417, at pp. 448 and 449 (1984).

48 *Sony Corp. of Am. v. Universal City Studios, Inc.*, 464 U.S. 417, at pp. 449 and 450 (1984).

49 *Sony Corp. of Am. v. Universal City Studios, Inc.*, 464 U.S. 417, at p. 450 (1984).

50 *Sony Corp. of Am. v. Universal City Studios, Inc.*, 464 U.S. 417, at p. 451 (1984).

51 *Sony Corp. of Am. v. Universal City Studios, Inc.*, 464 U.S. 417, at p. 450 (1984).

the copyrighted work. Actual present harm need not be shown; such a requirement would leave the copyright holder with no defense against predictable damage. Nor is it necessary to show with certainty that future harm will result. What is necessary is a showing by a preponderance of the evidence that some meaningful likelihood of future harm exists. If the intended use is for commercial gain that likelihood may be presumed. However, if it is for a non-commercial purpose, the likelihood must be demonstrated.[52]

Taken as a whole, the Supreme Court found the last factor favored Sony and that time-shifting was a non-commercial use.

Harper and Row   In *Harper and Row*, the Supreme Court held the unauthorized copying of President Gerald Ford's biography by *The Nation* was not fair use because it significantly impaired the rights of the copyright holder.[53] *Time Magazine* contracted with Harper and Row to publish sections of Ford's biography in anticipation of the work's release. Before *Time* published its story, however, *The Nation* made use of an illicitly obtained copy of Ford's manuscript to produce an article of its own. Once *The Nation* published its article, *Time* refused to pay under the contract. Harper and Row then sued for copyright infringement.[54] The district court held that copying by *The Nation* was not fair use and awarded damages. The Second Circuit reversed; it held Ford's manuscript contained mostly uncopyrightable facts, and reporting of politically significant material by *The Nation* was fair use.[55]

Before deciding whether the fair use defense was applicable to the article in *The Nation*, the Supreme Court made two preliminary findings. First, while the fair use defense can apply to the copying of an unpublished work, it weighs heavily against such a finding.[56]

Second, *The Nation* argued that its copying of the Ford work was protected by the First Amendment. The Supreme Court rejected this argument; it held:

> . . . that copyright's idea/expression dichotomy 'strike[s] a definitional balance between the First Amendment and the Copyright Act by permitting free communication of facts while still protecting an author's expression'. No author may copyright his ideas or the facts he narrates.[57]

---

52   *Sony Corp. of Am. v. Universal City Studios, Inc.*, 464 U.S. 417, at p. 451 (1984).

53   *Harper and Row, Publishers, Inc. v. Nation Enterprises*, 471 U.S. 539 (1985).

54   *Harper and Row, Publishers, Inc. v. Nation Enterprises*, 471 U.S. 539, at pp. 542 and 543 (1985).

55   *Harper and Row, Publishers, Inc. v. Nation Enterprises*, 471 U.S. 539, at pp. 543–545 (1985).

56   *Harper and Row, Publishers, Inc. v. Nation Enterprises*, 471 U.S. 539, at p. 554 (1985).

57   *Harper and Row, Publishers, Inc. v. Nation Enterprises*, 471 U.S. 539, at pp. 555 and 556 (1985).

In considering the first factor under section 107, "the purpose and character of the use", the Supreme Court found that the use by *The Nation* was presumptively unfair because it was commercial. *The Nation* argued that the presumption that a commercial use is unfair is inapplicable to news reporting. The Supreme Court disagreed:

> The Nation misses the point entirely. The crux of the profit/non-profit distinction is not whether the sole motive of the use is monetary gain but whether the user stands to profit from exploitation of the copyrighted material without paying the customary price.[58]

The Supreme Court found the illicit manner in which *The Nation* obtained Ford's work was relevant to its "character and purpose". According to the Supreme Court, "[f]air use presupposes 'good faith' and 'fair dealing'". In this matter, the Supreme Court found the use by *The Nation* was not in good faith:

> The Nation's use had not merely the incidental effect but the intended purpose of supplanting the copyright holder's commercially valuable right of first publication.[59]

Thus, because the use by *The Nation* was both commercial and not in good faith, the first factor weighed heavily against a finding of fair use.

The second factor of section 107, "the nature of the copyrighted work", also weighed against *The Nation*. Whether a work is published is one element of its nature. The use of any unpublished work is less likely to be fair because of the author's interest in confidentiality and creative control. The Supreme Court reasoned that the use by *The Nation* could not be characterized as fair because it violated Ford's irrefutable interest in confidentiality.[60]

The third factor, "the amount and substantiality of the portion used", evaluates the quantity and quality of the material copied from the original work. The Supreme Court found that, although the borrowing by *The Nation* was quantitatively small, it was qualitatively the most important part of the book. Moreover, the borrowed portion constituted the focal point of the article published by *The Nation*.[61] Thus, this factor weighed heavily against *The Nation*.

---

58 *Harper and Row, Publishers, Inc. v. Nation Enterprises*, 471 U.S. 539, at p. 562 (1985).

59 *Harper and Row, Publishers, Inc. v. Nation Enterprises*, 471 U.S. 539, at pp. 562 and 563 (1985) (quoting *Time Inc. v. Bernard Geis Assocs.*, 293 F. Supp. 130, at p. 146 (S.D.N.Y., 1968).

60 *Harper and Row, Publishers, Inc. v. Nation Enterprises*, 471 U.S. 539, at pp. 563 and 564 (1985).

61 *Harper and Row, Publishers, Inc. v. Nation Enterprises*, 471 U.S. 539, at pp. 564–566 (1985).

With respect to the fourth factor of section 107, the Supreme Court quoted *Nimmer on Copyright* for the proposition that:

> Fair use, when properly applied, is limited to copying by others which does not materially impair the marketability of the work which is copied.

The use by *The Nation* did not just impair the market for the work, it usurped it. *Time* cancelled its contract with Harper and Row because of the article in *The Nation*. The Supreme Court reasoned that, if the practice of unauthorized prepublication were to become widespread, it would impair copyright holders' rights of first serialization.[62] Based on this combination of factors, the Supreme Court concluded that the use by *The Nation* was not fair.

Campbell   *Campbell* is the Supreme Court's most recent case discussing fair use. The Supreme Court considered whether the defendant, 2 Live Crew's "commercial parody of Roy Orbison's song, 'Oh, Pretty Woman'" was a fair use.[63] The Supreme Court held that, while a parody can be fair, the effect of 2 Live Crew's song on rap derivatives of Orbison's original song must be further considered to determine whether 2 Live Crew's use was fair.[64]

In 1989, 2 Live Crew informed Acuff-Rose they created a parody of "Oh, Pretty Woman". 2 Live Crew offered to credit ownership of the original song and pay a fee. Acuff-Rose's agent refused permission and sued 2 Live Crew after they released the parody.[65] Relying on the Supreme Court's decision in *Sony*, the Sixth Circuit reversed, finding that 2 Live Crew's clearly commercial purpose prevented the use from being fair.[66]

According to the Supreme Court, one aspect of "the purpose and character of the use" is whether it is transformative. The more transformative a use, the more likely it is fair:

> [T]he goal of copyright, to promote science and the articles, is generally furthered by the creation of transformative works. Such works thus lie at the heart of the fair use doctrine's guarantee of breathing space within

---

62   *Harper and Row, Publishers, Inc. v. Nation Enterprises*, 471 U.S. 539, at pp. 566–568 (1985).

63   *Campbell v. Acuff-Rose Music, Inc.*, 510 U.S. 569, at pp. 571 and 572 (1994).

64   *Campbell v. Acuff-Rose Music, Inc.*, 510 U.S. 569, at pp. 593 and 594 (1994).

65   *Campbell v. Acuff-Rose Music, Inc.*, 510 U.S. 569, at pp. 572 and 573 (1994). The district court found 2 Live Crew's parody was fair use. It reasoned that, even though the use was commercial, 2 Live Crew took no more than was necessary to "conjure up" the original song, and the parody would not affect the market for the original. *Campbell v. Acuff-Rose Music, Inc.*, 510 U.S. 569, at p. 573 (1994).

66   *Campbell v. Acuff-Rose Music, Inc.*, 510 U.S. 569, at pp. 572 and 573 (1994).

the confines of copyright, and the more transformative the new work, the less will be the significance of other factors, like commercialism that may weigh against a finding of fair use.[67]

The Supreme Court reasoned that parody is transformative because "it can provide social benefit, by shedding light on an earlier work, and, in the process, creating a new one".[68] The Supreme Court was careful to distinguish parody, a transformative use, from satire, a non-transformative use. According to the Supreme Court, parody "is the use of some elements of a prior author's composition to create a new one that, at least in part, comments on that author's works", while satire "has no critical bearing on the substance or style of the original composition".[69]

According to the Supreme Court, 2 Live Crew's song was a parody because it "could be perceived as commenting on the original or criticizing it, to some degree".[70]

The Supreme Court also recognized that 2 Live Crew's use was commercial, and, under *Sony*, commercial use is presumptively unfair. Notwithstanding its statement in *Sony*, the Supreme Court held that fair use requires a sensitive balancing of interests:

> The Court of Appeals elevation of one sentence from Sony to a *per se* rule thus runs as much counter to Sony itself as to the long Common Law tradition of fair use adjudication. Rather, as we explained in Harper and Row, Sony stands for the proposition that the 'fact that a publication was commercial as opposed to non-profit is a separate factor that tends to weigh against a finding of fair use'. However that is all, and the fact that even the force of that tendency will vary with the context is a further reason against elevating commerciality to hard presumptive significance.

After finding that the second factor of section 107 failed to provide guidance in the case, the Supreme Court turned to the third factor of section 107.[71] In

---

67   *Campbell v. Acuff-Rose Music, Inc.*, 510 U.S. 569, at pp. 578 and 579 (1994).

68   *Campbell v. Acuff-Rose Music, Inc.*, 510 U.S. 569, at p. 579 and 573 (1994).

69   *Campbell v. Acuff-Rose Music, Inc.*, 510 U.S. 569, at p. 580 (1994).

70   *Campbell v. Acuff-Rose Music, Inc.*, 510 U.S. 569, at p. 583 (1994). Specifically, the Supreme Court stated: "2 Live Crew juxtaposes the romantic musings of a man whose fantasy comes true, with degrading taunts, a bawdy demand for sex, and sigh of relief from paternal responsibility. The later words can be taken as a comment on the naiveté of the original of an earlier day, as a rejection of its sentiment that ignores the ugliness of street life and the debasement that it signifies. It is this joinder of reference and ridicule that marks off the author's choice of parody from the other types of comment and criticism that traditionally have had a claim to fair use protection as transformative works . . .".

71   *Campbell v. Acuff-Rose Music, Inc.*, 510 U.S. 569, at p. 586 (1994).

considering "the amount and substantiality of the portion used in relation to the copyrighted work as a whole", the Supreme Court reasoned that:

> . . . the enquiry will harken back to the first of the statutory factors, for, as in prior cases, we recognize that the extent of permissible copying varies with the purpose and character of the use.[72]

The Supreme Court held that, because a parody must establish a link with the older work, some borrowing is necessary. At a minimum, the parodist is entitled to borrow enough to "conjure up" the original work. Borrowing beyond this, however, "will depend, say, on the extent to which the song's overriding purpose and character is to parody the original or, in contrast, the likelihood that the parody may serve as a market substitute for the original".[73] According to the Supreme Court, 2 Live Crew borrowed no more lyrics than necessary because they copied only the first line of Orbison's song and then significantly departed.[74]

The fourth factor requires an inquiry into not just the actual harm the plaintiff has suffered, but also the harm to potential markets for the original and derivative works. In the context of parodies, the Supreme Court found damage to markets for the original unlikely because parodies do not replace the original; rather, they create a new product. Therefore, the measurement of a parody's harm is limited to markets for derivative works.[75]

As a matter of law, the Supreme Court found that criticism or parodies of the original are not derivative works.[76] Therefore, the proper inquiry was whether 2 Live Crew's song harmed the market for a rap derivative of "Oh, Pretty Woman". Since neither of the courts below reached this question, nor did 2 Live Crew provide evidence on this point, the case was remanded to determine the effect of 2 Live Crew's song on rap derivatives.[77]

(v) Application of the Fair Use Defense in the United States Court of Appeals for the Ninth Circuit

In General   The Ninth Circuit has considered fair use in the context of developing technology. Specifically, *Sega Enterprises Ltd. v. Accolade, Inc.*,[78]

---

72   *Campbell v. Acuff-Rose Music, Inc.*, 510 U.S. 569, at pp. 586 and 587 (1994).

73   *Campbell v. Acuff-Rose Music, Inc.*, 510 U.S. 569, at p. 588 (1994).

74   *Campbell v. Acuff-Rose Music, Inc.*, 510 U.S. 569, at pp. 588 and 589 (1994). However, the Supreme Court ordered a remand to determine whether 2 Live Crew borrowed too much of Orbison's bass riff. *Campbell v. Acuff-Rose Music, Inc.*, 510 U.S. 569, at p. 589 (1994).

75   *Campbell v. Acuff-Rose Music, Inc.*, 510 U.S. 569, at pp. 590 and 592 (1994).

76   *Campbell v. Acuff-Rose Music, Inc.*, 510 U.S. 569, at p. 592 (1994).

77   *Campbell v. Acuff-Rose Music, Inc.*, 510 U.S. 569, at pp. 593 and 594 (1994).

78   *Sega Enterprises Ltd. v. Accolade, Inc.*, 977 F2d 1510 (9th Cir., 1992).

Recording Industry Association of America v. Diamond Multimedia Systems Inc.,[79] and *A&M Records, Inc. v. Napster, Inc.*[80] provide illustrations of the interplay between fair use to newer technologies.

Sega   In *Sega*, the Ninth Circuit sought to determine:

> . . . whether the Copyright Act permits persons who are neither copyright holders nor licensees to disassemble a copyrighted computer program to gain an understanding of the unprotected functional elements of the program.[81]

Ultimately, the Ninth Circuit found such acts constitute infringement, but are a fair use.[82] In doing so, the court confirmed that:

> . . . [w]hen technological change has rendered an aspect or application of the Copyright Act ambiguous, 'the Copyright Act must be construed in light of this basic purpose', which is 'to stimulate artistic creativity for the general public good'.[83]

Accolade was an independent unlicensed producer of game cartridges for Sega's Genesis game console. For Accolade to make its games compatible, it needed to understand how Sega game cartridges interfaced with the Genesis console. Accolade used a decompiler to convert the object code in Sega's game cartridges and in the Genesis console into human readable source code.[84]

---

79   *Recording Industry Association of America v. Diamond Multimedia Systems Inc.*, 180 F3d 1072 (9th Cir., 1999).

80   *FA&M Records, Inc. v. Napster, Inc.*, 239 F3d 1004 (9th Cir., 2001).

81   *Sega Enterprises Ltd. v. Accolade, Inc.*, 977 F2d 1510, at pp. 1513 and 1514 (9th Cir., 1992).

82   *Sega Enterprises Ltd. v. Accolade, Inc.*, 977 F2d 1510, at pp. 1517–1528 (9th Cir., 1992); *Sony Computer Entm't, Inc. v. Connectix Corp.*, 203 F3d 596 (9th Cir., 2000). The Ninth Circuit's opinion in *Sony Computer* is simply a better-written version of its prior opinion in *Sega*. The question presented in *Sony Computer* was whether the intermediate copying of BIOS, when done to gain access to the programs' functional elements, is a fair use. *Sony Computer Entm't, Inc. v. Connectix Corp.*, 203 F3d 596, at pp. 598, 599, and 602 (9th Cir., 2000). BIOS is the "basic input-output system" that operates the PlayStation. *Sony Computer Entm't, Inc. v. Connectix Corp.*, 203 F3d 596, at p. 598 (9th Cir., 2000). Just as in *Sega*, the court found the intermediate copying necessary to access the functional elements was a fair use. The court concluded that when the four fair use factors were "'weighed together, in light of the purposes of copyright'", Connectix's use was fair. *Sony Computer Entm't, Inc. v. Connectix Corp.*, 203 F3d 596, at p. 608 (9th Cir., 2000) (quoting *Campbell v. Acuff-Rose Music, Inc.*, 510 U.S. 569, at p. 578 (1994)).

83   *Sega Enterprises Ltd. v. Accolade, Inc.*, 977 F2d 1510, at p. 1527 (9th Cir., 1992) (quoting *Sony Corp. of Am. v. Universal City Studios, Inc.*, 464 U.S. 417, at p. 432 (1984)).

84   *Sega Enterprises Ltd. v. Accolade, Inc.*, 977 F2d 1510, at pp. 1514 and 1515 (9th Cir., 1992). A decompiler translates the binary format of object code to human readable source code. *Sega Enterprises Ltd. v. Accolade, Inc.*, 977 F2d 1510, at pp. 1514 and 1515 (9th Cir., 1992).

Accolade engineers located the interface specifications in Sega's source code, and used this information to make their own games compatible.[85] Sega sued Accolade for both trademark and copyright infringement.[86] The district court agreed with Sony that decompiling object code into source code constitutes copyright infringement, but it was not fair use.[87]

With respect to the first statutory factor, the court acknowledged that the particular circumstances of a commercial use could overcome the presumption of unfairness. According to the court, Accolade's decompilation of Sega's object code was for an "essentially non-exploitative purpose" because Accolade sought only to discover the unprotected functional elements of Sega's code.[88] Moreover, the court reasoned that Accolade's discovery of the functional elements created a public benefit because it "has led to an increase in the number of independently designed video game programs offered for use with the Genesis console". Taking these two considerations together, the court reasoned that Accolade overcame the presumption of unfairness.[89]

The court found the fourth factor, "the effect of the use on the potential market for or value of the copyrighted work", also supported Accolade. The court reasoned that, unlike the situation in *Harper and Row*, where the article in *The Nation* "usurped the market for the copyrighted work", Genesis owners often purchase more than one game. Thus, Accolade did not intend to "scoop" Sega's release of any particular game; rather, it sought only to become a legitimate competitor. The court reasoned that any financial impact on Sega would be minimal.[90]

The bulk of the court's analysis is dedicated to "the nature of the copyrighted work", the second factor. In the context of computer programs, this inquiry is particularly challenging because copyright protection does not extend to ideas and a work's functional elements.[91] Thus, to evaluate the nature of a copyrighted program, a court must remove the unprotected elements of the program from consideration.[92]

---

85   *Sega Enterprises Ltd. v. Accolade, Inc.*, 977 F2d 1510, at pp. 1514 and 1515 (9th Cir., 1992).

86   *Sega Enterprises Ltd. v. Accolade, Inc.*, 977 F2d 1510, at p. 1516 (9th Cir., 1992).

87   *Sega Enterprises Ltd. v. Accolade, Inc.*, 977 F2d 1510, at p. 1517 (9th Cir., 1992).

88   *Sega Enterprises Ltd. v. Accolade, Inc.*, 977 F2d 1510, at pp. 1522 and 1527 (9th Cir., 1992).

89   *Sega Enterprises Ltd. v. Accolade, Inc.*, 977 F2d 1510, at p. 1523 (9th Cir., 1992).

90   *Sega Enterprises Ltd. v. Accolade, Inc.*, 977 F2d 1510, at pp. 1523 and 1524 (9th Cir., 1992).

91   Section 102 of the United States Copyright Act provides: "In no case does copyright protection for an original work of authorship extend to any idea, procedure, process, system, method of operation, concept, principle, or discovery, regardless of the form in which it is described, explained, illustrated, or embodied in such work". 17 United States Code, section 102.

92   *Sega Enterprises Ltd. v. Accolade, Inc.*, 977 F2d 1510, at pp. 1524 and 1525 (9th Cir., 1992). To remove the unprotected elements of the program, the court adopted the Second Circuit's test in *Computer Association International v. Altai, Inc.*, 23 USPQ2d 1241, at pp. 1252 and 1253 (2d Cir., 1992). This test "breaks down a computer program into its component subroutines and sub-subroutines and then identifies the idea or core functional element of each". *Sega Enterprises Ltd. v. Accolade, Inc.*, 977 F2d 1510, at p. 1525 (9th Cir., 1992).

Even without the unprotected elements, the court found Accolade's conduct infringing, but did not end its inquiry there. Even though decompilation was infringement, the court found it was "necessary" to examine the uncopyrightable aspects of a program's object code. The court reasoned that while it was theoretically possible to study object code in its binary form, this method of study was so tedious that if decompilation were prohibited, the unprotected aspects of the program would receive *de facto* monopoly protection. This was impermissible because:

> To enjoy a lawful monopoly over the idea or functional principle underlying a work, the creator of the work must satisfy the more stringent standards imposed by the patent laws.[93]

In light of this conclusion, the court found the second factor of section 107 also weighed in favor of Accolade.[94] Without much explanation, the court found the third factor weighed against Accolade, but it was "of very little weight".[95]

Recording Industry Association of America   In *Recording Industry Association of America*,[96] the Ninth Circuit considered fair use as applied to MP3 technologies. The Recording Industry Association of America sued Diamond Multimedia Systems, a manufacturer of the "Rio" portable MP3 music player, alleging the player did not meet the requirements for digital audio recording devices under the Audio Home Recording Act of 1992 (the "Act"), because it did not employ a Serial Copyright Management System (SCMS) that sends, receives, and acts on information about the generation and copyright status of files that it plays.[97]

The question before the court was whether the Act covered the Rio.[98] The court found the plain language of the Act excluded the Rio, but nonetheless considered the Act's legislative history. According to the court, the purpose of the Act and SCMS was to facilitate personal use, and the operation of the Rio was consistent with this because it merely makes copies of recordings on users' hard drives. Thus, according to the court, such "space-shifting" was a fair use consistent with the Supreme Court's holding in *Sony*.[99]

---

93   *Sega Enterprises Ltd. v. Accolade, Inc.*, 977 F2d 1510, at p. 1526 (9th Cir., 1992).

94   *Sega Enterprises Ltd. v. Accolade, Inc.*, 977 F2d 1510, at p. 1526 (9th Cir., 1992).

95   *Sega Enterprises Ltd. v. Accolade, Inc.*, 977 F2d 1510, at pp. 1526 and 1527 (9th Cir., 1992).

96   *Recording Indus. Ass'n of Am. v. Diamond Multimedia Sys. Inc.*, 180 F3d 1072 (9th Cir., 1999).

97   *Recording Indus. Ass'n of Am. v. Diamond Multimedia Sys. Inc.*, 180 F3d 1072, at p. 1075 (9th Cir., 1999).

98   *Recording Indus. Ass'n of Am. v. Diamond Multimedia Sys. Inc.*, 180 F3d 1072, at p. 1075 (9th Cir., 1999).

99   *Recording Indus. Ass'n of Am. v. Diamond Multimedia Sys. Inc.*, 180 F3d 1072, at p. 1079 (9th Cir., 1999).

Napster *Napster*[100] is the primary case confronting Internet-based technologies in the context of fair use. Napster's technology enabled users to share copyrighted musical works in the form of MP3's over the Internet using a peer-to-peer (P2P) file sharing system. Napster's P2P system let users locate copyrighted musical works on other users' computers and download a copy of the work via the Internet. Various record labels sued Napster for copyright infringement.

Napster argued that its service as a whole, and the particular practices of sampling and space-shifting, were all fair uses. Napster contended its users downloaded files to sample them to decide whether to purchase a copy or not. Napster also maintained that the practice of space-shifting, when users download music they already own, was also a fair use.[101] The district court disagreed, finding Napster infringed the copyright holder's exclusive rights, and none of the uses was fair.[102]

In its analysis, the Ninth Circuit noted that the first factor of section 107, the purpose and character of the use, weighed against Napster. Citing *Campbell*, the court found Napster's use was not transformative. In considering whether the use was commercial, the court reasoned:

> . . . [d]irect economic benefit is not required to demonstrate a commercial use. Rather, repeated and exploitative copying of copyrighted works, even if the copies are not offered for sale, may constitute a commercial use.

Under this standard, Napster's use was clearly commercial, because it saved users the expense of purchasing copies.[103]

The second and third factors also weighed against Napster. Musical compositions are of a high creative value, and the copying thereof is less likely to constitute a fair use. Moreover, Napster users copied entire songs.[104]

With regard to the fourth factor, the court found that Napster harmed both present and future markets for the copyrighted works. As for present harm, the court credited the studies commissioned by A&M Records, which found college students purchased less music because of Napster. Likewise, the court found the music industry was unable to develop its own digital download system because:

> . . . [h]aving digital downloads available for free on the Napster system necessarily harms the copyright holders' attempts to charge for the same downloads.[105]

---

100 *A&M Records, Inc. v. Napster, Inc.*, 239 F3d 1004 (9th Cir., 2001).

101 *A&M Records, Inc. v. Napster, Inc.*, 239 F3d 1004, at p. 1014 (9th Cir., 2001).

102 *A&M Records, Inc. v. Napster, Inc.*, 239 F3d 1004, at pp. 1011–1014 (9th Cir., 2001).

103 *A&M Records, Inc. v. Napster, Inc.*, 239 F3d 1004, at p. 1015 (9th Cir., 2001).

104 *A&M Records, Inc. v. Napster, Inc.*, 239 F3d 1004, at p. 1016 (9th Cir., 2001).

105 *A&M Records, Inc. v. Napster, Inc.*, 239 F3d 1004, at p. 1017 (9th Cir., 2001).

The court further found the practice of so-called "sampling" via Napster was not a fair use.[106] The court reasoned that Napster users were not really sampling music because they downloaded full and free copies. In contrast, licensed sampling only involves short portions of the work, and the samples "time out" after a short time on the downloader's computer. Additionally, royalties are paid to the holder of the copyright. The court also found what Napster called sampling reduced the demand for CDs and prevented the development of a digital download market.

Likewise, Napster's claim that sampling actually stimulated overall demand for CDs was not supported by the evidence.[107] The court also distinguished Napster's version of space-shifting with that considered in *Recording Industry Association of America*, noting that:

> . . . the methods of shifting in [that case] did not also simultaneously involve distribution of the copyrighted material to the general public; the time or space-shifting [in Recording Industry Association of America] exposed the material only to the original user.[108]

The court also reasoned that *Sony* did not support Napster's position because the copying in *Sony* was done in the home.[109]

(vi) The Function of Fair Use

According to Professor Nimmer, as applied, the four-factor test of section 107 is essentially a "functional test".[110] The functional test examines:

> . . . the effect of the defendant's use on the potential market for or value of the plaintiff's work, a comparison must be made not merely of the media in which the two works may appear, but rather in terms of the function of each such work regardless of media.[111]

For example, as applied in *Harper and Row*, the functional test inquires "whether *The Nation* article adversely affected the value of any of the rights in the Ford manuscript whether or not the publisher had yet exercised those rights".[112] Under this test, the use by *The Nation* is clearly not fair; its article deprived *Time* of US $12,500.[113] Although the other factors of section 107

---

106 *A&M Records, Inc. v. Napster, Inc.*, 239 F3d 1004, at p. 1018 (9th Cir., 2001).

107 *A&M Records, Inc. v. Napster, Inc.*, 239 F3d 1004, at p. 1018 (9th Cir., 2001).

108 *A&M Records, Inc. v. Napster, Inc.*, 239 F3d 1004, at p. 1019 (9th Cir., 2001).

109 *A&M Records, Inc. v. Napster, Inc.*, 239 F3d 1004, at p. 1019 (9th Cir., 2001).

110 M. Nimmer and D. Nimmer, *Nimmer on Copyright*, at section 13.05(B)(1) (1994).

111 M. Nimmer and D. Nimmer, *Nimmer on Copyright*, at section 13.05(B)(1) (1994).

112 M. Nimmer and D. Nimmer, *Nimmer on Copyright*, at section 13.05(B)(2) (1994).

113 M. Nimmer and D. Nimmer, *Nimmer on Copyright*, at section 13.05(B)(2) (1994).

can be viewed through the functional test, the fourth factor appears to be the most reliable gauge of how a court will decide a case.

(b) European Law

(i) In General

While fair use is a doctrine unique to the United States, exceptions to the grant of copyrights are globally recognized.[114] Individual countries have long incorporated exceptions to the rights granted under copyright laws, striking a balance between the interests of the copyright owners and the public deemed appropriate by each respective country.

In contrast to the inherent flexibility of United States fair use, many countries provide for particular exceptions to copyrights by legislation. While some countries' laws allow some of the uses falling under the United States' fair use doctrine:

> . . . [m]ost other countries, particularly civil law countries, do not have a broad, judicially created doctrine that is analogous to the United States' fair use exception.[115]

(ii) United Kingdom Fair Dealing

The United Kingdom's treatment of limitations to copyrights bears similarities to that of United States' fair use. Like the United States, Common Law plays an important role in the United Kingdom. Like fair use, fair dealing is a concept developed by courts. In addition, the scope of fair dealing falls within that of fair use.

Fair dealing, however, is more narrowly defined by the United Kingdom Copyright, Designs, and Patents Act 1988.[116] Sections 29-50 of the 1988 Act delineate specific exceptions to copyright protections traditionally considered fair dealing.

In contrast, as discussed above, the United States' codified version of fair use set out a standard for determining fair uses, rather than a list of exceptions. Furthermore, fair dealing is less well developed by the United Kingdom courts than the doctrine of fair use in the United States. Consequently, United Kingdom courts have considered a more narrow range of activities in the context of fair dealing.

---

114 Newby, "What's Fair Here Is Not Fair Everywhere: Does the American Fair Use Doctrine Violate International Copyright Law?", 51 *Stan. L. Rev.* 1633, at p. 1642 (1999).

115 Newby, "What's Fair Here Is Not Fair Everywhere: Does the American Fair Use Doctrine Violate International Copyright Law?", 51 *Stan. L. Rev.* 1633, at p. 1642 (1999).

116 Copyright, Designs, and Patents Act 1988, sections 29–50 (c. 48).

Within that range, English courts have considered under what circumstances using extracts from a book[117] or clips from a television program[118] for purposes of comment, criticism, or review is fair dealing.

English courts also have addressed fair dealing in the context of using photographs for reporting current events.[119]

---

117 *Hubbard v. Vosper*, 2 Q.B. 84 (1972). The plaintiff, founder of the Church of Scientology, sued the defendant, a former member of the Church. The defendant used a number of extended extracts from the plaintiff's book to support critical theories of the Church. The court held the use of the extracts to be "fair dealing". In doing so, the court explained that it is impossible to define the exact scope of "fair dealing". Instead, the court reasoned that the determination must be a question of degree. Considerations for determining what constitutes fair dealing include the number and extent of the quotations and extracts: where the extracts considered together are many and long, the use may be unfair. It also is appropriate to consider the use made of the extracts: if the extracts are the basis for comment, criticism, or review, the use may be fair; whereas if the extracts are used to convey the same information in competition with the author, the use is likely to be unfair.

118 *Pro-Sieben Media AG v. Carlton United Kingdom Television Ltd.*, F.S.R. 43 (1998). Carlton Television made a program which criticized "checkbook journalism". Carlton included a 30-second video clip taken from a full television program by Pro Sieben. The clip included the logo of Pro Sieben. Substantial fees had been paid for the interview. It was claimed that Carlton obtained and spoiled the story, by showing the clip without contributing to the fees. The lower court looked at the motive of Carlton in including the particular clip, and concluded that the intent for using the clip was to defeat the economic interests of the plaintiffs. The Supreme Court of Appeal, however, held that this approach was too narrow and unanimously overturned the judge's decision. The Appeals Court held that the phrases "criticism or review" and "reporting current events" should be interpreted liberally, in the interests of freedom of speech. With respect to the defendants' purpose, it is sufficient for a program maker to sincerely, but misguidedly, believe that they were using another's copyright work for the purpose of criticism or review or for reporting a current event. Therefore, the court had to consider the impact of the derivative work on the audience. On this basis, the court decided that the purpose of the use of the extract was to criticize the works of checkbook journalism. The court noted, however, that the intentions and motives of the program maker are not completely irrelevant, but impact on the question of the fairness of the dealing. The court also held that the copying of the entire Pro Sieben program off air is likely to be a fair dealing if done for the purposes of deciding whether to use a clip from it and the actual use of the clip is a fair dealing.

119 *Hyde Park Residence Ltd. v. Yelland*, R.P.C. 604 (2000). *The Sun* published year-old pictures of Princess Diana and Dodi Al Fayed to dispute a current assertion by Mohammed Al Fayed in the *Daily Mirror* that the couple was making marriage arrangements. The pictures were taken from a video surveillance camera the day before the couple died. The security company that owned the videotape filed suit for infringement. *The Sun* alleged that the pictures were published for the purpose of reporting current events and, therefore, the fair dealing defense under section 30(2) of the 1988 Act applied. The lower court found publication by *The Sun* of the pictures to be fair dealing. The court reasoned that it was almost necessary to publish the pictures to refute Mr. Al Fayed's claims and the fact that *The Sun* paid the person who misappropriated the pictures did not weigh against the finding of fair dealing. The Supreme Court of Appeal, however, found the use unfair, noting that it is appropriate to consider the motives of the alleged infringer, in addition to considering whether the extent of the use was necessary for the purpose of reporting current events. Since the pictures did not establish that the couple was married, and only supported a minor fact stated in article in *The Sun* the extent of the use was unfair. Furthermore, the court noted that since the pictures had not been published, *The Sun* had prevented the copyright owner from exploiting the works.

Even with the enumerated exceptions stated in sections 29–50 of the Copyright, Designs, and Patents Act 1988, English courts, like United States courts, must carefully consider the circumstances of each case in concluding a particular use is fair. For example, when a court considers whether the use of a copyrighted work falls within one of the enumerated exceptions, the court will consider circumstances such as the extent of the particular use, the nature of the copyrighted work, the motivation of the user, and the effect of the use on the rights of the copyright owner.[120]

Moreover, the inflexible nature of specific statutory exceptions is not necessarily able to effectively balance potentially conflicting legal interests in all situations. In *Ashdown v. Telegraph Group Ltd.*,[121] the Supreme Court of Appeal considered the question of how protection afforded by the Copyright, Designs, and Patents Act 1988 and rights guaranteed by the Human Rights Act 1998 are to be balanced when in conflict.

Pursuant to article 10 of the European Convention, the 1998 Act guarantees the right to freedom of expression. In most circumstances, freedom of expression is protected by virtue of the fact that copyrights do not extend to the facts and ideas within a work. Therefore, publication of ideas and facts can occur without the need to copy the manner in which another expressed those facts and ideas. The court, however, noted that in rare circumstances it is in the public interest to publish the words of another without sanction. Accordingly, the court stated that although the 1988 Act does not contain a specific exception to copyright protection for public interest, section 171(3) of the 1988 Act permitted the defense of public interest to be raised. Section 171(3) provides that "[n]othing in this Part affects any rule of law preventing or restricting the enforcement of copyright, on grounds of public interest or otherwise".[122] As illustrated in *Ashdown*, specific exceptions may not readily provide the appropriate limits on copyrights under all circumstances.

(iii) Specific Exceptions

Most countries, however, have incorporated specific exceptions in their laws, rather than a standard for determining excepted uses. For example, European

---

120 *Pro-Sieben Media AG v. Carlton United Kingdom Television Ltd.*, F.S.R. 43 (1998) (considering the motives of the user); *Hyde Park Residence Ltd. v. Yelland*, R.P.C. 604 (2000) (considering the extent of the use, the fact that the work was unpublished, and the effect of the use on the rights of the copyright owner).

121 *Ashdown v. Telegraph Group Ltd.*, 4 All E.R. 666 (2001).

122 Ultimately, the appeal was dismissed. The court did not find that public interest or fair dealing as defined by the 1988 Act provided justification for the extent of the reproduction of the copyrighted work. The court reasoned that the work had been deliberately filleted to extract passages that were most likely to further the commercial interests of the defendant. Therefore, the court reasoned that article 10 did not allow the defendant to profit from the use of the copyright without paying compensation.

civil law countries, such as France and Germany, have enacted copyright legislation that includes exceptions similar to those in the United Kingdom's 1988 Act.[123] As the principles underlying the copyright laws of many European countries are based on the moral rights of authors, the exceptions to copyright protections tend to be narrower than those provided by fair use.

Japan and China, where formal copyright law is relatively new, also have opted for specific limits to copyrights.[124] The Copyright Law of Japan grants particular rights to the public, which, for example, permit uses for the development of education, art and culture, social welfare, and democratic systems.[125]

The Copyright Law of the People's Republic of China[126] limits the scope of copyrights in several ways. Copyright protection is not afforded to:

1. Laws;

2. Regulations;

3. Resolutions, decisions, and orders of State organs;

4. Other documents of a legislative, administrative, or judicial nature and their official translations;

5. News on current affairs; and

6. Calendars, numerical tables and forms of general use, and formulas.[127]

Furthermore Chinese law includes a list of specific exceptions to authors' rights.[128] Article 22 provides a list of 12 exceptions conditioned on mentioning

---

123 French Intellectual Property Code (*Code de la Propriete Intellectuelle*), article L 132-6; German Copyright Act (*Urheberrechtsgesetz*), articles 45–63.

124 Yamamoto, "The Wall Street Journal Case", *Copyright Update Japan 1998*, at http://www.cric.or.jp/cric_e/cuj/cuj98/cuj98_2.html (discussing the 27 October 1994 (*Hanrei Jihou* 1524-118) opinion of the Tokyo High Court and noting that Japan does not recognize a general principle of fair use).

125 Copyright Law of Japan, chapter II, section 3(5), articles 30–50. The purpose of the copyright protection system in Japan is to pursue the development of culture through ensuring the protection of authors' rights and other right holders. The Japanese government, however, recognizes other rights and values connected to the public welfare that are in contention with the protection of authors' rights. To provide a balance between copyright and other rights and values for the public welfare, the Copyright Law of Japan limits rights for limited and exceptional cases. The provisions are carefully established with strict and detailed conditions so that they do not unreasonably prejudice the interests of copyright owners.

126 Copyright Law of the People's Republic of China (2001), English translation, at http://www.chinaiprlaw.com/english/laws/laws10.htm.

127 Copyright Law of the People's Republic of China, article 5.

128 Copyright Law of the People's Republic of China, article 22.

the source of the exploited work and a lack of prejudice to the other rights enjoyed by the copyright owner. The exceptions include, for example:

> ... appropriate quotation from a published work in one's own work for the purposes of introduction to, or comments on, a work, or demonstration of a point; . . . reprinting by newspapers or periodicals, or rebroadcasting by radio stations, television stations, or any other media, of articles on current issues relating to politics, economics or religion published by other newspapers, periodicals, or broadcast by other radio stations, television stations or any other media except where the author has declared that the reprinting and rebroadcasting is not permitted; . . . translation, or reproduction in a small quantity of copies, of a published work for use by teachers or scientific researchers, in classroom teaching or scientific research, provided that the translation or reproduction shall not be published or distributed; . . . free-of-charge live performance of a published work and said performance neither collects any fees from the members of the public nor pays remuneration to the performers; [and] translation of a published work of a Chinese citizen, legal entity or any other organization from the Han language into any minority nationality language for publication and distribution within the country.[129]

A general public interest exception also is provided.[130]

The apparent scope of the exceptions between these countries and the United States fair use doctrine differs.[131] In light of the different principles underlying the copyright laws of different countries, it is likely that even where particular exceptions appear similar in scope, the exceptions are applied differently to promote different principles and/or promote distinct political or social policies.

While the examination of legislation lends insight into countries' limits on copyrights and is sufficient for purposes of this chapter, further

---

129 Copyright Law of the People's Republic of China, article 22.

130 Copyright Law of the People's Republic of China, article 4 ("Copyright owners, in exercising their copyright, shall not violate the Constitution or laws or prejudice the public interests").

131 For example, the United States doctrine of fair use provides the basis for permitting reverse engineering of computer software. While most consider reverse engineering legal under Japanese copyright law, the law does not contain a specific provision for reverse engineering. Sugiyama, "Japanese Copyright Law Development, Presentation at Fordham University IP Conference" (19 April 2001), at http://www.softic.or.jp/en/articles/fordham_sugiyama.html. In contrast, many Europeans have enacted laws specifically for the protection of computer programs to address issues of reverse engineering.

differences in those limits may be revealed on more detailed consideration of the application of those laws.[132]

5.05   International Treaties

(a) In General

As copyrights have increasingly become important assets in the global economy, treaties arose to provide a basic understanding of the scope of copyright laws among member countries. Each of the predominant multilateral treaties recognizes and provides for exceptions to the rights of copyright owners under the laws of the member states. As most international treaties allow individual states to define, within the confines of the treaty, their own exceptions to copyright protection based on domestic protections, the concept of fair use as it is known in the United States has not been widely adopted in the international community.

To date, there are a number of multilateral treaties related to copyrights. Two of the most prominent of those are the Berne Convention for the Protection of Literacy and Artistic Works (Berne Convention)[133] and the Agreement on Trade-Related Aspects of Intellectual Property Rights (TRIPS).[134]

(b) Berne Convention for the Protection of Literary and Artistic Works

As originally conceived, the Berne Convention was intended to promote five objectives:

(1) the development of copyright laws in favor of authors in all civilized countries;

(2) the elimination over time of basing rights on reciprocity;

(3) the end of discrimination in rights between domestic and foreign authors in all countries;

(4) the abolition of formalities for the recognition and protection of copyright in foreign works; and

---

132 In addition to the explicit exceptions listed in the legislation of various countries, it would be interesting to identify whether any other provisions of copyright laws or non-copyright laws serve to limit authors' rights and compare the application of such provisions with that of fair use. *Ashdown v. Telegraph Group Ltd.*, 4 All E.R. 666 (2001) (addressing the potential effect of the Human Rights Act 1998 on copyrights).

133 Berne Convention for the Protection of Literary and Artistic Works, 24 July 1971, S. Treaty Doc. Number 99-27 (1986) (hereinafter "Berne Convention").

134 Agreement on Trade-Related Aspects of Intellectual Property Rights, 15 April 1994, 33 *I.L.M.* 81 (hereinafter "TRIPS").

(5) ultimately, the promotion of uniform international legislation for the protection of literary and artistic works.[135]

At its inception, the Berne Convention embodied two underlying principles which are still vital today. The first is the idea of a union of states for the protection of the rights of authors in their literary and artistic works. The second is the rule of national treatment. With national treatment, authors receive in other countries the same protection for their works as those countries provide their own authors.

The Berne Convention has been revised five times, the most recent revision being the 1971 Paris Act of Berne, which contained revisions to accommodate developing countries.[136]

The copyright laws of those countries involved in developing the Berne Convention contained exceptions and limitations on authors' rights. Therefore, such ideas were incorporated into the Convention. In her historical analysis of exceptions and limitations to copyrights, Professor Okediji notes that:

> What was particularly problematic was that the recognized exceptions in the national legislation of each country were not rooted in a comprehensive philosophical perspective or policy with regard to copyright specifically, but instead tended to reflect broad themes within the socio-historical and political culture of the particular country. Thus, the initial set of limitations proposed... were not outgrowths of a particular doctrine or perspective on copyright *per se*. ... Consequently, the exceptions found throughout the Berne Convention do not necessarily reflect a common understanding or agreement as to the construction of each exception . . . .[137]

Currently, article 9(2) of the Berne Convention allows countries to:

> . . . permit the reproduction of [literary and artistic] works in certain special cases, provided that such reproduction does not conflict with a

---

135 House Report of the Berne Convention Implementation Act of 1988, H.R. Rep. Number 100-609 (1988). The Berne Convention was a European construct. Other countries, such as those in Africa, Asia, and Latin America, were not active participants in the development of the Convention. Okediji, "Toward and International Fair Use Doctrine", 39 *Colum. J. Transnat'l L.* 75, at p. 95 (2000).

136 H.R. Rep. Number 100-609. Other revisions of the Berne Convention include the 1908 Berlin Act (prohibiting formalities as a condition of the enjoyment and exercise of rights under the Convention); 1928 Rome Act (recognizing the "moral rights" of authors); 1948 Brussels Act (establishing the term of protection); and 1967 Stockholm Act (expressly establishing the implicit right of reproduction).

137 Okediji, "Toward and International Fair Use Doctrine", 39 *Colum. J. Transnat'l L.* 75, at p. 99 (2000).

normal exploitation of the work and does not unreasonably prejudice the legitimate interests of the author.[138]

The text of the Convention, however, does not provide insight into the meanings of "special case", "a normal exploitation of the work", or "legitimate interests of the author".

In addition to the general standard for exceptions, the Convention also lists particular purposes for which countries may legislate exceptions. For example, with certain conditions, countries may permit the use of a work to make quotations, to teach, or to report current events.[139]

(c) Agreement on Trade-Related Aspects of Intellectual Property Rights

TRIPS, article 13, incorporates language similar to that of article 9(2) of the Berne Convention.[140] Specifically, article 13 states:

> Members shall confine limitations or exceptions to exclusive rights to certain special cases which do not conflict with a normal exploitation

---

138 Berne Convention, article 9(2).

139 Article 10(1) of the Berne Convention states that "[i]t shall be permissible to make quotations from a work which has already been lawfully made available to the public, provided that their making is compatible with fair practice, and their extent does not exceed that justified by the purpose, including quotations from newspaper articles and periodicals in the form of press summaries". Article 10(2) is directed to teaching. Countries may "permit the utilization, to the extent justified by the purpose, of literary or artistic works by way of illustration in publications, broadcasts or sound or visual recordings for teaching, provided such utilization is compatible with fair practice". Article 10 *bis* (2) allows countries to determine the conditions under which works may be reproduced for the purpose of reporting current events.

140 The World Intellectual Property Organization Treaty, article 10, provides: "(1) Contracting Parties may, in their national legislation, provide for limitations of or exceptions to the rights granted to authors of literary and artistic works under this Treaty in certain special cases that do not conflict with a normal exploitation of the work and do not unreasonably prejudice the legitimate interests of the author. (2) Contracting Parties shall, when applying the Berne Convention, confine any limitations of or exceptions to rights provided for therein to certain special cases that do not conflict with a normal exploitation of the work and do not unreasonably prejudice the legitimate interests of the author". WIPO Copyright Treaty, *36 I.L.M. 65* (20 December 1996); WIPO Performances and Phonograms Treaty, *36 I.L.M. 76*, article 16(2) (20 December 1996) ("Contracting Parties shall confine any limitations of or exceptions to rights provided for in the Treaty to certain special cases which do not conflict with a normal exploitation of the performance or phonogram and do not unreasonably prejudice the legitimate interests of the performer or of the producer of the phonogram"); Universal Copyright Convention, 24 July 1971, *25 U.S.T. 1341*, *U.N.T.S. 178*. Article 4 *bis* of the Universal Copyright Convention provides that "any Contracting State may, by its domestic legislation, make exceptions that do not conflict with the spirit and provisions of this Convention, to the rights mentioned in paragraph 1 of this article. Any State whose legislation so provides, shall nevertheless accord a reasonable degree of effective protection to each of the rights to which exception has been made".

of the work and do not unreasonably prejudice the legitimate interests of the right holder.

Unlike the Berne Convention, TRIPS provides a mechanism for enforcement of its provisions. Accordingly, countries may challenge the laws of other countries pursuant to provisions of the Dispute Settlement Understanding.[141]

In 1999, the European Communities alleged that the United States Fairness in Music Licensing Act[142] failed to meet the standards of article 13 of TRIPS and requested the establishment of a World Trade Organization (WTO) Panel. The resulting WTO Panel Report provides some insight into the meaning of article 13, as well as article 9(2) of the Berne Convention.[143]

In construing the meaning of a "special case" under TRIPS, the Panel noted that an exception to copyright protection in a "special case" is not necessarily the same as an exception with a "special purpose".[144] The panel further held that to constitute a "special case", the exception must be clearly defined and narrow in scope.[145] In construing the phrase "normal exploitation" under TRIPS, the Panel held that normal exploitation includes actual and potential uses of a work. The Panel further noted that an exception for uses that do not come into economic competition with non-excepted uses would presumptively not conflict with the normal exploitation of a

---

141 Dispute Settlement Understanding, 15 April 1994, Marrakesh Agreement Establishing the World Trade Organization, Annex 2, *Legal Instruments — Result of the Uruguay Round,* volume 27, 33 *I.L.M.* 112 (1994). Questions regarding the consistency of fair use with the Berne Convention and article 13 of TRIPS have been raised by scholars. Okediji, "Toward and International Fair Use Doctrine", 39 *Colum. J. Transnat'l L.* 75, at pp. 114–123 (2000). Engle, "When Is Fair Use Fair?: A Comparison of EU and United States Intellectual Property Law", 15 *Transnat'l Law* 187, at pp. 222–225 (2002). It is beyond the scope of this chapter to address such issues. It is worth noting that fair use was an integral part of United States copyright law prior to the United States' membership to the Berne Convention or TRIPS. Furthermore, since the United States joined TRIPS, there has been no formal challenge to fair use.

142 17 United States Code, section 110(5).

143 WTO Panel Report on the United States — section 110(5) of the United States Copyright Act, 15 June 2000, WT/DS160/R, at http://www.wto.org/wto/ddf/ep/public.html (hereinafter Panel Report). Okediji, "Toward and International Fair Use Doctrine", 39 *Colum. J. Transnat'l L.* 75, at pp. 123–135 (2000); Gaubiac, "Exceptions and Limitations to Copyright within the Meaning of article 13 of TRIPS", *UNESCO Copyright Bulletin*, at http://portal.unesco.org/culture/en/ev.php-URL_ID=10018&URL_DO=DO_TOPIC&URL_SECTION=201.html.

144 WTO Panel Report on the United States — section 110(5) of the United States Copyright Act, 15 June 2000, WT/DS160/R, at http://www.wto.org/wto/ddf/ep/public.html.

145 WTO Panel Report on the United States — section 110(5) of the United States Copyright Act, 15 June 2000, WT/DS160/R, at http://www.wto.org/wto/ddf/ep/public.html.

work.[146] Without standards to apply to future cases, the meaning of article 13 (and article 9(2) of the Berne Convention) will remain ambiguous leaving countries little on which to base future challenges under article 13.[147]

5.06   Limitations on Copyrights in the Digital World

(a) In General

The Berne Convention and TRIPS allow countries to limit copyrights, but provide little guidance for such limits. Considering the differences between countries' approaches to limiting copyrights, there would be benefit to a standard to provide guidance for countries in their efforts to balancing the interests of copyright owners and the public in the face of new and developing technologies.

To determine the scope of such a standard, it is necessary to consider the challenges to balancing those interests presented by digital technologies and responses to those challenges.

(b) Challenges to Balancing the Interests of Copyright Owners and the Public: The Threat to Copyright Owners

There is no doubt that recent and constantly developing digital technologies have enabled easy and extensive infringement of copyrights. Many copyrighted works are or can be placed in a digital format. For example, music, images, and even entire libraries exist in digital formats. These works can be easily and quickly copied.

Furthermore, works in digital formats can be quickly and easily transmitted to anyone with access to the Internet. Accordingly, a person with a copyrighted work in a digital format can share that work with vast numbers of people quickly, easily, inexpensively, and, potentially, without their permission. It is clear that new and developing technologies present challenges to protections provided by copyright law and to the enforcement of those laws.

---

146 WTO Panel Report on the United States — section 110(5) of the United States Copyright Act, 15 June 2000, WT/DS160/R, at http://www.wto.org/wto/ddf/ep/public.html. The Panel Report provides some explanation of article 13, but is not particularly useful as a guide for countries to determine what legislation will be considered compliant. Similarly, the Panel Report does not provide much guidance to future Panels. The reasoning and factors on which the Panel based its decision indicate that compliance with article 13 must be determined on a case-by-case basis. Okediji, "Toward and International Fair Use Doctrine", 39 *Colum. J. Transnat'l L.* 75, at p. 130 (2000).

147 Okediji, "Toward and International Fair Use Doctrine", 39 *Colum. J. Transnat'l L.* 75, at p. 150 (2000).

The music industry's experience with new technologies is a prominent illustration of the threat that digital technologies present to copyright owners.[148] In addition to *Napster*, discussed above, other companies are using Peer-to-Peer (P2P) technologies which have enabled widespread copyright infringement.[149] Some of these new technologies have sparked prominent legal battles in the United States. The fate of such technologies remains unclear.

The most recent case is *Metro-Goldwyn-Mayer Studios, Inc. v. Grokster Ltd.*[150] This case was instituted by the music industry, along with other entertainment industries, against Grokster Ltd. and StreamCast Networks, Inc. Both Grokster Ltd. and StreamCast freely distribute P2P software that allows users to share computer files with each other, including digitized music and motion pictures. Metro-Goldwyn-Mayer Studios, Inc., and other copyright owners filed suit against Grokster and StreamCast, alleging liability for vicarious and contributory copyright infringement.

In contrast to *Napster*, the Ninth Circuit affirmed the district court's holding that neither Grokster nor StreamCast was liable for vicarious or contributory copyright infringement due in large part to the fact that Grokster and StreamCast exert very little control over the operation of their particular P2P.[151] Different P2P systems function in different ways to accomplish similar objectives. Napster's P2P system used a proprietary centralized indexing software architecture wherein an index of all available files was maintained on Napster-owned and operated servers. A user looking for a particular file on the Napster system sent a request to the Napster server. The Napster server, in turn, searched the index for the file and transmitted the search results to the user.

Where results showed that another user having the file was logged on, the user could connect to the other user's computer and download the file. Unlike Napster's system, Grokster's and StreamCast's systems avoid the use of a

---

148 Committee on Intellectual Property Rights in the Emerging Information Infrastructure, National Research Council, *The Digital Dilemma: Intellectual Property in the Information Age*, chapter 2 (2000), at http://www.nap.edu/html/digital_dilemma/ch2.html (stating that music is intellectual property's "canary in the digital coal mine").

149 In traditional P2P networks, computers were typically situated within relatively close physical proximity and ran similar networking protocols and software. Although one computer acted as a server at any given time, any of the computers within the P2P network could handle those responsibilities. In the past, individual computers accessing the internet (a client computer) were not sophisticated enough to be active parts of the internet, e.g., servers. As hardware and software technologies developed, this changed. In the modern version of P2P computing, P2P networks exist over the internet and each user's computer serves as both a client and a server.

150 *Metro-Goldwyn-Mayer Studios Inc. v. Grokster Ltd.*, 380 F3d 1154 (9th Cir., 2004).

151 *Metro-Goldwyn-Mayer Studios Inc. v. Grokster Ltd.*, 380 F3d 1154 (9th Cir., 2004).

central server. Under StreamCast's system, each user has an index of only the files that the user is making available to other users on the StreamCast P2P network. Grokster employs a "supernode" model where select computers on the network function as indexing servers. Any computer on Grokster's P2P network can function as a server if it meets certain technical requirements.[152] The Ninth Circuit acknowledged that it was undisputed that Grokster's and StreamCast's P2P systems had substantial non-infringing uses.[153] Due to the designs of systems, the Ninth Circuit reasoned that the defendants did not provide a site and facilities for infringement.[154]

Additionally, since the defendants do not keep a centralized index of files, the copyright owners' notices of infringing conduct on the systems were ineffective since, at the time the notices were received, the defendants were doing nothing to contribute to any infringement and could do nothing to stop the alleged infringement.[155] Furthermore, the court held that the defendants were not vicariously liable for infringement because Grokster and StreamCast lacked the right and ability to supervise users of their P2P networks. The Supreme Court, however, was to hear the case, and a decision was expected in July 2005.

(c) Responses to Digital Technologies

(i) In General

Industries and governments have reacted to new and developing digital technologies and the apparent threat that the technologies present to the rights of copyright owners. There have been two prominent responses. First, industries have developed technological controls for digital information, deemed digital rights management. Second, governments have enacted legislation to support industries' efforts to control information. The 1996 WIPO Copyright Treaty responded to the concerns of copyright owners that their works would be widely pirated with the development of digital technologies. The resulting United States legislation came in the form of the 1998 Digital Millennium Copyright Act.

In 2001, the European Parliament issued Directive 2001/29/EC, commonly known as the EU Copyright Directive. Digital rights management technologies

---

152 *Metro-Goldwyn-Mayer Studios Inc. v. Grokster Ltd.*, 380 F3d 1154, at pp. 1158–1160 (9th Cir., 2004).

153 *Metro-Goldwyn-Mayer Studios Inc. v. Grokster Ltd.*, 380 F3d 1154, at pp. 1161 and 1162 (9th Cir., 2004).

154 *Metro-Goldwyn-Mayer Studios Inc. v. Grokster Ltd.*, 380 F3d 1154, at p. 1162 (9th Cir., 2004).

155 *Metro-Goldwyn-Mayer Studios Inc. v. Grokster Ltd.*, 380 F3d 1154, at p. 1162 (9th Cir., 2004).

supported by law have changed, and they continue to change the flow of digital information and copyrighted works. As a consequence, the role of fair use in the United States, as well as that of exceptions to copyright protections outside the United States, has changed. As the responses to digital technologies continue to develop, it is the limitations on copyrights that may be in danger.

(ii) Digital Rights Management

Digital rights management technologies are aimed at increasing the kinds and/or scope of control that copyright owners can assert over their intellectual property assets. In that sense, digital rights management is similar to the copy protection technologies employed in the 1980s.[156]

Digital rights management systems protect the copyrights of data circulated by digital media, including the Internet, by enabling secure distribution and/or disabling illegal distribution of the data. Typically, a digital rights management system protects intellectual property by either encrypting the data so that it can only be accessed by authorized users or marking the content with a digital watermark or similar method so that the content cannot be freely distributed.[157]

Digital rights management technologies are still in development. Ultimately, digital rights management seeks to provide means to charge consumers for certain uses of copyrighted works and prohibit other uses, including piracy and free file sharing. Examples of proposed and/or developing technologies include: use of a computer code to program certain allowable uses directly onto the rule set that controls access to a digital file; use of key access where users apply for digital keys to access files and decisions to grant keys would be made by a person; and a combination of the first two methods where a code may prohibit certain uses, but a user could apply for an access key to use the file in a manner prohibited by the code.[158]

---

156 Examples of copy protection technologies included using floppy disks with holes punched out at precise locations, or, as with Lotus 1-2-3, a software program would write a code onto the floppy disk so that the disk could not be used to install the program onto any other hard drives unless one first used a utility on the floppy to remove the first hard drive installation. The copy protection technologies tended to be cumbersome to users and were eventually abandoned by many companies.

157 von Lohmann, "Electronic Frontier Foundation, Fair Use and Digital Rights Management: Preliminary Thoughts on the (Irreconcilable?) Tension between Them" (16 April 2002), at http://www.eff.org/IP/digital rights management/fair_use_and_drm.html.

158 Petrick, Berkman Center for Internet & Society at Harvard Law School, "Why DRM Should be Cause for Concern: An Economic and Legal Analysis of the Effect of Digital Technology on the Music Industry", *Research Publication Number 2004-09*, at pp. 7 and 8, at http://ssrn.com/abstract=618065 (Nov. 2004) (citing Burk and Cohen, "Fair Use Infrastructure for Rights Management Systems", 15 *Harv. J.L. & Tech.* 41, at p. 48 (Fall 2001)).

Considering the music industry's public battle with P2P technology over copyright infringement, it is no surprise that the music industry has made use of digital rights management.[159] For example, the Apple iTunes[160] employs digital rights management technologies in its successful on-line music store.[161]

Apple's digital rights management system, FairPlay, limits use of data in two ways. First, users are only permitted to download a purchased song once and are only able to use the song on five computers. Additionally, users can copy any given song to a CD an unlimited number of times, but can only copy the same playlist seven times. Second, only Apple's iPod products support FairPlay, and the iPod products only support the Advanced Audio Coding and MP3 standard rather than the dominant standard used by the other digital music services: Microsoft's Windows Media digital rights management for Windows Media Audio.[162] Thereby, Apple limits the interoperability of its technologies.[163]

Just as Apple's Fair Play limits the number of times a music file can be copied once it is purchased, digital rights management technologies could be developed to limit copying completely, regardless of the purpose for the copying. In theory, it is possible that digital rights management technologies could dictate all uses of the works they protect. As digital rights management technologies are still developing, their impact is not entirely apparent. It is clear, however, that digital rights management technologies will continue to

---

159 Gasser *et al.*, Berkman Center for Internet & Society at Harvard Law School, "iTunes: How Copyright, Contract, and Technology Shape the Business of Digital Media — A Case Study", Research Publication Number 2004-07, at http://ssrn.com/abstract=556802 (June 2004).

160 Unlike certain other internet music stores, Apple iTunes treats purchases like sales, rather than rentals. Consequently, the ability to play a purchased song is not contingent on remaining an Apple iTunes customer.

161 See http://www.apple.com/itunes/store/.

162 Gasser *et al.*, Berkman Center for Internet & Society at Harvard Law School, "iTunes: How Copyright, Contract, and Technology Shape the Business of Digital Media — A Case Study", Research Publication Number 2004-07, at http://ssrn.com/abstract=556802 (June 2004).

163 On 15 June 2004, Apple launched its iTunes Music Store in the United Kingdom, France, and Germany. In its first week, Apple outsold its closest competitor by a margin of 16 to one. Subsequently, on 26 October 2004, Apple launched its European Union version of the iTunes Music Store. Press Release, Apple, "Apple Launches EU iTunes Music Store" (26 October 2004), at http://www.apple.com/pr/library/2004/oct/26itmseu.html. The EU store serves Austria, Belgium, Finland, Greece, Italy, Luxembourg, The Netherlands, Portugal, and Spain. The European stores are nearly identical to the United States store, and they offer the same features as are offered in the United States. Notably, Apple describes its digital rights management as "groundbreaking personal use rights". Press Release, Apple, "Apple Launches EU iTunes Music Store" (26 October 2004), at http://www.apple.com/pr/library/2004/oct/26itmseu.html. Gasser *et al.*, Berkman Center for Internet & Society at Harvard Law School, "iTunes Europe: A Preliminary Analysis" (June 2004), at http://cyber.law.harvard.edu/media/uploads/82/itunes_europe_analysis.pdf.

exert control over the relationship between the public and copyright owners and will likely favor the interests of the copyright owners.

(iii) Legislation

In General The 1996 WIPO Copyright Treaty deals with the protection of literary and artistic works. It serves to update and supplement the major existing WIPO treaties on copyright and related rights, e.g., the Berne Convention, in response to developments in technology and in the marketplace. The WIPO Copyright Treaty directs countries to enact anti-circumvention laws and seeks to protect digital rights management.[164]

As a result, countries have passed legislation to meet their obligations under the Treaty. Below, this article considers the United States and European legislation pursuant to the Treaty.[165]

Digital Millennium Copyright Act In 1998, the United States passed the Digital Millennium Copyright Act to outlaw certain acts of circumvention and technologies designed to circumvent technical measures used to protect copyrighted works. The anti-circumvention provisions of the Digital Millennium Copyright Act are codified in section 1201 of the United States Copyright Act.[166] Congress enacted section 1201 in response to two pressures, namely:

1. Obligations imposed on the United States by the 1996 WIPO Copyright Treaty; and

2. Concerns of copyright owners that their works would be widely pirated with the development of digital technologies.

Section 1201 contains two distinct prohibitions, these being:

1. A ban on acts of circumvention; and

2. A ban on the distribution of tools and technologies used for circumvention.

First, the Digital Millennium Copyright Act prohibits the act of circumventing a technological measure used by copyright owners to control access to their works ("access controls").[167] For example, this provision makes it unlawful to defeat the encryption systems protecting works contained on DVDs.

---

164 World Intellectual Property Organization Copyright Treaty, 36 *I.L.M.* 65 (20 December 1996).

165 For Japan, see "On the Law to Partially Amend the Copyright Law", passed in the 145th session of the National Diet on 15 June 1999 and promulgated as Law Number 77 of 1999 on 23 June 1999.

166 17 United States Code, section 1201.

167 17 United States Code, section 1201(a)(1).

Second, the Digital Millennium Copyright Act prohibits the manufacture, sale, distribution, or trafficking of tools and technologies that make circumvention possible.[168] These provisions ban both technologies that defeat access controls, and also technologies that defeat use restrictions imposed by copyright owners, such as copy protections.

Section 1201 permits circumvention for certain limited activities, including security testing, reverse engineering of software, encryption research, and law enforcement.[169] These exceptions have been extensively criticized as being too narrow to be of any affect.[170] The Digital Millennium Copyright Act states that it is not intended to affect fair use as a defense to copyright infringement.[171] Fair use, however, is not a defense to violations of acts of circumvention prohibited by the Digital Millennium Copyright Act.

Directive 2001/29/EC of the European Parliament and the Council of May 2001   Directive 2001/29/EC of the European Parliament and of the Council of 22 May 2001 on the harmonization of certain aspects of copyright and related rights in the information society is the European counterpart to the United States Digital Millennium Copyright Act.[172]

Like the Digital Millennium Copyright Act, the EU Copyright Directive, as it is commonly known, protects technological measures that restrict the use of literary and other works in digital form based on instructions from their owners. The Directive requires member states to provide adequate legal protection prohibiting the "circumvention of any effective technological measures, which the person concerned carries out in the knowledge, or with reasonable grounds to know that he or she is pursuing that objective".[173] The EU Copyright Directive also requires states to have adequate legal protection prohibiting trafficking in circumventing technology.[174] The European Commission reported on the operation of the Directive in December 2004, after which amendments may be made by the Parliament and Council.

The EU Copyright Directive does require states to provide some exceptions. Member must take appropriate action to ensure that copyright owners

---

168 17 United States Code, section 1201(a)(2) and (b).

169 17 United States Code, section 1201(e)–(g).

170 Samuelson, "Intellectual Property and the Digital Economy: Why the Anti-Circumvention Regulations Need to Be Revised", 14 *Berkeley Technology L.J.* 519, at pp. 537–557 (1999), at http://www.sims.berkeley.edu/~pam/papers.html.

171 17 United States Code, section 1201(c)(1).

172 Directive 2001/29/EC of the European Parliament and of the Council on the harmonization of certain aspects of copyright and related rights in the information society, *O.J.* L 167/10-19 (22 May 2001) (hereinafter the "EU Copyright Directive").

173 Copyright Directive, article 6.

174 Copyright Directive, article 6.

adhere to certain limits on their rights. This should be understood to mean that owners will be required to give access to consumers who can claim one of the specified exemptions, but it is currently unclear how states will construe the EU Copyright Directive.[175] Additionally, states are not required to protect all exceptions. For example, copies for private use, reporting current events, and for criticism and review are not fully protected.[176]

Additionally, the exceptions apply only to the prohibition against circumvention, not the prohibition against trafficking in circumvention technology. Therefore, the practical effects of the exceptions are questionable since the only apparent way of legal circumvention is to privately develop and use circumvention technologies. Moreover, where works are made available by contract, states are not required to ensure that copyright owners respect the limitations to their copyrights.[177]

(iv) Effects of Digital Rights Management and Supporting Legislation on Limitations to Copyrights

By implementing digital rights management technologies to protect a copyrighted work, the copyright owner can dictate the rights a user has with respect to the work. Since, with limited exceptions, the Digital Millennium Copyright Act and the EU Copyright Directive prohibit the circumvention of digital rights management technologies, copyright owners are able to gain greater control over their works than provided by basic copyright laws.

In essence, the Digital Millennium Copyright Act and EU Copyright Directive have turned digital rights management into law, and copyright owners can, in effect, design the law that governs their copyrighted works. Moreover, copyright owners have the ability to significantly restrict fair uses or uses meeting an exception to the copyright protections afforded to their works. As stated by a critic of the Digital Millennium Copyright Act referring to digital rights management technologies as code:

> The controls built into the technology of copy and access protection become rules the violation of which also is a violation of the law. In this way, the code extends the law-increasing its regulation, even if the subject it regulates (activities that would otherwise plainly constitute fair use) is beyond the reach of the law. Code becomes law; code extends the law; code thus extends the control that copyright owners effect . . . .[178]

---

175 Brown, Foundation for Information Policy Research, "Implementing the EU Copyright Directive", at p. 18, at http://www.fipr.org/copyright/guide/ (last viewed 1/15/1905).

176 Copyright Directive, article 6(4).

177 Copyright Directive, article 6(4).

178 Lessig, *Free Culture: How Big Media Uses Technology and the Law to Lock Down Culture and Control Creativity*, at p. 160 (2004).

Together, digital rights management and the anti-circumvention laws that support it have significantly shifted the balance between the interests of copyright owners and the public.[179]

It is undeniable that certain technologies threaten the rights of copyright owners. It is equally clear that technologies, such as digital rights management, and legislative measures, such as the Digital Millennium Copyright Act and EU Copyright Directive, threaten the limits on copyright protections and, therefore, the interests of the pubic. To adequately serve the principles underlying copyright laws, copyright protections must be limited. Furthermore, in an increasingly information-based global economy and society, limits on copyright protections are essential to promoting free flow of information.

5.07   International Fair Use Standard

As noted above, in light of the differences between countries' approaches to limiting copyrights and the lack of effective guidance for determining appropriate limitations under various treaties, there would be benefit to an international standard for limitations on copyright protections. For the purposes of this chapter, such a standard is referred to an international fair use standard.[180] Below, this chapter identifies considerations for developing an international fair use standard, and suggests some general guidelines for such a standard.

Currently, the Berne Convention and TRIPS primarily provide a ceiling for limitations on copyrights. In other words, countries are prohibited from providing exceptions beyond what is set out in the Berne Convention and TRIPS. This approach makes sense, since limits on copyright protections should be narrow as compared to the grant of copyright protections.

The approach, however, does not exclude the possibility of a floor within an international fair use standard. The need for limits to copyright protections is universally recognized. Furthermore, there are many exceptions to copyrights that are recognized by all or a majority of countries. As noted above, limitations have been threatened by new technologies and supporting legislation.

---

179 In the early days of the Internet, tracking infringing activities was difficult. As technologies develop, however, infringing activities are ever easier to detect, contributing to a shift in favor of copyright owners' interests. Lessig, *FREE CULTURE: How Big Media Uses Technology and the Law to Lock Down Culture and Control Creativity*, at p. 160 (2004).

180 Okediji, "Toward and International Fair Use Doctrine", 39 *Colum. J. Transnat'l L.* 75, at p. 159 (2000) (noting that a standard, rather than a rule, is the more appropriate form).

Accordingly, a minimum floor to preserve certain exceptions to copyrights is warranted. The concept of requiring minimum limits on copyrights is not without precedent. As discussed above, the EU Copyright Directive requires countries to provide certain exceptions to copyright protections. To protect public welfare in information-based economies and societies, limits on copyrights cannot be overlooked or dismissed. At a minimum, certain activities related to education, scientific research, public comment or criticism, and security should be protected from sanctions under copyright laws.

It also is important to consider how a standard would accommodate current laws limiting copyrights, support principles underlying copyright laws, and provide relevant guidance in the future. A standard would be best accepted if it accommodated current differences in the limits to copyright protections provided by individual countries, as well as the current requirements of copyright-related treaties.

Additionally, since limitations to copyrights provide balance between the interests of copyright owners and the public, a standard would allow individual countries to balance those interests as legitimately needed. Thus, a standard could allow a country to balance interests in light of the principles underlying its own national copyright law; or it could allow developing countries to balance those interests to best promote development. Furthermore, a standard should be flexible enough to allow countries to adapt to changing circumstances presented by future technologies.

Professor Okediji has suggested that an international standard should require that a country base an exception on an established or identified public policy objective and that the exception be reasonably related to that stated objective.[181] As already acknowledged in treaties, another likely criterion is that an exception should not conflict with normal exploitation of the work. Whatever its substance, an international fair use standard should guide countries in maintaining a balance between the interests of copyright owners and the public.[182]

5.08   Conclusion

The increasing importance of intellectual property in local and global economies has placed focus on the laws protecting such property, including copyright laws. It is accepted that a primary function of copyright laws is to grant copyright owners rights over creative works. By way of limitations

---

181   Okediji, "Toward and International Fair Use Doctrine", 39 *Colum. J. Transnat'l L.* 75, at pp. 168 and 169 (2000).

182   Okediji, "Givers, Takers, and Other Kinds of Users: A Fair Use Doctrine for Cyberspace", 53 *Fla. L. Rev.* 107, at pp. 154 and 155 (2001).

and/or exceptions, copyright laws also serve the interests of the public. Such limitations and exceptions define the balance between the interests of copyright owners and those of the public and, therefore, are essential to underlying purposes and principles of copyright laws.

The current lack of an international standard for limitations to copyrights, as well as the focus on threats of new technologies to the interests of copyright owners, undermines such limitations. Accordingly, limits on copyrights are themselves open to threats presented by new and future technologies.

As the use and transfer of information becomes more and more dependent on digital technologies, those technologies exert greater control over the information. Technologies for restricting access to copyrighted works allow copyright owners greater protection than that provided by basic copyright laws. Additionally, past focus on the threat of digital technologies to the interests of copyright owners has lead to legislation buttressing restrictive technologies.

An international fair use standard is a means for preserving the balance between the interests of copyright owners and those of the public in light of new and developing technologies. Any such a standard would undoubtedly be the result of lengthy negotiations between countries. Certain considerations should guide the development of a standard, including: current laws and treaties regarding limiting copyrights, principles underlying various copyright laws, and the ability to adapt to future technologies.

Additionally, a standard should provide a ceiling for limitations on copyright protections in keeping with the idea that copyright laws are a grant of rights to copyright owners. However, in recognition that copyright laws must necessarily provide a balance between the interests of copyright owners and those of the public, a floor narrowly defining minimum exceptions to copyright protections is warranted.

CHAPTER 6

PATENTS: A GLOBAL PERSPECTIVE

David J. Simonelli
Clark Hill PLC
Detroit, Michigan, United States

6.01 Introduction

(a) In General

Because the patent is an often misunderstood legal device, this chapter will begin with a brief history and introduction into the patent. The legal backdrop will lead to the economic significance of the patent and how the terms of protection can foster economic growth for firms and the economies in which they participate.

Following this discussion is an offering of models that may be employed to overcome some hurdles that have recently grown out of the digital divide. Finally, certain realities require the consideration of limitations on the opportunities presented in the offered models.

(b) History

The patent is a device that has been devised to promote economic growth in a society.[1] The patent, like other vehicles used to promote economic growth, is a geopolitical concept, meaning that each country has its own rules and honors only patents that it issues. Patents that are issued in the United States are not recognized in any other country. Likewise, the United States does not recognize any patent issued by another country.

---

1   Poltorak, "Are Patents Bad for the Economy?", *New York Business Focus* (August 2002). "It is an undisputed fact among economists that the U.S. patent system has been the cornerstone of technological progress and economic prosperity of this country".

Patents are used by inventors and applicants to protect inventions, i.e., creations that are useful items (as opposed to creations that are merely new expressions of idea). In the United States, the term used to describe usefulness is "utility".[2] A patent protects a concept or invention that has utility. In addition, the invention must be new.[3] The government issuing the patent will only do so if the applicant is presenting something new to the body of knowledge from which the rest of the society can learn and grow.

In 1449, the King of England issued the first patent starting the first patent system to reward those who developed new technology. This first monopoly grant was given to John of Utynam for stained glass manufacture. King Henry VI granted the patent to help stem the tide of the importation of stained glass from other parts of Europe, most notably from Italy.[4]

The United States believed the concept of awarding patents was so important to a capitalistic society that it made specific provisions for patent law in its Constitution.[5] The concept of patents providing monopolies for entities that develop technology has been widely accepted in every corner of the world as most countries have active patent offices that issue and maintain patents. Some believe that economic gains occur without patents.[6] This is, however, a minority view, as many have invested heavily into the concept and assurances that the patent system offers.

Some countries believe the patent system should promote the societal benefit by publishing patent applications as soon as possible, allowing others the ability to read, understand, and further the technology as soon as possible. Other countries attempt to provide as much opportunity for the patent applicant to maximize its return on its investment in the technology.[7] Either way the patent system is developed, it is done to promote commerce

---

2   35 United States Code, section 101.

3   *Chisum on Patents*, section 2 (2005). "The first patent statute in the United States authorized patents for any useful art, manufacture, engine, machine, or device, or any improvement therein not before known or used", provided a designated group of executive officers (the Secretary of State, the Secretary of War, and the Attorney General) determined that the invention was "sufficiently useful and important".

4   See http://www.patent.gov.uk/about/reports/anrep2002/chapter3.pdf.

5   United States Constitution, article I, section 8, paragraph 8. "The Congress shall have Power . . . To promote the Progress of Science and useful Arts, by securing for limited Times to Authors and Inventors the exclusive Right to their respective Writings and Discoveries".

6   *The New York Times*, at C10, column 1 (29 September 2003).

7   Kotabe and Cox, *Business Horizons* (January–February 1993). "The American and Japanese systems . . . represent the ends of the continuum, with the United States placing the greatest emphasis on the rights of the inventor and Japan emphasizing the societal benefits of an invention".

through innovation allowing new products, and now services, to be introduced into the marketplace.[8]

Unlike other forms of protection for intellectual property, a patent protects the owner from others taking that idea.[9] It is a very powerful tool that can be used in various manners to obtain an edge in the marketplace. For example, the patent may be used to protect a specific embodiment of an incremental improvement on a known technology.[10] Alternatively, a patent may protect a broad concept of a new idea. Regardless of the scope of protection sought or obtained, the patent must protect something that is useful. Each country defines "useful" in its own way, but it being useful is a key component for a patent to be granted.

There are other forms of protection of intellectual property that are used to protect expressions, goodwill, and other pieces of knowledge that can be maintained as secret. Those forms of protection include copyright, trade marks, and trade secrets. These legal devices are discussed in greater detail elsewhere in this book. However, an important notion to understand with regard to the patent system is the fact that a patent grants someone or some entity an acknowledgement that they developed or invented something that has not been shown in public before and that the something is useful.

Other types of intellectual property protection protect expressions, the written word, reputation, names, logos, and the like. The patent is, however, the only legal device that protects an idea, its implementation, or an improvement on that idea. It is a very powerful tool to grow in economic success because a patentholder can develop a lawful monopoly for the technology claimed, requiring the purchasing public to go to that person or entity for the patented item.[11]

---

8   "From a theoretical perspective, patent law has the main aim of increasing the pool of technical knowledge of the United States by encouraging inventors to disclose to the country (and effectively to the world) the details of their inventions. In return for teaching the rest of the United States about new technologies and to make it financially worthwhile for inventors to disclose their inventions, the federal government grants the inventor a limited monopoly of 20 years from the time of applying for a patent". See http://iurtc.iu.edu/ott/inventors/032.html.

9   Article 28 of the Agreement on Trade-Related Aspects of Intellectual Property Rights, 15 April 1994, Marrakesh Agreement Establishing the World Trade Organization, Annex 1C, Legal Instruments — Results of the Uruguay Round, volume 31; 33 *I.L.M.* 1144, at p. 1197 (1994) [hereinafter TRIPs Agreement].

10 *Chisum on Patents* Scope, Glossary (2005). "An inventor may patent an improvement on an existing product or process (whether or not it is patented) if the improvement otherwise meets the standards of patentability. A patent on an improvement carries no right to practice the improvement in violation of the rights of the owner of a patent on a basic invention. Thus, basic and improvement patents may 'block' each other, and common subject matter may be used only with the concurrent authority of both patent owners . . . ."

11 *Image Technical Services, Inc. v. Eastman Kodak Co.*, 125 F.3d 1195 (9th Cir., 1997), *cert. denied*, 523 U.S. 1094 (1998).

(c) Patent Monopoly

A patent is often spoken of in terms of an absolute right. More specifically, the patent gives the patentholder the ability to control all things with regard to the disclosure in the patent. This simply is not the case.[12] One reason why patent rights are not absolute is because a capitalistic society neither wants nor trusts a monopoly. It is true that an entity may work hard toward success, which results in a lawful monopoly.[13] However, a capitalistic society is always cognizant of the monopoly and continues to attempt to place the marketplace in the hands of those that are most capable of creating the goods and services that are most wanted by the public. It wants the marketplace to determine what products are going to be offered, sold, and successful.

Inroads in the patent monopoly have been made in a few different ways. One example of this is in the United States, wherein a statute prevents a patent application from being published or a patent from issuing if it is considered a danger to national security.[14] If a patent is not issued, regardless of why it is prevented from issuing, it creates an opportunity for others to enter the market with products and services similar to those that might have been protected by a patent. Another example of an inroad into the patent monopoly is antitrust laws. More specifically, it would be inappropriate for a patent holder to use its patent to gain an advantage in another market with another non-patented product.[15]

Returning to the situation of national security, the opportunity to enter the marketplace may be limited, but the erosion of the monopoly has been created and provides the impetus for a government to use the rationalization of having one limit in the patent monopoly when considering the desire to make another limitation.

Another way in which government has reduced the effective monopoly granted pursuant to a patent is compulsory license statutes. Many countries have laws and statutes in place that create a compulsory license for a patented technology, wherein the patentholder is required to grant a license to the

---

12   Stern, *IEEE Micro Law*, at p. 9 (March-April 2000). "A major problem with the absolute right theory is that too many exceptions are already recognized for the theory of absolute rights to withstand scrutiny". See also Carrier, "Cabining Intellectual Property Through a Property Paradigm", 54 *Duke Law Journal* 1, 106 (2004).

13   *Smith v. Northern Mich. Hospitals*, 518 F.Supp. 644, at p. 648 (W.D. Mich., 1981). It is "well settled that there is no violation of antitrust laws if a monopoly grows and develops as a consequence of a superior product, business acumen, or historical accident".

14   35 United States Code, section 181.

15   *Image Technical Services, Inc. v. Eastman Kodak Co.*, 125 F.3d 1195 (9th Cir., 1997), at p. 1216, *cert. denied*, 523 U.S.1094 (1998).

country issuing the compulsory license or to a third-party national entity to allow the country or the third-party national entity to exploit the patent.[16]

That entity may utilize the technology in the patent to develop a market in that particular country should the patent owner fail to commercialize the patented technology in that country providing those domiciled in that country access to the invention.[17] One way to avoid being forced into a compulsory license is for a patent owner must "use" or "work" the patented technology by commercializing it in the country.[18] In addition to Bulgaria, a sampling of countries that have compulsory license laws include:

1. China;

2. Iceland;

3. Mexico; and

4. The United Kingdom.

While the list presented here is a small sampling, it does illustrate how countries, regardless of their economic status, believe it be important that their economies not suffer from non-participation in a particular industry just because a patent owner fails to enter that country with its product or service.

Statistics regarding the use of compulsory licenses are not readily available. It appears that few compulsory licenses outside the pharmaceutical industry are granted. Research has not developed an answer as to why this tool is not employed more by countries. One could hypothesize that a major reason why the compulsory license is not used often is because potential compulsory licensees may find that it is not economically beneficial to acquire these rights.

As stated above, a patent has a geopolitical quality inherent to its creation. It is only valid in the country in which it is issued. If one country grants a compulsory license, it is only a right to use the patent in that country. If a

---

16   Gillat, "Compulsory Licensing to Regulated Licensing: Effects on the Conflict between Innovation and Access in the Pharmaceutical Industry", 58 *Food Drug L.J.* 711, at p. 712 (2003).

17   Gillat, "Compulsory Licensing to Regulated Licensing: Effects on the Conflict between Innovation and Access in the Pharmaceutical Industry", 58 *Food Drug L.J.* 711, at p. 712 (2003).

18   "Any person concerned may request the Patent Office for grant of a compulsory license to work a patented invention, provided that at least one of the following conditions is met: 1. failure to use the invention for a period of four years from filing of the application for a patent or of three years from the grant of a patent, the time limit which expires last being applicable; 2. insufficient working of the invention to satisfy the needs of the national market, within the time limits set out in item 1, above, unless the patent owner gives valid reasons therefor . . . ." *Bulgarian Patentability Laws*, chapter III, section 32, at http://www.bpo.bg/en/law_patents.html).

prospective compulsory licensee wishes to export its product to another country, the patents in the other countries may bar it from such activity.[19]

Even when no issues regarding crossborder economics are involved, the compulsory license is not a preferred tool to be employed by those in developed countries. As such, the United States attempted to block the efforts of South Africa when they worked toward enacting legislation allowing for compulsory licenses for AIDS-related pharmaceutical,[20] even though it has statutes permitting compulsory licenses. By way of example, the United States permits compulsory licenses of patents necessary for the country's food supply,[21] patents developed through the research funds provided by the government,[22] and patents required to maintain the country's atomic energy needs.[23]

A third example of an inroad to the patent monopoly is the Agreement on Trade-Related Aspects of Intellectual Property Rights (TRIPs), a part of the General Agreement on Tariffs and Trade (GATT) in 1994.[24] The TRIPs Agreement provides an opportunity for underdeveloped countries for the ability to permissively infringe patents for a period of ten years to allow those members that are least-developed countries to develop private entities and economies to compete with first world countries.[25]

The period in which these permissive infringements could occur was for a period of time of which many have expired. Some time periods have,

---

19   Much of the discussion regarding compulsory licenses revolves around medicines and pharmaceuticals. For lack of alternatives, one may look to this "technology sector" for guidance in the information and communications technology sector. Love, "Access to Medicines: Solving the Export Problem Under TRIPs", *Bridges Between Trade and Sustainable Development* Year 6, Number. 4 (May 2002), at p. 3. "Korea, for example, is currently facing a request for a compulsory license on Gleevec, a drug that is very effective against two rare forms of cancer. Korea has a world-class pharmaceutical industry, and is now the most efficient global supplier for some important medicines. It would be possible, but not efficient, for Korea to manufacture Gleevec for its domestic market alone. This is so because, although it accounts for 15 to 20 per cent of all adult Korean leukemi a cases, chronic myelogenous leukemia afflicts only about 500 people each year. A much more efficient solution would be to allow generic producers to make Gleevec for sale in several countries where the combined markets would justify the fixed costs of pro duction".

20   Abbott, "The TRIPS-Legality of Measures Taken to Address Public Health Crisis: A Synopsis", 7 *Widener L. Symp. J.* 71, 72 (Spring 2001).

21   7 United States Code, section 2404.

22   35 United States Code, section 203.

23   42 United States Code, section 2183.

24   Agreement on Trade-Related Aspects of Intellectual Property Rights, 15 April 1994, Marrakesh Agreement Establishing the World Trade Organization, Annex 1C, Legal Instruments — Results of the Uruguay Round, volume 31; 33 *I.L.M.* 1144, at p. 1197 (1994) [hereinafter TRIPs Agreement].

25   TRIPs Agreement, article 66, paragraph 1.

however, been extended well into the future. For example, intellectual property rights for pharmaceutical products can be permissively infringed by less developed countries and least developed countries up to 1 January 2016.[26] The ability to infringe the intellectual property of another is given with the understanding that those Members will develop the necessary infrastructure to enforce the intellectual property rights of others in the future. In other words, it is the understanding of those members of the TRIPs Agreement that growing an economy is a vital step in having a member enter the global economy, with which comes the responsibilities of preparing for enforcing the intellectual property rights of those that want to introduce products and services into the member's economy with the expectation that those rights will be enforced.

These infringements on the patent monopoly find similarities in its sister bodies of law relating to other types of intellectual property. Exemptions from monopolies exist in trade mark law and copyright law. The United States has a Fair Use Exemption allowing non-copyright holders the right to copy works protected by another.[27]

In addition, depending on the country, trade mark rights are limited solely to the type of goods or services provided. Two identical marks can exist so long as they are associated with unrelated goods or services.[28] Across the board, monopolies are infringed or limited and it is because a monopoly interferes with the free flow of goods, services, and ideas that help grow an economy. These barriers also prevent those economies that fall behind in research and development any ability to catch up with other economies because the ability to make, use, and sell domestically and abroad becomes increasingly limited.

6.02 Is the Patent Monopoly Needed?

(a) In General

This portion of the chapter presents how the economy of a country is affected by the monopoly created by patents. To understand the diverging economic forces that are at play will set the stage to identify the opportunities available to use the inherent qualities of the various patent systems around the world to help foster growth of the economies of the least-developed countries.

---

26 Declaration on TRIPs Agreement and Public Health, WT/MIN (1) /DEC/2, at http://www.wto.org/english/thewto_e/minist_e/min01_e/mindecl_trips_e.htm.

27 17 United States Code, section 107.

28 "[J]ust because a trademark is arbitrary, if it is used only in a narrow area, others may use a similar mark for different goods without any trade mark infringement". *Sullivan v. CBS Corp.*, 385 F.3d 772, 776 (7th Cir., 2004), citing *McGraw-Edison Co. v. Walt Disney Prods.*, 787 F.2d 1163, 1170-71 (7th Cir., 1986).

It is the intention that the resulting opportunities presented herein will, in addition to fostering the growth of those economies that are weaker, provide opportunities for entities and countries outside the third and fourth worlds to experience growth through the growth of these economies. If a system is developed that creates a bar to the growth of those entities and countries that are well developed, the system will likely fail. Those countries and patentholders that have invested heavily in the patent system would surely prevent the upheaval of their expectations to claim their property rights.

Understanding that owning a patent is the result of spending a great deal of resources in research, development, and patent preparation and prosecution,[29] one appreciates why a patentholder does not want to acquiesce the very desirable position of owning the patent.

In mature industries, a patentable invention does not begin with an idea — it begins with a great number of ideas. Those ideas are distilled down to a few ideas, often based on great expenditures in research and/or development. Some ideas appear promising, but soon fall apart due to science — miscalculations in the technology — having the technology turn to already patented technology. In the pharmaceutical industry, side effects of a perfectly good drug may prevent the marketing of an otherwise promising product. This cost is great.

Some of the costs result from the preparation and prosecution of a patent application for the invention. The costs are high because they often involve taking time with a patent attorney to identify the invention, not in terms of how it is going to be sold, but in terms of how the innovation is different than what has been done before. These costs are proportionally higher in least developed countries.[30]

This process is time consuming for those involved with the development of the invention. In addition, fees paid to patent draftsmen, and the patent office in which the application is filed also add to the cost of the patent application. Once filed, the prosecution oftentimes adds as much or more cost as the preparation of the original filing because arguments need to be presented to the examiner reviewing the patent application to convince the examiner that what is claimed as an invention in the patent application is deserving of a patent and the associated monopoly.

---

29   Prosecution is the advocacy before a national or international patent office required by a patent applicant to further a patent application through the patent office to include a condition for allowance and the subsequent issuance into a patent.

30   The costs for patents are considered high, even in developed countries by those firms of the developed countries. See comments of Professor Alain Pompidou, President, EPO, at EPO Information Day, 30 March 2005, at http://events.european-patent-office.org/2005/0330/itre_comm/President_to_ITRE_en_red.pdf.

(b) Need for an Economy to Grow

Whether a society is run by a dictator, monarchy, prime minister, philosopher, king, or through a democratic body, the society can succeed as a capitalistic society only if there is growth in the economy.[31] Assuming this to be true, one must understand the economy to know whether it is growing. There are several facets to an economy; it includes industries, sectors of industries, populations, natural resources, products and services distinctive to a region, and borders.

Interestingly, borders to a country's economy now exist primarily for political reasons. In the past, borders were drawn by geography, cultures, tribes, and nations. When something affected one economy, it was typically limited largely to that economy, depending of course on what happened. As more economies began to rely on each other, economies acted more in unison.[32] Now, if a major tragedy befell one country, it affects the economies of its neighbors. As transportation became mainstream and affordable, geography had less of an impact in isolating an economy. As communication technologies and media permeate societies, understanding of currencies and products provided by those societies aids in the introduction of imports. Exports too are in more demand.

Since economies amalgamated into their current status, a "global economy", political events and decisions tighten the integration of nations and regions advancing the flow of technology and investment.[33]

While it is true that natural disasters, such as the Great Tsunami of 2004, affect the global economy in deep and long-lasting ways, those natural occurrences are no longer limited to just one country's economy. In addition, to have a global economy means more than just selling more products and services to more people. With a global economy comes a global responsibility.[34]

---

31 "Capitalism, on the other hand, grows by an ever expanding market, the innovation of new technology, and the ever-growing world population". Warner, *The Perpetual Wheel*, at http://people.ucsc.edu/~yle/papers/SocCapRep.html.

32 "The effect of globalization on business and industry has been profound. Innovations created in one country are routinely manufactured in a second country, often mobilizing capital from several countries . . . . No national economy is now an island. And every nation state is as interdependent as it is independent". Comments by Robin Cook at the Annual Meeting for the Trilateral Commission, at http://www.trilateral.org/annmtgs/trialog/trlgtxts/t55/coo.htm.

33 Maskus, "The Role of Intellectual Property Rights in Encouraging Foreign Direct Investment and Technology Transfer", *9 Duke J. Comp. & Int'l L.* 109, at p. 110 (1998).

34 "Those businesses most active in the globalizing economy must show the greatest global responsibility in stabilizing the global climate". Comments by Robin Cook at the Annual Meeting for the Trilateral Commission, at http://www.trilateral.org/annmtgs/trialog/trlgtxts/t55/coo.htm.

The fostering of lesser developed economies grows out of the communication lines that crisscross the forests, plains, and deserts of the lesser developed countries.

The peoples living in these lands now have access to images of lifestyles and wealth that are difficult to comprehend. Whole villages perceive huge riches, new products, and different life styles. With these new perceptions, first world countries must take on the responsibility to help these lesser developed economies into a more developed state to allow them the opportunity to achieve these new standards of livings if they so choose.

The stalling of the global economy in lesser developed countries is quite evident in Africa.[35] If a large investment in the economy of Africa was made earlier, there would not be the need for the massive investment required now to bring aid to their struggling economies.[36] The need for economic growth in the far reaches of the globe is similar.

If a large investment is made now to help jump-start the economies of lesser developed countries, less bridge-building will be needed later. Fewer people and societies will choose to not participate and will be able to participate in the global economy on terms with which they are comfortable. Those that are jealous of the haves will be confronted with the opportunity to change their condition in ways that they want through economic growth in themselves — and not through the violent means. In addition, through the additional growth, greater strides in the global economy will exist because whole cultures will be better educated, wealthier, and healthier. As more diversity enters the marketplace, more opportunities for choice, and growth through choice, exist. This will only contribute to the overall continued growth of the global economy.

(c) Why the Patent Monopoly Facilitates Economic Growth

Studies have attempted to qualify the effects of a patent system on a society. These studies have limited results due to the nature of the problem. When determining whether more money is being invested in research and development in countries with strong patent rights (and intellectual property rights in general), it is difficult to determine whether the strong patent rights result in more research and development investment or whether the strong research

---

35   Maskus, "The Role of Intellectual Property Rights in Encouraging Foreign Direct Investment and Technology Transfer", *9 Duke J. Int'l L.* 109, at p. 115 (1998).

36   "In every aspect of Africa's complex plight an ounce of prevention will be worth a ton of treatment. In recent years America gave a negligible $4m a year to Ethiopia to boost agricultural productivity, but then responded with around $500m in emergency food aid in 2003 when the crops failed", Sachs, "Doing the Sums on Africa", *The Economist*, at p. 19 (22 May 2004).

and development investment is sought to be protected by a society that inherently values strong research and development.[37]

Having said this, it is clear that several industries benefit from the patent system, the computer industry being one of those industries.[38] The economics of the benefits are less tenable, yet well recognized.[39]

Regardless of whether data can be empirically determined, the patent system provides a measure of confidence when investing in research and development and so that there will be a means to help gain a return on that investment. In the computer industry, so many advancements are made so rapidly that one would think that an investment in patent protection would be worthless due to the pendency of patent applications maintaining averages nearly 36 months.[40]

However, the advancements made are advancements to technologies that might last for years. The incremental improvements may render the principle or underlying technology "obsolete", but without the underlying technology, there would be no foundation for the improvements and, hence, there is value in protecting the underlying computer technology.[41]

---

37   Merrill, Levin and Myers, *A Patent System for the 21st Century*, at p. 40 (2004).

38   "One may legitimately question whether the impact of patenting on innovation and its consequences for social welfare are, on balance, positive outside of a handful of industries, such as pharmaceuticals, biotechnology, medical devices, and specialty chemicals where the benefits are well established, and possibly to a lesser extent, computers and auto parts", Merrill, Levin and Myers, *A Patent System for the 21st Century*, at p. 41 (2004).

39   "[It is] emphasized that from an economic point of view, it is very difficult to make normative statements or explicit comments on the economic development impact of [intellectual property rights] protection. Intellectual property rights are very difficult, hugely interrelated processes. Empirical work by economists on this topic has, so far, been mostly inconclusive, although there is some consensus that [intellectual property rights] protection have a moderately positive effect on international business (i.e., mainly international trade and foreign direct investment). One major difficulty economists face in evaluating the effects of [intellectual property rights] is that the causation between [intellectual property rights] and such international transactions often runs two-way. Moreover, [intellectual property rights] are an endogenous variable — not only with respect to the level of economic development, but also with respect to a country's culture". Intellectual Property Rights and Economic Development: An Agenda for The World Bank Group, at http://www.worldbank.org/html/fpd/technet/sem-sums/march5.htm.

40   In the United States Patent and Trade Mark Office, the pendency for technologies related to the communication arts is nearly 42 months. See http://www.uspto.gov/web/offices/com/annual/2004/060404_table4.html.

41   *Noll v. O.M. Scott & Sons Co.*, 467 F.2d. 295, at p. 301 (6th Cir., 1972), citing *Temco Elec. Co. v. Apco Mfg. Co.*, 275 U.S. 319, at p. 328, 48 S. Ct. 170, at p. 173 (1928). "It has long been recognized that an improver operating under a subsequently issued patent can not appropriate the basic patent of another and that the improver without a license is an infringer and may be sued as such".

The protection of computer technology helps advance the industry by allowing those that are in a position to invest in research and development to do so with an understanding that a larger firm will not be able to immediately take the fruits of its labor and compete against the firm developing the technology. Hewlett Packard did as much in the 1980s when they embarked on the development of the inkjet printer. Hewlett Packard made an enormous effort to patent every technology it developed in its research and development of the inkjet printer:

> Citizen engineers trying to develop print heads learned H-P had some 50 patents covering how ink travels through the head. 'It's like being in a maze: You go down this path and suddenly you're into an area that may infringe on their main patents and you must back up and start over'.[42]

As such, it became very difficult for the competition to obtain a foothold in the newest technology for the printer business. In addition, by the time the competition of Hewlett Packard did manage to produce a product that could compete with it, Hewlett Packard's "H-P" trade mark was almost synonymous with inkjet printers. For 20 years, patent protection has afforded Hewlett Packard with a commanding share of the printer business worldwide.

As a minor side note, the social welfare of a society that employs strong patent laws grows the economy in indirect ways. If there are strong patent laws, legal teams must be employed to assert and defend the rights of the parties. Legal teams often employ more than attorneys; they employ paralegals, secretaries, and clerks. These teams require resources such as offices, computers, copiers, paper, printers, electricity, and the like.

These components to the patent legal system aid in the development of an economy. The fees paid to patent offices in the filing and prosecuting of patents employs those that ensure the patent office runs properly. These minor, indirect ways in which monies are spent to protect inventions through the patent system help build and sustain an economy through employment and consumption. Thus, to say that the patent system financially overburdens a lesser-developed country[43] is to look only at direct costs while ignoring the benefits in the capital redistribution that occurs by having such infrastructures in place and funded.

---

42   *The Wall Street Journal*, at p. A6 (8 September 1994).

43   AIPPI, *AIPPI Contribution to the Patent Agenda*, at p. 9 (15 February 2002). "It is true that for some applicants the cost of obtaining patents is an obstacle, particularly for applicants who are individual inventors with scarce economic resources, such as some [small and medium-sized enterprises]. This problem is greater in developing countries, less-developed countries and countries in transition where the proportion of these kind of applicants is higher".

6.03   Patents and Their Obstructive Ways

(a) In General

As alluded to above, it is quite common for a technology to be protected through layers of patents based on layers of technological advances. One can appreciate that the development of products based on technology does not progress in a linear fashion. Research and development may go in several different directions. The resulting product may be vastly different from initial product concept.

This is common in the development of software and communications products used on the Internet. Unlike an automobile, physics is not a factor in many of the issues faced by those looking to sell a software product. This is less true for hardware, where size, shape, heat generation, and energy consumption are variables in design that may dictate certain parameters of the product design. However, once these issues are dealt with, the product may take on many different functions, some of which may not have even been contemplated at the initiation of a project due to other advances in technology made by others operating parallel to one another.

(b) Research and Development Factors

The entities that are developing products for use in the digital arena must consider the fact that others may have incurred large expenditures in research and development for a particular product. The product developed may never make it to the marketplace. Reasons for failure to make it to market include failure of technology, failure of packaging the technology in a viable end product, i.e., missing or unnecessary features, software bugs, and technology obsolescence before final development.[44]

Even if a product never made it to the marketplace, the investment in the technology developed has been incurred, and firms treat the research and development in a technology as an asset. In addition, if it is determined that the asset has value, regardless of whether the technology is to be incorporated into a product to be eventually sold, it may have value sufficient to warrant protection. If the decision is made to protect the investment, patents may be applied for and obtained on the non-marketed invention. A firm may do this for future freedom of practice.[45] Alternatively, a firm may patent non-marketed technology so that those that are successful in bringing the technology to market will have to seek licenses from the entity that first developed the technology.

---

44 Mangione, "Software Project Failure: The Reasons, The Costs", *CIO Information Network* (3 January 2003), at http://www.cioupdate.com/reports/article.php/1563701.

Whether or not a particular technology is included in a product currently in the marketplace it is very difficult for a firm, much less a firm domiciled in a lesser developed country, to be able to research and develop a product only to find out protection for that product or underlaying technology was obtained by another firm.[46] It is more difficult to discover this when the firm owning the patent(s) is not utilizing that technology because the lesser developed country firm may improperly believe it has no reason to investigate whether patents have issued on the non-marketed technology.

Adding to this problem is the fact that most firms filing patent applications do not file patent applications in lesser developed countries. For example, Microsoft owns more than 3,600 patents[47] that have issued in the United States. They own substantially fewer patents in lesser developed countries. Therefore, while a lesser developed country firm may have freedom to produce a product in the country in which it is domiciled, it may have difficulty when its product is transported to another country or region where patent protection may have been obtained. These products are referred to as "parallel imports".[48]

Because the nature of the digital divide relates to information and communication technologies, including software and hardware relating to communications, the Internet, and electronics, it is easy to understand that these types of products, especially software, are easily transportable. If the product were to cross

---

45   *Manildra Milling Corp. v. Ogilvie Mills*, 76 F.3d 1178, at p. 1183 (Fed. Cir., 1996). "The freedom to practice an invention without fear of suit by the patentee is a valuable commercial benefit. By removing the potential threat of the patentee instituting an infringement action, the competitor necessarily alters the patentee's subsequent behavior to his benefit".

46   Nottenburg, Pardey, and Wright, "Accessing Other People's Technology: Do Non-Profit Agencies Need It? How to Obtain It", Environment and Production Technology Division, International Food Policy Research Institute, *Discussion Paper Number 79*, at p. 34 (September 2001). "But it would be hazardous to assume general freedom to operate; mistakes could result in catastrophic legal liability. To reliably implement a strategy of obtaining intellectual property only where necessary, those that make research commitments must have access to adequate information on patent rights, and to expert legal counsel. Such access is not widely available at present on an international basis, and does not exist for most [lesser developed country] researchers and research institutions".

47   Electronic search for "Microsoft" on the website www.uspto.gov on 15 January 2005. No other entity name was searched so the number of patents owned my Microsoft Corporation could be larger, depending on the corporate structure(s) employed thereby.

48   Maskus, "Parallel Imports in Pharmaceuticals: Implications for Competition and Pricing in Developing Countries", Final Report to the World Intellectual Property Organization (April 2001). "Parallel imports . . . are goods produced genuinely under protection of a trademark, patent or copyright, placed into circulation in one market, and then imported into a second market without the authorization of the local owner of the intellectual property right".

into a country that has a patent covering some or all of the technology in the product, the value of the product is reduced. If a lesser developed country firm cannot export its products, the economy of the lesser developed country cannot grow as much as it could have if the product did not infringe any patent in any country, thus allowing it to be freely exported and enjoy a balanced economy.[49]

(c) Exportation of Information and Communication Technology Products

The exportation of a product relating to information and communication technologies is a concern that should be addressed in earnest. An economy can grow when it exports to other countries.[50] The money that is infused into the economy of the lesser developed country will help the lesser developed country lose its lesser developed status so that it can reinvest the capital received from other economies into its own so that more can be produced and more can be consumed. Exportation of products relating to information and communication technologies is such a concern because it is possible to export with little infrastructure investment.

In other words, a lesser developed country firm could export products with minimal investment due to the nature of many of the products utilized in the digital economy. A creator of software could be uplinked and downloaded anywhere there is Internet access.[51] The creator need only a computer to create the software and obtain access to the Internet to distribute it. Any lesser developed country firm with access to the Internet could ship software anywhere in the world. There would not have to be warehousing, trucking, inventorying, and the like.

Much of the hardware used in the digital economy is small, which further facilitates the exportation of those products. Investments in huge warehouses, factory equipment, inventory tracking systems, and transportation via any means is not necessary. In short, the business model of any lesser developed country firm attempting to build a business in the digital economy should and must include steps to promote the exportation of its products to other nations to infiltrate as many economies as possible to reach as many consumers as possible.

Therefore, it becomes imperative for lesser developed country firms to have the freedom to export products in a seamless fashion, meaning that the

---

49 Friedman and Friedman, "The Case for Free Trade", *Hoover Digest*, Number 4 (1997).

50 Maskus, "The Role of Intellectual Property Rights in Encouraging Foreign Direct Investment and Technology Transfer", *9 Duke J. Comp. & Int'l L.* 109, at p. 112 (1998).

51 Internet access is not an assumption, as it is very much a problem with lesser developed country firms and their ability to operate in the digital economy.

lesser developed country firm can be free to produce a product and sell that version of the product anywhere in the world, allowing that firm to maximize its revenue collection. It is obvious that a lesser developed country firm would be hindered and its ability to generate revenue diminished should it be required to develop different versions of a product for different nations based on the position patentholders may have in those various nations.

6.04   How to Treat Patents, Patent Owners, and Infringers from Lesser Developed Countries

(a) In General

Patents have diverging effects on the economies in which they issue. On the one hand, they promote the dissemination of information relating to science and manufacture. This grows the societal pool of information, which may be used to grow an economy by the development of new products and services.[52] On the other hand, however, patents have a deleterious effect on an economy because they prevent those that may be able to develop a competitive product from entering the marketplace with that product because to do so would be an infringement of the patent. Monopolies interfere with the ability of others that want to compete from entering the marketplace.

In the case of a patent, potential competitors with new and possibly better ideas cannot do so for the legal ramifications of another owning the patent rights to the underlying technology. In the situation where there is no patent, a monopoly results from having a large percentage, more than 60 per cent, of the sales associated with the product or service. This allows the monopoly holder the ability to use its shelf-space and pricing to prevent others from competing successfully with newer products and services.

In either instance, the monopoly prevents the advancement of a society by inhibiting the ability to purchase newer, better, and/or cheaper products, creating additional jobs, and allowing the dominant player in the product or service the ability to rest on its laurels. The dominant player will not be driven to reinvest in its product or service, which further stymies the advancement of technology.

---

52   *Grant v. Raymond*, 31 U.S. 218, at p. 247 (U.S., 1832) "The third section requires, as preliminary to a patent, a correct specification and description of the thing discovered. This is necessary in order to give the public, after the privilege shall expire, the advantage for which the privilege is allowed, and is the foundation of the power to issue the patent".

(b) Facilitating Patent Infringers from Lesser Developed Countries

Given it is a desire for the global economy to foster development of the global economy from all sectors and all economies, something must be done to facilitate the ability for patent infringers from lesser developed countries to enter the global economy with some degree of freedom. It might be questioned why anyone should be permitted to infringe a patent. As stated above, patentholders will be less likely to invest in new technologies if they will not be able to enjoy the benefits of a monopoly; a monopoly that ensures them the ability to obtain a return on their investment in the research and development of the new technology.[53]

With firms from lesser developed countries, there are obviously limited funds for investment in the development of products. There are also limitations in the surrounding infrastructure that supports the development of technology. Raw materials may be limited. Research facilities are limited and may be too difficult to reach. Research resources also may be limited, especially when there are more life-threatening issues to which government funds are being directed.

This limits the ability of these lesser developed country firms from investigating whether they will infringe on the rights of others.[54] Those resources may be spent on developing some of the necessary business components of providing a successful product in the global economy. For example, resources which, in a firm founded in a developed country, could be earmarked for research and development, may need to be spent on packaging, translations of user manuals, development of distribution networks, or facilities to protect inventory. The list is large and these are but a few of the possible uses for funds that would not be needed to be spent on freedom to practice studies in multiple countries.

Another reason for allowing a lesser developed country firm to infringe the patent rights of another is that a lesser developed country firm could spend less of their resources on unproven products. If a product is successful in the marketplace, a lesser developed country firm may be able to capitalize on its success and develop similar products that also may be successful. For a lesser developed country firm to miscalculate on the needs of the marketplace and spend its resources on the development of products that will not be well received can be catastrophic for a lesser developed country firm and the lesser developed country in which it is domiciled.

---

53 Bagchi, "Compulsory Licensing and the Duty of Good Faith in TRIPS", *55 Stan. L. Rev.* 1529, at p. 1531 (May 2003).

54 Nottenburg, Pardey and Wright, "Accessing Other People's Technology: Do Non-Profit Agencies Need It? How to Obtain It", Environment and Production Technology Division, International Food Policy Research Institute, *Discussion Paper Number 79*, p. 34 (September 2001).

It is difficult to appreciate how a lesser developed country firm could be able to pirate ideas and patented technology while still having the goal of a viable global economy in our sights. However, it is quite reasonable to suggest that such actions will result in a stronger global economy because some products produced by lesser developed country firms may introduce lesser developed country markets to the products provided by the patentholder.[55] In fact, a more competitive marketplace would exist in the economies in which the lesser developed country firm is permitted to infringe with the introduction of its products.

6.05   Models for Solving the Patent Problem

(a) In General

To say that a lesser developed country firm could permissively infringe any patent in the name of growing a sector of the global economy without any limitations would be cavalier. Limitations have been a part of the compulsory license since the Paris Convention.[56] Limitations have been a part of the compulsory license since the Paris Convention.[57] Unbound, it would greatly inhibit the desire of those participating in the research and development of products incorporating information and communication technologies.[58]

This is especially true for these product and service sectors because information and communication technologies may so readily be transported to nations having patents issued that cover them. In fact, it would be safe to say that such a wholesale and unencumbered permissive infringement would never be accepted by the governments of the developed countries.

---

55   The "patentholder" is considered to be the firm that owns the patent and/or the rights to manufacture product, or sell services that would be covered by the patent(s). Therefore, the patentholder may be a licensee and not the owner of the patent. In some instances, this will change who may bring suit for patent infringement.

56   Article 5 of the Paris Convention for the Protection of Industrial Property, March 1883, as last revised at Stockholm, July 1967 and as amended September 1979, 828 U.N.T.S. 305 [hereinafter Paris Convention].

57   Article 5 of the Paris Convention for the Protection of Industrial Property, March 1883, as last revised at Stockholm , July 1967 and as amended September 1979, 828 U.N.T.S. 305 [hereinafter Paris Convention].

58   Any research and development that does occur may never be implemented for fear of its use by its competitors. Black, "The Cure for Deadly Patent Practices: Preventing Technology Suppression and Patent Shelving in the Life Sciences", 14 Alb. L.J. Sci. & Tech. 397, at p. 398 (2004) "Companies will suppress new technology if the technology threatens to disrupt the profits in a market. Under most circumstances, the delay of public access only costs the consumer money or inconvenience".

(b) Limitations on Infringement

A model of limitations must be developed to define the relationship between patentholders and the lesser developed country firms that wish to obtain the permissions to infringe information and communication technologies patents. A model of limitations must be used for a couple of reasons. The first reason a model of limitations is desirable is to allow the patentholders that made the investment in the research and development, which eventually resulted in the patent(s), to maintain the ability to seek a return on its investment in the information and communication technologies that it patented.

This is a basic tenet[59] that should never be overlooked when contemplating the consideration of a compulsory license scheme for information and communications technologies. In other words, any system that prevents any return on an investment by the firm that makes the investment will surely fail. If it is known that there will be little opportunity for a return, a firm will forego any investment in the technology, information, and communication technologies or otherwise.

While it is desirable to have a lesser developed country firm have the ability to help foster economic growth in its sector of the global economy, it cannot be done to the detriment of those firms that are based in developed countries. This would be ill-received and, if instituted, would introduce a higher level of risk in the success of those patentholders. This would, in turn, adversely affect those developed countries to a level that would offset any benefit gained by having a lesser developed country firm enter the marketplace successfully.

A second reason to have limitations on the ability of a lesser developed country firm to permissively infringe a patent or group of patents is the resulting development associated with the permission. It is expected that as a lesser developed country firm becomes more successful, partly due to its permissive infringement, it will have enough resources to develop technologies, products and/or services that will be able to be both successful in the marketplace, and non-infringing.[60]

---

59   Article 30 of the TRIPs Agreement provides: "Members may provide limited exception to the exclusive rights conferred by a patent, provided that such exceptions do not unreasonably conflict with a normal exploitation of the patent and do not unreasonably prejudice the legitimate interests of the patent owner, taking account of the legitimate interests of third parties".

60   This limitation in time seems to be similar to that which is found in article 31(c) of the TRIPs Agreement. However, the reasoning has less to do with urgent matters and national emergencies, as set forth in article 31(b) of the TRIPs Agreement, and more to do with fostering a growth in a lesser developed country.

Once a lesser developed country firm can successfully wean itself off technology, products, and services that are patented by another, the lesser developed country firm may be able to invest in protecting its own advancements in and to the technology. This would provide an additional income stream of royalty payments in addition to the sale of products and service, and further the lesser developed country firm and the lesser developed country toward its goal of leaving its status as a lesser developed country.[61]

Yet another reason for limiting the rights of lesser developed country firms is to have successful lesser developed country firms develop their own technology which they will want to protect.[62] This protection will require the enforcement of intellectual property laws. The desire will be to strengthen the intellectual property laws and enforce them so that there will be more certainty in the marketplace as the lesser developed countries enter the global economy.

(c) First Selected Model

In the United States, there has been an acknowledgement that some firms have a greater difficulty participating in the market than others. Typically, those that are successful have largely been operating in the business sector for a long period of time. These firms are owned and operated by those that are considered to be a part of the majority in the United States.

Minorities have made inroads into a business sector, but it appears to take longer before a minority-owned business can become successful. This breeds a discontentment and social unrest undesirable on many levels, the least of which is an economic level.

To overcome this perception and reality, and to further those firms owned and operated by the disadvantaged, there is a network of federal laws[63] and programs,[64] as well as state laws[65] and programs.[66] within the United States providing benefits to those that operate their respective firms by purchasing

---

61 This desire is reflected in the objectives of the TRIPs Agreement, which are ". . . the promotion of technological innovation and to the transfer and dissemination of technology, to the mutual advantage of producers and users of technological knowledge and in a manner conducive to social and economic welfare, . . .". TRIPs Agreement, article 7.

62 Again, this is similar to the intent of the TRIPs Agreement. Maskus, "Intellectual Property Challenges for Developing Countries: An Economic Perspective", *2001 U. Ill. L. Rev.* 457 (2001).

63 49 Code of Federal Regulations, Part 26.

64 National Minority Supplier Development Council, at www.nmsdcus.org.

65 Oregon State Rules, section 200.

66 Minnesota Minority Business Development Council, at http://www.mmbdc.org.

the goods and services they need from an entity that has been certified as a disadvantaged or minority business enterprise. A firm must prove its status as a minority business enterprise. Once proven, it can engage in contractual relationships at preferred terms to help it grow.

A system for lesser developed country firms could be developed that would mirror the minority business enterprise laws of the United States. This system, hereinafter referred to as a lesser developed country Patent Infringement Permissive Program, provides a vehicle for lesser developed country firms to register for a status that would allow them to obtain permissions to infringe patents so that such firms could enter into a particular technological sector in the marketplace of the global economy.

A comprehensive study of various lesser developed countries and technology sectors could clarify which lesser developed country firms would be eligible to participate in the lesser developed country Patent Infringement Permissive Program. The eligibility of lesser developed country firms would depend on the type of technology or technologies they would implement under the program and the lesser developed country in which it is domiciled. The technology would be studied to determine if it were appropriate to foster the development of the technology in the lesser developed country in which the lesser developed country firm is domiciled.

Factors to determine such activity include how the technology can be manufactured, sold, and exported. This would be important because if the marginal gain to an economy is trivial, the comparative gain may not be worth the detriment to the patentholder by losing its monopoly for the technology.

The lesser developed country Patent Infringement Permissive Program would periodically review the status of the lesser developed country firm. Participation in the lesser developed country Patent Infringement Permissive Program by a firm could be terminated over time based on the success in fostering economic growth in the lesser developed country.

By generating revenue, the lesser developed country firm participating in the Program would eventually be able to reinvest the revenue back into the lesser developed country firm to develop products that would not be infringing any other patent. In this manner, the lesser developed country firm may slowly be able to move away from the manufacture and sale of infringing products while still operating as a viable and contributing firm in the economy to which it is domiciled.

While this model for reducing the Digital Divide is based on the lesser developed country firm, it also could be based on the lesser developed country. In this alternative model, a particular lesser developed country would be able to obtain a set number of permissions. As lesser developed country firms domiciled within that lesser developed country seek permission to infringe a patent, it would seek the permission through its home government. The lesser developed country might be able to foster the growth of industry therein by clustering its permissions around a particular industry it may deem important for its own economy. The lesser-developed country could act as a clearinghouse to obtain the necessary certificates to facilitate the growth of a desired industry.[67]

For information and communication technologies, it is quite possible that the development of a technology and the resulting product or service would infringe several patents should the product or service reach the countries in which these patents have been issued. The weave of studies to determine what is and what is not being infringed would likely bankrupt a lesser developed country firm. In the latter model, where the lesser developed country government obtains the permissions, the lesser developed country government takes on the role of a clearing house. It clears the way for a lesser developed country firm to step in and make a product that would read on several patents.

The Lesser Developed Country Patent Infringement Permissive Program may be too decentralized to effectively work. It would seem that there is a large opportunity for the governments of the various parties to weigh in on each opportunity sought by a lesser developed country firm. Such governmental involvement will most probably add too much time to the process and, with the information and communication technologies advancing rapidly, opportunities would be lost in bureaucracy.

(d) Second Selected Model

(i) In General

Nature of Compulsory License　　The compulsory license was described above. It is a device implemented by many countries that enables a particular country to have its economy benefit from the manufacture, use, and/or sale of patented technology. The country typically must wait for a predetermined period of time before it can issue a compulsory license. The time period is used to prove an underutilization of the patent, a concept which dates back to the Paris Convention.[68] The TRIPs Agreement also has provisions for a compulsory license;[69] however, it may limited to situations that catastrophic in nature.[70]

67　The lesser developed country would act in a manner similar to the Kansai Patent Center. Kukkonen, "The Use of a Patent Licensing Center as an Intermediary for Facilitating the Licensing of Commercially Viable, Unused Patents", 3 *Va. J.L. & Tech* 10 (Fall 1998).

68　Paris Convention, article 5(A)(4).

69　TRIPs Agreement, article 31.

70　TRIPs Agreement, article 31(b).

This time period is designed to give the patentholder an opportunity to enter the economy with the particular patented technology. After the time period, typically three to five years, it will authorize the licensing of the patent to a third party posed to market the product in the country.

The compulsory license is a device that seems worthy. The people of a particular country have the freedom to help their economy, and the country is able to keep up with developed countries by having every technology available to the marketplace at its disposal. Yet, contrary to the well-intentioned legislation, the compulsory license is not in wide use. It is believed that China has yet to grant a compulsory license to a third party.[71] There are two possible reasons for this.

Lack of Need to Seek Compulsory License One explanation for the lack of activity with compulsory licenses is simply that firms do not need to seek compulsory licenses. Typically, the countries in which a compulsory license may come into play are lesser developed countries that are on the cusp of bettering their economies. In this instance, the patentholder may believe there is enough future growth opportunities in the country that warrants potential protection of its technological development for the 20-year period, but does not believe there is enough current economic potential to warrant an immediate investment in the country.

Thus, while it will patent its technology in that lesser developed country, it will not produce or import it because the profit margins do not justify this investment. In these countries, one could make the generalization that the laws regarding intellectual property are lacking in quality and attention. More specifically, a country that is just developing a growth-oriented economy may have little on the legislative books relating to intellectual property.[72] In addition, even if a country has a substantial body of law regarding intellectual property, and in particular patents, it may have little resources to enforce those laws.

This leaves lesser-developed-country firms within such a country with a choice. A lesser developed country firm looking to market a patented technology may seek a license from the patentholder; it may seek a compulsory

---

71 A statement was made by Maria C. H. Lin, an expert on Chinese intellectual property, during the Patent Law Day Conference 2004, Michigan State University College of Law, that she was not aware of China issuing a single compulsory license. Currently, there are no accessible public channels for individuals to reach information about the issuance of compulsory licenses in China. A telephone call was placed in February 2005 directly with the State Intellectual Property Office (SIPO) of China wherein it was stated that there have been no compulsory licenses issued in China.

72 Maskus, "Intellectual Property Challenges for Developing Countries: An Economic Perspective", *2001 U. Ill. L. Rev.* 457 (2001).

license should the patentholder decline to entertain a license; or it may ignore the patent completely. Economically, the best choice for the third party may be the latter of those described above. If the patentholder has no intention on being active in the country's economy, and has little or no concern for parallel imports it may chose to ignore such activity.

If the patentholder chooses to ignore the infringing activity, there is no need for the third party to request a compulsory license. Other than the resulting economic gains, the government has no stake in the compulsory license, so there is no incentive to police such activities. If the patentholder does recognize the infringement and notifies the country of the infringing activity, there is again little incentive to enforce the compulsory license law because to do so would further hinder the fragile economy the government is trying so hard to nurture.

Global Economy Conflicts   Another reason why so little economic activity is based on a compulsory license is dictated by the very conflict between countries and the global nature of the economy. Each country promulgates its own laws and, absent a treaty between countries, does not recognize the laws of any other country. This is why each country has a patent system and issues its own patents. While the third party may be able to obtain a compulsory license in the country in which it is currently domiciled or operating, the compulsory license only extends to the borders of the country in which the government issues the compulsory license.

If a non-patentholder third party is looking to develop a product or service, it would look for alternatives to the patented technology so that it could sell the same product or service in other countries. In the case of information and communication technologies, which are highly mobile technologies in the sense that a software package can operate easily anywhere and can be distributed via the Internet, a compulsory license would provide little advantage. The third party could enjoy the market in one country, but its permission is only for that particular country.

Exporting the technology to other countries would expose the third party to patent infringement claims once the technology crossed a border into another country where a compulsory license has not been obtained or is not available because the country does not recognize it or because the patentholder is operating in the country. Therefore, the compulsory license in its current form is not an acceptable model in which to encourage entities to invest in the economies of lesser developed countries because each country has its own laws on parallel imports and the exhaustion of intellectual property rights.[73]

---

73   Maskus and Chen, "Vertical Price Control and Parallel Imports: Theory and Evidence", at p. 5, at http://wbln0018.worldbank.org/research/workpapers.nsf/0/c36b5a43b69c9 c47852569690050bf33/ $FILE/wps2461.pdf.

(ii) Benefits from Compulsory Licensing

The compulsory license model for encouraging economic growth is not entirely improper. There are four accepted reasons for issuing compulsory licenses with the first relating to the exploitation of the patented technology.[74] The compulsory license could spark economic growth in a lesser developed country if one was sought by a third party domiciled in the lesser developed country. To a lesser extent, the economy would experience growth if a third party entity, domiciled outside the lesser developed country, were to invest in the economy of the lesser developed country by promoting its product therein.

In the case of information and communication technologies, the compulsory license would, however, be much more effective if it represented a licensing scheme that reflected the international flavor of the global economy and the borderless flavor of the information and communication technologies.

(iii) Required Modifications in Compulsory Licensing

In General   The compulsory license needs to be modified. It needs to be an international vehicle. To bridge the Digital Divide and give the ability of growing digital economies to lesser developed countries, the lesser developed country firms need to directly engage the patentholder and obtain the right to place products and services in the marketplace that are capable of being bought and sold anywhere in the world.

For a patentholder to provide anything less than a regional or global license is providing a handicap to the third-party licensee which may eventually minimize the contribution to the economy of the lesser developed country by the lesser developed country firm. After all, the value of information and communication technologies is greatly reduced if it can only be used in those countries in which no patent exists or only in the country in which the compulsory license was issued.

There are three necessary components to a modified compulsory license that would allow the third party to help the economy of the lesser developed country in which it is domiciled and to further reduce the digital divide between those better developed countries and the lesser developed countries. It is believed that the three components are equally vital to the success of the modified compulsory license as a device that is to help the lesser developed countries enter the digital age and compete with the better developed countries. The three components are:

1. The modified compulsory license should be a regional, if not global, in scope;

---

74   Baca, "Compulsory Patent Licensing in Mexico in the 1990s: The Aftermath of NAFTA and the 1991 Industrial Property Law", *IDEA The Journal of Law and Technology*, at p. 184 (1994).

2. It must be limited, either temporally or in terms of output; and

3. It must be exclusive of terms relating to copyright infringement.

This is because having all three components will further the overall desire to have whole economies enter the Digital Age without having to sacrifice the capitalistic nature of the economy to the point where the support for the lesser developed country and its economy is falsely supported and doomed for subsequent failure.

International Scope   A key factor to a modified compulsory license is that it must be international in scope. For a lesser developed country firm to be as competitive as possible in a licensing arrangement, with a product or service that incorporates information and communication technologies, Internet, or electronics fields, it must be able to be marketed across the boundaries of countries. Many of these products are portable and must be free of encumbrances should the purchaser travel. Other products may engage in activity outside the lesser developed country without the lesser developed country firm ever leaving home.

Another reason why the modified compulsory license needs to be international in scope is a result of the recent trends in labor. With the advances in technology and transportation efficiencies, jobs in manufacturing continue to move around the globe to markets that have inexpensive work forces.[75] If a lesser developed country firm finds itself with an expensive work force, it might move production of an electronic good to another country. If their compulsory license is not international, limitations on where the manufacturing process can be moved are limited. In addition, such limitations could hinder the lesser developed country firm's ability to grow and contribute to the global economy.

More important than lower job costs is the cost of manufacturing. The production of products and services depending on information and communication technologies have dropped in price. Modern factories, robots, and automation have forced the costs of production down. Staying competitive in these industries has resulted in the savings in production, which are passed on to the consumer. Therefore, prices in products and services have dropped drastically.

To stay as competitive as the competition, many firms that have less efficient manufacturing facilities meet the downward price pressures by reducing the profit margin in their products and services. Regardless of the patent position that a firm may enjoy, the competition oftentimes has a similar product that

---

75   Gumpert, "An Atlas of Offshore Outsourcing", *Business Week Online* (18 February 2004), at http://www.businessweek.com/smallbiz/content/feb2004/ sb20040218_6502.htm.

may avoid the patents owned by the firm. So, the firm must compete in pricing of the product or service. In situations where the margin of profits is so small, the way a firm succeeds is by growing its purchasing class.

In some markets, that means selling to everyone in a particular class within a country. In other markets, it requires sales to so many entities, firms, or people that no single country can satisfy the requirements of the firm, especially when the state is a lesser-developed country. Sales across a country's borders become a necessity, and this becomes a driving force in why the value of any compulsory license will be measured by its freedoms to cross those borders to reach as many consumers as possible.

In short, the modified compulsory license must be an international document allowing the lesser developed country firm to reach as many consumers as possible so that the lesser developed country firm will not fail for having prices too high. If the lesser developed country firm cannot sell its products and services globally, it cannot compete with the patentholder due to the price elevation by having only one nation's population to which the lesser developed country firm can sell.

The third reason why the modified compulsory license needs to be international in geographic scope is because the lesser developed country firm cannot truly become a viable entity unless it can compete side-by-side with the patentholder. Most patentholders would find this proposal adverse to their interests, but the competition is what capitalistic societies thrive on — competition is the life blood of the capitalistic society. It is this competition that drives consumers to the marketplace to purchase better products and services and more competitive pricing.

The competition will help teach the lesser developed country firm how it needs to compete in an unrestrained market. The marketplace will teach the lesser developed country firm lessons that will help grow the lesser-developed country firm and help it compete better. The products and services provided by the lesser developed country firm will become better over a shorter period of time, or the lesser developed country firm will be limited to undesirable markets of limited growth potential. The patentholder will learn to be more competitive as well. The licensing terms will include some royalty scheme so that the patentholder will always have a slight edge over the lesser developed country firm representative of recognition of its contribution to the world's information and knowledge.

Impact of Compulsory License   Further to this point, it would be the hope that as the lesser-developed country firm matures, it will not require the assistance of a modified compulsory license, and the time under the modified compulsory license in which it competes in some or all geographic markets against a few competitors will teach the lesser-developed country firm about producing efficiently and leanly and bringing to the consumer something for which the consumer is looking. Mere production capacity is no insurance of success in any manufacturing process.

One need only look to the difficulties and loss in market share that the automotive manufactures in Detroit have experienced to understand that manufacturing is an ongoing discipline that cannot be thrust on a lesser developed country firm with the expectation that, after a time of enjoying protected market share, it will be able to thrive and succeed in a completely free marketplace. Many factors, including quality, perception, marketing, and design, all must be dealt with to have a successful product rollout. Hence, the sooner the lesser-developed country firm experiences a competitive marketplace, the sooner it will develop into a firm that requires no assistance to contribute to the global economy.

(e) Limitations on Permissive Patent Infringement

(i) In General

If left unchecked, the modified compulsory license could possibly do more harm to the global economy than help it. A patentholder unexpectedly finding itself in competition with its own product in a global sense may expose itself to failure with regard to that product. The exposure could be so significant that the patentholder may fail as a result of the competition.

Failure of a patentholder to benefit a lesser developed country firm is not a result that is desired because, simply put, it is the goal of the modified compulsory license to bring more stability into the global economy and not disrupt the current status of the global economy. It may be that a failed patentholder in a developed country can be more easily absorbed into the global economy but, depending on the size of the patentholder, this may not be the case.

Therefore, some limitations should be put placed on a lesser developed country firm and the modified compulsory license to satisfy those that become patentholders so that they will not be undermined by the modified compulsory license.[76] Assuming other economic factors do not come into play, a patentholder should always be able to enjoy a return on its investment in the research and development of a particular product or service, regardless of whether a lesser developed country firm chooses to attempt to market similar products and/or services which an independent claim of a patent reads thereon.[77] Stability and

---

76   Limitations are expected in compulsory license arrangements. see the Paris Convention, article 5, where limitations were presented for compulsory licenses.

77   A claim of a patent "reads on" a product or service when all of the elements and limitations of an independent claim are found in the product or service. Infringement occurs when the product or service reads on independent claims of the patent. If the patent discloses the product, but the claims do not read on the product or service, there is no infringement.

growth in the global economy, especially with lesser developed countries and the economy associated with the Digital Age, cannot come at the price of some established patentholders.

(f) Modified Compulsory License — Exclusive or Non-Exclusive

(i) In General

Once a lesser developed country firm decides to enter into a particular market with a product or service based on a patented technology, it may produce the product or provide the service so long as there is no patent in any of the countries in which the lesser developed country firm is operating.

In the arena of information and communication technologies, the goods and services may quickly cross into countries where patents exist. Once this occurs, an infringement of the patent or patents occurs.

At this point, the lesser developed country firm may be an infringer of the patent(s) of the patentholder. The lesser developed country firm is an infringer if it is directly responsible for the exportation of the product or service into the country. Regardless of whether the lesser developed country firm is responsible or not, it will have to make the decision on whether to clear the way for the distribution of the goods in that country.

Should the lesser developed country firm make the decision to work for greater proliferation of its goods into that and potentially other countries, it will have to seek permission via a license from the patentholder or look to change the product to avoid infringement of the patents that include claims that read on the goods. Should the process determine that a design around[78] is not possible, it must look to the patentholder to negotiate a license arrangement therewith.[79]

(ii) Standard Agreement

There is always the possibility that the relationship between the lesser developed country firm and the patentholder can be resolved with the standard compulsory license arrangement should the legislation in the country to which the products are flowing provide for this. In this situation, the patentholder is obliged to enter into a license agreement with the lesser

---

78 A "design around" is where an entity specifically designs a product or service that does not infringe the claims of a patent by focusing on what the patent does claim and purposefully designing the product around or outside the scope of coverage provided by the patent so the patent does not read on the product or service.

79 Article 31(b) of the TRIPs Agreement requires the potential licensee to seek a voluntary license prior to taking steps which will result in a compulsory license relationship.

developed country firm. There are no third-party entanglements because the compulsory license relationship is designed to work in the situation where there is no activity regarding the patent position of the patentholder in the that country. While it is understood that the compulsory license is designed to be implemented in the situation where there exists no activity in the country regarding the patent, the compulsory license will be non-exclusive allowing subsequent parties to enter the market.[80]

One of the requirements allowing a lesser developed country firm to force the compulsory license on the patentholder is inactivity on the part of the patentholder in that particular country.[81] But for the rights to the patent, the patentholder has no interest in the country or its economy. As stated above, this relationship is not, however, a compelling one for the lesser developed country firm. The lesser developed country firm will have only the right to operate within that country, which is difficult for the lesser developed country firm when the products and services relate to information and communication technologies and are so easily transportable across a country's boundaries.

The standard compulsory license relationship may work for a nascent lesser developed country firm. In fact, the relationship may satisfy such a lesser developed country firm for a period of time. After a period of time, the lesser developed country firm may require growth that requires it to consider exporting its licensed technology. It certainly will be in the best interest of the host country's economy that the lesser developed country firm export the products.[82]

As the country has more lesser developed country firms exporting products, its economy grows and the standard of living improves. The problem with this situation is that the lesser developed country firm may have no rights other than other countries outside its country where no patents have issued or compulsory licenses are available.[83] Hence, the lesser developed country firm may be prevented from exporting its product to significant markets due to the patent position held by the one or more patentholders in other countries.

---

80   Paris Convention, article 5; TRIPs Agreement, article 31(d).

81   Paris Convention, article 5.

82   Maskus, "The Role of Intellectual Property Rights in Encouraging Foreign Direct Investment and Technology Transfer", 9 *Duke J. Comp. & Int'l L.* 109, at p. 112 (1998).

83   One could argue that a lesser developed country firm could export product produced pursuant to a compulsory license into countries which have laws permitting parallel imports. It could be argued that the product is produced legitimately under authority of law and, hence, not infringing or counterfeit product.

(iii) Other Agreement Options

In General   Once a lesser developed country firm determines that the standard compulsory license, if available, is not going to suit its needs due to the technology, or the requirements for growth and export, the lesser developed country firm needs to see what options it has in the region or in terms of global expansion. Should the lesser developed country firm require a license, and one is economically available, the lesser developed country firm need merely strike a bargain with the patentholder or patentholders, allowing it the expansion it needs to flourish in the digital economy.

The economy of the lesser developed country will benefit by the influx of funds as the lesser developed country firm competes in new markets. The lesser developed country, the region surrounding the lesser developed country, and the lesser developed country firm all become more stable and the global economy grows.

The scenario above is rather simplistic and rarely occurs. The reason it rarely occurs is mainly due to the fact that patentholders in the information and communication technologies space all tend to manufacture their inventions, which makes it difficult to enter into licensing relationships with the patentholder. Therefore, it is unrealistic to think a lesser developed country firm can grow in a global sense with a simple license avoiding the only ownership-related encumbrance. The patentholder is surely going to desire the monopoly in the countries to which it holds a patent.

After all, the patentholder bargained with the government and disclosed its new technology hold a monopoly in the countries of its desire. The patentholder is not going to appreciate the competition it must face, even when it receives a royalty from the lesser developed country firm, if its marketing strategy was based on a monopoly. If the modified compulsory license is going to be successful, lesser developed country rights will need to be phased into existence in such a manner as to allow patentholders to adjust the rationale for patents and the expected return on the investment for obtaining patents. This phase-in period can be temporal or geographic.

Phasing a patentholder into the concept of having to relinquish its monopoly in one or more countries may be a tall order, given that this particular technology sector is such a fast moving one. It would not benefit the lesser developed country firm at all to make it wait for a period of time so that the patentholder could adjust its operations and business model to take into account the fact that another will be in the same space with the same product.

Geographic Phase-In   It is suggested that any phase-in of a lesser developed country firm into the marketplace currently occupied by a patentholder be done geographically and not temporally. Obviously, the lesser developed country firm could enter markets with no legal ramifications where the patentholder does not have a patent position.

After those markets are saturated with as much product as the economy can handle, then the lesser developed country firm can "announce" its need to enter regions and countries where the patentholder currently holds a legal monopoly. In addition, this invasion into monopolistic regions can be done systematically over time if so required as long as both the patentholder and the lesser developed country firm are not unduly prejudiced.

There are at least two benefits for temporarily preventing the lesser developed country firm from selling its product globally when the patentholder is doing so well. In the first instance, it provides a buffer to the patentholder so that it can adjust to the *entrée* of the lesser developed country firm into its domain. In the economies of the twenty-first century, a patentholder will not be able to sustain competition for identical or similar product, if it is not planned for at the outset. Allowing the patentholder this time to adjust will maintain the patentholder in a condition as stable as it was prior to the emergence of the lesser developed country firm.

Additionally, the prohibition of a lesser-developed country firm from immediately attempting to reach the entire global economy at once will force it into a growth scheme that is gradual, if not systematic. The lesser developed country firm will learn through gradual growth how to deal with the issues that confront a firm as it grows through each stage of development. By providing a system wherein the growth is required to be systematic and gradual, the lesser developed country firm will have a greater chance at growing in stability as well as revenue.

Obviously, there are situations where more rapid growth of a lesser developed country firm may be required. If such a situation were to exist, additional considerations must be taken into account. However, first and foremost, the stability of the patentholder cannot be compromised for the benefit, growth, and stability of the lesser developed country firm. Looking well into the business and technical plans of the lesser developed country firm should reveal options that were not seen or contemplated which may facilitate a mutual benefit for all parties. A discussion below will address the notion of the review process and with whom that responsibility should lie.

Thus far, only strictly bilateral relationships have been examined, i.e., the relationship between the patentholder and the lesser developed country firm. There is a simplicity to this relationship because one firm can figuratively look the other firm in the eye and strike bargains, deals, and potentially mutually beneficial relationships that could exist long after the lesser developed country firm is no longer eligible to obtain benefits by operating under the umbrella of the modified compulsory license.

Multilateral Relationships   The relationship becomes much more complex when more than the two firms are at the table. When this occurs, multiple competing interests may require more care to ensure all parties concerned have acceptable outcomes with the introduction of a lesser developed country firm to the table.

The modified compulsory license cannot be an exclusive arrangement when the patentholder has already entered into licensing relationships with third parties. On the one hand, the patentholder is in a better position to deal with a lesser developed country firm in this instance because it already can appreciate the role it takes on as a licensor. Having another party in the mix may be financially rewarding with the patentholder adding minimal infrastructure to deal with a license relationship. The real difficulty arises, however, when the prior licensee external to the modified compulsory license is an exclusive licensee.

The exclusive licensee may not have contemplated the fact that its exclusivity may be encroached upon by a lesser developed country firm that comes into the relationship after all economic decisions have been mapped out and negotiated between it and the patentholder. If a lesser developed country firm is allowed to permissively infringe in a country where an exclusive licensee has already established itself, will the patentholder be liable to the exclusive licensee for breach of contract? Legislation should be crafted to avoid this potential. It would be appropriate for the legislation to require the participation of the third-party exclusive licensee in the negotiation process of the modified compulsory license.

Because the exclusive licensee is in every way similar to ownership, the exclusive licensee should be treated as the patentholder. In most exclusive license arrangements, the exclusive licensee has every right the patentholder has, including the right to sue for infringement and to collect damages. Therefore, as with much of the discussion throughout this chapter, the exclusive licensee is considered to be in the same position as the patentholder.

In addition, the exclusive licensee is not helpless in this situation. Experienced representation on behalf of the exclusive licensee will successfully shift the burden that a lesser developed country firm may place on the economics of the production and sale of the invention from the exclusive licensee to the patentholder.

Or, what is more likely (and more reasonable) will be the negotiation of contract terms in the license agreement which shifts the burdens imposed by a lesser developed country firm to a shared burden borne by the patentholder and the exclusive licensee. In both instances, the exclusive license agreement should recognize the possibility that a lesser developed country firm may seek rights to the licensed invention. In the former instance, if a royalty payment clause is based on a lump sum fee, it could include language such as:

> As consideration for the license herein granted, exclusive licensee shall pay Patent holder a royalty of 1 million euros, payable in ten equal annual installments of 100,000 euros, less one-quarter of any remaining scheduled royalty payment should a lesser developed country firm enter into a modified compulsory license with the patent holder.

If, on the other hand, the royalty clause is based on a percentage of revenue or a "net selling price" per unit sales, the clause could include the following language:

> As consideration for the license herein granted, licensee shall pay patent holder a royalty of 7 per cent of the net selling price of each product sold by licensee and its sub-licensee under this agreement which are covered by, or made with methods or apparatus covered by licensed patents, less 50 per cent of any royalty received by patent holder from lesser developed country firm for each product sold by lesser developed country firm, should a lesser developed country firm enter into a modified compulsory license with the patent holder.

Obviously, the licensee engaging in a license agreement with the above terms must have the ability to audit the patentholder so that it can guarantee that it is receiving the appropriate rebate for sales of the lesser developed country firm. The terms may vary based on how likely it will be that a lesser developed country firm will want to seek a modified compulsory license that would affect the business model of the licensee.

Because the relationship between the patentholder and a lesser developed country firm is one that will most likely be global in scope, it does not seem practical to rely on legislation to provide answers for the questions surrounding contractual obligations. While each country that issues patents should recognize the existence of the modified compulsory license and what it means to force a patentholder into a license obligation with a lesser developed country firm, it is not expected that each country would pass legislation specifically as to what patentholders are to do contractually.

The relationship is far too complex, and depends on variables such as type of product sold, the amount of similar products currently in the marketplace, revenue streams required by the patentholder and the lesser developed country firm to be successful, and the like. To rely on legislation to dictate how an economic relationship is to exist is to doom the modified compulsory license before it can do any appreciable good to lesser developed countries and the firms therefrom.

The creation and regulation of the modified compulsory license must have flexibility built in so that it can respond to the various relationships that might be confronted by this legislation.

(g) Limitations on the Number of Lesser Developed Country Firms

(i)   In General

With all the lesser developed countries in the world, it is conceivable that multiple lesser developed country firms from one or more lesser developed countries may seek the opportunity to permissively infringe a patent or set of patents. If multiple lesser developed country firms seek the same rights, the patentholder would be required to organize several different license arrangements in multiple jurisdictions.

Coordinating these rights would take a great deal of resources. In addition, there might be a tendency for the patentholder to divide the rights to the lesser developed country firms based on geography. This could possibly run afoul of antitrust laws. Therefore, a limit as to how many lesser developed country firms can seek modified compulsory licenses should be contemplated. However, setting the limit to one may unnecessarily prevent an opportunity to another lesser developed country firm that may be able to grow without hindering the patentholder and the first lesser developed country firm that entered into a modified compulsory license.

In a vacuum, it is difficult to determine what a limit should be. Each specific technology sector may have different nuances to its market that multiple lesser developed country firms operating in a single country may not hinder the ability of any party to maximize their return while still allowing the patentholder to reach for its maximum return on its investment in the patented technology in as much of the global economy that it can based on its patent position. In other instances, even two lesser developed country firms seeking licenses from the patentholder may prove to be economically disastrous for the patentholder and/or the two lesser developed country firms.

Quite frankly, even a single lesser developed country firm having a modified compulsory license that extends across the globe may prove so unsettling for the patentholder that a qualification might be required before a patentholder can be forced into modified compulsory license. Such qualifications may relate to geography, output, language, and the like. In addition, to the extent that a patentholder can be required by law to enter into a modified compulsory license, there should exist requirements that protect the patentholder. Otherwise, additional instabilities will be forced on the patentholder which will do more damage to the patentholder and the global economy than would be benefits from allowing an unfettered modified compulsory license to be put into place.

(ii) Loss of Confidence

One form of instability that would inflict the global economy should a patentholder be denied a reasonable opportunity to make the best of the research and development is the loss of confidence in the patent process. If patents are going to be weakened to the point that the patentholder can expect nothing more than a modest return for its massive monies invested in the research and development, then there will be such a huge discouraging effect on the global economy that technological advancement will be stifled. Stifling the technological advancement will stagnate whole economies, and this will adversely affect the global economy. Basically, eroding the patent protections too far will foster the instability that the modified compulsory license is trying to reduce and eliminate.

Therefore, while a hard fast rule as to how many, if any, lesser developed country firms are able to obtain modified compulsory licenses for a particular patent or set of patents, steps should be developed to measure or estimate the economic gain of a patentholder by maintaining its monopoly and how its economic position will be hindered or improved by the presence of one or more lesser developed country firms.[84]

It is not the purpose of this chapter to engage in a discussion of which business model or economic factors are best to measure to attempt to reach the best answer on a case-by-case basis, but to suggest that a thorough model will be required to maximize the growth and stability of the global economy while adversely affecting as many firms as possible.

(h) Copyrights and Patents

(i)   In General

It is extremely important to understand that the modified compulsory license is a model for growing an economy that has been minimized by those in the world that have done so much better. To do so is to dismiss short-term gains for strides that produce benefits over the long term. In addition, it is commonly held that short-term "fixes" do little to help truly fix a problem. To paraphrase an old saying: if one gives a fish to a hungry person, that person will eat for the day; but teach that person to fish, and he will eat for a lifetime.

Taking this concept and transposing it into the problem for the Digital Divide, it must be the goal to foster an economic growth in a lesser developed country

---

84   It should be noted that the economic position of the patentholder may be improved by the licensing of the patent to a lesser developed country firm through a modified compulsory license. In such a circumstance, the lesser developed country firm may be exposing markets that the patentholder cannot feasibly reach. The development of those markets may prove beneficial to the patentholder in more ways than just receiving a royalty for sales. That particular market may develop more rapidly than the lesser developed country firm can develop. If the market matures faster than the lesser developed country firm, the market may seek out the patentholder for an additional, more sophisticated product, or the next generation of the product should one be developed.

so that it will be able to sustain itself in future times, regardless of the direction in which its economy grows. A typical economic environment cycles through good times and bad, and through periods of expansion, contraction, recession, and depression. While it would be futile to think any firm were impervious to every economic situation, it would be the desire to grow the global economy and the stability of lesser developed countries as best as possible.

One possible way in which a lesser developed country firm can withstand economically difficult times is to diversify. While diversification is typically discussed in terms of product or service offerings, diversification for a lesser developed country firm should be discussed principally in terms of skills. The lesser developed country firm cannot merely sell a product or service and expect to grow. A modified compulsory license for a patent may provide an advantage in a particular marketplace, especially if it is the only modified compulsory license and it is exclusive, but it is never to be considered a guarantee for financial success. The only guarantee, if one exists, is the ability to understand want is needed in the marketplace, and having the skill to execute a business plan to efficiently provide the product or service to the marketplace in a timely manner.

As a partial solution to the above problem is to provide as few shortcuts to a lesser developed country firm. This will position the lesser developed country firm into working on solutions as a matter of survival. It should be remembered that it is not the intent of this chapter to provide as much of a "free ride" as possible. It is to introduce a lenience into the patent question when a lesser developed country firm is attempting to produce, sell, and potentially export a product or service so that the lesser developed country in which the firm is domiciled will be able to introduce a greater level of stability into its economy. It is not to allow a lesser developed country firm to pirate technology.

(ii) Copyright Infringement

One way to ensure a lesser developed country firm is working in a healthy manner is to prevent such shortcuts as copyright infringement. In information and communication technologies, copying a work could allow another party to have a complete product or service. This would be a disservice on many levels. First, it does not provide assurances to the patentholder, who also is a copyright holder that their product will be distinguished in any way from the offering of a lesser developed country firm. This is tantamount to the taking of a reputation. Trade marks may be infringed.

Additionally, the buying public may be confused as to the source or origin of a product based on its complete similarity in its look and feel. The instability introduced into the marketplace by this confusion does not offset the minimal short-term gains received by a lesser developed country firm should they be allowed to engage in this type of commercial activity.

A second reason for preventing the infringement of copyrights even though permissive infringement is granted through a modified compulsory license is because it is simply a short-term solution to an economic problem that needs long-term solutions. If a lesser developed country firm is permitted to infringe copyrights that are critical to the functioning of a patented product or service, the lesser developed country firm is doing little by way of development of a suitable alternative to the offering of the patentholder. The lesser developed country firm does not need to take into account building an infrastructure to develop new products and services from those offered by the patentholder.

If the lesser developed country firm does not build itself into an entity that can perform some level of research and/or development, it may become nothing more than a small-scale operation, depending on the product or service being sold. While these sized firms are valuable to any economy, it would be the goal of the issuance of a modified compulsory license to help develop an economy capable of more resiliency than that.

It would be the desire to empower a lesser developed country firm to grow to a size sufficient to develop its own technologies, employ several people, require peripheral services from others in its community, and even seek and obtain its own patent portfolio so that it can grow through passive income, i.e., royalty payments that the lesser developed country firm can infuse back into its own firm or into its community to enhance the position of the community and the lesser developed country. This is how an economy of a lesser developed country will stabilize and grow.

A third reason why it is important that copyright infringement should not be permitted when patent infringement is permitted through a modified compulsory license is that a capitalistic society looks to innovation for growth. If copyright infringement were permitted, there would be no market differentiation in products and services — no real choice for the consumer, but price. The lesser developed country firm will have an unfair advantage over the patentholder and will have no incentive to do anything more than to take as much market share away from the patentholder as possible while investing little into itself and its surrounding community.

Understanding that it is a desire to have lesser developed country firms to be able to sell products and services in their country of domicile and to possibly export to other countries, it also is a desire for the lesser developed country firm to develop into something more than a minimal firm that does little to the surrounding community in terms of stabilization and growth. By requiring the lesser developed country firm to develop its own products, albeit infringing of the patent(s), the lesser developed country firm will be required to engage the community in its business activities more than if it were merely an authorized pirate.

Finally, by permitting infringement of copyrights is to allow stagnation in product development. The mantra of a capitalistic society is growth through development. If the global economy is to grow through development, an opportunity is lost by having even the smallest lesser developed country firm copy something only because it can. If all lesser developed country firms that enter into modified compulsory licenses were able to merely copy a portion of a patented product or service, if not the whole product or service, there will be many lost opportunities for growth.

Economic gains would be shallow and easily disrupted. The consumers will not benefit because they will have no choice other than price. They will not be able to select more desirable features or stripped-down versions based on their specific needs and economic condition. The shallow economic gains by a lesser developed country will be especially true if more than one lesser developed country firm were able to enter into modified compulsory licenses for the same patent or set of patents.

The resulting economic growth would shift to the lesser developed country firm that has the smallest margin and the cheapest workforce. This may effectively create more instability than it creates stability because a situation can be envisaged where one lesser developed country firm invests in product production and distribution only to find a second lesser developed country firm with a cheaper work force or government subsidies that can undercut the price of the first lesser developed country firm.

The undercutting of price is the only differentiator between the two products because both would be virtual copies of the offering by the patentholder. The first lesser developed country firm would lose its opportunity to compete because it would not have the simple economic advantages the second lesser developed country firm had. If nothing was done to the product to differentiate it from the patentholder, it stands to reason that junior parties will have nothing to differentiate their products either.

In addition, in the end, supply is merely shifted from one lesser developed country firm to another, which may have a devastating effect on lesser developed country firms that lose their business opportunity. By preventing copyright infringement, roots in an economic growth in a lesser developed country firm and its lesser developed country will take hold and at the same time provide opportunity to the consuming class to purchase a variety of products without the consuming class being confused about who provided the product or service.

(i) Economic Engagement by Patentholder

(i) In General

Another limitation that should be considered when determining whether a lesser developed country firm is capable of entering into a modified compulsory license is whether the patentholder has engaged the lesser developed country in some economic way. This is a similar hurdle that is faced by potential licensees in the traditional compulsory license arrangement.[85] The Digital Divide is the result of first world countries advancing technology and selling products and services to others in the first world countries. Whole generations of technology are non-existent to many of the lesser developed countries.

Because this phenomenon creates such difficulties for lesser developed country firms entering into the global economy a solution must be sought for the lesser developed country firms and their domicile countries in their attempts to reach for economic stability by tapping into these markets with products and services that may not only have a patent that prevents them from doing so, but multiple layers of patents on several successive stages of development.

If a patentholder has, however, participated in the economy of the lesser developed country, the solution of striving to bridge the Digital Divide has been achieved. Empowering a lesser developed country firm with the ability to force the patentholder into a modified compulsory license would pose greater harm to the growth and stabilization of the economy of the lesser developed country. Determining what level of participation is required by a patentholder to prevent lesser developed country firms from seeking licenses is one that requires some thought.

It may not be enough that the patentholder merely open a sales office in the lesser developed country. It may be that a sales office and extending the patent portfolio covering the particular product or service into that lesser developed country would be enough. Or, if there are more functions being performed on behalf of the patentholder by the offices in the lesser developed country, it would suffice the requirement to prevent modified compulsory licenses from being invoked.

(ii) Ramifications of Borderless Modified Compulsory Licensing

An interesting dilemma emerges from this issue. If the modified compulsory license is to be a pseudo-borderless concept, it will provide the lesser developed country firm the ability to export products, resulting in money entering the economy of the lesser developed country. If another lesser developed country firm from another country engages in the modified compulsory license process with the patentholder, it may be able to export to the country in which the patentholder has engaged on its own.

The end result is that firms from the lesser developed country in which the patentholder has entered are prevented from engaging in economic activity

---

85   Paris Convention, article 5.

relating to the particular product other than what is provided by the patentholder, whereas another lesser developed country firm from another country is able to obtain licensee status and can enter the lesser developed country and minimize the economy of the lesser developed country by having imports grow while preventing the exportation of this type of product or service.

One possible solution may be to prevent lesser developed country firms from obtaining modified compulsory licenses should the patentholder be within its country. Another possible solution is to allow the lesser developed country firm the ability to enter into a modified compulsory license, but prevent the lesser developed country firm from entering any country in which the patentholder has an economic interest therein. Granted, these potential solutions seem to be one-dimensional, but there must be some consideration to the patentholder and the lesser developed country.

Anything more forgiving on the part of the non-domiciled lesser developed country firm may result in more erosion of patent rights for the patentholder. In addition, the multiple parties entering a lesser developed country with imports may further hinder the lesser developed country in its ability to better its economic position. In both situations, a clearing house of sorts could regulate where lesser developed country firms would be able to enter and where current activity by the patentholder or another lesser developed country firm would prohibit their entry therein.

It may be useful to have such information readily available to provide a lesser developed country firm the ability to see if a product or service has potential to reap the necessary gains to make the development of such more practical. If it were to be determined that the lesser developed country firm would be limited to a patchwork of countries, it may determine that distribution may be too difficult.

(j) Reciprocity of Infringing Status

An interesting scenario could occur during the life of a modified compulsory license. What would happen if a lesser developed country firm, while operating under a modified compulsory license, developed a companion feature for the product that enhanced the product? In addition, what if the lesser developed country firm sought patent protection for those technological advances?

It would be somewhat of a success if this were to occur. The lesser developed country firm has developed in such a manner that it is not only becoming an economic survivor, but an economic contributor. It is contributing to its economy and community. The lesser developed country firm is capable of generating such economic activity that it can seek protection for its new technologies. This begins to elevate the lesser developed country firm to the level of first world firms. It can plan for years into the future and reap the benefits through its continued development or its collection of royalty payments.

If the lesser developed country firm is still a party to a modified compulsory license, considerations should be given to the patentholder because there are opportunities for the lesser developed country firm that would not have been available if the patentholder did not first develop the technology and invest in protecting that technology.

One consideration would be to give the patentholder the option to terminate the modified compulsory license. This is an extreme response and may be detrimental for the lesser developed country firm even though it is patenting its own technology. After all, the lesser developed country firm may still need rights in and to the underlying patented technology to continue selling its newly improved technology.

Another option would be to convert the modified compulsory license into a standard license agreement whereby the patentholder and the lesser developed country firm would enter into a relationship that is normally bargained for between parties when technology is involved. This would be an ideal situation because the lesser developed country firm has grown to the point where it can operate without the assistance of subsidies such as the modified compulsory licenses.

A third, less desirable, option in this situation is to force the lesser developed country firm and the patentholder into a mandatory cross-licensing relationship.[86] Here, the modified compulsory license would be maintained for its terms. However, as long as the modified compulsory license were to remain in effect, the lesser developed country firm would have to provide a license to the patentholder. This new license could mirror the terms of the modified compulsory license.

One difference in the newly required license would be that there would be no royalty payments contemplated. The new license would be similar to a grant back clause in a standard license providing a licensor the right to make and use all developments by the licensee during the development and use of the licensor's property. The lesser developed country firm can accept these terms because it will be receiving rights in the modified compulsory license that it would not have otherwise received.

---

86   This concept resonates in the traditional compulsory license relationship where one invention cannot be practiced without the permission of a first patent. In this situation, if the patentholder of the first patent is required to enter into a compulsory license, it is entitled to a cross license for the technology claimed in the second patent. TRIPs Agreement, article 31(l)(ii).

(k) Time Limits for Licensees of Modified Compulsory Licenses

Throughout this discussion of the modified compulsory license, there has been an underlying current that this will only work if it is beneficial to all parties concerned. It was spoken of in terms of economics, growth, and stability. For a patentholder to acquiesce some of its rights on which it has spent resources to obtain can only be done when safeguards are in place. Without the safeguards, the patentholder will be put at risk resulting in no net gain, globally speaking. In fact, it might be a net loss. Governments will understand this.

Developed countries will surely prevent such legislation from being passed should the safeguards not be in place — and rightfully so.

All patent rights exist for a limited time.[87] Therefore, there is a window of opportunity for the patentholder to garner a return on its investment. In reality, this window of opportunity is even more reduced in the information and communication technologies because those technologies develop and advance so rapidly. One way in which a patentholder may have some protection in its property is to limit the time period in which the modified compulsory license may be in force.

The limited time period may be technology specific so that any lesser developed country firm starting the process will be able to have a reasonable time period to recoup its costs in starting up production or in laying network materials. If system infrastructure is required, the time period for the modified compulsory license would need to be greater than that for something like a software package.

Regardless of the technology, the modified compulsory license can only have a fractional life of the patent into which the modified compulsory license is entered. Depending on the technology that the patent relates to, the term of the modified compulsory license would be dictated by the remaining term of the patent. In some situations, the patentholder may entertain the notion of extending the term of the modified compulsory license to something greater than what would be considered acceptable under the terms of these types of licenses.

In these situations, the patentholder may believe it appropriate that an extension of the term may prove beneficial to the patentholder to help mature a market. If this were the case, it might be contemplated that the two parties would enter into a standard license agreement that would start on the termination of the modified compulsory license.

---

87 Again, referring to the traditional compulsory license arrangement, the time allotted for the permissive infringement is always limited. TRIPs Agreement, article 31(c).

It is hard to put a number on a ratio between the term of the patent with respect to the term of the modified compulsory license. All attempts to define this ratio seem capricious due to a lack of information as to the technology, the products, and the economic position of the parties involved. As a starting point in a discussion that would have to evolve based on data collected, it would seem appropriate to limit the term of the modified compulsory license to one third of that which remains on the patent.

The remaining patent term should be calculated based on the date on which an application for the modified compulsory license is made by the lesser developed country firm. This would provide an incentive for all parties concerned to resolve the modified compulsory license efficiently by counting the time that would be consumed by the bureaucratic procedures that must be followed to create the relationship between the two parties.

(l)   Export Limitations for Lesser Developed Country Firms

Another means in which the patentholder can be protected so that it would continue to develop and disclose new technologies is to limit the export potential for a lesser developed country firm. If a patentholder has built a business plan around maximizing its penetration into specific countries, the presence of a lesser developed country firm with a modified compulsory license may disrupt the patentholder's business plan.

Therefore, trade offs must be accepted by both parties. Other than a mutual agreement to target different sectors of the same market through the providing of different offerings that may have different price points, there must be a limit as to how much a lesser developed country firm can penetrate a particular market. As stated above, there can always be an agreement allowing a lesser developed country firm more opportunity, but that can only come from the patentholder because the patentholder has no intention to develop a particular market and only stands to gain by greater sales on the part of the lesser developed country firm in that market.

There is no magic ratio between domestic sales and exports that would be suitable for an overall target. Too many variables would have to be set before one could create a model which would be helpful in any way to determine what the ratio would be. After making gross assumptions as to variables, the resulting model may have little reality left. However, a percentage could be set to somewhat put the brakes on a lesser developed country firm in its attempts to export heavily to the detriment of the patentholder.

Another reason why it is important to limit exports based on a ratio of domestic sales is to reduce the number of firms attempting to illegitimately take advantage of the opportunity a modified compulsory license may afford. It is conceivable that a firm not originally domiciled in a lesser developed country may establish a meager presence in the lesser developed country to take advantage of an opportunity to sell products elsewhere.

By requiring exports from a particular country to be tied to the number of sales within the country will limit the number of those firms that will attempt to take advantage of these provisions; firms that have no reason to be in competition with the patentholder because it will make no real effort to grow and stabilize the economy of the lesser developed country.

This proposition of having a ratio of exports based on domestic sales is problematic, however, because it presupposes a domestic market that can sustain a lesser developed country firm as it grows. It may be the plan of a lesser developed country firm to maximize sales through exporting. In the situation of little domestic sales, domestic sales will never meet the requirements of the plan for exports. This situation cannot be adequately satisfied through the modified compulsory license as it is contemplated because it is designed to help a lesser developed country firm bring products and services to the lesser developed country and to help sustain the bridging of the digital divide through the aid of exporting a percentage of its product and/or services.

It is not designed to aid a lesser developed country firm from reaping benefits in a business model that may maximize the profits of the lesser developed country firm with little opportunity for increased products and services being offered to the people of the lesser developed country from which the lesser developed country firm is domiciled. Therefore, it is important to maintain some relationship between the domestic sales and exports to ensure the benefit of the modified compulsory license remains focused on the result of doing as much as possible to have as many in a lesser developed country to have an opportunity to obtain the tools necessary to understand, become comfortable, and use all things digital.

6.06 Who Would Oversee Permissive Infringement by Lesser Developed Country Firms?

A coordinating body will be needed to administer the modified compulsory license because the rights of all parties involved in these agreements will have to be determined and to a certain extent regulated. It is conceivable that many patentholders will not appreciate being forced into these types of relationships.

In addition, it is for this reason that the lesser developed country firm will need to go through a regulatory body to ensure it gets the rights it is entitled to based on the legislation that provides for the modified compulsory license. The coordinating body will be able to monitor the patents, the remaining period of enforceability, who has obtained a modified compulsory license and whether there is an opportunity for additional lesser developed country firms to obtain rights under the same patent or patents. The coordinating body could also act as a clearing house should a particular product require rights under many patents that are not co-owned.

The most likely candidate to act as the coordinating body is the World Trade Organization (WTO). It has the infrastructure to bring parties together and resolve disputes. The World Intellectual Property Organization (WIPO) can be tapped to provide data on the patents and the patent activity in the various countries.

The WTO and the WIPO have cooperative agreements in place with respect to intellectual property.[88] Therefore, it would be appropriate to augment the responsibilities of these two organizations to develop a database of technologies, parties, royalties, lesser developed country firms. and licensing activity in selected lesser developed countries so that the modified compulsory license can be monitored to determine whether the results in the economies of the various lesser developed countries are improving in response, at least in part, by the ability of the members of the lesser developed countries to participate in the Digital Age by incorporating information and communication technologies into their products and services.

Additionally, counseling could be provided to certified lesser developed country firms to aid them in their endeavors on entering and growing in the global economy. Many issues present themselves when products and services are reaching a global market which will find many, if not all, lesser developed country firms ill-equipped to handle.

The coordinating body could help facilitate this type of counseling so that the lesser developed country firm does not experience unnecessarily fatal situations. Of course, a lesser developed country firm could seek help from any institution it sees fit, but issues relating specifically to the modified compulsory license could be fielded by the coordinating body.

Finally, the coordinating body could review a lesser developed country firm to determine whether continued activity under the modified compulsory license is warranted. Certainly, on the lesser developed country firm becoming a truly viable firm, its permissions to infringe patents should be limited or scaled back gradually until it no longer may obtain permissions based on its status as an entity from a lesser developed country. These actions would be detailed steps in the modified compulsory license, and the "early" termination of the modified compulsory license would follow the terms thereof.

---

88 Agreement Between the World Intellectual Property Organization and the World Trade Organization, at http://www.wto.org/english/tratop_e/trips_e/wtowip_e.htm.

It should be noted that on the termination of the modified compulsory license, a lesser developed country firm has the opportunity to enter into a standard license agreement should the parties reach a mutual agreement as to the terms of the relationship. In addition, as always, a lesser developed country firm that loses its rights under a modified compulsory license will be able to continue to market their products and software in countries in which the patentholder has failed to obtain patent protection. Therefore, a lesser developed country firm is not without opportunities if it fails to create new products that will not infringe others' patents as it moves forward in its attempts to become a firm that does not need to rely on normal business dealings to be successful.

6.07   Conclusion

In this attempt to bridge the Digital Divide and help lesser developed countries in their quest to enter the Digital Age, it is the hope that more lesser developed countries gain an appreciation for intellectual property rights. As more lesser developed country firms seek assistance via a modified compulsory license, they will only stand to gain by having intellectual property rights in their host lesser developed countries strengthened and enforced more vigorously.

In addition, this will prompt those lesser developed country firms to encourage their respective governments to provide new legislation where needed or enforce existing legislation to bring more certainty to those that stand to gain by investing resources in products and services that will better the economies of the lesser developed countries and eventually move those countries into better positions such that they will no longer be considered a member of the lesser developed countries.

Modifying patent laws to accommodate the modified compulsory license on a worldwide basis must be done with care. If done improperly or inconsistently, the probability that instability will grow instead of stability will increase, if done properly; however, the world has much opportunity to gain in stability, growth, and prosperity.

CHAPTER 7

INTERNET REGULATION

Julian Ding
First Pinciples Sdn Bhd
Kuala Lumpur, Malaysia

7.01 Introduction

(a) In General

This chapter discusses what the Internet and the World Wide Web are and the forms of regulation that are applied to them.

Obviously, the scope of Internet regulatory frameworks has many connections with topics such as gambling, crime, and pornography. It is too enormous a task to examine all of these subjects in this chapter.

The remaining parts of this chapter examine the regulatory frameworks applicable to:

1. Internet Protocol Address assignments;
2. Internet access;
3. Online content; and
4. Spam.

(b) What Is the Internet?

(i) In General

The Internet, in its simplest form, comprises the connection of many different computers located in many different places in the world. The connection is through the use of physical cables (i.e., wires) and, traditionally, this has been provided through the use of telecommunication cables. Now, wireless connectivity is rising and may become a substitute for wire for Internet connection.

In a sense, the Internet is the name given to the global information network which grew through cooperation among individuals rather than one which was developed by any single person or entity or country. It spans the world and connects anyone who has a computer, or access device, with a modem and an Internet access account.

Historically, the Internet grew up in the United States as part of the department of defense project (ARPA). A key element of the Internet was the development of the Transmission Control Protocol/Internet Protocol (TCP/IP) standard for communication. This breakthrough enabled the efficient use of networks to send and receive large quantities of data almost instantaneously.

Furthermore, ICANN's Strategic Priorities[1] succinctly identify three things about the Internet which makes it important, namely:

1. The Internet has been engineered with an open architecture, designed to allow new protocols and services to be readily integrated.

2. It is an aggregate of data networks that can operate over and support varied data technologies and applications.

3. [This is done by] maintaining a set of core protocols that are kept very stable. This core includes the Internet Protocol (IP), the routing system, and the domain name system.

These three elements — open architecture, capability to support varied data technologies/applications, and stable core protocol — make the Internet what it is today.

The next major breakthrough (where ordinary individuals were able to access the Internet and its content) is the development of the browser, which enabled simple "point and click" operations for anyone. This coincided with the simplification of the computers through the use of graphical user interfaces, i.e., technology started to become domesticated.

(ii) Differences between the Internet and the World Wide Web

While the terms "Internet" and the "World Wide Web" (or "Web") are sometimes used interchangeably, there are, in fact, differences between the two. These differences are:

1. The Internet is a "massive network of networks, a networking infrastructure. It connects millions of computers together globally, forming a network in which any computer can communicate with any other computer";[2]

---

1   Available at http://www.icann.org/strategic-plan/strategic-plan-sec2-16nov04.pdf, accessed on 5 February 2005.

2   Webopedia, at http://www.webopedia.com/DidYouKnow/Internet/2002/Web_vs_Internet.asp, accessed on 1 February 2005.

2. The information traveling across the Internet uses a variety of protocols, such as file transfer protocol (FTP), email (SMTP), and instant messaging;

3. Different protocols are used that enable connections to occur;

4. The Web "is a way of accessing information over the medium of the Internet. It is an information-sharing model that is built on top of the Internet. The Web uses the HTTP protocol, [which is] only one of the languages spoken over the Internet, to transmit data. Web services, which use HTTP to allow applications to communicate to exchange business logic, use the Web to share information";[3] and

5. The Web uses browsers (such as Mozilla and Internet Explorer) to access Web pages (documents built using html programming language).

Therefore, the Web is one of the ways by which information is accessed, and it is not the Internet. The Internet enables other activities, such as sending and receiving emails or accessing information contained in newsgroups or remote diagnosis of computers.

This distinction enables a proper appreciation of what should be regulated, and provides a context when one considers what Internet regulation is all about. In addition, by specifically identifying the differences between the Internet and the World Wide Web, it is hoped that the reader will appreciate that regulating the Internet and the World Wide Web are two different activities.

(III) Meaning of Regulation

Regulation, as it is commonly understood, refers to the imposition of standards and legally enforceable controls. Licensing regulation is one example of the imposition of a legally enforceable control.

The effectiveness of a regulation requires that there is a body (which all participants either explicitly or tacitly recognize) that is able to enforce the rules. This body is usually the nation-state, and the exercise of the authority is over those entities which are within its jurisdiction. This, however, is merely a description of regulation. There is no clear definition of regulation. One definition is:

> Regulation is the process by which government induces, requires or prohibits certain actions by individuals, private institutions and sometimes public institutions, often through the efforts of specially designated regulatory agencies.[4]

---

3   Webopedia, at http://www.webopedia.com/DidYouKnow/Internet/2002/Web_vs_Internet.asp, accessed on 1 February 2005.

4   Gow, "Business and Government as Regulation", in Colebatch, Prasser, and Nethercote (eds.), *Business-Government Relations: Concepts and Issues* (1997).

Another definition is:

> . . . the imposition of constraints (backed by government authority) which are intended to influence the behavior of individuals or industry.[5]

Alternative forms of regulation exist, for example, as between members *inter se* of a club or association. A breach of the rules does not result in any legal enforcement by the state. Instead, their enforcement is brought about by the club's internal disciplinary process, which may result in the expulsion of the member from the club or association. The "public shame" of being expelled from the club provides sufficient incentive for individuals to comply with the rules. This is considered as a form of self-regulation.

By identifying the characteristics of regulation, a better means by which the concept of Internet Regulation can be provided or addressed. Consequently, regulation (whether as commonly understood or in the form of self-regulation) possesses these characteristics:

1. It seeks to ensure a particular behavior is developed, adhered to, or maintained;

2. There is some penalty for non-observance;

3. It applies to all participants;[6] and

4. There is some form of enforcement to ensure compliance.

(iv) Reasons for Regulating

In General   There are four theoretical perspectives why Governments regulate an activity, namely:

1. Market failure;

2. Public interest;

3. Life cycle; and

4. Private interest.[7]

Market Failure   Market failure occurs when the market is unable to deal with structural problems, such as lack of competition (or monopolies), negative

---

5   Savage Report on the Review of Queensland Business Regulation, 1986.

6   A participant is an entity (whether as an individual person or a legal person, i.e., corporations) who is involved in the sector which is subjected to the regulation. This may be, for example, the travel agency business, which is subjected to licensing requirements (to start the business), consumer protection laws (to protect consumers), and anticompetitive or unfair trade practice laws.

7   Gow, "Business and Government as Regulation", in Colebatch, Prasser, and Nethercote (eds.), *Business-Government Relations: Concepts and Issues* (1997).

externalities (e.g., smoke-stack emissions affect quality of life of nearby residents), asymmetric information (where a consumer has insufficient information to determine whether to buy a product or not), and the provision of a public good (e.g., street lighting), thus necessitating governmental intervention through regulation.

Public Interest   Public interest emphasizes the collective good rather than individual good, which may be superior and necessary. Examples of public interest are the establishment of standard weight and measures, economic management, or collective amenity.

Life Cycle   The life cycle theory of regulation argues "that, while the initial regulation may have been intended to serve a particular public interest, regulation in time comes to serve a private interest".

Private Interest   The private interest theory argues that regulation is sought by private firms to accumulate the resource of the State to prevent others from entering their market space.

Other Reasons for Regulation   Other commentators[8] identify 12 reasons for regulation as set out in Table 1, below.

Table 1 — Reasons for Regulation

Rationale	Main Aims of Regulation	Example
Monopolies and natural monopolies	Counter tendency to raise prices and lower output Harness benefits of scale economies Identify areas genuinely monopolistic	Utilities
Windfall profits	Transfer benefits of windfalls from firms to consumers or taxpayers	Firm discovers unusually cheap source of supply
Externalities	Compel producer or consumer to bear full costs of production rather than pass on to third parties or society	Pollution of river by factory
Information inadequacies	Inform consumers to allow market to operate	Pharmaceuticals, food and drinks labeling

---

8   Baldwin and Cave, *Understanding Regulation: Theory, Strategy, and Practice* (1999), at pp. 9–17.

Rationale	Main Aims of Regulation	Example
Continuity and availability of service	Ensure socially desired (or protect minimal) level of "essential" service	Transport service to remote region
Anticompetitive and behavior predatory pricing	Prevent anticompetitive behavior	Below-cost pricing in transport
Public goods and moral hazard	Share costs where benefits of activity are shared but free-rider problems exist	Defense and security services. Health services
Unequal bargaining power	Protect vulnerable interests where market fails to do so	Health and safety at work
Scarcity and rationing	Public interest allocation of scarce commodities	Petrol shortages
Distribution justice and social policy	Distribute according to public interest. Prevent undesirable behavior or results	Victim protection
Rationalization and coordination	Secure efficient production where transaction costs prevent market from obtaining network gains or efficiencies of scale. Standardization	Disparate production in agriculture and fisheries
Planning	Protect interests of future generations. Coordinate altruistic intentions	Environment

Table: *Regions for Regulating [source: Baldwin and Cave (1999)]*

(v) Why Regulate the Internet?

Telecommunications is regarded as an essential service in most countries in the world. Until the 1980s, this service was provided by the government (or the public sector) rather than the private sector (with the exception of the United States). The 1980s saw the rise of privatization, led by the United Kingdom, which pursued privatization as a means of introducing economic efficiencies into an otherwise inefficient enterprise.

Once privatization occurred, governments soon realized that it was necessary to introduce regulation to ensure that the former state-owned enterprise did not behave improperly and to ensure that new entrants were allowed to participate. This created the licensing structure by which governments could enable a competitive market to emerge.

For access to the Internet to occur, it is necessary that a user subscribe to an entity which provides Internet access, known as an Internet Service Provider or

Internet Access Provider (ISP or IAP, respectively). Assuming that users have telephone connections to their home or office, the ISP or IAP will usually be an entity licensed or permitted by the government of the country in which the users reside to offer Internet access, email, or newsgroups as a service to them.

It is highly unlikely that a user will subscribe to an ISP or IAP located in another country because of the prohibitive cost of making an international call over a long period of time, just to get access to the Internet, although it is possible.

The technology that has enabled the Internet is fundamentally a "disruptive technology" (i.e., it changes the way things were done in a dramatic form). Examples of disruptive technology are the printing press and television.

Previously, one needed different devices to watch television (television set), communicate verbally (telephone), or process data (computer). Today, all of these activities can be performed by a single device, the personal computer connected to the Internet.

Government concerns relating to the Internet are based on issues dealing with:

1. National security;

2. Protection of minors;

3. Protection of human dignity;

4. Economic security;

5. Protection of information;

6. Protection of privacy;

7. Protection of reputation; and

8. Protection of intellectual property.[9]

Furthermore, it has been pointed out that today cyberspace (i.e., the Internet and the Web) is, in fact, subject to various forms of regulation.[10] There are:

> . . . four things that regulate cyberspace [namely]: laws (by government sanction and force), social norms (by expectation, encouragement, or embarrassment), markets (by price and availability), and architecture (what the technology permits, favors, dissuades, or prohibits).[11]

---

9   Peng, "How Countries Are Regulating Internet Content", at http://cad.ntu-kpi.kiev.ua/events/inet97/B1/B1_3.htm, accessed on 5 February 2005.

10 Lessig, "The Laws of Cyberspace", cited in Reagle, "Why the Internet is Good", at http://cyber.law.harvard.edu/people/reagle/regulation-19990326.html accessed on 30 November 2004.

11 Lessig, "The Laws of Cyberspace", cited in Reagle, "Why the Internet is Good", at http://cyber.law.harvard.edu/people/reagle/regulation-19990326.html, accessed on 30 November 2004.

Examples are:

1. Architectural structure of Internet Protocol Addresses — No one would consider using an Internet Address (i.e., an Internet Protocol Address used on the Internet as opposed to a private network) outside the standard structure, (i.e., the numeric range of 0 to 255), because of the possible impact to the stability of the core protocol. Consequently, it is necessary for there to be a proper, fair, and efficient management and administration system for allocating Internet Protocol Addresses. This is undertaken through various non-governmental bodies.

2. Market regulation — This is where rules that are set in a market environment apply to participants in that market. Examples of such market regulation are the online market places, business-to-business supply markets, and online auctions.

3. Social norms — This is perhaps the most widespread. It exists in all online communities, newsgroups, or other forms of membership-based organizations. Each group or community is subjected to certain norms or standards of behavior to which all adhere. The standards are made known at the outset, and individuals who continue to subscribe are deemed to have acceded to them. Breach of the norms does not result in penal sanctions but, in most cases, continued membership is prevented.

4. Laws — Legislation, by its very nature, requires the use of the state's coercive power to bring about a particular behavior. It is usual that laws are applied to such areas as the licensing of Internet access or the control of online content. The difficulty is with the enforcement of the laws, especially if the individual concern is beyond the geographical jurisdiction of the state.

(vi) Scope of Internet Regulation

The scope of Internet regulation falls within four categories, namely:

1. "Scarce resource" and public goods, i.e., bandwidth allocation and the quality of communal spaces;

2. Efficiency, i.e., anti-fraud regulation;

3. Interoperability, i.e., open standards, open source, and protocol and name registration; and

4. Behavior, i.e., prohibition of obscene speech.[12]

This categorization is a useful starting point, but it is by no means exhaustive or comprehensive. Governments are at various stages of evolution and are of

---

12 Reagle, "Why the Internet is Good", at http://cyber.law.harvard.edu/people/reagle/regulation-19990326.html, accessed on 30 November 2004.

different types. Some are democratically elected, while others are totalitarian regimes; yet, others are absolute monarchies. The Internet now enables knowledge to be shared by many individuals at a fraction of the costs. The concern of governments is that such access to knowledge may affect their political power and position. This concern is what drives these governments to sometimes ban or prevent access to the Internet totally. This is not regulation but outlawing, and is not considered in this chapter.

(c) Issues Affecting Regulation of the Internet

(i) In General

The rules and laws that govern human behavior have traditionally been limited by the geographical boundaries of the state. With the Internet, these geographical boundaries, to a great extent, have disappeared. Accordingly, there is uncertainty as to how to regulate the Internet.

It is necessary to distinguish between rules affecting the Internet and rules affecting the activity which uses the Internet. An example of the former would be the control of Internet access by a country, whereas an example of the latter would be the sale of books online by a commercial outlet. The sale of books is subject to existing laws on operating a business, content censorship or control, and taxation which are applicable to the vendor based on the geographical nexus of the vendor to the state.

These laws apply regardless of the fact that the activity occurs in cyberspace. The issue surrounding the activity and which is a problem for governments is one of enforcement. It is difficult to enforce the rules prohibiting sale of certain types of content if the vendors are physically outside the country seeking such enforcement.

In the first instance, in 2000, La Ligue successfully sued Yahoo! Inc. in France and obtained an order that imposed a daily fine of US $13,000 if Yahoo! did not block access to the Nazi content on its portal. Subsequently, La Ligue sought to enforce the French court's order in the United States and, there, the court of first instance ruled that Yahoo! was not subject to the French court order in the United States. This decision was appealed and the United States 9th Circuit Court decided that Yahoo! was so subject. Thereafter, Yahoo! filed a suit to seek a rehearing of the United States 9th Circuit Court's decision.[13] The United States Court of Appeals decided in 2005 that the original United States court order against Yahoo! in 2004 must be subjected to a rehearing because the issue of free speech and the right of a foreign state to impose a financial penalty were at play.

---

13   *Yahoo! Inc. v. La Ligue Contre le Racisme et L'antisemitisme and Another*, United States Court of Appeals for the 9th Circuit [Appeal Number 1-17424].

The *Yahoo!* case typifies the complexity of the issues affecting the Internet and content available thereat. Material which is considered acceptable in one country, but is available using the Internet or the Web, becomes unacceptable in another country. In such a situation, how should such material be treated? Is it illegal in the recipient country and, if so, can the "provider" be subjected to legal fines enforceable against it in its home country. The outcome of the rehearing would be of significant interest as it may provide some guidance on how the United States would treat the provision of content which is inappropriate by other countries laws by its companies.

What these evidence is the importance of the concept of national sovereignty. With national sovereignty, a nation-state is able to pass laws within its territory and deal with its citizens and businesses. Consequently, the recognition of national sovereignty by other nation-states has led to the conventions and norms for the dealings between them. Effectively, such dealings are undertaken on the basis of peers, as opposed to primary and secondary relationships.

From this concept, the evolution and creation of international institutions has been enabled. One must look at the preamble to the United Nations Charter,[14] which brought the United Nations into existence and which states:

> We the Peoples of the United Nations Determined:
>
>> to save succeeding generations from the scourge of war, which twice in our lifetime has brought untold sorrow to mankind, and
>>
>> to reaffirm faith in fundamental human rights, in the dignity and worth of the human person, in the equal rights of men and women and of nations large and small, and
>>
>> to establish conditions under which justice and respect for the obligations arising from treaties and other sources of international law can be maintained, and
>>
>> to promote social progress and better standards of life in larger freedom,
>
> And for These Ends:
>
>> to practice tolerance and live together in peace with one another as good neighbors, and
>>
>> to unite our strength to maintain international peace and security, and
>>
>> to ensure, by the acceptance of principles and the institution of methods that armed force shall not be used, save in the common interest, and
>>
>> to employ international machinery for the promotion of the economic and social advancement of all peoples,

---

14   United Nations Charter, at http://www.un.org/aboutun/charter/index.html, accessed on 12 February 2005.

Have Resolved to Combine Our Efforts to Accomplish These Aims:

> Accordingly, our respective Governments, through representatives assembled in the city of San Francisco, who have exhibited their full powers found to be in good and due form, have agreed to the present Charter of the United Nations and do hereby establish an international organization to be known as the United Nations.

The preamble clearly identifies that it is the people, through their respective governments, that have agreed to establish the United Nations. The choice of the words is material because it establishes that:

1. The governments represent their people;

2. Each government is sovereign; and

3. Each government is equal.

Without such recognition of national sovereignty and the peer-status of each government and country, the basis for setting up the United Nations would not exist. Furthermore, the arena of public international law, the prohibition of the enforcement of penal and revenue statutes or laws of one country in another country, and the need for the existence of extradition treaties before extradition proceedings in one country can be commenced all reinforce the principle of national sovereignty.

This legal legacy by which the world functions today finds difficulty in providing solutions to the borderless world of the Web. In such a situation, how does one exercise control of or regulate the Web?

There are, in fact some, simple solutions. Contractual arrangements made via the Web are no different than contractual arrangements made via telex or facsimile. Laws have evolved to recognize such contractual arrangements[15] and, accordingly, such evolution will occur to recognize contracts made via the Web simply because it is necessary to recognize such transactions which business people undertake.

The contrary would be unthinkable as it would cause immense commercial difficulty. Lord Wilberforce, in *Brinkibon v. Stahag Stahl und Stahlwarenhandelsgesellschaft mbH* (1983),[16] said that the approach to be taken to resolve these issues is by reference to the intention of the parties, by sound business practices and in some cases by a judgment where the risk should lie, indicating that courts do take a pragmatic approach to resolving some of these issues.

---

15 *Entores Ltd. v. Miles Far East Corporation* [1955] 2 Q.B. 327; [1955]2 All E.R. 493; *Brinkibon v. Stahag Stahl und Stahlwarenhandelsgesellschaft mbH* [1983] 2 A.C. 34; [1982] 1 All E.R .293.

16 *Brinkibon v. Stahag Stahl und Stahlwarenhandelsgesellschaft mbH* [1982] 1 All E.R. 293 (*per* Lord Wilberforce, at p. 296d-e).

While national sovereignty has been the basis for the evolution of the political and legal institutions today, it is necessary for governments to determine what exactly they want to regulate when it comes to the Internet and the Web. The lack of identification of where the problems are or the areas that need regulation has resulted in the perception that the Internet is beyond regulation.

7.02   Applicable Regulatory Frameworks

(a) In General

It is appropriate now to explore the structure of regulatory frameworks used by various countries affecting four areas, namely:

1. Regulating Internet Protocol Addresses;

2. Regulating Internet access;

3. Regulating online content; and

4. Regulating spam.[17]

(b) Regulating Internet Protocol Addresses

(i)   In General

In order for the Internet to function, there are certain pre-requisites as summarized below:

1. There is a need for every device that is connected to the Internet to have a unique and particular number, i.e., the Internet Protocol Address;

2. There must be a mechanism by which software can resolve these Internet Protocol Addresses, a process which is now undertaken by root servers located in three major areas in the world; and

3. There must be a system by which human recognizable names are managed (referred to as domain names) to which the Internet Protocol Address resolution must occur.

The Domain Name System relies on each domain name being assigned a unique identifier or number. *Webopedia* defines Internet Protocol Addressing as follows:

> An identifier for a computer or device on a TCP/Internet Protocol network. Networks using the TCP/Internet Protocol route messages based on the Internet Protocol Address of the destination. The format of an Internet Protocol Address is a 32-bit numeric address written as four numbers separated by periods. Each number can be zero to 255. For

---

17   Other areas, such as privacy, the issue of domain names and trade marks (and cybersquatting), e-contracting, and digital signatures are dealt with elsewhere in this publication.

example, 1.160.10.240 could be an Internet Protocol Address. Within an isolated network, you can assign Internet Protocol Addresses at random as long as each one is unique. However, connecting a private network to the Internet requires using registered Internet Protocol Addresses (called Internet Addresses) to avoid duplicates. The four numbers in an Internet Protocol Address are used in different ways to identify a particular network and a host on that network. Four regional Internet registries — ARIN, RIPE NCC, LACNIC, and APNIC — assign Internet Addresses from the following three classes:

Class A — supports 16-million hosts on each of 126 networks

Class B — supports 65,000 hosts on each of 16,000 networks

Class C — supports 254 hosts on each of 2-million networks

The number of unassigned Internet Addresses is running out, so a new classless scheme called CIDR is gradually replacing the system based on classes A, B, and C and is tied to adoption of IPv6.[18]

(ii) Who Assigns Internet Protocol Numbers?

Internet Protocol Numbers are required to be unique and are today assigned by non-governmental groups. These include IANA,[19] which has overall responsibility for assigning Internet Protocol Addresses to Regional Internet Registries (RIRs); each RIR, in turn, allocates Internet Protocol Addresses to local Internet registries or large end-users within their respective geographical jurisdictions. There are currently four RIRs, namely:

1. APNIC is a company incorporated under the laws of Australia,[20] and its official corporate name is APNIC Pty. Ltd. It's function according to APNIC's brochure is to ensure the fair distribution and responsible management of Internet Protocol Addresses and the related numeric resources which are required for stable and reliable operation of the Internet globally,[21] but not the domain name system. The countries that fall within APNIC's jurisdiction are Afghanistan, American Samoa, Australia, Bangladesh, Bhutan, British Indian Ocean Territory, Brunei Darussalam, Cambodia, China, Christmas Island, Cocos Keeling Islands, Comoros, Cook Islands, East Timor, Fiji, French Polynesia, French

---

18 *Webopedia*, at http://www.webopedia.com/TERM/I/Internet Protocol_address.html, accessed on 4 August 2004.

19 IANA stands for Internet Assigned Numbers Authority, at http://www.iana.org.

20 The memorandum of association of APNIC Pty. Ltd. is at http://www.apnic.org/docs/corpdocs/MoAhtm, and the articles of association of APNIC Pty. Ltd. are at http://www.apnic.org/docs/corpdocs/AoAhtm, accessed on 30 November 2004.

21 APNIC, at http://www.apnic.org/info/brochure/apnicbroc.pdf, accessed on 28 December 2004.

Southern Territories, Guam, Hong Kong, India, Indonesia, Japan, Kiribati, North Korea, South Korea, Laos, Macau, Madagascar, Malaysia, Maldives, Marshall Islands, Mauritius, Mayotte, Micronesia, Mongolia, Myanmar, Nauru, Nepal, New Caledonia, New Zealand, Niue, Norfolk Island, Northern Mariana Islands, Pakistan, Palau, Papua New Guinea, Philippines, Pitcairn, Reunion, Samoa, Seychelles, Singapore, Solomon Islands, Sri Lanka, Taiwan, Thai land, Tokelau, Tonga, Tuvalu, Vanuatu, Vietnam, Wallis and the Fortuna Islands.

2. ARIN, or the American Registry for Internet Numbers, Ltd., is a company incorporated under the Virginia Non-Stock Corporation Act and is domiciled in the State of Virginia, United States.[22] ARIN is responsible for such countries as the Bahamas, Barbados, Canada, the Cayman Islands, Mexico, South Africa, and the United States.[23]

3. LACNIC, or the Latin America and Caribbean Internet Addresses Registry, is a non-governmental, not-for-profit organization established under the laws of Uruguay. Its functions are to "administer Internet Protocol Addresses space, Autonomous System Numbers (ASN), reverse resolution and other resources of the Latin American and Caribbean region (LAC)".[24]

4. RIPE NCC (*Resaux Internet Protocol Europens Network Coordination Centre*)[25] is a non-profit association registered in Amsterdam, The Netherlands.[26] The RIPE NCC is responsible for countries in Europe, the Middle East, Central Asia, and Africa located north of the equator. RIPE NCC performs many functions and services, including managing, distributing, and registering public Internet Number Resources (i.e., Internet Protocol Addresses) within its region.

At the time of writing, a proposed new RIR for Africa, called AfriNIC,[27] received provisional recognition from ICANN[28] and is on the way to becoming

---

22   A copy of the articles of incorporation of ARIN is at http://www.arin.net/library/corp_docs/artic_incorp.pdf, accessed on 30 November 2004.

23   A complete list of countries within ARIN's jurisdiction is at http://www.arin.net/library/Internet_info/ARINcountries.htm.

24   Information about LACNIC is at http://lacnic.net/en/sobre-lacnic/estatuto/ and at http://lacnic.net/en/sobre-lacnic/, accessed on 30 November 2004.

25   General information about RIPE NCC is at http://www.ripe.net/.

26   A copy of the articles of association of RIPE NCC is at http://www.ripe.net/ripe/docs/articles-association.html, accessed on 28 December 2004.

27   Details about AfriNIC are at http://www.afrinic.net/.

28   AfriNIC received provisional recognition on 11 October 2004 from ICANN. A copy of the letter is at http://www.afrinic.net/documents/icann/Letter%20%20AfriNIC1.pdf.

the fifth RIR. AfriNIC is a company limited by guarantee, and it is incorporated under the Mauritius Companies Act 2001. It will have jurisdiction over those "African organizations that presently obtain Internet Protocol Address space from RIPE or ARIN".[29]

The RIRs are not controlled by any government, but are companies incorporated or societies organized under the laws of a selected country for convenience. Each RIR operates on a membership basis, and anyone can become a member of it. This is quite different from the way the International Telecommunications Union (ITU) is organized, where countries (represented by their governments) are members and these countries then allow their privatized telecommunications providers to attend.

Another entity that has overall responsibility for the Internet and the World Wide Web is ICANN, or the Internet Corporation of Assigned Names and Numbers.

ICANN is a corporation which is organized under the State of California Nonprofit Public Benefit Corporation Law for charitable and public purposes.[30] This makes ICANN a United States-domiciled company. Furthermore, ICANN is to ensure that the Domain Name System (DNS) works, as ICANN is responsible for managing and coordinating the DNS to ensure that every address is unique and that all users of the Internet can find all valid addresses. It does this by overseeing the distribution of unique Internet Protocol Addresses and domain names. It also ensures that each domain name maps to the correct Internet Protocol Address.[31]

According to the ICANN web site,[32] ICANN also is responsible:

> ... for Internet Protocol (IP) address space allocation, protocol identifier assignment, generic (gTLD) and country code (ccTLD) Top-Level Domain name system management, and root server system management functions. These services were originally performed under United States Government contract by the Internet Assigned Numbers Authority (IANA) and other entities. ICANN now performs the IANA function.

InterNIC is not a legal entity but a brand name owned by the United States Department of Commerce and managed by ICANN.[33]

---

29 AfriNIC's background information at http://www.afrinic.net/about.htm, accessed on 30 November 2004.

30 Articles of incorporation of ICANN, article 3, at http://www.icann.org/general/articles.htm, accessed on 30 November 2004.

31 See http://www.icann.org/faq/#WhatisICANN, accessed on 4 August 2004.

32 ICANN, at http://www.icann.org/general/, accessed on 30 November 2004.

33 See http://www.internic.org/index.html.

Therefore, IANA will allocate Internet Protocol Addresses from the pools of unallocated addresses to the RIRs according to their established needs. When an RIR requires more Internet Protocol Addresses for allocation or assignment within its region, a request is made and IANA makes an additional allocation to the RIR.[34] It should be noted that the functions of IANA are being transferred to ICANN.

APNIC, however, recognizes national Internet registries and defines them as:

> . . . [a] National Internet Registry (NIR) primarily allocates address space to its members or constituents, which are generally LIRs organized at a national level. NIRs are expected to apply their policies and procedures fairly and equitably to all members of their constituency. The policies in this document apply to NIRs; however, this document does not describe the entire roles and responsibilities of NIRs with respect to their formal relationship with APNIC. Such roles and responsibilities may be described in other documents and agreements, subject to APNIC Document review procedures.[35]

Taiwan, China, Vietnam, Indonesia, Japan, and Korea operate National Internet Registries. They receive bulk allocation of Internet Protocol Addresses from APNIC and are able to allocate individual Internet Protocol Addresses to users within their countries. The role played by these NIRs is to provide a degree of control over the allocation of Internet Protocol Addresses within their countries, as opposed to allow a non-governmental organization to do so. For example, in Vietnam, it is VNNIC that allocates Internet Protocol Addresses to those who require it in Vietnam whereas, in Thailand, APNIC allocates Internet Protocol Addresses. The rationale for governments taking over Internet Protocol Address allocations is to exercise some form of sovereignty over their use.

Malaysia has introduced regulatory provisions making the Malaysian Communications and Multimedia Commission the entity with overall responsibility for assigning Internet Protocol Addresses in Malaysia. However, this statutory duty has yet to be enforced whereby the Malaysian Communications and Multimedia Commission becomes Malaysia's National Internet Registry.

(iii) Process to Obtain Internet Protocol Addresses

According to IANA:

> [Internet Protocol] Addresses are assigned in a delegated manner. Users are assigned Internet Protocol Addresses by Internet Service Providers

---

34   See http://www.iana.org/ipaddress/ip-addresses.htm, accessed on 4 August 2004.

35   See http://www.apnic.net/docs/policy/add-manage-policy.html#4.1.2, accessed on 30 January 2005.

(ISPs). ISPs obtain allocations of Internet Protocol Addresses from a local Internet registry (LIR) or national Internet registry (NIR), or from their appropriate Regional Internet Registry (RIR).

According to RFC 2050, entitled "Internet Registry Internet Protocol Allocation Guidelines",[36] Internet Addresses (or Internet Protocol Addresses) are distributed with intent of meeting the following goals:

> Conservation: Fair distribution of globally unique Internet Address space according to the operational needs of the end-users and Internet Service Providers operating networks using this address space. Prevention of stockpiling to maximize the lifetime of the Internet Address space.

> Routability: Distribution of globally unique Internet Addresses in a hierarchical manner, permitting the routing scalability of the addresses. This scalability is necessary to ensure proper operation of Internet routing, although it must be stressed that routability is in no way guaranteed with the allocation or assignment of Internet Protocol Addresses.

> Registration: Provision of a public registry documenting address space allocation and assignment. This is necessary to ensure uniqueness and to provide information for Internet trouble shooting at all levels.

The guidelines do caution as to the possible conflict between conservation and routability and suggest that, in the final analysis, it is sound judgment which is to be relied on. To achieve these goals, an Internet registry with a hierarchical structure is created, whereby IANA has authority over all number spaces used on the Internet. IANA, in turn, allocates Internet Addresses to Regional Internet Registries, and RIRs, in turn, assign Internet Addresses to local Internet registries, ISPs, or large users (as defined in RFC 2050 *ante*).

Allocation of Internet Addresses entitles the "allocatee" to assign the Internet Numbers to users below it (remembering that the Internet registry structure is hierarchical). Assignments of Internet Addresses do not entitle the assignees to sub-allocate the Internet Addresses to other entities, and they may only use the Addresses for themselves.

An allocation of Internet Addresses is for a term of one year, renewable annually, if (a) "the original basis of the allocation or assignment remains valid"; and (b) ". . . address space is properly registered at the time of renewal".[37] However, compared to RIPE NCC, no such term is provided.[38]

---

36 The guideline was issued in November 1996, and is at http://www.isi.edu/in-notes/rfc2050.txt, accessed on 12 February 2005.

37 APNIC Policies for Internet Protocolv4 Address Space Management in the Asia Pacific Region, 16 August 2004, at http://www.apnic.net/docs/policy/add-manage-policy.html#8.3.

38 RIPE NCC Policy on Internet Protocolv4 Address Allocation and Assignment Policies for the RIPE NCC Service Region, Document RIPE 324, October 2004, at http://www.ripe.net/ripe/docs/ipv4-policies.html#ipv4.

The differences identified above indicate that the processes for allocating Internet Addresses by RIRs are not uniform.

(iv) Regulatory Issues

By ensuring a proper and orderly assignment of Internet Protocol Addresses, the uniqueness of the Internet Protocol Address system is preserved. This enables both origination and destination of messages to be known in cyberspace. Therefore, the management of Internet Protocol Addresses is an essential requirement to avoid clashes and confusion, and to create the stability needed for the Internet and the Web to function.

First, while recognizing the importance of Internet Protocol Addressing, the issue which governments are concerned about is why should this be undertaken by the private sector (meaning non-government entities).

Telecommunication regulation has been identified as:

> . . . one of the earliest examples of international regulatory cooperation between states . . . [b]ut in other respects . . . [regulation] is a story of territorial containment.[39]

This "cooperation between states" has not been pursued or given an opportunity to be pursued with respect to the allocation of Internet Addresses. It is assumed (rightly or wrongly) that having governments cooperate in this regard will be bad for the development of the Internet.

Furthermore, the right of ICANN[40] to allocate Internet Protocol Addresses to RIRs arises not because national governments have agreed to such an arrangement, but because the United States Department of Commerce has entered into a memorandum of understanding with ICANN. Consequently, it is necessary to ask whether the United States was authorized by other countries to do so. If not, what is the authority of the United States in entering an arrangement which affects all other countries?

The principal issue is one of national sovereignty — and whether a national government is perceived as being subordinate to another. These organizations owe their origin not to government cooperation, but to cooperation among a few individuals. The informality which existed at the time is argued to continue until today. Yet, these organization have become very formal in their organizational structure, their operations and functions, and their development of policies. Effectively, these organization perform quasi-governmental functions.

Second, the rise of United States political dominance and supremacy is of concern among other nation states. This rise is particularly manifested in the

---

39   Braithwaite and Drahos, "Telecommunications", *Global Business Regulation* (2000), at p. 322.
40   The functions and responsibilities of IANA are being transferred to ICANN.

administration and management of Internet Protocol Addresses. IANA's right to manage and administer Internet Protocol Addresses arises not because of cooperation among nation-states, but because of a contract that IANA has with the United States government. This arrangement alters the peer-to-peer relationship which exists among nation-states to one which is hierarchical, meaning that there are some states that are supreme (or primary) and some that are secondary.

Countries such as Taiwan, China, Vietnam, Japan, Indonesia, and Korea have taken steps towards reclaiming some degree of sovereignty by setting up NIRs to allocate Internet Protocol Addresses. However, the establishment of NIRs does not alter the main issue, i.e., that ICANN/IANA allocates Internet Protocol Addresses to RIRs which, in turn, allocate the addresses to NIRs. The entire hierarchical structure is based on RFC2050 of November 1996.

Furthermore, ICANN has set up a Governmental Advisory Committee[41] which:

> . . . should consider and provide advice on the activities of ICANN as they relate to concerns of governments and where they may affect public policy issues. The Advice of the Governmental Advisory Committee on public policy matters shall be duly taken into account by ICANN, both in the formulation and adoption of policies.

The central administration and management of the Internet Protocol Address system by a single entity of itself is not objectionable, simply because it is necessity to enable central coordination to occur. What is perhaps objectionable is that the authority granted to ICANN by the United States government indicates that all other governments are subordinate to the United States.

What is needed is for ICANN to seek approval from national governments for what it does. This may help to alleviate the concern that governments are being marginalized as to a resource (i.e., Internet Protocol Addresses) that is crucial for the effective participation in the knowledge economy and which is subject to United States control or dominance.

(c) Regulating Internet Access

The evolution of the Internet and the privatization of government-owned telecommunications providers created the environment that saw the rise of the Internet as a medium by which individuals anywhere in the world could communicate with one another at a fraction of the cost of a long-distance telephone call.

With this, governments began exploring ways and means by which Internet access could be regulated. Some governments viewed Internet access as a form of telecommunication service, while others did not. The approach by governments towards regulating Internet access has been piecemeal. Most

---

41   See http://194.78.218.67/web/index.shtml.

governments had in place telecommunication laws, and they used these laws to regulate access to the Internet.

However, since the 1990s, Internet access regulation has evolved. Governments today recognize that the Internet brings about a convergence of what were once separate and distinct functions or activities, i.e., telecommunications and broadcasting.

Table 2, below, summarizes the various types of Internet access regulation used by selected countries in regard to licensing of Internet Service Providers or Internet Access Providers. It is non-exhaustive but is representative of the dominant types of regulatory regimes.

Table 2 — Types of Internet Access Regulation

Country Name	No license required (Qualifications)	Individual license or concession required (Qualifications)	Class license required (Qualifications)
Anguilla		Yes	Yes (the regulator may decide that ISPs may be subject to a class license)
Australia	Yes (must comply with Schedule 2 of the Telecommunications Act 1997)		
Bahrain			Yes
Barbados		Yes	
Brunei Darulsalam			Yes (only registration required, and class license automatically applies)
Bulgaria	Yes		
China		Yes	
Cook Islands		Yes	
European Union			Yes (as a general authorization)
Germany		Yes	
Grenada		Yes (Internet Network/Services)	Yes (Internet Servic provision Type A Class License)

Country Name	No license required (Qualifications)	Individual license or concession required (Qualifications)	Class license required (Qualifications)
Hong Kong SAR			Yes
India		Yes	
Indonesia		Yes	
Jamaica		Yes	
Japan		Yes	
Korea		Yes (but apply by way of registration)	
Macau SAR		Yes	
Malaysia			Yes (only registration required)
New Zealand	Yes		
Russian Federation		Yes (Telemetric services license (to provide e-mail and hosting services if a company does not have its own lines). Data transmission and telematic services licenses (for companies that use their own external lines). Licenses for additional services (e.g., Internet Protocol (Internet Protocol telephone)	
Singapore[42]		Yes (applies to Public Internet Access Service)	Yes (Registration required; Internet based voice and data service)
South Africa		Yes	
Uganda		Yes	
United States	Yes		
Vietnam		Yes	
Zambia		Yes (including tele- centers)	

The licensing regimes as introduced in these countries can be grouped into three categories, as identified in Table 3, below.

---

42   See http://www.ida.gov.sg/idaweb/doc/download/I1301/SBO_Guidelines-8Sep2004.pdf, accessed on 12 January 2005.

Table 3 — Licensing Regimes

Licensing Regime	Description	Explanation
Group 1: A strict licensing regime (usually identified as an individual licensing regime)	Where the state authority reviews the formal license application and grants a license to operate an Internet service or access business. This is usually termed as an individual license regime.[43]	This regime is used by most countries when they first embark on allowing Internet access. The rationale is that the government is able to control the access point and is therefore able to continue to exercise influence over what people access. For example, Singapore requires providers of Public Internet Access Services to have an individual Service-Based Operator license.[44] The difference between countries using an individual license regime is the degree of transparency and bureaucratic discretion that exist. The greater the transparency and the less discretionary, the easier it is for businesses to operate.
Group 2: A less formal or more liberal licensing regime (usually identified as a class licensing regime)	Where the state authority permits entities wishing to offer Internet access to do so without the need for a formal license application. The license conditions are published, and individuals may either register or merely undertake the business and be deemed to be licensed.	This regime is used when a country determines that providing Internet access is a necessity to be able to participate in the knowledge economy. In addition, the economic philosophy of the country is a liberal and open market economy. If these elements are present, it is likely that a class licensing regime will be introduced. Class licensing regimes do not require formal license applications. The nature of being licensed varies, where some countries merely require entities to be registered with the national regulatory authority (i.e., a simple process to get licensed), whereas other countries deem entities that provide the service to be subjected to a class license (i.e., an automatic license).

---

43   Although this process lends itself to the grant of concessions by the government, which is usually adopted when the country does not have a clear set of regulations. The concession agreement sets out the rights and obligations of both the private enterprise and the government.

44   Guidelines For Submission of Application for Services-Based Operator License, Info-Comm Development Authority, at http://www.ida.gov.sg/idaweb/doc/download/I1301/SBO_Guidelines-8Sep2004.pdf accessed on 28 December 2004.

Licensing Regime	Description	Explanation
		In both situations, the conditions of the class licensed are published and entities are aware of the conditions that they must abide by.
		For example, in Malaysia, the provision of Internet access is a class-licensed activity (categorized as a class application service provision) and merely requires providers to be registered. The licensed conditions are gazetted and are publicly available.[45]
Group 3: No license required	Where the activity does not require a license from the state authority, but the provider may or may not be obligated to comply with certain rules and regulations.	The belief that the market can best discipline participants leads to the approach that there should be no requirement for licenses to provide access to the Internet. In this situation, the regulatory framework is viewed as imposing unnecessary burdens on a fledgling industry and the regulator.
		This belief has been proven accurate as evidenced by the rise of the number of Internet Access Providers and Internet users in countries such as Australia and the United States, where such a system is practiced.
		For example, the United States does not require Internet Service Providers or Internet Access Providers to be licensed as it considers them to be providers of "information services".[46] In Australia,[47] ISPs and IAPs are unlicensed, but they must comply with specific provisions in the Telecommunications Act 1997 and the Telecommunications (Consumer Protection and Service Standards) Act 1999.
		This does not mean that Internet Access Providers are totally unregulated. All it means is that there is no requirement for them to obtain a license before providing a service. They are subject to various regulations such as in Australia, where they are subjected to the Internet Content Code enforced by the Australian Broadcasting Authority.

---

45 Communications and Multimedia Act 1998 and the Communications and Multimedia (Licensing) Regulations 2000.

46 "Licensing Options for Internet Service Providers", at http://www.Internetpolicy.net/practices/licensing_options.pdf, accessed on 28 December 2004.

47 See http://Internet.aca.gov.au/Australian Communications AuthorityINTER2097602: STANDARD:1167708603:pp=PC_1621,pc=PC_1622, accessed on 28 December 2004.

There are various approaches taken by developing countries towards the regulation of Internet Service Providers, as set out in the tables, below.[48] The approach by developing countries towards regulating Internet service follows the same "tri-chotomy" as set out in Table 3, above, namely:

1. Requiring no licensing;
2. Requiring a simple licensing process (i.e., class license regime); or
3. Requiring a formal and strict licensing process (i.e., individual licensing regime).

Table 4 — Prior Approval Not Required

Country	Year Regulator Established	Approval Required for ISP to Start Operations	ISP Prices Regulated?
Brazil	1997	None	No
Bulgaria	1998	None	No
Chile	1977	None	No
El Salvador	1996	None	No
Moldova	N/A	None	No
Tanzania	1993	None	Yes

Table 5 — Only Notice Required

Country	Year Regulator Established	Approval Required for ISP to Start Operations	ISP Prices Regulated?
Bolivia	1995	Notification	No
Bosnia and Herzegovina	2001	Notification	N/A
Czech Repbulic	2000	Notification	No
Estonia	1998	Notification	No
Malaysia	1998	Notification	Yes (dial up)

---

48   Wallsten, "Regulation and Internet Use in Developing Countries", at http://www.aei-brookings.org/admiN/Authorpdfs/page.php?id=262, accessed on 12 December 2004.

Country	Year Regulator Established	Approval Required for ISP to Start Operations	ISP Prices Regulated?
Mexico	1996	Notification	No
Pakistan	1996	Notification	No
Poland	2000	Notification	No
Slovakia	1993	Notification	No

Table 6 — Approval Required

Country	Year Regulator Established	Approval Required for ISP to Start Operations	ISP Prices Regulated?
Argentina	1990	Formal	No
Barbados	2001	Formal	No
Colombia	1994	Formal	No
Costa Rica	1996	Formal	N/A
Côte d'Ivoire	1995	Formal	Yes
Dominican Republic	1998	Formal	No
Ecuador	1995	Formal	No
Ghana	1996	Formal	No
Guatamala	1996	Formal	No
Honduras	1995	Formal	No
Hungary	1990	Formal	No
India	1997	Formal	No
Jamaica	1997	Formal	No
Jordan	1995	Formal	Yes
Kenya	1999	Formal	No
Malawi	1998	Formal	Yes
Mongolia	1995	Formal	No
Panama	1996	Formal	No

Country	Year Regulator Established	Approval Required for ISP to Start Operations	ISP Prices Regulated?
Peru	1991	Formal	No
Romania	2001	Formal	No
South Africa	2000	Formal	No
Sri Lanka	1991	Formal	Yes
Venezuela	1991	Formal	No

Table 7 — Approval Not Available

Country	Year Regulator Established	Approval Required for ISP to Start Operations	ISP Prices Regulated?
Belize	1997	N/A	Yes
Latvia	1992	N/A	No
Morocco	1998	N/A	No
Thailand	2001	N/A	N/A
Turkey	2000	N/A	No
Uganda	1997	N/A	No

The use of formal licensing regimes arises partially because of the political concerns that the political elite has with permitting full access, namely the dangers (real or perceived) of political instability. As a result, the borderless nature of the Internet has not stopped governments from controlling access of its people to the Internet or the Web. Ultimately, what is important in developing a regulatory framework is that the framework must:

1. Enable the nation's goals or objectives to be achieved or materialized;

2. Be transparent;

3. Have a certain and fair process; and

4. Avoid the creation of unnecessary transactional costs.

It should be noted that the regulation of Internet Service Providers by national regulatory authorities is a highly contentious issue as it relates to economic and competition regulation. These areas are considered outside the scope of this chapter, but readers should bear in mind these other areas when considering the regulation of Internet Service Providers.

(d) Regulating Online Content

(i) In General

The concept of "content" in the Internet world encompasses anything that is created and would apply, from ordinary email to Web sites and weblogs. The wide scope of the word "content" provides a difficulty for governments when they consider content regulation. How far should such regulation go (i.e., a jurisdictional issue)? How wide should it reach (i.e., a scope issue)?

Control of content exists despite article 19 of the Universal Declaration of Human Rights, which provides that:

> ... [e]veryone has the right to freedom of opinion and expression; this right includes freedom to hold opinions without interference and to seek, receive and impart information and ideas through any media and regardless of frontiers.

The International Chamber of Commerce defines Internet content regulation as:

> ... any type of legislation by governments or regulatory authorities directed at:
>
> censoring information and communication on the Internet based on its subject matter, and
>
> controlling, or attempting to control, access to Internet sites based on subject matter.[49]

The control of access to particular Web sites based on their content is achieved by controlling access to the Internet. Hence, governments which advocate tight control of access to content tend to use individual licenses to control access to the Internet. In addition to tighter licensing controls, such governments tend to use filtering software or proxy server farms to manage access to content by blocking access based on the Internet Protocol Address of the server where the content is hosted. By controlling the providers of access, content which is prohibited can be similarly controlled.

The issue of regulating content is not a new one. It is part of an on-going debate between those who believe that the state has a role to ensure that harmful content is prohibited and those who believe that the individual must have a right to choose. The chasm between community rights and individual rights divides the debate over Internet content regulation. It has been pointed out that:

> ... [t]he key concern in the area of telecommunications regulation is not to attempt to alter or overlook these strictures in the drive to unleash market forces and economic growth through information technology. Rather, it should be to seek means to accommodate legal and

---

49   See http://www.iccwbo.org/home/statements_rules/statements/2002/Internet_content.asp, accessed on 5 February 2005.

cultural reservations about unfettered communications without building unnecessary new barriers to electronic commerce.[50]

While it is beyond the scope of this examination to consider all other laws that are applicable to content (whether online or otherwise), such as the law of defamation and publication of seditious material, the chapter will focus on identifying what some countries are doing with respect to regulating online content and will identify the regulatory approaches.

(ii) Regulatory Approaches

In General   It is possible to categorize various regulatory approaches taken by the selected countries as follows:

1. A legal prohibition regime, where providing or accessing certain types of content (whether online or not) is criminalized, requiring law enforcement authorities to monitor and prosecute offenders;

2. A legal prohibition regime and a technical "gatekeeper" system, where the legal regime prohibits the provision of or access to certain types of online content and the state controls access by means of filtering software and proxy server farms, where blocking techniques are used; and

3. A co-regulatory regime, where the Internet industry sets out the applicable rules in respect of controlling access to online content, and where the regulatory authority will only step in should the industry code not function adequately.

The choice of regime reflects the political views of the ruling elite. If they hold extremely conservative views or are less tolerant of dissent, it is more likely that they would employ the legal prohibition with a gatekeeper system. On the other hand, if the ruling elite recognizes that banning online content is difficult because of available software that allows one to by-pass such filters, coupled with the fact that it is necessary that knowledge be available so as to enable greater economic development, a co-regulatory regime will be adopted.

Approaches to Regulating Online Content   The choice of countries below reflects a broad spectrum as to the regulation of online content. The United States is excluded because attempts by government to introduce legislation (such as the Communications Decency Act or the Child Online Protection Act) to control access to certain types of content, especially those that affect minors, have been met with successful challenges in the courts.

---

50 Townsend, "Telecommunications Regulatory Issues for Electronic Commerce", Report to the International Telecommunication Union, 8th Regulatory Colloquium, at http://www.infodev.org/projects/ecommerce/341itu8/341.pdf, accessed on 12 February 2005.

Consequently, the approach of the United States is that online content should not be censored or controlled. Thus, the United States does not provide any appropriate means to consider how to control online content.

Singapore   Singapore has a three-prong approach to Internet content regulation,[51] as follows:

1. A light-touch, class license scheme, which provides minimum standards to safeguard values and promote healthy growth;

2. The encouragement of industry self-regulation; and

3. An active public education program to promote parental supervision.

The class license scheme is an automatic licensing scheme that requires IASPs and content providers to comply with an Internet Code of Practice. IASPs are not required to monitor or censor Internet content. They are, however, required to limit public access to 100 mass-impact pornography sites. Personal communications, such as email or Internet relay chat, personal websites, and corporate Internet use by employees or for business transactions, are not regulated.[52]

> Since its formation on 1 October 1994, the [Singapore Broadcasting Authority] has been tasked with the job of developing quality broadcasting, building a well-informed and culturally rich society and making Singapore a dynamic broadcasting hub. The SBA is, in addition to its various other functions, responsible for regulating Internet Service Providers and Internet Content Providers. This is done chiefly through the Internet Class License Scheme and the Internet Code of Practice which was first introduced in July 1996 via *Gazette* Notification Number 2400/96. The Internet Code of Practice was subsequently revised to remedy some of the shortcomings and perceived inadequacies of the earlier version of the Code as well as to take into account the recommendations made by the National Internet Advisory Committee (NIAC) in its report released in September 1997. The revised Code of Practice came into effect on 1 November 1997 via *Gazette* Notification Number 3810/97.[53]

Malaysia   Malaysia operates a co-regulatory scheme for Internet content, as set out in the Communications and Multimedia Act 1998. It requires a

---

51   UNPAN, "Singapore's Legal and Policy Environment for E-commerce", at http://unpan1.un.org/intradoc/groups/public/documents/APCITY/UNPAN002010.pdf, accessed on 5 February 2005.

52   SBA (Class License) Notification, 15 July 1996; SBA Internet Code of Practice, 1 November 1997.

53   Anil, "Re-Visiting the Singapore Internet Code of Practice", 2001(2) *Journal of Information, Law and Technology*, at http://elj.warwick.ac.uk/jilt/01-2/anil.html/, accessed on 5 February 2005.

designated industry group (the Communications and Multimedia Content Forum of Malaysia)[54] to develop a content code, with which members are to comply. The code is required to be registered with the Commission after it has undergone a public consultation process. However, once the code is registered, it affords any one who complies with it a defense to any action brought.

This provides the incentives for compliance. In addition, the Communications and Multimedia Commission may direct a licensee to comply with the content code, and a failure to do so is a breach of a legal instrument, with the possibility of criminal sanctions being imposed.

The code defines and describes the various types of prohibited content enabling content providers to have clearer guidance on what is prohibited and what is not. This arose because the previous regimes did not have any clear guidelines. By section 213 of the Communications and Multimedia Act 1998, the areas which are to be in the content code include model procedures for dealing with offensive or indecent content, as well as addressing such matters as:

1. The restrictions on the provision of unsuitable content;

2. The methods of classifying content;

3. The procedures for handling public complaints and for reporting information about complaints to the Commission;

4. The representation of Malaysian culture and national identity;

5. Public information and education regarding content regulation and technologies for the end user control of content; and

6. Other matters of concern to the community.

The need for the content code to explain and define the types of prohibited content exists because of the prohibition in the Communications and Multimedia Act 1998, which makes it an offense to provide content which is indecent, obscene, false, menacing, or offensive in character with intent to annoy, abuse, threaten, or harass any person. Consequently, the code elaborates in some detail what is indecent, obscene, false, menacing, or offensive content.

With respect to online content, the general approach is to place the responsibility for the content with the end-user. The end-user determines what he wants. The ISPs and other content hosts act as mere intermediaries and, hence, the concept of an "innocent carrier" is introduced. The "innocent carrier" concept introduced by the content code recognizes that IASPs are nothing more the carriers and that they do not have control over the content

---

54   See http://www.cmcf.org.my/.

which their subscribers access to. This inability to control, and the futility of imposing legal obligations on ISPs to control access, has produced this concept. However, once the IASP (including content hosts and aggregators) is aware of the type of content (and this is through a direction from the Complaints Bureau), the IASP (including content hosts and aggregators) is to remove the offending content.

Australia   According to the Australian Broadcasting Authority (ABA),[55] it administers a "co-regulatory" scheme for Internet content. The scheme aims to address community concerns about offensive and illegal material on the Internet and, in particular, to protect children from exposure to material that is unsuitable for them. The scheme is established under Schedule 5 of the Broadcasting Services Act 1992, which gives the ABA the following functions:

1. Investigation of complaints about Internet content and Internet gambling services;

2. Encouragement of development of codes of practice for the Internet industry, registering, and monitoring compliance with such codes;

3. Provision of advice and information to the community about Internet safety issues, especially those relating to children's use of the Internet;

4. Undertaking of research into Internet usage issues and informing itself and the Minister of relevant trends; and

5. Liaison with relevant overseas bodies.

In performing its role, the ABA is guided by principles laid down in legislation which have the aim of minimizing the financial and administrative burdens on industry and encouraging the supply of Internet services at performance standards that meet community needs. Furthermore:

> . . . the co-regulatory scheme for Internet content allows for and encourages the development of three codes of practice. . . one for Internet content hosts (ICHs) and two for Internet Service Providers (ISPs).

The codes are registered with the ABA, and compliance is voluntary, unless the ABA directs an ISP or Internet content host to comply with the code. Once this direction is given, if the directed entity fails to comply, it commits an offence under the Broadcasting Services Act 1992.

The Australian approach is one which is led by industry. Industry determines what it wishes to abide by, and the code is then developed. This code is then registered after it goes through a public consultation process. This form of "co-regulation" is seen as empowering industry to govern themselves, with the regulatory authority taking a back seat and only intervening when there has been a failure.

---

55   See http://www.aba.gov.au/Internet/.

China   China, in "1995, . . . began permitting commercial Internet accounts, [and] at least 60 sets of regulations have been issued aimed at controlling Internet content".[56] Some rules are directly aimed towards content control, such as:

1. The Decision of the Standing Committee of the National People's Congress on Maintaining Internet Security (2000);

2. The Measures for Managing Internet Information Services (2000);

3. The Provisional Rules for the Administration of the Operation of News Publication Services by Web Sites (2000);

4. The Rules for the Administration of Internet Bulletin Board System Services (2000);

5. The Rules for the Administration of Computer & Internet Bulletin Board System Services in the Colleges (2001); and

6. The Interim Provisions on the Administration of Internet Publication (2002).

Other rules are aimed at Internet cafes, state secrecy, network security, and encryption, but they also indirectly have a strong impact on Internet content regulation.

Article 15 of the Measures for Managing Internet Information Services provides that "[i]nformation that is detrimental to the honor and interests of the state" is banned on the Internet. Yet, an Internet user has no way of knowing what topics might be considered injurious. Online speech which only criticizes the current leaders or expresses some discontent with the government will perhaps be interpreted to violate this provision. Such obscurity gives the government wide discretion, and a stronger basis on which to arrest and punish persons who engage in such forms of expression. Sometimes, the result is unpredictable. The public notice at one chat room identifies what type of content is prohibited:

> Please take note that the following issues are prohibited according to Chinese law:
>
> 1. Criticism of the PRC Constitution
>
> 2. Revealing State secrets, and discussion about overthrowing the Communist government
>
> 3. Topics that damage the reputation of the State
>
> 4. Discussions that ignite ethnic animosity, discrimination or regional separatism

---

56   Li, "Internet Content Control in China", *International Journal of Communications Law and Policy*, Issue 8, Winter 2003/2004, at http://www.ijclp.org/8_2004/pdf/charlesli-paper-ijclp-neu.pdf, accessed on 12 February 2005.

5. Discussion that undermines the state's religious policy, as well as promotes evil cults and superstition

6. Spreading rumors, perpetrating and disseminating false news that promotes disorder and social instability

7. Dissemination of obscenity, sex, gambling, violence, and terror. Cyber-sex is not permitted within the English chat-room.

8. Humiliating or slandering innocent people

9. Any discussion and promotion of content which PRC laws prohibit.

"These rules grant various government authorities full power to monitor organizations and individuals on the Internet".[57] China spends a considerable amount of time and resources in implementing these content control rules and uses drastic enforcement measures to ensure compliance with them, such as arresting "Lin Hai, who was considered the first detained 'Internet dissident' in China".[58] The rules have shifted the:

> ... primary responsibility for control of the Internet from the government to ... Internet Service Providers. The regulations decentralize responsibility. As a result, content is not double- but triple-checked: at the gateway of the dominant connectors such as China Telecom, at the network responsible for delivering the content, and the receiver itself ... [which] is a very effective way to make Internet participants adhere to those norms beneficial to the Communist Party of China's control.[59]

All of these regulations make surveillance on the Internet legal in China.

There are other laws which apply to controlling access to or production of online content, such as:

1. The Measures on the Administration of Broadcasting Audio/Visual Programs over the Internet or Other Information Networks,[60] which impose a licensing requirement for any person who transmits audio/visual or news programs to the public via the Internet;

---

57 Li, "Internet Content Control in China", *International Journal of Communications Law and Policy*, Issue 8, Winter 2003/2004, at http://www.ijclp.org/8_2004/pdf/charlesli-paper-ijclp-neu.pdf, accessed on 12 February 2005.

58 Li, "Internet Content Control in China", *International Journal of Communications Law and Policy*, Issue 8, Winter 2003/2004, at http://www.ijclp.org/8_2004/pdf/charlesli-paper-ijclp-neu.pdf, accessed on 12 February 2005.

59 Li, "Internet Content Control in China", *International Journal of Communications Law and Policy*, Issue 8, Winter 2003/2004, at http://www.ijclp.org/8_2004/pdf/charlesli-paper-ijclp-neu.pdf, accessed on 12 February 2005.

60 See http://www.cecc.gov/pages/virtualAcad/cxp/explaws.php, accessed on 12 February 2005.

2. The Interim Provisions on the Administration of Internet Publishing, which require that Internet publishing activities can be done if prior permission be obtained; and

3. The Provisions on the Administration of Internet Electronic Bulletin Board Services, which require that bulletin board services be specifically set out when applying for the appropriate license, e.g., a commercial Internet Information Service License.[61]

Finally, China practices a gatekeeper system to control access to online content. This is done by strictly regulating the backbone network connections to the Internet outside China. By limiting the number of backbone network connections, China can effectively limit access to online content, thus controlling what its people are able to access.

Saudi Arabia   In Saudi Arabia, the online content rules are contained in the Council of Ministers Resolution of 2001,[62] which provides:

Publishing or accessing restricted data should be refrained;

Setting up websites or publishing Web pages must observe defined requirements as detailed below:

All Internet users in the Kingdom of Saudi Arabia shall refrain from publishing or accessing data containing some of the following:

1. Anything contravening a fundamental principle or legislation, or infringing the sanctity of Islam and its benevolent Shari'ah, or breaching public decency.

2. Anything contrary to the state or its system.

3. Reports or news damaging to the Saudi Arabian armed forces, without the approval of the competent authorities.

4. Publication of official state laws, agreements or statements before they are officially made public, unless approved by the competent authorities.

5. Anything damaging to the dignity of heads of states or heads of credited diplomatic missions in the Kingdom, or harms relations with those countries.

6. Any false information ascribed to state officials or those of private or public domestic institutions and bodies, liable to cause them or their offices harm, or damage their integrity.

---

61   The subject matter of the bulletin board is subject to prior approval. One is not allowed to provide a bulletin board on a subject which has not been approved. Bulletin board providers must monitor the content placed on the board and delete it if it is prohibited under article 9, retain records, and report to the authorities.

62   See http://www.al-bab.com/media/docs/saudi.htm, accessed on 13 February 2005.

7. The propagation of subversive ideas or the disruption of public order or disputes among citizens.

8. Anything liable to promote or incite crime, or advocate violence against others in any shape or form.

9. Any slanderous or libelous material against individuals.

Furthermore, certain trade directives stipulate that all companies, organizations, and individuals benefiting from the service may not:

1. Carry out any activity through the Internet, such as selling, advertising, or recruitment, except in accordance with the commercial licenses and registers in force;

2. Carry out any financial investment activity or offer shares for subscription, except when in possession of the necessary licenses to do so;

3. Promote or sell medicines or foodstuff carrying any medicinal claims, or cosmetics, except those registered and approved by the Ministry of Health;

4. Advertise or promote or sell substances covered by other international agreements to which the Kingdom is a party, except for those with the necessary licenses; and

5. Advertise trade fairs or organize trade delegations visits or tourist tours or trade directories, except those with the necessary licenses.

All private and government departments, and individuals, setting up websites or publishing files or pages, must:

1. Respect commercial and information conventions;

2. Have the approval of government authorities for setting up websites or publishing files or pages for or about themselves;

3. Have the approval of the Ministry of Information for setting up media-type websites which publish news on a regular basis, such as newspapers, magazines, and books;

4. Observe good taste in the design of websites and pages;

5. Assure the effective protection of data on websites and pages; and

6. Take full responsibility for websites and pages and the information contained therein.

The Resolution refers to a set of regulatory and technical procedures aimed at ensuring the safety of the constituents of the national network (the Internet inside the Kingdom) through effective programming and mechanical means. These include:

1. Service providers must determine Internet access eligibility through access accounts, user identification, and effective passwords for the use of the access point or subsequent points and linking that through tracing and investigation programs that record the time spent, addresses accessed or to which or through which access was attempted, and the size and type of files copied, when possible or necessary;

2. Anti-virus programs and protection against concealing addresses or printing passwords and files must be employed;

3. Providers must endeavor to avoid errors in applications that may provide loopholes that may be exploited for subversive activities or to obtain data not permitted for use for whatever reason;

4. Provision of Internet services must be restricted to the end-user through the Internet service unit at King Abdulaziz City for Science and Technology;

5. Providers must maintain a manual and electronic register with comprehensive information on end-users, their addresses, telephone numbers, purpose of use, and private Internet access accounts, and provide the authorities with a copy thereof, if necessary; and

6. Providers may not publish any printed directories containing subscriber and end-user names and addresses, without their agreement.

The government utilizes content-filtering technologies and proxy servers to maintain control over access to certain contents.[63] According to the Internet Services Unit (ISU) of the King Abdulaziz City for Science and Technology (KACST), the content-blocking policy[64] states that:

> A security committee chaired by the Ministry of Interior was [formed], with one of its tasks . . . is the selection of sites to be blocked and the oversight of this process. However, due to the wide-spread and diverse nature of pornographic sites, KACST was [requested] to directly block these types of sites. Other non-pornographic sites are only blocked based on direct requests from the security bodies within the government. KACST has no authority in the selection of such sites and its role is limited to carrying out the directions of these security bodies.

---

63 Zittrain and Edelman, "Documentation of Internet Filtering in Saudi Arabia", Berkmen Centre for Internet and Society, Harvard Law School, at http://cyber.law.harvard.edu/filtering/saudiarabia/, accessed on 12 February 2005.

64 See http://www.isu.net.sa/saudi-Internet/contenet-filtring/filtring-policy.htm, accessed on 12 February 2005.

Filtering is undertaken by passing all incoming Web traffic to Saudi Arabia through a proxy system operated by the ISU, which uses a content-filtering software to filter out prohibited content. Furthermore, a list of Internet Protocol Addresses for banned sites is maintained by the filtering system. The list is updated daily based on the content-filtering policy. However, individuals can report to the ISU and request that content from certain sites be blocked.[65]

The Philippines   The Philippines does not have any specific rules governing access to online content, and it relies on its general law that makes it an offence to provide obscene and pornographic material.[66] Furthermore, specific statutes are believed to provide adequate control of online content. These include:

1. Republic Act Number 7610, the Special Protection of Children Against Child Abuse, Exploitation, and Discrimination Act, 1992, which seeks "to provide special protection to children from all firms of abuse, neglect, cruelty exploitation and discrimination and other conditions" and makes criminally liable "any person who shall hire, employ, use, persuade, induce, or coerce a child to perform in obscene exhibitions and indecent shows, whether live or in video, or model in obscene publications or pornographic materials or to sell or distribute the said materials";[67]

2. Republic Act Number 6955 of 13 June 1990, which criminalizes the practice of establishing and carrying on businesses that match Filipino women for marriage to foreign nationals on a mail-order basis and other similar practices;[68] and

3. Republic Act Number 9208, the Act to Institute Policies to Eliminate Trafficking in Persons, Especially Women and Children, Establishing the Necessary Institutional Mechanisms for the Protection and Support of Trafficked Persons (the "Anti-Trafficking in Persons Act of 2003"),

---

65   See http://www.isu.net.sa/saudi-Internet/contenet-filtring/filtring-mechanism.htm, accessed on 12 February 2005.

66   Monte-Medina, "Policy Directions To Regulate Harmful Internet Content: The Philippine Experience", a Paper Presented at the Forum on ICTs and Gender, 20–23 August 2003, Kuala Lumpur, Malaysia, at http://www.globalknowledge.org/gkps_portal/view_file.cfm?fileid=1111, accessed on 11 February 2005.

67   Special Protection of Children Against Child Abuse, Exploitation, and Discrimination Act, 1992, section 9.

68   Section 2(a)(2) of Republic Act Number 6955 makes it unlawful "to advertise, publish, print, or distribute or cause the advertisement, publication, printing, or distribution of any brochure, flier, or any propaganda material" to promote the matching of Filipino women to foreign nationals for marriage on a commercial basis.

which specifically contemplates Internet content in defining "pornography" and the crime of trafficking in persons.[69]

United Kingdom   The United Kingdom's Internet Service Providers Association developed a Code of Conduct 1999 (amended 2002),[70] which its members agree to adopt on becoming a member. It is an industry-led regulatory framework in the form of industry self-regulation. In essence, the Code of Conduct, as it applies to online content, provides:

1.   Content must comply with United Kingdom law;

2.   Material ought not to be provided which incites violence, cruelty, or racial hatred; and

3.   Contents should not mislead by being inaccurate, ambiguous, exaggerated, omissive, or otherwise.

The Code refers to actions which may be taken by the Internet Watch Foundation (IWF),[71] such as where members of Internet Service Providers Association agree that:

> . . . where the IWF has notified them that Internet sites and Usenet news groups contain material which the IWF considers to be illegal child pornography, members will remove such materials, wherever it is technically possible to do so . . . . Where requested by the IWF (on behalf of a legitimate law enforcement authority), and where technically able to do so, members must retain copies of removed material for a reasonable period of time. . Members should take careful consideration of all other IWF notices and recommendations.

In effect, the use of a self-regulatory regime to control online content is seen as a more practicable approach than through legislation, although what is

---

69   Section 3(h) of the Anti-Trafficking in Persons Act defines "pornography" as any "representation, through publication, exhibition, cinematography, indecent shows, information technology, or by whatever means, of a person engaged in real or simulated explicit sexual activities or any representation of the sexual parts of a person for primarily sexual purposes". Section 5(c) of the Act makes it unlawful "to advertise, publish, print, broadcast, or distribute or cause the advertisement, publication, printing, broadcasting, or distribution by any means, including the use of information technology and the Internet, of any brochure, flyer, or any propaganda material that promotes trafficking in persons".

70   A copy of ISPA's Code of Conduct is available at http://www.ispa.org.uk/html/index3.html?frame=http%3A//www.ispa.org.uk/html/about_isp/ispa_code.html, accessed on 18 April 2005.

71   "The Internet Watch Foundation was formed in 1996 following an agreement between the government, police, and the Internet service provider industry that a partnership approach was needed to tackle the distribution of child abuse images (often referred to as child pornography) online". Internet Watch Foundation web site, available at http://www.iwf.org.uk/public/page.103.htm.

prohibited content is dependent on the local legislation. In the United Kingdom, for example, legislation exists which renders certain types of content prohibited, as shown in the table below.

Subject Matter	Prohibited Because
Child abuse images	Protection of Children Act 1978 Civic Government Act 1982 (Scotland) Sexual Offences Act 2003
Obscene Publications — There is no definition, other than it must be content which tends to "deprave and corrupt" those likely to read, see, or hear the matter contained or embodied in it. As the possible width of the words "deprave and corrupt", the IWF identifies as a guide and for ease the following types of content which are considered as obscene, "images featuring acts of extreme sexual activity such as bestiality, necrophilia, rape, or torture".	Obscene Publications Act 1959 and 1964
Racist Content — Content which stirs up racial hatred against a group of persons in Great Britain, by reference to color, race, nationality, ethnic or national origins.	Public Order Act 1936 (amended by the Race Relations Act 1976)

In two cases in the United Kingdom, *R. v. Bowden*[72] and *R. v. Jayson,*[73] the court in the former case held that pseudo-photo is sufficiently wide to include what appears to be a photo; hence, downloading an image from a web site would be within the ambit of "pseudo" for the purposes of the Protection of Children Act 1978. The wording in section 1 of the Act, as amended, was clear and unambiguous. The words "to make" had to be given their natural and ordinary meaning, and in the instant context, that was "to cause to exist; to produce by action, to bring about".

In the latter case, the Court of Appeal had to address the issue as to what constitutes "making" a photograph or "pseudo photograph" for the purposes of section 1(1)(a) of the Protection of Children Act 1978. It was held that "the act of voluntarily downloading an indecent image from a web page on to a computer screen is an act of making a photograph or

---

72   *R. v. Bowden* (2000) Cr. App. R. 438.
73   *R. v. Jayson* (2002) E.W.C.A. Crim. 683; see also *R. v. Smith* (2002) E.W.C.A. Crim. 683.

pseudo-photograph". The requisite *mens rea* is that the act of making should be a deliberate act with the knowledge that the image was, or was likely to be, an indecent photograph or pseudo-photograph of a child. No intention to store the image was required to satisfy the *mens rea* requirement. The case of *R. v. Smith* held that opening an email attachment containing an indecent image was sufficient to constitute "making" for the purposes of the Act.

These cases indicate the extent by which the United Kingdom courts are prepared to construe the word "making", so that activities such as downloading or opening of email attachments may become criminalized, unless before the person opened the attachment he was unaware that it contained, or was likely to contain, such an image.[74]

What is observable is that the United Kingdom uses both legislative and self-regulatory means by which online content is regulated. Laws are used to render certain activities offences and, at the same time, industry acts as a watch dog reporting the existence of such content to bodies such as INHOPE or to the law enforcement authorities. Yet, the question whether the online provider itself is exposed to liability needs to be addressed. According to European Directive 2000/31/EC, three areas are considered, i.e., hosting, caching, and mere conduit.[75]

Area	Scope of Defense/Exclusion of Liability
Mere conduit	No criminal liability for that transmission where the service provider: (a) did not initiate the transmission; (b) did not select the receiver of the transmission; and (c) did not select or modify the information contained in the transmission.
Caching	No criminal liability where caching is done because of technical purposes (e.g., making more efficient onward transmission of the information to other recipients of the service on their request) or does not modify the data.
Hosting	No criminal liability if the service provider was unaware of the content, or on becoming aware, act expeditiously to remove the content or the recipient was not acting under the control of the service provider.

---

74 *Atkins v. Director of Public Prosecution* (2000) 2 Cr. App. R. 248.

75 See sections 17, 18, and 19 of the E-Commerce Regulations which implement the Directive.

The scope of the Directive is to enable the concept of "innocent carrier" to exist and be a defense recognizing that it is impossible to impose any effective legislative restriction on service providers to act as gatekeepers, as the cost to do so is prohibitive.

United States The United States has several statutes dealing with child pornography, making it an offence to own, distribute, advertise, or persuade any child to participate in any pornographic act. These statutes are:

1. The Sexual Exploitation of Children Act 1977;

2. The Child Protection Act 1984;

3. The Child Sexual Abuse and Pornography Act 1986;

4. The Child Protection and Obscenity Enforcement Act 1988;

5. The Telecommunications Act of 1996; and

6. The Child Pornography Prevention Act 1996.

Furthermore, the Children's Internet Protection Act 2000 mandated schools and libraries to install Internet filters on all their computers as a condition for receiving federal funds. The law was upheld by the Supreme Court in June 2003.[76]

In addition, the United States Internet Service Providers Association[77] identifies some key principles in respect of illegal online/internet content.[78] These are summarized below:

1. The liability for content should lie with the creators, and not with an entity that retransmits, hosts, stores, republishes, or receives such content;

2. If ISPs are mere conduits, they should have no liability (this is the concept of "innocent carrier"); and

3. If ISPs are content hosts, they should not be liable for content created by others, but they should have the responsibility to disable access to such content.

Interestingly, the reference used is "illegal content", and this would appear to mean that the principles must be read with the existing legislation in the United States which renders a type of content as illegal. This eliminates the imposition of individual moral standards in an assessment of whether a particular type of content is or is not suitable.

---

76 *United States v. American Library Association*, 123 S.Ct. 2297 (2003).

77 The United States Internet Service Providers Association web site is at http://www.usispa.org/index.html.

78 See http://www.usispa.org/founding.html, accessed on 24 April 2005.

The United States attempted to introduce legislation that prohibited "Internet users from using the Internet to communicate material that, under contemporary community standards, would be deemed patently offensive to minors under the age of 18" (under the Communications Decency Act 1996). It was challenged by the American Civil Liberties Union as being contrary to the First Amendment to the United States Constitution. The challenge was upheld by the Supreme Court,[79] which declared the Communications Decency Act 1996 unconstitutional on the basis that:

> . . . [t]he CDA's 'indecent transmission' and 'patently offensive display' provisions abridge 'the freedom of speech' protected by the First Amendment.

The Supreme Court also found that:

> . . . the CDA differs from the various laws and orders upheld in [earlier] cases in many ways, including that it does not allow parents to consent to their children's use of restricted materials; is not limited to commercial transactions; fails to provide any definition of 'indecent' and omits any requirement that 'patently offensive' material lack socially redeeming value; neither limits its broad categorical prohibitions to particular times nor bases them on an evaluation by an agency familiar with the medium's unique characteristics; is punitive; applies to a medium that, unlike radio, receives full First Amendment protection; and cannot be properly analyzed as a form of time, place, and manner regulation because it is a content based blanket restriction on speech.

Subsequently, the United States government sought to introduce the Child Online Protection Act in 1998. The legislation was intended to protect minors from exposure to sexually explicit materials on the Internet. The Child Online Protection Act covers communications that are made for commercial purposes on the World Wide Web, and it requires commercial Web publishers to ensure that minors do not access "material harmful to minors" on their Web sites.

The Act was challenged as being unconstitutional in *Ashcroft v. ACLU* (2004).[80] The Supreme Court held that the Child Online Protection Act was inconsistent with the First Amendment and should be nullified.

---

79   Reno, *Attorney General of States, et al. v. American Civil Liberties Union et al.* (1997), available at http://supct.law.cornell.edu/supct/html/96-511.ZS.html.

80   See http://supct.law.cornell.edu/supct/search/display.html?terms=COPA&url=/supct/html/03-218.ZS.html for an extract of the case.

Regional Supervision   The Internet Hotline Providers in Europe Association (INHOPE),[81] a Dutch registered association, is concerned with:

1. Child pornography;

2. Commercial sites;

3. Morphed and edited images;

4. Chat rooms and abduction;

5. Pedophile rings;

6. Racism;

7. Adult pornography; and

8. Grooming and conditioning of individuals to accept certain sexual behavior.

INHOPE is, however, not a law enforcement agency but has as its purpose to "facilitate and coordinate the work of Internet hotlines in responding to illegal use and content on the Internet". This means that content which falls within the above-mentioned groups would be provided to law enforcement authorities in the countries where the content is located. INHOPE acts in some ways as a coordinating center for such exchange so that law enforcement authorities are able to take action in their respective countries.

Summary   Attempts to control access to online content have been varied and with different measures of successes. What is perhaps clear is that the cost to a country to control access to online content is perhaps much higher than not to do so. The impetus for controlling online content is more to do with political control than it is to do with protecting individuals.

Despite this, it is recognized that there must be some element of control of access, especially with respect to minors. The choice of regime is very much a reflection of the particular country's political development. Those countries who have moved out of a form of "paternalism" tend to be more liberal than those who have not.

(e) Co-Regulatory Regimes — A Comparative Analysis

The following section provides a comparative analysis of co-regulatory regimes in Australia, Malaysia, and Singapore in respect of controlling online content.

---

81   INHOPE's web site is available at http://www.inhope.org/en/index.html (for the English language version).

(i) *Comparative Analysis*

Country / Area	Singapore	Malaysia	Australia
Regulatory Instrument	Internet Code of Practice	Industry-developed content code Section 211, Communications and Multimedia Act 1998	Internet Industry Codes of Practice Schedule 5 of the Broadcasting Services Act 1992 (as amended)
Applies to	ISPs and Internet Content Providers	Providers of online content or those who provide access to online content, including Internet Access Service Providers (IASP), Internet Content Hosts, Online Content Developers, Online Content Aggregators, and Link Providers.	ISPs Internet Content Hosts
Type of content that is not allowed	**Prohibited Material** 4(1) Prohibited material is material that is objectionable on the grounds of public interest, public morality, public order, public security, national harmony, or is otherwise prohibited by applicable Singapore laws. (2) In considering what is prohibited material, the following factors should be taken into account:	Part 2 of the Code provides definitions and examples of the following types of content, which are prohibited: **2.0 — Indecent Content** 2.1 Indecent Content is material which is offensive, morally improper, and against current standards of accepted behavior. This includes nudity and sex. i) **Nudity** Nudity cannot be shown under any circumstances, unless approved by the Film Censorship Board.	**Prohibited or Potentially Prohibited Content.** **Schedule 5 defines prohibited content as being:** (a) the content has been classified "RC" (Refused Classification) or "X" by the Classification Board; or (b) the content has been classified "R" by the Classification Board and access to the content is not subject to a restricted access system.

Country Area	Singapore	Malaysia	Australia
	(a) whether the material depicts nudity or genitalia in a manner calculated to titillate; (b) whether the material promotes sexual violence or sexual activity involving coercion or non-consent of any kind; (c) whether the material depicts a person or persons clearly engaged in explicit sexual activity; (d) whether the material depicts a person who is, or appears to be, under 16 years of age in sexual activity, in a sexually provocative manner, or in any other offensive manner; (e) whether the material advocates homosexuality or lesbianism, or depicts or promotes incest, pedophilia, bestiality, and necrophilia; (f) whether the material depicts detailed or relished acts of extreme violence or cruelty; (g) whether the material glorifies, incites or endorses ethnic, racial, or religious hatred, strife, or intolerance. (3) A further consideration is whether the material has intrinsic medical, scientific, artistic, or educational value.	ii) Sex and Nudity Sex scenes and nudity cannot be shown under any circumstances, unless approved by the Film Censorship Board. 3.0 — Obscene Content 3.1 Obscene Content gives rise to a feeling of disgust by reason of its lewd portrayal and is essentially offensive to one's prevailing notion of decency and modesty. The test of obscenity is whether the Content has the tendency to deprave and corrupt those whose minds are open to such communication. Specific regard is to be had to: i) Explicit Sex Acts / Pornography Any portrayal of sexual activity that a reasonable adult considers explicit and pornographic is prohibited. The portrayal of sex crimes, including rape or attempted rape and statutory rape, as well as bestiality is not permitted, including the portrayal of such sexual acts, through animation and whether consensual or otherwise. ii) Child Pornography Child pornography, including the depiction of any part of the body of a	Potentially prohibited content is defined as being if the content has not been classified by the Classification Board, but if it were to be classified, there is a substantial likelihood that the content would be prohibited content. Australia applies the general law on classification of content as contained in the Classification (Publications, Films and Computer Games) Act 1995.

Area \ Country	Singapore	Malaysia	Australia
	(4) A licensee who is in doubt as to whether any content would be considered prohibited may refer such content to the Authority for its decision.	minor in what might be reasonably considered a sexual context, and any written material or visual and/or audio representation that reflects sexual activity, whether explicit or not, with a minor are strictly prohibited. iii) Sexual Degradation The portrayal of women, men or children as mere sexual objects or to demean them in such manner is prohibited. 4.0 — Violence 4.1 Violence occurs through the ravages of natural disaster, outrageous acts of terrorism, war, human conflict both in fact and through popular fiction, the antics of cartoon characters, (body) contact sports, and more. Violence is a reality and Code Subjects need to be able to reflect, portray, and report on it. 4.2 To deny narration or depiction of hard truths about the world would tantamount to a substantial disservice to understanding of the human condition. The portrayal of violence, with careful editorial justification, is permitted. 4.3 Violence, psychological, but especially physical or incitement to violence,	

Area	Country	Singapore	Malaysia	Australia
			should be portrayed responsibly, and not exploitatively. Presentation of violence must avoid the excessive, the gratuitous, the humiliating, and the instructional. The use of violence for its own sake and the detailed dwelling on brutality or physical agony, by sight or sound, is to be avoided. Programs involving violence should venture to present the consequences to its victims and perpetrators. Particular care should be exercised where children may see, or be involved in, the depiction of violent behavior. Specific considerations are as follows: i) Offensive Violence The portrayal of violence, whether physical, verbal, or psychological, can upset, alarm, and offend viewers. It can be accused of causing undue fear among the audience and of encouraging imitation. The portrayal of violence is permitted to the extent of news reporting, discussion, or analysis and in the context of recognized sports events. In these matters: a) The portrayal of violence, whether physical, verbal, or psychological, can	

Country / Area	Singapore	Malaysia	Australia
		upset, alarm, and offend viewers. It can cause undue fear among the audience and encourage imitation. b) Such public concerns require due consideration whenever violence, real or simulated, is portrayed. The treatment of violence must be appropriate to the context and audience expectations. c) Gratuitous and wanton presentation of sadistic practices and torture, explicit, and excessive imageries of injury and aggression, and of blood, are to be avoided. d) The portrayal of violence is permitted to the extent of news reporting, discussion, or analysis and in the context of recognized sports events in the following instances: i) Use of appropriate editorial judgment in the reporting of audio and visual representation of violence, aggression, or destruction within their content. ii) Exercise of caution and discretion in the selection of, and repetition of, Content which depicts violence. iii) Viewers are to be cautioned in advance of showing scenes of extraordinary	

Area / Country	Singapore	Malaysia	Australia
		violence, or graphic reporting on delicate subject matter, with appropriate warnings to audiences in the case of gore or actual scenes of executions or of people clearly being killed. **ii) Imitable Violence** Due consideration must be given to the fact that violence portrayed visually may be imitated in real life. The presentation of dangerous behavior, which is easily imitated, must be justified and, ideally, excluded. **iii) Sexual Violence** Graphic representations of sexual violence, such as rape or attempted rape or other non-consensual sex, or violent sexual behavior are not allowed. **iv) Violence and Young, Vulnerable Audiences** The susceptibility of younger audiences, particularly those impressionable minds, must be considered. **5.0 — Menacing Content** 5.1 Content that causes annoyance, threatens harm or evil, encourages or	

Area	Country	Singapore	Malaysia	Australia
			or incites crime, or leads to public disorder is considered menacing and is prohibited.

5.2 Hate propaganda, which advocates or promotes genocide or hatred against an identifiable group, may not be portrayed. Such material is considered menacing in nature and is not permitted.

5.3 Information which may be a threat to national security or public health and safety also is not to be presented.

Illustration

i) Making available instructions and guidance on bomb-making, illegal drug production, or counterfeit products;

ii) Disseminating false information with regards to outbreak of racial disturbances in a specific part of the country;

iii) Circulating information and statements with regards to possible terrorist attacks;

iv) Circulating or making available information with regards to the outbreak of a deadly or contagious diseases. | |

Area Country	Singapore	Malaysia	Australia
		6.0 — Bad Language 6.1 Bad language, including expletives and profanity, is offensive to many people. The use of crude words and derogatory terms is most likely to cause offense, especially if the language is contrary to audience expectation. Bad language includes the following: i) Offensive Language The use of disparaging or abusive words which is calculated to offend an individual or a group of persons is not permitted. ii) Crude References Words, in any language commonly used in Malaysia, which are considered obscene or profane are prohibited, including crude references to sexual intercourse and sexual organs. It is, however, permissible to use such words in the context of their ordinary meaning and not when intended as crude language. iii) Hate Speech Hate speech refers to any portrayal (words, speech, or pictures), which denigrates, defames, or otherwise devalues a person or group on the basis of race,	

Country Area	Singapore	Malaysia	Australia
		ethnicity, religion, nationality, gender, sexual orientation, or disability and is prohibited. In particular: *Descriptions of any of these groups or their members involving the use of strong language, crude language, explicit sexual references, or obscene gestures are considered hate speech.* **iv) Violence** Where the portrayal of violence is permitted with appropriate editorial discretion as in news reporting, discussion or analysis, and in the context of recognized sports events, care must be taken to consider the use of explicit or graphic language related to stories of destruction, accidents, or sexual violence, which could be disturbing for general viewing. **7.0 — False Content** **7.1** Content which contains false material and is likely to mislead, due among others to incomplete information, is to be avoided. Content providers must observe measures outlined in specific parts of this Code to limit the likelihood of perpetuating untruths via the communication of false content.	

Country Area	Singapore	Malaysia	Australia
		7.2 Content is false where, prior to communications, reasonable measures to verify its truth have not been adopted or taken. 7.3 Content which is false is expressly prohibited except in any of the following circumstances: (a) satire and parody; (b) where it is clear to an ordinary user that the content is fiction. 7.4 Code Subjects must take all necessary steps outlined in the specific parts of this Code to limit the likelihood of provision of false Content.	
Scope of Obligations / Responsibilities	Burden on ISPs to use best efforts to ensure that prohibited material is not broadcast via the Internet to users in Singapore.	To take down if aware, but Code subject possess a degree of immunity based on the concept of an "innocent carrier". There is a burden on users to exercise caution. The ultimate responsibility for content lies with content creators and providers	1. The primary focus is on controlling children's access to content. (a) Accounts for Minors ISPs cannot provide access accounts, or Internet Content Hosts cannot provide subscription accounts to persons below 18 years of age, unless parental or guardian's consent is obtained. ("Reasonable steps" are required, and these are identified in the code, albeit non-exhaustively.)

Country / Area	Singapore	Malaysia	Australia
			(b) Unsuitable Content for Children
			ISPs and ICHs who ers as subscribers to encourage contenthave content providers to use appropriate labeling system in respect of content likely to be considered unsuitable for children although such content is not prohibited or potentially prohibited content, including their responsibilities. This is satisfied by a link to the ABA.
			ISPs and ICHs must provide users with information (via a link to the ABA) about supervising and controlling children's access to Internet content.
			2. Supervision of others by ISPs and ICHs
			(a) Monitoring other Content Providers
			Once ISPs or ICHs are aware that an ICH (or a second ICH) is hosting prohibited content in Australia, they must advise the ICH about the fact and the existence of the prohibited content.
			(b) Duty to Inform
			ISPs and ICHs must inform subscribers that placing content on the Net may entail legal responsibilities. The manner of informing such people is a notice on the

Area	Country	Singapore	Malaysia	Australia
				ISP home page or a prominent Web page or, in the case of an ICH, via a relevant term in the hosting contract or in the acceptable use policy. **3. Complaint Process** ISPs must provide a complaint process for unsolicited commercial emails. ICHs must provide a link to tell users about the complaint process.
Power of regulator		Notify IASPs to bar access to specified sites and deny access to sites notified to them by the Authority as containing prohibited material.	The Malaysian Communications and Multimedia Commission has no authority to notify IASPs about particular sites because it amounts to censoring the Internet and is prohibited by section 3(3) of the Communications and Multimedia Act. However, the provision of content which is offensive, obscene, false, and menacing is a criminal offence under the Communications and Multimedia Act.	a) Notify ISP of prohibited or potentially prohibited content and, once notified, the ISP must provide for use a filter [technology] as prescribed in the code. (b) Notify an ICH if it is hosting prohibited or potentially prohibited content in Australia, upon which the ICH is to remove it; if it is R-rated content, the ICH must apply a restricted access system and take other action as may be prescribed. Furthermore, it must inform its customer that it is in breach of customer service conditions.

(f) Spamming

(i)   In General

The Internet has experienced phenomenal growth in terms of number of users — 687-million Internet users[82] and more than 240-million people who have email accounts with free email providers such as Hotmail and Yahoo!.

The large number of users is an incentive for businesses which wish to market their products. In addition to this "pull" factor, the ease by which such marketing can be done, and most importantly its low cost, make it a compelling case for businesses to undertake direct marketing using the Internet globally. Thus, such businesses use the simplest form of communication on the Internet — email — to send their marketing materials to potential buyers and customers.

(ii) What Is Spam?

In General   There is much debate[83] over the origins of the term "spam" in its use in respect of the Internet. Spam has come to be associated with the following:

1. "Electronic junk mail or junk newsgroup postings";[84]

2. "Unsolicited email";[85]

3. "Unsolicited commercial email (UCE) or unsolicited bulk email (UBE)";[86] and

4. Any email which the recipient did not ask for, but receives from senders whom the recipient does not know, but who wish to sell something to the recipient. It is usual for there to be many recipients of the same email.[87]

An industry definition of spam is an "unsolicited, commercial e-mail, usually sent in bulk".[88] Interestingly, spam does not mean "ads". It does not mean "abuse". It does not mean "posts whose content I object to".[89] This perspective identifies spam as a message which is repeatedly posted.

---

82   International Telecommunication Union Statistics as at 2003, available at http://www.itu.int/ ITU-2D/ict/statistics/at_glance/Internet03.pdf, accessed on 22 January 2005.

83   *Webopedia*, at http://www.webopedia.com/TERM/s/spam.html, accessed on 22 January 2005.

84   *Webopedia*, at http://www.webopedia.com/TERM/s/spam.html, accessed on 22 January 2005.

85   *Webopedia*, at http://www.webopedia.com/TERM/s/spam.html, accessed on 22 January 2005.

86   Indiana University Knowledge Base, at http://kb.indiana.edu/data/afne.html, accessed on 22 January 2005.

87   See http://email.about.com/library/weekly/aa090197a.htm, accessed on 22 January 2005.

88   Emigh, "Stomping Out Spam: The Spam Series 1", at http://www.esecurityplanet.com/ trends/article.php/2107121, accessed on 22 January 2005.

89   Southwick and Falk, "The Net Abuse FAQ", at http://www.cybernothing.org/faqs/ net-abuse-faq.html, accessed on 22 January 2005, and cited in Khong, "Spam Law for the Internet", *Journal of Information, Law, and Technology*, at http://elj.warwick.ac.uk/ jilt/01-3/khong.html#Southwick, accessed on 22 January 2005.

Malaysia The Malaysian Communications and Multimedia Commission proposed the following definition of spam:

> Spam may be elucidated as the activity of sending unsolicited messages (for example Internet emails or mobile short messages).[90]

The definition covers both the Internet and short messaging services using mobile telephones.

However, in Malaysia, there is no legislative prohibition on the sending of spam, other than a statutory prohibition against providing "content which is indecent, obscene, false, menacing, or offensive in character with intent to annoy, abuse, threaten, or harass any person".[91]

United States The United States CAN-SPAM (Controlling the Assault of Non-Solicited Pornography and Marketing) identifies spam as a "commercial electronic mail message" and which is defined in section 3 as "mean[ing] any electronic mail message the primary purpose of which is the commercial advertisement or promotion of a commercial product or service (including content on an Internet website operated for a commercial purpose)".

Australia In Australia, the definition is set out in the Spam Act 2003,[92] where spam is identified as "unsolicited commercial electronic messages" and covers both email as well as short message services provided by mobile phone service providers. Furthermore, section 6 of the Australian Spam Act 2003 defines commercial electronic messages as:

> . . . an electronic message, where, having regard to:
>
> (a) the content of the message; and
>
> (b) the way in which the message is presented; and
>
> (c) the content that can be located using the links, telephone numbers or contact information (if any) set out in the message;
>
> it would be concluded that the purpose, or one of the purposes, of the message is:
>
> (d) to offer to supply goods or services; or
>
> (e) to advertise or promote goods or services; or
>
> (f) to advertise or promote a supplier, or prospective supplier, of goods or services; or
>
> (g) to offer to supply land or an interest in land; or
>
> (h) to advertise or promote land or an interest in land; or

---

90 See http://www.mcmc.gov.my/Admin/FactsAndFigures/Paper/PC-SPAM-04.pdf, accessed on 22 January 2005.

91 Communications and Multimedia Act 1998, section 211.

92 See http://scaleplus.law.gov.au/html/comact/11/6735/top.htm.

(i) to advertise or promote a supplier, or prospective supplier, of land or an interest in land; or

(j) to offer to provide a business opportunity or investment opportunity; or

(k) to advertise or promote a business opportunity or investment opportunity; or

(l) to advertise or promote a provider, or prospective provider, of a business opportunity or investment opportunity; or

(m) to assist or enable a person, by a deception, to dishonestly obtain property belonging to another person; or

(n) to assist or enable a person, by a deception, to dishonestly obtain a financial advantage from another person; or

(o) to assist or enable a person to dishonestly obtain a gain from another person; or

(p) a purpose specified in the regulations.

South Africa   South Africa, which introduced the Electronic Communications and Transaction Act 2002,[93] provides in section 45 that unsolicited commercial messages can only be sent to persons who have subscribed for them.

It specifies that the sender must give the recipient an option to unsubscribe from the mailing list, and the sender must identify the source from which the sender obtained the recipient's personal information. If this is not provided, the sender commits an offence. It is interesting that there is no definition of unsolicited commercial messages in the Electronic Communications and Transaction Act 2002.

Summary   The table below summarizes the legal definition of spam.

	Malaysia	United States	Australia	South Africa
What is spam	The activity of sending unsolicited messages	Commercial electronic mail messages	Unsolicited commercial electronic messages	Unsolicited commercial messages

(iii) Characteristics of Spamming

From the various regulatory definitions of spam, there are certain characteristics attributable to spam, namely:

1. It is unsolicited by the recipient;

2. The same message is sent in bulk; and

---

93   See http://www.gov.za/gazette/acts/2002/a25-02.pdf, accessed on 30 January 2005.

3. The recipient's address is obtained not from the recipient voluntarily and the recipient did not knowingly provide it.

Spam, by definition, is not concerned with the content of the messages, rather with the fact that a message was sent to many people. Consequently, the focus by some regulatory authorities on the content of spam, as opposed to the activity of sending the same message to many people, may be misdirected.

(iv) Why Is Spam of Concern?

The easy way by which the problem of junk mail is resolved in the physical world may not necessarily extend to the online world. When an email is sent, it consumes network resources, it costs the recipient money (in connection time to download the messages), and possibly loss of income (if legitimate emails are "bounced back" because the mail box is full).

The Australian Communications Authority states that spam is a problem because:

> ... [s]pam now makes up more than 60 per cent of all email traffic, and is having a significantly negative effect on both businesses and individuals. The billions of unwanted email messages circulating across the Internet disrupt email delivery, clog up computer systems, reduce productivity, waste time, raise the cost of Internet access fees, irritate users, and erode their confidence in using email. Many spam messages also contain material that is offensive or fraudulent, and spam is sometimes used to spread computer viruses.[94]

A recent Working Group on Internet Governance[95] working paper on spam[96] states that:

> ... spam [was found to raise] different kinds of governance issues [such as:]
>
> Spam can be annoying or offensive to consumers and imposes various additional costs, especially on individuals who access the network through pay-per-use or low bandwidth connections, thereby hampering the development of Internet access.
>
> Spam imposes significant costs on organizations in the private, public and not-for-profit sectors, whose employees may spend substantial amounts of work time sorting through email messages to determine which are legitimately related to their work, and in deleting the rest.
>
> Spam also imposes significant costs on Internet Service Providers and other network operators, since it requires investment in a range of tools that are needed to counter spam, including anti-spam technologies (e.g., filtering

---

94 See http://Internet.aca.gov.au/Australian Communications AuthorityINTER3997752: STANDARD:731001197:pp=DIR2_12,pc=PC_1793,#problem, accessed on 22 January 2005.

95 See http://www.wgig.org/index.html.

96 "Draft Working Group on Internet Governance Issues Paper on Spam", at http://www.wgig.org/docs/WP-Spam.pdf, accessed on 5 February 2005.

technologies), server and transmission capacity, human resources, and anti-spam information sharing, cooperation, and regulatory structures. This is a particularly important concern in developing countries.

Spam provides a cover for spreading viruses, worms, trojans, spyware, etc., which typically are sent as attachments to e-mail messages, which may cause harm to individual consumers and user organizations, as well as to network operators and service providers.

As well causing inconvenience and reducing the utility of the Internet for consumers and users, spam may violate national law, e.g., if it constitutes an invasion of privacy (e.g., spyware), leads to malicious attacks on their personal property (e.g., viruses), or results in the unauthorized use of this property, possibly for illegal purposes (e.g., zombie networks).

Spam also provides a cover for other forms of cyber crime, such as identity theft through "phishing" and other forms of online fraud, which cause harm to individual consumers and impose costs on corporations (e.g., in the financial services sector), and government agencies (e.g., that issue licenses).

For all these reasons, there is growing concern that, if spam is not controlled, it will constitute a serious impediment to Internet use for consumers and users, and a significant roadblock to the development of e-commerce, e-government, and online public services, thereby reducing the "social value" of the Internet. This is of particular concern to government policymakers in developed and developing countries, although the specific concerns it presents may vary according to the level of technological and economic development within a country.

At the same time, it also is generally recognized that commercial e-mail, which does not raise the kinds of issues listed above, has a legitimate place in the development of e-commerce and the economy and that measures to control spam must distinguish between acceptable and unacceptable commercial e-mail practices. This is of particular concern to businesses in both developed and developing countries, which see the new commercial opportunities made possible by e-mail and want to avoid being subjected to overly onerous laws and regulations.

The United States CAN_SPAM Act exemplifies the United States concern with spamming and spam messages, as follows:

Section 2. Congressional Findings and Policy.

(a) Findings. — The Congress finds the following:

(1) Electronic mail has become an extremely important and popular means of communication, relied on by millions of Americans on a daily basis for personal and commercial purposes. Its low cost and global reach make it extremely convenient and efficient, and offer unique opportunities for the development and growth of frictionless commerce.

(2) The convenience and efficiency of electronic mail are threatened by the extremely rapid growth in the volume of unsolicited commercial electronic mail. Unsolicited commercial electronic mail is currently estimated to account for over half of all electronic mail traffic, up from an estimated seven percent in 2001, and the volume continues to rise. Most of these messages are fraudulent or deceptive in one or more respects.

(3) The receipt of unsolicited commercial electronic mail may result in costs to recipients who cannot refuse to accept such mail and who incur costs for the storage of such mail, or for the time spent accessing, reviewing, and discarding such mail, or for both.

(4) The receipt of a large number of unwanted messages also decreases the convenience of electronic mail and creates a risk that wanted electronic mail messages, both commercial and non-commercial, will be lost, overlooked, or discarded amidst the larger volume of unwanted messages, thus reducing the reliability and usefulness of electronic mail to the recipient.

(5) Some commercial electronic mail contains material that many recipients may consider vulgar or pornographic in nature.

(6) The growth in unsolicited commercial electronic mail imposes significant monetary costs on providers of Internet access services, businesses, and educational and non-profit institutions that carry and receive such mail, as there is a finite volume of mail that such providers, businesses, and institutions can handle without further investment in infrastructure.

(7) Many senders of unsolicited commercial electronic mail purposefully disguise the source of such mail.

(8) Many senders of unsolicited commercial electronic mail purposefully include misleading information in the messages' subject lines to induce the recipients to view the messages.

(9) While some senders of commercial electronic mail messages provide simple and reliable ways for recipients to reject (or "opt-out" of) receipt of commercial electronic mail from such senders in the future, other senders provide no such "opt-out" mechanism, or refuse to honor the requests of recipients not to receive electronic mail from such senders in the future, or both.

(10) Many senders of bulk unsolicited commercial electronic mail use computer programs to gather large numbers of electronic mail addresses on an automated basis from Internet websites or online services where users must post their addresses to make full use of the website or service.

. . .

(b) Congressional Determination of Public Policy — On the basis of the findings in subsection (a), the Congress determines that:

(1) there is a substantial government interest in regulation of commercial electronic mail on a nationwide basis;

(2) senders of commercial electronic mail should not mislead recipients as to the source or content of such mail; and

(3) recipients of commercial electronic mail have a right to decline to receive additional commercial electronic mail from the same source.

There are three different perspectives when considering spam, namely:

1. End-users (ultimate recipients);

2. Network administrators; and

3. Third, parties (innocent bystanders).[97]

The table below summarizes their respective concerns, and it identifies the possible costs.

Perspective of	Reasons for Concern	Possible Costs
End-users (recipients)	Spam fills mail boxes and hinders legitimate email in getting through. The user installs spam filters to mitigate the concern, but this has other effects.	Costs include those for connection, purchase of anti-spam filters, and loss of business if legitimate email is lost.
Network administrators (intermediaries)	Khong points out that "a deluge of emails to a mail server may severely cripple the network of an email service provider".[98]	Khong indicates that "spam increases the cost of support by 15 per cent to 20 per cent, administration by 20 per cent, incoming delivery by 10 per cent, disk space by 15 per cent, and overall equipment cost of 10 per cent to 15 per cent".[99] The intermediary suffers further loss of reputation and the burden of having to deal with customer complaints.

---

97   Khong, "Spam Law and Internet", 2001 (3) *Journal of Information, Law, and Technology*, available at http://elj.warwick.ac.uk/jilt/01-3/khong.html#2, accessed on 22 January 2005.

98   Khong, "Spam Law and Internet", 2001 (3) *Journal of Information, Law, and Technology*, available at http://elj.warwick.ac.uk/jilt/01-3/khong.html#2, accessed on 22 January 2005.

99   Khong, "Spam Law and Internet", 2001 (3) *Journal of Information, Law, and Technology*, available at http://elj.warwick.ac.uk/jilt/01-3/khong.html#2, accessed on 22 January 2005.

Perspective of	Reasons for Concern	Possible Costs
Third parties (innocent bystanders)	Their email addresses are hijacked by spammers without their knowledge or consent.	They receive angry emails, and the deluge of responses may have an impact on third-party systems.
Spammers (the sender)	Spammers are not concerned and view the sending of bulk email as a cost-effective way to market their products. Preparing and sending the email costs almost nothing.	

In the Hong Kong case of *Goetz Trading Limited v. Pacific Supernet Limited*,[100] the judge found that:

> ... spam could have come from the plaintiff's server in four ways. The first is "open relay", whereby spam from an outside transmitter is relayed by the server; it can be stopped by the use of an anti-spam program which will prevent the spam from coming into the server in the first place. The second is hacking, whereby an outside spammer obtains control of the server. The parties have agreed that neither of these in fact applied. The third way is wrongful use by someone within the plaintiff's network of the service to transmit the spam through the plaintiff's e-mail server. The fourth way is "IP forgery", i.e., the sending of messages by a third party which appear to come from a particular IP address when in fact they do not.

The Goetz case nicely summarizes how third parties may be innocent bystanders and be affected by the activities of spammers, including the costs incurred. Furthermore, the open relay system that is used in Internet email may be used by spammers to send emails with illegal content or to perpetrate a fraud.

Unlike junk postal mail, where the costs was borne by the sender (i.e., the costs of printing, paper, postage, and envelopes) and the recipient does not incur any costs, the situation with spam is the total reversal, i.e., senders incur no costs and recipients and intermediaries incur most of the costs. The reversal of the cost burden has not only made spamming a viable advertising option for businesses, but has become the subject of governmental action.

Spamming has become a method by which illegitimate activities are undertaken, such as bank fraud, spoofing (where one uses a legitimate email account but it is

---

100 *Goetz Trading Limited v. Pacific Supernet Limited* (2002), available at http://www.hklii.org/cgi-hklii/disp.pl/hk/jud/en/hkdc/2004/DCCJ005427%5f2002.html?query=%22spam%22, accessed on 30 January 2005.

not actually used), or the famous Nigerian scams. Essentially, spamming can be divided into two groups (from the sender's perspective), namely:

1. Spamming as a form of direct marketing by legitimate businesses (commercial); and

2. Spamming as a form of perpetrating fraud or some other scam (criminal).

(v) Regulatory Approach

In General   The nature of spam as unsolicited commercial messages or unsolicited bulk messages has meant that the focus of most regulatory approaches tries to balance two competing philosophies, i.e., the right of individual privacy and the right of businesses to market and promote their goods and services.

As a result of these competing philosophies, regulatory frameworks have been designed to achieve a balance between the two interests. However, the regulatory approach starts from the basis that spamming is a legitimate business activity (akin to junk mail). From this perspective, the solutions designed in regulatory frameworks have become known as the "opt-in" approach and the "opt-out" approach. These approaches are, however, unsuitable for non-commercial spam (or spam which is a step towards perpetrating a fraud).

Opt-In Approach   The opt-in approach is based on the primacy of the individual's right to privacy. Based on this primary right, regulation prohibits absolutely the sending of any commercial message to any person, whether such message is an email, SMS, or MMS. The only exception to the absolute prohibition is that before such emails are sent, the prospective recipients must have expressly chosen or consented to receive such emails.

If no such choice or consent is made (i.e., opt-in), the sender cannot send any messages. Express consent must be provided unless the sender and recipient have an existing customer relationship. The European Union adds that senders must clearly indicate the use of cookies or other tracking devices (including spyware)[101] so that recipients can make informed decisions.

Opt-Out Approach   The opt-out approach is based on the rights of a business to promote its activity, and it may use all available means to do so. However, once individual recipients have informed the business that they do not wish to receive any such messages, the business must remove their contact details from its databases.

Hence, this approach requires businesses to specifically state that recipients have the right to "unsubscribe" or be removed from the mailing list of the business enterprise, i.e., "opt-out".

---

101 See http://www.itu.int/osg/spu/spam/law.html#countries, accessed on 29 January 2005.

Combined Approach   Countries such as Finland have adopted a unique approach, whereby spamming individuals are subject to an opt-in requirement, while spamming corporations are subject to an opt-out requirement.

While this may enable marketing materials to be sent to corporations by legitimate spammers, it also may have a far greater effect if such spamming can critically affect the corporate network. This duality approach does not take into account the costs of spamming to corporate network administrators and the possible loss of legitimate business opportunities.

Opt-In and Opt-Out Problems   The problem with either the opt-in or opt-out approaches is that, while legitimate business enterprises will comply with the legislative environment, it is those enterprises which use spam for illegal activities, such as fraud or to spread viruses, where there is greater concern. This is the duality of spamming.

Australia addresses this duality of spamming by prohibiting the sending of unsolicited commercial messages (as prescribed in section 16 of the Spam Act 2003)[102] and by defining the phrase "unsolicited commercial messages" widely to encompass the assisting or enabling a person, by a deception, to dishonestly obtain property belonging to another person or to take financial advantage of another person. By comparison, the United States CAN-SPAM Act provides that:

1. False or misleading header information in emails is banned so as to be able to accurately identify the person who initiated the email;

---

102 Section 16 of the Spam Act 2003 provides: "(1) A person may not send, or cause to be sent, a commercial electronic message that: (a) has an Australian link; and (b) is not a designated commercial electronic message. (2) Subsection (1) does not apply if the relevant electronic account-holder consented to the sending of the message. (3) Subsection (1) does not apply if the person: (a) did not know; and (b) could not, with reasonable diligence, have ascertained that the message had an Australian link. (4) Subsection (1) does not apply if the person sent the message, or caused the message to be sent, by mistake. (5) A person who wishes to rely on subsection (2), (3) or (4) bears an evidential burden in relation to that matter. (6) A person may not send, or cause to be sent, a commercial electronic message to a non-existent electronic address if: (a) the person did not have reason to believe that the electronic address existed; and (b) the electronic message: (i) has an Australian link; and (ii) is not a designated commercial electronic message. (7) Subsection (6) does not apply if the person: (a) did not know; and (b) could not, with reasonable diligence, have ascertained; that the message had an Australian link. (8 A person who wishes to rely on subsection (7) bears an evidential burden in relation to that matter. (9) A person may not: (a) aid, abet, counsel or procure a contravention of subsection (1) or (6); or (b) induce, whether by threats or promises or otherwise, a contravention of subsection (1) or (6); or (c) be in any way, directly or indirectly, knowingly concerned in, or party to, a contravention of subsection (1) or (6); or (d) conspire with others to effect a contravention of subsection (1) or (6). (10) A person does not contravene subsection (9) merely because the person supplies a carriage service that enables an electronic message to be sent. (11) Subsections (1), (6), and (9) are civil penalty provisions".

2. The subject line cannot mislead the recipient about its contents or subject matter;

3. The email must enable recipients to opt-out from receiving future emails;[103]

4. One entity may not assist another to send email to that address; nor can another entity send email on the original spammer's behalf to that address;

5. Selling or transferring the email addresses of people who choose not to receive spam email is illegal; and

6. Commercial email must be identified as an advertisement and include the sender's valid physical postal address.[104]

The United States approach is to prescribe what must be stated in emails and, as most spammers of illegal or fraudulent activities do not specify genuine headers, these are subject to the general prohibition.

(vi) Jurisdictional Issues

Most spam that is received originates outside the recipient's home country. This raises the difficult issue of jurisdiction. Because spamming is an activity that can commence in one country and affect individuals in another country, the jurisdictional difficulties in enforcing anti-spam laws become acute. Traditional public international law rules do not allow penal statutes to be enforced in other countries, thus rendering the usefulness of anti-spam legislation nugatory. Spammers will simply locate to a "friendly jurisdiction" to undertake their activities or, worse still, they may use the many cyber cafes to launch their emails. The latter renders their identification almost untraceable, as they are only in the cyber cafe for a short while.

To permit the enforcement of anti-spam laws of one country against individuals of another country would be to go against the fundamental principle of national sovereignty. Hence, cross-jurisdictional issues are a major concern which may need international cooperation in the form of a treaty or multi-lateral arrangement, such as the trilateral memorandum[105] entered into by the United States, Australia, and the United Kingdom on 2 July 2004.

---

103 The opt-out method requires that a valid return email address or another Internet-based response mechanism that allows a recipient to ask that future email messages not be sent, which request must be honored. After receipt of an opt-out request, the sender has 10 business days to stop sending email to the requestor's email address.

104 See detail summary at http://www.ftc.gov/bcp/conline/pubs/buspubs/canspam.htm, accessed on 13 February 2005.

105 See http://www.ftc.gov/os/2004/07/040630spammoutext.pdf, accessed on 30 January 2005.

This memorandum of understanding on mutual enforcement assistance in commercial email matters provides for cooperation among Australia, the United Kingdom, and the United States by:

1. Sharing of evidence to facilitate enforcement of spam laws, coordination of investigations, and education and research; and

2. Informing each other as to developments in their respective countries.

Such cooperative approaches do help in mitigating the activities of spammers since these countries have formalized (albeit in a non-legally binding arrangement) their mutual cooperation and assistance. This approach is an example of what countries can do to militate against the activities of spammers, and overcome the jurisdictional issues.

(vii) Comparison of Anti-Spam Laws

The International Telecommunication Union, as at 1 January 2005,[106] has produced a list of legislative frameworks affecting the issue of spam.

Argentina   In 2001, anti-spam legislation (*Anteproyecto de Ley de Regulación de las Comunicaciones Publicitarias por Correo Electrnico*) was proposed to combat spam. In November 2003, the Federal Court heard its first spam case. The judge issued an injunction relying on the Personal Data Protection Act of 2000, particularly its article 25.

Under the injunction, the spammer on trial was ordered to stop sending e-mail after an opt-out was requested. It also was ordered that the spammer could not give the addresses to a third party under the Act.

In 2004, the national legislature introduced a new Bill allowing the government to block the Internet Protocols and cancel domain names of spammers. The Bill proposes an opt-out system (*Proyecto de ley para regular el Spam en Argentina*). The legal regime relevant to regulation of spam includes:

1. The Constitution, section 43;

2. Decree Number 995 of 2000; and

3. Decree Number 1558 of 2001.

Australia   The Spam Act 2003 and the Spam (Consequential Amendments) Act 2003 were passed by Parliament in 2003. The two Acts came into effect on 10 April 2004 and are due for review within two years.

Legislation will be administered by the Australian Communications Authority. In addition to a set of industry codes and standards, under the Spam Act,

---

106   The online version is available at http://www.itu.int/spam/.

the Australian Communications Authority has the ability to pursue a number of enforcement options.

As part of the changes, the National Office for the Information Economy becomes the Australian Government Information Management Office, with some functions transferring to the Department of Communications, Information Technology, and the Arts. Australia uses an opt-in approach. The legal regime relevant to regulation of spam includes:

1. The Spam Act 2003;

2. The Spam (Consequential Amendments) Act 2003; and

3. The Spam Regulations 2004.

Canada   The Privacy Commissioner of Canada is an Officer of Parliament who reports directly to the House of Commons and the Senate as an advocate for the privacy rights of Canadians. In May 2004, the Economic Development Agency of Canada for the Regions of Quebec launched an Anti-Spam Action Plan and announced the creation of a ministerial task with the Electronic Commerce Branch of Industry Canada to combat spam. The legal regime relevant to regulation of spam includes:

1. The Privacy Acts of 1980, 1981, 1982, and 1983; and

2. The Personal Information Protection and Electronic Documents Act, section 11.

European Union   The European Union uses an opt-in approach. The legal regime relevant to regulation of spam includes:

1. The E-Privacy Directive, Directive 2002/58/EC Concerning the Processing of Personal Data and the Protection of Privacy in the Electronic Communications Sector;

2. The E-Commerce Directive, Directive 2000/31/EC on Certain Legal Aspects of Information Society Services, in Particular Electronic Commerce, in the Internal Market;

3. The Telecommunications Privacy Directive, Directive 97/66/EC Concerning the Processing of Personal Data and the Protection of Privacy in the Telecommunications Sector (repealed and replaced by Directive 2002/58/EC);

4. The Distance Contracts Directive, Directive 97/7/EC on the Protection of Consumers in Respect of Distance Contracts; and

5. The Data Protection Directive, Directive 95/46/EC on the Protection of Individuals with Regard to the Processing of Personal Data and on the Free Movement of Such Data.

France The competent authority is the *Commission Nationale de l'Informatique et des Liberté*, an independent administrative agency which enforces the Data Protection Act of 1978 and other related laws. In July 2002, it created a Spam Mailbox to combat Spam. In July 2003, a Contact Group was established by the government within the *Direction du Développement des Médias* to fight against spam. France employs the opt-in approach. The legal regime relevant to regulation of spam includes:

1. Law Number 78-17 of 6 January 1978;

2. Decision Number 496 of 2004; and

3. Deliberation Number 2–075 of 24 October 2002.

Japan In April 2002, the Japanese government passed the Law on Regulation of Transmission of Specified Electronic Mail. This law addresses "specified electronic mail", which is defined as e-mail for advertisement purposes sent to users who have not opted in for the service.

The Law controls spam disseminated by anyone under the jurisdiction of the Ministry of Public Management, Home, Affairs, Posts and Telecommunications (MPHPT), which includes the entire country and the solitary islands. In July 2002, the MPHPT established the Japan Data Communications Association to determine appropriateness of sending specified e-mail messages. Japan uses the opt-out approach.

Ireland The Irish government has signed a law outlawing spam. The law gives effect to new EU regulations banning the sending of unsolicited e-mails or text messages to the general public.

Ireland passed the self-titled European Communities (Electronic Communications Networks and Services) (Data Protection and Privacy) Regulations 2003. Regulation 13 relates to spam, and it provides for mandatory opt-in for unsolicited spamming.

Regulation 19 grants enforcement powers to the Commission for Communications Regulation (the "Regulator" in the regulations). The Regulator, in consultation with the Data Protection Commissioner, also may specify the form and any other requirements regarding the obtaining, recording, and rescinding of consent of subscribers for the purposes of these Regulations. The punishment granted to the Commission is a warning. The legal regime relevant to regulation of spam includes:

1. The Data Protection Act, 1988; and

2. Statutory Instrument Number 535 of 2003, European Communities (Electronic Communications Networks and Services) (Data Protection and Privacy) Regulations 2003.

Italy   Italy has enacted an anti-spam law that makes spamming a criminal offense punishable by up to three years' imprisonment. The Italian Data Protection Authority is an independent agency created to ensure personal data protection and deal with Spam problems. Italy employs the opt-in approach. The legal regime relevant to regulation of spam includes:

1. Decree-Law Number 675/1996 on privacy protection;

2. Decree-Law Number 171/1998 on telecommunications privacy protection;

3. Decree-Law Number 185/1999 on customer protection in respect of long-distance contracts; and

4. Decree-Law Number 196/2003, the Personal Data Protection Code.

New Zealand   The Office of the Privacy Commissioner is an independent Crown entity established by the Privacy Act. The government has issued a discussion paper to outlaw unwanted Spam.

The Privacy Commissioner's principal powers and functions include promoting the objects of the Privacy Act 1993, monitoring proposed legislation and government policies, dealing with complaints at first instance, approving and issuing codes of practice and authorizing special exemptions from the information privacy principles, and reviewing public-sector information-matching programs.

Republic of Korea   The Korea Spam Response Center was constituted within the Korea Information Security Agency, which is an agency of the Ministry of Information and Communication, to deal with problems regarding spam. Korea uses an opt-out approach. The legal regime relevant to regulation of spam includes:

1. The Anti-Spam Regulations; and

2. The Act on Promotion of Information and Communication and Communications Network Utilization and Information Protection of 2001 and its 2002 Revisions.

United Kingdom   The United Kingdom Department for Trade and Industry implemented the Privacy and Electronic Communications (EC Directive) Regulation, a new anti-spam regulation based on EU Directive 58/2002, which came into force on 11 December 2003.

Enforcement is the responsibility of the Information Commissioner; however, considering that several issues relating to spam concern also consumer protection and trade, the Office of Fair Trading also is active in this field, in particular on the subject of online scams. The United

Kingdom uses the opt-in approach. The legal regime relevant to regulation of spam includes:

1. Statutory Instrument 2003 Number 2426, the Privacy and Electronic Communications (EC Directive) Regulations 2003;

2. The Data Protection Act 1998;

3. The Electronic Commerce (EC Directive) Regulations 2002;

4. The Control of Misleading Advertisements Regulations 1988 (amended 2000);

5. The Consumer Protection (Distance Selling) Regulations 2000;

6. The Ecommerce Regulations 2002; and

7. The Unfair Terms in Consumer Contracts Regulations (amended 2001).

United States On 1 January 2004, the CAN-SPAM Act came into effect in the United States. The law imposes specific requirements on senders of commercial e-mail and places enforcement in the hands of the Federal Trade Commission and State Attorneys General.

The Federal Trade Commission[107] summarizes the anti-spam law as follows:

> It bans false or misleading header information. Your emails "From", "To", and routing information — including the originating domain name and email address — must be accurate and identify the person who initiated the email.

> It prohibits deceptive subject lines. The subject line cannot mislead the recipient about the contents or subject matter of the message.

> It requires that your email give recipients an opt-out method. You must provide a return email address or another Internet-based response mechanism that allows a recipient to ask you not to send future email messages to that email address, and you must honor the requests. You may create a "menu" of choices to allow a recipient to opt out of certain types of messages, but you must include the option to end any commercial messages from the sender. Any opt-out mechanism you offer must be able to process opt-out requests for at least 30 days after you send your commercial email. When you receive an opt-out request, the law gives you 10 business days to stop sending email to the requestor's email address. You cannot help another entity send email to that address, or have another entity send email on your behalf to that address. Finally, it's illegal for you to sell or transfer the email addresses of people who choose not to receive your email, even in the form of a mailing list, unless

---

107 See http://www.ftc.gov/bcp/conline/pubs/buspubs/canspam.htm, accessed on 13 February 2005.

you transfer the addresses so another entity can comply with the law.

It requires that commercial email be identified as an advertisement and include the sender's valid physical postal address. Your message must contain clear and conspicuous notice that the message is an advertisement or solicitation and that the recipient can opt out of receiving more commercial email from you. It also must include your valid physical postal address.

7.03   International Activities

Since the commercial expansion of the Internet in the early 1990s, there have been many activities on the international front. These range from the Model Law on E-Commerce of the United Nations International Trade Law Commission (UNCITRAL) to the Hague Conference on Private International Law. Various regional groupings, such as the Association of South East Asian Countries (ASEAN) and the Asia-Pacific Economic Cooperation (APEC), also have focused on the issues affecting e-commerce.

Agency or Grouping	Activities
UNCITRAL	UNCITRAL developed a model law in 1996 on e-commerce.[108] UNCITRAL developed a model law in 2001 on electronic signatures.[109]
ASEAN	ASEAN developed the e-ASEAN initiative: "[which is to] facilitate the establishment of the ASEAN Information Infrastructure — the hardware and software systems needed to access, process and share information — and promote the growth of electronic commerce in the region".[110] The e-ASEAN initiative requires that: "[e]lectronic commerce will be facilitated through the adoption of laws and policies based on international norms that promote trust and confidence of the general population and, in particular, those who transact business over the Internet. This task will involve the establishment of a system of mutual recognition of digital signatures; secure electronic transactions, payments and settlements; protection of intellectual property rights arising from e-commerce; measures to promote personal data protection and consumer privacy; and dispute settlement mechanisms".

---

108 See http://www.uncitral.org/en-index.htm, accessed on 28 December 2004.

109 See http://www.uncitral.org/en-index.htm, accessed on 28 December 2004.

110 See http://www.aseansec.org/7659.htm, accessed on 29 December 2004.

Agency or Grouping	Activities
APEC	The Electronic Commerce Steering Group (ECSG) was created to provide a coordinating role for APEC e-commerce activities.[111] The ECSG is committed to promoting and facilitating the development and use of electronic commerce by creating legal, regulatory, and policy environments in the APEC region that are predictable, transparent, and consistent. In addition, the ECSG is working to promote mechanisms to increase trust and confidence of participants in electronic commerce to encourage greater use of the Internet to perform transactions. Finally, the ECSG is using information technology and electronic commerce methods to facilitate trade transactions among member economies.
ICANN	ICANN has developed gTLDs, such as .info; .firm; and .museum to enable new participants on the World Wide Web to have better choice of domain names.[112]
	ICANN has promoted the Internationalized Domain Name to enable a domain name in a language other than English to be recognized by the Domain Name System, without causing technical difficulties for existing operations.
World Intellectual Property Organization (WIPO)	WIPO has developed a Uniform Dispute Resolution Procedure to handle disputes about domain names and trade marks.[113]
	WIPO2 extends the UDRP to cover situations, such as "confusingly similar domain names, geographical locations, and identifications".
Hague Conference on Private International Law	The Hague Conference is examining the issues and concerns affecting e-commerce and designing and re-examining existing conventions to bring them in line with the requirements of the Information Society.[114]

Most international activities are centered around the sharing of information and experiences in order for there to be developed some form of "harmonized" regulatory framework affecting the Internet through e-commerce. The rationale is that, with such harmonization, the risks of conflicts between national laws may be reduced.

Other than the work of UNCITRAL on model laws, there has been little substantive development of international cooperative arrangements on, for example, anti-spam arrangements.

---

111 See http://www.apecsec.org.sg/content/apec/apec_groups/som_special_task_groups/ electronic_commerce.html, accessed on 29 December 2004.

112 See http://www.icann.org/.

113 See http://www.icann.org/committees/JWGW2/final-report/JWGW2-final-report-part 1.pdf.

114 See http://www.hcch.net/index_en.php?act=progress.listing&cat=9, accessed on 9 December 2004.

CHAPTER 8

DOMAIN NAMES: A GLOBAL VIEW

Fredrik Roos
Setterwalls
Göteborg, Sweden

8.01   Introduction

This chapter will provide an overview of the evolution of the Domain Name System and related legal issues, including the set of rules regulating the issuance of domain names and the resolution of disputes regarding domain names. The most important concerns will be discussed, and references will be provided to more specialized work for deeper studies.

This chapter also will provide a global perspective of the Domain Name System, discussing the importance of cultural differences, the role of Country Code Top Level Domains, the division of the Internet into different languages, and the need for the harmonization of systems for dispute resolution.

8.02   The Domain Name System

(a)   What are Domain Names?

Every computer connected to the Internet has an individual numerical address, referred to as an "IP Number", which enables a message from one computer to another to find its way on the Internet. The IP Numbers are naturally too difficult for a human being to memorize. We are more used to remembering addresses in the form of words and, therefore, a system that translates the IP Numbers into words has been created, the domain name system.

A typical domain name consists of a main-domain located in a top-domain and sub-domains attached to the main-domain. The appearance in an Internet browser window is sub-domain.main-domain.top-domain. An example is the address of my former department at the University "informatics.gu.se". Top-domains can be either generic, e.g., ".com", or belong to a country, e.g., "se" and are often referred to as Top-Level-Domains (TLDs). The main-domain name usually leads to the homepage,[1] of a website[2] such as "gu" (Gothenburg University), and then sub-domains are linked to the homepage, such as "informatics" (the Department of Informatics).

(b) Purpose of Trade Marks and Domain Names

Since the domain name is the address that enables people to find other people, companies, or organizations, it is very important. Today, there are more than 16 million ".com" domains, and this large interest alone proves its importance as an asset. However, what is of real importance is not just having a domain name, but rather that the domain name is a good one.

A good domain name is intuitive, easy to remember, and likely to be noticed on the Internet. For businesses, the commercial importance of domain names as trade marks can be tremendous.[3] The right to a domain name has become a form of proprietary brand asset. This right can provide a competitive advantage that contributes to the equity of the brand.[4] If the brand is already used as a trade mark, it is of great importance to the trade mark holder to also have the right to the domain name.

The Domain Name System (the "DNS") requires everyone on the Internet to have a unique domain name address; however, different companies in different countries, or different kinds of businesses, have similar or identical trade marks.

Previously, this has not been a problem since domains have not been competing for the same customers but, with the creation of the DNS and the widespread use of the Internet, potential conflicts have sprung up over the use of the same domain name. In conjunction with this are other related problems involving the DNS and trade mark law, in particular the practice of cybersquatting (acquiring a domain name and trying to sell it to the rightful owner).

(c) Evolution of the Domain Name System

(i) ICANN

To regulate policy for the DNS, the United States government proposed the creation of a not-for-profit entity based in the United States. This entity

---

1   "Homepage" is used here as the definition of the "first page" of a website, the page one is expected to first arrive to, as in "cocacola.com" or "microsoft.com".
2   "Website" is used here as the definition of a set of linked web pages belonging to, e.g., a company or an organization.
3   Lindqvist, "Domännamn — stöld, strategi och utveckling", *Centraltryckeriet* (1999).
4   Aaker, *Building Strong Brands*, at pp. 7–9 (1996).

would be devoted to the collective interest of the Internet as a whole, with a board to be composed of representatives of stakeholders on the Internet and charged with authenticating the policy decisions that the Internet Assigned Names Authority (IANA) was to make. In exchange, the United States government would give up the administration of the DNS and instead support the delegation in its transition to the Internet Corporation for Assigned Names and numbers (ICANN).

At the time, the creation of ICANN seemed a logical and obvious choice. A private entity would take up the tasks of the government, but it would not be the government *per se*. Nevertheless, almost five years after its creation, there are accusations that the corporation has failed to implement the principles and structures that would turn it into an e-government and that its role in relation to Internet governance, especially towards citizens and their rights, is rather ambiguous.

(ii)   History of ICANN

From 1994 to 1998, a series of attempts to move Internet administration into the private sector were made. The attempts began with the Internet Society (ISOC) in the United States, but gradually escalated as the ISOC realized that allies were needed to help it carry out this agenda.[5]

Prior to ICANN's creation, a string of authorities, corporations, and companies were responsible for the administration of the DNS; however, all of these authorities were directly or indirectly contingent on the intervention of and approval by the United States Department of Commerce. While the Internet was evolving and turning into a global medium, many governments around the world started questioning the United States government's influence and control of this exceptional interchange.

In June 1998, the United States Department of Commerce released a White Paper on the administration of Internet names and numbers, the ostensible purpose of which was to reposition the management of Internet domain names and IP addresses out from under the influence of the United States federal government and into the hands of a private, non-profit organization with international participation and representation.[6] In November 1998, the United States United States Department of Commerce officially recognized ICANN as the organization responsible for the administration and supervision of the domain name system.[7]

---

5   Mueller, "ICANN and Internet Governance: Sorting through the Debris of "Self-Regulation", *Journal of Policy, Regulation and Strategy for Telecommunications, Information and Media*, volume 1, number 6 (December 1999).

6   Department of Commerce, NTIA, "Management of Internet Names and Addresses", *Statement of Policy, Federal Register*, volume 63, number 111 (10 June 1998), at p. 31741.

7   See http://www.ntia.doc.gov/ntiahome/domainname/icann-memorandum.htm.

To justify this transmission and ease the concerns surrounding such an action, the United States Department of Commerce decided to adopt the "self-regulatory" model, a concept already tested and approved by other industry sectors. "Self-regulation" meant that the United States government would not be involved in the creation of the new organization or specifically define its power and structure.

Instead, it invited the private sector to form an entity that would be based on a broad consensus among industry stakeholders. Once the "private sector" came to the government with a formal proposal, the latter would delegate its assets and, after two years of supervision, the United States government would walk away. That, at any rate, was what was supposed to happen.

"Self-regulation" had been a *leitmotif* of other Clinton Administration efforts to privatize sectors of the digital economy; it characterized its approach to digital television broadcasting,[8] the protection of online privacy,[9] and content regulation.[10] "Self-regulation" also was a term easily affixed to the Internet itself, and it resonated rhetorically with the culture of the Internet's engineering and technical community, which needed to be convinced of the success of the process.

During the period that the United States Department of Commerce was drafting the White Paper that would eventually pave the way for ICANN's debut, ICANN started making its first moves. First, it laid down its bylaws and determined its board of directors while, at the same time, making clear to the other existing organizations that it would take up their tasks and would be the sole administrator of the Internet. As a result, as soon as ICANN was officially launched, the chores of the ISOC, IANA, and Network Solutions, Inc. (NSI) were incorporated into ICANN's duties.

Second, and occurring concurrently, while trade mark owners were pushing for the lion's share on the Internet, ICANN, instructed by the White Paper, asked the World Intellectual Property Organization (WIPO) to devise a

---

8   In December 1998, an Advisory Committee on Public Interest Obligations for Advanced Television recommended that the National Association of Broadcasters, acting as the representative of the broadcasting industry, draft an updated voluntary Code of Conduct to highlight and reinforce the public interest commitments of broadcasters, at http://www.benton.org/PIAC/.

9   The United States Department of Commerce, along with the Office of Management and Budget, was asked to report to President Clinton on industry efforts to establish self-regulatory regimes to ensure privacy online and to develop technological solutions to protect privacy. This led to its staff discussion paper, "Elements of effective self regulation for protection of privacy", at http://www.ntia.doc.gov/ntiahome/privacy/index.html.

10   The United States government has passed legislation to install the "V-chi'" and associated ratings systems in televisions and has encouraged the development of the Platform for Internet Content Selection (PICS) standard for Internet content.

dispute resolution procedure that would assist in resolving the conflicts between trade marks and domain names. After a period of consultation and debate, ICANN introduced the Uniform Domain Name Dispute Resolution Policy (UDRP) to the trade mark world.

ICANN's creation served two main purposes. The first one was to take the Internet out of the realm of United States domination and governmental control, and the second was to satisfy the desires and wishes of citizens. The tasks that ICANN was requested to carry out were specified in the White Paper. One of the principal catalysts behind the launching of ICANN was the need to de-monopolize the business of registering domain names.[11] Before ICANN's creation, Network Solutions, Inc. (NSI) was the sole registrar and had a *de facto* monopoly of all registrations in the generic Top Level Domains (gTLDs), based on its contract with the United States government. The purpose of ICANN's formation was to eliminate the NSI monopoly and allow other registrars to enter the market, thus stimulating competition.

A second task ICANN had to undertake was the formulation of a dispute resolution policy for potential conflicts between trade marks and domain names. The pre-existing policies had many deficiencies, and a number of citizens, the trade mark owners, were seriously dissatisfied. Consequently, one of the first concerns of ICANN was to somehow manage to satisfy two diverse groups of citizens: trade mark owners and domain name holders. Based on recommendations from WIPO, ICANN produced the Uniform Domain Name Dispute Resolution Policy, which allows conflicting parties, regardless of which jurisdiction they may operate under, to settle their disputes through a form of quasi-arbitration, thus providing an alternative option to the courts.

Moreover, ICANN took on board Jon Postel, the original creator of the DNS. In accordance with Postel's suggestions, ICANN introduced the country code Top Level Domain Names (ccTLDs).[12] Postel had made it clear from the beginning that, when it comes to ccTLDs, there should be no policy involved as the Internet community is not in a position to define what a country is or recognize a territory or other geographic unit as a "country".[13] ICANN's job in this case was to ensure that all ccTLDs are properly added to the authoritative root and thus enable all websites using ccTLDs to be visible on the World Wide Web (WWW).

---

11   Kleinwaechter, "Governance Systems in the Internet Age: ICANN between Technical Mandate and Political Challenges", at http://www.mcc.ruc.dk/aktuelt/2000/symp/kleinwaechter-paper.pdf.

12   Yu, "The Neverending ccTLD Story", *Public Law & Legal Theory Working Paper Series*, Research Paper Number 1-22, at http://ssrn.com/abstract=388980.

13   Kleinwaechter, "Governance Systems in the Internet Age: ICANN between Technical Mandate and Political Challenges", at http://www.mcc.ruc.dk/aktuelt/2000/symp/kleinwaechter-paper.pdf.

(iii) CcTLDs

Since no policy was created for the ccTLDs, their delegation became somewhat arbitrary. In many western countries, university employees introduced
the Internet, and at that time they were organized into different not-for-profit
Internet organizations; consequently, the governments' knowledge of the
Internet was very limited. As a result, the control of the ccTLD was in many
cases delegated to the not-for-profit organizations. In less technologically
developed countries, the control over the ccTLD was generally delegated to
the government, where it was not actively used until years later.

The not-for-profit organizations operated under the fundamental principle
that "the net should be free". However, in the second half of the 1990s, the
Internet began to be commercialized, and not only by universities and enthusiasts, but companies, consumers, and individuals began to take an interest in
domain names.

(d) Need for Regulation of the Domain Name System

The *laissez-faire* concept of an open market with many companies competing
to establish themselves is one whose practical application has not always
proven itself feasible. There are examples of scarce resources or instances
where a form of direction and regulation has been required. The DNS is a
classic example. It has a strict hierarchical structure and, as of yet, there is no
technical way to administer it without this hierarchy.

The domain names in a TLD must be unique. Subsequently, two different
interests may both have a legitimate claim to the name, or alternatively one of
them may have a more illegitimate motivation, such as the wish to extort others who wish to use the name (cybersquatting); yet, in either instance, they
will still be able to register the name in a TLD. Both situations will obviously
result in disputes; the only solution — someone must regulate the DNS. Some
TLDs have chosen to regulate the issuance of domain names, while others
have decided to create an independent mechanism for the purposes of arbitrating conflicts.

8.03   Issuance of Domain Names and Related Conflicts

(a) Issuance of Domain Names

(i)   First Come, First Served

The control of the majority of the TLDs is very liberal, and the "First come,
first served" principle is generally applied to the issuance of domain names,
i.e., the registration of a requested domain name is granted provided that the
name is not already registered. ICANN applies the "first come, first served"

principle to the generic top-level domains (gTLDs),[14] as is done with the German and United Kingdom TLDs.

That a country applies the "first come, first served" principle does not necessarily mean that the domain is completely available for registration. Many TLDs require the applicant to have a relation to the ccTLD, i.e., that they be a company, organization, or individual who is a resident in that country. Other restrictions include reserved names that for different reasons are not allowed to be registered as domain names.

An example is the Canadian TLD ".ca", which requires having a "Canadian Presence" to register a domain name, i.e., the applicant must be an individual or an organization with a connection to Canada (a Canadian citizen, corporation, or organization).[15] The German ".de", on the other hand, is an example of the more liberally controlled TLDs. To be allowed to register a domain name in Germany, the applicant is only required to have a contact person in Germany.[16]

(ii) Rules for Registration

Another attempt has been to control ccTLDs by applying more detailed rules to the registration of domain names. These systems typically require the applicant to have not only a connection to the relevant ccTLD, but also some form of documented connection to the specific domain name applied for. An example of such a documented connection is that the domain name is identical or very similar to a registered company name or trade mark held by the applicant.

The application of such rules for registration is an attempt to achieve a certain standard of registered domain names in the ccTLD and assure that the ccTLD is used in the desired way. The purpose being to ensure that what is published under a ccTLD is representative of, or at least has a connection with, the country related to the ccTLD.

The rules for registration have served their purpose well. TLDs applying such rules have traditionally had little or no problems with disputes (e.g., trade marks) concerning domain names. Consequently, there has been no need for an alternate dispute resolution system. The registered domain names also have been almost exclusively used by companies and organizations with a strong connection to the country related to the ccTLD.

However, there is a built-in problem with these systems based on the difficulty in registering domain names. Systems requiring that a domain name

---

14 Bryde-Andersen, *IT-retten, avsnitt* 11.5.c (2001).
15 CIRA Registration Rules, Version 2.2, at http://www.cira.ca.
16 See http://www.denic.de/de/bedingungen.html.

must reflect the exact registered name of a company exclude not only trade marks, personal names, and abbreviations of long or difficult company names, but also generic names as domain names. It is self-evident that every company and individual that is not granted the registration of a desired domain name will question the system.

Consequently, an international trend has been that the rules for registration have changed from being very restrictive to very accessible. They have undergone a liberalization process that started with allowing each company to register an unlimited number of domain names corresponding to the abbreviations of the company name and any registered trade marks. In recent years, many ccTLDs have taken the full step toward liberalization and implemented the first-to-file system. These ccTLDs include:

1. The Belgian ".be";

2. The Dutch ".nl";

3. The French ".fr";[17]

4. The Greek ".gr";

5. The Irish ".ie";

6. The Luxembourgian ".lu";

7. The Norwegian ".no";[18] and

8. The Swedish ".se".[19]

Another instigator behind the push for liberalization was that the rules for registration proved to restrain the popularity of a ccTLD, thereby causing a country's inhabitants and companies to register their domain names in other countries' ccTLDs or a gTLD, in effect counteracting the original purpose of applying these rules to create a ccTLD that was the natural domicile for the country's inhabitants and companies. Compounding this, of course, was the resultant loss of profit due to the relatively small number of registered domain names.

A striking example is the French ccTLD ".fr". Prior to liberalization, it had only 160,000 registered domain names.[20] Compare this with the German ".de", with more than 7-million registered names,[21] or the Danish ".dk", with 450,000 registered domain names. France has more than 10 times the

---

17   See http://www.nic.fr.

18   See http://www.norid.no/.

19   Roos "'First Come, Not Served': Domain Name Regulation in Sweden", *International Review of Law Computers & Technology*, volume 17, number 1 (2003).

20   See www.nic.fr/statistiques/afnic/afnic-repart.html.

21   See www.denic.de/DENICdb/stats/index.en.html#domaincount.

population of Denmark and an approximately comparative level of information technology development, yet the Danish ccTLD had three times as many registered domain names.[22]

(b) Disputes

(i) In General

Over time, the registration and use of domain names has resulted in a variety of disputes, and their legal implications have been discussed thoroughly. The most important issues will be discussed below, as well as the methods applied in different countries and for different TLDs in respect to dispute resolution.

(ii) Cybersquatting

Cybersquatting is perhaps the most well-known reason for disputes over domain names. Cybersquatting can be defined as occurring when a person, the "Cybersquatter", registers a domain name that rightfully "belongs" to someone else, e.g., someone registers a company's registered trade mark, and the registration is made for the purpose of extorting the trade mark holder (in "bad faith").

(iii) Reverse Domain Name Hijacking

Prior to the creation of ICANN and the UDRP, the gTLDs were provided by NSI,[23] and a policy was applied that allowed trade mark holders to place a domain name, identical with their registered trade mark, "on hold" pending resolution. The result of such an action, consequently, was that neither party could use the domain name.[24]

The applied policy, however, did not take into consideration the fact that trade mark rights do not apply to non-commercial use. Reverse domain name hijacking can be defined as when a trade mark holder manipulates an implemented policy so as to take action in respect to domain names that would not have been possible solely based on trade mark rights.[25] Reverse domain name hijacking must, to some extent, have lost its importance, at least regarding the gTLDs, following the implementation of the UDRP and with it the condition that a domain name must be registered in "bad faith" to be transferred or cancelled (see text, below).

---

22   See www.dk-hostmaster.dk/dkhostcms/bs?pageid=101&action=cmsview&language=da.

23   This was achieved through a private corporation in contractual agreement with NSF and the United States government.

24   Jones, "Protecting Your 'SportsEvent.com': Athletic Organizations and the Uniform Domain Name Dispute Resolution Policy", *West Virginia Journal of Law & Technology*, at http://www.wvu.edu/~wvjolt/Arch/Jones/Jones.htm.

25   Komaitis, "ICANN: Guilty as Charged?", *Journal of Information, Law and Technology* 2003(1).

Yet, due to the far-ranging interpretations of the UDRP-regulations performed by some panellists, reverse domain name hi-jacking is still being discussed.[26]

(iv) Misspellings

Misspelling is a form of cybersquatting that is done through the registration of a domain name similar to a popular domain name. As many people incorrectly spell or type the address in the web-browser, this registration is intended to capture traffic from the popular 'correct' domain name.

(v) Use of "Expired" Domain Names

Another method used to capture the traffic from a popular domain name is to renew its registration if the registration, intentionally or by mistake, has expired without being renewed. If the previous domain name holder does not have a trade mark right, there is almost no possibility of them recapturing the name.

(vi) Obscenities

In some cultures, the registration of words considered obscene is a large problem. The easy solution is to reserve words so that they cannot be registered. This might, however, be construed to be in conflict with the principle of freedom of speech; and it also must be understood that a word may have different, sometimes unfortunate, meanings in foreign cultures.

(vii) Defamation

Domain names can also be utilized in action opposed to a trade mark to express opinions regarding, for example, a company's behavior or policy. The most common example is the registration of ".sucks" domain names, i.e., a domain name constituting a company's name and the word "sucks" following it.

It has proven difficult to draw the line between cybersquatting and the freedom of expression, and panellists have interpreted the UDRP quite widely to close down ".sucks" sites. This has been criticized and has been considered contrary to the underlying purposes of the UDRP (see text, below).

(c) Dispute Resolution

As mentioned above, the "first to file" system is now the most common system for the issuance of domain names. Legal discussions regarding

---

26 See the *Barcelona.com* case, where the domain name was transferred from a travel agency to the city of Barcelona with the motivation that the city had better rights. WIPO Case Number D2000-0505.

domain names therefore tend to mainly concern disputes, predominantly in relation to trade mark interests, and how they should be resolved, rather than discussions concerning which conditions should apply for registration.

Advantages of the "first to file" system include its speed and the fact that it makes the registration process simple; yet these very same factors can result in difficulties as the applicants are solely responsible for the control of a name prior to registration.

The "first to file" system can therefore enable the registration of a name that interferes with, for example, trade mark rights, and hence a condition for the system to function properly is that the applicants take responsibility when registering a domain name. As a result, the system can easily be used for illegitimate purposes, or two parties may both think that they are entitled to the same domain name. In both cases, there is a need for an effective forum that an aggrieved party can turn to for resolution of the dispute.

(i) Public Courts and Interpretation of Existing Legislation

One solution, used by several ccTLDs, is to allow public courts to interpret existing legislation and apply it to domain name disputes. The interpretation of trade mark law in relation to the regulations regarding freedom of speech has, in Germany for example, been considered to function adequately and to provide fair judgements.[27]

Predictability in the rulings can be established through the use of precedents. The litigation process in public courts is, unfortunately, often too slow and costly to provide an effective solution.

(ii) New Legislation

A number of countries have considered domain name disputes as a basis with which to provide specific issues that need to be regulated by special legislation.

The most well-known example is the United States Anti-Cybersquatting Consumer Protection Act[28] that was created to prevent cybersquatting. The Anti-Cybersquatting Consumer Protection Act is applicable to registrations that are made in bad faith with the intent to profit from a protected trade mark (including a personal name) that is not registered to the applicant.

---

27   Papiri, "The Evolving System of Domain Name Dispute Resolution, section 99", *Skrifter utgivna av Institutet für Immaterialrätt och Marknadsrätt vid Stockholms Universitet*, number 115 (2002).

28   15 United States Code, section 1125(d).

(iii) Alternate Dispute Resolution Systems

To create an alternative to litigation in public courts, one that can resolve disputes quicker and less expensively, the majority of TLDs have chosen to implement special dispute resolution policies and alternative forums providing alternate dispute resolution systems (ADRs).

These ADRs are generally proceedings containing just one round of written pleadings that are made mandatory for all domain name registrants in the TLD. This is enforced by demanding that applicants for a domain name sign a contract ensuring that they must adhere to the ADR process.[29]

The most important ADR is ICANN's Uniform Domain Name Dispute Resolution Policy (the UDRP) that applies to all of the gTLDs. The principles behind the UDRP were drafted by the World Intellectual Property Organization (WIPO) and implemented by ICANN in October 1999. The UDRP allows trade mark holders to seek arbitration against cybersquatters with the potential remedies of having the offending name cancelled or transferred. The UDRP was not supposed to replace the courts but instead to create globally uniform rules to be applied only to the most obvious cases of cybersquatting.

Compared to the previously applied NSI policy, the UDRP did not allow for the possibility of putting a trade mark on hold during the dispute resolution process; it also required that a domain name be registered or used in bad faith in order for a trade mark holder to initiate proceedings.

(d) Evaluation and Criticism

(i) In General

The ".com" TLD is the most popular, and most of the discussion regarding the ADRs has thus far been focused on ICANN's dispute resolution system. This discussion has included important issues such as legitimacy, predictability, and freedom of speech, and has been too extensive to be thoroughly discussed here. A review of the various arguments and criticism follow below, with references to the most important decisions and work in the area.

(ii) Forum Shopping

The UDRP allows the complainant to choose from three different dispute resolution providers, the WIPO, the National Arbitration Forum (NAF), and the CPR Institute for Dispute Resolution (CPR). The UDRP has been criticized for enabling the complainant to choose the provider where it feels there

---

29　Geist, "Fair.com?: An Examination of the Allegations of Systematic Unfairness in the ICANN UDRP", at http://aix1.uottawa.ca/~geist/geistudrp.pdf.

is the greatest possibility of winning by studying the statistics from previous decisions. A study performed by Professor Geist in 2001 showed that the WIPO handled 58 per cent of the total disputes and, in 82 per cent of the cases, it decided in favor of the complainant; the NAF handled 34 per cent of the disputes with almost 83 per cent of its decisions in favor of the complainant; while the CPR had only been engaged in 1 per cent of the cases, with the complainants winning 59 per cent of them.[30] The study has led to intense discussion and criticism of the UDRP. A simple solution that was applied by many of the ccTLDs who implemented their own ADRs instead of joining the UDRP has been to allow only one dispute resolution provider.

Another point reviewed in Geist's study, and closely related to forum shopping, was the possibility of choosing from either a single panellist or a three-member panellist proceeding. In disputes decided by a single panellist, the complainant has won 83 per cent of the cases while, in three-member panels, they have only won 60 per cent of the time. Both parties have the right to opt for a three-member panel, yet in consequence that party must then carry the cost for the two extra panellists. As a note of reference, 90 per cent of the UDRP-cases are decided by single-member panels.

(iii) Lack of Predictability

The UDRP also has been criticized for lacking predictability.[31] The UDRP was initially supposed to be applied only to clear and obvious cases where a domain name was registered in "bad faith".

Many panellists have, however, applied the UDRP much more extensively and thus expanded the UDRP's area of application to cases that are more complex and demanding. The catalogue of behavior which constitutes bad faith is non-exclusive, and thus allows panellists to interpret it in a myriad of ways.

If the domain name has been registered for the purpose of "disrupting the business of a competitor", it is presumed to be registered in bad faith. In the decision *Dixons-online.com*, Mr. Abu Abdullah, a displeased consumer, was running a website that concerned a specific car dealer. It is noted in the UDRP decision that "there was no evidence to conclude the respondent is offering services or goods for any kind of commercial gain".[32] Nevertheless Mr. Abdullah was considered to be a "competitor" and, thus, his domain name was registered in bad faith.

---

30 Geist, "Fair.com?: An Examination of the Allegations of Systemic Unfairness in the ICANN UDRP", section 2 (2001), at http://aix1.uottawa.ca/~geist/geistudrp.pdf.

31 Mueller, "Success by Default, A New Profile of Domain Name Trade mark Disputes under ICANN's UDRP", A Study Prepared for the Convergence Center, at pp. 22–25, at http://dcc.syr.edu/markle/markle-report-final.pdf.

32 ICANN UDRP Decision D 2001-0843.

The panel justified this by referring to a previous decision where it had been held "that competitor has a wider meaning and is not confined to those who are selling or providing competing products. In this wider context it means, one who acts in opposition to another and the context does not demand any restricted meaning such as commercial or business competitor". This interpretation has been criticized for being unfair, contradictory to the legal and general definition of a "competitor", and as being a threat to the freedom of speech.[33]

Another example of the expansive interpretation of the UDRP has concerned the question of when a domain name is "identical or confusingly similar" to, e.g., a trade mark right, and thus can be transferred according to the UDRP. The most extensive interpretations and cases discussed involve a number of decisions regarding so-called ".sucks" domain names, e.g., websites with the primary purpose of expressing an opinion regarding a company or product and using a domain name which consists of said company's trade mark or company name and, most typically, the word "sucks" thereafter.

Examples of decisions regarding such domain names are Guinessreallysucks.com,[34] Wal-martsucks.com,[35] and Philpsucks.com.[36] All of these domain names were considered confusingly similar with the trade marks.[37]

(iv) Lack of Legitimacy

Regardless of the form the system applied to control a TLD takes, voices have been raised in criticism of both the systems and their controlling organizations, in the international and the national TLDs. The dialogues and retorts have so far focused on legitimacy and citizens' acceptance of the systems for the issuance of Domain names and dispute resolution. Legitimacy and acceptance can be obtained through many different methods, used not only by governments but also by the organizations controlling TLDs.

ICANN has been at the epicenter of these rebukes, with claims that it lacks legitimacy as well as acceptance. It has been argued that ICANN can rely on neither direct nor indirect public elections for legitimacy and that it also lacks the broad support of public opinion.

---

33   Mueller, "Success by Default, A New Profile of Domain Name Trade Mark Disputes under ICANN's UDRP", A Study Prepared for the Convergence Center, at pp. 22–25, at http://dcc.syr.edu/markle/markle-report-final.pdf.

34   ICANN UDRP Decision D2000-0996.

35   ICANN UDRP Decision D2000-0662.

36   ICANN UDRP Decision D2001-1195.

37   Other ".sucks" decisions include UDRP Decisions D2000-0584, D2000-0996, D2000-1015, D2000-0662, D2000-0477, D2001-0007, FA00102247, FA0097077, FA0097750, D2000-0636, D2001-1195, D2001-1195, D2001-0213, D2000-0681, D2000-0583, and D2000-1121.

As previously mentioned, the ICANN UDRP has been criticized for lacking independent panellists, and predictable regulations. In order for a system to be considered legitimate, the enforcement of powers must be clear and predictable and not give the impression of being arbitrary. Another shortcoming of the UDRP is its lack of a judicial review, as a judicial review would help bolster the commitment to process and rationality which becomes an important source for legitimacy.[38]

(e) Differences between Countries

The manner in which a TLD is controlled has a large effect on its popularity and its functionality. First-to-file systems have proven much more popular than systems requiring a registered right to a name prior to registration. This is, of course, simply a consequence of the cost and trouble connected with registering a domain name.

Although some of the ccTLDs who impose requirements have satisfied their intention of preventing both cybersquatters and companies or individuals without a presence in their country from registering their domain names, they have failed to become the natural TLD for their countries. Due to the comprehensive regulations applicable on registrations in the Swedish TLD ".se", for example, a majority of Swedish companies and individuals choose to register their name in the ".nu" TLD instead.

The Swedish TLD has now removed their requirements and are applying the First to file system. Another poignant example is the United States TLD ".us" that also previously applied rigorous requirements for the registration of its domain names, for example, registrations were only allowed under sub-domains that indicated the domicile of the registering company or individual. United States companies and citizens have chosen to primarily use the .com TLD instead of the United States TLD.[39]

8.04 Other Issues

(a) Country Code Top-Level Domains

Although the ".com" TLD is still the largest TLD in terms of registered domain names, ccTLDs are increasing in importance. One good example is the German TLD ".de" that today has more than 8-million registered domain names and is rapidly and continuously increasing.[40] While the ".com" TLD

---

38 Weinberg "ICANN and the Problem of Legitimacy", *Duke Law Journal*, volume 50, section 187, 2000.

39 See www.nic.us/faqs/index.html.

40 See http://www.denic.de/de/domains/statistiken/index.html, last visited March 2005.

was, just a few years ago, the only thinkable option for a commercial company, the ccTLD ".de" has now grown to become the number-one TLD for companies and organizations addressing the consumers and inhabitants of German-speaking countries.

This trend can be seen in ccTLDs all over the world, including smaller countries, but can of course be expected to have the largest impact in ccTLDs with large numbers of inhabitants. One example is the Chinese ".ch" that currently has only 430,000 registered domain names but is increasing steadily as Chinese inhabitants gain increased access to the Internet.[41]

The European Union (EU) announced its plan to introduce a new European ccTLD in 1999 but, due to the fact that the EU is not a "country" according to the ISO 3166-1 table, it could not be accepted as a ccTLD according to the ICANN ICP-1 policy document on country code delegations.

The EU Commission would not give up the idea of a European domicile on the Internet and, after extensive negotiations with the ICANN Board, the policy was changed. The ccTLD ".eu" is planned to be activated during 2005.[42]

A ccTLD domain name enables the holder to address the population in one particular country directly in its own language and with a website attuned to the relevant market. Paradoxically, the most interesting effect that the ccTLDs might have is that the once-global Internet could become divided into different languages or geographic areas.

(b) Government Take-Overs

A direct effect of the ccTLD's increased popularity is the growing interest from national governments. As a direct result of the universities' strong influence in the beginning of Internet development, independent organizations were often assigned the responsibility of the ccTLDs.

In most instances, governments were not interested in the ccTLD as a national resource or considered it best administered by academic or non-profit organizations run by experienced enthusiasts. The Swedish ccTLD ".se", for instance, was run for five years by a private citizen working at the Royal Institute of Technology. When the workload became too heavy, a non-profit organization was created to administer the TLD, draft rules for registration, and provide alternate dispute resolution.

---

41   15th Statistical Survey on the Internet Development in China (January, 2005), at http://www.cnnic.net.cn/en/index/0O/02/.

42   Von Arx and Hagen, "Sovereign Domains: A Declaration of Independence of ccTLDs from Foreign Control", 9 *Rich. J.L. & Tech*. 4 (Fall 2002), at http://www.law.richmond.edu/jolt/v9i1/article4.html.

Many ccTLDs are today still controlled by academic or non-profit organizations, but national governments have begun to realize their importance and started to interfere. The governments of Switzerland, Australia, and Canada have seized full or partial control of their ccTLDs, while, in The Netherlands,

a proposed bill would implicate an impending take over; and in Sweden the non-profit organization formerly in control of domain names has been forced, by the government, to change its rules for registration under the threat of a take over.

(c) "Generic" ccTLDs

Some ccTLDs have, primarily for economic reasons, chosen not to strive to become a national "zone" on the Internet, but instead to apply liberal rules for registration and to market their ccTLD towards other countries. In contrast to the government-controlled ccTLDs, which have a strong connection to a country's inhabitants or to a particular language, is the corporate-controlled ccTLDs who address a global market, or even the inhabitants of a totally different country.

Possibly the most interesting example is that of the Tuvalu ccTLD ".tv". Tuvalu is an island group in the South Pacific with a population of a bit more than 10,000. When Network Solutions first created the original ccTLDs, Tuvalu was abbreviated as ".tv". The commercial potential of this ccTLD was quickly noticed by the corporation WebTV before the Tuvalu government was even aware of its existence. WebTV applied for and managed to be appointed as the representative of ccTLD. This would, however, not last for long, as soon the Tuvalu government gained knowledge of the situation and claimed the right to the ccTLD. The IANA then transferred the control of the ccTLD to the Tuvalu government, but the government was not interested in administrating the ccTLD and, instead, auctioned it to the highest bidder. Today, it is controlled by the ".tv corporation" and has no other relationship with the Tuvalu government than of paying royalties for its use of the TLD.[43]

Other examples of ccTLDs which target markets other than their domestic market include the Niue ".nu" that is licensed to the United States corporation .NU Domain Ltd. and targets primarily the Nordic countries where "nu" translates as "now"; the Tonga ".to", controlled by the private corporation Tonic with the Crown Prince of Tonga as the majority owner and targeting the global market, the Moldovian ".md", controlled by the corporation Dot MD under a license from the government to issue domain names in English-speaking countries, primarily targeting medical doctors in the

---

43   See http://www.tv/.

United States; and the Samoan ".as", controlled by the government but targeting the Norwegian market (where "as" translates as Inc.).[44]

8.05 Conclusion

(a) In General

This chapter has dealt with the significant legal issues regarding the DNS. Several of these are of substantial importance, and jointly they are far too extensive to be discussed more thoroughly in this chapter.

One of the most interesting recent developments is the increasing importance of the ccTLDs. This also is the most pertinent issue in relation to the context of this chapter, and the discussion and conclusions will consequently focus on this issue.

(i) Increasing Importance of ccTLDs

The DNS, gTLDs, ICANN, and the connected dispute resolution system are all strongly influenced by western, particularly United States, interests. As a result of the United States advanced position in the development of information technology combined with its restrictive regulations for the issuance of domain names in the ccTLD ".us", the gTLDs, and particularly ".com", are dominated by United States companies and individuals.

Subsequently, as a reaction to this development, ccTLDs have gained in popularity, especially in countries where languages other than English are preferred in the contact with the domestic market and the citizens of the country; the fascinating popularity of the German ".de" is one example. Although many companies still operate from a central website divided into parts with different languages, generally registered in the ".com" TLD, it has become more common to also register the domain name in popular ccTLDs. This enables the domain name holder to address that country's market directly from a national website.

This increased popularity of ccTLDs is likely to continue. Developing countries will rapidly increase their presence on the Internet as technological developments advance. Differences in culture and religion, as well as the recognition of languages and geographical areas as separate distinct markets that need to be independently addressed, will contribute to evolve. One excellent example that illustrates this point is the planned ccTLD ".eu", whose issuance has been approved by ICANN following pressure from the EU.

---

44 "Location, Location, Location: The Geography of the Dot com Problem", *Environment and Planning B: Planning and Design* 2001, volume 28, at pp. 59–71.

Accordingly, domain names in ccTLDs have become advantageous in the communication with citizens of different countries and distinct markets. From a legal viewpoint, this provides new perspectives on the previously discussed questions regarding the issuance of domain names and dispute resolution.

(b) Issuance of Domain Names in ccTLDs

The recent trend with reference to the issuance of domain names in diverse ccTLDs is a transition from systems requiring naming-rights for registration, into more liberal systems that apply the first-to-file principle.

This change is in reaction to the failure of the successful implementation of such systems. One difficulty with such systems is that they must compete with the gTLDs as well as other ccTLDs; applicants who are not allowed to register their desired domain name in one ccTLD may simply choose to register their name in another TLD. This has resulted not only in a loss of profits but, moreover, the ccTLDs' position as a natural zone for domain names related to that country is undermined.

The recent developments have now afforded new opportunities for ccTLDs to control which domain names are approved for registration. As the importance of a ccTLD increases, the alternatives become less attractive; for instance, when targeting the German market, a ".de" domain name has become almost a necessity. Although the requirements for name rights are not likely to be re-introduced, other techniques are being utilized to align ccTLDs with a country's national interests, e.g., cultural traditions, religious values, or desire for a national connection.

Such techniques are requirements for the applicant to be domiciled in the country and the reservation of names that are either not allowed to be used as domain names or reserved for the potential use of a certain party. Reserved names often include religious words, names associated with royal courts or states, and city or government authorities.

(c) Dispute Resolution in ccTLDs

Weighed against trade mark applications, the registration of a domain name is an uncomplicated, quick, and inexpensive procedure. Consequently, the increased importance of ccTLDs has caused international companies to 'vacuum' ccTLDs for salient domain names as a part of their trade mark strategy. The registered domain names might not only be trade marks held by the applicant company, but also generic words, abbreviations, and potential trade marks.

Another dissimilarity to trade mark applications is the fact that the DNS does not provide the possibility for dividing names into different classes of goods and services; furthermore, the DNS is an international system that addresses every geographical area in the world. While one name can be used as a trade mark in many different fields of goods and services and in many different countries or regions, that name converted into a domain name in a ccTLD is a scarce resource, creating potential conflicts between different trade mark holders. Coalesce this with ccTLDs becoming new markets for cybersquatters, and these disputes over competing legitimate interests result in the systems for dispute resolution taking on even greater importance.

Alternate dispute resolution methods have provided an alternative to traditional court processes that have proven effective enough to decrease cybersquatting in gTLDs. Although ADR techniques have been implemented in several ccTLDs, the situation is somewhat different. The costs for alternate dispute resolution procedures are often partially financed through the earnings of domain name registration fees in the TLD; this has resulted in fees for a complainant wishing to initiate a procedure that are reasonably low, often as low as US $1,000.

In comparison to disputes over trade marks, this is very inexpensive but, conversely, there is rarely any possibility of transferring any of the cost to the opposing party, even if the decision is fully in favor of the complainant. If it is necessary to initiate procedures in several different ccTLDs, each having different rules for the resolution, costs both for the procedures and legal representation adds up to become quite substantial, and the administration become extensive.

The preferable solution would be a harmonization of all these many alternate dispute resolution methods, where a decision from any dispute resolution procedure would have a binding effect in all affiliated TLDs or a system where disputes would be resolved in one central alternate dispute organization, e.g., the ICANN UDRP. This concept is not a new one; the UDRP was created for the purpose of arbitrating not only disputes regarding domain names registered in gTLDs, but also in ccTLDs. WIPO published its ccTLD Best Practices for the Prevention and Resolution of Property Disputes back in 2001.[45] Despite the opportunity for ccTLDs to adopt the UDRP, a majority have instead opted to create their own ADR procedures; stating their motive as being the need to control the resolution of disputes related to their ccTLDs in accordance with differences in culture, religion, and differing views on trade marks, intellectual property rights, and freedom of speech.

---

45   See http://arbiter.wipo.int/domains/cctld/bestpractices/bestpractices.pdf, last visited March 2005.

As a concluding remark, it should be mentioned that the future evolution of the DNS, and most especially the ccTLDs, is of exceptional interest as the activities of emerging economies, major languages, and developing countries influence the Internet. Concurrently, Europe is striving to delineate a part for themselves by demanding a new TLD of their own.

(d) Policy Issues

(i) In General

Finally, and taking into account the knowledge and conclusions discussed in this chapter, it is appropriate to provide a few comments and suggestions regarding the policy issues for the regulation of TLDs. These suggestions are of foremost interest to developing countries that have not yet dealt with the regulation of their ccTLDs.

(ii) Issuance of Domain Names

Distinct Interests   The policy issues can be divided into two distinct areas, namely:

1. The regulation of the issuance of domain names; and

2. The dispute resolution of conflicts related to registered domain names.

The regulation of the issuance of domain names is dependent on which interests the policies aim to safeguard. The most fundamental interests to which a TLD may well give priority are:

1. Ensuring that registered names have a national connection;

2. Protecting trade marks;

3. Preventing disputes;

4. Ensuring that the right person has a particular domain name;

5. Profiting from registrations;

6. Ensuring usability and an uncomplicated registration process; and

7. Other specific interests, e.g., cultural or religious reasons for not allowing certain words to be registered.

Maximizing Profits   It is easy to conclude that, if the main purpose is to maximize the profit of the TLD, a first-to-file system that is totally open for registration should be implemented.

This is the generally applied policy in the generic TLDs, as well as in national TLDs, such as the Niue ".nu" and the Tuvalu ".tv" that have successfully turned their fortunate delegation of ccTLDs into good incomes.

Rules for Registration   If the policy aims to ensure that domain names have a national connection and to completely prevent disputes over trademark rights the solution is more complicated.

Systems with detailed rules for registration have, on the one hand, been proven to prevent disputes; on the other hand, they have been regarded as too bureaucratic and have caused applicants to choose alternative TLDs. These aspects need to be weighed against each other if the implementation of rules for registration are to be considered.

First-to-File System   Based on present experience, including the fact that most policies with rules for registration have failed and have converted to first-to-file systems, the best suggested solution is for the TLD to apply a liberal policy and implement a first-to-file system.

Reserved words may be used to prevent culturally and religiously sensitive words from being used as domain names and to assure that certain names can only be registered by a specially entitled party, e.g., a local government or city. To serve the purpose of preventing trade mark disputes, trade marks can be reserved for the benefit of the trade mark holder. Reserved words should be published on the registrars' website in order to inform potential applicants and create trust in the system.

(iii) Dispute Resolution

Distinct Interests   The policy issues related to domain name dispute resolution can in turn be divided into various areas where distinct interests may need to be safeguarded. Interests that need to be taken into account include:

1. Legitimacy;

2. Predictability;

3. Legal security;

4. Reasonably quick arbitration; and

5. Inexpensive arbitration.

Should a Policy Be Implemented?   As a first step, it must be decided if an alternate dispute resolution policy and an alternate dispute resolution forum on the whole should be implemented or if disputes should be settled by public courts relying on existing or newly implemented legislation.

If the main objective is to safeguard the legitimacy, predictability and legal security of the system the dispute resolution may well be left to the public courts. In countries with established trade mark laws and experienced courts, this option has been proven to provide well-balanced and generally accepted decisions. Public courts do, however, have the severe disadvantage of being very costly and relatively slow. At least for uncomplicated and relatively clear disputes, a quicker and cheaper alternative in the form of an alternate dispute resolution procedure is preferable.

(iv) Is Special Legislation Necessary?

The problem of solving disputes over domain names has existed in many countries for almost a decade. Some have chosen to implement special legislation, one example being the United States Anti-Cybersquatting Act, but others have instead relied on their general trade mark legislation and precedents. Both options have turned out well. Issues that cause difficult considerations and that can be solved through legislation include:

1. Creating a legal ground for the transfer of a domain name to the rightful owner (trade mark law generally only offers the possibility to impose prohibitions against use); and

2. Establishing the grounds for intervening against a domain name that has been registered in bad faith but which has not yet been used.

Decisions made by alternate dispute resolution procedures should preferably not be based on trade mark law but on a special, simpler, dispute resolution policy.

Adherence to the UDRP?   If the TLD chooses to use alternate dispute resolution, it must decided whether to implement an existing policy, e.g., the ICANN UDRP, or to create its own policy. Developing countries implementing a new policy for dispute resolution can, with certain advantage, adhere to ICANNs UDRP.

Although the UDRP has been criticized, e.g., for lacking legitimacy and predictability, it has proven that it provides a practical working alternative for the resolution of trade mark disputes and is well known to domain name applicants on the global market. Consequently, despite its flaws, the UDRP will help provide trust in the TLD. Instead of attempting to create their own perfect systems, countries implementing alternate dispute resolution procedures should adhere to the UDRP and engage in the process of revising and improving it.

Arbitration Institute   A TLD also must decide whether a new dispute resolution forum should be implemented or if one or all of the existing institutes for dispute resolution should be given the task. Based on the discussion related to arbitration, it can be concluded that the most important issue to address is the problem of forum shopping.

This problem can, however, easily be avoided by using only one arbitration institute. Whether one of ICANNs designated institutes is chosen or a national institute is created is of less importance. Competent arbitrators can surely be found in either case. What is important is that every measure is taken to guaranty that the arbitrators are independent, in order to provide just decisions and legitimacy.

Transfer of Costs   If the TLD has implemented an alternate dispute resolution procedure, the cost for the dispute resolution may be as low as US $1,000, and many alternate dispute resolution procedures also reward the applicant with a reimbursement of half the cost if the claim is successful. The process generally consists of only one written statement, which helps to minimize the legal expenses and provide for a very inexpensive dispute resolution process as compared to a court process.

Despite these factors, the costs are not negligible and are definitely not for smaller companies and individuals; as a result, a market for "low-budget cybersquatting" can arise, i.e., cybersquatters demand an amount that is just under the cost for dispute resolution. In order to solve this problem, some TLDs, including the Dutch ".nl", have implemented policies that allow the successful party to transfer legal expenses to the other party. This solution can be recommended, under the prerequisite that a relatively low limit for the allowed legal expenses is applied.

CHAPTER 9

CRYPTOGRAPHY AND ELECTRONIC SIGNATURES

Maury D. Shenk, Stewart A. Baker, and Winnie Chang
Steptoe & Johnson LLP
London, England and Washington, DC, United States

9.01   Introduction

The use of mathematical and other techniques to scramble and unscramble information — known as cryptography or encryption — has a long and fascinating history. One of the better-known examples of early cryptography is the Caesar cipher, a simple method that Julius Caesar is said to have used to secure confidential communications to his army.

While protecting access to secret information is still a major reason for using cryptography today, cryptographic techniques also are increasingly used to authenticate the identity of individuals and to ensure data integrity (i.e., the assurance that information has not been altered in storage or transit between a sender and intended recipients).

Modern encryption technology is based on several types of mathematical algorithms — primarily symmetric algorithms, asymmetric algorithms, and hash algorithms. Although these algorithms are highly complex, a brief description is appropriate.

Symmetric algorithms (such as AES, DES, and Blowfish) allow confidential communications using a secret "key" shared by the sender and recipient. Asymmetric algorithms (such as RSA, ElGamal, and Diffie-Hellman) involve two mathematically related keys, one of which is usually public. Asymmetric algorithms can be used both for confidentiality (via encryption with the recipient's public key and decryption with the recipient's private key) and digital signature (via signature with the sender's private key and verification with the sender's public key). Hash algorithms (such as SHA-1 and MD5) take a variable-length message (as short as a sentence or as long as a book) and produce a unique, fixed-length "digest" that can be used to confirm that the message has not been changed.

Particular practical applications of encryption (on the Internet, other networks, and otherwise) often involve complex combinations of these encryption algorithms into encryption "protocols", such as SSL (for secure connections over the World Wide Web), S/MIME (for secure email), IPSec (for securing Internet TCP/IP traffic), and others.

9.02   Regulation of Encryption: Export, Import, and Use

(a) In General

With the growth of the Internet as a global communications infrastructure, encryption has become the subject of debate and government regulation in recent years. On the one hand, encryption software and hardware allow individuals to send and receive secure, authenticated communications, thus providing important benefits that include protection of legitimate privacy interests and enhanced viability of electronic commerce.

On the other hand, there is ongoing concern that encryption could potentially allow criminals, terrorists, and unfriendly governments to hide their communications and illegal activities. As a result, many countries tend to apply strict regulation to encryption products.

(b) Types of Encryption Regulation

(i)   General Principles and Exceptions

Confidentiality vs. Authentication   As mentioned above, encryption can be used to provide confidentiality (i.e., the assurance that only authorized persons have access to secret information) and/or authentication (i.e., a trusted way to verify the identity of a particular person who sent a specific message, commonly through the use of electronic signatures).

Most countries today only restrict items that use encryption for confidentiality.

Temporary Import and Export   Many countries exempt temporary encryption import and export for "personal use" (usually including business uses), allowing travelers to carry personal laptops loaded with encryption software into and out of the country without any special license or authorization.

Intangible Transfers   The United States and many European Union (EU) member states control intangible transfers (i.e., Internet downloads and uploads) of encryption technology quite aggressively. In the recent climate of heightened electronic vigilance, other countries (e.g., Singapore) have decided to follow suit.

However, some countries (mainly in South America, Africa, and the Middle East) do not extend import and export controls to intangible transfers of encryption software, and generally due to the focus of their customs laws on physical items.

(ii) Export

Established in July 1996, the Wassenaar Arrangement was designed to increase the transparency and responsibility in global transfers of conventional arms and dual-use goods and technologies.[1] It is one of several worldwide non-proliferation regimes created near the end of the Cold War. Other principal regimes are the Nuclear Suppliers Group, the Australia Group, and the Missile Technology Control Regime, and they are mainly directed against the proliferation of weapons of mass destruction and missiles. The 33 participating countries of the Wassenaar Arrangement are:

1. Argentina;
2. Australia;
3. Austria;
4. Belgium;
5. Bulgaria;
6. Canada;
7. Czech Republic;
8. Denmark;
9. Finland;
10. France;
11. Germany;
12. Greece;
13. Hungary;
14. Ireland;
15. Italy;
16. Japan;
17. Korea, Republic;

---

1   See http://www.wassenaar.org.

18. Luxembourg;

19. The Netherlands;

20. New Zealand;

21. Norway;

22. Poland;

23. Portugal;

24. Romania;

25. Russian Federation;

26. Slovakia;

27. Spain;

28. Sweden;

29. Switzerland;

30. Turkey;

31. Ukraine;

32. United Kingdom; and

33. United States.

Membership is open on a global and non-discriminatory basis to countries meeting certain criteria. In particular, a country must:

1. Be a producer or exporter of arms or associated dual-use goods and technology;

2. Maintain non-proliferation policies and appropriate national policies (including adherence to international non-proliferation regimes and treaties); and

3. Implement fully effective export controls.

The member countries agreed to control all items on the Wassenaar Arrangement Munitions and Dual-Use lists, with the aim of preventing unauthorized transfers or re-transfers of those items. These lists are reviewed periodically to take into account technological advances or other changes. The Dual-Use List consists of a basic list (tier 1) and annexes of sensitive (tier 2) and very sensitive (sub-set of tier 2) items. Most encryption hardware, software and technology are in tier 1, although cryptanalytic items (i.e., those designed for "breaking" encryption codes) are designated as sensitive items.

Although the Wassenaar Arrangement sets out the minimum standards for export regulations for military and dual-use goods (including encryption items), member countries are allowed to authorize exports according to their own policies and discretion.

With respect to encryption controls, the Wassenaar Arrangement explicitly provides exclusions for mass-market products, weak encryption (with key length up to 56 bits), mobile telephones, personalized smart cards, digital signature products, equipment used for banking transactions, copy protection software, and other items.

National Practices Australian, Canadian, EU, Japanese, and United States export controls are closely based on Wassenaar controls.

Although Hong Kong and Singapore are not signatories to the Wassenaar Arrangement, they implement encryption regulations that generally follow Wassenaar guidelines. Other countries, including China, Israel, and Kazakhstan, apply various *ad hoc* controls.

(iii) Import

There are various types of import controls on encryption products. Some countries (including China, Tunisia, and certain former Soviet Union republics, such as Russia, Kazakhstan, and Uzbekistan) apply blanket import restrictions encryption items.

Some countries, such as Hong Kong and certain new EU members, such as the Czech Republic, Latvia, Lithuania, and Slovakia, apply Wassenaar restrictions to imports. Countries that do not implement encryption-specific import restrictions (e.g., Malaysia) may impose import and equipment type-approval requirements on telecommunication products (including any embedded encryption software or hardware).

(iv) Use

There also are various types of controls on the use of encryption products. Countries that apply blanket import prohibitions on encryption items (such as China, Tunisia, and Russia) usually have broad restrictions on encryption use. Certain countries (e.g., India) apply encryption-use restriction in particular applications (e.g., telecommunications and the Internet).

Other countries (including Israel and South Africa) implement restrictions on particular activities (e.g., commercial supply and development of encryption products and services) or pursuant to specified license conditions.

(c) Global Regulation

(i) In General

This section describes the encryption laws and policies of a sample of several countries (and the EU). The countries covered include leading producers of encryption products, important markets for encryption products, and other countries whose laws illustrate the nature of global encryption regulation.

(ii) United States

United States export and re-export controls are administered by the Bureau of Industry and Security of the United States Department of Commerce. The Export Administration Regulations,[2] which contain rules governing exports of encryption items, apply to most products using encryption for confidentiality, except to certain products decontrolled under the Wassenaar Arrangement and products using "short-range wireless encryption".

However, Bureau of Industry and Security regulations do not apply to encryption used for authentication, digital signature, or access control, or to exports to Canada. Exports of publicly available source code also are substantially decontrolled.

The strictest export treatment applies to encryption technology, proprietary source code, and open cryptographic interfaces exported to countries other than the favored countries (EU member states, plus Australia, Japan, New Zealand, Norway, and Switzerland).

Most encryption products are exportable under a license exception. Qualification for most license exceptions requires submission of a "review request" to the Bureau of Industry and Security. The request, which also is reviewed by the National Security Agency, is submitted on a Bureau of Industry and Security form and should also include a letter of explanation and technical specifications. A few encryption items — primarily network infrastructure and certain other products exported to foreign government entities and open cryptographic interfaces and encryption technology to non-favored countries — continue to require licenses from Bureau of Industry and Security.

Application procedures are similar to those for review requests, but license applications are reviewed by the Bureau of Industry and Security, the National Security Agency, the Federal Bureau of Investigation, the Department of State, and the Department of Defense.

Processing of review requests by the US government generally takes approximately four to eight weeks, although most products may be exported either immediately on submission of a review request or 30 days after the request is registered by the Bureau of Industry and Security. Processing times for license applications vary depending on complexity. The Bureau of Industry and Security requires post-export reporting for many encryption exports (as well as re-exports from Canada), but there are a variety of significant exceptions.

2　　15 Code of Federal Regulation, sections 730–774.

The United States does not restrict the import or use of encryption products, although US legislation regarding wiretaps can affect use of encryption. For example, United States law enforcement agencies can, with appropriate judicial authorization, conduct electronic surveillance of electronic communications, under both federal and state law. This authority was significantly broadened by the USA PATRIOT Act,[3] which was passed in response to the 11 September 2001 terrorist attacks on the United States.

To facilitate such electronic surveillance, telecommunications carriers are required by the Communications Assistance for Law Enforcement Act[4] to build their networks in a way that facilitates wiretapping of publicly available telecommunications services. The use of encryption on telecommunications carrier networks may be affected by the obligations of Communications Assistance for Law Enforcement Act.

(iii) European Union

Majority Position The EU Dual-Use Regulation,[5] originally passed in 2000 and modified several times since, has removed almost all restrictions on the intra-Community transfer of encryption products and technology, allowing the unlicensed shipment between EU member states of all encryption goods except cryptanalytic items.

Under the Regulation, the export of encryption goods or technology with key lengths greater than 56 bits generally requires authorization for all destinations outside the EU, though there are some significant exceptions to this rule. Among the primary exceptions, exports of all encryption products, except cryptanalytic items, are permitted under a General License to a group of seven favored countries: Australia, Canada, Japan, New Zealand, Norway, Switzerland, and the United States.

In addition, mass-market encryption products, regardless of key length, may be freely exported outside the EU, and no restrictions apply to the export of encryption goods and technology that are used for basic scientific research that provide the minimum information necessary for patent applications, or that are in the public domain. However, EU member states may impose additional controls on the products listed in the EU export control lists (even those deemed acceptable for intra-Community transfers) "to safeguard public policy or public security". All encryption goods and technology not exempted from control must be licensed prior to export from any EU member state.

---

3   Pub. Law Number 107-56 (2001).
4   Pub. Law Number 102-414 (1994).
5   Regulation 1334/2000/EC.

An individual export authorization is generally required for the export of controlled encryption goods and technology outside the EU. Notably, the EU Dual-Use Regulation provides for General Licenses and other simplified procedures for the export of dual-use goods to the seven states listed above. The EU also permits global authorizations to be issued to a particular exporter for a type or category of dual-use goods and technology that may be eligible for export to one or more specified countries. The member states, and not the EU, have the authority to issue export licenses.

However, the EU has identified a number of factors that member states must take into account when issuing export authorizations, including commitments under other international agreements on non-proliferation and control of sensitive goods, international sanctions obligations, national security considerations, and considerations concerning the intended end-use and risk of diversion of the goods and/or technology to be exported.

Under the EU regime, exporters are required to keep detailed records of consignments of dual-use goods and technology for at least three years. In addition, exporters who engage in intra-Community trade of controlled dual-use items must provide competent authorities with their names and the addresses where records relating to the transaction can be inspected.

The majority of EU member states do not control the import or use of encryption hardware, software, or technology. However, certain EU legislation, while not restricting the use of encryption, may ultimately have an impact on how encryption goods and technology are used, and on the types of requirements that are placed on providers of encryption-related services. This legislation includes:

1. The Data Protection Directive — The Data Protection Directive[6] may limit the types of national controls that can be placed on encryption technology. In addition, there may be circumstances in which the Data Protection Directive mandates the use of encryption or digital signature services to ensure the protection of personal information, or implies particular security requirements for the provision of cryptographic services.

2. The Electronic Signatures Directive — The Electronic Signatures Directive[7] recognizes that divergent member state rules with respect to the legal recognition of electronic signatures and the accreditation of certification service providers may create a significant barrier to the use of electronic communications and electronic commerce within the EU (see text, below).

---

6   Directive 95/46/EC.
7   Directive 99/93/EC.

3. The Electronic Commerce Directive — The Electronic Commerce Directive[8] supports the elimination of national restrictions on the availability and use of encryption technology.

Each of the EU Directives has been implemented by most individual EU member states, and the specifics of the national implementations of the directives can differ (in most cases, in relatively minor respects).

France France has traditionally placed very tight controls on all but the weakest of encryption products. In addition to being a member state of the EU and the Wassenaar Arrangement and regulating exports of encryption accordingly, France has its own system of controls, which include restrictions on not only the import, export, and use of encryption, but also on the "supply" (i.e., sale or distribution to third parties) of encryption products. French encryption controls are administered by the *Direction Centrale de la Sécurité des Systèmes d'Information* (DCSSI), which reports to the Prime Minister through the *Secrétariat Général de la Défence Nationale.*

In June 2004, France passed the Digital Economy Law (*Loi pour la Confiance dans l'économie Numérique*),[9] becoming the last of the original 15 EU member states to implement the EU Electronic Commerce Directive. The Digital Economy Law liberalizes the supply of encryption products in France, while tightening the rules on the transfer of encryption products outside of France. Among other things, the Digital Economy Law replaces strict authorization requirements for import and use of encryption products with declaration requirements. However, as of February 2005, the implementing Decree for the encryption provisions of the Digital Economy Law had not yet been adopted. It was expected that the Decree would be issued in the summer of 2005.

Czech Republic As a member of the EU and the Wassenaar Arrangement, the Czech Republic regulates the export of encryption products and technology in accordance with EU law and Wassenaar recommendations. However, unlike most EU member states, the Czech Republic also regulates the import of encryption products.

In particular, Act Number 21/1997 (as amended by Act Number 204/2002) and Decrees Number 397/2003 and Number 398/2003 regulate the import of dual-use goods in the Czech Republic. Under these laws, any firm or individual seeking to import a controlled encryption product from a non-EU country to the Czech Republic under a General Import License must first register with the Ministry of Industry and Trade.

---

8   Directive 2000/31/EC.
9   Law Number 2004-575.

Importers wishing to import very sensitive encryption products are required to obtain an Individual or Individual Open License from the Ministry of Industry and Trade. The Ministry of Industry and Trade will also issue Individual Import Licenses or International Import Certificates when required by officials in the country of origin of a controlled item.

Other States　　Some other new EU members, such as Latvia, Lithuania, and Slovakia, also tend to have stricter rules than original 15 EU members (except for those of France).

(iv) China

Mainland China　　China regulates the import and export of all hardware and software products "for which their intended functions cannot be fulfilled without implementing encryption or decryption functionality".

Controlled encryption products require government approval by the State Encoding Control Commission (also known as the State Encryption Management Commission) prior to import or export, pursuant to the Regulations on Commercial Encryption. In addition, the import or export of certain restricted items or technologies requires a license issued by the Ministry of Commerce. Despite several policy clarifications, the approval process to export, import, or use encryption in China remains an extremely *ad hoc* system.

The Regulations on Commercial Encryption do not provide vehicle for distribution of foreign encryption in China. It is illegal for Chinese nationals to use foreign encryption products, although foreign entities or individuals and "foreign-invested enterprises" in China may use foreign encryption for their corporate internal use after registering and obtaining approval from the State Encoding Control Commission.

Hong Kong　　Hong Kong became a Special Administrative Region (HKSAR) of the People's Republic of China on 1 July 1997. Despite this reversion to Chinese jurisdiction, Hong Kong remains an independent trading entity and a separate customs territory.

The Basic Law of the HKSAR, which went into effect on the date of Hong Kong's transfer from British to Chinese control, puts forth the principle of "One Country, Two Systems", meaning that (for the time being) Hong Kong will retain its capitalist system of government and law. Thus, the Hong Kong Government continues to preside over its own economic and trade matters, including the implementation of export and import controls.

Currently, Hong Kong does not restrict the domestic use of cryptography. However, Wassenaar-like licensing restrictions apply to both export and import of encryption hardware and software under the HKSAR strategic trade control system. Specifically, the import or export of cryptographic items over 56 bits is regulated by the Trade and Industry Department, unless a license exception (e.g., personal use or mass market exception) applies.

(v) Russia

Generally, Russia has the strictest rules in the world regarding encryption. In addition to controls on the import, use, and export of encryption products, the Russian Federation imposes broad controls on the development, distribution, technical maintenance, and manufacture of all encryption products (including hardware, software, and technical materials), as well as the supply of encryption-related services.

Each encryption-related activity requires a license, and there are no significant exceptions from the licensing requirement for particular uses of encryption (e.g., authentication) or particular sectors (e.g., financial institutions). The Federal Security Service has licensing authority for all encryption-related activities. Intangible transfers (e.g., Internet downloads and uploads) of encryption software also are controlled in the country.

(vi) India

Pursuant to the Foreign Trade (Development & Regulations) Act of 1992, India uses a so-called "negative list" which sets forth those products whose import and export are controlled. Because encryption items are not currently listed on the "negative list", their import and export are not explicitly restricted.

However, encryption software could possibly be controlled as a result of the tangible form in which it is transported to India. Although India does not control encryption software stored on CD-ROMs, floppy discs, or magnetic tapes, other storage mechanisms may be subject to licensing requirements. The Department of Telecommunications of the Ministry of Communications and Information Technology controls import of voice encryption products and communications jamming equipment, as well as the export of encryption-based telemetry equipment.

India applies a patchwork of restrictions to the use of encryption. Many uses of encryption (particularly for internal corporate use) are not restricted. However, restrictions could apply to encryption products if used in connection with services interconnected to a public network, or services operated pursuant to an Indian telecoms license. Specifically, there are restrictions under Indian telecommunications law on provision of encryption functionality by certain types of telecommunications service providers.

The standard license (a contract with the government) issued for provision of voice mail and unified messaging services prohibits the licensee from using encryption equipment for bulk encryption of communications. Likewise, the standard license for Internet Service Providers (ISPs) and the Guidelines for Internet Service issued by the Department of Telecommunications provide that ISPs may use only up to 40-bit encryption (or equivalent level of encryption) as part of the services that they provide.

(vii) Israel

There are import, use, and export licensing restrictions in Israel. Israeli law does not provide exemptions for particular types of encryption products (e.g., encryption products providing authentication functions only) or encryption products of particular key lengths (e.g., products with key lengths less than 56-bits). However, there is a broad exception for the internal use of encryption by a business or an individual.

Under this exception, a license is not required by businesses or individuals for internal or personal use of commercial encryption products acquired in Israel from an entity licensed to sell and distribute them or downloaded from the Internet to be used either for authentication (i.e., to create a digital signature) or to secure information for "self-use" (i.e., internal or personal use). Nevertheless, a license is still required when encryption software is downloaded from the Internet for integration into an encryption product or for encryption development or manufacturing purposes.

Furthermore, imports of encryption items for commercial use (e.g., imports by a retailer for sale and distribution in Israel) continue to require an import license (as well as a license to sell and distribute the encryption items in Israel).

Export controls — although they have been strictly imposed in the past — have been liberalized, and the export licensing process has been streamlined. Under a September 2000 policy, all encryption products are eligible for a restricted license authorizing exports to all non-government end-users in all countries (except for certain countries against which Israel maintains embargoes) after a technical review.

(viii) South Africa

Although South Africa restricts the import and export of encryption products that are destined for a military end-user, it does not presently restrict the export of encryption products that are intended for non-military end-users.

Under the Electronic Communications and Transactions Act 2002, no person is allowed to provide cryptography products or services in South Africa without registering with the Department of Communications.

The Electronic Communications and Transactions Act also establishes a voluntary accreditation scheme for authentication products and services. However, the registration requirement under the Electronic Communications and Transactions Act is currently not in force since the government has not yet released regulations that set out the detailed requirements for registering encryption products or services, the registration process and costs.

(d) Legal and Regulatory Trends

The general global trend in encryption policies has been one of moderately rapid deregulation of encryption items. As stronger encryption protocols have been developed, governments have continued to ease restrictions on the import, export, and use of products that utilize encryption protocols with lower key lengths.

However, after 11 September 2001, this trend changed to a significant extent. Overall, developed countries (e.g., EU member states and the United States) have continued to relax the regulatory restrictions on encryption products, albeit at a slightly slower pace. In developing countries, however, regulation appears to be increasing.

(e) Policy Issues

Government encryption regulation, as it has been since the advent of encryption regulation, is driven primarily by two distinct, but related, interests, namely:

1. A foreign intelligence interest in collecting all information that implicates national security; and

2. A law enforcement interest in collecting evidence of criminal activity.

The prospect of widely available strong encryption threatens both these interests. The global survey above shows that governments have taken different policy approaches in their efforts to contain the threat they see posed by encryption.

What is the best approach to encryption export, import, and use regulation? Governments can choose between overt domestic regulation, as in China, France, and Russia, and the export-focused policies that now prevail in the domestic markets of the United States and EU.

While countries with advanced encryption industries may have a stronger basis for export controls, other countries that wish to restrict access to information or have aggressive national security structures may have a stronger basis for import/use controls. Certain developing countries might even choose not to control encryption at all if they believe that domestic use of encryption has not become widespread and that they have not had cause to focus on the need for controls. Thus, the answer to the question above may be different for developed countries (particularly those with leading technology and software industries) and developing countries.

However, technological advances and commercial realities have increasingly made strong encryption an essential component of the international infrastructure for electronic commerce. The ability of sophisticated companies and savvy encryption users and developers around the world to sidestep government controls on the export, import, and use of encryption is likely to frustrate the unilateral efforts of individual governments to restrict global availability of strong encryption or to prevent the emergence of secure international communications. While this may call for a new international approach to encryption controls, any international effort without closely coordinated and monitored enforcement is unlikely to succeed.

9.03 Regulation of Electronic Signatures

(a) Types of Electronic Signature Legislation

(i) In General

There are several different approaches that have been taken to electronic signature legislation, varying according to the degree of specificity regarding use of particular signature technologies. The legislative schemes can generally be classified as prescriptive, enabling, or hybrid.

(ii) The Prescriptive Approach

The earliest electronic signature legislation took the approach of prescribing that particular technology must be used, generally requiring the use of digital signatures based on public key encryption technology.

For example, this approach was taken by the German Digital Signature Law adopted in 1997,[10] and the statutes adopted in the United States states of Utah in 1995[11] and Washington in 1997.[12]

The prescriptive approach has the significant disadvantage that it eliminates flexibility regarding implementation of electronic signature technology. In the fast-changing e-commerce technology environment, such a lack of flexibility is usually commercially unacceptable. As a result, the prescriptive approach to electronic signatures has largely been abandoned.

(iii) The Enabling Approach

Under the enabling approach, all electronic signatures are potentially valid. That is, a signature may not be denied effect solely because it is in electronic form — although in certain cases there are exceptions for particular types of

---

10   *Informations-und Kommunikationsdienste-Gesetz*, BT-Drs. 13/7934, 11 June 1997.

11   Utah Digital Signature Act, Utah Code, section 46.

12   Washington Electronic Authentication Act, R.C.W. 19.34.

transaction that must be "on paper" (e.g., real property or notarial transactions). The weight that is attached to a particular electronic signature under the enabling approach is an evidentiary issue to be decided in court (to the extent a signature is challenged).

For example, the writing of the author's name in an email (or even the mere sending of an email) could be construed as a valid electronic signature. If such a signature were challenged, the recipient or other party asserting the validity of the signature would need to prove facts sufficient to establish its validity, such as facts relating to the computer systems over which the email was sent and received.

The enabling approach is the one that has been taken in the United States, including in the Uniform Electronic Transactions Act (a model law which has now been adopted by almost all United States states) and the federal Electronic Signatures in Global and National Commerce Act. These statutes are discussed in further detail below.

The enabling approach has the significant advantage of placing no barriers on development of technology. Some signature technologies may succeed in the market because they provide heightened indicia of reliability, while others may succeed because of ease of use. Furthermore, the requirement to prove signature validity is a familiar issue for courts and has arisen often in the context of handwritten signatures.

(iv) The Hybrid Approach

The hybrid approach combines the enabling and prescriptive approaches, seeking to realize the benefits of both. It incorporates the enabling approach, but also provides that electronic signatures using particular technologies are entitled to a special presumption of validity. For example, this is the approach taken by the EU Electronic Signatures Directive[13] (see text, below).

The hybrid approach has most of the advantages of the enabling approach, but does provide technological guideposts for high-reliability digital signatures. The latter feature of the hybrid approach has both advantages and disadvantages. On the one hand, it identifies signatures that will be deemed valid with significantly reduced requirements of evidentiary proof in court. On the other hand, it suffers a disadvantage analogous to the prescriptive approach, i.e., that it confines development of technologies for high-reliability digital signatures.

(b) Global Survey of Regulation

(i) European Union

The EU Electronic Signatures Directive recognizes that divergent member state rules with respect to the legal recognition of electronic signatures and

---

13   Directive 1999/93/EC.

the accreditation of Certification Service Providers (CSPs) may create a significant barrier to the use of electronic communications and electronic commerce within the EU.

Aimed at creating a "clear Community framework regarding conditions applying to electronic commerce [in order to] strengthen confidence in, and general acceptance of, the new technologies", the Electronic Signatures Directive provides for the legal recognition of electronic signatures and the establishment of national CSP accreditation schemes.

The Electronic Signatures Directive adopts the hybrid approach to electronic signature legislation. It does not set particular requirements for the legal recognition of electronic signatures.[14] Under the Electronic Signatures Directive, no electronic signature may be denied legal effectiveness or admissibility in legal proceedings solely on the grounds that it is in electronic form.[15]

However, "advanced electronic signatures",[16] based on "qualified certificates" and created by a "secure-signature-creation device", will receive heightened evidentiary consideration (and are deemed the legal equivalent of hand-written signatures).[17] The Electronic Signatures Directive's three Annexes set the requirements for qualified certificates, Certification Service Providers issuing qualified certificates, and secure-signature-creation devices.

The Electronic Signatures Directive also takes other steps to eliminate obstacles to the establishment of a single "electronic" market. It prohibits mandatory CSP accreditation schemes and the discriminatory treatment of CSPs based in other member states, and it sets standards for the recognition of qualified certificates issued by CSPs in third countries.[18] It also sets minimum liability standards for CSPs that issue qualified certificates or guarantee their certificates to the public and reaffirms the obligation of CSPs to comply with the EU requirements concerning the transfer of personal data.[19]

(ii)   United States

As mentioned above, the enabling approach has been adopted by both the Uniform Electronic Transactions Act of 1999 and the federal Electronic Signatures in Global and National Commerce Act of 2000 (E-SIGN Act),[20] these

---

14   Electronic signatures are defined in article 2(1) of the Directive as "data in electronic form which are attached to or logically associated with other electronic data and which serve as a method of authentication".

15   Electronic Signatures Directive, article 5(2).

16   Electronic Signatures Directive, article 2(2).

17   Electronic Signatures Directive, article 5(1).

18   Electronic Signatures Directive, articles 3, 4, and 7.

19   Electronic Signatures Directive, article 8(1).

20   15 United States Code, sections 7001 *et seq.*

having adopted a minimalist approach to enabling the use and recognition of electronic signatures without mandating use of specified technology (e.g., the operation of public key infrastructures).

The Uniform Electronic Transactions Act is technologically-neutral model legislation that gives legal effect to electronic signatures, contracts, and other transactional records. The Uniform Electronic Transactions Act does not require any particular technology to be used for an electronic signature, and allows parties to prove the validity of an electronic signature by demonstrating that it was "executed or adopted by a person with the intent to sign the electronic record".

Under the Uniform Electronic Transactions Act, an electronic signature can be proven "in any manner" to be attributed to a particular person, including by reference to the security procedure used to create the signature. The effect of an electronic signature attributed to a particular person is to be determined from the "context and surrounding circumstances at the time of its creation", including any agreement that the parties have entered into concerning the use of electronic signatures.

As of January 2005, 46 states, the District of Columbia, and the United States Virgin Islands had adopted the Uniform Electronic Transactions Act. The E-Sign Act has similar effect in the few United States states that have not yet adopted the Uniform Electronic Transactions Act.

(iii) Canada

The federal Personal Information Protection and Electronic Documents Act defines an "electronic signature" as:

> . . . a signature that consists of one or more letters, characters, numbers or other symbols in digital form incorporated in, attached to or associated with an electronic document.

The Personal Information Protection and Electronic Documents Act provides that legal signature requirements under certain listed federal legislation are satisfied if the regulations have been complied with. However, certain types of electronic documents (e.g., sworn statements, witnessed documents, originals, and sealed documents) require a "secure electronic signature", defined in the Personal Information Protection and Electronic Documents Act as an "electronic signature that results from the application of a technology or process prescribed by regulations".

In February 2005, the Canadian government issued the Secure Electronic Signature Regulations pursuant to the Personal Information Protection and Electronic Documents Act and the Canada Evidence Act. The Secure Electronic Signature Regulations require the use of digital signatures created using public key encryption and specify that a secure electronic signature is trustworthy only if it is created using a "digital signature certificate" issued by a reliable certification authority (i.e., an authorized certification authority that has been verified by the President of the Treasury Board of Canada as having the capacity to issue digital signature certificates in a secure and reliable manner).

In addition, the Secure Electronic Signature Regulations provide that an electronic document signed with a digital signature for which a certificate was issued by an authorized certification authority would carry a rebuttable presumption that the electronic document is attributable to the person identified by the digital signature certificate.

(iv) Singapore

Under section 8 of the Singapore Electronic Transactions Act 1998, secure electronic signatures are given full legal effect as a signature. The Singapore Electronic Transactions Act is based largely on the Model Law on Electronic Commerce issued by the United Nations Commission on International Trade Law (UNCITRAL) and certain United States legislation.

According to the Singapore Electronic Transactions Act, any letters, characters, numbers, or other symbols in digital form used by a person with the intention of authenticating an electronic record can constitute an "electronic signature".

Recognizing that electronic signatures may be easily forged, the Singapore Electronic Transactions Act provides that a "secure electronic signature" is an electronic signature that can be verified, by a secure procedure prescribed by the Singapore Electronic Transactions Act (i.e., the use of digital signatures and public key encryption) or commercially reasonable security procedure agreed by the parties involved, to be:

1. Unique to the signatory;

2. Capable of identifying such a person as the signatory;

3. Created in a manner or using a means under the sole control of the person using it; and

4. Linked to the associated electronic record so that any tampering with such record can be detected.

Specific legal presumptions apply to a secure electronic signature — it is presumed that it is the signature of the signatory and that the signatory intended to maintain the authenticity and integrity of the electronic record signed with a secure electronic signature. This would prevent the signatory from easily repudiating a validly signed electronic document. With a non-secure ordinary electronic signature, no such legal presumptions can be made.

(v) South Africa

Under the Electronic Communications and Transactions Act, which came into effect on 2 August 2002, no person is allowed to provide cryptography products or services in South Africa without registering with the Department of Communications. The Electronic Communications and Transactions Act also establishes a voluntary accreditation scheme for authentication products and services.

The South African Accreditation Authority established under the Electronic Communications and Transactions Act has the responsible for assessing applications and accrediting certain electronic signatures as "advanced electronic signatures".

The Department of Communications issued draft Accreditation Authority Regulations and Cryptography Regulations for public consultation in July and September 2004, respectively. The proposed Cryptography Regulations contain detailed requirements for registering encryption products or services, the registration process, and costs. However, the registration requirement under the Electronic Communications and Transactions Act has yet to be fully implemented since the government had not yet released finalized Cryptography Regulations.

(vi) Thailand

The UNCITRAL Model Law on Electronic Commerce (1996) and the UNCITRAL Model Law on Electronic Signatures (2001) were used as guidelines in drafting Thailand's Electronic Transactions Act. Under the Thailand Electronic Transactions Act, which came into effect in April 2002, an electronic signature constitutes a valid and binding legal signature in Thailand.

The Thailand Electronic Transactions Act defines "electronic signature" in a similar way to Singapore's Singapore Electronic Transactions Act. The Thailand Electronic Transactions Act also specifically provides that any data or record may not be denied legal effect and enforceability solely because it is in electronic form. This is to ensure that Thailand has an effective legal framework to successfully enforce electronic contracts and to allow the courts to accept evidence in the form of electronic documents.

(vii) Ukraine

The Law of Ukraine on Electronic Digital Signature came into effect on 1 January 2004. While the Law gives legal effect to electronic signatures (so that they are equivalent to handwritten signatures and corporate seals that are commonly used in Ukraine), a related Law of Ukraine on Electronic Documents and Electronic Circulation of Documents provides legal effect to documents in electronic commerce environment.

The Ministry of Transport and Communications of Ukraine was assigned the role of a "centralized" certification authority with responsibility to issue digital certificates and accredit entities involved in the certification of digital signatures, pursuant to the Cabinet of Ministers of Ukraine Resolution Number 1451 on Approving the Regulations of the Central Certifying Body of 28 October 2004.

(viii) United Nations Commission on International Trade Law

In July 2001, UNCITRAL adopted the Model Law on Electronic Signatures (the "2001 Model Law"). The 2001 Model Law was designed to assist national legislatures in developing a modernized, harmonized, and fair legislative framework to facilitate the use of electronic signatures. By encouraging nations around the world to adopt the 2001 Model Law, UNCITRAL hoped to foster economy and efficiency in international trade.

Created as an extension of the UNCITRAL Model Law on Electronic Commerce (1996), the 2001 Model Law offers practical standards against which the technical reliability of electronic signatures may be measured, and it does not favor the use of any particular technology. Specifically, the Model Law states that an electronic signature is considered "reliable" if it is:

1. Uniquely linked to the signatory;

2. Created in a manner that is under the sole control of the person using it;

3. Incapable of being altered without detection; and

4. Linked, when required by law, to the associated electronic record so that any alteration to the record can be detected.

In addition to these criteria, the Model Law establishes basic rules of conduct that are to be observed by the various parties involved in the electronic signature process (including the signatory, the relying party, and any trusted third party).

(c) Public Key Infrastructure

"Public key infrastructure" (PKI) refers to rules, technologies, and physical infrastructure that allow digital signature and encryption use public key encryption technology. Because PKI offers the possibility for digital signatures to be used broadly by a large group of individuals, it offers major potential benefits for electronic commerce and electronic government.

However, these benefits have been widely advertised for roughly a decade, with fairly limited achievements in practice — as a result of limitations and risks of PKI technologies that have become increasingly apparent. Nevertheless, in the last few years PKI has seen substantial growth in controlled environments.

PKI essentially provides a means in which the "public keys" used to verify digital signatures of particular individuals (or to send encrypted messages to those individuals) are widely available on the Internet or another network. The technological details of how this works are beyond the scope of this chapter. However, it is possible to identify three general legal and procedural requirements for an effective PKI.

First, there must be legal recognition of digital signatures performed using PKI. This requirement is fulfilled by the electronic signature laws discussed above. Second, there must be a trusted party — often called a Certification Authority (CA) or Certification Service Provider (CSP) — that issues and verifies public keys. Third, there must be defined procedures regarding how signing parties use their keys and how relying parties may rely on such signatures.

It is not too difficult to develop software, hardware, and procedures that theoretically satisfy these requirements. However, the devil, as it is often said, is in the details. A number of significant practical difficulties have emerged in deployment of PKIs:

1. Certification Authority liability — It is necessary to specify the extent to which a CA bears liability for improperly issuing a certificate. Many prospective CAs are unwilling to bear sufficient liability to make their certificates appropriate for use in high-value transactions.

2. Standards and interoperability — Because of the high degree of specificity of PKI implementations, there have been significant difficulties in ensuring interoperability of electronic signatures, even among users implementing the same technology. A particular problem in this area is that available PKI standards are insufficiently precise. For example, the leading x.509 v3 for digital certificates, developed by the International Telecommunication Union (ITU), allows for significant variation among certificates.

3. Certificate revocation — To ensure that a particular certificate is valid, it is typically necessary to check the "certificate revocation lists" of the CA that issued the certificates. Effective means to do so in the context of a public PKI have developed slowly.

4. Security — There are numerous security risks associated with PKIs. These include the possibility that individual users fail to secure their "private keys" that are used in the signature process, and the possibility that the facilities of a CA or other signature infrastructure could be compromised. These security risks are related to the risks of CA liability and certificate revocation.

The combined effect of these risks is that there has been extremely slow development of broadly available public PKIs. These have been successful only in narrow applications.

For example, Secure Sockets Layer (SSL) certificates are widely deployed to identify web sites for secure transactions. This application only requires that the certificate associate a particular public key with the web site that a user has accessed. In this application, many of the issues noted above are significantly reduced.

VeriSign and a few other companies sell low-cost certificates via the Internet, which offer minimal liability protection and which are generally suitable only for low-value transactions or transactions with entities or individuals that are independently trusted.

With respect to use of PKIs in higher-risk situations, the trend is for development of purpose-specific "private" PKIs, rather than widely interoperable PKIs. For example, PKI technology is beginning to be widely used by banking networks, and various multinational companies are deploying PKIs to support their global operations. A few countries (generally not including large industrialized economies) have also explored use of PKI as the basis for national identification systems (e.g., on PKI-based identity cards).

(d) Policy Issues

What is the best approach to electronic signature regulation? Of the general approaches to electronic signature regulation described above, the prescriptive approach has clearly been discredited. Between the enabling and hybrid approaches, these authors believe there are arguments on both sides. Although the hybrid approach is now the majority view (outside the United States), the risk of constraining development of high-security electronic signatures is in our view significant.

In the EU, where the hybrid approach has been adopted by the Electronic Signatures Directive, few entities have chosen to implement advanced electronic signatures. However, this may change if EU governments and other entities begin to require that advanced electronic signatures be used to perform particular types of transactions and interactions — and the hybrid approach does offer the benefit of a degree of standardization for high-security signatures used in such circumstances. In addition, in any event, the hybrid approach is likely to remain the legal reality in the EU, Canada, and elsewhere.

As noted above, an absolute prerequisite to promoting use of electronic signatures and PKI is the passage of law ensuring the validity of electronic signatures. This has already occurred in most of the developed world, and significant parts of the developing world.

Beyond this, these authors believe that development of electronic signatures and PKI should be largely left to the market. Thus, entities considering the use of electronic signatures in particular applications, including governments considering their use for e-government applications, should assess the benefits and costs of the particular use, considering issues including the risk factors that are addressed above. Over time, it appears likely that use of electronic signatures and deployment of PKI will increase, including because techniques will gradually be developed to deal with the above risk factors.

It is certain that the near- and medium-term potential for PKI has periodically been exaggerated by those with an interest in promoting its development. In large part, proponents of PKI have under-weighted risk factors like those noted above. However, in the longer term, benefits of PKI will certainly outweigh risks in a variety of applications. As discussed above, this is already occurring fairly broadly in corporate and other "closed" PKI applications.

CHAPTER 10

EFFECTIVE FORMATION OF CONTRACTS BY ELECTRONIC MEANS: DOES THE WORLD NEED A UNIFORM REGULATORY REGIME?

Karen Mills
KarimSyah Law Firm
Jakarta, Indonesia

10.01 Introduction

A conference was held on electronic commerce in Sydney, Australia, in November 2000,[1] at which the author presented a paper on the self topic covered in this chapter.

At the time, with the rise of electronic commerce at a relatively early stage, it was clear that there were still far more questions than answers in arriving at any effective mechanism to ensure validity of contracts entered into through electronic means and that, as electronic commerce evolves, it will give rise to as many more legal questions as it will solve business problems. Five years later, some of these questions have been addressed, but others still remain.

In addition, regardless of the extent to which the new e-conomy really does change the way business is done, it will certainly require the world to seek new paradigms in many facets of the law.[2]

---

1   Third Asian Financial Law Conference of the International Bar Association Asia Pacific Forum, at Sydney, Australia, 18–21 November 2000, paper published in *Online Contract Formation*, Kinsella and Simpson, eds. (1st ed., 2004.

2   The author was assisted in the preparation of this paper by several associates of the firm, including Ilman F. Rakhmat, Luna Amanda, Fifiek N. Woelandara, and N. Pininta Ambuwaru (the last two having since left the firm).

As electronic technology has continued to evolve in the intervening years, most jurisdictions have addressed some of the questions in new legislation or, for Common Law based legal systems, in court decisions in cases heard. International organizations which support international business, such as the United Nations Commission on International Trade Law (UNCITRAL) and the International Chamber of Commerce (ICC), also have expended considerable effort to offer solutions to the business world through standard model legal provisions and contractual terms and conditions which can be utilized by any and all nations in drafting their legislation or by parties in formulating contracts, respectively.

Nonetheless, the validity of a contract will depend in each instance not only on the facts and intention of the parties but also on the law under which such contract is to be interpreted, governed, and eventually enforced. As long as the laws of each jurisdiction differ in material ways from that of others, questions will continue to arise in interpretation and enforcement where there is any crossborder element of an electronic transaction. In addition, is not the "borderless" as well as the "paperless" nature of electronic commerce through the Internet the very essence of electronic commerce?

Of course, transactions themselves, and the substantive commercial provisions embodied in transactional contracts, do not change, or should not, in any material way simply because the contract is formed electronically. What has changed, and will continue to evolve, are primarily the means by which the parties, or their counsel, will communicate in establishing those contracts.

There still are, and will continue to be, buyers and sellers and lenders and borrowers just as there will continue to be contracts negotiated and concluded for the purchase of goods and services, financing of assets and projects, issuance and transfer of stocks and bonds, provision and perfection of security, and payment and repayment of principal, interest, and other compensation, as well as the failure to make such payments, thereby requiring rights and obligations to be pursued through legal means. The only totally new form of transaction in any sense is the licensing of the use of software which is delivered directly by downloading from the Internet.

In e-commerce, not only are contracting parties not necessarily situate within, or subject to the jurisdiction of, the courts of a single geographical area, but in some situations there may be no way to determine exactly where one or more of the parties are situate. Communication through the Internet can take any form the transmitting party desires. Letterheads can be created and any name can be affixed to an electronic message, so how can one ascertain with certainly who is the originator of a communication? Documents transmitted electronically can be edited and revised seamlessly by a recipient, or anyone else having access to such document; thus, how can one be sure what the communication originally said?

How does one determine or, more importantly, prove when an agreement has been reached and what are the terms of that agreement? What law will apply to that agreement, and what governing body has jurisdiction over that agreement and/or the parties thereto? These are some of the questions which arise when one considers how a contract effectively can be formed by electronic means. Although many of these questions are being addressed by the various lawmakers in their own way all over the world today, it appears patently clear that because of the borderless nature of electronic commerce, the same can be regulated smoothly, safely, and consistently on an international scale only if there is a single universal framework within which all legal systems will eventually operate, in short, a universal law of cyberspace.

10.02   Electronic Commerce

The easy question to address is: what does one mean by electronic commerce? At least for the purposes of this chapter, the author refers to transactions effected via the Internet, and one might consider that these fall into two basic categories, namely:

1. Transactions where the Internet is the operative element in concluding the contract, or where one party offers goods or services openly on the Internet, to anyone interested, and any party wishing to obtain such goods and services places its order by clicking a box or filling out a form, or similar, on the website or by responding to a bulk email offer, and the contract is thereby established — Delivery can be made by shipping the goods or downloading the product, such as computer software, directly via the Internet, and payment is invariably made via credit card with the details and authorization made on order, also on the Internet. This kind of contract is often referred to as a "click-wrap" contract or, where relating to downloading of software, "browse-wrap" contract, but a more universal term for these basically retail contracts is "simple sales contracts".

2. Other types of contracts are those where the parties negotiate for the terms via email, passing draft language back and forth until the terms are all agreed, and the sum of the messages themselves may become the contract; or a full electronic document may be prepared containing all of the agreed-on terms, and this document is confirmed and, perhaps also "signed" online. These types of contracts may be referred to as "negotiated contracts".

10.03   The Contract

(a) In General

Before one can consider how any contract may effectively be formed online, one must first examine the larger question of what legally constitutes a "contract".

From a legal point of view, by "contract" one must assume a legal, binding, and enforceable agreement which binds each of the parties thereto to the obligations which are assigned to it in such contract. The legal force of a contract will depend on the law that governs the contract itself, while its enforceability will depend on the law of the place in which one is attempting to enforce it.

Although some jurisdictions may require contracts to be in writing to be binding, others, theoretically, and subject to certain exceptions, may not. There are numerous other differences found among various legal systems and some of these may have a considerable impact on the validity and enforceability of an electronic contract in or under the laws of the country or countries applying such system. Most legal systems in the world adhere, to a greater or lesser degree, to one of two basic concepts, namely:

1. The Common Law system, based on English law and practiced in the United Kingdom, the United States, Canada, Australia, New Zealand, and other countries once under the influence of the United Kingdom, or other Common Law jurisdictions, such as Hong Kong, Singapore, Malaysia, India, and parts of Africa and the Pacific Islands, in which the applicable law consists not only of written legislation but also of the body of case decisions rendered by learned judges over the centuries to interpret such written legislation; and

2. The Civil Law system, practiced in most European countries and those jurisdictions once under their influence, including many South American countries, and a few others as well, such as Indonesian and Japan.[3]

Civil Law does not view its body of court decisions as an integral part of its binding law. While some cases may take on importance as guidance, or jurisprudence, Civil Law is based primarily on written laws and regulations only, combined with an underlying duty of good faith.

Civil Law and Common Law based jurisdictions tend to apply different criteria to determine whether, or when, a binding contract exists.

(b) Common Law v. Civil Law Contracts

(i)   In General

Under the Common Law, as a general rule, a contract is said to be formed where the parties have made clear their intention to be bound, or to create legal obligations between or among them. This is normally characterized in terms of one

---

3   Civil Law does not view its body of case law as an integral part of its binding law. While some cases may take on importance as guidance, or jurisprudence, Civil Law is based primarily on written laws and regulations only, combined with an underlying duty of good faith.

party making an offer, with the contract formed when the other party accepts such offer. The second party may not accept the offer in its entirety, but may propose deletions of or revisions to some provisions or additions of others.

Such a counter proposal is considered a counter offer, which becomes the offer on the table, and it is up to the other party to accept this, as acceptance, or put forward yet another counter proposal, which proposal then becomes the offer on the table at that time. This kind of back and forth negotiation will continue until the terms proposed by one party, being the offer at that stage, are accepted in their entirety by the other, thereby constituting the acceptance and, generally, at that point the contract is deemed to have been formed.

Thus, in a nutshell, Common Law sees a contract as a mutual declaration of an intention to be bound to stated, agreed terms, as evidenced by an offer by one party which is, eventually or immediately, accepted by the other(s). Some jurisdictions have specific requirements for the form such offer or acceptance must take or that the contract must be embodied in a writing signed by both parties and, for certain contracts, there may be additional evidentiary requirements such as legalization of the execution or registration of notice or of the contract itself in some regulatory archive or similar.

Likewise questions often arise as to how long an offer is effective, i.e., how long the offeror is bound to honor its offer and perform if the other party accepts later on and, as a corollary, whether an offer may be rescinded at any time prior to acceptance and, if so, the time frame allotted for that.

Civil Law jurisdictions generally consider that a contract becomes binding as soon as the formal requirements for establishment of a contract have been complied with. These requirements generally will look more to such issues as whether the parties voluntarily intended to bind themselves to specific terms, whether those terms are sufficiently clear to create binding obligations, as well as such matters as the legality of the obligations assumed and the capacity and authority of the parties to bind themselves, or their principals. Each country will have its own legislation setting out the formal requirements for a contract, and for the most part they will address the above issues. Other differences include the Common Law requirement of consideration (*quid pro quo*), not usually present in the Civil Law regime, and the Civil Law duty of good faith, not specifically required under Common Law (see text, below).

As a general principle, all jurisdictions look towards the intention of the parties, as expressed in the manner as prescribed by the provisions of its respective laws, to determine:

1. Whether and when the parties bound themselves to certain obligations to the other party or parties, and

2. What those obligations are.

(ii) Simple Sales Contracts

As mentioned above, the most common form of electronic simple sales contracts are generally referred to as "click-wrap" contracts, where one party purchases goods or services from another over the Internet. The purchasing party will click boxes indicating the item(s) it wishes to purchase, or the program it wishes to download, and usually another set of boxes to indicate method of payment and possibly delivery. Payment is made, normally by the purchaser providing its credit card information, in another set of dialogue boxes.

Normally, it is only after the order and payment information have been provided on line, and confirmed by the selling party, that the purchasing party is provided with the standard terms and conditions, or possibly only a link thereto, with further dialogue boxes which the purchaser will click on to indicate his agreement therewith, usually by clicking "accept" or "agree", which then is supposed to consummate the transaction.

Even with software which is offered free, the offerors of the software will require a click to indicate agreement to their "fine print" terms of software license. One can see that questions can easily arise as to exactly at which point a click wrap agreement is formed: exactly what constitutes an offer and what the acceptance?

Courts in some jurisdictions have already looked into such questions, and the United States court has in at least one instance recognized that click-wrap contracts do create legal obligations.[4] However, it is still early, and time will tell whether the courts of different jurisdictions will view these questions similarly.

Such questions may become even more difficult to determine with respect to what are sometimes referred to as "browse-wrap" contracts. This refers to some websites which require acceptance of their standard terms and conditions, normally the license and attendant restrictions on use and reproduction, from every user that signs on to its website, whether goods or services are available for purchase, or for free, thereon or for access to the information available on the site.

Whether, and when, such terms and conditions are communicated to the prospective user and in what manner, if any, such user accepts such terms, is even more likely to give rise to differing views by courts of different jurisdictions. One United States court has already found that where a website did not give sufficient notice of the terms of its license agreement, the user was not bound to such agreement simply because it had downloaded the software offered.[5]

---

4   *Hotmail Corp. v. Van Money Pie Inc.*, 47 U.S.P.Q. 2d 1020 (1998) (N.D. Cal).

5   *Specht v. Netscape Communications Corp.*, 150 F. Supp. 2d 585, United States Dis. LEXIS 9073, 45 U.C.C. Rep. Serv. 2d (CBC) 1 (S.D.N.Y., 2001), in Bouchard, "Canada", *Online Contract Formation*, Kinsella and Simpson, eds. (2004).

For analysis of electronic formation of simple sales contracts, the first, and for the most part the primary, question is what constitutes an offer and what an acceptance. Terms and conditions are generally standard and not negotiable, so that the only question is whether or not the parties are bound whereby many of the questions which arise with regard to negotiated contracts, in particular identifying binding terms, governing law, enforcement, capacity to contract and the like, do not often arise in this kind of transaction.

Not only can the seller ascertain through the credit card company whether the party's credit is current and the billing address corresponds with the requested shipping address, but normally a mechanism of order confirmation will be applied, whereby a "click" to order an item is followed by a request for a second confirming click, and in some cases even a third. Goods will normally not be shipped until the credit is authorized.

(iii) Offer or Offer to Treat?

Thus, the primary issue which appears to arise with regard to formation of these simple sales contracts is based more on the Common Law view of offer and acceptance. The question which appears to arise most frequently in cases and published discussions is whether, when, or to what extent, an advertisement for sale of goods or services posted on an Internet website or sent by bulk email constitutes a firm offer.

Some jurisdictions consider that such an advertisement is an offer and, when a prospective purchaser places its order in reliance on that advertisement, such order constitutes acceptance, upon which the contract arises. However, other jurisdictions take the opposite view, i.e., that an open advertisement is not an offer, but is considered as an "offer to treat", or an invitation to make an offer. In that scenario, the order by the prospective purchaser becomes the offer, and only when that order is confirmed as accepted by the seller do contractual obligations arise.

Where the advertisement is considered an offer, the question then arises as to how long is that offer valid — how long is the offeror bound to perform in the event that another party accepts? If the advertiser, being deemed an offeror, declines to perform or deliver the goods or services advertised once a prospective purchaser accepts the offer by placing an order (in this case over the Internet), will the accepting party have a cause of action for breach?

In the event of such a dispute, such as, if a purchasing party placed an order in response to a posting on the Internet, believing that the sale was thereby consummated, but the selling party was not able to fulfill it and the purchasing party was thereby prejudiced or suffered damages due to the failure to receive the goods, the courts would have to look to whether a contract was ever effected between them: whether the advertisement was an offer or an offer to treat, and therefore whether the order was an acceptance or an offer.

There is unlikely to be any choice of governing law nor forum for resolution of disputes in such a situation and, where the parties reside in different jurisdictions, usually at least the purchaser will not be aware of the domicile or location of the seller. Thus, unless all jurisdictions view this question similarly, one can see that courts in different locations might find exactly the opposite on the matter in question. Unfortunately, however, there is no uniform view of this question. Different jurisdictions appear to take different views.

There is some attempt at uniformity offered in the language of the United Nations Convention on the International Sale of Goods (the "Vienna Convention"), which states, in article 14:

> (1) A proposal for concluding a contract addressed to one or more specific persons constitutes an offer if it is sufficiently definite and indicates the intention of the offeror to be bound in case of acceptance. A proposal is sufficiently definite if it indicates the goods and expressly or implicitly fixes or makes provision for determining the quantity and the price.

> (2) A proposal other than one addressed to one or more specific persons is to be considered merely as an invitation to make offers, unless the contrary is clearly indicated by the person making the proposal.

More than 60 countries have ratified the Vienna Convention, but many have included various reservations, which in the aggregate would tend to vitiate much of the uniformity provided. Although the convention seeks to look to the intention of the parties, by the language it would appear that an advertisement sent by email would likely be construed as an offer, whereas one simply posted on the Internet would be considered as an offer to treat, Of course, as there were no electronic commerce media, except perhaps telefax, in existence when this Convention was drafted, what would have been intended by its drafters, or even its signatories, as to offers or advertisements on the Internet cannot be ascertained.

Brazil and Malaysia generally view an advertisement as a binding offer, at least for a reasonable period of time. Brazil views contracts differently in accordance with whether or not the parties are face to face when making them. Parties face to face can discuss the terms, an offer can be changed or withdrawn at that time, and the contract is either made immediately or not made and is not binding until agreed by the other party. In such a case, the contract is considered as entered into *inter praesentes*. Where the parties do not have face to face, direct access to each other, and therefore cannot discuss terms, the contract is considered to be concluded *inter absentes*.

Where the parties are *inter absentes*, Brazil considers that an advertise-ment is binding on the advertiser at least long enough for other parties to consider whether to accept and will not be free to renege or change the terms once the advertisement is posted.[6]

Canada makes a similar distinction, but also recognizes that where a contract is entered into by parties via a "chat line" or some system of electronic conferencing, the parties may be considered to be *inter praesentes*, whereas where the advertisement is made through an email or posted on a website, the parties are *inter absentes* and the advertiser is considered as an offeror and is bound to the terms of the offer for a reasonable time in which to expect acceptance/response from the offeree or from the public in general.

Switzerland recognizes an offer on the Internet as an offer *inter absentes*, and it views it as a binding offer for the amount of time it is reasonable to expect an acceptance to be made.

Hungary and the United Kingdom, on the other hand, generally view adver-tisements as offers to treat, but the United Kingdom also requires that an open offer may be revoked at any time before acceptance, but such revoca-tion must be communicated to the offeree. Singapore and, for the most part, the United States, will look beyond the face of the question and apply other tests, such as intention of the parties, where ascertainable, what other terms or time limits are imposed, what is a reasonable time limit for an offer to be considered as open, and form of revocation, although, absent other clarifying elements, they tend to lean towards seeing an advertisement as an offer to treat and not a clear offer.

Clearly, then, with exactly the same facts before them, courts in different jurisdictions might well render exactly opposite decisions.

(c) Standard Terms and Conditions

(i) In General

A question which may arise even more often than what has constituted an offer and whether it has been accepted in general, is to what extent standard terms and conditions set out by the "offeror" (or offeror to treat) will be binding on the offeree, or purchaser of the goods or services.

Most courts which have examined this issue in cases of normal paper con-tracts have taken the logical view, seeking to determine whether the terms and conditions in question were effectively communicated to the purchaser, whether this was before or after acceptance was indicated (or order placed),

---

6   Momsen, Leonardos & Cia, "Brazil", *Online Contract Formation*, Kinsella and Simpson, eds. (2004).

whether there was some acknowledgement of agreement thereto and whether any of such conditions are unreasonable or onerous. It is reasonable to assume that the courts will apply the same reasoning for click-wrap and browse-wrap contracts executed electronically.

Beyond the above questions, however, by far the majority of problems faced with simple sales contracts over the Internet relate not to whether and when contracts are formed but to fraud of one sort or another, which is an issue beyond the scope of this chapter. The author is more concerned here with formation of a valid and binding contract, and that question arises far more frequently in the case of negotiated contracts.

(ii) Negotiated Contracts

In General   While Common Law jurisdictions generally apply the offer and acceptance test to determine the underlying validity of a contract, the prevailing legislation in Civil Law jurisdictions normally sets out formal requirements which must be met.

As Indonesia is the jurisdiction in which the writer practices, the requirements under Indonesian law as an example of the Civil Law regime will be considered, although in one form or another many of these issues also will arise under Common Law regimes as well. Indonesia's basic law of obligations is virtually identical to mid-twentieth-century Dutch law[7] which, like most Civil Law legislation, was based on the Napoleonic Code, and thus is typical of Civil Law.

Article 1338 of the Indonesian Civil Code is the basic provision of Indonesian law affording freedom of contract. The article provides, *inter alia*, that a contract has the force of law as between or among the parties who have validly and legally entered into it.

A contract is legally concluded when it fulfills the required conditions set out in article 1320 of the Civil Code. Those conditions[8] are:

1. The parties must each have the legal capacity to conclude a contract. All persons are deemed to have such legal capacity except: (i) minors (under 21 years old, unless married)[9] and (ii) persons under official custody;[10]

---

7   Most Dutch laws in force at the time of Indonesia's independence, in 1945, were adopted and, except to the extent subsequently repealed or superseded by new laws, remain in effect.

8   Note: these are enumerated here in an order different from that provided in the Civil Code.

9   Indonesian Civil Code, article 330.

10   Indonesian Civil Code, article 433. Legal entities must be represented by someone with the authority to bind that entity, either an actual corporate authority or authority granted by such an authorized person through power-of-attorney.

2. The subject matter must be clearly defined and, if possible, the quality and quantity thereof should be specified;[11]

3. The contract must be for a permissible legal purpose, i.e., no obligation or performance may be contrary to the law, public order, or public morality; and

4. There must be a meeting of minds, by free consent, without any coercion, error, or deceit.

Where there is lack of legal capacity, or of free consent on the part of a party, the contract is voidable, and annulment may be requested from the court. In cases of ambiguity about the subject matter or illegal cause, the contract is null and void *ab initio*, and the court must, *ex officio*, so declare.

A contract which fulfills the requirements mentioned above comes into existence as a legally binding obligation the moment there is an agreement between or among the parties[12] (whether or not the same is in writing) and cannot be terminated unilaterally (or, in some cases, even bilaterally, such as ante-nuptial settlements) without judicial intervention.[13] Every contract must be performed in good faith.[14]

Legal Capacity   With traditional contract negotiation, the parties are generally known to each other, at least sufficiently for each to determine the approximate age and mental capacity of the other(s). However, how does one determine that the person who is making a commitment through the Internet has legal capacity? How does one even determine what constitutes such legal capacity in the jurisdiction to which such party is subject or, in many cases, even what jurisdiction that may be?

A contractual commitment might easily be made over the Internet by an underage child or even, for that matter, an insane person or incarcerated criminal. At least in Indonesia, a court should rule that an underage child will not be held liable for breach of contract. More importantly, how can a party intending to contract with a corporation or similar legal entity in another jurisdiction ascertain that the person with whom he is dealing is in fact authorized to represent that legal entity?

A mechanism to determine exactly with whom one is contracting, and what is that person's authority so to act, is clearly in order. Asking for such information as a preliminary measure may suffice, provided the responding party provides accurate information. However, how can one determine that? Electronic signatures, discussed below, may solve this difficulty to some extent.

---

11   Indonesian Civil Code, article 1333. The obligations of each of the parties must be clear.

12   Indonesian Civil Code, article 1338.

13   Indonesian Civil Code, article 1266.

14   Indonesian Civil Code, article 1338.

Certainly of Obligations   While the subject matter of an Internet-based simple sales contract is immediately identifiable, as it is the product being advertised or offered, in negotiated contracts there are likely to be many, more complicated, contractual obligations to be assumed. Where the contract is to be formed through electronic commerce, the terms finally agreed on will usually be embodied in a series of negotiating correspondences sent through e-mail, or through a combination of telephone conversations, e-mail, telefax, and perhaps other means as well.

Where drafts are exchanged through the Internet and, when all of the terms are finally agreed on, a hard copy is produced for execution, one can be reasonably secure that the terms set out in that hard copy will correctly represent the agreement of the parties, particularly where, as in Indonesia and some other Civil Law jurisdictions such as France, the parties initial each page. However, what of contracts that are constituted by the exchange of e-mails only? How does one determine at what stage the contract has been concluded and which of the set of e-mails constitutes the final terms?

In addition, what about integrity of content? How does one ensure that the electronically created document which one party has sent to another is not edited and revised? How does one prove that the terms of the contract which are negotiated through the Internet and finally agreed on will not be adjusted just that little bit when presented as evidence, or for enforcement?

Legal Purpose   There are certain activities which would be legal in some jurisdictions but are contrary to law and/or public policy in others. Gambling is one example, which concept may be deemed to extend to the holding of raffles, sweepstakes, or lotteries. In some jurisdictions, such as Monaco, Macau, and even some states of the United States, such as Nevada, all forms of gambling are legal, while in others, such as Indonesia, any gambling is prohibited.

The laws of other jurisdictions may fall somewhere in between. How the prohibition against an Indonesian resident entering, and winning, for example, a foreign state lottery, could be put into effect is difficult to contemplate. However, it is clear that any action submitted to an Indonesian court to enforce a gambling obligation would almost certainly be rejected on the basis of illegality. This would apply regardless of how the obligation were incurred — in person or electronically.

The legality question of course brings up other issues, such as those relating to computer fraud and crime, but these, again, are well beyond the scope of this chapter.

Free Consent — "Signing" a Contract   As mentioned above, under Indonesian law, and that of at least some other Civil Law jurisdictions, the contract is deemed to come into existence the moment both parties have come to agreement on their respective rights and obligations. Thus, one must ensure not only that such rights and obligations are clear, but that they have in fact been agreed to. Traditionally, this would be indicated by the parties affixing their signature to the end of the agreement (and, as mentioned above, their initials to each page in jurisdictions where the same is either the law or the practice.)

Probably the major difficulty faced by the legal profession in ensuring effective formation of contracts through electronic means stems from the requirements of many jurisdictions that contracts need be in writing and signed by the parties if they are to be enforceable. This requirement differs in some Common Law and Civil Law jurisdictions. Common Law jurisdictions often have strict requirements of writing through legislation such as statutes of frauds.[15] Civil law jurisdictions vary. Normally, the requirement of a signed writing is not as stringent as in many Common Law jurisdictions, and it is a matter of evidentiary value rather than one of validity.

Under Indonesian law, although theoretically a contract need not be committed to writing so long as the formal requirements are met, as a practical matter where there is no writing, compliance with these requirements will be difficult to prove if contested. Furthermore, the requirements under Indonesian law and practice, as well as that of some other jurisdictions, for proving the authenticity of a signature are quite stringent, normally requiring two witnesses or a notarial legalization.

10.04   The Questions

(a) In General

As mentioned at the outset, the questions that arise in evaluating the validity and enforceability of any contract, but in particular those entered into electronically without the parties having direct personal contact, can, in lay parlance, be broken down into the age-old categories of who, when, where, what, and why?

(b) Who?

(i)   In General

First, one must identify the parties to the contract. Where parties sit together and execute a paper document, they can show each other their identifying documentation and, where relevant, corporate authority, and will actually see each other execute the final contract, and may even have witnesses or a notarial legalization. How can the parties to an electronic contract assure these matters?

---

15   United Kingdom Property Act of 1989, section 2; United States Uniform Commercial Code, article 2-201.

With the advent of scanners and pdf files, documents indicating corporate authority and, to some extent, legal capacity, can be provided electronically. Fraud and forgery are, of course, possible, but that risk is not much greater for a scanned certified document than for an "original". More importantly, one must establish that a party sought to be bound by an electronically generated contract has really agreed to it.

(ii) Electronic Signature

To this problem one is beginning to see solutions emerge through the advances of technology. An example is the "electronic signature", which was quite early on approved by then-United States President Clinton who, in 2000, signed a bill — electronically, of course — giving full legal effect to electronic signatures in the United States. Hong Kong and New Zealand have legislation recognizing electronic signatures, and presumably most other jurisdictions have, or soon will have, enacted similar legislation to comply with market conditions, although thus far many, in particular Civil Law jurisdictions, impose additional requirements to ensure authenticity of such electronic signatures.

In December 2001, UNCITRAL issued, by Resolution of the General Assembly, a Model Law on Electronic Signatures (the "2001 Model Law"), offered to any and all states that may wish to adopt it, and intended to be adopted together with UNCITRAL's Model Law on Electronic Commerce (the "1996 Model Law"), discussed below. The 2001 Model Law defines an Electronic Signature as:

> . . . data in electronic form in, affixed to or logically associated with, a data message, which may be used to identify the signatory in relation to the data message and to indicate the signatory's approval of the information contained in the data message . . . .[16]

Jurisdictions which adopt the 2001 Model Law, preferably together with the 1996 Model Law, will have accepted electronic signatures as, more or less, the equivalent of a physical signature on paper. However, the Model Laws do not provide any guidance as to how the electronic signature may be created to meet the requirements. One such mechanism is offered in the General Usage for International Digitally Ensured Commerce (GUIDEC), issued by the ICC. GUIDEC applies the term "ensure" to indicate the method by which a sender of a message may authenticate, or ensure, the message. An ensured message is one that is: "(1) intact and unaltered since ensured, and (2) identified with its ensurer".[17]

---

16   UNCITRAL Model Law on Electronic Signatures, 2001, article 2(a). The full text can be found on the UNCITRAL website at http://www.uncitral.org and provides, in article 6(1), that: "Where the law requires a signature of a person that requirement is met in relation to a data message if an electronic signature is used that is as reliable as was appropriate for the purpose of which the data message was generated or communicated, in the light of all the circumstances, including any relevant agreement".

17   GUIDEC, article 2, section VII, at http://www.iccwbo.org/home/guidec/guidec.asp.

The method suggested by which parties may ensure involves a combination of a private and a public key, with third-party certification, and it is described in some detail in the GUIDEC.[18] GUIDEC is not intended for use in simple Internet sales, but only for negotiated contracts and similar instruments by which a party may be bound.

Many technology companies offer encryption software, often bundled with Internet browsers, which can legally certify a signatory. However, how is fraud to be avoided? Does the electronic signature stay with the computer in which the software is installed, or can a person apply it from any computer? In either case, how can one protect it against hacker, or even co-worker, break-in? GUIDEC refers to this problem and provides that a sender of an ensured message is not to be held responsible for such message if the same is forged. It does not advise how to avoid hacking and forgery, however; nor could it be expected to do so.

Another solution is offered by a Japanese company through a device which enables electronic documents to be signed with a fingerprint. This is a field that will certainly continue to evolve in the near future. However, each time a "foolproof" system is developed, will it only be a very short matter of time before the code is broken?

The issue becomes more complicated where contracts are entered into, or obligations assumed, by means of "electronic agents". This term has been used to refer to certain computer programs or other electronic means which may be used to communicate electronically and initiate action or respond to electronic "offers". Theoretically, two electronic agents could contract together with no actual person even participating in such transaction at the time it is contracted for.

At least recent Canadian legislation recognizes such contracts in cases in which it can be established that such an electronic agent was in fact authorized by the party to enter into such contracts, for example, if a computer is programmed to make or accept offers in predetermined circumstances the intention of the programmer or user to create legal relations may be reasonably inferred.[19]

Electronic agents may be utilized in systems such as electronic data interchanges (EDI). These are closed, or private, information systems through which contracting parties both, or all, utilize a specific dedicated software

---

18   A very clear description of the working of an electronic signature can be found in Lockett, "United Kingdom" in *Online Contract Formation*, Kinsella and Simpson, eds. (2004), at p. 303.

19   Sookman, *Computer, Internet and Electronic Commerce Law* (Release 3) (2002), a p. 10-18.6, quoted by Bouchard, "Canada", *Online Contract Formation*, Kinsella and Simpson, eds. (2004), at p. 50.

application installed in their computer which links their information systems together and allows them to execute a contract via an encrypted electronic data interchanges message which is decipherable only by the information systems of these private participants.

Electronic data interchanges is defined in the UNCITRAL Model Law on Electronic Commerce as ". . . the electronic transfer from computer to computer of information using an agreed standard to structure the information".[20] In a sense, it might be considered a private Internet membership club used for the purpose of establishing contractual relations. As the scope of electronic data interchanges is limited to individual participants in such systems, further discussion of electronic data interchanges is outside the scope of this Chapter.

(iii) Satisfying Formal Requirements Electronically

Some contracts require a higher standard of execution. Under many laws, for example, and those of Civil Law jurisdictions in particular, certain contracts must be taken as notarial deeds, thereby being entitled to official status or force of law. Examples might include contracts for the sale of land or registered seagoing vessels, establishment of companies, or the creation of certain security interests over property.

The contracting parties to such deeds must appear before a notary public, who in some jurisdictions must read out to them the text of the deed, and certify their acknowledgement that those are the terms to which they have agreed. Such a deed is then executed in the presence of the notary. Can this type of contract be consummated through electronic means? It appears clear that it cannot, at least not unless and until a jurisdiction with authority over such deeds adopts an entirely new paradigm for such authentic government-regulated documentation.

In addition, at least for the foreseeable future, regardless of what facilities are being offered for electronic contracts, if the legal profession wishes to ensure the integrity and enforceability of negotiated contracts, and be sure that such contracts will meet the test for validity and enforceability in any jurisdiction in which it may be disputed, it would still be wise to commit the final copy to paper and have each party sign it in the traditional way and exchange original executed copies by post or courier, not only via the Internet.

(c) When?

(i)   When Is a Contract Formed?

In negotiated contracts, as in simple sales contracts mentioned above, the point at which a contract is concluded, or deemed concluded, may be

---

20   United Nations International Trade Law Commission Model Law on Electronic Commerce, 1996, article 2(b).

relevant for a number of purposes, the most important of which is to know when and whether the parties have agreed to be bound with each other, and to identify what are the terms to which they have agreed. We have discussed offer and acceptance in the section on simple sales contracts, above, but with negotiated contracts the question may take on further complexities.

Common Law generally deems the contract to have been concluded when an offer is accepted, and such acceptance is communicated to the offeror. Civil Law generally deems the contract to be concluded the moment the formal requirements, as set out in the relevant legislation, are met. One can imagine, without looking much further, that it is possible that these two concepts may not always result in the same legal conclusion, particularly where the parties are themselves subject to different legal regimes and no specific governing law has been designated.

Where contracts are executed on paper by the parties, in particular where they sit together for such execution, it is clear that the contract is formed on such execution, even if, in some cases, the contract may recite that it becomes effective at or as of an earlier, or even later, time. As a written signature is not always required for a contract to be valid (see text, above), other principles must be looked to for determining when the contract came into effect.

Common Law looks to when an acceptance is made and communicated to the offeror. However, even this seemingly simple test has given rise to disputes the world over, as different jurisdictions may have different views as to when an acceptance is deemed to be made or received. Some laws state that the acceptance is effective on its leaving the control of the sender, whereas others state that it becomes effective only when it is received by the offeror or when it is in a situation in which the offeror has control of it and ability to know of it (such as arrival into the email box of the offeror), whether or not the offeror actually sees it at that time. Of course, the offeror may designate the form or means which an acceptance may take, and as long as the prospective acceptor has due notice of such requirement, most jurisdictions will recognize it, but possibly not all where additional legal requirements are imposed.

(ii)   When Is a Revocation of an Offer Effective? When Does a Breach Occur?

Questions also arise as to the validity of a contract where the offeror seeks to revoke an offer prior to receipt of acceptance but where notice of acceptance has been dispatched. Since views on when contracts are formed differ from jurisdiction to jurisdiction, clearly this issue too can create legal uncertainty where such notices are sent over the Internet.

In addition, where there are requirements for notice to cure or attempt at amicable settlement, before a breach can be declared or action therefor may be commenced, the appropriate legal regime must be consulted to determine whether such time limits have been complied with and thus whether or not a party may have a cause of action. All of these questions may be treated differently by the legislative regime and/or the courts of differing jurisdictions.

(d) Where?

(i)   In General

Many questions arise in this category and, because of the borderless nature of electronic commerce and the territorial nature of legislation, clearly some of the major difficulties in finding uniform solutions will arise in these areas.

(ii) Where Are the Parties Situate? Where Is the Contract Entered into and Where Is It Deemed to Be Performed?

Parties that contract via the Internet may do so from virtually anywhere in the world, provided there is some telephonic or other communications service available at such locality. However, the Internet provides no facility to determine where is the website visited, or where a party to or from whom an email is addressed is either domiciled or situate at the time.

Most website and email addresses are not location specific. Unless both parties are domiciled in the same jurisdiction or the parties designate a law to govern their relationship, what law would one look to for determining the ramifications of this? Clearly, conflict of laws legislation in any jurisdiction in which a party might seek to enforce its contractual rights would come into play if these matters were not made clear in the contract or ancillary matters thereto. However, the conflict of laws rules differ from one jurisdiction to another and thus, again, different answers will result from application to different courts or recourse to laws in different jurisdictions.

(iii) Tax Ramifications

These questions become particularly relevant in determining which jurisdiction's taxing authority may tax the transaction, or the income derived therefrom. Most countries tax on a combination of the bases of:

1. Source of income (where the activity giving rise to the income takes place); and

2. Destination of income (where the recipient of the income is domiciled or resident.)

How then does one determine which taxing authority may tax any given electronic transaction? A product may be produced, or service rendered, in one or more countries through a facility owned by a resident of another but under license from the IPR owner located in a third country, marketed by a marketing company located in one or more fourth countries through the Internet, and purchased by buyers in any number of fifth countries. Goods may be stored in warehouses in one or more sixth countries and shipped to all buyers from there, and the purchase price may be paid by credit card to a bank in a seventh country and credited to the account of a subsidiary of the seller located in an eighth country.

What taxing authority determines the taxes that are due and payable; who is responsible to pay them; and to which taxing authority must they be paid? [21]

(iv) What Is the Governing Law?

How are international electronic contracts to be interpreted where the laws of each relevant jurisdiction (to the extent such jurisdictions can be determined) differ? In addition, which country or countries will have jurisdiction to enforce a contract entered into in cyberspace?

Certainly, it is to be recommended that parties clearly designate the place of performance and, more importantly, their choice of governing law in any electronic contract. Of course, in simple sales contracts the parties are unlikely to use counsel and thus are even less likely to consider the issue. How does one establish what law is to govern their electronic transaction?

In traditional paper contracts, where the governing law is not clear, general principles of private international law would normally apply the law of the place where the contract is concluded and/or the law of the place in which the contract is performed. In a transaction contracted electronically, neither of these factors may be able to be ascertained and thus neither of such general rules can be applied. The contract may be concluded in cyberspace and/or may be performed in more than one, or in indeterminable, jurisdictions, just as in our taxation example, above.

Legal control — the right to make and enforce laws — has always been based on the territorial control of the geographical area so governed. If the Internet is either domiciled everywhere, or nowhere, what laws can effectively govern activities conducted within or through it, i.e., transactions which occur in cyberspace. Is this not the great metaphysical question of our age: Just where is cyberspace located?

There is no government with the jurisdiction to govern or regulate cyberspace. Only if all governments adopt the same laws to govern "e-conomic"

---

21   These questions were posed by Indonesia's then Director of Income Tax, Dr. Gunadi, in his paper for the International Fiscal Association's compilation of national reports on taxation of electronic commerce. Dr. Gunadi concluded that electronic commerce forces one to seek new paradigms in the legal regulation of business transactions. However, no country can do this alone. It will require cooperation among all countries for the questions posed in this chapter and those questions yet to emerge meaningfully and consistently to be answered.

transactions will there be the possibility of an even playing field and effective, transparent, flow of business through the Internet. Otherwise, a transaction may be subject to too many conflicting, laws or perhaps to none at all.

(v) Where Can the Contract Be Enforced?

Again, unless a choice of jurisdiction or designation of an alternative means of dispute resolution, such as arbitration in a certain venue or under specific institutional rules or administration, are incorporated into the contract, the courts in the domicile of the party against which the aggrieved party wishes to proceed may be the only forum in which the contract can effectively be enforced, assuming such domicile can be determined.

If the place of domicile or residence of a party is known, the other party may bring an action in the court which has *in personam* jurisdiction over the party to be claimed against. If such domicile is not known, whether the court of the domicile of the complaining party has jurisdiction over the subject matter will depend on the laws of the complainant's jurisdiction, and such laws do vary from state to state.

However, even if the laws of the state in which a case may be brought recognize the court's jurisdiction, those of the state in which the defendant may reside or maintain assets may not recognize judgments of the courts of other countries, or at least those of the country in which the judgment was issued.

Where the parties have in their contract designated arbitration as the means to resolve any disputes which may arise thereunder, some of these problems may be less difficult to resolve. Most arbitration rules and some laws enabling arbitration make it clear that an arbitral tribunal has the jurisdiction to decide on its own jurisdiction over the subject matter of and parties to a dispute and, absent designation by the parties, also to decide on the seat, or venue of the arbitration.

Although arbitration laws and rules may differ on these and other points, as long as both the state in which the arbitration is held and that in which the award eventually rendered is sought to be enforced are signatories to the 1958 United Nations Convention on the Recognition and Enforcement of Arbitral Awards (the "New York Convention"), enforcement should not present difficulty, as an award rendered in any contracting state may be enforced in any other.

The issue may not be quite as clear, however, if an arbitration is held electronically. Many arbitration laws require that to be valid an arbitral award must state where the award was rendered and must be signed by all arbitrators. Both of these requirements can cause difficulties where the arbitration is held in cyberspace and rendered electronically. Some arbitration rules and laws have different requirements for procedures, registration, and/or enforcement, depending on whether the arbitration is domestic or international.

Where the arbitrators do not hold hearings in a single location but sit in different places, as do the parties, where can the arbitration be deemed to be held and where is the award rendered? Only if the parties can agree that the arbitral reference will be deemed to be held, and/or the award rendered, in a specific geographic location will cyber-arbitrations be feasible where either of the parties resides or maintains assets in a jurisdiction with such requirements. Cyberspace is not a signatory to the New York Convention.

Where the award is required to be signed by the arbitrators, and/or registered in the courts, unless the 1996 Model Law has been adopted in the jurisdiction in which the award is sought to be enforced and unless such jurisdiction recognizes electronic signatures or ensured signatures as provided in the 2001 Model Law or the GUIDEC, the original award will have to be printed out in hard copy and sent around to the full tribunal for signature. For the present, this is a precaution which it is probably wise to take in any arbitration unless the parties have specifically agreed, in a signed writing, to the contrary.

(e) What?

The terms and conditions which will bind each of the parties to a negotiated Contract are generally negotiated through meetings, conversations, drafts passing back and forth, and similar communications, until a point is reached at which both, or all, parties are sufficiently satisfied with the language included in a particular draft to agree thereto. The final version, with all terms and conditions agreed on by the parties, is normally embodied in a set of hard copy originals executed by the parties, with each one retaining an identical original signed at least by the other(s).

Such negotiations can almost as easily be conducted through electronic messages, such as email and perhaps even video conferencing. However, when all of the terms have been agreed on (or, in the parlance of Common Law, when the final offer is accepted), how do the parties indicate their agreement and intention to be bound to these electronically? In addition, perhaps more importantly, is there a mechanism to ensure that an instrument embodying the full and final terms can be obtained, reviewed, and perhaps used as evidence in case of an eventual dispute?

Some contracts are not committed to a single writing but are embodied in a series of letters or, in the case of a contract negotiated and formed electronically, a series of emails. The questions that arise here include: how can each party ensure that the other has the same understanding of the totality of the rights and obligations as he has and that the same messages are considered to constitute their agreement, and that the other party will not revise any of the text of the emails, thereby adjusting the terms previously agreed to?

(f) Why?

(i) Why Do the Parties Wish to Contract? What Is the Consideration? Is Consideration Required?

One issue that indeed will vary from jurisdiction to jurisdiction is the necessity for consideration for a contract to be recognized as valid. Most Common Law jurisdictions require that each party receive some benefit from a contract and do not recognize one-sided obligations as binding.

Some may require that the benefits are more or less in balance, where others will be satisfied even with nominal consideration, or simply the recital that there has been consideration without specifying what it is. Many Civil Law jurisdictions have no such requirement and recognize even a patently unfair and unbalanced contract as valid as long as it complies with the formal requirements set by its laws.

(ii) Recognition of Electronic Obligations

The above are some of the factual questions which the parties should keep in mind, and these should be able to be clarified with diligent practice. However, we must also look to the laws of the jurisdictions in which the contract may at any point need to be enforced, and the law governing the contract itself, to ensure those laws recognize contractual obligations formed in this way as valid, and will enforce them.

Some jurisdictions will still require a hard copy signed writing to recognize the obligations as binding on a party. Others now recognize electronic communications, but require confirmation, either by email as well or in hard-copy writing. Thus, even when the terms have all been agreed on, parties would be wise to look to the laws that might at any point be deemed relevant to ensure that the contract, and its means of execution, are recognized.

As mentioned above, although the formal requirements for a contract do not necessarily require it be committed to writing, a verbal contract can create innumerable evidentiary difficulties whenever the obligations of the parties are disputed. Thus, for all practical purposes, we must assume that a "writing" is required to establish contractual obligations. Can that writing be in electronic form?

(g) Solutions

(i) In General

Over the past years, since electronic commerce began to show itself as a force for the future conduct of all manner of business, and as the questions raised herein and many others have emerged, not only have individual states been seeking solutions to such questions, but so have international organizations which support trade. The ICC and UNCITRAL organizations, which appear to be the first to address so many international commercial issues, have been mentioned above.

Primarily, UNCITRAL creates draft legislation which it offers to all governments to adopt, or adapt, and encourages as many as possible to do so in the interests of standardizing the legal regime for international trade, thereby eliminating the many divergences in laws which lead to uncertainty and sometimes injustice today.

Although sometimes UNCITRAL offers tools for the private sector, such as its rules of arbitration for use by any private parties in *ad hoc* arbitral references as well as by arbitral institutions which wish to bring their rules into synchronization with that of other bodies, primarily UNCITRAL's efforts are directed at the public sector. The ICC, on the other hand, addresses more the private sector, creating draft terms for private contracts, although the ICC Court of Arbitration is more in the line of a public sector facility, as it replaces a court of law where the parties have so designated.

Thus, as seen above, UNCITRAL has created the Model Law on Electronic Signatures, 2001, and the ICC has offered its GUIDEC to help private parties implement such a law where passed, or even where it is not in effect. UNCITRAL also has offered its Model Law on Electronic Commerce, 1996, to countries wishing to utilize it as their law on such matters; the 1996 Model Law recognizes electronic messages as the equivalent of written ones, while one of the most recent products offered by the ICC are "eTerms 2004", offering draft language which any party may include in their contracts to facilitate the acceptance of such electronic messages.

(ii) ICC eTerms 2004

The eTerms themselves address many, although by no means all, of the questions posed in this chapter above. The eTerms are expressed as follows:

Article 1 — E-commerce agreement

The parties agree:

1.1 that the use of electronic messages shall create valid and enforceable rights and obligations between them; and

1.2 that to the extent permitted under the applicable law, electronic messages shall be admissible as evidence, provided that such electronic messages are sent to addresses and in formats, if any, designated either expressly or implicitly by the addressee; and

1.3 not to challenge the validity of any communication or agreement between them solely on the ground of the use of electronic means, whether or not such use was reviewed by any natural person.

Article 2 — Dispatch and Receipt

2.1 An electronic message is deemed to be:

(a) dispatched or sent when it enters an information system outside the control of the sender; and

(b) received at the time when it enters an information system designated by the addressee.

2.2 When an electronic message is sent to an information system other than that designated by the addressee, the electronic message is deemed to be received at the time when the addressee becomes aware of the message.

2.3 For the purpose of this contract, an electronic message is deemed to be dispatched or sent at the place where the sender has its place of business and is deemed to be received at the place where the addressee has its place of business.[22]

(iii) UNCITRAL 1996 Model Law

UNCITRAL has been prescient enough to provide a suggested solution to many of the above enumerated problems in its Model Law on Electronic Commerce of 1996 (as supplemented in 1998). As with its model arbitration law, UNCITRAL offers the 1996 Model Law to all jurisdictions to adopt, or adapt, in this case in support of the commercial use of international contracts in electronic commerce. The 1996 Model Law has already been adopted in more than 20 jurisdictions and has influenced legislation in others, including most of the states of the United States. Article 11(1) of the 1996 Model Law states:

> In the context of contract formation, unless otherwise agreed by the parties, an offer and the acceptance of an offer may be expressed by means of data messages. Where a data message is used in the formation of a contract that contract shall not be denied validity or enforceability on the sole ground that a data message was used for that purpose.

Article 11(2) allows certain types of contracts to be excluded from the scope of this article 11(1), at the option of the issuing body. "Data message" is defined as:

> . . . information generated, sent, received or stored by electronic, optical or similar means including, but not limited to, electronic

---

22 ICC Department of Policy and Business Practices, Commission on Commercial Law and Practice; Commission on E-Business, IT and Telecoms, Task Force on Electronic Contracting, ICC eTerms 2004, ICC Guide to Electronic Contracting, ICC Document 460-22/3rev3, 28 May 2004. The ICC eTerms 2004 should be available on the ICC website by the time of publication of this chapter, although they was not posted at the time of writing.

data interchanges. (electronic data interchanges), electronic mail, telegram, telex or telecopy.[23]

Generally the solutions offered by the 1996 Model Law provide that documents, instruments, or other units of information will not be denied legal effect, validity, or enforceability solely on the grounds that the same is in the form of a data message. The 1996 Model Law has been well drafted to set new paradigms for the transaction of business in a manner compatible with the unique borderless, paperless nature of electronic commerce. This is made clear in its Introduction. Paragraph 2 of section A, Objectives, states:

> The use of modern means of communication such as electronic mail and electronic data interchange for the conduct of international trade transactions has been increasing rapidly and is expected to develop further as technical supports such as information highways and the Internet become more widely accessible. However, the communication of legally significant information in the form of paperless messages may be hindered by legal obstacles to the use of such messages, or by uncertainty as to their legal effect or validity. The purpose of the Model Law is to offer national legislators a set of internationally acceptable rules as to how a number of such legal obstacles may be removed, and how a more secure legal environment may be created for what has become known as "electronic commerce". The principles expressed in the Model Law are also intended to be of use to individual users of electronic commerce in the drafting of some of the contractual solutions that might be needed to overcome the legal obstacles to the increased use of electronic commerce.

Indeed, coordination of legislation is even more essential in the regulation of electronic commerce than of arbitration laws and rules, as addressed by the UNCITRAL's Model Law on Arbitration and its Rules of Arbitration. Most arbitrations, except where conducted electronically, are usually conducted in a single jurisdiction and, thus, the hardship of such jurisdiction having different laws from others is not as severe. Electronic commerce is, by its very nature, borderless, encompassing any number of different jurisdictions for any single transaction. If each jurisdiction views the transaction differently from a legal point of view, how can any such business effectively be concluded?

Jurisdictions which have adopted, or which will adopt, the 1996 Model Law will now have a basis for recognition and admissibility of electronically created and/or transmitted contractual and other documentation. This will mean, among other things, that within such jurisdictions where a regulatory authority does not wish to recognize electronic "data messages", it will have to take affirmative action, i.e., promulgate legislation which specifically and categorically excludes it.

---

23   UNCITRAL Model Law on Electronic Commerce, 1996, article 2(a).

The requirement of execution as a deed before a notary would certainly constitute such legislation. Otherwise, the mere fact that a message is contained in electronic media will not cause such message to be viewed as being inferior to a written document.[24]

Thus, one can see that UNCITRAL and the ICC, through UNCITRAL's 1996 and 2001 Model Laws and the ICC's GUIDEC and eTerms, respectively, are already laying the basis for a uniform international standard of recognition and application of electronic contractual data. The 1996 and 2001 Model Laws address validity of electronic messages and signatures, while GUIDEC addresses protection of their integrity and eTerms provides uniform language for implementation.

Jurisdictions that do not adopt the Model Laws or apply the system offered by the ICC will have to find their own way in navigating across these troublesome shoals. However, it is clear that because electronic commerce can cut across any number of jurisdictional borders, consistent regulation can only be effected if all countries apply the same, or at least a similar, regulatory framework. The 1996 and 2001 Model Laws have been created for just such a purpose, and it is hoped that, with time, they will be adopted by most, if not all, jurisdictions.

10.05   Conclusion

Concurrent with, although not arising out of, the economic chaos which reigned in the last few years of the 20th century came the rise of electronic commerce. As financial markets struggle to restructure debt obligations and rebuild ailing economies, a new universal Internet e-conomy is emerging which pays no heed to geographical borders or long-established commercial traditions. The job of the legal practitioner has changed, and is changing, and one must establish new paradigms to address the myriad of questions and pitfalls one is encountering every step of the way.

Because there is no single governing body with the power and authority to regulate borderless commerce, we can no longer expect business practices to comply with the laws and regulations established in any one jurisdiction or by any one government. International organizations such as UNCITRAL and ICC are seeking to offer global solutions. It is up to each government individually, as well as all governments collectively, to remove the stumbling blocks which its old regulatory framework may have, over the years, set in the way of new business trends.

---

24   The full text of the 1996 Model Law, with explanatory material and a guide to its use, can be found on the UNCITRAL website, at http://www.UNCITRAL.org.

CHAPTER 11

VENDOR'S LIABILITY FOR DEFECTIVE SOFTWARE IN A GLOBAL MARKET

Sakari Aalto, Lauri Mertala, and Leena Kerppilä
Roschier Holmberg, Attorneys Ltd.
Helsinki and Tampere, Finland

11.01 Introduction

(a) In General

Most of the functionalities of and practically all services available in a modern communications network are based on computer software. Consequently, laws applicable to software and transactions involving software have significant impact on the development of communications networks and services based on the use of such networks.

Similarly, as with other aspects of law governing activities related to communications networks, the software-related aspects also would need international solutions for trade in software across borders without undue legal barriers.

The work to establish internationally accepted regime governing software has only begun recently and, thus far, any development has mainly concentrated on the legal protection of software, primarily through copyright.

(b) Scope

Legal issues related to licensing and delivery of software have not been addressed to any significant extent in any international instrument. This chapter seeks to shed light on one of the key aspects related to software deliveries, namely, the allocation of liability for defective software between the vendor and the purchaser of software.

The authors have selected France, Germany, Finland, and the United States and made a comparison of the regimes these countries apply to the liability

427

for defective software. The allocation of liability in a delivery chain between the vendor, any distributors or resellers, and the purchaser for the defects in a software product will not be covered.

This overview focuses on laws that have a direct impact on software delivery contracting. The authors have, therefore, limited themselves to the substantive laws applicable to determining the liability of the vendor and excluded dealing with rules of procedural law, although procedural questions, such as evaluation of proof and practices related to assessment of damages, may substantially affect the overall picture of vendor's liability.

The chapter will address only the civil liability issues arising in relation to business-to-business relationships. On civil liability, it will cover both tort and contractual liability although, for issues covered in this chapter, the importance of the contractual liability is predominant.

In terms of the nature of the software, the authors will only assess liability issues arising out of delivery of ready-made software. The liability structures related to provision of custom software or consultancy work resulting in software are significantly different and would justify a separate chapter on those topics.

(c) Why the Vendor Is Liable for Defects in Software

If a vendor and purchaser have agreed on a delivery of software, all of the western legal systems protect the purchaser's expectation that the software will be delivered in accordance with the agreement. Liability for defects is a part of the system enforcing this protection.

Liability serves a reparative function in compensating the purchaser for the damage caused by the vendor not fulfilling the expectations. In addition, the liability has a preventive function since the threat of liability gives the vendor an incentive to deliver in accordance with the agreement.

Both the reparative and preventive function should be taken into account when evaluating the legal regimes on vendor's liability for software defects. Especially, the preventive function should be emphasized as, often after completed delivery and commissioning of particular software, its removal and replacement with other software is extremely costly in comparison to the value of the software delivered.

(d) Market Practices on Contractual Limitations of Liability

Vendors of software typically seek to limit their liability for software defects extensively through the use of general terms and conditions, which are often in the form of end-user license agreement, or individually negotiated limitation of liability clauses.

Examples of extensive liability limitations and warranty exclusion are not hard to find. More often than not, general terms and conditions for standard software include clauses limiting vendor's liability solely to cover liability for defects in the media on which the software is provided. In addition, common is a clause expressly stating that the vendor does not represent or warrant that the software is error or virus free or that any errors will be corrected.

The software industry justifies extensive liability limitations by the fact that no software is error free and that it is impossible to make sure that software is free from viruses. These statements have certain truth to them but, unfortunately, the world is not quite so simple. In theory, software could be made error free, but this would require much more rigorous testing than what is the current practice in the information technology industry.

(e) Distinction between Responsibility for Testing and Liability for Defects

To a large extent, the software industry is used to testing its products on customers, also beyond any express alpha and beta testing. Generally, the software industry relies heavily on getting feedback from its customers, e.g., relating to bugs in the software, and fixing sometimes even critical bugs in some cases years after the first release of the software.

Arguably, the users of software have benefited from this practice through the availability of more extensive functionalities for an affordable price, or simply through lower prices.

However, although the authors would accept that it is beneficial for both the software vendor and purchaser at large that the purchaser performs some of the testing of the software for defects and bugs in the course of using the software, this does not necessarily justify the total exclusion of liability of the vendor for such defects in the general terms and conditions.

The vendor of software should generally have an incentive to develop and test the software so as to minimize the amount of defects in the code. It is the vendor who knows and has access to the code and, therefore, has much better means to assess eventual defects in the software and also take precautions against and remedy any defects in the software.

With wide liability limitation and warranty exclusions, it could be even beneficial to the vendor not to fix known bugs if the cost of repair would be higher than the limited liability exposure under its agreements with the purchasers constituting efficient breach or, in case of wide warranty exclusion, no breach at all.[1]

---

[1] Mercuro and Medema, *Economics and the Law, from Posner to Post-Modernism* (1997), at pp. 74 and 75.

As a standard practice, the purchaser does not get the source code of a standard software product. Furthermore, although the purchaser would have access to the source code, in most cases it could not with reasonable efforts gain such understanding of the code that would be sufficient to assess the potential risks caused by defects in the code, let alone avoid or fix such defects.

On the other hand, a vendor of software is usually not in the position to evaluate even the direct damages that a defect in the software could cause to a particular purchaser. In addition, in many instances it is impractical and would result in unbearable transactions costs if the vendor would even attempt to assess the purchaser's liability exposure in sufficient detail.

Consequently, black and white solutions either way in the allocation of liability are not likely to result in satisfactory solutions. The appropriate level of liability and the allocation thereof should be assessed case-by-case and, in a perfect world, would be agreed on by the parties for each case. As we are not living in a perfect world, this does not happen and the parties end up with standard contractual clauses which may be unfit to govern the relationship between them.

11.02   General Questions

(a) Applicable Statutes

(i)   In General

Although financial interests related to software are increasingly important, there are, with the exception of the Uniform Computer Information Transactions Act (UCITA) which has been enacted in a few states in the United States, no specific statutes or provisions on software contracts in force in any of the jurisdictions covered.[2]

In the absence of specific legislative instruments, the software contracts are governed mainly by the respective general contract law and analogies to the existing law on sale and lease of movable property in each jurisdiction. In this section, the main applicable statutes in each of the jurisdictions will be described.

The contract laws in Germany, France, and Finland are built on the principle of freedom of contract subject to a varying number of limitations based on mandatory law. Consequently, the parties are in principle free to determine allocation of liability for defects in the software as they deem

---

2   In the United States, the National Conference of Commissioners on Uniform State Laws approved in 1999 the Uniform Computer Information Transactions Act (UCITA), including specific provisions concerning transactions in the information society and recommended its enactment by the states. To date, only two states have enacted the law at least in some form, i.e., Maryland and Virginia. The basic set of rules governing also software transactions in the United States is thus the Uniform Commercial Code (UCC).

appropriate. However, each of the countries has at least some mandatory rules governing the issue of liability. In addition, the contract laws provide content of the legal relationship between the parties on issues the parties have not agreed on in their agreement.

(ii) Germany

In Germany, rules concerning, for example, the sale and lease of goods, are contained in the German Civil Code (*Bürgerliches Gesetzbuch* — BGB). After the reform of the law of obligations in Germany,[3] the substantive provisions most relevant for this discussion can be found in the German Civil Code as the Act on the Regulation of General Business Terms (*Gesetz zur Regelung des Rechts der Allgemeinen Geschäftsbedingungen*, AGBG) was incorporated in the Civil Code.[4]

Since most of the standard software is provided under general business terms, the provisions found earlier in the Code, severally limiting the enforceability of limitations of liability contained in such clauses, are very significant with respect to the subject matter of this article.

Under the German Civil Code, software contracts for the provision of standard software would usually be treated in accordance with the rules of the Civil Code covering sale or lease of movable property. In exceptional cases, also a separate category covering work-for-hire situations could be applied. The categorization of the software contract in one of the three categories for the application of the Civil Code has crucial importance in determining the parties' responsibilities and, for example, the applicable warranties.[5]

It appears to be clear that, in the case of standard software being sold against a one-off payment for an unlimited term, the software contract falls under the provisions of sale (see text, below). However, if one of said criteria is not present, the contract could be considered a lease or a contract for provision of work rather than sale.[6]

---

3   Effective as of 1 January 2002.

4   Those provisions are now found, as amended, in sections 305–310 of the German Civil Code. Section 307 of the Civil Code sets forth a detailed list of conditions under which a clause in a standard business contract may be invalid. In general, according to the Civil Code, individually negotiated terms take precedence over standard business terms.

5   For example, under German law, the lessor/licensor is obligated to repair defects at no charge for the entire duration of the term of the lease. This may lead to interesting questions with respect to maintenance and support agreements concluded in connection with a software license agreement.

6   Marly, *Softwareüberlassungsverträge 3. Auflage* (2000, 4. Auflage, 2004), at pp. 74 *et seq*. In addition, the parties may conclude a leasing contract for software. On individual and modified standard software in general, see Redeker, "Anpassung von Standard-Software", in Redeker (ed.), *Handbuch der IT-Verträge I* (2004). and Witte.

(iii) France

The French Civil Code is, for the purposes of the discussion in this chapter, similar in scope to the German Civil Code, and it includes rules concerning sale, lease, and work-for-hire related to goods. According to the French Civil Code, sale is defined as a contract in which a party undertakes to deliver an object (*chose*) and the other to pay for the object,[7] resulting in a transfer of title in the object from the first party to the other party.

In principle, the provisions of the Civil Code governing sales contract are applicable to contracts for the supply of goods regardless of the nature of the objects of such transactions. To the extent a software contract is construed to constitute a sale of software, such contract is not subject to any special regime and the general provisions of the Civil Code, along with consumer protection rules (*Code de la consummation*), appear to apply to the contract.[8]

The French legal regime is different from the corresponding regimes in Germany and Finland in that businesses may under certain conditions enjoy the protection provided by the consumer protection laws. Thus, a purchaser may benefit from consumer protection with unenforceable liability limitations and statutory warranties in business-to-business relations.

The notion of "professional of the same specialty" (*professionnel de la même spécialité*) has been developed in French courts to determine the scope of application of the consumer protection in business-to-business relationships. The French Supreme Court (*Cour de cassation*) has ruled that, when a contract is concluded between two entrepreneurs representing different fields of activity, and which are, therefore, not considered as "professionals of the same specialty", the consumer protection rules become applicable to the benefit of the purchaser.[9] Thus, when a software supplier enters into a sales agreement or license with a non-software company, there is in principle a risk that consumer protection laws are applied.

In the light of the most recent case law from the *Cour de cassation*, the risk that consumer protection rules would be applied to a software contract between a software vendor and a non-software company appears more limited.

In a case involving software for the management of the customer relationships of a business, the *Cour de cassation* expressly excluded from the consumer protection the purchasers who utilized the software in direct relation with its business operations, although the purchaser operated in a different field of specialty than the software supplier.[10]

---

7   French Civil Code, article 1592.

8   Le Tourneau, *Contrats informatiques et électroniques* (3rd ed., 2004), at pp. 6 and 7.

9   Le Tourneau, *Contrats informatiques et électroniques* (3rd ed., 2004), at pp. 40 and 41.

10   A company purchasing software destined for use in the management of its clientele information was assimilated to the professional of the same specialty by the *Cour de cassation*.

(iv) Finland

Finnish courts and legal scholars appear to agree that the Sale of Goods Act (*Kauppalaki*) applies widely to the software contracts involving licensing of off-the-shelf software. In addition, in most cases, determining whether the Sale of Goods Act applies directly to a contract involving a delivery of software is mostly of academic interest.

This is, first, because the provisions of the Sale of Goods Act are applied widely outside the scope of the Act by analogy and, second, because the parties may contractually agree to exclude the applicability of the Sale of Goods Act in whole or in part. Consequently, it is safe to assume that, as there are no special acts or statutes governing software deliveries, the Sale of Goods Act is applicable unless the parties have agreed otherwise.[11]

In addition to the Sale of Goods Act, the principles of the largely uncodified, general Finnish contract law also are applicable to a contract involving software delivery. The general contract law provides, for example, the rules on determining the amount of damages awarded, the obligation to mitigate damages, and the order in which the purchaser could resort to different remedies in case of defect in a software delivery.

For the purposes of determining a vendor's liability for defective software, the provision of the Finnish Contracts Act empowering a court to adjust or declare unenforceable contract terms that are deemed to be unreasonable or that lead to unreasonable consequences relevant may, in some circumstances, be relevant.[12]

In practice, the courts have been reluctant to intervene in contracts between two business entities. The right to rewrite contracts has been used only in a handful of cases where the agreement has been entered into in a situation where there has been extreme imbalance between the parties' negotiation powers, or if an unexpected change in the circumstances renders the agreement significantly unreasonable.

(v) United States

United States contract law is largely state rather than federal law. There are separate statutes in the area of contract law but largely it is based on the Common Law. Despite the initial diversified appearance, contract law differs from one state to another mostly only in detail.[13] The Uniform Commercial Code is a central codification in the area of commercial law, widely implemented in the

---

11   Routamo and Ståhlberg, *Suomen vahingonkorvausoikeus* (4th ed., 2000), at p. 14; Halila and Hemmo, *Sopimustyypit* (1996), at pp. 28 and 29.

12   Finnish Contracts Act, section 36; Ramberg, *Kauppalain kommentaari* (1997), at p. 29.

13   Farnsworth, *An introduction to the Legal System of the United States* (3rd ed.), at p. 122.

states of the United States, which applies generally to the sale of goods. It also is considered to be applicable to the sale of off-the-shelf software.

In addition, the *Restatement of the Law 2nd*, "Contracts",[14] codifies case law and Common Law rules with significance to the contract practices of the software industry, as well.

A special statute, the Uniform Computer Information Transactions Act, lays down specific provisions for transactions in the information society. The Uniform Computer Information Transactions Act is a proposed uniform law that would create new rules for software licensing, online access, and other computer information transactions, supplementing and substituting those of the Uniform Commercial Code. However, only two states to date, Maryland and Virginia, have adopted the Uniform Computer Information Transactions Act at least in some form.[15] The Uniform Computer Information Transactions Act has evoked significant controversy, for example, due to allegedly shifting the balance of existing contract law dramatically in favor of software vendors. Although an interesting topic, the Uniform Computer Information Transactions Act is not discussed further in this chapter due to its limited implementation and significance.

(vi) Summary

As may be concluded from the above, none of the jurisdictions dealt with have, with the exception of the Uniform Computer Information Transactions Act in a few United States states, specific legislation covering the software contracts. It appears that the courts in each of the countries would most likely apply the rules established for sale and purchase of movable property and perhaps in some special circumstances, the rules regarding lease, either directly or through analogy.

None of the systems is necessarily well equipped to deal with the reasonable expectation of the parties related to software deliveries. In addition, the application of many of the rules to situations involving a software delivery may take place in general courts and require a great deal of interpretation, and the consequences of the application are not necessarily predictable for the parties to a contract.

---

14   The *Restatement of the Law 2nd*, "Contracts", is maintained and published by the American Law Institute (at http://www.ali.org/). Although not official and not binding on the courts, the *Restatements* is nevertheless accorded a great deal of deference because of the reputations of its reporters and advisers. The *Restatements* is generally considered to be an authoritative work of legal scholars. The *Restatements* presents the general Common Law of the United States, not a discussion of its jurisdictional variations or the law of a particular jurisdiction.

15   The opposition to Uniform Computer Information Transactions Act has been strong in the United States, as three states have enacted laws that render void governing law clauses that refer to the Uniform Computer Information Transactions Act.

(b) United Nations Convention on Contracts for International Sale of Goods

The United Nations Convention on Contracts for International Sale of Goods (the "Vienna Convention") may be applicable to international sale of software, as outlined below, depending on the interpretation and circumstances at hand in each case. Applicability being casuistic, the topic would deserve an elaborate study of its own. For the purposes of comparison, some basic principles of how the Vienna Convention may become applicable to an international contract for the sale of software have been outlined below.

The Vienna Convention provides a legal framework for sale and purchase of goods across borders where the parties are domiciled in different countries and both of the countries are parties to the Convention. The Vienna Convention also may apply if the connecting-factor rule of international civil law leads to applicability of the law of a country signatory to the Convention. Parties to an agreement are free to agree otherwise than what is stated in the Convention or exclude it altogether.

Since the Vienna Convention is perceived to be rather purchaser friendly, blanket exclusions of the Convention are fairly common in software contracts. If the parties have already defined the content of their relationship in detail in an agreement, applying the Vienna Convention could lead to unexpected consequences.

If, for example, the parties would have agreed on a process for repairing the delivered software in case of a defect without return obligations for the purchaser, applying the returning obligations of the Vienna Convention would not appear to be appropriate. To avoid such situations, excluding the application of the Vienna Convention may be justified.

Even if an agreement regarding the delivery of software would meet the criteria concerning the international aspects and the domicile of the parties and would not contain an exclusion of the Vienna Convention, it is not clear whether the Convention would be applicable. As set forth in article 1 of the Convention, its provisions are applicable to sale and purchase of "goods", and there are arguments both for and against considering software as "goods" within the meaning of the Convention.

By its own terms, the Convention applies solely to sale of goods, excluding its applicability to the provision of services. However, the Convention provides no positive definition for "sale" or "goods". Articles 2 and 3 further define the scope by expressly excluding its applicability to certain intangibles (such as electricity, shares of stock, and securities), while applicability to software is neither excluded nor confirmed.

A widely agreed view defines a "good" under the Vienna Convention as an "essentially movable and identifiable separate object".[16] The applicability of

---

16   Cox, "Chaos Versus Uniformity: The Divergent Views of Software in the International Community", at http://cisgw3.law.pace.edu/cisg/biblio/cox.html#iii.

the Vienna Convention to international software sales is subject to scholarly debate and divergent judgments.

It appears that the prevailing view on this point currently in the court practice and the works of the commentators is to regard software that is provided on a tangible media as goods within the meaning of article 1 of the Convention.[17]

However, the Vienna Convention provides little guidance on whether it applies to software contracts where the software is delivered electronically and, although it appears questionable to treat software differently depending on the way it is delivered, the issue remains unsolved to date.[18] At least one commentator[19] is firmly, and fairly, of the opinion that the Vienna Convention should be applied to software, no matter what the delivery form.

(c)   Software — Sale or Lease, Goods or Service?

The contracts for the delivery of software do not fit into the legal framework regulating any of the contract types established in the laws of any of the countries covered without a varying degree of difficulty.

In each of the examined jurisdictions, above, qualification of a contract providing for the supply of software as a sales contract has raised scholarly debates and was earlier rejected by the courts. Instead, the courts have tended to apply the provisions in the respective contract law governing lease or provision of services.

However, to date, the case law, along with positions taken by the scholars, shows a trend towards a different construction regarding standard software contracts more often under the provisions governing sale of goods contracts.[20]

---

17   Lookofsky, "In Dubio Pro Conventione? Some Thoughts about Opt-outs, Computer Programs and Preemption under the 1980 Vienna Sales Convention", *Duke J. of Comp. & Int'l L.* 263, at http://www.law.duke.edu/shell/cite.pl?13+Duke+J+Comp.+&+Int%27l+L+0263.

18   Cox, "Chaos Versus Uniformity: The Divergent Views of Software in the International Community", at http://cisgw3.law.pace.edu/cisg/biblio/cox.html#iii.

19   Lookofsky, "In Dubio Pro Conventione? Some Thoughts about Opt-outs, Computer Programs and Preemption under the 1980 Vienna Sales Convention", *Duke J. of Comp. & Int'l L.* 263, at http://www.law.duke.edu/shell/cite.pl?13+Duke+J+Comp.+&+Int%27l+L+0263.

20   Le Tourneau, *Contrats informatiques et électroniques* (3rd ed., 2004), at p. 161; Lipovetsky, "Les clauses limitatives de responsabilité et de garantie dans les contrats informatiques. Approche comparative France/Etats-Unis — quelles limitations?", at http://www.kahnlaw.com/france/newsjob/publications/clauses_limitatives_sl.htm. See also the judgement of the *Cour d'appel de Montpellier* (2ème ch. A, 2 July 1991, *Caisse Régionale de Crédit Agricole et autres v. Sté Sud Conseil Services*, no. 88-2421), where the court expressly declined to apply the regime of *vente* to a software "sale" contract by basing its argumentation on the fact that proprietary rights to the software sold under the contract were not transferred to the purchaser in full. Siivola, "Tietokoneohjelmissa kaksinumeroisesta vuosiluvusta 2000-luvulla aiheutuvan ongelman oikeudellinen vastuu", *Defensor Legis* (6/1997), at pp. 903–913.

The difficulty in placing software contracts under any existing provisions of contract law lies with the special nature of the contract, deriving from the unique nature of software itself. First, although often referred to as a sales contract, the contract providing for supply of standard software does not transfer the title to the software, but only to a copy of the software and to the tangible storage medium on which the software is provided, if any.

Since the title and proprietary rights to the software remain with the vendor, the vendor's primary obligation under such contract typically consists of granting a license to use the software. Therefore, it appears fair to question whether the "sale" of software should be brought under the general rules governing sales contracts. The traditional solution to these hesitations has been to treat the contract as a lease or, in certain cases, as a contract for the provision of services rather than a sale.[21]

In both German and Finnish case law, the courts have set certain criteria for applying the rules concerning sale of movable property to software contracts involving the delivery of software. The courts have found that off-the-shelf (standard) computer programs which are embodied in a tangible medium and delivered to resellers, distributors, and end users against a one-off payment for an unlimited term constitute object of a sale and are not to be construed as a lease.[22]

In Finland, it remains unsolved under these interpretations whether the sale of standard software online would be construed as a sale of goods — and whether a distinction should be drawn based on how, on a tangible disk or electronically via Internet, the software is delivered. Under German law, there is a consensus that software delivered both on tangible media and in electronic format is to be regarded as a good for the purposes of determining the applicable German Civil Code provisions. The German Supreme Court (*Bürgerliches Gerichtshof*) indirectly reached this conclusion in one of its judgments based on the intention of the party acquiring the software. According to the German Supreme Court, the absence of a disk does not change the intentions of the parties. Thus, electronic software should be treated equally to software on a disk.[23]

The French case law appears somewhat less established. It is clear that, under French law, the software protected as intellectual property may be treated

---

21   Le Tourneau, *Contrats informatiques et électroniques* (3rd ed., 2004), at pp. 160 *et seq.*

22   Finnish Supreme Court, KKO 2003:88. The ruling follows previous practice in Europe. See, for example, the decisions of the Court of Appeal of Munich (12 February 1998), 28U 5911/97, and the Court of Appeal of Frankfurt am Main (3 November 1998), 11U 20/98.

23   Cox, "Chaos Versus Uniformity: The Divergent Views of Software in the International Community", at http://cisgw3.law.pace.edu/cisg/biblio/cox.html#iii.

differently from the media through which it is transmitted. Standard software licenses as such have traditionally been treated as licenses or leases (*louage*) under French law.

However, it also has been maintained that, in "sale" of standard software, the parties do not intend to limit the term of contract in time (as is the case with licenses under French law, which does not acknowledge licenses — or any contracts — in perpetuity), which would lead rather to the conclusion that such contracts should be regarded as sale.[24]

The applicability of the Civil code's provisions governing sales seems, in a majority of cases where a contract has been construed by a French court as a sales contract (*contrat de vente*), to be determined by the fact that the contract in question concerns not only supply of software, but also transfers title to certain pieces of hardware, storage medium, or other such tangible objects related to the software.

In applying the principle of indivisibility of contract, both French and Finnish courts tend to hold that the object of the sale must be construed as consisting of all the material sold under the contract, including not only the copy of the program itself, but also the tangible storage medium on which the software is provided, support and maintenance services, as well as the related documentation and the hardware, where any piece of hardware is provided under the contract.

The terminology employed in a number of software-related judgments in France describes the object of the sale as an indivisible "information technology-based functionality or entity" (*tout informatique*) and places contracts involving the delivery of such entity under the regime for *contrat de vente*.[25]

The same reasoning has been retained by a number of Finnish scholars as well to justify the application of the provisions of the Finnish Sale of Goods Act.[26] The French courts also have, not quite convincingly, employed the "theory of accessories" (*théorie de l'accessoire*), suggesting that the program itself should be regarded as an accessory to the tangible material sold under the contract to place it within the scope of application of the provisions on sales contracts.[27]

---

24   Le Tourneau, *Contrats informatiques et électroniques* (3rd ed., 2004), at p. 161.

25   Lipovetsky, "Les clauses limitatives de responsabilité et de garantie dans les contrats informatiques. Approche comparative France/Etats-Unis — quelles limitations?", at http://www.kahnlaw.com/france/newsjob/publications/clauses_limitatives_sl.htm; Le Tourneau, *Contrats informatiques et électroniques* (3rd ed., 2004), at pp. 160 and 161.

26   Routamo and Ståhlberg, *Suomen vahingonkorvausoikeus* (4th ed., 2000); Ramberg, *Kauppalain kommentaari* (1997), at p. 15.

27   Trezeguet, "Débat: Peut-on appliquer la garantie contre les vices cachés en matière de logiciels?", at http://www.cejem.com/article.php3?id_article=131, 2003.

The majority of court decisions in the United States on this topic have found that software and related licensing constitute a sale of goods transaction under the Uniform Commercial Code. The sale of off-the-shelf software has been consistently regarded by the courts as a sale of goods under article 2 of the Uniform Commercial Code.[28]

The sale of custom software is, as in the European systems, seen more often in the United States as a sale of services not covered by the Uniform Commercial Code, but rather by Common Law rules. However, several courts appear to have applied the Uniform Commercial Code even in cases where the essence of the contract is service.[29]

As has been seen, the sale of pre-existing packaged standard software appears to be construed as a sale rather than lease in each country studied.[30] While the legal nature of software within the existing legal framework remains somewhat unclear, a further question open to interpretation has been whether software should be categorized as goods or services.

However, this question appears to be of relevance only in cases of furnishing tailored software. The supply of tailored software remains outside of the scope of this chapter, but the interpretations appear more established for software contracts involving the delivery of tailored software and that the courts do not generally hesitate to deem contracts for the supply of tailored software as service provision contracts.[31]

11.03 Defective Software

(a) Definition of "Defect" in the Context of Software — Defect in Quality

The essential question is whether the software meets the requirements set forth in the agreement or in the applicable statutes.

---

28   See, however, Lemley *et al.*, *Software and Internet Law* (2nd ed.), at pp. 312 *et seq* and the cited case law where it is argued that a sale of standard software could be seen as license in the case of a bargained agreement.

29   One goal of the Uniform Computer Information Transactions Act is to bring the goods and service aspects related to software transactions closer together.

30   Le Tourneau, *Contrats informatiques et électroniques* (3rd ed., 2004), at pp. 160 and 161. Le Tourneau refers to the following judgments where the applicability often appears to be presupposed by the respective court: *Cour de cassation*, com. (22 January 1991), Giso, *Dr. informatique et telecoms* 1993/2, at p. 40; *Cour d'appel d'Aix-en-Provence* (21 May 1997), *J.C.P.E.* 1998, I, at p. 845; *Cour d'appel de Besançon* (9 April 1999), St, Lacroix, *Gaz. Pal.*; 2000, 1, at p. 820; *Cour d'appel de Bastia* (19 November 2002), *Comm. com. électr.* 2003, no. 123. The United States courts appear to treat software as goods as well. The most recent cases have extended the scope to customized software. Phillips, "When Software Fails: Emerging Standards of Vendor Liability under the Uniform Commercial Code", *Business Lawyer* (November 1994), at p. 3.

31   Le Tourneau, *Contrats informatiques et électroniques* (3rd ed., 2004), at pp. 162 *et seq*.

In the legal systems covered, a vendor, by a contract of sale, is bound to hand over the product to the purchaser and to transfer the ownership of the product. The vendor must deliver the product to the purchaser in a state that is free from defects as to quality.[32]

Before it is possible to assess the liability of a vendor for defects in software, one must consider what constitutes such a defect that triggers the liability. In practice, the notion of "defect" is one of the most difficult issues related to determining the liability for software problems. The extremes are clear enough: if it is not possible to boot the software in the agreed hardware and software environment, the software is defective and, on the other hand, if the software functions in accordance with a detailed acceptance criteria set forth in the agreement, it is difficult to argue that it would be defective.

Unfortunately, the real-life cases are rarely that simple. How often may a software program crash or is the software defective if the cursor is red instead of blue. Practical difficulties relate often also to the interaction between the software provided with other software or hardware. The parties are likely to have very divergent views on which of the systems are defective when the interaction does not work.

As discussed above, issues related to software deliveries have not been dealt with in specific statutes in the legal systems covered, and the case law is still developing. Consequently, the notion of a defect in each country covered must be construed in accordance with the rules established to deal with the sale or lease of movable property or general principles of contract law. None of these sets of rules is particularly well equipped to resolve the issue.

Software vendors often state in their standard terms and conditions that the software delivered is not warranted to be free from "defects" in the sense that the software contains bugs or errors in code which may cause unexpected or unwanted functioning of the software or interruptions in the use of the software. Depending on the interpretation of this statement, it may be considered either self-evident or quite unreasonable.

If a word processing program crashes in daily use once per year, it does probably contain a bug, but the bug is probably immaterial to most users. However, if the same word processing program changes every "a" into a random character every time a document is saved, the bug defies the purpose of using the program, and releasing the vendor from liability based on the warranty exclusion requires probably more justifications.

More appropriate limitations of warranties are the ones based on limiting the warranty with the words "substantially" or "materially". The warranty

---

32   Finnish Sale of Goods Act, section 18; German Civil Code, section 433.

language could read ". . . the vendor warrants that the software functions substantially in accordance with the specifications . . .". This limitation, although being often subject to heavy negotiations, follows closely the traditions of the statutory warranties applicable to the sale of goods, where the warranties typically cover only defects that are material for the purchaser's use or the value of the sales object.

The close alignment with the traditional structures makes the situation easier if the existing regime for the sale of goods must be applied on top of the contractual provisions, than in case of the exclusion for a warranty on uninterrupted and error-free operation of the software.

The primary contractual obligation imposed on the vendor is the duty of conformity, i.e., the obligation to deliver the goods in conformity with what is agreed. In the context of software sales, the object of the transaction, i.e., the software, is typically thoroughly specified in detailed specification documents describing the functionalities and properties of the software.

This is of course the case when the supplied software is tailored or developed specifically to meet the requirements set forth by the purchaser. When such specification documentation has not been included in the contract between vendor and purchaser, determining what has actually been agreed to be delivered becomes more difficult. In cases where the sold software can be categorized as standard software, the object of the transaction is typically determined by referring to a specific version and type of software and the software is accompanied by a user manual or the like.

In either case, the accompanying documentation typically forms a part of the delivery as a whole; the user documentation is an essential part of the software without which the use of the software is in most cases barely (or not at all) possible. Thus, the documentation amounts to a primary obligation and the lack of documentation or delivery of poor documentation leads to a failure in the performance of the contract by the vendor.[33]

In Germany, there are, for example, warranty obligations in the law for misleading, confusing or otherwise insufficient manuals and assembly instructions. In short, if the assembly information for a product "meant to be assembled after the purchase" is defective, the purchaser is entitled to the same remedies as if the product itself were defective, provided that he does not manage to build the product properly as a result of the poor information.

---

33 Redeker, "Anpassung von Standard-Software", in Redeker (ed.), *Handbuch der IT-Verträge I* (2004), at p. 22. Actually drawing a line between the duty of information and the delivery itself becomes somewhat hazy — the accompanying documentation may well be seen as a product description stating the qualities of the product in question; on the other hand, the documentation may be seen as an inseparable part of the delivery and a prerequisite for the contracted functioning (use) of the product.

It remains to be seen whether these rules also will apply to user manuals relating to the installation of software.[34]

The vendor's statutory warranty against defects in quality provides purchasers with protection against defects which are inherent to the object sold, but invisible at the moment of conclusion of the contract (latent defect). To fall within the scope of latent defect, such defect must render the object unfit for its intended use, or restrict such use to the extent that the purchaser would not have purchased the object at all, or would only have paid a reduced price for it, had he been aware of the defect.

However, typically, the vendor is not liable for such defects that the purchaser could reasonably have noticed before the conclusion of the contract. As held by the French courts in software-related cases, software defects, such as bugs or errors in programming which result in unwanted functionalities, are regarded as latent defects or defects in quality.[35]

In the jurisdictions examined, a product is typically considered defective in respect of quality if, at the time of passing of risk, it is inconsistent with what was agreed between the parties or if it is not fit for the purpose specified in the contract or, as is the case in Finland and the United States, for a particular purpose if the vendor was aware of such purpose at the time of conclusion of the contract. Furthermore, a product is defective if it is not fit for its normal use and its quality does not correspond to the quality of products of the same kind and to what can be expected by the purchaser by virtue of the product's nature.[36] It is further expressly stated in the Uniform Commercial Code that implied warranties may arise from course of dealing or usage of trade.[37] Although not expressly stated in the Sale of Goods Act, usage of trade in Finland also may lead to an implied warranty. Typically, in the jurisdictions at hand, the delivery by the vendor of a different product or a product of lesser amount (in case of software, rather, lack in capacity, or absent functionalities or features) also constitutes a defect.

When determining defect in the absence of an explicit agreement between the parties regarding the quality of the product, the legal systems covered in this chapter are fairly close to each other. In such cases, objective criteria are decisive, such as the questions: what quality can an ordinary purchaser of that

---

34   Retzer, "The New German Contract Law — Impact on Information Technology Contracts", at http://www.mofo.com/news/general.cfm?MCatID=9156&concentrationID=&ID=700 &Type=5.

35   *Cour d'appel de Bastia*, civ. (19 November 2002), *SARL Girashi voyages v. SA. Téchnique et développement informatique et éditions*, SA. Arius, SA. BNP Lease, *Banque Populaire Toulouse Pyrénées*, no. 2002/00772.

36   Finnish Sale of Goods Act, section 17; German Civil Code, section 434.

37   Uniform Commercial Code, section 2-314(3).

type of product reasonably expect the product to possess, or what quality and description is a common standard?

(b) Defect in Information

(i) Pre-Contractual Disclosure

All the legal systems covered above acknowledge the binding effect of information provided as regards qualities and functioning of the software. The information provided by the vendor concerning the software forms part of its contractual obligations. In the jurisdictions examined, the duty of information in terms of software sales could be construed as obligating the supplier of software to provide the purchaser with due information concerning the software by describing its qualities and technical specifications so as to provide the purchaser with adequate information for the making of a purchase decision.

If the software is described "by reference", the contractual terms that the software must conform with are determined on the basis of the information provided by the software vendor in marketing or promotion materials and like documents describing the qualities or functionalities of the software.[38]

The duty of information derives from the general principles of contract law or, more accurately, from the duty of loyalty between contractual parties. The French construction of the duty of information that the vendor owes *vis-à-vis* the purchaser appears to be extreme among the legal systems covered. Under French law, the vendor is under a duty to actively provide the purchaser with relevant information relating to qualities of the object of the transaction, including the risks that the vendor is aware of and could be reasonably understood to be relevant to the purchaser's decision to enter into the agreement.

The duty of information further obligates the vendor to inform the purchaser about the fitness for a particular purpose, when such purpose is identified by the purchaser, provided that the vendor is in possession of such information.[39]

The French case law has attached considerable importance to provision of information by the vendor both prior to and after the conclusion of the contract and has imposed an extensive duty on the vendor. The rationale of this approach lies, according to French courts, with the increasing complexity of the information technology systems, and related services and equipment.[40]

---

38   Le Tourneau, *Contrats informatiques et électroniques* (3rd ed., 2004), at p. 107; *Cour d'appel de Paris* (10 May 1989), *Expertises* (1998), at p. 398.

39   Le Tourneau, *Contrats informatiques et électroniques* (3rd ed., 2004), at p. 17; Verbiest and Dervaux, *L'Obligation d'information du prestataire informatique à l'égard de son client* (30 December 2004).

40   *Cour de cassation*, com. (6 May 2003) *U.G.M.R. v. Proland, Expertises* (2003), at p. 262.

The supplier has a broad obligation to establish the needs of the purchaser, to ascertain the compatibility of the software with the purchaser's information system, and further recommend, when this may be necessary, appropriate products to the purchaser.[41]

In the light of French case law, it can be concluded that the duty of information under French law consists not only of a general duty to inform as such, but also of a duty to advise (*obligation de conseil*), as well as a duty to warn with respect to the possible problems and risks relating to the software (*obligation de mise en garde*).[42]

The courts have applied an interestingly broad interpretation of these obligations. The *Cour de cassation* has, in its recent case law, expressly confirmed that the vendor's duty to inform the purchaser in the field of information technology applies not only to the more obvious supply of tailored software but also to supplying standard software. A supplier of software has an obligation to inform not only *vis-à-vis* consumers but also, to a certain extent, *vis-à-vis* more skilled or well-informed purchasers and even professionals in the field of information technology.

The German law establishes liability for statements in public made by the vendor, the producer, or someone on their behalf. Product descriptions, advertisement, and the like may form part of the warranted quality of the product. This includes in particular statements in advertisements, unless the vendor was not aware of such statement nor ought to have been aware of such statement.[43]

The vendor can, however, attempt to exclude the liability for statements in public, but the subject matter (specifications for the software) should be expressly included in the contract and liability for public statements expressly excluded. Absent contractual specifications for standard software, an express exclusion of liability for public statements would be interpreted narrowly and only partially upheld.[44]

---

41 Chauleur, "Le passage à l'an 2000 dans les contrats informatiques", *Les Notes bleues de Bercy*, no. 126 (1998), at http://www.finances.gouv.fr/archives/an2000/documentation/appendum/nbb126.htm; Le Tourneau, *Contrats informatiques et électroniques* (3rd ed., 2004), at pp. 17–19; Verbiest and Dervaux, *L'Obligation d'information du prestataire informatique à l'égard de son client* (30 December 2004).

42 Le Tourneau, *Contrats informatiques et électroniques* (3rd ed., 2004), at pp. 17–22; Chauleur, "Le passage à l'an 2000 dans les contrats informatiques", *Les Notes bleues de Bercy*, no. 126 (1998), at http://www.finances.gouv.fr/archives/an2000/documentation/appendum/nbb126.htm.

43 German Civil Code, section 434(1).

44 Redeker, "Anpassung von Standard-Software", in Redeker (ed.), *Handbuch der IT-Verträge I* (2004), at pp. 26 and 27.

Liability for publicly made statements under both German and Finnish law is excluded if the description or the advertisement or other public statement has not influenced the purchaser's decision to purchase the product, or if the given information has already been corrected at the time the contract is concluded and, furthermore, if the product is installed correctly in spite of the misleading installation instructions.

In Finland, this principle is expressly stated in section 18 of the Sale of Goods Act, which provides that a product is considered defective if it is not in conformity with information relating to its properties or use that was disclosed by the vendor when marketing the product or otherwise before the conclusion of the contract. The product also must possess the qualities of goods which the vendor has held out as a sample or model. However, the applicability is subject to proof of a causal link between the information given and the purchase decision;[45] if the faulty information has no effect on the purchase decision, the vendor is not liable.

The importance of the information provided by the vendor is further elaborated in section 19 of the Finnish Sale of Goods Act, which provides that if a product is sold subject to an "as is" clause — as is the case in many standard software contracts — or a similar general reservation as regards the quality, the product is, nevertheless, considered defective if the product does not conform to information relating to its properties or as specified by the vendor prior to the conclusion of the contract.

The same applies when the vendor failed to disclose to the purchaser facts relating to the properties or the use of the product which the vendor could not have been unaware of and which the purchaser reasonably could expect to be informed about. This is, however, applicable only if the information given or the failure to disclose the facts presumably had an effect on the contract. In addition, the product will be held defective if it is in essentially poorer condition than the purchaser reasonably could expect taking into account the price and other circumstances, including information submitted.[46]

The United States system does not, in light of the provisions of the Uniform Commercial Code, appear to differ that much from the Finnish or German systems. Any affirmation of fact or promise made by the vendor which relates to the software in question and becomes, or any description, sample, or model which is made "a part of the basis of the bargain" creates an express warranty that the software must conform to the affirmation or promise. However, an affirmation made by the vendor merely as to the value of the

---

45 Finnish Sale of Goods Act, section 18.
46 Finnish Sale of Goods Act, section 19.

software or a statement, purporting to be merely the seller's opinion or commendation of the goods, is not regarded as creating a warranty.[47]

The German, Finnish and United States legal systems do not appear to require the vendor to actively track down the purchaser's needs save under exceptional circumstances where a lay purchaser particularly seeks professional assistance and has reasonably justifiable grounds to rely on the vendor's expertise. A more extensive duty of information also may arise when the purchaser expressly requests for information, recommendation, or advice. However, in cases where exceptionally wide advice is requested, it is likely that the vendor is inclined to propose a consultancy agreement.[48] With respect to off-the-shelf software, this is not common in a pre-contractual situation, but could come into question post-contractually in the form of a support agreement.

In addition, case law shows that, in sales of standard software between businesses, the purchaser is typically not regarded as a lay person but an entity with knowledge, bargaining power, and the possibility to refer to counsel.

In cases of false representation by the vendor, in the United States, an important fact to keep in mind is that the misrepresentation may be interpreted differently in different states. Misrepresentation can be innocent, negligent, or fraudulent and may lead to liability in tort. If the vendor, for example, knows or believes that the matter is not as he represents it to be, a misrepresentation is fraudulent. If, in addition, the purchaser in justifiable reliance on such statement chooses the course of its business and incurs damages, then such damages are recoverable in tort.

The states of the United States widely allow suing for fraud (and recovering punitive damages) in cases of fraudulent misrepresentation, and damages can exist separately from any recovery based on a warranty breach.[49] In cases of negligent misrepresentation in the United States, the duty is to exercise the care or competence of a reasonable person who is communicating information. The states of the United States vary in the degree to which they allow a negligent misrepresentation suit.[50]

(ii) Post-Contractual Duty to Inform

In addition to the pre-contractual obligations described above, the vendor is under an obligation to provide the purchaser with information needed and

---

47   Uniform Commercial Code, section 2-313.

48   Marly, *Softwareüberlassungsverträge* (4th ed., 2004), at pp. 284 *et seq*.

49   Uniform Commercial Code, section 2-721. Fraud is a state law claim, however, and thus there are variations among states.

50   For misrepresentation see also *Restatement of the Law 2nd*, "Contracts", sections 159–173.

useful for the proper installation and use of software unless otherwise agreed. Provision of information need not always be based on a separate contract (such as a consultation agreement), but it may be, and to a certain extent is, part of the delivery of the product itself.

For example, in the case of software sales, the user documentation is an essential part of the software without which the use of the software is barely (or not at all) possible. Thus, the provision of the documentation in each of the legal systems covered amounts to a primary obligation of the contractual relationship, and the lack of documentation or delivery of poor documentation leads to a failure in performance.[51]

The post-contractual duty of information does typically not include any obligation to give training unless so agreed. Duties also are dependent on the purchaser's expertise in the field of software. As a rule, the German and Finnish legal systems do not require the software vendor to provide a purchaser with extensive information after the conclusion of the contract. For example, providing a lay person with a typical user manual that is understandable to a layman is sufficient.[52]

In the legal systems covered, the seemingly extensive scope of the vendor's duty of information is essentially dependent on the skills and knowledge of the purchaser and is, therefore, basically determined on a case-by-case basis, evaluating the transaction as a whole, i.e., the more skilled the purchaser, the less extensive is the vendor's duty of information.[53] In France, however, the vendor may be held strictly liable on the basis of breach against the duty of information (see text, above).

The post-contractual duty to provide a purchaser of software with information relevant for the use of the software appears in the United States to relate largely to product liability and, thus, such aspects of the software that are relevant for the safe use of the software.

(c) Third-Party Claims

The object of a sale is deemed to contain a defect if it or its use is subject to a third-party right or claim and the purchaser is not, under the contract, required to tolerate the restrictions resulting from such claim or if the vendor has not excluded such warranty. Although a third-party claim may be based

---

51 In Germany, for example, if not agreed to the contrary, the documentation must be in the German language and, in France, respectively, in the French language. Redeker, "Anpassung von Standard-Software", in Redeker (ed.), *Handbuch der IT-Verträge I* (2004), at p. 22.

52 Marly, *Softwareüberlassungsverträge* (4th ed., 2004), at pp. 321–323.

53 *Tribunal de commerce de Créteil* (16 June 1998), *Expertises* (1998), at p. 316.

on other rights than intellectual property rights, copyright and other intellectual property rights are predominantly the cause for third-party claims related to software. As a rule, a *bona fide* purchaser is entitled to be compensated for losses incurred as a result of a third-party claim under the laws of Germany, France, Finland, and the United States.

Applying the provisions on third-party claims to software deliveries involves certain distinct difficulties. First, it may be that combining the software to another software or hardware results in a combination that is infringing third-party rights, although neither of the components is infringing. The authors are not aware of any case law involving this point but, in contracting practice, the problem is well known and often a difficult one to solve.

The vendor argues as a standard practice that it cannot control the combination that the purchaser makes and at the same time attempt to limit practically any use of the software outside its liability. The purchaser typically rejects this argument by explaining how it is going to use the software and by requiring the vendor to confirm that this does not constitute an infringement. In contracting practice, the issue is resolved in different ways, depending on the respective negotiation positions of the parties.

Second, since software can commonly be used for different purposes and only some of these purposes are infringing, it is unclear whether the purchaser or the vendor should be responsible for a third-party claim caused by a particular use. In principle, the purchaser decides on the use of the software and this would support the proposition that the purchaser should bear the liability for possible infringement. On the other hand, in many cases, the vendor is in a better position to judge which kind of use is infringing and which is not and, thus, would be the more natural party to take responsibility for possible infringement.

Third, software is regularly modified by the vendor in the form of maintenance updates. If the software is infringing only in its modified form, are the parties' respective liabilities the same as they would be in cases where the original product is infringing?

Each jurisdiction studied within this chapter contains provisions protecting purchasers against third-party claims violating purchasers' rights to the object purchased. It appears that the content of the applicable provisions in force in French, German, Finnish, and United States contract law is essentially the same.[54] The simple general rule is that vendor must deliver the software free of any third-party claims unless otherwise agreed. If the software is subject to such claims that the purchaser has not agreed to tolerate, the software is defective, and the vendor is in breach of contract.

---

54 French Civil Code, article 1626; German Civil Code, section 435; Finnish Sale of Goods Act, section 41.

In the French Civil Code, third-party claims are regulated through providing for a statutory warranty against third-party claims (*garantie d'éviction*). The applicability of the provision to intellectual property infringements has been expressly confirmed by the *Cour de cassation*.[55]

In the Uniform Commercial Code, an implied warranty against third party claims arises out of section 2-312(1), where it is stated that a sales contract contains a warranty by the seller that the title conveyed must be good and its transfer rightful and, furthermore, that goods must be delivered free from any encumbrance of which the buyer at the time of contracting has no knowledge.

In contrast, it is not clear whether section 41 of the Sale of Goods Act, defining a defect in title under Finnish law, applies to intellectual property right infringements. In the light of its legislative history, section 41 could be construed as expressly excluding the vendor's liability for third-party intellectual property rights infringements. However, it appears likely that, if the parties have failed to address the issue in the contract text, the general principles of Finnish contract law that are in line with article 42 of the Vienna Convention, providing for an implied warranty against third-party claims, would be applicable.[56]

11.04 Bases of Liability

(a) Contractual Liability

As generally with all the western jurisdictions, civil liability in the examined countries may be based either on contractual liability or on non-contractual liability (liability in tort). Although this fundamental distinction between the two bases of liability is far from clear,[57] it is of more than academic interest since the legal requirement for and the content of the two liability types have significant differences.

The question of whether liability is based on a contract or on delict may be of importance owing to the fact that different liability types lead to the

---

55 Le Tourneau, *Contrats informatiques et électroniques* (3rd ed., 2004), at pp. 128 *et seq.*

56 Routamo and Ståhlberg, *Suomen vahingonkorvausoikeus* (4th ed., 2000); Finnish Supreme Court, KKO 1990:147. See article 42 of the United Nations Convention on Contracts for International Sale of Goods: "The vendor must deliver goods which are free from any right or claim of a third-party based on industrial property or intellectual property, of which at the time of the conclusion of the contract the vendor knew or could not have been unaware provided that the right or claim is based on industrial property or intellectual property".

57 Hemmo, "Sopimus ja delikti: Tutkimus vahingonkorvausoikeuden vastuumuodoista", *Lakimiesliiton kustannus* (1998), at pp. 328 *et seq.*

application of distinct bodies of law and ultimately to different outcomes. Furthermore, the legislators and courts in Germany, France, and Finland have taken a restrictive view on using alternative types of liability to justify liability for the same act or omission; in principle a claim must be based on either one.[58]

The United States legal system appears to differ in this respect from the European systems and allows easier access to either of these different but parallel claims.

A pre-condition for the applicability of the rules on contractual liability is a valid contract between the parties and that the damage results from breach of an obligation arising out of the contract. To clarify the scope of the contractual liability regime and the line between the two co-existing liability regimes, the *Cour de cassation* has introduced a principle of non-cumulation (*non-cumul des responsabilités contractuelle et délictuelle*) to French law. This judge-made principle expressly excludes the right of the non-breaching party to make a choice between the different liability bases; the claim must be based on the rules governing contractual liability for a claim based on a breach of an obligation arising out of a contact.[59]

For the purposes of this chapter, the authors have assumed a valid contractual relationship between the vendor and the purchaser of software. In addition, any general contractual terms referred to in this chapter are assumed to be validly incorporated into the contract.

(b) Non-Contractual Liability

Each of the jurisdictions falling within the scope of this chapter provides for separate liability regimes for contractual and tort liability. Where the contractual liability is based on the non-execution of contractual obligations and therefore requires a contract between the parties, the tort liability bases on the damage caused by the tortfeasor by his negligent conduct.[60]

The general principles of tort law are practically the same in each of the European legal orders examined here, and the regime for non-contractual liability is construed as being secondary to the contractual liability regime in Germany, France, and Finland. When combined with the above

---

58   For discussion on the concurrence of claims (*Anspruchskonkurrenz*) and the two "schools" of interpretation in Germany, see Medicus, *Schuldrecht I. Allgemeiner Teil. 15 Auflage* (2004), at pp. 179 and 180.

59   Jourdain, *Les principes de la responsabilité civile* (5th ed., 2000), at p. 36.

60   French Civil Code, articles 1382 and 1383; Finnish Torts liability Act (*Vahingonkorvauslaki*), chapter 2, section 1.

mentioned rule that, in principle, a vendor is not allowed to choose between the liability type it seeks to enforce this means that a vendor may not resort to non-contractual liability where a damage relates to the performance of an obligation under a contract.

Naturally, it is possible that the purchaser suffers harm due to an extra-contractual cause which is attributable to the vendor, and which does not relate to performance of the contractual obligations of the vendor. The vendor's liability in such event would obviously be based on the tort liability regime.

In addition to the general civil liability provisions, a vendor's civil liability may be based on special provisions or statutes. A vendor may be held liable for defective software, for example, on the basis of the product liability legislation. The product liability laws in force in France, Germany, and Finland provide the purchaser with compensation for damage caused by a defective product on persons and personal property other than the defective product itself. These rules are not discussed here in detail since they apply to the relationship between the vendor and the purchaser in a business-to-business software contract only in exceptional cases.

Basing claims in tort in the United States is, to a European lawyer, a somewhat complex area since the law of torts varies from state to state and is mostly based on Common Law and not statute. It may be, for example, that a total disclaimer of warranties leaves the purchaser with no effective contractual remedies, thus opening the door for a tort action[61] whereas, in Finland and Germany, the contract would be adjusted as unreasonable.

Restructuring a contract claim into a tort claim may affect warranty and liability disclaimers included in the contract as well as allow punitive damages and nullify choice of law and forum clauses. United States courts appear to be reluctant to allow tort claims without a *bona fide* tort basis, and the Uniform Commercial Code is seen as the proper framework for recovery of economic losses. Most torts can be divided into three broad categories, depending on whether liability is based on intent, negligence or absolute (strict) liability with no requirement of either intent or negligence.[62] For purposes of this chapter, intentional misrepresentation and negligence cases would be the most important bases of non-contractual liability since strict liability is largely the basis for product liability for manufacturers and sellers of defective products which falls outside the scope of this article.

---

61   This is the case in Florida. See *Interface Inc. v. Pioneer Technologies Group and KSH Systems Inc.*, 774 F. Supp. 1355 (M.D. Fla., 1991).

62   Farnsworth, *An introduction to the Legal System of the United States* (3rd ed.), at p. 126.

11.05　Liability Standards and Recoverable Damage

(a)　Liability Standards

If the software is found to be defective and this causes damage to the purchaser, the question remains if the vendor should compensate such damage. The rules on civil liability in France, Germany, Finland, and the United States are essentially based on fault and, furthermore, on the presumption of fault in case of a breach of contract. The vendor can release himself from liability by proving that the damage was not caused by his negligent or intentional act or omission.

Traditionally, liability not requiring fault (strict liability) has only been applied to certain special cases, such as employer-employee relationships. Departing from the fault-based liability, legislators in all the jurisdictions examined have more recently also adopted product liability rules, including the strict liability of the vendor. Furthermore, in France, the extensive duty of information (see text, above) imposed by the *Cour de cassation* on suppliers operative in the information technology field is essentially based on the strict liability rule, i.e., the vendor's failure to fulfill its duty to inform the purchaser on a rather extensive list of facts results in liability for damages irrespective of the degree of fault on the part of the vendor.[63]

In French law, the liability standard applied to the vendor's liability for any defects in quality of software is exculpatory, whereby the vendor's liability is presumed.[64] The Finnish Sale of Goods Act applies the control liability rule and the burden of proof lies with the vendor as well, although control liability is viewed stricter and thus closer to strict liability. Under Finnish law, the vendor is, however, held strictly liable for defects in title and third-party claims.[65] Likewise, under German law, a vendor assumes strict liability for defects in title (*Rechtsmängel*). The same applies also to so-called initial incapability (*anfängliche Unvermögen*).

(b)　Recoverable Damage

Software defects may result in a plethora of different types of damages. Probably the most obvious damage caused by a defect in software is the repair and replacement cost for the software. However, repairing and replacing standard software also may not be a straightforward exercise.

63　Viney and Jourdain, *Traité de droit civil Les effets de la responsabilité* (2nd ed., 2001), at pp. 175 *et seq.*

64　Viney and Jourdain, *Traité de droit civil Les effets de la responsabilité* (2nd ed., 2001), at pp. 175 *et seq.*

65　Finnish Sale of Goods Act, section 41.

Anyone who installed updates or reinstalled a program knows that, even with relatively simple and widely used software, such as office programs installations of updates or re-installing the program requires at worst significant time and may result in unexpected difficulties with the interaction with other software and hardware.

The second type of damage in relation to software results from the down time of the software or, worse, a wider system requiring the software to run. If an operating system is defective in a way that it does not boot or crashes repeatedly, for example, this effectively prevents the use of the whole system, including the hardware. These examples are illustrative of the second type of loss, i.e., loss of use. Loss of use often causes difficult questions as to the amount of damage because it is not necessarily clear what is the amount of damage for a system being down unless there is a substitute system that is used during down time.

The third typical software-related damage type is loss of data. Loss of data arises when a defect in a software results in corruption of files or crashes, during which unsaved data is lost. The damage caused by loss of data is often even more difficult to measure than the damage for loss of use, but it is relatively easy to construe that the damages are considerable. The liability caused by loss of data typically relates inseparably to the question on the content of the agreement as to how and by whom back-up copies of data are to be made.

Lastly, software defects may cause the same types of damages as a sale or lease of a movable property typically causes, such as loss of profit, cost for substitute products, and legal fees.

If the vendor is liable to compensate the purchaser for the damage that defective software has caused, the parties almost invariably disagree on the amount of such damage. In all western jurisdictions, there is a well-established body of law on the principles determining the amount of recoverable damages. All of the legal systems falling within the scope of this chapter are based on the principle of full compensation. Accordingly, the damages for compensating the injured party for its loss should in principle cover the loss, irrespective of its nature, in full.

Since the liability in Germany, France, Finland, and the United States is based on fault, the causal link between damage and the vendor's conduct is required. The rule applied in determining this causal connection is based on the principle of foreseeability in all four jurisdictions. Despite different wordings in the applicable regulations or rules in each country, the main rule is the same: to be recoverable, concrete harm must be foreseeable in a way that is based on the factors that the non-breaching party ought to have known at the time of conclusion of the contract. This results in excluding the purchaser's right to compensation for the loss suffered if such damage is extraordinary or objectively unforeseeable to the vendor.

As a rule, the actual scope of the different types of loss to be compensated is not regulated exhaustively. Although the Finnish Sale of Goods Act provides a non-exhaustive list of recoverable types of damage,[66] the full scope of the damage to be compensated is not regulated in detail in the Finnish contract law, but rather assessed in the light of general tort law principles.[67] Briefly, the compensation is provided in Germany, Finland, and the United States in accordance with the theory of expectation interest. Accordingly, the awarded compensation aims at putting the plaintiff into the position she or he would have been in had the contract been performed in accordance with its terms.

In other words, the law compensates for any gains which the plaintiff expected to realize as a result of the performance but which he has not received on account of the defendant's breach. The plaintiff is, thus, entitled to compensation for, e.g. lost profit, or payment of damages for the cost of substitute performance. In contrast to German, Finnish, and United States law, the approach adopted in France aims at recovering negative interest of the injured party, i.e., to put the plaintiff into the position he would have been in if he had never concluded the contract. Applying this theory, which also is referred to as the "theory of reliance interest", in practice results in, e.g., compensating the plaintiff for expenditures made towards performance of the contract.

It should be noted that, according to the Finnish Sale of Goods Act, a vendor's liability to compensate for indirect damage follows stricter rules than is the case with direct damage. The purchaser is, under Finnish law, entitled to damages for direct losses that he suffers as a result of a defect in the software, unless the vendor proves that there was an impediment beyond its control which he could not reasonably be expected to have taken into account at the time of the conclusion of the contract.[68]

In contrast to direct damage, liability for indirect damage is based on the vendor's fault. The Finnish Sale of Goods Act defines indirect loss as including loss due to reduction or interruption in production or turnover; other loss arising because the goods cannot be used as intended, loss of profit arising because a contract with a third party has been lost or breached, loss due to damage to property other than the goods sold, and other similar loss that is difficult to foresee. However, the compensation for loss suffered by

---

66 Finnish Sale of Goods Act, section 67. See also Routamo and Ståhlberg, *Suomen vahingonkorvausoikeus* (4th ed., 2000).
67 Routamo and Ståhlberg, *Suomen vahingonkorvausoikeus* (4th ed., 2000).
68 Finnish Sale of Goods Act, section 27.1.

purchasers may be limited if the result would otherwise be unreasonable to the vendor or if the damages are extraordinary or unforeseeable.

(c) Purchaser's Liability to Mitigate Damages

The law in all the legal systems treated here enforces a contractual duty of loyalty where the participants may not act solely in their own interest at the expense of the other party.

Deriving inherently from this duty of loyalty, the law imposes on the contracting parties a general duty to mitigate the loss suffered as a result of breach of contract. Accordingly, the injured party in the contractual relationship is obliged to take all reasonable measures which may be needed to limit the damage suffered.[69]

In the case of a purchase of defective software, the purchaser's duty to limit the extent of losses incurred may, in practice, require the purchaser to take measures aiming, for example, at replacing the defective software without undue delay to limit the damage to its business operations. The contributory fault of the purchaser also may be construed on the basis of an omission to call the attention of the vendor to danger of unusually high damage that the vendor neither knew of nor should have known of.

The duty to mitigate the damages has been codified both into the German Civil Code and the Finnish Sale of Goods Act, with practically the same content. Section 70 of the Sale of Goods Act specifically provides that, if a party who has suffered damage as a result of a breach fails to take all the reasonable measures to mitigate the loss, the vendor's liability is reduced by the amount that could have been avoided had the purchaser mitigated the damage. Section 254 of the German Civil Code also includes a rule defining the relevant factors to be taken into consideration in assessing the respective attribution and the liability of the parties.

The *Restatement of the Law 2nd*, "Contracts", section 350, describes this as damages that could have been avoided without undue risk, burden, or humiliation; damages that a non-breaching party could have reasonably avoided cannot recover.[70]

Germany, France, Finland, and the United States appear to take a holistic case-by-case assessment as a starting point for determining the liabilities of each party. Clear-cut lines are hard to draw and universally applicable rules of course hard to establish, and the actual scope and the limits of the purchaser's duty are

---

69   Le Tourneau, *Contrats informatiques et électroniques* (3rd ed., 2004), at p. 45.

70   See also Uniform Commercial Code, sections 2-712 and 2-715, for the approach of the Uniform Commercial Code.

obviously difficult to define at a general level. However, a purchaser's duty does not extend to averting or calling the vendor's attention to a fact that is unreasonable taking into account the possibilities of the purchaser to foresee and prevent the loss.

(d) Purchaser's Contributory Action

In all of the four jurisdictions, a purchaser may not passively wait for vendor's performance, but instead has a duty of collaboration.[71] One of the illustrations of this duty is the above-discussed duty to mitigate damages. In Finland, this duty is expressly codified in section 50.1 of the Sale of Goods Act, which states that a party's failure to cooperate constitutes a ground for rescission of the contract. However, the Finnish Sale of Goods Act does not clearly state anything about the purchaser's contributory action and whether the purchaser's acts or omissions increasing the amount of damages affects the vendor's liability and appraisal for damages.

Particularly in French tort law, the non-breaching party's duty to mitigate damages suffered is strengthened through the fact that considerable attention is paid to the contributory negligence of the victim. In the light of French case law, the contributory negligence is taken into account as a mitigating factor when appraising the party's negligence in tort and leads, thus, to a proportional division of responsibility between the parties (*partage de la responsabilité*).

Such allocation of liability between vendor and purchaser consists, in practice, of lowering the amount of damages to be paid to the purchaser.[72] However, as is the case in general with establishing civil liability, the causal link between the negligent act and the damage suffered must be proved — in addition to establishing the presence of negligence and the damage. Thus, the negligent action committed by the purchaser has no legal relevance where the causal link between his action and the damage suffered is missing.

In cases where the purchaser's negligent action or omission is intentional and there is no negligence on the part of the vendor, the vendor has no liability for the damage. The same applies, according to French case law, to cases where the purchaser itself is actually the sole cause of the damage, and the damage was unforeseeable and insurmountable for the vendor. The United States approach appears to be similar, i.e., contributory negligence affects a vendor's liability by either barring a damages claim completely or lowering the amount of damages.

---

71 Le Tourneau, *Contrats informatiques et électroniques* (3rd ed., 2004), at p. 173.
72 Jourdain, *Les principes de la responsabilité civile* (5th ed., 2000), at pp. 163–165.

(e) Punitive Damages and Contractual Penalties

Punishments by law related to contract law are more or less fundamentally rejected in all of Germany, France, and Finland. Without going into detail in analyzing the differences in doctrine between the countries, the purpose of granting damages to the injured party serves the compensatory purpose and does not strive for punishment or deterrence in any of the European jurisdictions examined.

Accordingly, in these countries, punitive damages are not available under contract or tort law, the underlying ideologies of which are compensation: compensation awarded for the non-breaching or suffered party aims at restoring the situation and achieving the situation as it would be if the cause giving rise to the damage had not occurred at all.

As the *Cour de Cassation* has, in French case law, consistently pointed out, the courts are not allowed to take into consideration the absence of fault, the degree of fault, or other such moral aspects on the side of the breaching party and the assessment of damages must be carried out independently of such factors.[73]

However, the recent case law shows a certain trend towards attenuation in this respect and some judgments may fairly be regarded as not only fulfilling the function of providing the aggrieved party with a full compensation for the damage suffered, but also measuring damages with the view of sanctioning the defendant. This trend is materializing through the use of the discretionary powers of the judges to estimate the scope of damage as particularly broad in the case of a gross negligence.[74]

Liquidated damages setting the damages payable to a predefined damage amount representing a fair estimate of the foreseeable damages for a breach are enforceable with little limitations in each of the three countries. The French law departs from the principle of freedom of contract in relation to liquidated damages by providing that such limitations, through agreeing on the sum of damages, are permissible only to the extent that they do not lead to limiting non-contractual liability, setting a floor to the amount of liquidated damages. In addition, French courts could intervene and adjust the amount of liquidated damages if the amount is considered to be excessive or unreasonably low in comparison to the actual damages.[75]

Contractual penalties providing for a contractually agreed damage amount in excess of an estimate of the damages resulting from a breach are in

---

73 *Cour de cassation,* civ., 8 May 1964 ("L'indemnité nécessaire pour compenser un préjudice subi doit être calculée en fonction de la valeur do dommageé sans que lag gravité de la faute puisse avoir aucune influence sur le montant de ladite indemnité").

74 Le Tourneau, *Contrats informatiques et électroniques* (3rd ed., 2004), at pp. 9–11; Jourdain, *Les principes de la responsabilité civile* (5th ed., 2000), at pp. 156–159.

75 Jourdain, *Les principes de la responsabilité civile* (5th ed., 2000), at pp. 163–165.

principle permissible in all of the three countries, but in each three with some mandatory limitations. The limitations are the strictest in Germany, where contractual penalties are unenforceable in certain cases, including mostly contractual penalties set forth in general terms and conditions.

Based on the case law, the unenforceability of contractual penalties also appears to extend to business-to-business relationships. In addition, German courts tend to regularly adjust the amounts of contractual penalties.[76]

The French and the Finnish law basically only include the latter of these intervention mechanisms, and the courts could adjust the amount of such penalties if it is deemed unreasonable. Especially in Finland this would appear to require a very significant imbalance between the damage and the penalty and some special circumstances for the courts to intervene.

Although not unfamiliar to the United States legal system, punitive or exemplary damages are generally not awarded in commercial contract cases in the United States.[77] However, they may be awarded in limited circumstances.[78] According to the Uniform Commercial Code, section 2-718, the parties may, for breach by either party, liquidate damages in the agreement, but only at an amount which is reasonable in light of the anticipated or actual harm caused by the breach, the difficulties of proof of loss, and the inconvenience or non-feasibility of otherwise obtaining an adequate remedy.

Most importantly, section 2-718 of the Uniform Commercial Code renders void the use of liquidated damages if the amount of liquidated damages is unreasonably large. Liquidated damages clauses may be enforceable if the damages for contractual breach were difficult to ascertain or estimate at the time of conclusion of the contract and the amount agreed for liquidated damages is considered a reasonable forecast of compensatory damages in the case.[79] No actual pecuniary damages need be shown if the above prerequisites are met for the liquidated damages to be received.

(f) Enforceability of Liability Limitations and Exclusions

In business-to-business contracts, freedom of contract prevails and the parties are, as a general rule, free to agree on exclusions of warranties or

---

76   Medicus, *Schuldrecht I. Allgemeiner Teil. 15 Auflage* (2004), at pp. 223 *et seq.*

77   Restatement *of the Law 2nd*, "Contracts", section 356.

78   According to the *Restatement of the Law 2nd*, "Contracts", section 355, punitive damages are only recoverable if the breach also is a tort for which punitive damages are recoverable.

79   Unreasonable liquidated damages would be construed as a penalty and, therefore, held unenforceable on grounds of public policy; see *Restatement of the Law 2nd*, "Contracts", section 356, and Uniform Commercial Code, section 2-718.

limitations of liability. In fact, the limitation clauses, addressing typically, for example, limitations of actions or caps to indemnities, are an essential part of contracts in business-to-business sales.

Outside the scope of consumer protection, the common principles of contract law, most importantly the principles of loyalty and the requirement for balance of the rights and obligations between the parties to the contractual relationship, as well as regulations aiming to preserve the loyalty in the contractual relationship, set boundaries to the enforceability of liability limitation clauses. The conduct of the vendor, primarily the presence or absence of good faith, is one of the essential factors determining the enforceability of contractual liability limitations.[80]

Consequently, unreasonable limitations are not enforceable. As an example, contractual clauses may set forth a cap limiting the amount of indemnities where such caps are found unreasonable since they are construed as constituting a clause of non-liability and therefore regarded as void.[81]   Another expression of the rule, which appears to be found in all of the legal systems examined here, is the Uniform Commercial Code ban on limitation of remedies where such limitation leads to avoidance of liability for failure of essential purpose.[82]

The vendor's right to limit its liability in none of the jurisdictions examined extends to limiting liability for damage resulting from its intentional acts or omissions. Limiting liability for gross negligence in all legal systems covered in this chapter also is unenforceable.[83] However, liability for harm resulting from simple negligence appears to be enforceable when the software contract is concluded between businesses.

Limitation of liability clauses regarding damages caused by simple negligence may still be invalid under German law, if contained in general terms and conditions to the extent their application would lead to a result that would defy

---

80   Lipovetsky, "Les clauses limitatives de responsabilité et de garantie dans les contrats informatiques. Approche comparative France/Etats-Unis — quelles limitations?", at http://www.kahnlaw.com/france/newsjob/publications/clauses_limitatives_sl.htm.

81   Le Tourneau, *Contrats informatiques et électroniques* (3rd ed., 2004), at p. 41; Lipovetsky, "Les clauses limitatives de responsabilité et de garantie dans les contrats informatiques. Approche comparative France/Etats-Unis — quelles limitations?", at http://www.kahnlaw.com/france/newsjob/publications/clauses_limitatives_sl.htm. 2000; Sédallian, "Garanties et responsabilités dans les logiciels libres", http://www.juriscom. net/pro/2/da20020901.pdf, 2002, p. 9. See also *Cour de cassation* 1ère civ. (22 October 1996), *Chronopost*, D 1997, at p. 121, where the court held that a clause limiting the liability of the contractor is not permissible when it leads to abolition of the material obligations of the professional contractor.

82   Uniform Commercial Code, section 2-719(2).

83   It appears that in the United States it is possible to also exclude gross negligence by way of an express contractual limitation.

the purpose of the contract: a provision is held invalid if it limits essential rights or obligations of a party.[84]

The French law takes another step in limiting the freedom of contract. In French civil law, liability limitation clauses — whether included in consumer contracts or in business-to-business contracts — are only enforceable to the extent they aim at limiting the contractual liability of a party and, following the constant case law of *Cour de Cassation*, liability based on tort is a matter of public policy (*d'ordre public*) and cannot therefore be contractually excluded or limited.[85]

In Germany, in case of contractual liability, it is a question of interpretation whether a provision of contract concerning limitation of liability would cover also delict-based liability. It is generally acceptable if and to the extent the limitation has only marginal effect. Case law sets another requisite for limitation of liability through standard terms and conditions: such a limitation must be clearly expressed.[86]

The French courts also appear to have reserved themselves fairly large discretionary powers to limit the extent of clauses limiting software suppliers' liability on a case-by-case basis.[87] Thus, the judge-made rule of "professional of the same specialty" discussed above is of the essence when assessing the enforceability of the liability limitation clauses.[88]

This rule also provides justification why under French law consumer protection rules may become applicable even to business-to-business contracts. It should be noted that, in accordance with settled case law, the professional vendors of software cannot in consumer contracts validly exclude liability for any defects in quality (*vices cachés*), third-party claims or for any of the essential obligations of the vendor.[89]

With respect to legal defects, the German commentaries have pointed out that liability may be limited with moderate liability caps. Such a cap in an agreement must be in a reasonable proportion to the damages so incurred.

---

84   Redeker, "Anpassung von Standard-Software", in Redeker (ed.), *Handbuch der IT-Verträge I* (2004), 2001, 1.2, at p. 95; German Civil Code, section 307, paragraph 2, number 2.

85   Sédallian, "Garanties et responsabilités dans les logiciels libres", http://www.juriscom.net/pro/2/da20020901.pdf; Lipovetsky, "Les clauses limitatives de responsabilité et de garantie dans les contrats informatiques. Approche comparative France/Etats-Unis — quelles limitations?", at http://www.kahnlaw.com/france/newsjob/publications/clauses_limitatives_sl.htm.

86   Medicus, *Schuldrecht I. Allgemeiner Teil. 15 Auflage* (2004), at pp. 178 and 180.

87   Le Tourneau, *Contrats informatiques et électroniques* (3rd ed., 2004), at p. 168; *Cour de cassation*, 3ème civ., 27 September 2000; *Cour de cassation*, com., 14 March 2000.

88   *Cour de cassation*, civ., 24 January 1995; *Tribunal de Grande Instance de Versailles*, 2 July 2004.

89   *Cour de cassation*, com., 15 May 2001, *Cedig informatique*, *Expertises* (2001), at p. 349.

With respect to a limitation of liability in case of third-party claims, the German scholars have set three other prerequisites, namely:

1. The vendor may not have been aware of the third-party rights;

2. The vendor must offer the purchaser help in legal defense; and

3. The vendor must hold the purchaser harmless from the third-party claims.[90]

Finnish law also accepts liability caps in principle only with the limitation of reasonableness and a mandate of the courts to rewrite or invalidate unreasonable liability caps.

In Finland, if standard terms include an exemption clause that is onerous and unexpected, it will only become a part of the contract if it was especially emphasized when concluding the contract. An exemption clause limiting the amount of damage compensated is not automatically an onerous clause, but the evaluation of the content of the whole contract is needed. An exemption clause also may lose its binding force through the adjustment of the contract. Relevant factors, when evaluating the reasonableness of an exemption clause, include:

1. The price the vendor has received;

2. The possibilities to avoid the damages and to be protected against them; and

3. The overall view of the creditor's remedies and the content of the breach of contract.

The ambiguity rule (*in dubio contra stipulatorem*) is an interpreting principle that may narrow the meaning of an exemption clause if the debtor has written the clause.

In the United States legal system, the Uniform Commercial Code, section 2-316(1), expressly provides that an express warranty cannot be disclaimed. On the other hand, disclaimers to exclude an implied warranty of merchantability are permitted. To be effective, however, such disclaimer must be conspicuous and consistent with the requirements laid down in the Uniform Commercial Code.[91]

---

90 Marly, *Softwareüberlassungsverträge 3. Auflage* (2000, 4. Auflage, 2004), at pp. 489 and 490.

91 For the definition of "conspicuous", see Uniform Commercial Code, section 1-201(10). The definition puts weight on the appearance of the disclaimer. The disclaimer must be so "written, displayed, or presented that a reasonable person against which it is to operate ought to have noticed it". See also Uniform Commercial Code, section 2-316(2) and (3), for exclusion or modification of warranties.

For example, an "as is" clause effectively disclaims all implied warranties unless the circumstances indicate otherwise.[92] Liability limitations may, under the Uniform Commercial Code, be challenged on two grounds, namely:

1. Unconscionability;[93] and

2. Failure of essential purpose.

Commercial transactions courts will traditionally place the burden on the party seeking to invalidate an allegedly unconscionable contract or contract term.[94] Although the "failure of essential purpose" doctrine varies from state to state, it appears fair to conclude that, if the exclusive remedy available in the case of defective software is repair and the software for some reason cannot be repaired, it would appear likely that such remedy fails its essential purpose. The unconscionability rule applies also expressly to consequential damages. Under United States law, consequential damages may thus be excluded unless regarded as unconscionable.[95]

In each of the four countries, the party who has breached the contract deliberately or by an act or omission of gross negligence loses his possibility to appeal to the exemption clause almost without exception. If the breach of contract is due to the gross fault of a third person, whom the vendor has engaged to perform the whole or a part of the contract, there is a greater chance that the exemption clause is binding.

11.06 System of Remedies in Defective Software

Each legal system covered in this chapter provides several remedies for the purchaser if the software delivered is found to be defective. In addition, the parties to a contract may have agreed remedies that either add on to or replace the remedies available by law.

The statutory remedies available to a purchaser include the right to have the vendor repair or replace the defective software with non-defective software, to have the price of the software reduced, termination of the agreement, or

---

92 This appears, in light of the statutes, to be similar to the Finnish equivalent in the Sale of Goods Act, section 192 .

93 Uniform Commercial Code, section 2-302.

94 Courts have rejected such claims in commercial settings with arguments such as that the transaction was between "large, sophisticated merchants"; familiarity and understanding of the nature of contract; expert review of the contract; and equal bargaining power.

95 Uniform Commercial Code, section 2-719(3). The courts appear to deal with the unconscionability of limitation of consequential damages differently, depending on the court's view as to whether the limitation of consequential damages should fall or be upheld together with limitation of remedies.

withholding payment of the purchase price. The exact content of these remedies is not the same in each of the countries.

Supply of defective software triggers the vendor's contractual liability. However, the purchaser needs to take certain practical steps to enforce the remedies for defects in the software. Such practical steps typically include inspecting and testing the software on receipt or shortly after receipt, and providing notice of any defects to the vendor without undue delay after becoming aware of the defect. The rules on these practical steps may be based on laws, but also on provisions in the contract between the parties. These practical steps could have significant impact on the parties' relevant positions in case of a software defect, but a discussion on the exact content of the requirements for the practical steps is outside the scope of this chapter.

The usual method of enforcement of contractual obligations is by compensation for losses caused by their breach, but claim for performance *in natura* also is generally recognized in each country covered by this chapter. In fact, although pecuniary damages remain the most common means for remedying the loss suffered by the purchaser, specific performance is regarded as primary to pecuniary damages in all the contract laws reviewed, with the exception of the United States.

The range of remedies at the purchaser's disposal is essentially the same in Germany, France, and Finland. The available remedies include redelivery, repair, price reduction, rescission of the contract, withholding payment and, finally, claim for damages and compensation. As a rule, any defect in quality or third-party claim allows the purchaser to repair the defect and, at the purchaser's discretion, to require the vendor either to replace the goods or to attempt to correct the defect. Thus, the purchaser basically has the choice between claiming for performance *in natura* either in the form of repair of the defective product or delivery of a new product.[96]

A purchaser's right to performance *in natura* can only be limited on certain conditions, such as in cases where the performance of the contract turns out to be unreasonable or impossible. It should be noted that performance *in natura* also may be impossible or unreasonable only with respect to a particular part of the vendor's performance. In such cases, the purchaser also is respectively partly entitled to rely on other forms of remedies.[97]

---

96 German Civil Code, sections 437, item 1, and 439. In the United States, it appears that the purchaser's option to invoke remedies may be limited by the contract. However, the limitation of remedies to only one remedy may result in the so-called failure of essential purpose problem where the only allowed remedy is, in practice, not applicable. Such situation may arise where the software is simply not repairable so that it would meet its purpose. In such cases, the courts may deem the essential purpose of the remedy to have failed and, as a consequence, may consider the limitation (or the disclaimer as the case may be) unenforceable as it would leave the customer without any practical remedies.

97 German Civil Code, section 439(3).

Accordingly, courts are basically not entitled to refuse the vendor's right to specific performance, such as right to have a bug affecting the software fixed by the vendor, if such performance is possible and can be considered to satisfy the purchaser.

If the seller fails to replace the goods or correct the deficiency, the buyer may rescind the contract or obtain a reduction of the price paid. The French law shows a somewhat diverging trend in this respect, since it places the choice between specific performance and pecuniary damages at the purchaser's sole discretion. In Germany, there is an explicit statutory obligation to take measures to repair defects (*Nacherfüllung*) in accordance to which the vendor may only refuse to repair the defect when it is unreasonable considering all the relevant circumstances, e.g., when cost of the item is low in comparison to the repair costs. In addition, the buyer may claim any damages that have been caused by a negligent or intentional act.[98]

The systems of remedies in the United States legal order differs to some extent from the European systems examined here, mostly in that specific performance is clearly not used as much in the European systems. If the seller fails to make delivery or repudiates or the buyer rightfully rejects acceptance, the buyer may cancel and, whether or not he has done so, may, in addition to recovering the amount of the price as has been paid, "cover" and damages as to all the goods affected or recover damages for non-delivery. If the seller fails to deliver or repudiates, the buyer also may, if the goods have been identified, recover them or, in a proper case, obtain specific performance or replevy the goods.[99]

Finally, it should be noted that the provisions in force, e.g., in Finland, specifically reserve the vendor the right, even in the absence of the purchaser's request, to remedy the defect or to deliver substitute goods at its own expense when this may take place without substantial inconvenience to the purchaser. In contrast to the Finnish approach, a vendor's right to remedy the defect in France is subject to discretionary assessment by the competent court.

11.07   Comparative Aspects

(a)   Major Differences in Legislation

The legal regimes are significantly different on the liability of vendors of software. A good example of this is the enforceability of liability limitations and warranty exclusions; under French law, the enforceability of liability

---

98   Retzer, "The New German Contract Law — Impact on Information Technology Contracts", at http://www.mofo.com/news/general.cfm?MCatID=9156&concentration ID=&ID=700&Type=5.

99   Uniform Commercial Code, section 2-711.

limitations and warranty exclusions is overshadowed by affording certain businesses essentially the same protection as consumers. In Germany, the dividing line appears to be whether the limitations of liability or the warranty exclusions are included in a standard form contract or individually negotiated agreement and, in addition, such clauses could be unenforceable if the agreement would lose its essential purpose. The Finnish system limits the enforceability of contractual clauses through a reasonableness standard. However, between businesses, the courts have been reluctant to rule that certain clauses would be unenforceable.

Enforceability of liability limitations and warranty exclusions is not the only issue where the legal regimes are different. There appear to be differences in almost all the key aspects of the law covering vendor's liability, although each of the systems is an implementation of the principle that contracts should be honored and a breach should be remedied so that the non-breaching party is economically at the position it would have been if the other party had not breached.

(b) Impact of Choice of Forum and Law on Vendor's Liability

Despite the fact that it is a simple matter to declare that the laws on vendor's liability for software defect are different, it is not easy to determine which of the laws are beneficial or detrimental to a vendor or purchaser with respect to a particular software contact. Providing more guidance on this issue would require a more in-depth analysis of each of the laws covered. Merely outlining the laws does not give the full picture because the court practices on evaluating proof and the amount of damages awarded varies significantly.

In practice, in contract negotiation, the parties agree on the choice of law and dispute resolution provisions of an agreement last after everything else, including where the testing, repair, and liability provisions related to software defects have already been agreed. Based on the differences outlined above as to the rules regarding liabilities of the parties in case of software defects, it would make much more sense to agree on the applicable law and dispute resolution before agreeing on the liability provisions. However, it appears unlikely that the choice of law and dispute resolution sections of an agreement would be discussed anything but last in practice.

(c) Need for International Treaties on Liability for Defective Software

International harmonization in the field of liability for software defects would be welcome. The existing systems are fundamentally different and make assessment of crossborder transactions involving software difficult. However, the differences stem from differences in the basic principles underlying the contract law in each country. Short-term success in international harmonization in questions where the diverging approaches are so closely tied to the fundaments of national contract laws is unlikely to materialize.

The first step towards more a harmonized system of vendor's liability for defective software would be raising awareness of the differences and their consequences among researchers, governments, and practitioners. Legal differences are not going to stop the globalization of the markets related to delivery of software, but legal differences could cause unnecessary difficulties in special circumstances (such as treatment of liability limitations for open-source software).

(d) National Choices Related to Liability for Defective Software

Regulation at a national level could result in further fragmentation of the applicable laws as, absent international harmonization policies, national legislators in each country will be put into a situation where they will have to draft their legislation based on their own circumstances. Countries with a strong software industry could provide a more favorable environment for this industry through more limitations on liability, while countries with a weak or non-existing software industry could attempt to establish regimes onerous for software vendors.

However, the national choices related to the vendor's liability for software defects are not, and should not be, determined only by the strength of the domestic software industry. The liability regime will have an impact on the availability and pricing of software products available in a country. The most obvious result is that the vendors will seek to increase the prices for their products to take into account the increased liability exposure. Generally, most vendors may effectively provide different prices for different markets and prohibit parallel imports by using license terms that are restricted to a single market. Consequently, the practical effects of the liability regime on pricing will very much depend on the competition in the market affected by the liability regime.

The liability regime also could have a significant impact on the development and availability of new products and technologies. If the liability regime is very strict, this may inhibit the development of new technologies where the technology could result in significant liability exposure. This is especially true as the software industry commonly accepts the fact that products released will contain bugs, and the bugs may be repaired through new versions and patches after the products are already on the market. In addition, if software vendors are uncomfortable with the liability regime of a certain country, they could decide not to make a certain product available in a certain market at all or do so only after the software has been tested in other markets.

On the other hand, a country making choices as to liability for defects in software should properly take into account that the purchaser of a software product typically has no practical way to verify the quality of the software, either through testing or reviewing it before making the purchase decision. A regime that allows vendors to escape all liability for defects reduces the incentive of the vendors to provide good products. The vendors also have, of course, an incentive to provide products of acceptable quality based on the market realities, but intensifying this incentive through the liability regime may have a positive impact on the quality of the software on market.

This examination of the liability regimes for defective software in the limited number of jurisdictions specified here likely provides significant issues for legislators to consider on both the international and national level. National legal tradition and practical realities may result in rather diversified liability regimes, both in structure and in content. For parties engaged in software-related transactions, this examination has demonstrated that choice of law provisions in the contract, and possibly the country of establishment of the parties, have a significant impact on the parties' liabilities and anyone contracting at an international level must pay due attention to this impact.

CHAPTER 12

RESOLVING DISPUTES OVER INFORMATION TECHNOLOGY TRANSFERS

Mark A. Nadeau
Squire, Sanders & Dempsey, LLP
Phoenix, Arizona, United States

12.01 Introduction

Phase I of the United Nations World Summit on the Information Society, held in Geneva in December 2003, culminated in the adoption of a Declaration of Principles and comprehensive Plan of Action, which addressed many broad themes concerning the Information Society.[1]

Fundamentally, the World Summit on the Information Society and the Plan of Action seek to extend access to the Information Society to the citizens of the world and utilize the Information Society to ease problems such as poverty, hunger, and environmental concerns and attendant problems, such as access to education and medical services and gender inequalities.[2] Likewise, the delegates of the United Nations consider it fundamental to a stable world economy

---

1 World Summit on the Information Society Declaration of Principles (World Summit on the Information Society-03/GENEVA/DOC/0004) and Plan of Action (World Summit on the Information Society-03/GENEVA/DOC/0005); see http://www.itu.int/wsis (3 February 2005). The author acknowledges Andrew L. Marcom, Kate E. Frenzinger, Jolana N. Berchin, and Patricia A. Kelly for their time and effort in developing this chapter and bringing the project to a close.

2 World Summit on the Information Society Declaration of Principles (WSIS-03/GENEVA/DOC/0004) and Plan of Action (WSIS-03/GENEVA/DOC/0005), at http://www.itu.int/ wsis (3 February 2005). (World Summit on the Information Society-03/ GENEVA/DOC/0005); see http://www.itu.int/wsis (3 February 2005), at paragraph A(91), B(4)–(6).

that developing countries obtain access to the tools of the Information Society that may advance their own health, welfare, and education.

In the Second Phase of the World Summit on the Information Society, scheduled to be held in Tunis in November 2005, efforts were to be made to "put the Plan of Action in motion", and working groups were to endeavor to find solutions and reach agreements in the fields of Internet governance and financing mechanisms.[3]

The benefits derived from increasing worldwide access to the Information Society are great. However, increased participation in the Information Society will inevitably result in a greater number of disputes related to information technology. In particular, disputes related to the intellectual property aspect of information technology will likely increase.

In fact, business leaders identified the protection of intellectual property rights, need for harmonization of intellectual property rights among nations, and the establishment of secure and consistent legal institutions to protect these rights as potential barriers to reaching the goals of the World Summit on the Information Society that must be addressed.[4]

Other intellectual property disputes that are likely to increase with greater access to the Information Society include piracy and infringement of information technology. Increasing access to the Information Society, by its very definition, results in a proliferation of intellectual property related to information and communication technology. Moreover, as intellectual property and the technology created therefrom is "transferred" into developing nations to increase access to the Information Society, there will be a greater concern about State protection of these rights. Such disputes will implicate treaty, as well as national, intellectual property law.

3　See the World Summit on the Information Society web site for more information about Phase II of the World Summit on the Information Society, at http://www.itu.int/wsis. The topics of Internet governance and financing mechanisms are outside the scope of this chapter.

4　Hassan, "Actions for Governments to Undertake to Attract Private Sector Investments in ICT", *Remarks at the Coordinating Committee of Business Interlocutors, Intersessional Meeting*, 16 July 2003; see http://www.iccwbo.org (visited 26 January 2005); see also Danish, "Intellectual Property, Standards, Security, and Other Issues", *Remarks, Coordinating Committee of Business Interlocutors Intersessional Meeting*, 15 July 2003, transcript available at http://www. iccwbo.org (visited 26 January 2005); Wintrebert, "Enabling Environment and Infrastructure Issues, Remarks", *Coordinating Committee of Business Interlocutors Intersessional Meeting*, 15 July 2003, transcript available at http://www. iccwbo.org (visited 26 January 2005); Leca, "Investment", *Remarks at the Coordinating Committee of Business Interlocutors Intersessional Meeting*, 15 July 2003, transcript available at http://www. iccwbo.org (visited 26 January 2005).

Information and communication technology-related disputes will inevitably increase with the proliferation of online contracts, software licensing agreements among foreign entities, and other crossborder transactions involving information technology-related intellectual property. These disputes may arise solely between private parties or between States and private parties. Such contracts are often entered online and have minimal formalities; thus, disputes will often implicate jurisdictional and choice of law problems, among others. In circumstances where formalities are set forth in print, they may be ignored and a commercially acceptable recourse for prosecution of violators must be found.

Intellectual property-related and other disputes (e.g., contract disputes) arising from information and communication technology transfers themselves also will increase. The private sector has been a philanthropic contributor in the past, but commercial reality dictates that economic interests will ultimately be the drivers of true advancement of the Information Society into developing countries.

Much of the fundamental groundwork necessary to springboard the less fortunate into the world of the Information Society will occur through transfers of technology. However, these information and communication technology transfers also can increase the number of disputes related to piracy, infringement, or the abuse and misuse of a private entity's intellectual property rights. Disputes relating to the investor's infrastructure of technology also may increase. As above, these disputes may involve private parties and/or states.[5]

This chapter outlines the history of intellectual property rights protection, including why the protection of intellectual property rights has been, and remains, such a controversial issue for the global community. The chapter then outlines the currently available methods of international dispute resolution for these type of disputes, identifying the benefits and drawbacks of each, as well as analyzes specific case studies highlighting particular problems with current dispute resolution methods.

Based on the foregoing, it is apparent that the current methods of international dispute resolution are inadequate to cope with the expected onslaught of information and communication technology-related disputes arising from increased participation in the Information Society.

Finally, the chapter concludes with some possible solutions to improve current methods of international dispute resolution to make them more amenable to the need targeted by the World Summit on the Information Society.

---

5   These are the three types of disputes within the scope of this chapter, but it is by no means an exhaustive list.

Proposed solutions will focus primarily on modification of current treaties and conventions, but also will suggest, as an alternative, a new international forum to deal specifically with these types of disputes.

12.02 Global Nature of Intellectual Property

(a) History of Intellectual Property Protection

The increasingly global nature of intellectual property is a critical issue in international dispute resolution today. With the explosive growth of the Internet, digital technology, and peer-to-peer networks, intellectual property rights are at the heart of today's ever-expanding world market. This "internationalization of intellectual property", however, is not a new development.[6]

Since the late 19th century, countries have understood the importance of safeguarding intellectual property rights beyond their borders.[7] There has been a growing trend toward developing international standards for protecting these rights in the last century.[8]

One of the earliest treaties born out of the "desire for international consensus on intellectual property rights" was the Paris Convention for the Protection of Industrial Property.[9] Drafted in 1883, the Paris Convention endeavored to create a system that would provide for international protection of patents.[10]

In addition to providing for national treatment and procedural coordination, the Paris Convention established some minimum substantive standards for protecting patents and industrial designs; however, it did not require any minimum level of protection.

The Berne Convention for the Protection of Literary and Artistic Works was another important early treaty. Effectuated in 1886, the Berne Convention

---

6   Cheek, "The Limits of Informal Regulatory Cooperation in International Affairs: A Review of the Global Intellectual Property Regime", 33 *Geo. Wash. Int'l L. Rev.* 277, at p. 284 (2001).

7   "The need for international protection of intellectual property became evident when foreign exhibitors refused to attend the International Exhibition of Inventions in Vienna in 1873 because they were afraid their ideas would be stolen and exploited commercially in other countries". World Intellectual Property Organization, General Information, at http://www.wipo.int/about-wipo/en/gib.htm#P29_4637 (visited 14 July 2004).

8   Long, "The Protection of Information Technology in a Culturally Diverse Marketplace", 15 *J. Marshall J. Computer and Info. L.* 129, at p. 134 (1996).

9   Cheek, "The Limits of Informal Regulatory Cooperation in International Affairs: A Review of the Global Intellectual Property Regime", 33 *Geo Wash. Int'l L. Rev.* 277, at p. 289 (2001).

10 Yosick, Note, "Compulsory Patent Licensing for Efficient Use of Inventions", 2001 *U. Ill. L. Rev.* 1275, at p. 1284 (2001). See also *Paris Convention for the Protection of Industrial Property*, 5 September 1970, 21 U.S.T. 1583, 828 U.N.T.S. 305.

acted as a "driving force in the development of international protection norms" in the area of copyright.[11] Member states to the Convention were required to grant copyright holders national treatment, i.e., to provide the same level of protection for copyrights to both domestic and foreign owners.[12]

In addition to requiring national treatment, and in contrast to the Paris Convention, the Berne Convention mandated minimum standards of protection from all signatories. For example, the Berne Convention established that member countries must grant domestic and foreign copyright owners the following rights:

1. Copyright protection for certain defined categories of "literary and artistic works";

2. A term of protection of no less than the life of the author, plus 50 years for most copyrighted works; and

3. The right to control the reproduction of their works, the creation of translations of such works, and the public distribution, performance, and display of such works.[13]

Together, the Berne and Paris Conventions acted as the "cornerstones of international intellectual property law throughout most of the twentieth century".[14] However, the rapid growth of technology and global trade precipitated the need to revise the Conventions.[15]

Ultimately, the World Intellectual Property Organization (WIPO) was founded to administer these Conventions and provide a forum for international discussion on intellectual property matters.[16] Despite WIPO's goal of fostering international

---

11 Long, "The Protection of Information Technology in a Culturally Diverse Marketplace", 15 J. Marshall J. Computer and Info. L. 129, at p. 151 (1996).

12 Long, "The Protection of Information Technology in a Culturally Diverse Marketplace", 15 J. Marshall J. Computer and Info. L. 129, at p. 151 (1996).

13 Long, "The Protection of Information Technology in a Culturally Diverse Marketplace", 15 J. Marshall J. Computer and Info. L. 129, at p. 151 (1996); Berne Convention for the Protection of Literary and Artistic Works, 24 July 1974, 828 U.N.T.S., articles 7–9, 11 bis–11 ter).

14 Cheek, "The Limits of Informal Regulatory Cooperation in International Affairs: A Review of the Global Intellectual Property Regime", 33 Geo. Wash. Int'l L. Rev. 277, at p. 289 (2001).

15 Cheek, "The Limits of Informal Regulatory Cooperation in International Affairs: A Review of the Global Intellectual Property Regime", 33 Geo. Wash. Int'l L. Rev. 277, at p. 289 (2001).

16 The history of the World Intellectual Property Organization is beyond the scope of this chapter; however, the predecessor to the World Intellectual Property Organization, the United International Bureau for the Protection of Intellectual Property, was formed in 1893 and governed international intellectual property rights until 1967, when the United International Bureau for the Protection of Intellectual Property became the World Intellectual Property Organization following the Convention Establishing the World Intellectual Property Organization. WIPO, General Information, at http://www.wipo.int/about-wipo/en/gib.htm#P61_9104 (visited 14 July 2004).

cooperation and harmonizing intellectual property laws and procedures, the treaties that it administers, including the Paris and Berne Conventions, do not guarantee minimum levels of protection for intellectual property.[17]

While WIPO treaties make it easier for intellectual property owners to "satisfy procedural hurdles to obtaining protection in member countries" by requiring "national treatment", WIPO member states have discretion regarding the substantive law of these treaties and independently determine their own level of enforcement.[18] Thus, problems arise, and the hopes of global cooperation are frustrated, when a country becomes a signatory to a WIPO treaty but refuses to enforce intellectual property rights within its borders.

The limitations of the WIPO Convention led to the development of other significant treaties. In 1994, the Uruguay Round of the General Agreement on Tariffs and Trade (GATT) concluded with the signing of the agreement establishing the World Trade Organization (WTO).[19] One of the WTO Agreements — the Agreement on Trade Related Aspects of Intellectual Property Rights (TRIPS) — provided the first multilateral trade forum in which to discuss international protection of intellectual property rights.[20]

This Agreement marked a major advance in the effort to establish uniform requirements for protecting intellectual property rights because it was the first treaty to mandate minimum levels of protection and provide a binding enforcement mechanism for dispute resolution for all aspects of intellectual property in a single agreement.[21] The Paris and Berne Conventions acted as the starting point in satisfying these goals and, where these and other WIPO treaties fall short, TRIPS adds additional higher standards of protection.[22]

---

17 Cheek, "The Limits of Informal Regulatory Cooperation in International Affairs: A Review of the Global Intellectual Property Regime", 33 *Geo. Wash. Int'l L. Rev.* 277, at pp. 290 and 297.

18 Cheek, "The Limits of Informal Regulatory Cooperation in International Affairs: A Review of the Global Intellectual Property Regime", 33 *Geo. Wash. Int'l L. Rev.* 277, at p. 297.

19 World Trade Organization, Legal Texts, at http://www.wto.org/english/docs_e/legal_e/ legal_e.htm (visited 15 February 2005). The treaty establishing the WTO and most of the WTO Agreements were signed in Marrakech, Morocco, in April 1994.

20 Goldberg, Comment, "Who Will Raise the White Flag? The Battle between the United States and the European Union over the Protection of Geographical Indications", 22 *U. Pa. J. Int'l Econ. L.* 107, at p. 116 (2001). See also *Agreement on Trade-Related Aspects of Intellectual Property Rights, including Trade in Counterfeit Goods, Annex IC to the Agreement Establishing the World Trade Organization*, 15 April 1994, Marrakech, Morocco [hereinafter TRIPS].

21 Effron, "Secrets and Spies: Extraterritorial Application of the Economic Espionage Act and the TRIPS Agreement", 78 *N.Y.U. L. Rev.* 1475, at p. 1493 (2003).

22 World Trade Organization, "Intellectual Property: Protection and Enforcement", at http://www.wto. org/english/thewto_e/whatis_e/tif_e/agrm7_e.htm#basic (visited 15 July 2004).

For example, TRIPS extends the Berne Convention to protect certain computer programs and databases, and clarifies that patent protection under the Paris Convention includes inventions "in all fields of technology".[23] TRIPS is part of the WTO Agreement, which means that any state seeking to become a WTO member is required to sign TRIPS.[24]

Since 1995, 147 nations have become signatories to TRIPS and committed themselves to narrowing the gap in the way intellectual property rights are protected around the world.[25] However, TRIPS only acts as a "floor", such that member states are free to establish their own levels of protection and enforcement mechanisms beyond the required minimum standards.[26]

However, TRIPS does not require a waiver of sovereign immunity and, thus, the member states are generally immune from their own failures to enforce TRIPS standards.[27]

Likewise, there is no requirement that state courts be reformed to assure transparency of process and adherence to the statutorily adopted "floor" for intellectual property rights protection.[28]

The TRIPS agreement and other international treaties attempted to address the shift in attitude toward intellectual property that occurred in the mid-1980s.[29] At that time, the high-tech and entertainment industries were rapidly growing, and developed countries (particularly the United States) faced an alarming increase in international piracy along with inconsistent international enforcement of intellectual property rights.[30]

---

23 Long, "The Protection of Information Technology in a Culturally Diverse Marketplace", 15 *J. Marshall J. Computer and Info. L.* 129, at p. 151 (1996), *supra* note 9 at 154.

24 Effron, "Secrets and Spies: Extraterritorial Application of the Economic Espionage Act and the TRIPS Agreement", 78 *N.Y.U. L. Rev.* 1475, at p. 1482 (2003).

25 World Trade Organization, at http://www.wto.org/english/thewto_e/ whatis_e/tif_e/ agrm7_e.htm (visited 15 July 2004).

26 Effron, "Secrets and Spies: Extraterritorial Application of the Economic Espionage Act and the TRIPS Agreement", 78 *N.Y.U. L. Rev.* 1475, at p. 1477 (2003).

27 TRIPS does not contain any provision requiring a waiver of sovereign immunity). However, TRIPS membership requires states to subject themselves to the jurisdiction of the WTO's Understanding on Dispute Settlement.

28 World Trade Organization, at http://www.wto.org/english/thewto_e/ whatis_e/tif_e/agrm7_e.htm (visited 15 July 2004). (TRIPS does not contain any such requirements). In the context of the Understanding on Dispute Settlement, however, states may be motivated to reform state courts under certain circumstances.

29 Cheek, "The Limits of Informal Regulatory Cooperation in International Affairs: A Review of the Global Intellectual Property Regime", 33 *Geo. Wash. Int'l L. Rev.* 277, at p. 285 (2001).

30 Cheek, "The Limits of Informal Regulatory Cooperation in International Affairs: A Review of the Global Intellectual Property Regime", 33 *Geo. Wash. Int'l L. Rev.* 277, at pp. 284 and 285 (2001).

Businesses were concerned about lost market share, and protection of intellectual property became a key element of trade strategy for developed nations such as the United States, which saw intellectual property become a large percentage of its exports by mid-decade.[31]

With the rise of multinational corporations and international trade in the 1980s, the need to protect intellectual property rights was never greater, and the inconsistent levels of protection in countries around the world resulted in considerable economic costs to those developing intellectual property.[32]

Without a uniform, international system to govern and enforce intellectual property rights, piracy became a chief concern among nations that were investing in and producing intellectual property.[33] During the 1980s, countries that afforded minimal intellectual property rights protection became havens for piracy,[34] and foreign companies in these countries were able to deliver pirated goods to the world market at drastically reduced prices.[35]

Companies that copy products without permission of the originator do not invest in the research and development of the intellectual property and do not pay royalty fees to the owners; thus, they are able to charge far less for the pirated product than the original, resulting in an adverse economic impact on the company owning the intellectual property rights.[36]

Even with a "full panoply of rights" in its home country, a company may be unable to stop foreign competitors from engaging in piracy without international cooperation and enforcement.[37] Currently, there remains no

---

31   Cheek, "The Limits of Informal Regulatory Cooperation in International Affairs: A Review of the Global Intellectual Property Regime", 33 *Geo. Wash. Int'l L. Rev.* 277, at p. 285 (2001); Callen, *Pirates on the High Seas: The United States and Global Intellectual Property Rights* 10 (1998).

32   Cheek, "The Limits of Informal Regulatory Cooperation in International Affairs: A Review of the Global Intellectual Property Regime", 33 *Geo. Wash. Int'l L. Rev.* 277, at p. 285 (2001).

33   Cheek, "The Limits of Informal Regulatory Cooperation in International Affairs: A Review of the Global Intellectual Property Regime", 33 *Geo. Wash. Int'l L. Rev.* 277, at p. 285 (2001).

34   Long, "The Protection of Information Technology in a Culturally Diverse Marketplace", 15 *J. Marshall J. Computer and Info. L.* 129, at p. 149 (1996).

35   Cheek, "The Limits of Informal Regulatory Cooperation in International Affairs: A Review of the Global Intellectual Property Regime", 33 *Geo. Wash. Int'l L. Rev.* 277, at p. 285 (2001).

36   Cheek, "The Limits of Informal Regulatory Cooperation in International Affairs: A Review of the Global Intellectual Property Regime", 33 *Geo. Wash. Int'l L. Rev.* 277, at p. 285 (2001).

37   Cheek, "The Limits of Informal Regulatory Cooperation in International Affairs: A Review of the Global Intellectual Property Regime", 33 *Geo. Wash. Int'l L. Rev.* 277, at p. 285 (2001).

worldwide system to govern intellectual property rights, and drafters of intellectual property law are faced with the challenge of protecting the rights of intellectual property holders while encouraging technological innovation and competition.[38]

Given the increase in international trade and rapid development in information technology, the modification of existing treaties and/or drafting of new treaties which increase the level of protection for intellectual property rights protection remain important.

(b) Treatment of Intellectual Property by Developed and Developing Countries

A primary issue impacting intellectual property rights exchanges is the differing levels of protection that occur between so-called developed and developing countries. During the global trade boom of the 1980s, it became clear that inconsistent protection of intellectual property rights can result in serious economic harm for nations that produce and export intellectual property[39]

In addition, intellectual property owners became acutely aware that they were not granted the same rights in developing countries as they were in developed countries.[40] The ease of infringement of intellectual property and inconsistent enforcement of intellectual property rights in developing countries increased piracy concerns among industrialized nations.[41]

---

38 Mann, "Balancing Issues and Overlapping Jurisdictions in the Global Electronic Marketplace: The Ucita Example", 8 *Wash. U. J. L and Pol'y* 215, at p. 236 (2002).

39 Cheek, "The Limits of Informal Regulatory Cooperation in International Affairs: A Review of the Global Intellectual Property Regime", 33 *Geo. Wash. Int'l L. Rev.* 277, at p. 286 (2001); 4 *Comm. Daily* 6 (16 May 1994) (citing then-Paramount Senior Vice President Lawrence Levinson, who stated that the International Intellectual Property Alliance estimated US $7.6-billion in losses from foreign piracy of films, records, music, computer programs, and books). More recently, in May 2004, Eric Smith, International Intellectual Property Alliance President, stated that, in 2003, losses to the United States economy due to copyright piracy amounted to more than US $10-billion, and more than US $20-billion globally. Press Release, International Intellectual Property Alliance, "International Intellectual Property Alliance Concerned about Pace and Progress of Copyright Developments in Key Markets Like Russia, Thailand, Brazil, China, Poland, Israel, Spain" (3 May 2004), available at http://www/iipa/com/pressreleases (visited 14 February 2005).

40 Cheek, "The Limits of Informal Regulatory Cooperation in International Affairs: A Review of the Global Intellectual Property Regime", 33 *Geo. Wash. Int'l L. Rev.* 277, at p. 286 (2001).

41 Cheek, "The Limits of Informal Regulatory Cooperation in International Affairs: A Review of the Global Intellectual Property Regime", 33 *Geo. Wash. Int'l L. Rev.* 277, at p. 290 (2001).

The reasons for these differing approaches are complex, and they often implicate economic, political, and cultural disparities between industrialized and emerging nations.[42] One of the keys to developing an international consensus on the scope of protection for intellectual property rights, which must be understood to include transfers of technology, rests in understanding these differences, and incorporating that understanding into treaty negotiations.

One reason for the differing level of protection of intellectual property rights afforded by various nations is simply a matter of language. Definitional problems plague efforts to reach agreements on intellectual property issues. As no uniform definitions exist for the various forms of intellectual property, the words themselves carry a host of philosophical and cultural meanings and assumptions that are often lost in translation.[43]

Often, a concept may have a "rough equivalent" in another language, but it may not fully encompass the legal and ideological precepts of the original.[44] The author uses the word "copyright" as an example of how differences in language can result in difficulties when trying to create a set of international definitions for legal concepts.

Even the word "property" represents significantly different concepts in divergent cultures, particularly between those of Eastern and Western ideology. For example, whether intellectual property rights constitute intangible "property" over which the creator or right holder has a right to control is a subject of significant debate among various nations.[45] Thus, even the preliminary steps of developing uniform, international standards of protection are hampered by such language barriers.

Cultural and ideological distinctions between so-called developed and developing nations also play a role in frustrating efforts to build an international consensus on intellectual property rights. Differences in attitude regarding the role of intellectual property in a growing economy translate into difficulties at the negotiating table when crafting international treaties.[46]

---

42 Long, "The Protection of Information Technology in a Culturally Diverse Marketplace", 15 *J. Marshall J. Computer and Info. L.* 129, at p. 132 (1996).

43 Long, "The Protection of Information Technology in a Culturally Diverse Marketplace", 15 *J. Marshall J. Computer and Info. L.* 129, at p. 148 (1996).

44 Long, "The Protection of Information Technology in a Culturally Diverse Marketplace", 15 *J. Marshall J. Computer and Info. L.* 129, at p. 148 (1996).

45 Long, "The Protection of Information Technology in a Culturally Diverse Marketplace", 15 *J. Marshall J. Computer and Info. L.* 129, at p. 148 (1996).

46 Cheek, "The Limits of Informal Regulatory Cooperation in International Affairs: A Review of the Global Intellectual Property Regime", 33 *Geo. Wash. Int'l L. Rev.* 277, at p. 286 (2001). The author cites India and Brazil as examples of developing countries that refused to provide intellectual property protection unless the technology benefited their citizens. Braga, "The Economics of Intellectual Property Rights and the GATT: A View from the South", 22 *Vand. J. Transnat'l L.* 243, at p. 253 (1989).

For example, the problem of attempting to enforce intellectual property rights in China may be traced to the Confucian view that information should be shared without receiving compensation.[47] In addition, tribal cultures such as New Zealand's Maori have a "community view" of property that does not easily integrate with the more individualistic approach to intellectual property of Western, industrialized countries.[48] In general, developing nations often believe that intellectual property is for the "public good" and belongs to the "common heritage of mankind", which is an ideological perspective that makes developing a uniform standard of rights challenging.[49]

In addition to cultural differences, the discrepancy between the legal institutions and enforcement methods of developed and developing nations contributes to the difficulty of creating international standards of protection for intellectual property. Despite the presence of these standards under treaties such as TRIPS and the Paris and Berne Conventions, enforcement is still largely the responsibility of the domestic legal institutions of the member states.[50]

Many industrialized nations with well-developed common law systems have civil enforcement mechanisms in place to protect intellectual property rights, whereas many developing nations offer little or no enforcement of these rights, or turn to criminal sanctions as a means of enforcement.[51] This problem of enforcement in developing countries is one of the major roadblocks for creating uniform standards on intellectual property protection today.[52]

For example, China enacted its intellectual property laws in 1996, and they generally comply with the minimum substantive requirements of the Berne Convention. Nevertheless, an alleged failure to enforce those requirements led many copyright owners in the United States to claim billions of dollars in losses.[53]

---

47   Wang, *The Chinese Traditions Inimical to the Patent Law*, 14 N.W.J. Int'l L. and Bus. 15, at p. 17 (1993).

48   Long, "The Protection of Information Technology in a Culturally Diverse Marketplace", 15 *J. Marshall J. Computer and Info. L.* 129, at p. 157 (1996).

49   Long, "The Protection of Information Technology in a Culturally Diverse Marketplace", 15 *J. Marshall J. Computer and Info. L.* 129, at p. 163 (1996).

50   Long, "The Protection of Information Technology in a Culturally Diverse Marketplace", 15 *J. Marshall J. Computer and Info. L.* 129, at p. 157 (1996).

51   Long, "The Protection of Information Technology in a Culturally Diverse Marketplace", 15 *J. Marshall J. Computer and Info. L.* 129, at pp. 157 and 158 (1996).

52   Long, "The Protection of Information Technology in a Culturally Diverse Marketplace", 15 *J. Marshall J. Computer and Info. L.* 129, at p. 158 (1996).

53   Long, "The Protection of Information Technology in a Culturally Diverse Marketplace", 15 *J. Marshall J. Computer and Info. L.* 129, at pp. 158 and 159 (1996).

Thus, without adequate enforcement, uniform standards on intellectual property protection become meaningless. In this context, any effort by the World Summit on the Information Society to advance the exchange of technology among developed and lesser developed nations is doomed to fail absent acknowledged and accepted methods for the protection of technology and agreed paths for resolving disputes that will surely arise.

Understanding the divergent economic and development strategies of so-called developed and developing nations is crucial to building an international consensus on intellectual property protection. The first step is to examine the purpose of the intellectual property in these countries. In developing nations, intellectual property rights promote the dissemination of technology whereas, in developed nations, intellectual property rights focus on protecting such nations from piracy.[54]

Often, this means that the intellectual property laws of developing nations will be weaker or less consistently enforced than their industrialized counterparts. Weak intellectual property laws indicate a preference for a system based on competition; one that makes goods available to the greatest number of people at the lowest price.[55] These nations essentially have no choice but to depend on industry competition because they lack the resources of industrialized countries to invest in the research and development of new technology.[56]

Nonetheless, they still seek to furnish their populations with these new products and, for that reason, they are often resistant to enacting strict, uniform standards of intellectual property protection that they regard as barriers to their nation's domestic economic development.[57] Indeed, some scholars argue that the strict standards and "protectionist" intellectual property regimes of self-interested industrialized nations can harm the growth of developing nations.[58] This argument goes so far as to suggest that the wealth enjoyed in developed countries is improperly insulated by legal protectionism resulting in a lack of competition.

As opposed to the competition-based system of developing nations, countries that offer greater protection of intellectual property rights and stricter laws

---

54 Cheek, "The Limits of Informal Regulatory Cooperation in International Affairs: A Review of the Global Intellectual Property Regime", 33 *Geo. Wash. Int'l L. Rev.* 277, at p. 286 (2001).

55 Effron, "Secrets and Spies: Extraterritorial Application of the Economic Espionage Act and the TRIPS Agreement", 78 *N.Y.U. L. Rev.* 1475, at p. 1479 (2003).

56 Effron, "Secrets and Spies: Extraterritorial Application of the Economic Espionage Act and the TRIPS Agreement", 78 *N.Y.U. L. Rev.* 1475, at p. 1479 (2003).

57 Effron, "Secrets and Spies: Extraterritorial Application of the Economic Espionage Act and the TRIPS Agreement", 78 *N.Y.U. L. Rev.* 1475, at p. 1479 (2003).

58 Reichman, "Global Competition Under TRIPS", 29 *N.Y.U.J. Int'l. L. and P.* 23, at pp. 24–26 (1996).

favor a system based on innovation, where the works of the mind are viewed as valuable to the individual creator and therefore deserving of protection.[59]

Moreover, other developed nations, particularly those with common law systems like the United States and Great Britain, follow an "economic property view" of intellectual property that focuses on economic returns and incentives.[60]

In these countries, research and development costs can be so great, particularly in fields of high-level technology, that the only way these costs will be incurred is if the creators of the intellectual property have some level of assurance that the fruit of their efforts will be protected.[61]

Invention and creativity will be stymied in a country that develops intellectual property without adequate protection and enforcement of intellectual property rights.[62] If creators of a new product were given absolute dominion over the intellectual property and the power to monopolize their industry, prices for the product would soar, quality would be compromised, and efforts to bring better and cheaper alternatives to a wider market would be prevented.

Respecting the intellectual property rights of creators is important, for there would be little incentive to invent new products without some assurances of protection; however, "the law recognizes exceptions that allow for the study of, and improvement on, discoveries that have been committed to the public domain, in all realms of intellectual property protection".[63]

Due to the difference in economic perspective between developed and developing nations, reaching an agreement on transfers of technology and uniform standards for intellectual property protection will not be without its

---

59   Effron, "Secrets and Spies: Extraterritorial Application of the Economic Espionage Act and the TRIPS Agreement", 78 *N.Y.U. L. Rev.* 1475, at p. 1479 (2003).

60   Long, "The Protection of Information Technology in a Culturally Diverse Marketplace", 15 *J. Marshall J. Computer and Info. L.* 129, at p. 157 (1996).

61   Effron, "Secrets and Spies: Extraterritorial Application of the Economic Espionage Act and the TRIPS Agreement", 78 *N.Y.U. L. Rev.* 1475, at p. 1479 (2003).

62   The movement to harmonize intellectual property standards and enforcement methods has, in large part, focused on increasing the level of protection for creators of intellectual property and the holders of intellectual property rights. However, a competing force has always been to promote innovation, investment, and improvements in intellectual property through competition so as to build on our collective knowledge. Uhrich, "The Economic Espionage Act, Reverse Engineering and the Intellectual Property Public Policy", 7 *Mich. Telecomm and Tech. L. Rev.* 147, at p. 155 (2001).

63   Uhrich, "The Economic Espionage Act, Reverse Engineering and the Intellectual Property Public Policy", 7 *Mich. Telecomm and Tech. L. Rev.* 147, at p. 155 (2001). Reverse engineering, which involves the detailed study of a product to understand how it operates so that a similar or superior product can be created to compete with the original, is such an exception.

challenges. The governments of many countries, such as Taiwan, China, South Korea, India, and Brazil, are often unwilling to provide greater protection for foreign intellectual property at the risk of having to sacrifice jobs for their citizens by closing certain industries.[64]

Accordingly, some commentators argue that these nations lack a commitment to enforcing intellectual property rights, and thus are not seen as having the same goal as developed countries.[65] This is because developing nations arguably benefit from weak intellectual property laws (and indeed, from piracy) as they do not possess much of their own intellectual property and, therefore, rely on the intellectual property of other nations to promote their own economic development.[66]

As a result, these countries view pressure to adopt strict international standards on intellectual property as a "direct threat to their ability to play a significant role in the world economy".[67]

The United States, for instance, has responded to the perceived weakness of intellectual property laws and enforcement of rights in developing nations. In an attempt to stem the loss of billions of dollars from inconsistent intellectual property enforcement and piracy abroad, the United States pursued an aggressive foreign policy campaign to establish minimum standards for the protection of intellectual property.[68]

This led to the enactment of the Omnibus Trade and Competitiveness Act of 1988 ("the Act"), which gave the United States Trade Representative authority to unilaterally act against countries that failed to protect American intellectual property.[69]

Under the Act, the United States Trade Representative had the authority to investigate the practices of foreign countries and label them as a "Priority Foreign Country" if they failed to sufficiently protect intellectual property

---

64   Cheek, "The Limits of Informal Regulatory Cooperation in International Affairs: A Review of the Global Intellectual Property Regime", 33 *Geo. Wash. Int'l L. Rev.* 277, at p. 316 (2001).

65   Cheek, "The Limits of Informal Regulatory Cooperation in International Affairs: A Review of the Global Intellectual Property Regime", 33 *Geo. Wash. Int'l L. Rev.* 277, at p. 316 (2001).

66   Long, "The Protection of Information Technology in a Culturally Diverse Marketplace", 15 *J. Marshall J. Computer and Info. L.* 129, at p. 162 (1996).

67   Long, "The Protection of Information Technology in a Culturally Diverse Marketplace", 15 *J. Marshall J. Computer and Info. L.* 129, at p. 163 (1996).

68   Cheek, "The Limits of Informal Regulatory Cooperation in International Affairs: A Review of the Global Intellectual Property Regime", 33 *Geo. Wash. Int'l L. Rev.* 277, at p. 287 (2001).

69   Omnibus Trade and Competitiveness Act of 1988, Pub. L. No. 100-418, 102 stat. 1107 (1988).

rights. The United States Trade Representative could then impose trade sanctions if the country did not improve its intellectual property laws and enforcement mechanisms.[70] Many nations were critical of this unilateral approach, particularly developing nations that felt threatened into adopting strict standards for intellectual property protection that favored the United States and other industrialized nations.

The international community also has responded to weaken intellectual property standards in developing nations, but sought a more multilateral approach. Despite the appeal of WIPO as a forum for multilateral negotiation, many developed nations looked elsewhere due to WIPO's slow progress on harmonization of intellectual property laws, the voluntary nature of many WIPO conventions, and WIPO's failure to revise the Paris Convention in the 1980s.[71]

The industrialized nations turned to the ongoing trade negotiations in the Uruguay Round of the GATT.[72] A precursor to the WTO, the GATT requires member states to commit to free trade in goods and ensures that countries treat each other equally in trade agreements.[73]

With regard to establishing uniform substantive laws concerning intellectual property rights, GATT is more favorable than WIPO because an agreement within GATT commits all signatories to minimum substantive standard.[74]

Including intellectual property rights in GATT, the emphasis on procedural uniformity found in WIPO treaties transformed into emphasis on minimum levels of substantive protection of intellectual property rights.[75]

The TRIPS Agreement, which emerged from the Uruguay Round in 1994, represented a sea of change in the multinational recognition and protection of intellectual property rights, particularly in developing countries.[76]

70　Omnibus Trade and Competitiveness Act of 1998, Pub. L. Number 100-418,102 stat. 1107 (1988).

71　Cheek, "The Limits of Informal Regulatory Cooperation in International Affairs: A Review of the Global Intellectual Property Regime", 33 *Geo. Wash. Int'l L. Rev.* 277, at pp. 297 and 298.

72　Cheek, "The Limits of Informal Regulatory Cooperation in International Affairs: A Review of the Global Intellectual Property Regime", 33 *Geo. Wash. Int'l L. Rev.* 277, at p. 287.

73　Mann, "Balancing Issues and Overlapping Jurisdictions in the Global Electronic Marketplace: The Ucita Example", 8 *Wash. U. J. L. and Pol'y* 215, at p. 226 (2002).

74　Cheek, "The Limits of Informal Regulatory Cooperation in International Affairs: A Review of the Global Intellectual Property Regime", 33 *Geo. Wash. Int'l L. Rev.* 277, at p. 288 (2001).

75　Cheek, "The Limits of Informal Regulatory Cooperation in International Affairs: A Review of the Global Intellectual Property Regime", 33 *Geo. Wash. Int'l L. Rev.* 277, at p. 291 (2001).

76　Cheek, "The Limits of Informal Regulatory Cooperation in International Affairs: A Review of the Global Intellectual Property Regime", 33 *Geo. Wash. Int'l L. Rev.* 277, at p. 292 (2001).

TRIPS requires that WTO members "(1) provide minimum intellectual property rights protection through domestic laws; (2) provide effective enforcement of those rights; and (3) agree to submit disputes to the WTO dispute settlement system". TRIPS eliminated the limitations of its voluntary WIPO predecessors by mandating minimum levels of substantive protection, and requiring all signatories to commit to significant domestic reform.[77] The United States itself had to draft new laws to comply with the TRIPS Agreement.[78]

The effect of TRIPS on developing nations is viewed by some as a major victory for developed nations in their fight to protect intellectual property rights worldwide.[79] Developing nations that seek entrance into the WTO and sign TRIPS must enact substantive laws and create domestic enforcement systems to comply with the Agreement.[80]

These countries are given more time to introduce the necessary changes than developed nations,[81] and the WIPO has signed an agreement with the WTO to assist these emerging countries in satisfying their obligations under TRIPS.[82]

Member nations must meet the minimum level of substantive protection for intellectual property rights, but are free to develop their own methods and strategies for satisfying the requirements.[83] Thus, the gap in intellectual property protection between developed and developing nations is closing as a result of the TRIPS Agreement.

---

77 Cheek, "The Limits of Informal Regulatory Cooperation in International Affairs: A Review of the Global Intellectual Property Regime", 33 *Geo. Wash. Int'l L. Rev.* 277, at p. 294 (2001).

78 Cheek, "The Limits of Informal Regulatory Cooperation in International Affairs: A Review of the Global Intellectual Property Regime", 33 *Geo. Wash. Int'l L. Rev.* 277, at p. 292 (2001).

79 Effron, "Secrets and Spies: Extraterritorial Application of the Economic Espionage Act and the TRIPS Agreement", 78 *N.Y.U. L. Rev.* 1475, at p. 1493 (2003).

80 Cheek, "The Limits of Informal Regulatory Cooperation in International Affairs: A Review of the Global Intellectual Property Regime", 33 *Geo. Wash. Int'l L. Rev.* 277, at p. 295 (2001).

81 TRIPS, articles 65–66. Developing countries are divided into two groups for determining time frame compliance. Developing countries have five years to satisfy the minimum standards set forth in TRIPS, while the least developed nations have 10 years. Effron, "Secrets and Spies: Extraterritorial Application of the Economic Espionage Act and the TRIPS Agreement", 78 *N.Y.U. L. Rev.* 1475, at p. 1494 (2003).

82 Cheek, "The Limits of Informal Regulatory Cooperation in International Affairs: A Review of the Global Intellectual Property Regime", 33 *Geo. Wash. Int'l L. Rev.* 277, at p. 298 (2001).

83 Otten and Wager, "Compliance with TRIPS", 29 *Vand. J. Transnat'l L.* 391, at p. 394 (1996).

Many developing nations, however, feel pressured by developed countries to take an even more protectionist stance than is required by TRIPS. Such steps are often inconsistent with the domestic economic agenda of the developing nations and, as a result, TRIPS is not the ultimate solution to this issue.[84]

The distinction between developed and developing countries with regard to protection of intellectual property rights is a product of numerous factors. Language, ideology, culture, and economics play a role in how each country views intellectual property rights and the level of enforcement for intellectual property rights. Thus, to build a truly uniform standard of intellectual property rights on which all member nations agree, these differences must be understood and incorporated into the international dialogue.

Significant steps have been taken through treaties such as TRIPS to build a global consensus on intellectual property rights. Notwithstanding, further advances must be made as technology continues to develop, and emerging nations look forward to joining the world marketplace and Information Society.

12.03 Current Forums for Dispute Resolution Are Inadequate

(a) In General

Globalization of the world's economy brings new challenges to the world of information technology, and intellectual property specifically. Increasingly, people across the globe are communicating and transacting business with each other, which will seemingly expand geometrically as more people gain access to the Information Society. Disputes inevitably arise, but resolution is complicated by different national and international laws.

In particular, cases where the dispute arises entirely over the Internet present unique issues of electronic contract formation, authentication, security, jurisdiction, and enforceability of judgments, among others.[85]

Moreover, as steps are taken to enhance access to the Information Society, disputes arising from licensing agreements, joint venture agreements, business acquisition agreements or employment contracts related to the

---

84 Effron, "Secrets and Spies: Extraterritorial Application of the Economic Espionage Act and the TRIPS Agreement", 78 *N.Y.U. L. Rev.* 1475, at p. 1495 (2003).

85 "In e-commerce, not only are contracting parties not necessarily situate within, or subject to the jurisdiction of, the courts of a single geographical area, but there may be no way to determine exactly where one or more of the parties are situate". Mills, Firmansyah, and Woelandara, *Effective Formation of Contracts by Electronic Means and Dispute Resolution in the New E-conomy* (2000).

transfer of technology to developing nations, as well as a wealth of intellectual property issues, will surely increase.[86]

As discussed above, nations protect intellectual property differently, and different national and international laws may conflict over the level of protection afforded. Consider the following hypothetical, which illustrates the effect that these varying levels of protection may have on a nation's intellectual property laws and the innovators themselves:

> . . . [S]ometimes Country B's decision not to protect an innovation, or to protect it less strongly than A, has spillover effects for country A. Country B's decisions may, moreover, attract domestic and foreign investments . . . . [C]ountry A may not always be able to prevent products developed in country B from entering its market. Unless country A can persuade all nations to harmonize on its higher-protection rule, a lower-protection rule in even one jurisdiction may undermine A's rule. Innovators may either have protection everywhere (because A persuaded all nations to adopt its rule) or effectively nowhere (because the lower-protection rule undermines A's rule).[87]

Generally, it is said that highly developed nations have greater protections for intellectual property than do lesser developed countries.[88] Resolving disputes such as those contemplated in this chapter is complicated by questions such as: Under which nation's laws does a patent holder seek the protection? In what forum does that patent holder seek recourse? How is a judgment from one nation enforced in a foreign nation? This chapter proceeds to highlight such challenges with an overview of the current forums available for the resolution of international disputes and the advantages and drawbacks of each forum.

(b) National Court Systems

(i) In General

Although a nation's court system may appear to be a logical choice of forum, seeking recourse in a national court system often raises difficult

---

86 Blessing, "Arbitrability of Intellectual Property Disputes", 12 *Arb. Int'l* 191, section II(b) (1996); Benton and Rogers, "The Arbitration of International Technology — Disputes under the English Arbitration Act 1996", 13 *Arb. Int'l* 361, section II (1997). Intellectual property disputes arising from information and communication technology transfers may involve both contractual and non-contractual issues (i.e., disputes over domain names and patent, trade mark, and copyright infringement).

87 Samuelson, "Intellectual Property Arbitrage: How Foreign Rules Can Affect Domestic Protections", 71 *U. Chi. L. Rev.* 223, at p. 225 (2004).

88 Mills, "Alternative Dispute Resolution in International Intellectual Property Disputes", 11 *Ohio St. J. on Disp. Resol.* 227, at p. 232 (1996).

questions regarding jurisdiction, choice of law, neutrality, speed, and enforceability of a decision. Although an adversarial system is efficient in that a final judgment resolves the rights of the parties in a single, win-or-lose situation,[89] an adversarial system also generally distances the parties from each other.[90]

Communication channels divert from commercial business personnel to lawyers and advocates, thus cutting off the life line of business interests that may well have driven the parties towards each other in the first instance. Complex court procedures often further aggravate the parties' frustrations due to inherent delays and incomprehensibility of litigation procedures.[91]

Litigation in a national court is not well-suited to maintaining positive relationships between the parties. Indeed, some commentators assert that ultimately the battle escalates to the point that the parties throw "more time and money into 'winning' rather than solving the problems".[92]

Thus, the adversarial system can create hostility between parties, and is a better solution when the parties do not desire to maintain friendly relationships. Of course, even if the parties would like to part company and forget they were ever introduced, such a result may not be in the best interest of the country and its other residents who may be advantaged by continuity of the relationship.

(ii) Jurisdiction and Choice of Law

Determining which court has jurisdiction over a dispute and which substantive and procedural law to apply to a dispute is often a challenging task. "Jurisdiction over a person is generally based on that person's physical presence or commission of acts within given geopolitical boundaries."[93]

Once the appropriate forum is determined, the state judge then must determine which procedural and substantive law to apply. The determination of choice of law often requires analysis of where an act was committed, where the parties reside or where a document was signed.[94] Furthermore, if litigants

---

89 Ciaraco, "Forget the Mechanics and Bring in the Gardeners", 9 *U. Balt. Intell. Prop. J.*, 47, at p. 54 (2000).

90 Ciaraco, "Forget the Mechanics and Bring in the Gardeners", 9 *U. Balt. Intell. Prop. J.* 47, at p. 57 (2000).

91 Ciaraco, "Forget the Mechanics and Bring in the Gardeners", 9 *U. Balt. Intell. Prop. J.* 47, at p. 57 (2000).

92 Ciaraco, "Forget the Mechanics and Bring in the Gardeners", 9 *U. Balt. Intell. Prop. J.* 47, at p. 58 (2000).

93 Donahey, "Dispute Resolution in Cyberspace", 15 *J. Int'l Arb.* 127, at pp. 127 and 128 (1998).

94 Donahey, "Dispute Resolution in Cyberspace", 15 *J. Int'l Arb.* 127, at pp. 127 and 128 (1998).

bring an international case in a particular State's court, even if the parties included a choice of law provision in their contract, the judge also may have to determine whether foreign mandatory rules of law apply or do not apply.

If foreign mandatory rules of law apply, the judge must interpret the foreign laws.[95] Variability in national laws has particular impact on the adjudication of intellectual property issues. Although people across the world may have access to a patent holder's invention, as discussed in detail above, each nation protects intellectual property to varying degrees. For instance, some national laws reserve "exclusive jurisdiction over the validity of intellectual property rights registered in that country", particularly with respect to patent and trade mark rights.[96] Additionally, national laws still vary considerably on two issues, namely:

1. By what means are related protective rights to be acquired; and

2. To what level is the protection granted to be extended.[97]

In the realm of information and communication technology transfers, choice of law and jurisdiction may further complicate contract negotiations between the private party and the state receiving the technology transfer, particularly if the receiving state is a developing nation. The private party may not wish to subject itself to the jurisdiction and laws of the developing nation which, as discussed above, may be less favorable than that of a developed nation.

At the same time, however, if the parties contract for jurisdiction in another state, there is no guarantee that state courts will abide by the contractual agreement, and each party runs the risk that the state will claim sovereign immunity should it have any hand in the alleged violation of law.

Disputes that arise online further complicate jurisdiction and choice of law issues because the dispute may have arisen entirely over the Internet. As described above, a court's jurisdiction over a person is generally based on the person's physical presence or commission of acts within certain geographic boundaries.[98] Similarly, choice of law often requires analysis regarding where an act was committed, the parties' residence, or where a contract or other governing document was signed.[99]

---

95 Blessing, "Arbitrability of Intellectual Property Disputes", 12 *Arb. Int'l* 191, section IV(a) (1996).

96 Blessing, "Arbitrability of Intellectual Property Disputes", 12 *Arb. Int'l* 191, section III(f) (1996). *Id*. Section III(f).

97 Blessing, "Arbitrability of Intellectual Property Disputes", 12 *Arb. Int'l* 191, section II(a) (1996).

98 Donahey, "Dispute Resolution in Cyberspace", 15 *J. Int'l Arb*. 127, at pp. 127 and 128 (1998).

99 Donahey, "Dispute Resolution in Cyberspace", 15 *J. Int'l Arb*. 127, at pp. 127 and 128 (1998).

Increasingly, however, contracts are formed and transactions take place entirely over the Internet such that there is no physical place where a document was signed, where acts were committed, or where the dispute arose. It is commonly understood that the rationale supporting the above distinctions is that a party who purposefully avails itself of a particular jurisdiction must expect the laws of that jurisdiction to apply and should become familiar with and follow those laws.

Such distinctions become less clear within the borderless realm of the Internet. The question then becomes whether, by simply doing business on the Internet, do customers and businesses avail themselves of the laws of foreign countries with which they otherwise have no connection? In addition, third-party providers often supply the technology underlying and supporting these business transactions. Locating the web site host or the wireless Internet provider that acted as an intermediary can be a complex undertaking. The question of internet "jurisdiction" has been answered differently by courts who have addressed it.[100]

(iii) Neutrality of Forum

If disputants seek recourse in a national court system, national bias may prevent a fair trial. "Parties typically prefer to accept a neutral forum over the uncertainties of minefields [in] foreign laws and the risk of bias by foreign courts."[101] Accordingly, many parties generally turn to an alternative form of dispute resolution to resolve international intellectual property disputes such as arbitration.[102]

(iv) Futility of Foreign Judgments

On its face, the concept of recognizing foreign judgments appears to be a fairly fundamental one to implement. However, commentators have opined that the process "masks profound value conflicts" based on diverging national sentiments regarding jurisdiction, procedure, and substantive law.[103]

In addition, culture and politics play a significant role in this arena, with some nations resistant to the idea of having their citizens and courts bound

---

100 Donahey, "Dispute Resolution in Cyberspace", 15 *J. Int'l Arb*. 127, at pp. 127 and 128 (1998).

101 Benton and Rogers, "The Arbitration of International Technology — Disputes under the English Arbitration Act 1996", 13 *Arb. Int'l* 361, section II(a) (1997); Najar, "The Inside View: Companies in Need of Arbitration", 12 *Arb. Int'l* 362 (1996).

102 Benton and Rogers, "The Arbitration of International Technology — Disputes under the English Arbitration Act 1996", 13 *Arb. Int'l* 361, section II (1997).

103 Perez, "The International Recognition of Judgments; The Debate between Private and Public Law Solutions", 19 *Berkeley J. Int'l L*. 44, at p. 46 (2001).

by the decisions of another country. This can result in political pressure both at home and abroad, with:

> . . . [i]nternational tensions ris[ing] if foreign judgments are not recognized and domestic tensions ris[ing] if they are recognized in defiance of national values.[104]

Nevertheless, numerous attempts to increase the recognition and enforcement of foreign judgments have been made, although these have largely been unsuccessful.

One of the problems facing this area is that some nations are more willing to recognize foreign judgments than others. The United States, for example, is "generally receptive to enforcing foreign judgments", while other nations are not so inclined.[105]

This is an incongruous result as it is the United States that has steadfastly refused to sign the Hague Convention for the Recognition and Enforcement of Foreign Judgments.[106]

This "perceived asymmetry" between the United States and the rest of the world is based on the belief that foreign courts are less likely to recognize and enforce American judgments.[107] This is not to say that foreign judgments have been or will always be enforced in the United States. Indeed, when the United States Supreme Court first addressed this issue more than 100 years ago in *Hilton v. Guyot*, the Court declined to give effect to a French judgment because of a lack of reciprocity on the part of the French courts.[108]

Since an American judgment was going to be reviewed again on the merits in a French court, the United States Supreme Court held that the principle of

---

104 Perez, "The International Recognition of Judgments; The Debate Between Private and Public Law Solutions", 19 *Berkeley J. Int'l L.* 44, at p. 46 (2001).

105 Perez, "The International Recognition of Judgments; The Debate Between Private and Public Law Solutions", 19 *Berkeley J. Int'l L.* 44, at p. 57 (2001); Lau, "Update on the Hague Convention on the Recognition and Enforcement of Foreign Judgments", 6 *Ann. Surv. IntT'l and Comp. L.* 13, at p. 14 (2000).

106 Juenger, "A Hague Judgments Convention?", 24 *Brooklyn J. Int'l L.* 111, at p. 123 (1998); Chao and Neuhoff, "Enforcement and Recognition of Foreign Judgments in United States Courts: A Practical Perspective", 29 *Pepp. L. Rev.* 147, at p. 148 (2001).

107 Perez, "The International Recognition of Judgments; The Debate between Private and Public Law Solutions", 19 *Berkeley J. Int'l L.* 44, at p. 57 (2001).

108 *Hilton v. Guyot*, 159 U.S. 113, at pp. 130 and 131 (1895); Traynor, "An Introductory Framework for Analyzing the Proposed Hague Convention on Jurisdiction and Foreign Judgments in Civil and Commercial Matters: US and European Perspectives", 6 *Ann. Surv. Int'l and Comp. L.* 1, at p. 4 (2000).

reciprocity dictated a similar position.[109] Other factors emerged from the *Hilton* decision that American courts must consider when confronted with a foreign judgment, such as whether that court had proper jurisdiction and whether it conducted a fair proceeding free from fraud or prejudice.[110]

Notwithstanding, United States courts now primarily recognize foreign judgments based on the principle of comity.[111] Thus, while certainly not all foreign judgments will be given effect in American courts, the United States remains one of the most generous nations with regard to enforcing the judgments of other nations.

The failure to enforce foreign judgments is an issue that does not belong to the United States alone. Many other nations face the same challenges, and wish to see the judgments of their courts upheld in foreign jurisdictions. Historically, some effort has been made to address the issue. Namely, the Hague Conference on Private International Law has tried for many years to establish some form of international consensus. In 1971, the Convention on the Recognition and Enforcement of Foreign Judgments in Civil and Commercial Matters concluded to require that decisions rendered in one of the member states would be entitled to recognition and enforcement in another member state.[112] Only four nations signed the Convention: Cyprus, The Netherlands, Portugal, and Kuwait.[113]

The failure of this Convention to adequately address the concerns and demands of members and ultimately attract signatories has led the Hague Conference to re-commence its efforts in recent years. Since 1992, member nations have been actively negotiating a new Convention on foreign judgment enforcement. However, progress has been slow, and commentators

---

109 *Hilton v. Guyot*, 159 U.S. 113, at p. 131 (1895); Perez, "The International Recognition of Judgments; The Debate Between Private and Public Law Solutions", 19 *Berkeley J. Int'l L.* 44, at p. 58 (2001). This requirement of reciprocity has been roundly criticized by commentators, primarily because it is not grounded on any Constitutional principles, such as the Full Faith and Credit Clause that mandates recognition of judgments among the 50 states of the United States. Yet, *Hilton* remains the only instance where the Supreme Court has addressed the issue.

110 Traynor, "An Introductory Framework for Analyzing the Proposed Hague Convention on Jurisdiction and Foreign Judgments in Civil and Commercial Matters: US and European Perspectives", 6 *Ann. Surv. Int'l and Comp. L.* 1, at p. 4 (2000).

111 *De la Mata v. Am. Life Ins. Co.*, 771 F. *Supp.* 1375, at p. 1380 (Del., 1991) (recognizing foreign judgments based on principles of comity is contrasted to any constitutional requirement, such as the Full Faith and Credit Clause).

112 Hague Conference on Private International Law, Convention on the Recognition and Enforcement of Foreign Judgments in Civil and Commercial Matters, article 4, at http://www.hcch.net/e/conventions/text16e.html (visited 23 July 2004) [hereinafter Hague Convention].

113 Statute of the Hague Conference on Private International Law, at http://www.hcch.net/e/status/stat16e.html (visited 22 July 2004).

believe that the attempt will fail once again, largely because the proposed Convention continues to be reduced in scope and several important substantive areas are being severely limited, including intellectual property.[114]

Moreover, given the concerns of countries such as the United States regarding the protection of intellectual property rights, it is unlikely that these countries will become signatories to such an agreement. Thus, while the international community works to find a solution to the dilemma of foreign judgment recognition, the problem continues, and agreements will need to be reached as global trade continues to flourish and more nations join the world economy.

(c) Traditional Alternative Dispute Resolution

(i) In General

Traditional alternative dispute resolution mechanisms generally provide some relief from the challenges that arise when litigating cases in national courts. By definition, traditional alternative dispute resolution is a format where:

> . . . a third party listens to disputants and makes a decision as a judge would, except that in an arbitration process, the parties often decide the rules of procedure, rights of appeal, whether or not the arbitration decision will be binding, and, most important, who the arbitrator(s) will be.[115]

This chapter will consider three methods of traditional alternative dispute resolution, namely:

1. Arbitration;

2. Mediation; and

3. Negotiation.

Proponents believe that:

> . . . the use of [alternative dispute resolution], with arbitrators and mediators with experience in the technical field at issue, will save time and effort and will likely lead to more equitable results.[116]

Scholars also opine that, at present, traditional forms of alternative dispute resolution are typically preferred in international dispute resolution.[117]

---

114 Perez, "The International Recognition of Judgments; The Debate between Private and Public Law Solutions", 19 *Berkeley J. Int'l L.* 44, at pp. 67–70 (2001); Dreyfuss and Ginsburg, "Draft Convention on Jurisdiction and Recognition of Judgments in Intellectual Property Matters", 77 *Chi-Kent. L. Rev.* 1065 (2002).

115 Ciaraco, "Forget the Mechanics and Bring in the Gardeners", 9 *U. Balt. Intell. Prop. J.* 47, at p. 53 (2000).

116 Mills, "Alternative Dispute Resolution in International Intellectual Property Disputes", 11 *Ohio St. J. on Disp. Resol.* 227, at pp. 227 and 228 (1996).

117 Wahab, "The Global Information Society and Online Dispute Resolution: A New Dawn for Dispute Resolution", 21 *J. Int'l Arb.* 143, section IV (2004).

(ii) Arbitration

Arbitration offers several advantages over litigation in national court systems. One advantage is that parties choose their arbitrator. Due to the highly technical nature of many intellectual property disputes, in particular, the ability to select an arbitrator with experience in the field at issue rather than being forced to litigate disputes before judges who are largely unfamiliar with these issues is of significant worth, saving time, expense, and arguably leading to more equitable results.[118]

Commentators also maintain that arbitration is generally faster and less costly than litigation and that the rules of procedure and evidence are often less rigid.[119]

Time is a particularly sensitive issue in information technology and intellectual property disputes because, as technology evolves quickly, protection is needed immediately, rather than months or years later.[120]

The confidentiality provided by alternative dispute resolution is another important advantage, particularly with respect to parties in intellectual property disputes involving trade secrets and other protected technologies.[121] Moreover, arbitration of international disputes provides for greater neutrality than national court systems where litigants face potential bias. Such neutrality is particularly important for international disputes involving intellectual property and information technology "which often involve transactions between purchasers in developed Western countries and suppliers in developing Asian countries, and often involve cultural as well as legal clashes".[122]

Notwithstanding the above benefits, arbitration is not without its challenges. First, arbitration is subject to national as well as international regulation,[123]

---

118 Mills, "Alternative Dispute Resolution in International Intellectual Property Disputes", 11 *Ohio St. J. on Disp. Resol.* 227, at pp. 227 and 228 (1996); Arnold, *et al., Patent ADR Handbook*, section 5.02 (1991).

119 "Traditional alternative dispute resolution mechanisms . . . have been increasingly preferred to court proceedings due to their procedural flexibility, speediness, absence of jurisdiction/related problems, as well as other difficulties associated with in-court dispute resolution processes". Wahab, "The Global Information Society and Online Dispute Resolution: A New Dawn for Dispute Resolution", 21 *J. Int'l Arb.* 143, section I (2004).

120 For example, one scholar notes that often "patents and the technology being disputed may actually become obsolete before a matter reaches the litigation stage", Mills, "Alternative Dispute Resolution in International Intellectual Property Disputes", 11 *Ohio St. J. on Disp. Resol.* 227, at p. 231 (1996).

121 Mills, "Alternative Dispute Resolution in International Intellectual Property Disputes", 11 *Ohio St. J. on Disp. Resol.* 227, at p. 231.

122 Benton and Rogers, "The Arbitration of International Technology — Disputes under the English Arbitration Act 1996", 13 *Arb. Int'l* 361, section II(a) (1997).

123 Wahab, "The Global Information Society and Online Dispute Resolution: A New Dawn for Dispute Resolution", 21 *J. Int'l Arb.* 143, section I (2004), *supra* note 119, Section IV.

which may lead to conflicting laws. Other shortcomings associated with traditional arbitration include choosing the place of arbitration, the language in which the arbitration will take place, the jurisdiction of the arbitration, the law governing the arbitration and the substance of the dispute, and ensuring enforceability of the award.[124]

As arbitration becomes increasingly popular, some of the advantages over litigation diminish. Indeed, today, arbitration can be a costly forum in which to bring less complicated disputes.[125] The number of smaller claims in international arbitration has grown with the increased participation of small to medium-sized companies in international commerce.[126]

Moreover, more complex and legalistic disputes are being arbitrated now than ever before.[127] As a result of these new concerns caused by greater demands on the international arbitration system, providers of arbitration services have developed new arbitration rules particularly aimed at reducing the time and costs spent on the proceedings. These new rules also are known as "fast-track" arbitration rules.[128]

Fast-track arbitration rules focus on reducing cost and time spent on resolving disputes and provide the greatest benefits to the resolution of smaller, less complex disputes.[129] A number of organizations, including without limitation, the American Arbitration Association (AAA), WIPO, the Japan Commercial Arbitration Association (JCAA), the China International Economic Arbitration Commission (CIETAC), and the Geneva Chamber of Commerce and

---

124 Schneider and Kuner, "Dispute Resolution in International Electronic Commerce", 14 *J. Int'l Arb*. 5, section III (1997). Issues regarding uncertainty in the law applicable to an arbitration, jurisdiction of the courts providing legal support to the proceeding, and potential review and enforcement of the award are minimized in legal systems that have adopted the Swiss concept of the "seat" of arbitration. The "seat" is a legal concept that is independent of the physical place of arbitration and serves to connect the arbitration to a specific legal system. This concept has also been adopted in the 1996 English Arbitration Act, and the arbitration agreement can specify the seat of arbitration at the outset. Schneider and Kuner, "Dispute Resolution in International Electronic Commerce", 14 *J. Int'l Arb*. 5, section III(B) (1997).

125 Müller, "Fast-Track Arbitration: Meeting the Demands of the Next Millennium", 15 *J. Int'l Arb*. 5, sections I and II (1998). At least one commentator has also questioned whether arbitration actually leads to speedier resolution of disputes. Müller, "Fast-Track Arbitration: Meeting the Demands of the Next Millennium", 15 *J. Int'l Arb*. 5, sections I and II (1998).

126 Müller, "Fast-Track Arbitration: Meeting the Demands of the Next Millennium", 15 *J. Int'l Arb*.. 5, sections I and II (1998).

127 Müller, "Fast-Track Arbitration: Meeting the Demands of the Next Millennium", 15 *J. Int'l Arb*.. 5, section IV (1998).

128 Müller, "Fast-Track Arbitration: Meeting the Demands of the Next Millennium", 15 *J. Int'l Arb*.. 5, section 1 (1998).

129 Müller, "Fast-Track Arbitration: Meeting the Demands of the Next Millennium", 15 *J. Int'l Arb*.. 5, section 11(2) (1998).

Industry (GMAC) have devised rules for fast-track arbitration.[130] Even so, the rules differ regarding applicability to arbitration proceedings, the time frame for rendering award, nature of the hearing, documents submitted, and procedural limitations.[131]

One disadvantage of fast-track arbitration rules is that courts may be more likely to set aside awards over due process concerns. For instance, limitations on hearings under certain fast-track arbitration rules may raise due process concerns in some jurisdictions. Many rules provide for limited time of hearings.[132] The AAA and JCAA, for example, provide that the hearing must be completed within one day.[133]

In many nations, including the United States, however, the hearing symbolizes the parties' right to present a case and is viewed at the core of the dispute settlement procedure. Under United States federal law, for instance, failure to grant parties an oral hearing is regarded as a violation of due process.[134]

This distinction, among others, may cause some courts concern that fast-track arbitration rules do not give parties a chance to fairly and fully present their case.[135] Of particular concern to some courts is that the application of fast-track arbitration rules is linked to a threshold in some arbitration institutions such that, having subscribed to the rules of a particular arbitral institution, parties automatically consent to the application of fast-track arbitration procedures when the amount claimed does not reach a certain threshold.[136]

---

130 Müller, "Fast-Track Arbitration: Meeting the Demands of the Next Millennium", 15 *J. Int'l Arb*. 5, section 111(3) (1998).

131 Müller, "Fast-Track Arbitration: Meeting the Demands of the Next Millennium", 15 *J. Int'l Arb*. 5, section 111(3) (1998).

132 Müller, "Fast-Track Arbitration: Meeting the Demands of the Next Millennium", 15 *J Int'l Arb*. 5, section 111(5) (1998).

133 Müller, "Fast-Track Arbitration: Meeting the Demands of the Next Millennium", 15 *J. Int'l Arb*. 5, section 111(5) (1998) (citing article 56 of the American Arbitration Association Rules and article 58 of the JCAA Rules). Both rules, however, provide for an extension of the hearing, if necessary. The CIETAC Rules, as well as those of the China Maritime Arbitration Commission (CMAC) and the Arbitration Institute of the Stockholm Chamber of Commerce (SCC), do not require any restrictions on time but do provide that to have a hearing, the arbitrator must deem it appropriate, as is stated by the CIETAC and CMAC or necessary as in the SCC. Müller, "Fast-Track Arbitration: Meeting the Demands of the Next Millennium", 15 *J. Int'l Arb*. 5, section 111(5) (1998) (citing article 67 of the CIETAC and CMAC Rules and article 16 of the SCC Rules).

134 Müller, "Fast-Track Arbitration: Meeting the Demands of the Next Millennium", 15 *J. Int'l Arb*. 5, section 111(5) (1998).

135 Müller, "Fast-Track Arbitration: Meeting the Demands of the Next Millennium", 15 *J. Int'l Arb*. 5, section III(2) (1998).

136 This principle is true with respect to the CIETAC, CMAC, JCAA, and AAA Rules. The WIPO, CCIG, and SCC Rules, on the contrary, require the parties' express consent to fast-track arbitration. Müller, "Fast-Track Arbitration: Meeting the Demands of the Next Millennium", 15 *J. Int'l Arb*. 5, section 111(2) (1998).

As a result, some courts may be concerned that parties are limiting their rights without specific and actual voluntary waiver of that right or notice of the same. As a result, some courts may be concerned that parties are limiting their rights without specific and actual voluntary waiver of that right or notice of the same.[137] Accordingly, due process concerns are less prevalent in cases where the parties agree on the rules of procedure before a dispute arises, but present increased challenges in cases where the parties did not agree beforehand to the accelerated processes and procedures the accelerated processes and procedures.[138] Due process concerns may thus be ameliorated if the parties agree at time of contracting to the particular dispute mechanism and the rules of procedure, including, in particular, whether fast-track arbitration is a permissible option whether fast-track arbitration is a permissible option.[139]

Regardless of whether the form of arbitration chosen is traditional or fast-track, one problem that continues to plague arbitration is the disparate enforcement of arbitral awards. The New York Convention on the Recognition and Enforcement of Foreign Arbitral Awards[140] was promulgated by the United Nations in 1958 to address this issue. Today, approximately 136 states are signatory parties to that treaty, including many developing nations.[141]

In essence, the treaty requires all contracting states to recognize and enforce arbitral awards made in the territory of another state, as well as domestic arbitral awards.[142] The Convention further outlines certain minimum requirements for enforcement of awards, such as requiring the arbitration agreement to be an "agreement in writing", which includes either a written arbitration clause or agreement signed by the parties or contained in an exchange of letters or telegrams.[143]

The New York Convention also permits a state to refuse to recognize and enforce an award under certain circumstances, including the following:

1. When the agreement is not valid under the law to which the parties or the contract is subject or the law of the place where the award was rendered;

---

137 Müller, "Fast-Track Arbitration: Meeting the Demands of the Next Millennium", 15 J. Int'l Arb. 5, section 111(5) (1998).

138 Müller, "Fast-Track Arbitration: Meeting the Demands of the Next Millennium", 15 J. Int'l Arb. 5, section 111(2) (1998).

139 Müller, "Fast-Track Arbitration: Meeting the Demands of the Next Millennium", 15 J. Int'l Arb. 5, section 111(2) (1998).

140 New York Convention on the Recognition and Enforcement of Foreign Arbitral Awards, 10 June 1958, 21 U.S.T. 2517; Reichman, "Global Competition Under TRIPS", 29 N.Y.U.J. Int'l. L. and P. 23, at pp. 24–26 (1996); 330 U.N.T.S. 38 [hereinafter New York Convention].

141 New York Convention, article I; United Nations Treaties at http://untreaty.un.org/ENGLISH/bible/englishinternetbible/partI/chapterXXII/treaty1.asp (visited 15 February 2005).

142 New York Convention, article I; United Nations Treaties at http://untreaty.un.org/ENGLISH/bible/englishinternetbible/partI/chapterXXII/treaty1.asp (visited 15 February 2005).

143 New York Convention, article II.

2. When a party was not given proper notice or was otherwise unable to present its case;

3. When the award deals with a dispute outside the scope of the arbitration agreement;

4. When the composition of the arbitral panel or the arbitration procedure was not that contemplated by the parties, or violated the law in which the arbitration took place; or

5. When the award is not yet binding on the parties, or was suspended or set aside by a competent authority in which the award was made.[144]

Many other issues arise from language in articles I and IV of the Convention which affect the enforcement of arbitral awards. First, states differ on how to determine where an award was "made". Primarily, this could affect whether the award will be enforced, because some states have declared under article I(3) that they will only recognize and enforce awards made in another contracting state.

Differences among states' determination of where awards are "made" affect the classification of an arbitral award as foreign or domestic. For example, Panamanian law deems an arbitration award to be "foreign" if it is issued outside of Panama, or issued within Panama pursuant to an international commercial arbitration taking place in Panama. Dissimilarly, in the United States, the nature of the award depends on the nationality of the parties in the case.[145] The classification of an award as foreign or domestic may determine how the award will be enforced. For example, in Brazil, if the award is domestic, the losing party must file an annulment action to oppose its enforcement whereas, if the award is foreign, the loser must simply challenge the award in the winner's action to enforce the award.[146]

States also differ on what it means to have an agreement "in writing" under the New York Convention, although many national laws and other international conventions contain provisions which require forum selection or arbitration agreements to be in writing.[147] In particular, this issue implicates

---

144 New York Convention, article V.

145 Mason, "Seven Keys to Arbitration in Latin America", 19-2 *Mealey's Intl. Arb. Rep.* 11, section 2, paragraph 6 (2004).

146 Mason, "Seven Keys to Arbitration in Latin America", 19-2 *Mealey's Intl. Arb. Rep.* 11, section 2, paragraph 6 (2004).

147 For example, the Brussels and Lugano Conventions require a written form for prorogation agreements and the New York Convention requires "a writing" for arbitration agreements. Schneider and Kuner, "Dispute Resolution in International Electronic Commerce", 14 *J. Int'l Arb.* 5, section III(A) (1997).

contracts entered into on the Internet. Many domestic laws do not consider an agreement to be "in writing" when it is recorded by electronic means.[148]

Indeed, the language of the New York Convention (authored in 1958) does not include any reference to agreements recorded by electronic means.[149] An alternative to a signed writing under the New York Convention is an exchange of letters or telegrams; however, some states might not consider an exchange of emails in the same light as an exchange of letters or telegrams.[150] Moreover, the Convention does not address agreements that might be contained in a transcript of an online chat exchange.

Issues of sovereignty also continue to plague arbitration proceedings and enforcement of arbitral awards. When a private party chooses to contract with a state, the party invariably runs the risk that the state may decline to

---

148 Shah, "Using ADR to Resolve Online Disputes", 10 *Rich. J.L. and Tech* 25, section V(D) (2004) (citing Friedman, "Alternative Dispute Resolution and Emerging Online Technologies: Challenges and Opportunities", 19 *Hastings Comm. and Ent. L.J.* 695 (1997)). To exemplify, Dutch law requires "a writing" (Dutch Civil Procedure Law, article 1021); Italian Civil Procedure Law's definition of "a writing" only references telegrams and telexes. Schneider and Kuner, "Dispute Resolution in International Electronic Commerce", 14 *J. Int'l Arb.* 5, section III(A) (1997) (citing Italian Civil Procedure Law, article 807 (amended in 1994)). Moreover, German law requires arbitration agreements to be in writing (*Schriftform*), which means "written on paper", unless the parties are considered to be merchants (*Vollkauflettte*) under the meaning of the Commercial Code. Schneider and Kuner, "Dispute Resolution in International Electronic Commerce", 14 *J. Int'l Arb.* 5, section III (1997) (citing German Civil Procedure Law, article 1027(1) and (2) and German Commercial Code, article 4). Other national laws are more flexible regarding the writing requirement. Swiss law, for instance, provides that an international arbitral agreement "may take any form which permits it to be evidenced by a text" such that electronically transmitted arbitral agreements are arguably valid. Schneider and Kuner, "Dispute Resolution in International Electronic Commerce", 14 *J. Int'l Arb.* 5, section III (1997). Indonesia also recognizes e-mail as a form of writing, although it requires, at a minimum, a record of receipt. Mills, Firmansyah, and Woelandara, Effective Formation of Contracts by Electronic Means and Dispute Resolution in the New E-conomy (2000), at p. 10 (citing the authors' unofficial translation of Indonesian Law Number 30 of 1999, article 4).

149 "The term 'agreement in writing' shall include an arbitral clause in a contract or an arbitration agreement, signed by the parties or contained in an exchange of letters or telegrams". New York Convention, article II(2). Despite expressed inclusion of electronic arbitration agreements in the New York Convention, some scholars interpret the Convention's language and aims to implicitly include such agreements. Wahab, "The Global Information Society and Online Dispute Resolution: A New Dawn for Dispute Resolution", 21 J. *Int'l Arb.* 143, section IV(A) (2004); Arsic, "International Commercial Arbitration on the Internet", 14 *J. Int'l Arb.* 209 (Number 3, 1997); Hill, "Online Arbitration: Issues and Solutions", 15 *Arb. Int'l* 199 (Number 2, 1999), at http://www.umass.edu/dispute/hill.htm (visited 2 February 2005); Schellekens, "Online Arbitration and E-Commerce", 9 *Electronic Communication L. Rev.* 119 (2002).

150 Japan, for example, requires that the agreement be contained in hard copy documents. Ohno and Tsunematsu, *Commentary to the Arbitration Law of Japan*, section I, at http://www.klumerarbitration.com (visited 27 January 2005).

submit to the jurisdiction of the arbitral tribunal, or the state may plea sovereign immunity when the private party attempts to enforce the award. Some states have addressed this issue with domestic legislation, case law, or regional agreements. For example, the European Union Convention on State Immunity[151] provides that when a contracting state has agreed in writing to submit to arbitration, it may not claim sovereign immunity from jurisdiction in any proceeding relating to the validity of the agreement or enforcement of the award.[152]

The scope of these treaties, legislation, and case law, however, is limited. Other states persist in using sovereign immunity as a bar to arbitration proceedings or enforcement of awards against the state. For example, in a recent International Chamber of Commerce arbitration proceeding involving a contract dispute between a private party and an entity of the state of Brazil, the state intervened to suspend the proceeding, stating that a state entity may only use arbitration in their contracts if they are granted explicit statutory authority to do so.[153] Similar cases in Brazil punctuate the problems with attempting to contract with entities of the state in Brazil — yet, Brazil is a party to the New York Convention.[154]

Finally, regional or local bias may affect the enforcement of arbitral awards, placing arbitration on the same footing as national courts. For example, commentators note concern that, in China, some courts do not enforce arbitral awards against local entities due to bias.[155]

(iii) Mediation

Mediation is a traditional, non-binding form of alternative dispute resolution with its own set of advantages and disadvantages. Mediation is:

> . . . the process by which the participants, together with the assistance of a neutral person or persons, systematically isolate disputed issues to develop options, consider alternatives, and reach a consensual settlement that will accommodate their needs will accommodate their needs.[156]

---

151 European Convention on State Immunity (E.T.S. Number 74) (entered into force 11 June 1976) at http://www.server.law.wits.ac.za/humanrts/euro/ets74.html.

152 European Union Convention on State Immunity, article 12(2).

153 Mason, "Seven Keys to Arbitration in Latin America", 19-2 *Mealey's Intl. Arb. Rep.* 11, section 1(b), paragraph 6 (2004).

154 Mason, "Seven Keys to Arbitration in Latin America", 19-2 *Mealey's Intl. Arb. Rep.* 11, section 2, paragraph 1 (2004).

155 Harpole, "Factors Affecting the Growth (or Lack Thereof) of Arbitration in the Asia Region", 20(1) *J. Int'l Arb.* 89, at p. 95 (2003).

156 Ciaraco, "Forget the Mechanics and Bring in the Gardeners", 9 *U. Balt. Intell. Prop. J.*, 47, at p. 53 (2000); Folberg and Taylor, *Mediation — A Comprehensive Guide to Resolving Conflicts Without Litigation* (1984), at p. 7.

Successful mediation depends on the relationship between mediator and the parties as mediation resolves problems by focusing on parties' relations, and not the rights involved.[157]

This philosophy differs fundamentally from right-determinative forums such as arbitration and traditional court forums, which solve disputes in one case. Settlement through compromise, however, affords the parties the opportunity to understand each other better and aids in maintaining relationships. Furthermore, as in arbitration, mediators with technical expertise may help reduce costs by making the proceedings more time efficient.[158] Mediation and arbitration differ in many respects:

> Arbitration has often been criticized because disputants have frequently treated arbitration as a means for attaining individual goals, rather than as a forum for resolving disputes without confrontation. The result of this misuse of the arbitration process is that today's arbitration sessions take on all the trappings of litigation: lawyers, transcripts, formal rules of evidence and procedures, and their associated costs.[159]

On the other hand, the flexibility of:

> ... mediation adapts to parties and their interests.[160] The arbitration system ... is still strongly connected to the adversarial system and puts considerable weight on rights as opposed to interests. Mediation, however, is designed to be more concerned with addressing interests rather than rights.[161]

Mediation is not appropriate for all types of international intellectual property disputes, however. Disputes involving piracy and counterfeiting are inappropriate for mediation, because they may require immediate injunctive relief, or are strictly rights-based such that a party may wish to depend on legal precedent.[162]

Moreover, one party may be unwilling to participate in good faith, in which case the procedure will be stalled or ultimately lead to a court proceeding.[163]

---

157 Mills, "Alternative Dispute Resolution in International Intellectual Property Disputes", 11 *Ohio St. J. on Disp. Resol.* 227, at pp. 231 and 232 (1996).

158 Mills, "Alternative Dispute Resolution in International Intellectual Property Disputes", 11 *Ohio St. J. on Disp. Resol.* 227, at p. 232 (1996).

159 Ciaraco, "Forget the Mechanics and Bring in the Gardeners", 9 *U. Balt. Intell. Prop. J.*, 47, at pp. 62 and 63 (2000).

160 Ciaraco, "Forget the Mechanics and Bring in the Gardeners", 9 *U. Balt. Intell. Prop. J.*, 47, at p. 60 (2000).

161 Ciaraco, "Forget the Mechanics and Bring in the Gardeners", 9 *U. Balt. Intell Prop J.* 47, at pp. 56 and 57 (2000).

162 Plant, "Some Aspects of Mediating Intellectual Property Disputes", Panelist, Conference on Mediation, 29 March 1996, Geneva, Switzerland, at http://arbiter.wipo.int/events/conferences/1996/plant.html (visited 1 February 2005).

163 Plant, "Some Aspects of Mediating Intellectual Property Disputes", Panelist, Conference on Mediation, 29 March 1996, Geneva, Switzerland, at http://arbiter.wipo.int/events/conferences/1996/plant.html (visited 1 February 2005).

Such tactics, in turn, can serve to actually increase the costs of dispute resolution, making them greater than if the parties had turned initially to the national court system.[164] Finally, mediation is typically non-binding, thus again opening up the possibility of resort to the national court system, and increased costs.

(iv) Negotiation

Negotiation is a form of traditional arbitration that focuses, even more heavily than mediation, on the relations between, rather than the rights of, the parties. Negotiation is a collaborative dispute resolution process where parties communicate, directly or indirectly, about "the form of any joint action which they might take to manage and ultimately resolve the differences between them".[165] Negotiation is advantageous because parties work together, which leads to a compromise. This process thus benefits "disputants who seek to maintain their relationship or resolve disputes with multiple issues".[166]

In today's business world, formal dispute resolution is abhorred by most and negotiation is the precursor relied on by those who wish to resolve differences rather than fight about them. However, it is apparent that negotiations will only succeed when parties want to work together to find a solution. As with mediation, negotiation may be inappropriate for some disputes. Moreover, because negotiation lacks a neutral third-party mediator, the problems associated with mediation may be exacerbated.

(d) Online Dispute Resolution

Online dispute resolution is the newest form of alternative dispute resolution. Online dispute resolution introduces technology to the advantages of alternative dispute resolution.[167]

While not without its faults, online dispute resolution has already begun to have utility in resolving certain types of disputes (e.g., business-to-business and business-to-consumer disputes concerning goods exchanged over the Internet) and holds the promise of improving for potential use in more complex disputes

---

164 Plant, "Some Aspects of Mediating Intellectual Property Disputes", Panelist, Conference on Mediation, 29 March 1996, Geneva, Switzerland, at http://arbiter.wipo.int/events/conferences/1996/plant.html (visited 1 February 2005).

165 Ciaraco, "Forget the Mechanics and Bring in the Gardeners", 9 *U. Balt. Intell. Prop. J.* 47, at p. 53 (2000).

166 Ciaraco, "Forget the Mechanics and Bring in the Gardeners", 9 *U. Balt. Intell, Prop. J.* 47, at p. 54 (2000). Heinze, "Patent Mediation: The Forgotten Alternative in Dispute Resolution", 18 *A.I.P.L.A. Q.J.* 333, at p. 339 (1991).

167 Wahab, "The Global Information Society and Online Dispute Resolution: A New Dawn for Dispute Resolution", 21 *J. Int'l Arb.* 143, section I (2004).

with increased use and improved technology. Moreover, online dispute resolution may be an efficient solution for international disputes because it offers an international, or private, as opposed to sovereign, solution.[168]

Scholars have categorized online dispute resolution mechanisms into three groups, namely:

1. Technology-assisted online dispute resolution mechanisms used to resolve existing disputes;

2. Technology-based online dispute resolution mechanisms to resolve existing disputes; and

3. Technology-facilitated online dispute prevention that arguably aids in reducing the risk of potential e-disputes.[169]

Technology-assisted online dispute resolution mechanisms include assisted e-negotiation, e-mediation, e-arbitration,[170] online ombudsmen proceedings, and cyber-courts.[171]

The role of technology in this mechanism is primarily to facilitate communication between the parties (e.g., electronic mail communication, chat rooms,

---

168 Donahey, "Dispute Resolution in Cyberspace", 15 *J. Int'l Arb*. 127, at pp. 127 and 128 (1998).

169 Wahab, "The Global Information Society and Online Dispute Resolution: A New Dawn for Dispute Resolution", 21 *J. Int'l Arb*. 143, section I (2004).

170 The Virtual Magistrate Project (VMAG) was one of the first online alternative dispute resolution projects. Commentators have described VMAG as a "classic illustration of how online alternative dispute resolution failed, as well as a good example from which to learn for future alternative dispute resolution service providers". Shah, "Using ADR to Resolve Online Disputes", 10 *Rich. J.L. and Tech* 25, section II(A). VMAG would arbitrate any online disputes submitted to it. Arbitrators were appointed and trained by the American Arbitration Association. Friedman and Gellman, "An Information Superhighway 'On Ramp' for Alternative Dispute Resolution", 68 *N.Y.S.T.B.J*. 38, at p. 41 (1996). The primary purpose of VMAG was to "demonstrate that online technology could be used to resolve online disputes in a quick, cost-effective and accessible means" through arbitration, Shah, "Using ADR to Resolve Online Disputes", 10 *Rich. J.L. and Tech* 25, section II(A) (citing Chicago-Kent College of Law, Illinois Institute of Technology, VMAG: Online Dispute Resolution, at http://www.vmag.org (visited 15 February 2005). VMAG proceedings were held via e-mail, and decisions were required within three business days once the initial complaint was received. Shah, "Using ADR to Resolve Online Disputes", 10 *Rich. J.L. and Tech* 25, section II(A). It has been said that VMAG was largely unsuccessful because several types of complaints were not within its jurisdiction, the project was not widely advertised or used, and VMAG lacked the ability to enforce its decisions. In fact, in the only decision that VMAG rendered, one of the parties (the alleged offender) did not participate. *Tierney v. Email America*, VM Docket Number 96-001 (8 May 1996) (noting that the full text of the decided case is "coming soon"), available at http://www.vmag.org/sample.html (visited 1 February 2005); Ponte, "Throwing Bad Money after Bad: Can Online Dispute Resolution Really Help Deliver the Goods for the Unhappy Internet Shopper?", 3 *Tul. J. Tech. and Intell. Prop*. 55, at p. 64 (2001).

171 Wahab, "The Global Information Society and Online Dispute Resolution: A New Dawn for Dispute Resolution", 21 *J. Int'l Arb*. 143, section I (2004).

audio and video conferencing, message posting, and traditional offline means); secure the exchange of information; store data; house an efficient electronic filing system; and ensure the confidentiality and security of the proceedings.[172]

Technology-based online dispute resolution mechanisms include automated negotiation, multi-variable resolution optimization programs, solution-set databases, and the electronic virtual judge system.[173] Online negotiation and meditation companies allow parties to confidentially enter offers or demands online and, if the parties' offers are within a certain identified range, the dispute is settled for the median.[174]

The comparison process and other logistics, such as the number of bids allowed and settlement calculations, vary based on the programs used.[175] If the claimant is unwilling to negotiate and accept less than the actual or initial amount of the claim, however, automated negotiation may not be a feasible alternative. Other technology-based online dispute resolution mechanisms, such as multi-variable resolution optimization programs, provide the parties the ability to set forth their disputed issues and then weigh their importance.[176]

Such programs allow a party to develop different proposals to present to the opposing party and, after several proposals, the program will deliver a mathematically optimal solution to the disputes based on the parties' stated preferences and interests.[177] This process may involve a human facilitator who uses the computer analysis to help the parties weigh issues, build consensus, and objectively evaluate the issues prior to commencing settlement negotiations.[178]

---

172 Wahab, "The Global Information Society and Online Dispute Resolution: A New Dawn for Dispute Resolution", 21 *J. Int'l Arb.* 143, section II (2004).

173 Wahab, "The Global Information Society and Online Dispute Resolution: A New Dawn for Dispute Resolution", 21 *J. Int'l Arb.* 143, section II (2004).

174 Wahab, "The Global Information Society and Online Dispute Resolution: A New Dawn for Dispute Resolution", 21 *J. Int'l Arb.* 143, section II (2004).

175 Online negotiation and mediation providers include Cybersettle, MARS, Intersettle, SmartSettle, Dispute Manager, Esettle.co.uk, WeCanSettle, and SettleOnline. Wahab, "The Global Information Society and Online Dispute Resolution: A New Dawn for Dispute Resolution", 21 *J. Int'l Arb.* 143, section II (2004).

176 Such programs include Computer Aided Negotiation-Web International Network (CAN-WIN) and Smart Settle. Wahab, "The Global Information Society and Online Dispute Resolution: A New Dawn for Dispute Resolution", 21 *J. Int'l Arb.* 143, section II (2004).

177 Wahab, "The Global Information Society and Online Dispute Resolution: A New Dawn for Dispute Resolution", 21 *J. Int'l Arb.* 143, section II (2004); Rule, *Online Dispute Resolution for Business* 47, at p. 58 (2002).

178 Wahab, "The Global Information Society and Online Dispute Resolution: A New Dawn for Dispute Resolution", 21 *J. Int'l Arb.* 143, section II (2004).

It should be obvious, but perhaps its needs saying, that intellectual property rights disputes are — by their very nature — not often susceptible to resolution by mere mathematical equation. Indeed, the value of intellectual property rights is often in the "perceived advantage" of exclusivity and the revenue that can be derived from that exclusivity over time. For this reason, most contractual undertakings will contain remedial provisions that acknowledge a dispute may not be resolved by "money damages", and each party agrees an injunction may be the appropriate remedy. It follows that an online dispute resolution methodology may not achieve the "cease and desist" focus that is often the main thrust of any intellectual property rights owner in adversarial proceedings.

Online dispute prevention programs, on the other hand, work to help prevent e-disputes. Such programs include trustmark schemes, i-escrow, credit card charge backs, feedback ratings, and evaluations systems.[179] These programs work to enhance security to online transactions and minimize the risk of e-disputes. For example, i-escrow is similar to a documentary letter of credit and protects buyers' and sellers' interests in online transactions against fraud and non-performance.[180]

E-Bay, a popular web-based auction service, recommends the use of an i-escrow service for merchandise of US $500 or more.[181] Scholars assert that post-dispute online dispute resolution systems may draw their binding force from Online Dispute Prevention mechanisms that create incentives to perform (such as trustmark schemes and feedback rating systems) or self-enforcing mechanisms (including i-escrow services and credit card charge-back mechanisms).[182]

Online dispute resolution is most useful to resolve e-commerce disputes over small amounts of money or inexpensive goods that arise from business-to-business contracts or business-to-consumer contracts initiated on the Internet.[183] Online dispute resolution may be particularly well-suited to resolving these type of disputes because the parties presumably already have

---

179 Wahab, "The Global Information Society and Online Dispute Resolution: A New Dawn for Dispute Resolution", 21 *J. Int'l Arb*. 143, section III (2004).

180 Wahab, "The Global Information Society and Online Dispute Resolution: A New Dawn for Dispute Resolution", 21 *J. Int'l Arb*. 143, section III (2004).

181 Wahab, "The Global Information Society and Online Dispute Resolution: A New Dawn for Dispute Resolution", 21 *J. Int'l Arb*. 143, section III (2004); eBay, http://pages.ebay.com/help/community/escrow.html (visited 1 February 2005).

182 Wahab, "The Global Information Society and Online Dispute Resolution: A New Dawn for Dispute Resolution", 21 *J. Int'l Arb*. 143, section III (2004).

183 Wahab, "The Global Information Society and Online Dispute Resolution: A New Dawn for Dispute Resolution", 21 *J. Int'l Arb*. 143, section I (2004).

some familiarity with operating the Internet, have e-mail facilities, and the parties have an online financial relationship.[184]

In such cases, disputants may not otherwise have a forum to resolve disputes due in part to the expense and time involved in litigation and alternative dispute resolution.[185] Online dispute resolution also has achieved marked success in the realm of domain name disputes. WIPO is the primary accredited domain name dispute resolution provider pursuant to the Uniform Domain Name Dispute Resolution Policy (UDRP) adopted by the Internet Corporation for Assigned Names and Numbers (ICANN).[186]

Registrants agree to resolve disputes related to domain names under UDRP at the time a domain name is registered.[187] Scholars assert that this policy provides for efficient and quick resolution of "cases involving 'bad faith' use of domain name confusingly similar or identical to those of trade marks in which the complainant has a right".[188] Indeed, WIPO touts its process as taking only 14 days. So far, experienced lawyers report that it is working and that it may be safe to observe this as one of the most expedient services available for focused disposition of domain name controversies.

In general, online dispute resolution appears to be most useful in resolving monetary disputes as certain online dispute resolution programs may facilitate the bargaining process between the parties and encourage more expedient resolutions to disputes.[189] Online dispute resolution has many advantages over national court systems or traditional alternative dispute resolution methods, including lower costs, speed of resolution, neutrality of forum, and the offer of a non-confrontational means to resolve disputes.[190]

---

184 Shah, "Using ADR to Resolve Online Disputes", 10 *Rich. J.L. and Tech*. 25, section III(A) (2004). For example, online dispute resolution may be used to resolve disputes concerning delivery of products, enforcing warranties, guaranteeing productions, and billing issues, among others.

185 Wahab, "The Global Information Society and Online Dispute Resolution: A New Dawn for Dispute Resolution", 21 J. *Int'l Arb*. 143, section I (2004).

186 Shah, "Using ADR to Resolve Online Disputes", 10 *Rich. J.L. and Tech* 25, section II(A), *supra* note 151, Section II (C).

187 Shah, "Using ADR to Resolve Online Disputes", 10 *Rich. J.L. and Tech* 25, section II(A), *supra* note 151, Section II (C).

188 Appleton and Troller, "Domain Name Arbitrations — A Review of Selected Decisions", 18 *ASA Bull*. 716, 1 (2000). Despite its criticisms, the Policy does not always result in a win for the "big guy". For instance, the singer Sting lost the rights to "sting.com" to a party who argued that "sting" is a common English word, and that he had used the word in video games since the mid-90's. Many other similar examples exist and, as one author notes, "[o]ften it is cases where the 'big guy' loses that raise the most interesting policy questions".

189 Shah, "Using ADR to Resolve Online Disputes", 10 *Rich. J.L. and Tech* 25, section II(A).

190 Shah, "Using ADR to Resolve Online Disputes", 10 *Rich. J.L. and Tech* 25, section IV.

Some scholars have also suggested that online dispute resolution may diminish the jurisdictional and choice-of-law problems inherent in a borderless Internet.[191] However, it also must be noted that issues related to choice of substantive law will remain even when parties include a choice of law provision in the online agreement to submit to arbitration via an online provider.[192]

Online dispute resolution is not without its disadvantages, however, including some that are novel to the forum (e.g., lack of personal interaction/ miscommunication, inadequate confidentiality and security, inadequate authenticity and insufficient accessibility and user sophistication).[193] Obstacles to online dispute resolution also arise in several other areas relevant to arbitration law. Online arbitration agreements, in particular, may face problems with their validity pursuant to the "in writing" requirement.[194]

Many national and international laws require arbitration agreements to be in writing, however, many national laws do not consider agreements recorded by electronic means to be "in writing".[195] Consequently, it may be difficult to enforce online arbitration awards in jurisdictions that do not recognize online arbitration agreements as being "in writing".[196]

Even if online arbitration agreements are considered to satisfy the "in writing" requirement under many laws, such agreements may still face enforceability problems. For example, the arbitration laws of some nations disallow arbitration where the parties have significantly unequal positions in bargaining power as void against public policy to protect consumers.[197] This may be a particular obstacle in resolving disputes arising from business-to-consumer transactions wherein consumers do not generally have an opportunity to negotiate terms of arbitration agreements.

---

191 Lide, "ADR and Cyberspace: The Role of Alternative Dispute Resolution in Online Commerce, Intellectual Property, and Defamation", 12 *Ohio St. J. Disp. Resol.* 193, at p. 200 (1996).

192 See Lide, "ADR and Cyberspace: The Role of Alternative Dispute Resolution in Online Commerce, Intellectual Property, and Defamation", 12 *Ohio St. J. Disp. Resol.* 193, at p. 200 (1996); see also Shah, "Using ADR to Resolve Online Disputes", 10 *Rich. J.L. and Tech* 25, section II(A).

193 Shah, "Using ADR to Resolve Online Disputes", 10 *Rich. J.L. and Tech*. 25, section V.

194 Shah, "Using ADR to Resolve Online Disputes", 10 *Rich. J.L. and Tech*. 25, section IV(D).

195 Shah, "Using ADR to Resolve Online Disputes", 10 *Rich. J.L. and Tech* 25, section V.

196 Shah, "Using ADR to Resolve Online Disputes", 10 *Rich. J.L. and Tech* 25, section V(D).

197 Shah, "Using ADR to Resolve Online Disputes", 10 *Rich. J.L. and Tech*. 25, section V(D) (2004); Schultz, "Online Arbitration: Binding or Non-Binding?, *ADR Online Monthly*, at http://www.ombuds.org/center/adr2002-11-schultz.html (visited 2 February 2005).

If this is so, it follows that transfers of technology from the "haves" to the "have-nots" may involve unequal bargaining power on the face of the documents. In such circumstances, the owner of the intellectual property rights can take little comfort in a document that provides it with substantial enforcement rights where the fundamental public order of a state may declare the agreement void.

Another roadblock to enforcement of online awards is that many national and international arbitration laws require an arbitration award to state where the award was rendered and require the signature of the entire tribunal. Online arbitration presents problems if the members of the tribunal arbitrate from different jurisdictions, or the award is signed electronically. To minimize the potential effect of this issue, some scholars suggest that online arbitration awards should be printed and a hard copy of the award signed by all of the members of the tribunal to better ensure enforceability of the award.[198]

Moreover, the circumvention of a state's jurisdiction or choice of law that is advantageous in online dispute resolution also may promote difficulties in enforcing awards.[199] Indeed, the very circumvention of a state's jurisdiction or laws may be unjust to the party against whom enforcement is sought and thus be contrary to the enforcing state's public policy.[200]

It also may be difficult to locate another party on the Internet or the location of a party's assets from which the award will be satisfied.[201] The above issues related to enforceability of online arbitration agreements and awards, among others, may decrease confidence in online dispute resolution to resolve more complex, international disputes, including those related to information and communication technology transfers or intellectual property, if they are not addressed.

(e) Case Studies: How Problems with Current Forums May Depress the World Summit on the Information Society's Goals

(i) National Courts

Pursuing intellectual property claims in the domestic courts of developing nations can be time-consuming, expensive, and lead to inconsistent results, in part because the law is often in flux and courts are not always informed

---

198 Mills, Firmansyah, and Woelandara, *Effective Formation of* Contracts by Electronic Means and Dispute Resolution in the New E-conomy 1, at p. 12 (2000).

199 Shah, "Using ADR to Resolve Online Disputes", 10 *Rich. J.L. and Tech* 25, section V(F).

200 Krause, "Do You Want to Step Outside? An Overview of Online Alternative Dispute Resolution, 19 *J. Marshall J. Computer and Info. L.* 457, at p. 475 (2001).

201 Shah, "Using ADR to Resolve Online Disputes", 10 *Rich. J.L. and Tech* 25; Perritt, Jr., "Economic and Other Barriers to Electronic Commerce", 21 *U. Pa. J. Int'l. Econ. L.* 563, at pp. 571 and 572 (2000).

regarding changes in the law.[202] For example, the pharmaceutical company Eli Lilly recently sued a Chinese company in Chinese court for patent violations.[203]

The lower court found no patent violation, but based its decision, in part, on a procedural error in which it did not permit Eli Lilly to cross-examine the defendant's witnesses. Eli Lilly appealed to the Supreme People's Court, which overturned the lower court's decision, and remanded the case for decision.[204] As of December 2004, the case was not yet resolved.[205]

Although the Supreme Court ultimately overturned the lower court's decision, Eli Lilly was still forced to engage in protracted foreign litigation to protect its rights. Moreover, Eli Lilly's troubles may not yet be over. Practitioners note that, in China, even if parties can track down the violating companies and get a favorable decision in a national court, local judges will often refuse to enforce the rulings.[206]

China acceded to the WTO in 2001.[207] Judge Jiang of the People's Supreme Court asserts that since then, Chinese courts are improving at enforcing intellectual property rights.[208] In fact, there is a concerted effort to improve the enforcement of intellectual property rights in China, through training of judges and prosecutors.[209] However, some private companies, such as Eli

---

202 Luh, "Let 100 Capitalists Bloom; China pries open some of its rules and regulations ahead of the WTO timetable. However, that's still not enough", 10 *Corp. Counsel* 132 (2003).

203 Ning, "Judicial Protection of Intellectual Property Rights in China, Courts More Cognizant of Intellectual Property Rights", *China Daily*, available at http://www.chinaiprlaw.com (visited 3 February 2005). Liu, Shen and Associates, list of intellectual property cases, at http://www.liu-shen.com/news02_en.asp (visited 4 February 2005).

204 Ning, "Judicial Protection of Intellectual Property Rights in China, Courts More Cognizant of Intellectual Property Rights", *China Daily*, available at http://www.chinaiprlaw.com (visited 3 February 2005); Liu, Shen and Associates, List of Intellectual Property Cases, at http://www.liu-shen.com/news02_en.asp (visited 4 February 2005).

205 Guogiang, "Injunctive Relief in China: A Judicial Perspective, China Intellectual Property Focus 2004", at http://www.legalmediagroup.com/Mintellectual property/default.asp?Page=1&SID=2227&ImgName=chinaintellectual propertyfocus04.gif&=F=F (visited 4 February 2005).

206 Luh, "Let 100 Capitalists Bloom; China pries open some of its rules and regulations ahead of the WTO timetable. However, that's still not enough", 10 *Corp. Counsel* 132 (2003).

207 World Trade Organization, Accessions, at http://www.wto.org (visited 7 February 2005).

208 Ning, "Judicial Protection of Intellectual Property Rights in China, Courts More Cognizant of Intellectual Property Rights", *China Daily*, available at http://Iwww.chinaiprlaw.com (visited 3 February 2005).

209 Luh, "Let 100 Capitalists Bloom; China pries open some of its rules and regulations ahead of the WTO timetable. However, that's still not enough", 10 *Corp. Counsel* 132 (2003).

Lilly, may find that the prospect of facing Chinese court proceedings chill their desire to invest in China.[210]

(ii) International Arbitration

The current system of arbitration pursuant to bilateral investment treaties and the International Center for Settlement of Investment Disputes also has failed in some instances concerning investment-related disputes. For example, in two recent arbitrations before *ad hoc* International Center for Settlement of Investment Disputes tribunals, the tribunals reached opposite conclusions on the question of the tribunals' jurisdiction over the claims, even though jurisdiction was alleged under virtually identical bilateral investment treaties provisions.

In *Société Générale v. Pakistan*,[211] the claimant, a Swiss company (*Société Générale de Surveillance SA*) entered into a contract with Pakistan. When a dispute arose between the parties, *Société Générale de Surveillance SA* pursued arbitration through International Center for Settlement of Investment Disputes pursuant to a 1995 bilateral investment treaty between Switzerland and Pakistan.[212]

The claims included pure contract claims that were not based on an alleged violation of the treaty. *Société Générale de Surveillance SA* argued that the tribunal had jurisdiction over the pure contract claims because of the presence of an "umbrella clause" in the bilateral investment treaty, stating that:

> ... [e]ither Contracting Party shall constantly guarantee the observance of commitments it has entered into with respect to the investments of the other Contracting Party.[213]

The Tribunal rejected this argument and found that it did not have jurisdiction over the pure contract claims. The Tribunal opined that the bilateral investment treaty's umbrella clause could not be read to extend to disputes beyond those involving a breach of international law without

---

210 Luh, "Let 100 Capitalists Bloom; China pries open some of its rules and regulations ahead of the WTO timetable. However, that's still not enough", 10 *Corp. Counsel* 132 (2003). Specifically, this article cites the problems with enforcement of rights as a reason why biomedical companies are reluctant to build research and development facilities in China.

211 *Société Générale de Surveillance SA v. Islamic Republic of Pakistan*, International Center for Settlement of Investment Disputes Case Number ARB/01/13 (2003), available at http://ita.law.uvic.ca.

212 Agreement between the Swiss Confederation and the Islamic Republic of Pakistan on the Promotion and Reciprocal Protection of Investments, 11 July 1995 [hereinafter Switzerland–Pakistan Bilateral Investment Treaty].

213 Switzerland–Pakistan Bilateral Investment Treaty, article 11.

clear and convincing evidence that the parties to the treaty, i.e., Switzerland and Pakistan, so intended.[214]

On the other hand, in the later case of *Société Générale de Surveillance SA v. Philippines*,[215] *Société Générale de Surveillance SA* entered into a contract with the Philippines. When a dispute arose between the two parties, *Société Générale de Surveillance SA* again pursued arbitration through the International Center for Settlement of Investment Disputes pursuant to a 1999 bilateral investment treaty between Switzerland and The Philippines.[216]

As in *Société Générale de Surveillance SA v. Pakistan*, the claims included pure contract claims. In this case, however, the tribunal determined that it did have jurisdiction to hear the contract claim, despite the fact that its jurisdiction was based in the bilateral investment treaty and the contract claim did not involve claims of a breach of international law. In this case, the bilateral investment treaty's umbrella clause provided that:

> . . . [e]ach Contracting Party shall observe any obligation it has assumed
> with regard to specific investments in its territory by investors of the
> other Contracting Party.[217]

The tribunal read "any obligation" to be more expansive than the Switzerland–Pakistan bilateral investment treaties umbrella clause, and concluded that it included pure contract disputes in addition to violations of international law.[218]

Although both arbitrations took place under the guise of the International Center for Settlement of Investment Disputes and included similar service contracts and virtually identical bilateral investment treaty umbrella clauses, the results were entirely inconsistent. Such disputes arising from investment contracts between a private party and a state will only increase with efforts to enhance participation in the Information Society.

However, absent reform, a party's ability to pursue arbitration of these types of disputes under the International Center for Settlement of Investment Disputes

---

214 *Société Générale de Surveillance SA v. Islamic Republic of Pakistan*, International Center for Settlement of Investment Disputes Case Number ARB/01/13 (2003), available at http://ita.law.uvic.ca.

215 *Société Générale de Surveillance SA v. Philippines*, International Center for Settlement of Investment Disputes Case Number ARB 2/6 (2003), available at http://ita.law.uvic.ca.

216 Agreement on the Promotion and Reciprocal Protection of Investments, 31 March 1997, Switzerland-Philippines (in force 23 April 1999) [hereinafter Switzerland–Philippines Bilateral Investment Treaty].

217 Switzerland-Philippines Bilateral Investment Treaty, article II.

218 *Societé Genérale de Surveillance S.A. v. Philippines*, International Center for Settlement of Investment Disputes Case Number ARB 2/6 (2003), available at http://ita.law.uvic.ca.

pursuant to its nation's bilateral investment treaties may be unclear and force such parties into other arbitration institutions or national court systems.

12.04 Prescription for a Remedy

(a) In General

The inconsistencies and problems of current forums as described above lead to the question of whether these and other current methods of dispute resolution are adequate, or whether there may exist a better solution. This author concludes that the current methods for resolving disputes of the nature discussed in this chapter are insufficient and that one or more proposed alternatives may better equip the global community to handle the panoply of disputes that will inevitably arise with efforts to increase participation in the Information Society.

Given the problems of enforcement of foreign judgments and issues of neutrality, the best solution may be to remove these disputes from the national courts. However, relegating these disputes to traditional alternative dispute resolution methods, commercial arbitration in particular, also is problematic because it presupposes that parties have agreed to arbitrate disputes and that such agreements are enforceable. Thus, simply recognizing that arbitration may be the best overall solution for these disputes does not address the issues of jurisdiction, arbitrability, and enforcement, among other issues raised above.

Creating a default forum for these disputes, from which parties presumably could opt out, much like parties can opt out of legal proceedings in domestic courts through arbitration agreements, will aid in the efficiency of dispute resolution and harmonize procedures and outcomes such that private entities (and states) can be assured that any intellectual property or other disputes arising from an information and communication technology transfer will, at the very least, be resolved according to generally agreed upon procedural principles.

Moreover, granting a panel and subsequent domestic or foreign court jurisdiction over a state against whom an award is rendered better assures the party seeking to contract with that state enforcement of an award in the event of a dispute. A default forum also will help stem some of the rising costs related to disputes over jurisdiction. However, to address these and other concerns, and to create such a default forum, some type of modification to the current arbitration reality is required.

(b) United Nations Involvement

The United Nations has taken a lead role in the movement to increase participation in the Information Society as evidenced, in part, by the World Summit on the Information Society. The participation of the United Nations began in 1998 when the International Telecommunications Union (ITU), an organization within the United Nations system, instructed its Secretary-General to place the question of holding a World Summit on the Information Society on the agenda of the United Nations Administrative Committee on Coordination (ACC).[219]

When the idea of such a summit was favorably received, the ITU went forward with the concept under the patronage of the United Nations Secretary-General, with ITU taking the lead role in preparations. The United Nations General Assembly then endorsed the Summit, and preparations for the World Summit on the Information Society, to be held in two phases, began.[220]

The World Summit on the Information Society Plan of Action, developed at the Geneva Summit, states that:

> ... [t]he commitment of the private sector is important in developing and diffusing information and communication technologies . . . , for infrastructure, content, and applications. The private sector is not only a market player but also plays a role in a wider sustainable development context.[221]

The Plan of Action plainly memorializes the commonly held belief that the private sector and its economic resources are invaluable to carrying out the World Summit on the Information Society's goals. Recognizing the private sector's concerns about, among other things, legal protection of its intellectual property rights and infrastructure invested in developing nations, the Plan of Action also includes, as a goal:

> ... [e]ncourag[ing] the ongoing work in the area of effective dispute settlement systems, notably alternative dispute resolution . . . , which can promote settlement of disputes.[222]

In addition to its expertise regarding the Information Society and its past experience in conceiving, bringing to fruition, and governing other dispute resolution international forums,[223] the multi-national nature of the United

---

219 The United Nations Administrative Committee on Coordination is now the United Nations System Chief Executive Board, CEB.

220 Background information on the World Summit on the Information Society is available at http://www.itu.int/wsis/basic/background.html (visited 24 January 2005).

221 World Summit on the Information Society Plan of Action (WSIS-03/GENEVA/DOC/0005), at http://www.itu.int/wsis (3 February 2005), paragraph A(3)(b).

222 World Summit on the Information Society Plan of Action (WSIS-03/GENEVA/DOC/0005), at http://www.itu.int/wsis (3 February 2005), paragraph C6(k).

223 These include the International Court of Justice, the International Criminal Court, and the International Criminal Tribunal for the Former Yugoslavia, and the International Criminal Tribunal for Rwanda.

Nations is, on its face, a substantial benefit to its involvement in improving dispute resolution methods for intellectual property rights and related information and communication technology issues.

One need only briefly review the controversy over domain name and other Internet governance issues to understand why so many would prefer to imbue the responsibility of an international forum in a multi-national body such as the United Nations.[224]

The credibility of the United Nations as a sponsor of advances in the Information Society must be distinguished from its oft-perceived lack of credibility as a regulator or enforcement mechanism of rights. Moreover, the United Nations has, in recent times, lost some of its credibility as a consensus-builder or, at least, its ability to include the United States in its consensus building. These issues do not merely permeate the highly publicized area of conflicts over nuclear proliferation, but have even infested the World Summit on the Information Society.

For example, the United States, which currently and for the foreseeable future maintains at least indirect control over the administration of domain names through ICANN, is not a member of the World Summit on the Information Society's Working Group on Internet Governance (WGIG).[225] Moreover, pure "consensus building" of the type generally pursued by the United Nations, will not necessarily represent the concerns of the private parties who will be the primary investors/losers in information and communication technology transfer, in particular, *vis-à-vis* intellectual property rights.

(c) Expanding TRIPS Dispute Settlement Procedures to Private Parties

One potential, but limited, solution is to expand the WTO's Understanding on Dispute Settlement procedures to private party claims. This solution would be limited in scope, as it would only be available for the resolution of claims brought by private parties to the effect that states are not protecting their intellectual property rights according to the minimum rights under TRIPS.

Therefore, it would not resolve the problems associated with pure private party disputes (such as intellectual property infringement, piracy, and private

---

224 The United States indirectly controls domain name administration via ICANN; however, many states, among them Brazil, India, Singapore, South Korea, Tunisia, and several European countries, contest this, and have called for United Nations or other inter-governmental control. Barrett, "Few Said to Fear United Nations Takeover of Internet, Washington Internet Daily", Volume 6, Number 12, 19 January 2005, available at http://www.wgig.org/docs (visited 23 January 2005).

225 WGIG Members, http://www.wgig.org/members.html (visited 2 February 2005).

party Internet transactions), because the responding private parties do not have obligations under the treaty.[226] Moreover, such a solution is limited to disputes that involve states who are TRIPS signatories because states who are not signatories to TRIPS would not have any obligations under the treaty.

Private parties could, however, bring claims against a state (as signatory to the treaty) if the state itself infringed its intellectual property rights, or if a private party infringed its intellectual property rights and the state failed to properly enforce its own intellectual property law, or failed to enact intellectual property protections pursuant to TRIPS, therefore permitting private parties to infringe intellectual property rights with impunity.

The WTO added TRIPS and the Understanding on Dispute Settlement during the Uruguay Round. The government of each state determines whether a claim should be made to the WTO's Dispute Settlement Board (DSB). Allowable claims include violations of the TRIPS agreement, which include the incorporated sections of the Berne Convention. There are two types of TRIPS claims, a violation complaint and a non-violation complaint.

A violation complaint involves a claim that a benefit under TRIPS is nullified or impaired by the laws or other measures taken by another member state.[227] A non-violation complaint involves a claim that an objective of TRIPS is impeded as a result of a measure taken by another member state, regardless of whether that measure actually violates TRIPS.[228]

A finding that the state has violated TRIPS can lead to recommendations by the DSB that violators must conform with the treaty, pay compensation to the complaining state, allow the complaining party to suspend trade concessions granted to the violating state, or other trade obligations.[229]

There is great debate over private party standing under the Understanding on Dispute Settlement, the full reach of which is outside the scope of this chapter. However, it is helpful to highlight some of the advantages and disadvantages

---

226 World Trade Organization Understanding on Rules and Procedures Governing the Settlement of Disputes, Annex 2 to the Agreement Establishing the World Trade Organization, (1994) article 1.

227 Dreyfuss and Lowenfeld, Symposium: "Intellectual Property Law in the International Marketplace — Trade-Related Aspects of International Property Rights — Enforcement and Dispute Resolution - Principle Paper: Two Achievements of the Uruguay Round: Putting TRIPS and Dispute Settlement Together", 37 *Va. J. Int'l L.* 275, at p. 283 (1997).

228 Dreyfuss and Lowenfeld, Symposium: "Intellectual Property Law in the International Marketplace — Trade-Related Aspects of International Property Rights — Enforcement and Dispute Resolution - Principle Paper: Two Achievements of the Uruguay Round: Putting TRIPS and Dispute Settlement Together", 37 *Va. J. Int'l L.* 275, at p. 283 (1997).

229 World Trade Organization Understanding on Rules and Procedures Governing the Settlement of Disputes, Annex 2 to the Agreement Establishing the World Trade Organization (1994), articles 19 and 22.

of allowing private party standing under the Understanding on Dispute Settlement to give the reader a taste of the debate, and place it in the context of information and communication technology transfer. There are several benefits to permitting a private party to bring claims against TRIPS member states.

First, permitting private party actions gives private party investors a degree of security that they will be able to enforce an already accepted legal minimum standard of protection for their intellectual property rights. They will thus not be subject to a lower standard at the national level if the state has not yet implemented TRIPS provisions. Nor will they find themselves without remedy if the state has infringed their intellectual property rights, but has claimed sovereign immunity in a domestic action.[230]

Furthermore, if the private party has pursued an action on the domestic level against a state, but has been unsuccessful because the state either did not enact the minimum level of protection or did not enforce it, the private party will have recourse, at least against the state. This security may motivate the private sector to engage in information and communication technology transfers, furthering the World Summit on the Information Society's goals. Likewise, a suit against the state may cause the state to seek compliance from offending persons in its jurisdiction. State leverage against private persons and entities may be much more substantial than ordinary litigation brought within the jurisdiction by a foreigner.

Second, private party standing may increase treaty enforcement. States may be hesitant to bringing an action against another state for TRIPS violations because of diplomatic relations which are completely unrelated to intellectual property, or any aspect of trade.[231] For instance, a state may refuse or delay effort to enforce TRIPS against another state for fear of jeopardizing its diplomatic relationship relevant to some other trade or military concern.

On the other hand, a private party is not constrained by the same political pressures.[232] Furthermore, a state can distinguish between actions filed by a private party and actions filed by other states.[233]

---

230 A member state subjects itself to the jurisdiction of the Understanding on Dispute Settlement; in fact, it cannot join the WTO with a reservation to the Understanding on Dispute Settlement. WTO, Introduction to the WTO dispute settlement system, Module 1.3: "Functions, objectives and key features of the dispute settlement system", at http://www.wto.org (visited 2 February 2005).

231 Schleyer, "Power to the People: Allowing Private Parties to Raise Claims before the WTO Dispute Resolution System", 65 *Fordham L. Rev.* 2275, at p. 2277 (1996–1997).

232 Schleyer, "Power to the People: Allowing Private Parties to Raise Claims before the WTO Dispute Resolution System", 65 *Fordham L. Rev.* 2275, at p. 2277 (1996–1997).

233 Schneider, "Democracy and Dispute Resolution: Individual Rights in International Trade Organizations", 19 *U. Pa. J. Int'l Econ. L.* 587, at p. 634 (1998).

Thus, if a private party is permitted to file complaints against states that violate TRIPS, it will have the positive effect of increasing treaty enforcement without jeopardizing diplomacy. A state also may be cautious about bringing a claim against another state for a TRIPS violation for fear that it will, in turn, be implicated for its own TRIPS or other treaty violations.[234] Private party actions can overcome this collusion or impasse, causing not only the direct effect of forcing the state against whom they have brought their claim to conform to TRIPS, but also potentially causing the indirect effect of forcing their own state to conform to treaty provisions.

For all of the advantages, there also are several problems with permitting private party standing under the Understanding on Dispute Settlement. Initially, permitting such standing is contrary to the structure of the WTO, which is akin to a global representative democracy wherein states represent their constituent citizens.[235]

This, however, could be said about any treaty or international agreement. Moreover, even in a representative democracy, private citizens maintain the ability to hold their governments "in check" through the judiciary.[236] Given that private parties would only be given standing to enforce treaties, not negotiate them, there is little danger that private parties will "make" the law, rather, they will simply enforce it.

Some commentators also argue that granting private parties standing will limit their own government's ability to choose which claims to bring. This problem is two-fold. Some scholars argue that private party actions might ultimately harm the domestic industry. For example, governments are most likely to bring claims that have the greatest significance to trade.[237] As such, on a domestic level, private parties who could not afford to bring a claim themselves can pool their resources with similarly situated parties to lobby their government to bring a claim on their behalf.

Allowing private parties to bring claims directly could result in only well-funded parties, whose interests may not reflect the domestic majority, asserting claims against non-complying governments. However, it appears likely that the

---

234 Waincymer, "Transparency of Dispute Settlement within the World Trade Organization", 24 *Melb. U. L. Rev.* 797, at pp. 831 and 832 (2000).

235 Professor Philip M. Nichols argues that governments best represent their constituencies, and that the values to be balanced in this "representative democracy" should be held closely to the local level. Nichols, "Extension of Standing in the World Trade Organization Disputes to Non-Government Parties", 17 *U. Pa. J. Int'l Econ. L.* 295, at pp. 310–313 (1996).

236 For example, in the United States, private citizens can challenge state, local, or federal legislation or executive branch actions in state and federal courts.

237 Waincymer, "Transparency of Dispute Settlement within the World Trade Organization", 24 *Melb. U. L. Rev.* 797, at p. 831 (2000).

above-mentioned well-funded party is likely to have great influence with its own government, and could convince the government to bring a claim on its behalf. Prohibiting private party actions, therefore, likely does not prevent the problem of a single party imposing its interests on others in the industry.[238]

In addition, as noted above, permitting private party standing could divest states of their power to negotiate often delicate trade policies, which in turn prevents the government from using another state's non-compliance as a bargaining tool. Such a tool may force the state to comply with other WTO requirements, and/or prevent government from using another state's non-compliance as a means of diverting attention away from its own non-compliance to TRIPS or other WTO provisions. These concerns, however, ignore the argument that treaty enforcement is one of the primary goals of permitting private party standing in support of independent enforcement actions. If the by-product of a private party action against a foreign state is treaty enforcement in its own state, this is ultimately a positive side effect.

Another argument against private party standing in the Understanding on Dispute Settlement is that the remedies available thereunder do not account for correcting an injured private party's harm.[239] For example, a private party cannot force its own state to suspend concessions until the violating state has changed its laws or methods of enforcing TRIPS, but mere compensation may be insufficient to remedy the private party's harm. Thus, the Understanding on Dispute Settlement would need to reconsider available remedies to make them appropriate for the purpose envisioned.

(d) A New Merged Forum

Another potential solution lies in creating an entirely new international forum with original jurisdiction over all of these disputes. As outlined above, the problem with existing dispute resolution forums is that they do not provide sufficient legal protection, in the nature of bilateral investment treaties[240] or otherwise, to escape local protectionism and a lack of transparency in state courts that depress the goals of the World Summit on the Information Society summit. An international forum for these disputes, one that is acknowledged

---

238 Nichols, "Extension of Standing in the World Trade Organization Disputes to Non-Government Parties", 17 *U. Pa. J. Int'l* Econ. L. 295, at pp. 310-313 (1996).

239 Carmody, "Remedies and Conformity under the WTO Agreement", *J. Int'l Econ. L.* 307, at p. 316 (2002).

240 In addition, although bilateral investment treaties can help to increase information and communication technology transfers through consistent rules and a forum for disputes from which a state cannot excuse itself through sovereign immunity, they actually create an inconsistent patchwork system, as noted above in the discussion of the *Société Générale de Surveillance SA* cases.

and approved by all nations, can transcend the lack of credibility in national courts, the burdens and inefficiencies of existing alternative dispute resolution, and the questioned legitimacy of online dispute resolution.

There are several advantages to such a forum. First, it provides default jurisdiction for these disputes, along with consistent procedural and evidentiary rules. Furthermore, it will create a body of consistent jurisprudence that will produce precedent for future actions, thereby providing all parties involved with some insight, before they enter a contract, into how a potential dispute will be resolved.

Finally, scholars identify several benefits to specialized intellectual property and technology forums, including experienced judges who can provide reasoned and consistent decisions, an ability to focus resources on specific training and knowledge of current developments in the field, and, as noted, a consistent body of law on which parties can rely.[241]

For all of its advantages, this solution also presents many hurdles, many of which are logistical. For example, given the range of disputes related to the Information Society, it is inevitable that parties to these disputes will run the gamut from developed states, to developing states, to private parties. The question arises whether it is appropriate to open one forum as a venue for disputes to which both states and private parties may bring claims. Notwithstanding this legitimate concern, other international forums do permit some private party disputes in addition to state party disputes.

For example, private parties may bring claims against states under the North American Free Trade Agreement (NAFTA)[242] and the Convention for the Protection of Human Rights and Fundamental Freedoms (the "Human Rights Convention"),[243] which established the European Court of Human Rights. In general, these treaties permit private parties to bring actions against states for violations of international law.[244]

A second challenge concerns the range of disputes that will be under the jurisdiction of this court. The range of disputes highlighted in this chapter

---

241 International Bar Association, Draft, International Survey of Specialized Intellectual Property Courts — 2004 article 11, at http://www.iba.org (visited 30 January 2005) [hereinafter Draft IBA survey].

242 North American Free Trade Agreement (1994), available at http://www.mac.doc.gov/nafta/naftatext.html [hereinafter NAFTA].

243 Convention for the Protection of Human Rights and Fundamental Freedoms, as amended by Protocol Number 11, ETS # 155, 4 November 1950 (as amended by Protocol Number 11 on 11 May 1994) [hereinafter Human Rights Convention].

244 Human Rights Convention, as amended by Protocol Number 11, ETS 155, 4 November 1950 (as amended by Protocol Number 11 on 11 May 1994). (1994), available at http://www.mac.doc.gov/ nafta/naftatext.html.

includes intellectual property infringement and piracy by private individuals and states, as well as other intellectual property and non-intellectual property issues related to technology transfer disputes between private parties or private parties and states. Thus, these disputes could be simple contract claims, treaty violation claims, complex intellectual property infringement claims, or a variety of other claims related to information and communication technology transfers (i.e., tort claims).

The question remains, is it appropriate to create a forum to hear all of these claims, and no others? If, on the other hand, the nature of allowable claims is limited, for example, to claims relating to intellectual property or information technology issues only, what happens when parties have multiple claims arising from information and communication technology transfers, but only one or two of them are directly related to intellectual property or information technology? This could increase the costs to private parties because they will be forced to pursue their claims in multiple jurisdictions, decreasing their motivation to engage in information and communication technology transfers and depressing the World Summit on the Information Society's goals.

Moreover, such a specialized forum may be expensive to maintain, and the potential caseload may overrun it. In addition, a specialized court may increase travel costs and diminish parties' flexibility and decreased costs associated with selecting a local forum.[245] Other logistical challenges include where such a forum should be located[246] and which rules of procedure and evidence to apply, among others.

Another significant issue that remains unresolved is the lack of harmonization in international intellectual property law. Treaties such as TRIPS and the Berne Convention create minimum standards of protection required by the laws of the member states, but they do not create a standard for private behavior or affect laws in non-member states. Until intellectual property law is successfully harmonized, the problems of inconsistent outcomes and un-remedied intellectual property claims will persist, even in a new forum.

Finally, there remains a question of remedies and enforcement. In intellectual property and technology disputes, remedies in the form of compensation and/or injunction are appropriate, depending on the nature of the claim.[247]

---

245 Draft International Bar Association Survey, article 13, at http://www.iba.org (visited 30 January 2005).

246 For example, in the Hague, like the World Court and the International Criminal Court, or perhaps with regional offices, to facilitate resolution of disputes in developing nations. This could address the above-noted concerns about travel costs.

247 Lemley, "I'll Make Him an Offer He Can't Refuse: A Proposed Model for Alternative Dispute Resolution in Intellectual Property Disputes", 37 *Akron L. Rev.* 287, at pp. 290–292 (2004).

Injunctions are generally a vital form of relief.[248] The obstacle is whether an international forum such as this would have the power to grant, and then enforce, injunctive relief against either a private party or state.

Various forms of non-monetary relief and methods of enforcement do occur in other international tribunals. For example, in contentious cases before the International Court of Justice, relief is generally in the form of declaratory relief, i.e., a statement that the responding state is or is not in violation of treaty law, and a direction to conform, generally in some specific way.[249]

States are expected to abide by International Court of Justice decisions according to their obligations under the United Nations Charter.[250] If a state fails to abide by an International Court of Justice judgment, the other state can seek to enforce it via the Security Council. In addition, under the WTO's Understanding on Dispute Settlement, remedies come in the form of a declaration that the responding state has violated one of the Agreements and a direction to conform.[251] The Understanding on Dispute Settlement also may direct the responding state to compensate the complaining state. Furthermore, it may allow the complaining state to suspend trade concessions granted to the violating state, or other trade-related obligations.[252]

In this proposed new forum, if the disputes are between two states, similar remedy and enforcement mechanisms could be applied. However, if one or more of the parties is a private party, the above provisions are not applicable. For example, a private party who brings a claim cannot singularly abrogate trade concessions, or seek enforcement of its judgment through the Security Council. Moreover, if a judgment is against another private party, there is no place for assuring compliance with such remedies.

Even if it is determined that this new forum may provide for injunctive relief as well as compensation, enforcing awards remains a challenge. Private parties would likely need to seek enforcement of these judgments in a national court, similar to the methods by which enforcement of international arbitration awards occur today. The document creating this new forum should

---

248 Moore and Parisi, Symposium on Constructing International Intellectual Property Law: "The Role of National Courts: Thinking Forum Shopping in Cyberspace", 77 *Chi-Kent. L. Rev.* 1325, at p. 1350, note 56; Kesan and Ulen, Symposium: "Intellectual Property Challenges in the Next Century", 2001 *U. Ill. L. Rev.* 57, at p. 66 (2001).

249 Case Concerning Aveno and other Mexican Nationals (*Mexico v. United States*), International Court of Justice Case Number 128 (28 March 2003), available at http://www.icj-cij.org.

250 United Nations Charter, article 94.

251 World Trade Organization, Understanding on Dispute Settlement, article 19; Carmody, "Remedies and Conformity under the WTO Agreement", *J. Int'l Econ. L.* 307, at p. 316 (2002).

252 World Trade Organization, Understanding on Dispute Settlement, articles 19 and 22.

therefore contain a provision requiring all states to recognize and enforce judgments of this new forum as against both state and private parties. States would similarly waive their sovereign immunity *vis-à-vis* national proceedings to enforce judgments.

Then, a private party could enforce judgments against both states and private parties. One problem with this solution is that it fails to diminish expensive and drawn-out proceedings because, after conclusion of the proceedings in this proposed new forum, the private party must still then submit the award to a national court for enforcement. However, presumably, the national court would not require the parties to litigate the award's validity, as might be necessary with an international arbitration award. Likewise, waiver of sovereign immunity is not likely to receive favorable consideration without some restriction or recompense for meritless claims that could inundate nations that unwittingly waive that immunity.

Another obstacle to creating such a new forum is that it fails to solve the problem of enforcing awards against a reticent state. Under the WTO, the possibility of losing trade concessions or other trade-related retaliatory action appears to be successful in inducing states to settle with the complaining state or comply with DSB decisions.[253]

However, as noted above, a private party cannot, on its own, abrogate trade concessions. One possible solution is to create a registry of states against whom private party investors have obtained judgments that remain open due to some act or failure to act by the state against whom the party has obtained the judgment.[254]

While this approach may have seemed unwieldy in the past, the age of the Internet and computer advancement allow central registration and updating with relative ease. Potential investors could access this registry to determine whether the state with which they are considering executing an information and communication technology transfer contract is likely to avoid enforcement of

---

253 Carmody, "Remedies and Conformity under the WTO Agreement", *J. Int'l Econ. L.* 307, at p. 316 (2002).

254 This could be similar to the U.S.T.R.'s Special 301 "Watch List", published annually, which creates a list of countries in which piracy is especially prevalent, or governments are less likely to enforce intellectual property rights. This list purports to "warn a country of [the U.S.T.R.'s] concerns. In addition, it warns potential investors in that country that their intellectual property rights are not likely to be satisfactorily protected". U.S.T.R., The Work of United States Trade Representative and Intellectual Property, http://www.ustr.gov/Trade_Sectors/Intellectual_Property/The_Work_of_U.S.T.R_-_Inte llectual_Property.html (visited 2 February 2005). This system has yielded success for US interests. Yu, "From Pirates to Partners: Protecting Intellectual Property in China in the Twenty-First Century", 50 *Am. U. L. Rev.* 131, at p. 140 (2000); Newby, "Effectiveness of Special 301 in Creating Long Term Copyright Protections for U.S. Companies Overseas", 21 *Syracuse J. Int'l L. and Com.* 29 (1995).

any judgment rendered against it. This places the threat of decreased investment over that state and, although not as biting as actual retaliatory actions, it would at least provide a modicum of security that awards will be enforced.

(e) Multilateral Treaty Vesting Jurisdiction of Certain Disputes in the International Center for Settlement of Investment Disputes

A third potential solution, which is again limited in scope, involves the creation of a multilateral treaty which places intellectual property-related information and communication technology transfer disputes under the jurisdiction of the International Center for Settlement of Investment Disputes.

The International Center for Settlement of Investment Disputes was established under the Convention on the Settlement of Investment Disputes between states and Nationals of Other States (the Convention), which came into force on 14 October 1966.[255] Investment contracts between governments of member states and investors from other member states generally provide for arbitration under the International Center for Settlement of Investment Disputes.

Furthermore, advance consents by governments to submit investment disputes to International Center for Settlement of Investment Disputes arbitration also can be found in approximately 20 investment laws and in more than 900 bilateral investment treaties.[256] Arbitration under the International Center for Settlement of Investment Disputes also is one of the primary mechanisms for the settlement of investment disputes under four multilateral trade and investment treaties (NAFTA, the Energy Charter Treaty, the Cartagena Free Trade Agreement, and the Colonia Investment Protocol of Mercosur).[257]

All International Center for Settlement of Investment Disputes Contracting states, whether or not parties to the dispute, are required by the Convention to recognize and enforce International Center for Settlement of Investment Disputes arbitral awards.[258]

Currently, disputes arising from transfers of technology subject to a bilateral investment treaties are generally subject to the jurisdiction of the International Center for Settlement of Investment Disputes (provided that in the bilateral

---

255 International Center for Settlement of Investment Disputes, see http://www.worldbank.org/ icsid/about/about.htm (visited 30 January 2005).

256 International Center for Settlement of Investment Disputes, see http://www.worldbank.org/ icsid/about/about.htm (visited 30 January 2005).

257 International Center for Settlement of Investment Disputes, at http://www.worldbank.org/ icsid/about/about.htm (visited 30 January 2005).

258 International Center for Settlement of Investment Disputes, at http://www.worldbank.org/ icsid/about/about.him (visited 30 January 2005); Convention on the Settlement of Investment Disputes Between States and Nationals of Other States, 14 October 1966.

investment treaty definition of "investment" is sufficiently broad).[259] A multilateral treaty, however, could cover disputes between states and parties that are not subject to bilateral investment treaties (either because the transaction is outside the scope of the bilateral investment treaty or because there is no bilateral investment treaties in place).

As noted, this solution is limited in its scope. It will likely not cover intellectual property-related Internet transactions unless they arise from information and communication technology transfer contracts between a private party and a state; nor will it provide for the resolution of general intellectual property infringement or piracy disputes. According to the International Center for Settlement of Investment Disputes Convention, the Center is intended to resolve investment disputes between private parties and states.[260]

The benefits of creating such a treaty are similar to those of the solutions above. This will provide a default forum, with a consistent set of rules and a body of precedent to which panelists could look for guidance.[261]

The disadvantages to relegating these disputes to the International Center for Settlement of Investment Disputes are the converse of the advantages to creating a new forum. That is, while the International Center for Settlement of Investment Disputes is currently the forum of choice for investment disputes,[262] it is not a specialized intellectual property or technology forum. So, while this solution gains the benefit of established legitimacy and a broad caseload to sufficiently fund the court and give its panelists varied perspective, it loses the benefits of an intellectual property or technology-specific forum.[263]

Numerous prior attempts at drafting multilateral investment treaties, however, have failed.[264] Most recently, the Organization for Economic

---

259 As an example, see the 2004 United States Model Bilateral Investment Treaty, article 1, available at http://www.ustr.gov ("An investment is every asset that an investor owns or controls, directly or indirectly that has the characteristic of an investment . . .").

260 International Center for Settlement of Investment Disputes Convention, articles 1 and 25. Disputes between states are referred to the International Court of Justice.

261 Thereby avoiding the divergent outcomes of *Société Générale de Surveillance SA v. Philippines and Société Générale de Surveillance SA v. Pakistan*, which resulted from different language in bilateral investment treaties.

262 By its nature, the transfer of technology to a developing country or an entity located in a developing country is correctly considered an "investment", although it may or may not involve transfers of negotiable instruments. This is particularly so in circumstances where the so-called return on the investment is speculative or long-term. It is clear that without substantial investment in the technological infrastructure of developing countries, the upswing in demand for technology and sophisticated products is unlikely to follow.

263 Unless, of course, this treaty created an intellectual property-specific procedure, perhaps as an addendum to the International Center for Settlement of Investment Disputes Convention.

264 Muchlinski, "The Rise and Fall of the Multilateral Agreement on Investment: Where Now?", 34 *Int'l L.* 1033, at pp. 1034–1037 (2000).

Cooperation and Development (OECD) attempted to draft and promulgate a multilateral investment agreement. Although it was generally supported by developed nations (such as the United States and members of the European Union), it ultimately failed.[265] There are a variety of reasons for its failure, but scholars point primarily to the negotiating environment and certain provisions of the treaty as its major roadblocks.[266]

For example, the OECD is seen to have failed to include NGOs and developing nations in the negotiations.[267] Problems with specific provisions of the treaty included the definitions of "investor" and "investment", the large number of country-specific exceptions, and the inability to reach consensus on most-favored nation and national treatment issues, performance requirements for entry and establishment, expropriation and taxation, and the dispute resolution proceedings.[268] Regarding dispute resolution proceedings, some NGOs were concerned that permitting private parties to bring claims against states for violation of the treaty allowed these investors to "neutralize legitimate national laws and regulations".[269]

Because this new proposed multilateral treaty would presumably be far more limited in scope than a general multilateral investment treaty, however, these issues may not arise. For example, the definitions of "investor" and "investment" would be specifically limited to those envisioned by the World Summit on the Information Society. Moreover, because many of these disputes are specifically related to intellectual property and technology issues, questions of most-favored nation and national treatment may be resolved according to the current efforts to harmonize intellectual property rights. Furthermore, the issue with dispute resolution giving citizens power to challenge legitimate laws is not new — the methods provided are identical to those already provided for in numerous bilateral investment treaties.

This new multilateral treaty must clearly define the disputes within its scope, to prevent a rash of jurisprudence on the subject. Furthermore, the treaty could be over-ridden by subsequent bilateral investment treaties (if the bilateral investment treaties so states) or existing bilateral investment treaties (as long as the contracting state so signifies when acceding to the treaty).

---

265 Muchlinski, "The Rise and Fall of the Multilateral Agreement on Investment: Where Now?", 34 *Int'l L.* 1033, at p. 1039 (2000).

266 Muchlinski, "The Rise and Fall of the Multilateral Agreement on Investment: Where Now?", 34 *Int'l L.* 1033, at p. 1038 (2000).

267 Muchlinski, "The Rise and Fall of the Multilateral Agreement on Investment: Where Now?", 34 *Int'l L.* 1033, at pp. 1039 and 1040 (2000).

268 Muchlinski, "The Rise and Fall of the Multilateral Agreement on Investment: Where Now?", 34 *Int'l L.* 1033, at p. 1038 (2000).

269 Muchlinski, "The Rise and Fall of the Multilateral Agreement on Investment: Where Now?", 34 *Int'l L.* 1033, at p. 1046 (2000).

Moreover, the terms could be over-ridden by contract terms, as long as it is clear from the contract that the parties so intended.

To further the goals of the World Summit on the Information Society through the methods outlined in this chapter, namely, harmonizing resolution of these disputes to motivate the private sector to invest in information and communication technology transfers in developing nations, some changes to the International Center for Settlement of Investment Disputes will be necessary.

First, because the jurisdiction of the International Center for Settlement of Investment Disputes is generally invoked pursuant to a bilateral investment treaty, and the disputes involve an alleged violation of a state's obligations under the bilateral investment treaty, the bilateral investment treaties itself generally provides the standards for performance. The International Center for Settlement of Investment Disputes panels also can hear contract disputes between a private party and a state that do not allege treaty violations.[270]

The contract investment between the parties will generally decide the law to be applied but, failing a choice of law provision, the International Center for Settlement of Investment Disputes panel will apply the substantive law of the state in which the private party invested.[271] Thus, absent a bilateral investment treaty that creates the standards of protection of intellectual property, or a provision in the contract that creates the standards of protection of intellectual property, the International Center for Settlement of Investment Disputes panel will apply the intellectual property protections of the state in which the private party invested (i.e., the state that was on the receiving end of the technology transfer).

This could be problematic; if the parties do not agree on a choice of law provision in their contract, or if the arbitral panel finds it defective, the private party may be forced to apply the law of the state in which it has invested.[272]

In the context of intellectual property, as earlier described, this is not always favorable to the private party, especially in the context of the World Summit

---

270 Gill, *et al.*, "Contractual Claims and Bilateral Investment Treaties: A Comparative Review of the Société Générale de Surveillance SA Cases", *J. Int'l Arb.* 2004, available at http://www.kluwerarbitration.com.

271 International Center for Settlement of Investment Disputes Convention, article 42.

272 Indeed, this is a specific circumstance where the definition of "investment" becomes difficult. When focused on the World Summit on the Information Society's objectives, a right of "access" to technology may amount to an investment by the party allowing such access. In the context of web sites that today contain compilations of data and proprietary narratives (such as a medical advice or treatment site), the mere access is sufficiently dangerous to the web provider's exclusivity or uniqueness so that it may considerably off-set intended benefits, such as sales or advertising revenues. If a party who has access to the technology can essentially conscript it for personal or commercial use without international accountability, the World Summit on the Information Society objectives are likely to be squelched until protection of the proprietary materials is assured.

on the Information Society's goals because the state will likely be a developing nation.[273] Accordingly, although harmonization of intellectual property law is outside the scope of this chapter, it is a necessary step to increasing participation in the Information Society if for no other reason than to motivate the private sector to invest technology. Moreover, absent a choice of law provision from a bilateral investment treaty or contract, the arbitral panel will apply the arbitration law of the state party to the dispute.

Again, this could be problematic for a private party because it may find particular aspects of the arbitration law unfavorable (such as the validity of the agreement or arbitrability of intellectual property claims).[274] Many of these concerns, however, can be addressed in the language of the new multilateral treaty itself.

Additionally, jurisdiction should be extended to disputes between a private party investor and a private party acting for the state (i.e., one that has received concessions from the state).[275] As such, states will not be able to avoid their responsibilities to private parties by "farming out" their information and communication technology development.

Lastly, the International Center for Settlement of Investment Disputes permits states to indicate which disputes are and are not arbitrable under the Center;[276] thus, to be effective, the International Center for Settlement of Investment Disputes must be clear that states may not decline arbitrability for information and communication technology transfer-related disputes.

(f) New York Convention on the Recognition and Enforcement of Foreign Arbitral Awards

Another potential solution, which may, in fact, simply be an interim solution while a new treaty or forum is debated, is to modify the New York Convention to improve the efficacy of current international arbitration.

---

273 World Summit on the Information Society World Summit on the Information Society Plan of Action (WSIS-03/ GENEVA/DOC/0005), at http://www.itu.int/wsis (3 February 2005).

274 Some states do not permit certain intellectual property disputes to be arbitrated. Arfazadeh, "Arbitrability under the New York Convention: the Lex Fori Revisited", 17 *Arb. Int'l* 73 (2001), available at http://www.kluwerarbitration.com, stating that such states permit arbitration of intellectual property disputes only were the arbitration panel must simply determine whether a party has violated an intellectual property right created by a contract between the parties. Baron and Liniger, "A Second Look at Arbitrability Approaches to Arbitration in the United States, Switzerland, and Germany", *Arb. Int'l* 2003, available at http://www.kluwerarbitration.com; Blessing, "Arbitrability of Intellectual Property Disputes", 12 *Arb. Int'l* 191 (1996), available at http://www.kluwerarbitration.com. In the absence of specific contract provisions in an information and communication technology transfer agreement between a private party and the state, this treaty would be the gap-filler that gives the panel jurisdiction.

275 *Salini and Italstrade v. Kingdom of Morocco*, International Center for Settlement of Investment Disputes Case Number ARB/00/4 (2002), available at http://www.kluwerarbitration.com.

276 International Center for Settlement of Investment Disputes Convention, article 25(4).

First, an addendum could be added to the New York Convention that distinguishes intellectual property disputes related to information technology and other identified disputes relating to information and communication technology transfers from other types of disputes resolved through arbitration. These disputes would be so designated with the express purpose of furthering the goal of increasing participation in the Information Society, to bridge the "digital divide". This addendum could then either specify a particular forum into which these disputes should be resolved or simply outline specific rules and procedures to be applied to the enforcement of awards rendered in existing arbitral forums.

Second, the addendum should include a modified definition (which is not limiting) of "a writing" that includes electronic documents.[277] Furthermore, the term "signed by both parties" should be defined (but not limited) to include the methods by which willing parties to contracts entered electronically deem to be "signed". A careful survey of current accepted business practice must be undertaken before this addendum is added.

Third, this addendum should define a method by which a court enforcing the award may determine where the award is rendered to reflect current accepted business practice. This is particularly important where arbitration has been conducted via telecommunication methods (e.g., via email or video-conferencing).

Fourth, a provision should be incorporated wherein each contracting state waives its sovereign immunity and subjects itself to the jurisdiction of the arbitral tribunal and the contracting state in which the award is to be enforced for the specific purposes identified under the so-called "World Summit on the Information Society Addendum". Such a proviso would be a major departure from the existing treaty as it would compel signatories to likewise submit themselves, through an express waiver of sovereign immunity, to the arbitral process in these circumstances. If the award is to be enforced in a state other than that of the state-party, this will still leave unresolved the obvious problem of enforcement in a state that is not a party.[278]

---

277 For example, soft copy word processing documents, electronic forms, or email.

278 This is, of course, the problem that exists today in commercial disputes resolved by international arbitration. Ultimately, the World Summit on the Information Society objectives can advance the objectives of the 1958 New York Convention and reach even further to newly developing countries in need of technology transfers, such as those contemplated by the World Summit on the Information Society objectives. In this scenario, each is complimentary of the other. If a new and developing country seeks access to technology, the first step is accountability for the lawful protection of such an investment. To achieve that end, the waiver of sovereign immunity and the adherence to both the commercial dispute resolution procedures of the New York Convention, coupled with the same avowal to support the World Summit on the Information Society Addendum will go a long way to advancing the objectives of the international community.

Finally, a special provision should be added that reinforces the jurisdiction of the default forum to which disputes arising from information and communication technology transfer-related transactions that lack a choice of forum clause or dispute resolution agreement are subject. This should specifically address the domestic constitutionality of a default forum, i.e., can the state abrogate private parties' rights to pursue their claim in a court of law?[279] Because these disputes are limited to international intellectual property infringement, intellectual property disputes related to international information and communication technology transfers and potential other disputes stemming from information and communication technology transfers, therefore implicating problems with personal jurisdiction that cannot be constitutionally overcome, states will likely find that the treaty does not violate domestic constitutional provisions.

There are several advantages to modifying this treaty, as opposed to creating a new treaty or an entirely new forum. First, many states, including many developing nations, have already acceded to the New York Convention.[280] Furthermore, this solution merely acts to modify the current method of enforcing an arbitral award and is not a major upheaval of the current arbitration forums.

Thus, no action, other than conforming national laws or rules that conflict with the new provisions of the treaty, are necessary by states or arbitral institutions. Third, such an addendum provides parties with considerable flexibility and freedom of choice in resolving their disputes; parties may resort to any arbitral body and be assured that the award will be enforced.

There are, however, disadvantages and obstacles to successful modification of the New York Convention. First, if the treaty is not clear that the specific definitions advised are not exhaustive, a panel's discretion to interpret the terms may be too limited. Second, some states may not wish to give up their sovereignty in the area of intellectual property and technology for public policy or other reasons. It also may be awkward to limit these new provisions to

---

279 A "default" is critical to the success of such an addendum. It is a foreseeable consequence of the Information Society that transactions will occur in electronic and digital circumstances devoid of typical contract formalities. When this occurs, the state must have already provided the regulatory "default" to international arbitration. Likewise, the state itself must be subject to this default so that appropriate political leverage between the state and its constituent citizens may occur. The targeted government defendant in an international arbitration may find itself more willing to influence disreputable citizens in its borders than a state that is merely a bystander to theft of intellectual property or other technology.

280 More than 135 nations are parties to the New York Convention. Parties to the Convention on the Recognition and Enforcement of Foreign Arbitral Awards (as of 23 December 2003), http://arbiter.wipo.int/arbitration/ny-convention/parties.html (visited 2 February 2005).

the disputes highlighted in this chapter, as that may lead to greater inconsistency within any given single contract dispute. Finally, some developing states are not parties to the New York Convention. Thus, the question arises: what is the reasonable prognosis for capturing developing nations? Moreover, what is the value of such a change when some developing countries lack stability and may change regimes overnight?

Developing nations must recognize that to motivate information and communication technology transfer and increase investment in the Information Society by private entities from developed nations, they must give some security to these private entities. Private entities that fear a loss of control over their intellectual property, or fear that they will have no recourse in the event of a breach of contract by a state or private entity within the developing nation, will be less motivated to "share the wealth".[281]

For example, during the Intercessional Meetings of July 2003 of the Coordinating Committee of Business Interlocutors, representatives from the private sector around the globe gave their thoughts on the first phase of the World Summit on the Information Society. Common themes among the speakers included the need for transparency and predictability in the legal environments of developing nations and sufficient protection of intellectual property rights.[282] Thus, those developing nations that refuse to become a party to the New York Convention (or any proposed treaty) may find themselves at the end of the line to receive investments of technology, replaced by those developing nations that can provide security for private entities.

---

281 Hassan, "Actions for Governments to Undertake to Attract Private Sector Investments in ICT, Remarks at the Coordinating Committee of Business Interlocutors", *Intersessional Meeting*, 16 July 2003, at http://www.iccwbo.org (visited 26 January 2005); Danish, "Intellectual Property, Standards, Security, and Other Issues", *Remarks, Coordinating Committee of Business Interlocutors Intersessional Meeting*, 15 July 2003, transcript available at http://www.iccwbo.org (visited 26 January 2005); Wintrebert, "Enabling Environment and Infrastructure Issues", *Remarks, Coordinating Committee of Business Interlocutors Intersessional Meeting*, 15 July 2003, transcript available at http'//www.iccwbo.org (visited 26 January 2005); Leca, "Investment", *Remarks, Coordinating* Committee of Business Interlocutors Intersessional Meeting, 15 July 2003, transcript available at http://www,iccwbo.org (visited 26 January 2005).

282 Hassan, "Actions for Governments to Undertake to Attract Private Sector Investments in ICT", *Remarks at the Coordinating Committee of Business Interlocutors, Intersessional Meeting*, 16 July 2003; see http://www iccwbo.org (visited 26 January 2005); Danish, "Intellectual Property, Standards, Security, and Other Issues", *Remarks, Coordinating Committee of Business Interlocutors Intersessional Meeting*, 15 July 2003, transcript available at http://www.iccwbo.org (visited 26 January 2005); Wintrebert, "Enabling Environment and Infrastructure Issues", *Remarks, Coordinating Committee of Business Interlocutors Intersessional Meeting*, 15 July 2003, transcript available at http://www.icewbo.org (visited 26 January 2005); Leca, "Investment", *Remarks, Coordinating* Committee of Business Interlocutors Intersessional Meeting, 15 July 2003, transcript available at http://www iccwbo.org (visited 26 January 2005).

The effect of the current political climate, on the other hand, may not be so easily solved by such a simple theory of market economics. Clearly, a state in flux cannot be relied on to submit itself to the jurisdiction of any tribunal, or enforce any award, even if an earlier regime has signed the treaty. In addition, there is no doubt that such states are likely in the most dire need of investment, as such instability leads to greater poverty, which in turn can widen the digital divide.[283]

On the other hand, developed nations have accepted reasonable risk in other areas of international investment. Thus, developed nations may be independently motivated to accept reasonable risk to extend markets opened by the extension of information and communication technology transfers. While it is true that risk will remain, even in transfers among constituents in "stable government and economic systems", the more narrow the spectrum of risk as a whole, the greater the ability to accept significant risk in limited circumstances. The objectives of the World Summit on the Information Society conventions cannot be altruistic solutions.

Rather, the objectives are, to be blunt, accelerated segues from the back road to the digital superhighway. No participant in the Tunis Convention expects or demands this segue occur without problems or uncertainty. Each knows only too well that the existing world is a patchwork of legal accountability and that enforcement is not predictable. In such times, the effort of the United Nations Summit must focus on narrowing the field of potential problems to encourage the risk and rewards that will flow from our Information Society during the legitimate and necessary exchange of information among the "Haves" and the "Have-Nots".

12.05 Conclusion

The Plan of Action from the first phase of the World Summit on the Information Society recognized that the private sector is necessary to increasing participation in the Information Society. It also recognized that the protection of intellectual property rights and improving dispute resolution methods are an integral part of wooing the private sector to participate.

The above solutions may be a starting point for improving dispute resolution methods *vis-à-vis* intellectual property disputes related to information and communication technology transfer, Internet contracts, and the general rise of piracy and infringement that will result from the increase in information and communication technology users. The methods suggested in this paper

---

283 World Summit on the Information Society World Summit on the Information Society Declaration of Principles (WSIS-03/GENEVA/DOC/0004) and Plan of Action (WSIS-03/GENEVA/DOC/0005), at http://www.itu.int/wsis (3 February 2005).

may, when combined with a concerted effort to harmonize intellectual property rights, help to achieve the important goals of the World Summit on the Information Society.

APPENDIX I

DECLARATION OF PRINCIPLES BUILDING THE INFORMATION SOCIETY: A GLOBAL CHALLENGE IN THE NEW MILLENNIUM

APPENDIX I

DECLARATION OF PRINCIPLES BUILDING THE INFORMATION SOCIETY: A GLOBAL CHALLENGE IN THE NEW MILLENNIUM

World Summit on the Information Society
Geneva 2003 — Tunis 2005
12 December 2003

A. Our Common Vision of the Information Society

1. We, the representatives of the peoples of the world, assembled in Geneva from 10–12 December 2003 for the first phase of the World Summit on the Information Society, declare our common desire and commitment to build a people-centered, inclusive and development-oriented Information Society, where everyone can create, access, utilize and share information and knowledge, enabling individuals, communities and peoples to achieve their full potential in promoting their sustainable development and improving their quality of life, premised on the purposes and principles of the Charter of the United Nations and respecting fully and upholding the Universal Declaration of Human Rights.

2. Our challenge is to harness the potential of information and communication technology to promote the development goals of the Millennium Declaration, namely the eradication of extreme poverty and hunger; achievement of universal primary education; promotion of gender equality and empowerment of women; reduction of child mortality; improvement of maternal health; to combat HIV/AIDS, malaria and other diseases; ensuring environmental sustainability; and development of global partnerships for development for the attainment of a more peaceful, just and prosperous world. We also reiterate our commitment to the achievement of sustainable development and agreed development goals, as contained in the Johannesburg

Declaration and Plan of Implementation and the Monterrey Consensus, and other outcomes of relevant United Nations Summits.

3. We reaffirm the universality, indivisibility, interdependence and interrelation of all human rights and fundamental freedoms, including the right to development, as enshrined in the Vienna Declaration. We also reaffirm that democracy, sustainable development, and respect for human rights and fundamental freedoms as well as good governance at all levels are interdependent and mutually reinforcing. We further resolve to strengthen respect for the rule of law in international as in national affairs.

4. We reaffirm, as an essential foundation of the Information Society, and as outlined in Article 19 of the Universal Declaration of Human Rights, that everyone has the right to freedom of opinion and expression; that this right includes freedom to hold opinions without interference and to seek, receive and impart information and ideas through any media and regardless of frontiers. Communication is a fundamental social process, a basic human need and the foundation of all social organization. It is central to the Information Society. Everyone, everywhere should have the opportunity to participate and no one should be excluded from the benefits the Information Society offers.

5. We further reaffirm our commitment to the provisions of Article 29 of the Universal Declaration of Human Rights, that everyone has duties to the community in which alone the free and full development of their personality is possible, and that, in the exercise of their rights and freedoms, everyone shall be subject only to such limitations as are determined by law solely for the purpose of securing due recognition and respect for the rights and freedoms of others and of meeting the just requirements of morality, public order and the general welfare in a democratic society. These rights and freedoms may in no case be exercised contrary to the purposes and principles of the United Nations. In this way, we shall promote an Information Society where human dignity is respected.

6. In keeping with the spirit of this declaration, we rededicate ourselves to upholding the principle of the sovereign equality of all States.

7. We recognize that science has a central role in the development of the Information Society. Many of the building blocks of the Information Society are the result of scientific and technical advances made possible by the sharing of research results.

8. We recognize that education, knowledge, information and communication are at the core of human progress, endeavor and well-being. Further, Information and Communication Technologies (ICTs) have an immense impact on virtually all aspects of our lives. The rapid progress of these technologies opens completely new opportunities to attain higher levels of development.

The capacity of these technologies to reduce many traditional obstacles, especially those of time and distance, for the first time in history makes it possible to use the potential of these technologies for the benefit of millions of people in all corners of the world.

9. We are aware that ICTs should be regarded as tools and not as an end in themselves. Under favorable conditions, these technologies can be a powerful instrument, increasing productivity, generating economic growth, job creation and employability and improving the quality of life of all. They can also promote dialogue among people, nations and civilizations.

10. We are also fully aware that the benefits of the information technology revolution are today unevenly distributed between the developed and developing countries and within societies. We are fully committed to turning this digital divide into a digital opportunity for all, particularly for those who risk being left behind and being further marginalized.

11. We are committed to realizing our common vision of the Information Society for ourselves and for future generations. We recognize that young people are the future workforce and leading creators and earliest adopters of ICTs. They must therefore be empowered as learners, developers, contributors, entrepreneurs and decision-makers. We must focus especially on young people who have not yet been able to benefit fully from the opportunities provided by ICTs. We are also committed to ensuring that the development of ICT applications and operation of services respects the rights of children as well as their protection and well being.

12. We affirm that development of ICTs provides enormous opportunities for women, who should be an integral part of, and key actors, in the Information Society. We are committed to ensuring that the Information Society enables women's empowerment and their full participation on the basis on equality in all spheres of society and in all decision-making processes. To this end, we should mainstream a gender equality perspective and use ICTs as a tool to that end.

13. In building the Information Society, we shall pay particular attention to the special needs of marginalized and vulnerable groups of society, including migrants, internally displaced persons and refugees, unemployed and underprivileged people, minorities and nomadic people. We shall also recognize the special needs of older persons and persons with disabilities.

14. We are resolute to empower the poor, particularly those living in remote, rural and marginalized urban areas, to access information and to use ICTs as a tool to support their efforts to lift themselves out of poverty.

15. In the evolution of the Information Society, particular attention must be given to the special situation of indigenous peoples, as well as to the preservation of their heritage and their cultural legacy.

16. We continue to pay special attention to the particular needs of people of developing countries, countries with economies in transition, Least Developed Countries, Small Island Developing States, Landlocked Developing Countries, Highly Indebted Poor Countries, countries and territories under occupation, countries recovering from conflict and countries and regions with special needs as well as to conditions that pose severe threats to development, such as natural disasters.

17. We recognize that building an inclusive Information Society requires new forms of solidarity, partnership and cooperation among governments and other stakeholders, i.e. the private sector, civil society and international organizations. Realizing that the ambitious goal of this Declaration-bridging the digital divide and ensuring harmonious, fair and equitable development for all-will require strong commitment by all stakeholders, we call for digital solidarity, both at national and international levels.

18. Nothing in this Declaration shall be construed as impairing, contradicting, restricting or derogating from the provisions of the Charter of the United Nations and the Universal Declaration of Human Rights, any other international instrument or national laws adopted in furtherance of these instruments.

B. An Information Society for All: Key Principles

19. We are resolute in our quest to ensure that everyone can benefit from the opportunities that ICTs can offer. We agree that to meet these challenges, all stakeholders should work together to: improve access to information and communication infrastructure and technologies as well as to information and knowledge; build capacity; increase confidence and security in the use of ICTs; create an enabling environment at all levels; develop and widen ICT applications; foster and respect cultural diversity; recognize the role of the media; address the ethical dimensions of the Information Society; and encourage international and regional cooperation. We agree that these are the key principles for building an inclusive Information Society.

1)   The role of Governments and All Stakeholders in the Promotion of ICTs for Development

20. Governments, as well as private sector, civil society and the United Nations and other international organizations have an important role and responsibility in the development of the Information Society and, as appropriate, in decision-making processes. Building a people-centered Information Society is a joint effort which requires cooperation and partnership among all stakeholders.

2)   Information and Communication Infrastructure: An Essential
      Foundation for an Inclusive Information Society

21. Connectivity is a central enabling agent in building the Information Society. Universal, ubiquitous, equitable and affordable access to ICT infrastructure and services, constitutes one of the challenges of the Information Society and should be an objective of all stakeholders involved in building it. Connectivity also involves access to energy and postal services, which should be assured in conformity with the domestic legislation of each country.

22. A well-developed information and communication network infrastructure and applications, adapted to regional, national and local conditions, easily-accessible and affordable, and making greater use of broadband and other innovative technologies where possible, can accelerate the social and economic progress of countries, and the well-being of all individuals, communities and peoples.

23. Policies that create a favorable climate for stability, predictability and fair competition at all levels should be developed and implemented in a manner that not only attracts more private investment for ICT infrastructure development but also enables universal service obligations to be met in areas where traditional market conditions fail to work. In disadvantaged areas, the establishment of ICT public access points in places such as post offices, schools, libraries and archives, can provide effective means for ensuring universal access to the infrastructure and services of the Information Society.

3)   Access to Information and Knowledge

24. The ability for all to access and contribute information, ideas and knowledge is essential in an inclusive Information Society.

25. The sharing and strengthening of global knowledge for development can be enhanced by removing barriers to equitable access to information for economic, social, political, health, cultural, educational, and scientific activities and by facilitating access to public domain information, including by universal design and the use of assistive technologies.

26. A rich public domain is an essential element for the growth of the Information Society, creating multiple benefits such as an educated public, new jobs, innovation, business opportunities, and the advancement of sciences. Information in the public domain should be easily accessible to support the Information Society, and protected from misappropriation. Public institutions such as libraries and archives, museums, cultural collections and other community-based access points should be strengthened so as to promote the preservation of documentary records and free and equitable access to information.

27. Access to information and knowledge can be promoted by increasing awareness among all stakeholders of the possibilities offered by different software models, including proprietary, open-source and free software, in order to increase competition, access by users, diversity of choice, and to enable all users to develop solutions which best meet their requirements. Affordable access to software should be considered as an important component of a truly inclusive Information Society.

28. We strive to promote universal access with equal opportunities for all to scientific knowledge and the creation and dissemination of scientific and technical information, including open access initiatives for scientific publishing.

4)   Capacity Building

29. Each person should have the opportunity to acquire the necessary skills and knowledge in order to understand, participate actively in, and benefit fully from, the Information Society and the knowledge economy. Literacy and universal primary education are key factors for building a fully inclusive information society, paying particular attention to the special needs of girls and women. Given the wide range of ICT and information specialists required at all levels, building institutional capacity deserves special attention.

30. The use of ICTs in all stages of education, training and human resource development should be promoted, taking into account the special needs of persons with disabilities and disadvantaged and vulnerable groups.

31. Continuous and adult education, re-training, life-long learning, distance-learning and other special services, such as telemedicine, can make an essential contribution to employability and help people benefit from the new opportunities offered by ICTs for traditional jobs, self-employment and new professions. Awareness and literacy in ICTs are an essential foundation in this regard.

32. Content creators, publishers, and producers, as well as teachers, trainers, archivists, librarians and learners, should play an active role in promoting the Information Society, particularly in the Least Developed Countries.

33. To achieve a sustainable development of the Information Society, national capability in ICT research and development should be enhanced. Furthermore, partnerships, in particular between and among developed and developing countries, including countries with economies in transition, in research and development, technology transfer, manufacturing and utilization of ICT products and services are crucial for promoting capacity building and global participation in the Information Society. The manufacture of ICTs presents a significant opportunity for creation of wealth.

34. The attainment of our shared aspirations, in particular for developing countries and countries with economies in transition, to become fully-fledged members of the Information Society, and their positive integration into the knowledge economy, depends largely on increased capacity building in the areas of education, technology know-how and access to information, which are major factors in determining development and competitiveness.

5)   Building Confidence and Security in the Use of ICTs

35. Strengthening the trust framework, including information security and network security, authentication, privacy and consumer protection, is a prerequisite for the development of the Information Society and for building confidence among users of ICTs. A global culture of cyber-security needs to be promoted, developed and implemented in cooperation with all stakeholders and international expert bodies. These efforts should be supported by increased international cooperation. Within this global culture of cyber-security, it is important to enhance security and to ensure the protection of data and privacy, while enhancing access and trade. In addition, it must take into account the level of social and economic development of each country and respect the development-oriented aspects of the Information Society.

36. While recognizing the principles of universal and non-discriminatory access to ICTs for all nations, we support the activities of the United Nations to prevent the potential use of ICTs for purposes that are inconsistent with the objectives of maintaining international stability and security, and may adversely affect the integrity of the infrastructure within States, to the detriment of their security. It is necessary to prevent the use of information resources and technologies for criminal and terrorist purposes, while respecting human rights.

37. Spam is a significant and growing problem for users, networks and the Internet as a whole. Spam and cyber-security should be dealt with at appropriate national and international levels.

6)   Enabling Environment

38. An enabling environment at national and international levels is essential for the Information Society. ICTs should be used as an important tool for good governance.

39. The rule of law, accompanied by a supportive, transparent, pro-competitive, technologically neutral and predictable policy and regulatory framework reflecting national realities, is essential for building a people-centered Information Society. Governments should intervene, as appropriate, to correct

market failures, to maintain fair competition, to attract investment, to enhance the development of the ICT infrastructure and applications, to maximize economic and social benefits, and to serve national priorities.

40. A dynamic and enabling international environment, supportive of foreign direct investment, transfer of technology, and international cooperation, particularly in the areas of finance, debt and trade, as well as full and effective participation of developing countries in global decision-making, are vital complements to national development efforts related to ICTs. Improving global affordable connectivity would contribute significantly to the effectiveness of these development efforts.

41. ICTs are an important enabler of growth through efficiency gains and increased productivity, in particular by small and medium sized enterprises (SMEs). In this regard, the development of the Information Society is important for broadly-based economic growth in both developed and developing economies. ICT-supported productivity gains and applied innovations across economic sectors should be fostered. Equitable distribution of the benefits contributes to poverty eradication and social development. Policies that foster productive investment and enable firms, notably SMEs, to make the changes needed to seize the benefits from ICTs, are likely to be the most beneficial.

42. Intellectual Property protection is important to encourage innovation and creativity in the Information Society; similarly, the wide dissemination, diffusion, and sharing of knowledge is important to encourage innovation and creativity. Facilitating meaningful participation by all in intellectual property issues and knowledge sharing through full awareness and capacity building is a fundamental part of an inclusive Information Society.

43. Sustainable development can best be advanced in the Information Society when ICT-related efforts and programs are fully integrated in national and regional development strategies. We welcome the New Partnership for Africa's Development (NEPAD) and encourage the international community to support the ICT-related measures of this initiative as well as those belonging to similar efforts in other regions. Distribution of the benefits of ICT-driven growth contributes to poverty eradication and sustainable development.

44. Standardization is one of the essential building blocks of the Information Society. There should be particular emphasis on the development and adoption of international standards. The development and use of open, interoperable, non-discriminatory and demand-driven standards that take into account needs of users and consumers is a basic element for the development and greater diffusion of ICTs and more affordable access to them, particularly in developing countries. International standards aim

to create an environment where consumers can access services worldwide regardless of underlying technology.

45. The radio frequency spectrum should be managed in the public interest and in accordance with principle of legality, with full observance of national laws and regulation as well as relevant international agreements.

46. In building the Information Society, States are strongly urged to take steps with a view to the avoidance of, and refrain from, any unilateral measure not in accordance with international law and the Charter of the United Nations that impedes the full achievement of economic and social development by the population of the affected countries, and that hinders the well-being of their population.

47. Recognizing that ICTs are progressively changing our working practices, the creation of a secure, safe and healthy working environment, appropriate to the utilization of ICTs, respecting all relevant international norms, is fundamental.

48. The Internet has evolved into a global facility available to the public and its governance should constitute a core issue of the Information Society agenda. The international management of the Internet should be multilateral, transparent and democratic, with the full involvement of governments, the private sector, civil society and international organizations. It should ensure an equitable distribution of resources, facilitate access for all and ensure a stable and secure functioning of the Internet, taking into account multilingualism.

49. The management of the Internet encompasses both technical and public policy issues and should involve all stakeholders and relevant intergovernmental and international organizations. In this respect it is recognized that:

a) Policy authority for Internet-related public policy issues is the sovereign right of States. They have rights and responsibilities for international Internet-related public policy issues;

b) The private sector has had and should continue to have an important role in the development of the Internet, both in the technical and economic fields;

c) Civil society has also played an important role on Internet matters, especially at community level, and should continue to play such a role;

d) Intergovernmental organizations have had and should continue to have a facilitating role in the coordination of Internet-related public policy issues;

e) International organizations have also had and should continue to have an important role in the development of Internet-related technical standards and relevant policies.

50. International Internet governance issues should be addressed in a coordinated manner. We ask the Secretary-General of the United Nations to set up a working group on Internet governance, in an open and inclusive process that ensures a mechanism for the full and active participation of governments, the private sector and civil society from both developing and developed countries, involving relevant intergovernmental and international organizations and forums, to investigate and make proposals for action, as appropriate, on the governance of Internet by 2005.

7)   ICT Applications: Benefits in All Aspects of Life

51. The usage and deployment of ICTs should seek to create benefits in all aspects of our daily life. ICT applications are potentially important in government operations and services, health care and health information, education and training, employment, job creation, business, agriculture, transport, protection of environment and management of natural resources, disaster prevention, and culture, and to promote eradication of poverty and other agreed development goals. ICTs should also contribute to sustainable production and consumption patterns and reduce traditional barriers, providing an opportunity for all to access local and global markets in a more equitable manner. Applications should be user-friendly, accessible to all, affordable, adapted to local needs in languages and cultures, and support sustainable development. To this effect, local authorities should play a major role in the provision of ICT services for the benefit of their populations.

8)   Cultural Diversity and Identity, Linguistic Diversity and Local Content

52. Cultural diversity is the common heritage of humankind. The Information Society should be founded on and stimulate respect for cultural identity, cultural and linguistic diversity, traditions and religions, and foster dialogue among cultures and civilizations. The promotion, affirmation and preservation of diverse cultural identities and languages as reflected in relevant agreed United Nations documents including UNESCO's Universal Declaration on Cultural Diversity, will further enrich the Information Society.

53. The creation, dissemination and preservation of content in diverse languages and formats must be accorded high priority in building an inclusive Information Society, paying particular attention to the diversity of supply of creative work and due recognition of the rights of authors and artists. It is essential to promote the production of and accessibility to all content-educational, scientific, cultural or recreational-in diverse languages and formats. The development of local content suited to domestic or regional

needs will encourage social and economic development and will stimulate participation of all stakeholders, including people living in rural, remote and marginal areas.

54. The preservation of cultural heritage is a crucial component of identity and self-understanding of individuals that links a community to its past. The Information Society should harness and preserve cultural heritage for the future by all appropriate methods, including digitization.

9)   Media

55. We reaffirm our commitment to the principles of freedom of the press and freedom of information, as well as those of the independence, pluralism and diversity of media, which are essential to the Information Society. Freedom to seek, receive, impart and use information for the creation, accumulation and dissemination of knowledge are important to the Information Society. We call for the responsible use and treatment of information by the media in accordance with the highest ethical and professional standards. Traditional media in all their forms have an important role in the Information Society and ICTs should play a supportive role in this regard. Diversity of media ownership should be encouraged, in conformity with national law, and taking into account relevant international conventions. We reaffirm the necessity of reducing international imbalances affecting the media, particularly as regards infrastructure, technical resources and the development of human skills.

10) Ethical Dimensions of the Information Society

56. The Information Society should respect peace and uphold the fundamental values of freedom, equality, solidarity, tolerance, shared responsibility, and respect for nature.

57. We acknowledge the importance of ethics for the Information Society, which should foster justice, and the dignity and worth of the human person. The widest possible protection should be accorded to the family and to enable it to play its crucial role in society.

58. The use of ICTs and content creation should respect human rights and fundamental freedoms of others, including personal privacy, and the right to freedom of thought, conscience, and religion in conformity with relevant international instruments.

59. All actors in the Information Society should take appropriate actions and preventive measures, as determined by law, against abusive uses of ICTs, such as illegal and other acts motivated by racism, racial discrimination, xenophobia, and related intolerance, hatred, violence, all forms of child abuse, including pedophilia and child pornography, and trafficking in, and exploitation of, human beings.

11) International and Regional Cooperation

60. We aim at making full use of the opportunities offered by ICTs in our efforts to reach the internationally agreed development goals, including those contained in the Millennium Declaration, and to uphold the key principles set forth in this Declaration. The Information Society is intrinsically global in nature and national efforts need to be supported by effective international and regional cooperation among governments, the private sector, civil society and other stakeholders, including the international financial institutions.

61. In order to build an inclusive global Information Society, we will seek and effectively implement concrete international approaches and mechanisms, including financial and technical assistance. Therefore, while appreciating ongoing ICT cooperation through various mechanisms, we invite all stakeholders to commit to the "Digital Solidarity Agenda" set forth in the Plan of Action. We are convinced that the worldwide agreed objective is to contribute to bridge the digital divide, promote access to ICTs, create digital opportunities, and benefit from the potential offered by ICTs for development. We recognize the will expressed by some to create an international voluntary "Digital Solidarity Fund", and by others to undertake studies concerning existing mechanisms and the efficiency and feasibility of such a Fund.

62. Regional integration contributes to the development of the global Information Society and makes strong cooperation within and among regions indispensable. Regional dialogue should contribute to national capacity building and to the alignment of national strategies with the goals of this Declaration of Principles in a compatible way, while respecting national and regional particularities. In this context, we welcome and encourage the international community to support the ICT-related measures of such initiatives.

63. We resolve to assist developing countries, LDCs and countries with economies in transition through the mobilization from all sources of financing, the provision of financial and technical assistance and by creating an environment conducive to technology transfer, consistent with the purposes of this Declaration and the Plan of Action.

64. The core competences of the International Telecommunication Union (ITU) in the fields of ICTs-assistance in bridging the digital divide, international and regional cooperation, radio spectrum management, standards development and the dissemination of information-are of crucial importance for building the Information Society.

C. Towards an Information Society for All Based on Shared Knowledge

65. We commit ourselves to strengthening cooperation to seek common responses to the challenges and to the implementation of the Plan of Action, which will realize the vision of an inclusive Information Society based on the Key Principles incorporated in this Declaration.

66. We further commit ourselves to evaluate and follow-up progress in bridging the digital divide, taking into account different levels of development, so as to reach internationally agreed development goals, including those contained in the Millennium Declaration, and to assess the effectiveness of investment and international cooperation efforts in building the Information Society.

67. We are firmly convinced that we are collectively entering a new era of enormous potential, that of the Information Society and expanded human communication. In this emerging society, information and knowledge can be produced, exchanged, shared and communicated through all the networks of the world. All individuals can soon, if we take the necessary actions, together build a new Information Society based on shared knowledge and founded on global solidarity and a better mutual understanding between peoples and nations. We trust that these measures will open the way to the future development of a true knowledge society.

Appendix II

Plan of Action

APPENDIX II

PLAN OF ACTION

World Summit on the Information Society
Geneva 2003 — Tunis 2005
12 December 2003

A. Introduction

1. The common vision and guiding principles of the Declaration are translated in this Plan of Action into concrete action lines to advance the achievement of the internationally-agreed development goals, including those in the Millennium Declaration, the Monterrey Consensus and the Johannesburg Declaration and Plan of Implementation, by promoting the use of ICT-based products, networks, services and applications, and to help countries overcome the digital divide. The Information Society envisaged in the Declaration of Principles will be realized in cooperation and solidarity by governments and all other stakeholders.

2. The Information Society is an evolving concept that has reached different levels across the world, reflecting the different stages of development. Technological and other change is rapidly transforming the environment in which the Information Society is developed. The Plan of Action is thus an evolving platform to promote the Information Society at the national, regional and international levels. The unique two-phase structure of the World Summit on the Information Society (WSIS) provides an opportunity to take this evolution into account.

3. All stakeholders have an important role to play in the Information Society, especially through partnerships:

   a) Governments have a leading role in developing and implementing comprehensive, forward looking and sustainable national e-strategies. The private sector and civil society, in dialogue with governments, have an important consultative role to play in devising national e-strategies.

   b) The commitment of the private sector is important in developing and diffusing information and communication technologies (ICTs), for infrastructure, content and applications. The private sector is not only a market player but also plays a role in a wider sustainable development context.

c) The commitment and involvement of civil society is equally important in creating an equitable Information Society, and in implementing ICT-related initiatives for development.

d) International and regional institutions, including international financial institutions, have a key role in integrating the use of ICTs in the development process and making available necessary resources for building the Information Society and for the evaluation of the progress made.

B. *Objectives, Goals and Targets*

4. The objectives of the Plan of Action are to build an inclusive Information Society; to put the potential of knowledge and ICTs at the service of development; to promote the use of information and knowledge for the achievement of internationally agreed development goals, including those contained in the Millennium Declaration; and to address new challenges of the Information Society, at the national, regional and international levels. Opportunity shall be taken in phase two of the WSIS to evaluate and assess progress made towards bridging the digital divide.

5. Specific targets for the Information Society will be established as appropriate, at the national level in the framework of national e-strategies and in accordance with national development policies, taking into account the different national circumstances. Such targets can serve as useful benchmarks for actions and for the evaluation of the progress made towards the attainment of the overall objectives of the Information Society.

6. Based on internationally agreed development goals, including those in the Millennium Declaration, which are premised on international cooperation, indicative targets may serve as global references for improving connectivity and access in the use of ICTs in promoting the objectives of the Plan of Action, to be achieved by 2015. These targets may be taken into account in the establishment of the national targets, considering the different national circumstances:

a) to connect villages with ICTs and establish community access points;

b) to connect universities, colleges, secondary schools and primary schools with ICTs;

c) to connect scientific and research centers with ICTs;

d) to connect public libraries, cultural centers, museums, post offices and archives with ICTs;

e) to connect health centers and hospitals with ICTs;

f) to connect all local and central government departments and establish websites and email addresses;

g) to adapt all primary and secondary school curricula to meet the challenges of the Information Society, taking into account national circumstances;

h) to ensure that all of the world's population have access to television and radio services;

i) to encourage the development of content and to put in place technical conditions in order to facilitate the presence and use of all world languages on the Internet;

j) to ensure that more than half the world's inhabitants have access to ICTs within their reach.

7.   In giving effect to these objectives, goals and targets, special attention will be paid to the needs of developing countries, and in particular to countries, peoples and groups cited in paragraphs 11-16 of the Declaration of Principles.

C.   Action Lines

C1. The Role of Governments and All Stakeholders in the Promotion of ICTs for Development

8.   The effective participation of governments and all stakeholders is vital in developing the Information Society requiring cooperation and partnerships among all of them.

a) Development of national e-strategies, including the necessary human capacity building, should be encouraged by all countries by 2005, taking into account different national circumstances.

b) Initiate at the national level a structured dialogue involving all relevant stakeholders, including through public/private partnerships, in devising e-strategies for the Information Society and for the exchange of best practices.

c) In developing and implementing national e-strategies, stakeholders should take into consideration local, regional and national needs and concerns. To maximize the benefits of initiatives undertaken, these should include the concept of sustainability. The private sector should be engaged in concrete projects to develop the Information Society at local, regional and national levels.

d) Each country is encouraged to establish at least one functioning Public/Private Partnership (PPP) or Multi-Sector Partnership (MSP), by 2005 as a showcase for future action.

e) Identify mechanisms, at the national, regional and international levels, for the initiation and promotion of partnerships among stakeholders of the Information Society.

f) Explore the viability of establishing multi-stakeholder portals for indigenous peoples at the national level.

g) By 2005, relevant international organizations and financial institutions should develop their own strategies for the use of ICTs for sustainable development, including sustainable production and consumption patterns and as an effective instrument to help achieve the goals expressed in the United Nations Millennium Declaration.

h) International organizations should publish, in their areas of competence, including on their website, reliable information submitted by relevant stakeholders on successful experiences of mainstreaming ICTs.

i) Encourage a series of related measures, including, among other things: incubator schemes, venture capital investments (national and international), government investment funds (including micro-finance for Small, Medium-sized and Micro Enterprises (SMMEs), investment promotion strategies, software export support activities (trade counseling), support of research and development networks and software parks.

C2. Information and Communication Infrastructure: An Essential Foundation for the Information Society

9.   Infrastructure is central in achieving the goal of digital inclusion, enabling universal, sustainable, ubiquitous and affordable access to ICTs by all, taking into account relevant solutions already in place in developing countries and countries with economies in transition, to provide sustainable connectivity and access to remote and marginalized areas at national and regional levels.

a) Governments should take action, in the framework of national development policies, in order to support an enabling and competitive environment for the necessary investment in ICT infrastructure and for the development of new services.

b) In the context of national e-strategies, devise appropriate universal access policies and strategies, and their means of implementation, in line with the indicative targets, and develop ICT connectivity indicators.

c) In the context of national e-strategies, provide and improve ICT connectivity for all schools, universities, health institutions, libraries, post offices, community centers, museums and other institutions accessible to the public, in line with the indicative targets.

d) Develop and strengthen national, regional and international broadband network infrastructure, including delivery by satellite and other systems, to help in providing the capacity to match the needs of countries and their citizens and for the delivery of new ICT-based services. Support technical, regulatory and operational studies by the International Telecommunication Union (ITU) and, as appropriate, other relevant international organizations in order to:

   i) broaden access to orbital resources, global frequency harmonization and global systems standardization;

   ii) encourage public/private partnership;

   iii) promote the provision of global high-speed satellite services for underserved areas such as remote and sparsely populated areas;

   iv) explore other systems that can provide high-speed connectivity.

e) In the context of national e-strategies, address the special requirements of older people, persons with disabilities, children, especially marginalized children and other disadvantaged and vulnerable groups, including by appropriate educational administrative and legislative measures to ensure their full inclusion in the Information Society.

f) Encourage the design and production of ICT equipment and services so that everyone, has easy and affordable access to them including older people, persons with disabilities, children, especially marginalized children, and other disadvantaged and vulnerable groups, and promote the development of technologies, applications, and content suited to their needs, guided by the Universal Design Principle and further enhanced by the use of assistive technologies.

g) In order to alleviate the challenges of illiteracy, develop affordable technologies and non-text based computer interfaces to facilitate people's access to ICT,

h) Undertake international research and development efforts aimed at making available adequate and affordable ICT equipment for end users.

i) Encourage the use of unused wireless capacity, including satellite, in developed countries and in particular in developing countries, to provide access in remote areas, especially in developing countries and countries with economies in transition, and to improve low-cost connectivity in developing countries. Special concern should be given to the Least Developed Countries in their efforts in establishing telecommunication infrastructure.

j) Optimize connectivity among major information networks by encouraging the creation and development of regional ICT backbones and Internet exchange points, to reduce interconnection costs and broaden network access.

k) Develop strategies for increasing affordable global connectivity, thereby facilitating improved access. Commercially negotiated Internet transit and interconnection costs should be oriented towards objective, transparent and non-discriminatory parameters, taking into account ongoing work on this subject.

l) Encourage and promote joint use of traditional media and new technologies.

C3. Access to Information and Knowledge

10. ICTs allow people, anywhere in the world, to access information and knowledge almost instantaneously. Individuals, organizations and communities should benefit from access to knowledge and information.

a) Develop policy guidelines for the development and promotion of public domain information as an important international instrument promoting public access to information.

b) Governments are encouraged to provide adequate access through various communication resources, notably the Internet, to public official information. Establishing legislation on access to information and the preservation of public data, notably in the area of the new technologies, is encouraged.

c) Promote research and development to facilitate accessibility of ICTs for all, including disadvantaged, marginalized and vulnerable groups.

d) Governments, and other stakeholders, should establish sustainable multi-purpose community public access points, providing affordable or free-of-charge access for their citizens to the various communication resources, notably the Internet. These access points should, to the extent possible, have sufficient capacity to provide assistance to users, in libraries, educational institutions, public administrations, post offices or other public places, with special emphasis on rural and underserved areas, while respecting intellectual property rights (IPRs) and encouraging the use of information and sharing of knowledge.

e) Encourage research and promote awareness among all stakeholders of the possibilities offered by different software models, and the means of their creation, including proprietary, open-source and free software, in order to increase competition, freedom of choice and affordability, and to enable all stakeholders to evaluate which solution best meets their requirements.

f) Governments should actively promote the use of ICTs as a fundamental working tool by their citizens and local authorities. In this respect, the international community and other stakeholders should support capacity building for local authorities in the widespread use of ICTs as a means of improving local governance.

g) Encourage research on the Information Society, including on innovative forms of networking, adaptation of ICT infrastructure, tools and applications that facilitate accessibility of ICTs for all, and disadvantaged groups in particular.

h) Support the creation and development of a digital public library and archive services, adapted to the Information Society, including reviewing national library strategies and legislation, developing a global understanding of the need for "hybrid libraries", and fostering worldwide cooperation between libraries.

i) Encourage initiatives to facilitate access, including free and affordable access to open access journals and books, and open archives for scientific information.

j) Support research and development of the design of useful instruments for all stakeholders to foster increased awareness, assessment, and evaluation of different software models and licenses, so as to ensure an optimal choice of appropriate software that will best contribute to achieving development goals within local conditions.

C4. Capacity Building

11. Everyone should have the necessary skills to benefit fully from the Information Society. Therefore capacity building and ICT literacy are essential. ICTs can contribute to achieving universal education worldwide, through delivery of education and training of teachers, and offering improved conditions for lifelong learning, encompassing people that are outside the formal education process, and improving professional skills.

a) Develop domestic policies to ensure that ICTs are fully integrated in education and training at all levels, including in curriculum development, teacher training, institutional administration and management, and in support of the concept of lifelong learning.

b) Develop and promote programs to eradicate illiteracy using ICTs at national, regional and international levels.

c) Promote e-literacy skills for all, for example by designing and offering courses for public administration, taking advantage of existing facilities such as libraries, multipurpose community centers, public access points and by establishing local ICT training centers with the cooperation of all stakeholders. Special attention should be paid to disadvantaged and vulnerable groups.

d) In the context of national educational policies, and taking into account the need to eradicate adult illiteracy, ensure that young people are equipped with knowledge and skills to use ICTs, including the capacity to analyze and treat information in creative and innovative ways, share their expertise and participate fully in the Information Society.

e) Governments, in cooperation with other stakeholders, should create programs for capacity building with an emphasis on creating a critical mass of qualified and skilled ICT professionals and experts.

f) Develop pilot projects to demonstrate the impact of ICT-based alternative educational delivery systems, notably for achieving Education for All targets, including basic literacy targets.

g) Work on removing the gender barriers to ICT education and training and promoting equal training opportunities in ICT-related fields for women and girls. Early intervention programs in science and technology should target young girls with the aim of increasing the number of women in ICT careers. Promote the exchange of best practices on the integration of gender perspectives in ICT education.

h) Empower local communities, especially those in rural and underserved areas, in ICT use and promote the production of useful and socially meaningful content for the benefit of all.

i) Launch education and training programs, where possible using information networks of traditional nomadic and indigenous peoples, which provide opportunities to fully participate in the Information Society.

j) Design and implement regional and international cooperation activities to enhance the capacity, notably, of leaders and operational staff in developing countries and LDCs, to apply ICTs effectively in the whole range of educational activities. This should include delivery of education outside the educational structure, such as the workplace and at home.

k) Design specific training programs in the use of ICTs in order to meet the educational needs of information professionals, such as archivists, librarians, museum professionals, scientists, teachers, journalists, postal workers and other relevant professional groups. Training of information professionals should focus not only on new methods and techniques for the development and provision of information and communication services, but also on relevant management skills to ensure the best use of technologies. Training of teachers should focus on the technical aspects of ICTs, on development of content, and on the potential possibilities and challenges of ICTs.

l) Develop distance learning, training and other forms of education and training as part of capacity building programs. Give special attention to developing countries and especially LDCs in different levels of human resources development.

m) Promote international and regional cooperation in the field of capacity building, including country programs developed by the United Nations and its Specialized Agencies

n) Launch pilot projects to design new forms of ICT-based networking, linking education, training and research institutions between and among developed and developing countries and countries with economies in transition.

o) Volunteering, if conducted in harmony with national policies and local cultures, can be a valuable asset for raising human capacity to make productive use of ICT tools and build a more inclusive Information Society. Activate volunteer programs to provide capacity building on ICT for development, particularly in developing countries.

p) Design programs to train users to develop self-learning and self-development capacities.

C5. Building Confidence and Security in the Use of ICTs

12. Confidence and security are among the main pillars of the Information Society.

a) Promote cooperation among the governments at the United Nations and with all stakeholders at other appropriate fora to enhance user confidence, build trust, and protect both data and network integrity; consider existing and potential threats to ICTs; and address other information security and network security issues.

b) Governments, in cooperation with the private sector, should prevent, detect and respond to cyber-crime and misuse of ICTs by: developing guidelines that take into account ongoing efforts in these areas; considering legislation that allows for effective investigation and prosecution of misuse; promoting effective mutual assistance efforts; strengthening institutional support at the international level for preventing, detecting and recovering from such incidents; and encouraging education and raising awareness.

c) Governments, and other stakeholders, should actively promote user education and awareness about online privacy and the means of protecting privacy.

d) Take appropriate action on spam at national and international levels.

e) Encourage the domestic assessment of national law with a view to overcoming any obstacles to the effective use of electronic documents and transactions including electronic means of authentication.

f) Further strengthen the trust and security framework with complementary and mutually reinforcing initiatives in the fields of security in the use of ICTs, with initiatives or guidelines with respect to rights to privacy, data and consumer protection.

g) Share good practices in the field of information security and network security and encourage their use by all parties concerned.

h) Invite interested countries to set up focal points for real-time incident handling and response, and develop a cooperative network between these focal points for sharing information and technologies on incident response.

i) Encourage further development of secure and reliable applications to facilitate online transactions.

j) Encourage interested countries to contribute actively to the ongoing United Nations activities to build confidence and security in the use of ICTs.

C6. Enabling Environment

13. To maximize the social, economic and environmental benefits of the Information Society, governments need to create a trustworthy, transparent and non-discriminatory legal, regulatory and policy environment. Actions include:

a) Governments should foster a supportive, transparent, pro-competitive and predictable policy, legal and regulatory framework, which provides the appropriate incentives to investment and community development in the Information Society.

b) We ask the Secretary General of the United Nations to set up a working group on Internet governance, in an open and inclusive process that ensures a mechanism for the full and active participation of governments, the private sector and civil society from both developing and developed countries, involving relevant intergovernmental and international organizations and forums, to investigate and make proposals for action, as appropriate, on the governance of Internet by 2005. The group should, *inter alia*:

i) develop a working definition of Internet governance;

ii) identify the public policy issues that are relevant to Internet governance;

iii) develop a common understanding of the respective roles and responsibilities of governments, existing intergovernmental and international organizations and other forums as well as the private sector and civil society from both developing and developed countries;

iv) prepare a report on the results of this activity to be presented for consideration and appropriate action for the second phase of WSIS in Tunis in 2005.

c) Governments are invited to:

i) facilitate the establishment of national and regional Internet Exchange Centers;

ii) manage or supervise, as appropriate, their respective country code top-level domain name (ccTLD);

iii) promote awareness of the Internet.

d) In cooperation with the relevant stakeholders, promote regional root servers and the use of internationalized domain names in order to overcome barriers to access.

e) Governments should continue to update their domestic consumer protection laws to respond to the new requirements of the Information Society.

f) Promote effective participation by developing countries and countries with economies in transition in international ICT forums and create opportunities for exchange of experience.

g) Governments need to formulate national strategies, which include e-government strategies, to make public administration more transparent, efficient and democratic.

h) Develop a framework for the secure storage and archival of documents and other electronic records of information.

i) Governments and stakeholders should actively promote user education and awareness about online privacy and the means of protecting privacy.

j) Invite stakeholders to ensure that practices designed to facilitate electronic commerce also permit consumers to have a choice as to whether or not to use electronic communication.

k) Encourage the ongoing work in the area of effective dispute settlement systems, notably alternative dispute resolution (ADR), which can promote settlement of disputes.

l) Governments, in collaboration with stakeholders, are encouraged to formulate conducive ICT policies that foster entrepreneurship, innovation and investment, and with particular reference to the promotion of participation by women.

m) Recognizing the economic potential of ICTs for Small and Medium-Sized Enterprises (SMEs), they should be assisted in increasing their competitiveness by streamlining administrative procedures, facilitating their access to capital and enhancing their capacity to participate in ICT-related projects.

n) Governments should act as model users and early adopters of e-commerce in accordance with their level of socio-economic development.

o) Governments, in cooperation with other stakeholders, should raise awareness of the importance of international interoperability standards for global e-commerce.

p) Governments, in cooperation with other stakeholders, should promote the development and use of open, interoperable, non-discriminatory and demand-driven standards.

q) ITU, pursuant to its treaty capacity, coordinates and allocates frequencies with the goal of facilitating ubiquitous and affordable access.

r) Additional steps should be taken in ITU and other regional organizations to ensure rational, efficient and economical use of, and equitable access to, the radio-frequency spectrum by all countries, based on relevant international agreements.

C7. ICT Applications: Benefits in All Aspects of Life

14. ICT applications can support sustainable development, in the fields of public administration, business, education and training, health, employment, environment, agriculture and science within the framework of national e-strategies. This would include actions within the following sectors:

15. E-government

a) Implement e-government strategies focusing on applications aimed at innovating and promoting transparency in public administrations and democratic processes, improving efficiency and strengthening relations with citizens.

b) Develop national e-government initiatives and services, at all levels, adapted to the needs of citizens and business, to achieve a more efficient allocation of resources and public goods.

c) Support international cooperation initiatives in the field of e-government, in order to enhance transparency, accountability and efficiency at all levels of government.

16. E-business

a) Governments, international organizations and the private sector, are encouraged to promote the benefits of international trade and the use of e-business, and promote the use of e-business models in developing countries and countries with economies in transition.

b) Through the adoption of an enabling environment, and based on widely available Internet access, governments should seek to stimulate private sector investment, foster new applications, content development and public/private partnerships.

c) Government policies should favor assistance to, and growth of SMMEs, in the ICT industry, as well as their entry into e-business, to stimulate economic growth and job creation as an element of a strategy for poverty reduction through wealth creation.

17. E-learning (see section C4)

18. E-health

a) Promote collaborative efforts of governments, planners, health professionals, and other agencies along with the participation of international organizations for creating a reliable, timely, high quality and affordable health care and health information systems and for promoting continuous medical training, education, and research through the use of ICTs, while respecting and protecting citizens' right to privacy.

b) Facilitate access to the world's medical knowledge and locally-relevant content resources for strengthening public health research and prevention programs and promoting women's and men's health, such as content on sexual and reproductive health and sexually transmitted infections, and for diseases that attract full attention of the world including HIV/AIDS, malaria and tuberculosis.

c) Alert, monitor and control the spread of communicable diseases, through the improvement of common information systems.

d) Promote the development of international standards for the exchange of health data, taking due account of privacy concerns.

e) Encourage the adoption of ICTs to improve and extend health care and health information systems to remote and underserved areas and vulnerable populations, recognizing women's roles as health providers in their families and communities.

f) Strengthen and expand ICT-based initiatives for providing medical and humanitarian assistance in disasters and emergencies.

19. E-employment

a) Encourage the development of best practices for e-workers and e-employers built, at the national level, on principles of fairness and gender equality, respecting all relevant international norms.

b) Promote new ways of organizing work and business with the aim of raising productivity, growth and well-being through investment in ICTs and human resources.

c) Promote teleworking to allow citizens, particularly in the developing countries, LDCs, and small economies, to live in their societies and work anywhere, and to increase employment opportunities for women, and for those with disabilities. In promoting teleworking, special attention should be given to strategies promoting job creation and the retention of the skilled working force.

d) Promote early intervention programs in science and technology that should target young girls to increase the number of women in ICT carriers.

20. E-environment

a) Governments, in cooperation with other stakeholders are encouraged to use and promote ICTs as an instrument for environmental protection and the sustainable use of natural resources.

b) Government, civil society and the private sector are encouraged to initiate actions and implement projects and programs for sustainable production and consumption and the environmentally safe disposal and recycling of discarded hardware and components used in ICTs.

c) Establish monitoring systems, using ICTs, to forecast and monitor the impact of natural and man-made disasters, particularly in developing countries, LDCs and small economies.

21. E-agriculture

a) Ensure the systematic dissemination of information using ICTs on agriculture, animal husbandry, fisheries, forestry and food, in order to provide ready access to comprehensive, up-to-date and detailed knowledge and information, particularly in rural areas.

b) Public-private partnerships should seek to maximize the use of ICTs as an instrument to improve production (quantity and quality).

22. E-science

a) Promote affordable and reliable high-speed Internet connection for all universities and research institutions to support their critical role in information and knowledge production, education and training, and to support the establishment of partnerships, cooperation and networking between these institutions.

b) Promote electronic publishing, differential pricing and open access initiatives to make scientific information affordable and accessible in all countries on an equitable basis.

c) Promote the use of peer-to-peer technology to share scientific knowledge and pre-prints and reprints written by scientific authors who have waived their right to payment.

d) Promote the long-term systematic and efficient collection, dissemination and preservation of essential scientific digital data, for example, population and meteorological data in all countries.

e) Promote principles and metadata standards to facilitate cooperation and effective use of collected scientific information and data as appropriate to conduct scientific research.

C8. Cultural Diversity and Identity, Linguistic Diversity and Local Content

23. Cultural and linguistic diversity, while stimulating respect for cultural identity, traditions and religions, is essential to the development of an Information Society based on the dialogue among cultures and regional and international cooperation. It is an important factor for sustainable development.

a) Create policies that support the respect, preservation, promotion and enhancement of cultural and linguistic diversity and cultural heritage within the Information Society, as reflected in relevant agreed United Nations documents, including UNESCO's Universal Declaration on Cultural Diversity. This includes encouraging governments to design cultural policies to promote the production of cultural, educational and scientific content and the development of local cultural industries suited to the linguistic and cultural context of the users.

b) Develop national policies and laws to ensure that libraries, archives, museums and other cultural institutions can play their full role of content-including traditional knowledge-providers in the Information Society, more particularly by providing continued access to recorded information.

c) Support efforts to develop and use ICTs for the preservation of natural and, cultural heritage, keeping it accessible as a living part of today's culture. This includes developing systems for ensuring continued access to archived digital information and multimedia content in digital repositories, and support archives, cultural collections and libraries as the memory of humankind.

d) Develop and implement policies that preserve, affirm, respect and promote diversity of cultural expression and indigenous knowledge and traditions through the creation of varied information content and the use of different methods, including the digitization of the educational, scientific and cultural heritage.

e) Support local content development, translation and adaptation, digital archives, and diverse forms of digital and traditional media by local authorities. These activities can also strengthen local and indigenous communities.

f) Provide content that is relevant to the cultures and languages of individuals in the Information Society, through access to traditional and digital media services.

g) Through public/private partnerships, foster the creation of varied local and national content, including that available in the language of users, and give recognition and support to ICT-based work in all artistic fields.

h) Strengthen programs focused on gender-sensitive curricula in formal and non-formal education for all and enhancing communication and media literacy for women with a view to building the capacity of girls and women to understand and to develop ICT content.

i) Nurture the local capacity for the creation and distribution of software in local languages, as well as content that is relevant to different segments of population, including non-literate, persons with disabilities, disadvantaged and vulnerable groups especially in developing countries and countries with economies in transition.

j) Give support to media based in local communities and support projects combining the use of traditional media and new technologies for their role in facilitating the use of local languages, for documenting and preserving local heritage, including landscape and biological diversity, and as a means to reach rural and isolated and nomadic communities.

k) Enhance the capacity of indigenous peoples to develop content in their own languages.

l) Cooperate with indigenous peoples and traditional communities to enable them to more effectively use and benefit from the use of their traditional knowledge in the Information Society.

m) Exchange knowledge, experiences and best practices on policies and tools designed to promote cultural and linguistic diversity at regional and sub-regional levels. This can be achieved by establishing regional, and sub-regional working groups on specific issues of this Plan of Action to foster integration efforts.

n) Assess at the regional level the contribution of ICT to cultural exchange and interaction, and based on the outcome of this assessment, design relevant programs.

o) Governments, through public/private partnerships, should promote technologies and R&D programs in such areas as translation, iconographies, voice-assisted services and the development of necessary hardware and a variety of software models, including proprietary, open source software and free software, such as standard character sets, language codes, electronic dictionaries, terminology and thesauri, multilingual search engines, machine translation tools, internationalized domain names, content referencing as well as general and application software.

C9. Media

24. The media-in their various forms and with a diversity of ownership-as an actor, have an essential role in the development of the Information Society and are recognized as an important contributor to freedom of expression and plurality of information.

a) Encourage the media-print and broadcast as well as new media-to continue to play an important role in the Information Society.

b) Encourage the development of domestic legislation that guarantees the independence and plurality of the media.

c) Take appropriate measures-consistent with freedom of expression-to combat illegal and harmful content in media content.

d) Encourage media professionals in developed countries to establish partnerships and networks with the media in developing ones, especially in the field of training.

e) Promote balanced and diverse portrayals of women and men by the media.

f) Reduce international imbalances affecting the media, particularly as regards infrastructure, technical resources and the development of human skills, taking full advantage of ICT tools in this regard.

g) Encourage traditional media to bridge the knowledge divide and to facilitate the flow of cultural content, particularly in rural areas.

C10. Ethical Dimensions of the Information Society

25. The Information Society should be subject to universally held values and promote the common good and to prevent abusive uses of ICTs.

  a) Take steps to promote respect for peace and to uphold the fundamental values of freedom, equality, solidarity, tolerance, shared responsibility, and respect for nature.

  b) All stakeholders should increase their awareness of the ethical dimension of their use of ICTs.

  c) All actors in the Information Society should promote the common good, protect privacy and personal data and take appropriate actions and preventive measures, as determined by law, against abusive uses of ICTs such as illegal and other acts motivated by racism, racial discrimination, xenophobia, and related intolerance, hatred, violence, all forms of child abuse, including pedophilia and child pornography, and trafficking in, and exploitation of, human beings.

  d) Invite relevant stakeholders, especially the academia, to continue research on ethical dimensions of ICTs.

C11. International and Regional Cooperation

26. International cooperation among all stakeholders is vital in implementation of this plan of action and needs to be strengthened with a view to promoting universal access and bridging the digital divide, *inter alia*, by provision of means of implementation.

  a) Governments of developing countries should raise the relative priority of ICT projects in requests for international cooperation and assistance on infrastructure development projects from developed countries and international financial organizations.

  b) Within the context of the UN's Global Compact and building upon the United Nations Millennium Declaration, build on and accelerate public-private partnerships, focusing on the use of ICT in development.

  c) Invite international and regional organizations to mainstream ICTs in their work programs and to assist all levels of developing countries, to be involved in the preparation and implementation of national action plans to support the fulfillment of the goals indicated in the declaration of principles and in this Plan of Action, taking into account the importance of regional initiatives.

D.   *Digital Solidarity Agenda*

27. The Digital Solidarity Agenda aims at putting in place the conditions for mobilizing human, financial and technological resources for inclusion of all

men and women in the emerging Information Society. Close national, regional and international cooperation among all stakeholders in the implementation of this Agenda is vital. To overcome the digital divide, we need to use more efficiently existing approaches and mechanisms and fully explore new ones, in order to provide financing for the development of infrastructure, equipment, capacity building and content, which are essential for participation in the Information Society.

D1. Priorities and Strategies

a) National e-strategies should be made an integral part of national development plans, including Poverty Reduction Strategies.

b) ICTs should be fully mainstreamed into strategies for Official Development Assistance (ODA) through more effective donor information-sharing and co-ordination, and through analysis and sharing of best practices and lessons learned from experience with ICT-for-development programs.

D2. Mobilizing Resources

a) All countries and international organizations should act to create conditions conducive to increasing the availability and effective mobilization of resources for financing development as elaborated in the Monterrey Consensus.

b) Developed countries should make concrete efforts to fulfill their international commitments to financing development including the Monterrey Consensus, in which developed countries that have not done so are urged to make concrete efforts towards the target of 0.7 per cent of gross national product (GNP) as ODA to developing countries and 0.15 to 0.20 per cent of GNP of developed countries to least developed countries.

c) For those developing countries facing unsustainable debt burdens, we welcome initiatives that have been undertaken to reduce outstanding indebtedness and invite further national and international measures in that regard, including, as appropriate, debt cancellation and other arrangements. Particular attention should be given to enhancing the Heavily Indebted Poor Countries initiative. These initiatives would release more resources that may be used for financing ICT for development projects.

d) Recognizing the potential of ICT for development we furthermore advocate:

   i) developing countries to increase their efforts to attract major private national and foreign investments for ICTs through the creation of a transparent, stable and predictable enabling investment environment;

ii) developed countries and international financial organizations to be responsive to the strategies and priorities of ICTs for development, mainstream ICTs in their work programs, and assist developing countries and countries with economies in transition to prepare and implement their national e-strategies. Based on the priorities of national development plans and implementation of the above commitments, developed countries should increase their efforts to provide more financial resources to developing countries in harnessing ICTs for development;

iii) the private sector to contribute to the implementation of this Digital Solidarity Agenda.

e) In our efforts to bridge the digital divide, we should promote, within our development cooperation, technical and financial assistance directed towards national and regional capacity building, technology transfer on mutually agreed terms, cooperation in R&D programs and exchange of know-how.

f) While all existing financial mechanisms should be fully exploited, a thorough review of their adequacy in meeting the challenges of ICT for development should be completed by the end of December 2004. This review shall be conducted by a Task Force under the auspices of the Secretary-General of the United Nations and submitted for consideration to the second phase of this summit. Based on the conclusion of the review, improvements and innovations of financing mechanisms will be considered including the effectiveness, the feasibility and the creation of a voluntary Digital Solidarity Fund, as mentioned in the Declaration of Principles.

g) Countries should consider establishing national mechanisms to achieve universal access in both underserved rural and urban areas, in order to bridge the digital divide.

E)   Follow-Up and Evaluation

28. A realistic international performance evaluation and benchmarking (both qualitative and quantitative), through comparable statistical indicators and research results, should be developed to follow up the implementation of the objectives, goals and targets in the Plan of Action, taking into account different national circumstances.

a) In cooperation with each country concerned, develop and launch a composite ICT Development (Digital Opportunity) Index. It could be published annually, or every two years, in an ICT Development Report. The index could show the statistics while the report would present analytical work on policies and their implementation, depending on national circumstances, including gender analysis.

b) Appropriate indicators and benchmarking, including community connectivity indicators, should clarify the magnitude of the digital divide, in both its domestic and international dimensions, and keep it under regular assessment, and tracking global progress in the use of ICTs to achieve internationally agreed development goals, including those of the Millennium Declaration.

c) International and regional organizations should assess and report regularly on universal accessibility of nations to ICTs, with the aim of creating equitable opportunities for the growth of ICT sectors of developing countries.

d) Gender-specific indicators on ICT use and needs should be developed, and measurable performance indicators should be identified to assess the impact of funded ICT projects on the lives of women and girls.

e) Develop and launch a website on best practices and success stories, based on a compilation of contributions from all stakeholders, in a concise, accessible and compelling format, following the internationally-recognized web accessibility standards. The website could be periodically updated and turned into a permanent experience-sharing exercise.

f) All countries and regions should develop tools so as to provide statistical information on the Information Society, with basic indicators and analysis of its key dimensions. Priority should be given to setting up coherent and internationally comparable indicator systems, taking into account different levels of development.

F) Towards WSIS Phase 2 (Tunis)

29. Recalling General Assembly Resolution 56/183 and taking into account the outcome of the Geneva phase of the WSIS, a preparatory meeting will be held in the first half of 2004 to review those issues of the Information Society which should form the focus of the Tunis phase of the WSIS and to agree on the structure of the preparatory process for the second phase. In line with the decision of this Summit concerning its Tunis phase, the second phase of the WSIS should consider, *inter alia*:

a) Elaboration of final appropriate documents based on the outcome of the Geneva phase of the WSIS with a view to consolidating the process of building a global Information Society, and reducing the Digital Divide and transforming it into digital opportunities.

b) Follow-up and implementation of the Geneva Plan of Action at national, regional and international levels, including the United

Nations system, as part of an integrated and coordinated approach, calling upon the participation of all relevant stakeholders. This should take place, *inter alia*, through partnerships among stakeholders.

Appendix III

UNCITRAL Model Law
on Electronic Commerce with
Guide to Enactment of 1996

WITH ADDITIONAL ARTICLE 5bis, AS ADOPTED IN 1998

Contents

Paragraphs

Guide to Enactment of the UNCITRAL Model Law on Electronic Commerce

Purpose of this Guide

Resolution adopted by the General Assembly

[on the report of the Sixth Committee (A/51/628)]

51/162 Model Law on Electronic Commerce adopted by the United Nations Commission on International Trade Law

The General Assembly,

Recalling its resolution 2205 (XXI) of 17 December 1966, by which it created the United Nations Commission on International Trade Law, with a mandate to further the progressive harmonization and unification of the law of international trade and in that respect to bear in mind the interests of all peoples, in particular those of developing countries, in the extensive development of international trade,

Noting that an increasing number of transactions in international trade are carried out by means of electronic data interchange and other means of communication, commonly referred to as "electronic commerce", which involve the use of alternatives to paper-based methods of communication and storage of information,

Recalling the recommendation on the legal value of computer records adopted by the Commission at its eighteenth session, in 1985, and paragraph 5(b) of General Assembly resolution 40/71 of 11 December 1985, in which the Assembly called upon governments and international organizations to take action, where appropriate, in conformity with the recommendation of the Commission,[1] so as to ensure legal security in the context of the widest possible use of automated data processing in international trade,

Convinced that the establishment of a model law facilitating the use of electronic commerce that is acceptable to states with different legal, social, and economic systems, could contribute significantly to the development of harmonious international economic relations,

Noting that the Model Law on Electronic Commerce was adopted by the Commission at its twenty-ninth session after consideration of the observations of governments and interested organizations,

Believing that the adoption of the Model Law on Electronic Commerce by the Commission will assist all states significantly in enhancing their legislation

---

1   See *Official Records of the General Assembly*, Fortieth Session, Supplement Number 17 (A/40/17), chapter VI, section B.

governing the use of alternatives to paper-based methods of communication and storage of information and in formulating such legislation where none currently exists,

1. Expresses its appreciation to the United Nations Commission on International Trade Law for completing and adopting the Model Law on Electronic Commerce contained in the annex to the present resolution and for preparing the Guide to Enactment of the Model Law;

2. Recommends that all states give favorable consideration to the Model Law when they enact or revise their laws, in view of the need for uniformity of the law applicable to alternatives to paper-based methods of communication and storage of information;

3. Recommends also that all efforts be made to ensure that the Model Law, together with the Guide, become generally known and available.

85th plenary meeting

16 December 1996

UNCITRAL Model Law on Electronic Commerce

[Original: Arabic, Chinese, English, French, Russian, Spanish]

Part 1. Electronic commerce in general

Chapter I. General provisions

Article 1. Sphere of application[2]

This Law[3] applies to any kind of information in the form of a data message used in the context[4] of commercial[5] activities.

---

2   The Commission suggests the following text for states that might wish to limit the applicability of this Law to international data messages: "This Law applies to a data message as defined in paragraph (1) of article 2 where the data message relates to international commerce".

3   This Law does not override any rule of law intended for the protection of consumers.

4   The Commission suggests the following text for states that might wish to extend the applicability of this Law: "This Law applies to any kind of information in the form of a data message, except in the following situations: [. . .]".

5   The term "commercial" should be given a wide interpretation so as to cover matters arising from all relationships of a commercial nature, whether contractual or not. Relationships of a commercial nature include, but are not limited to, the following transactions: any trade transaction for the supply or exchange of goods or services; distribution agreement; commercial representation or agency; factoring; leasing; construction of works; consulting; engineering; licensing; investment; financing; banking; insurance; exploitation agreement or concession; joint venture and other forms of industrial or business cooperation; and carriage of goods or passengers by air, sea, rail. or road.

Article 2. Definitions

For the purposes of this Law:

(a) "Data message" means information generated, sent, received or stored by electronic, optical, or similar means including, but not limited to, electronic data interchange (EDI), electronic mail, telegram, telex or telecopy;

(b) "Electronic data interchange (EDI)" means the electronic transfer from computer to computer of information using an agreed standard to structure the information;

(c) "Originator" of a data message means a person by whom, or on whose behalf, the data message purports to have been sent or generated prior to storage, if any, but it does not include a person acting as an intermediary with respect to that data message;

(d) "Addressee" of a data message means a person who is intended by the originator to receive the data message, but does not include a person acting as an intermediary with respect to that data message;

(e) "Intermediary", with respect to a particular data message, means a person who, on behalf of another person, sends, receives, or stores that data message or provides other services with respect to that data message;

(f) "Information system" means a system for generating, sending, receiving, storing or otherwise processing data messages.

Article 3. Interpretation

(1) In the interpretation of this Law, regard is to be had to its international origin and to the need to promote uniformity in its application and the observance of good faith.

(2) Questions concerning matters governed by this Law which are not expressly settled in it are to be settled in conformity with the general principles on which this Law is based.

Article 4. Variation by agreement

(1) As between parties involved in generating, sending, receiving, storing, or otherwise processing data messages, and except as otherwise provided, the provisions of chapter III may be varied by agreement.

(2) Paragraph (1) does not affect any right that may exist to modify by agreement any rule of law referred to in chapter II.

Chapter II. Application of legal requirements to data messages

Article 5. Legal recognition of data messages

Information shall not be denied legal effect, validity, or enforceability solely on the grounds that it is in the form of a data message.

Article 5 bis. Incorporation by reference

(as adopted by the Commission at its thirty-first session, in June 1998)

Information shall not be denied legal effect, validity, or enforceability solely on the grounds that it is not contained in the data message purporting to give rise to such legal effect, but is merely referred to in that data message.

Article 6. Writing

(1) Where the law requires information to be in writing, that requirement is met by a data message if the information contained therein is accessible so as to be usable for subsequent reference.

(2) Paragraph (1) applies whether the requirement therein is in the form of an obligation or whether the law simply provides consequences for the information not being in writing.

(3) The provisions of this article do not apply to the following: [. . .].

Article 7. Signature

(1) Where the law requires a signature of a person, that requirement is met in relation to a data message if:

 (a) a method is used to identify that person and to indicate that person's approval of the information contained in the data message; and

 (b) that method is as reliable as was appropriate for the purpose for which the data message was generated or communicated, in the light of all the circumstances, including any relevant agreement.

(2) Paragraph (1) applies whether the requirement therein is in the form of an obligation or whether the law simply provides consequences for the absence of a signature.

(3) The provisions of this article do not apply to the following: [. . .].

Article 8. Original

(1) Where the law requires information to be presented or retained in its original form, that requirement is met by a data message if:

 (a) there exists a reliable assurance as to the integrity of the information from the time when it was first generated in its final form, as a data message or otherwise; and

(b) where it is required that information be presented, that information is capable of being displayed to the person to whom it is to be presented.

(2) Paragraph (1) applies whether the requirement therein is in the form of an obligation or whether the law simply provides consequences for the information not being presented or retained in its original form.

(3) For the purposes of subparagraph (a) of paragraph (1):

(a) the criteria for assessing integrity shall be whether the information has remained complete and unaltered, apart from the addition of any endorsement and any change which arises in the normal course of communication, storage, and display; and

(b) the standard of reliability required shall be assessed in the light of the purpose for which the information was generated and in the light of all the relevant circumstances.

(4) The provisions of this article do not apply to the following: [. . .].

Article 9. Admissibility and evidential weight of data messages

(1) In any legal proceedings, nothing in the application of the rules of evidence shall apply so as to deny the admissibility of a data message in evidence:

(a) on the sole ground that it is a data message; or,

(b) if it is the best evidence that the person adducing it could reasonably be expected to obtain, on the grounds that it is not in its original form.

(2) Information in the form of a data message shall be given due evidential weight. In assessing the evidential weight of a data message, regard shall be had to the reliability of the manner in which the data message was generated, stored or communicated, to the reliability of the manner in which the integrity of the information was maintained, to the manner in which its originator was identified, and to any other relevant factor.

Article 10. Retention of data messages

(1) Where the law requires that certain documents, records, or information be retained, that requirement is met by retaining data messages, provided that the following conditions are satisfied:

(a) the information contained therein is accessible so as to be usable for subsequent reference; and

(b) the data message is retained in the format in which it was generated, sent, or received, or in a format which can be demonstrated to represent accurately the information generated, sent or received; and

(c) such information, if any, is retained as enables the identification of the origin and destination of a data message and the date and time when it was sent or received.

(2) An obligation to retain documents, records, or information in accordance with paragraph (1) does not extend to any information the sole purpose of which is to enable the message to be sent or received.

(3) A person may satisfy the requirement referred to in paragraph (1) by using the services of any other person, provided that the conditions set forth in sub-paragraphs (a), (b), and (c) of paragraph (1) are met.

Chapter III. Communication of data messages

Article 11. Formation and validity of contracts

(1) In the context of contract formation, unless otherwise agreed by the parties, an offer and the acceptance of an offer may be expressed by means of data messages. Where a data message is used in the formation of a contract, that contract shall not be denied validity or enforceability on the sole ground that a data message was used for that purpose.

(2) The provisions of this article do not apply to the following: [. . .].

Article 12. Recognition by parties of data messages

(1) As between the originator and the addressee of a data message, a declaration of will or other statement shall not be denied legal effect, validity, or enforceability solely on the grounds that it is in the form of a data message.

(2) The provisions of this article do not apply to the following: [. . .].

Article 13. Attribution of data messages

(1) A data message is that of the originator if it was sent by the originator itself.

(2) As between the originator and the addressee, a data message is deemed to be that of the originator if it was sent:

(a) by a person who had the authority to act on behalf of the originator in respect of that data message; or

(b) by an information system programmed by, or on behalf of, the originator to operate automatically.

(3) As between the originator and the addressee, an addressee is entitled to regard a data message as being that of the originator, and to act on that assumption, if:

(a) in order to ascertain whether the data message was that of the originator, the addressee properly applied a procedure previously agreed to by the originator for that purpose; or

(b) the data message as received by the addressee resulted from the actions of a person whose relationship with the originator or with any agent of the originator enabled that person to gain access to a method used by the originator to identify data messages as its own.

(4) Paragraph (3) does not apply:

(a) as of the time when the addressee has both received notice from the originator that the data message is not that of the originator, and had reasonable time to act accordingly; or

(b) in a case within paragraph (3)(b), at any time when the addressee knew or should have known, had it exercised reasonable care or used any agreed procedure, that the data message was not that of the originator.

(5) Where a data message is that of the originator or is deemed to be that of the originator, or the addressee is entitled to act on that assumption, then, as between the originator and the addressee, the addressee is entitled to regard the data message as received as being what the originator intended to send, and to act on that assumption. The addressee is not so entitled when it knew or should have known, had it exercised reasonable care or used any agreed procedure, that the transmission resulted in any error in the data message as received.

(6) The addressee is entitled to regard each data message received as a separate data message and to act on that assumption, except to the extent that it duplicates another data message and the addressee knew or should have known, had it exercised reasonable care or used any agreed procedure, that the data message was a duplicate.

Article 14. Acknowledgement of receipt

(1) Paragraphs (2)–(4) of this article apply where, on or before sending a data message, or by means of that data message, the originator has requested or has agreed with the addressee that receipt of the data message be acknowledged.

(2) Where the originator has not agreed with the addressee that the acknowledgement be given in a particular form or by a particular method, an acknowledgement may be given by:

(a) any communication by the addressee, automated or otherwise, or

(b) any conduct of the addressee, sufficient to indicate to the originator that the data message has been received.

(3) Where the originator has stated that the data message is conditional on receipt of the acknowledgement, the data message is treated as though it has never been sent, until the acknowledgement is received.

(4) Where the originator has not stated that the data message is conditional on receipt of the acknowledgement, and the acknowledgement has not been received by the originator within the time specified or agreed or, if no time has been specified or agreed, within a reasonable time, the originator:

(a) may give notice to the addressee stating that no acknowledgement has been received and specifying a reasonable time by which the acknowledgement must be received; and

(b) if the acknowledgement is not received within the time specified in subparagraph (a), may, upon notice to the addressee, treat the data message as though it had never been sent, or exercise any other rights it may have.

(5) Where the originator receives the addressee's acknowledgement of receipt, it is presumed that the related data message was received by the addressee. That presumption does not imply that the data message corresponds to the message received.

(6) Where the received acknowledgement states that the related data message met technical requirements, either agreed upon or set forth in applicable standards, it is presumed that those requirements have been met.

(7) Except insofar as it relates to the sending or receipt of the data message, this article is not intended to deal with the legal consequences that may flow either from that data message or from the acknowledgement of its receipt.

Article 15. Time and place of dispatch and receipt of data messages

(1) Unless otherwise agreed between the originator and the addressee, the dispatch of a data message occurs when it enters an information system outside the control of the originator or of the person who sent the data message on behalf of the originator.

(2) Unless otherwise agreed between the originator and the addressee, the time of receipt of a data message is determined as follows:

(a) if the addressee has designated an information system for the purpose of receiving data messages, receipt occurs:

(i) at the time when the data message enters the designated information system; or

(ii) if the data message is sent to an information system of the addressee that is not the designated information system, at the time when the data message is retrieved by the addressee;

(b) if the addressee has not designated an information system, receipt occurs when the data message enters an information system of the addressee.

(3) Paragraph (2) applies notwithstanding that the place where the information system is located may be different from the place where the data message is deemed to be received under paragraph (4).

(4) Unless otherwise agreed between the originator and the addressee, a data message is deemed to be dispatched at the place where the originator has its place of business, and is deemed to be received at the place where the addressee has its place of business. For the purposes of this paragraph:

(a) if the originator or the addressee has more than one place of business, the place of business is that which has the closest relationship to the underlying transaction or, where there is no underlying transaction, the principal place of business;

(b) if the originator or the addressee does not have a place of business, reference is to be made to its habitual residence.

(5) The provisions of this article do not apply to the following: [. . .].

Part 2. Electronic commerce in specific areas

Chapter I. Carriage of goods

Article 16. Actions related to contracts of carriage of goods

Without derogating from the provisions of part 1 of this Law, this chapter applies to any action in connection with, or in pursuance of, a contract of carriage of goods, including but not limited to:

(a) (i) furnishing the marks, number, quantity, or weight of goods;

   (ii) stating or declaring the nature or value of goods;

   (iii) issuing a receipt for goods;

   (iv) confirming that goods have been loaded;

(b) (i) notifying a person of terms and conditions of the contract;

   (ii) giving instructions to a carrier;

(c) (i) claiming delivery of goods;

   (ii) authorizing release of goods;

   (iii) giving notice of loss of, or damage to, goods;

(d) giving any other notice or statement in connection with the performance of the contract;

(e) undertaking to deliver goods to a named person or a person authorized to claim delivery;

(f) granting, acquiring, renouncing, surrendering, transferring, or negotiating rights in goods;

(g) acquiring or transferring rights and obligations under the contract.

Article 17. Transport documents

(1) Subject to paragraph (3), where the law requires that any action referred to in article 16 be carried out in writing or by using a paper document, that requirement is met if the action is carried out by using one or more data messages.

(2) Paragraph (1) applies whether the requirement therein is in the form of an obligation or whether the law simply provides consequences for failing either to carry out the action in writing or to use a paper document.

(3) If a right is to be granted to, or an obligation is to be acquired by, one person and no other person, and if the law requires that, in order to effect this, the right or obligation must be conveyed to that person by the transfer, or use of, a paper document, that requirement is met if the right or obligation is conveyed by using one or more data messages, provided that a reliable method is used to render such data message or messages unique.

(4) For the purposes of paragraph (3), the standard of reliability required shall be assessed in the light of the purpose for which the right or obligation was conveyed and in the light of all the circumstances, including any relevant agreement.

(5) Where one or more data messages are used to effect any action in subparagraphs (f) and (g) of article 16, no paper document used to effect any such action is valid unless the use of data messages has been terminated and replaced by the use of paper documents. A paper document issued in these circumstances shall contain a statement of such termination. The replacement of data messages by paper documents shall not affect the rights or obligations of the parties involved.

(6) If a rule of law is compulsorily applicable to a contract of carriage of goods which is in, or is evidenced by, a paper document, that rule shall not be inapplicable to such a contract of carriage of goods which is evidenced by one or more data messages by reason of the fact that the contract is evidenced by such data message or messages instead of by a paper document.

(7) The provisions of this article do not apply to the following: [. . .].

Guide to Enactment of the UNCITRAL Model Law on Electronic Commerce (1996)

Purpose of this Guide

1. In preparing and adopting the UNCITRAL Model Law on Electronic Commerce (hereinafter referred to as "the Model Law"), the United Nations

Commission on International Trade Law (UNCITRAL) was mindful that the Model Law would be a more effective tool for states modernizing their legislation if background and explanatory information would be provided to executive branches of governments and legislators to assist them in using the Model Law. The Commission was also aware of the likelihood that the Model Law would be used in a number of states with limited familiarity with the type of communication techniques considered in the Model Law. This Guide, much of which is drawn from the *travaux prparatoires* of the Model Law, also is intended to be helpful to users of electronic means of communication as well as to scholars in that area. In the preparation of the Model Law, it was assumed that the draft Model Law would be accompanied by such a guide. For example, it was decided in respect of a number of issues not to settle them in the draft Model Law but to address them in the Guide so as to provide guidance to states enacting the draft Model Law. The information presented in this Guide is intended to explain why the provisions in the Model Law have been included as essential basic features of a statutory device designed to achieve the objectives of the Model Law. Such information might assist states also in considering which, if any, of the provisions of the Model Law might have to be varied to take into account particular national circumstances.

I. Introduction to the Model Law

A. Objectives

2. The use of modern means of communication, such as electronic mail and electronic data interchange (EDI), for the conduct of international trade transactions has been increasing rapidly and is expected to develop further as technical supports, such as information highways and the Internet become more widely accessible. However, the communication of legally significant information in the form of paperless messages may be hindered by legal obstacles to the use of such messages, or by uncertainty as to their legal effect or validity. The purpose of the Model Law is to offer national legislators a set of internationally acceptable rules as to how a number of such legal obstacles may be removed, and how a more secure legal environment may be created for what has become known as "electronic commerce". The principles expressed in the Model Law are also intended to be of use to individual users of electronic commerce in the drafting of some of the contractual solutions that might be needed to overcome the legal obstacles to the increased use of electronic commerce.

3. The decision by UNCITRAL to formulate model legislation on electronic commerce was taken in response to the fact that in a number of countries the existing legislation governing communication and storage of information is inadequate or outdated because it does not contemplate the use of electronic

commerce. In certain cases, existing legislation imposes or implies restrictions on the use of modern means of communication, for example, by prescribing the use of "written", "signed", or "original" documents. While a few countries have adopted specific provisions to deal with certain aspects of electronic commerce, there exists no legislation dealing with electronic commerce as a whole. This may result in uncertainty as to the legal nature and validity of information presented in a form other than a traditional paper document. Moreover, while sound laws and practices are necessary in all countries where the use of EDI and electronic mail is becoming widespread, this need also is felt in many countries with respect to such communication techniques as telecopy and telex.

4. The Model Law also may help to remedy disadvantages that stem from the fact that inadequate legislation at the national level creates obstacles to international trade, a significant amount of which is linked to the use of modern communication techniques. Disparities among, and uncertainty about, national legal regimes governing the use of such communication techniques may contribute to limiting the extent to which businesses may access international markets.

5. Furthermore, at an international level, the Model Law may be useful in certain cases as a tool for interpreting existing international conventions and other international instruments that create legal obstacles to the use of electronic commerce, for example, by prescribing that certain documents or contractual clauses be made in written form. As between those states parties to such international instruments, the adoption of the Model Law as a rule of interpretation might provide the means to recognize the use of electronic commerce and obviate the need to negotiate a protocol to the international instrument involved.

6. The objectives of the Model Law, which include enabling or facilitating the use of electronic commerce and providing equal treatment to users of paper-based documentation and to users of computer-based information, are essential for fostering economy and efficiency in international trade. By incorporating the procedures prescribed in the Model Law in its national legislation for those situations where parties opt to use electronic means of communication, an enacting State would create a media-neutral environment.

B. Scope

7. The title of the Model Law refers to "electronic commerce". While a definition of "electronic data interchange (EDI)" is provided in article 2, the Model Law does not specify the meaning of "electronic commerce". In preparing the Model Law, the Commission decided that, in addressing the subject matter before it, it would have in mind a broad notion of EDI,

covering a variety of trade-related uses of EDI that might be referred to broadly under the rubric of "electronic commerce" (see A/CN.9/360, paragraphs 28-29), although other descriptive terms could also be used. Among the means of communication encompassed in the notion of "electronic commerce" are the following modes of transmission based on the use of electronic techniques: communication by means of EDI defined narrowly as the computer-to-computer transmission of data in a standardized format; transmission of electronic messages involving the use of either publicly available standards or proprietary standards; and transmission of free-formatted text by electronic means, for example, through the Internet. It was also noted that, in certain circumstances, the notion of "electronic commerce" might cover the use of techniques such as telex and telecopy.

8. It should be noted that, while the Model Law was drafted with constant reference to the more modern communication techniques, e.g., EDI and electronic mail, the principles on which the Model Law is based, as well as its provisions, are intended to apply also in the context of less advanced communication techniques, such as telecopy. There may exist situations where digitalized information initially dispatched in the form of a standardized EDI message might, at some point in the communication chain between the sender and the recipient, be forwarded in the form of a computer-generated telex or in the form of a telecopy of a computer print-out. A data message may be initiated as an oral communication and end up in the form of a telecopy, or it may start as a telecopy and end up as an EDI message. A characteristic of electronic commerce is that it covers programmable messages, the computer programming of which is the essential difference between such messages and traditional paper-based documents. Such situations are intended to be covered by the Model Law, based on a consideration of the users' need for a consistent set of rules to govern a variety of communication techniques that might be used interchangeably. More generally, it may be noted that, as a matter of principle, no communication technique is excluded from the scope of the Model Law since future technical developments need to be accommodated.

9. The objectives of the Model Law are best served by the widest possible application of the Model Law. Thus, although there is provision made in the Model Law for exclusion of certain situations from the scope of articles 6, 7, 8, 11, 12, 15, and 17, an enacting State may well decide not to enact in its legislation substantial restrictions on the scope of application of the Model Law.

10. The Model Law should be regarded as a balanced and discrete set of rules, which are recommended to be enacted as a single statute. Depending on the situation in each enacting State, however, the Model Law could be implemented in various ways, either as a single statute or in several pieces of legislation (see below, paragraph 143).

C. Structure

11. The Model Law is divided into two parts, one dealing with electronic commerce in general and the other one dealing with electronic commerce in specific areas. It should be noted that part 2 of the Model Law, which deals with electronic commerce in specific areas, is composed of a chapter I only, dealing with electronic commerce as it applies to the carriage of goods. Other aspects of electronic commerce might need to be dealt with in the future, and the Model Law can be regarded as an open-ended instrument, to be complemented by future work.

12. UNCITRAL intends to continue monitoring the technical, legal, and commercial developments that underline the Model Law. It might, should it regard it advisable, decide to add new model provisions to the Model Law or modify the existing ones.

D. A "framework" law to be supplemented by technical regulations

13. The Model Law is intended to provide essential procedures and principles for facilitating the use of modern techniques for recording and communicating information in various types of circumstances. However, it is a "framework" law that does not itself set forth all the rules and regulations that may be necessary to implement those techniques in an enacting State. Moreover, the Model Law is not intended to cover every aspect of the use of electronic commerce. Accordingly, an enacting State may wish to issue regulations to fill in the procedural details for procedures authorized by the Model Law and to take account of the specific, possibly changing, circumstances at play in the enacting State, without compromising the objectives of the Model Law. It is recommended that, should it decide to issue such regulation, an enacting State should give particular attention to the need to maintain the beneficial flexibility of the provisions in the Model Law.

14. It should be noted that the techniques for recording and communicating information considered in the Model Law, beyond raising matters of procedure that may need to be addressed in the implementing technical regulations, may raise certain legal questions, the answers to which will not necessarily be found in the Model Law, but rather in other bodies of law. Such other bodies of law may include, for example, the applicable administrative, contract, criminal, and judicial-procedure law, which the Model Law is not intended to deal with.

E. The "functional-equivalent" approach

15. The Model Law is based on the recognition that legal requirements prescribing the use of traditional paper-based documentation constitute the main obstacle to the development of modern means of communication. In the

preparation of the Model Law, consideration was given to the possibility of dealing with impediments to the use of electronic commerce posed by such requirements in national laws by way of an extension of the scope of such notions as "writing", "signature", and "original", with a view to encompassing computer-based techniques. Such an approach is used in a number of existing legal instruments, e.g., article 7 of the UNCITRAL Model Law on International Commercial Arbitration and article 13 of the United Nations Convention on Contracts for the International Sale of Goods. It was observed that the Model Law should permit states to adapt their domestic legislation to developments in communications technology applicable to trade law without necessitating the wholesale removal of the paper-based requirements themselves or disturbing the legal concepts and approaches underlying those requirements. At the same time, it was said that the electronic fulfillment of writing requirements might in some cases necessitate the development of new rules. This was due to one of many distinctions between EDI messages and paper-based documents, namely, that the latter were readable by the human eye, while the former were not so readable unless reduced to paper or displayed on a screen.

16. The Model Law thus relies on a new approach, sometimes referred to as the "functional equivalent approach", which is based on an analysis of the purposes and functions of the traditional paper-based requirement with a view to determining how those purposes or functions could be fulfilled through electronic-commerce techniques. For example, among the functions served by a paper document are the following: to provide that a document would be legible by all; to provide that a document would remain unaltered over time; to allow for the reproduction of a document so that each party would hold a copy of the same data; to allow for the authentication of data by means of a signature; and to provide that a document would be in a form acceptable to public authorities and courts. It should be noted that in respect of all of the above-mentioned functions of paper, electronic records can provide the same level of security as paper and, in most cases, a much higher degree of reliability and speed, especially with respect to the identification of the source and content of the data, provided that a number of technical and legal requirements are met. However, the adoption of the functional-equivalent approach should not result in imposing on users of electronic commerce more stringent standards of security (and the related costs) than in a paper-based environment.

17. A data message, in and of itself, cannot be regarded as an equivalent of a paper document in that it is of a different nature and does not necessarily perform all conceivable functions of a paper document. That is why the Model Law adopted a flexible standard, taking into account the various layers of existing requirements in a paper-based environment: when adopting the

"functional-equivalent" approach, attention was given to the existing hierarchy of form requirements, which provides distinct levels of reliability, traceability and unalterability with respect to paper-based documents. For example, the requirement that data be presented in written form (which constitutes a "threshold requirement") is not to be confused with more stringent requirements such as "signed writing", "signed original" or "authenticated legal act".

18. The Model Law does not attempt to define a computer-based equivalent to any kind of paper document. Instead, it singles out basic functions of paper-based form requirements, with a view to providing criteria which, once they are met by data messages, enable such data messages to enjoy the same level of legal recognition as corresponding paper documents performing the same function. It should be noted that the functional-equivalent approach has been taken in articles 6 to 8 of the Model Law with respect to the concepts of "writing", "signature", and "original", but not with respect to other legal concepts dealt with in the Model Law. For example, article 10 does not attempt to create a functional equivalent of existing storage requirements.

F. Default rules and mandatory law

19. The decision to undertake the preparation of the Model Law was based on the recognition that, in practice, solutions to most of the legal difficulties raised by the use of modern means of communication are sought within contracts. The Model Law embodies the principle of party autonomy in article 4 with respect to the provisions contained in chapter III of part 1. Chapter III of part 1 contains a set of rules of the kind that would typically be found in agreements between parties, e.g., interchange agreements or "system rules". It should be noted that the notion of "system rules" might cover two different categories of rules, namely, general terms provided by communication networks and specific rules that might be included in those general terms to deal with bilateral relationships between originators and addressees of data messages. Article 4 (and the notion of "agreement" therein) is intended to encompass both categories of "system rules".

20. The rules contained in chapter III of part 1 may be used by parties as a basis for concluding such agreements. They also may be used to supplement the terms of agreements in cases of gaps or omissions in contractual stipulations. In addition, they may be regarded as setting a basic standard for situations where data messages are exchanged without a previous agreement being entered into by the communicating parties, e.g., in the context of open-networks communications.

21. The provisions contained in chapter II of part 1 are of a different nature. One of the main purposes of the Model Law is to facilitate the use of modern communication techniques and to provide certainty with the use of such techniques where obstacles or uncertainty resulting from statutory provisions could not be

avoided by contractual stipulations. The provisions contained in chapter II may, to some extent, be regarded as a collection of exceptions to well-established rules regarding the form of legal transactions. Such well-established rules are normally of a mandatory nature since they generally reflect decisions of public policy. The provisions contained in chapter II should be regarded as stating the minimum acceptable form requirement and are, for that reason, of a mandatory nature, unless expressly stated otherwise in those provisions. The indication that such form requirements are to be regarded as the "minimum acceptable" should not, however, be construed as inviting states to establish requirements stricter than those contained in the Model Law.

G. Assistance from UNCITRAL Secretariat

22. In line with its training and assistance activities, the UNCITRAL secretariat may provide technical consultations for governments preparing legislation based on the UNCITRAL Model Law on Electronic Commerce, as it may for governments considering legislation based on other UNCITRAL model laws, or considering adhesion to one of the international trade law conventions prepared by UNCITRAL.

23. Further information concerning the Model Law, as well as the Guide and other model laws and conventions developed by UNCITRAL, may be obtained from the secretariat at the address below. The secretariat welcomes comments concerning the Model Law and the Guide, as well as information concerning enactment of legislation based on the Model Law.

International Trade Law Branch
Office of Legal Affairs
United Nations Vienna International Centre
P.O. Box 500
A-1400, Vienna, Austria
Telephone: (43-1) 26060-4060 or 4061
Telefax: (43-1) 26060-5813
E-mail: uncitral@uncitral.org
Internet: http://www.uncitral.org

II. Article-by-Article Remarks

Part 1. Electronic commerce in general

Chapter I. General provisions

Article 1. Sphere of application

24. The purpose of article 1, which is to be read in conjunction with the definition of "data message" in article 2(a), is to delineate the scope of

application of the Model Law. The approach used in the Model Law is to provide in principle for the coverage of all factual situations where information is generated, stored, or communicated, irrespective of the medium on which such information may be affixed. It was felt during the preparation of the Model Law that exclusion of any form or medium by way of a limitation in the scope of the Model Law might result in practical difficulties and would run counter to the purpose of providing truly "media-neutral" rules. However, the focus of the Model Law is on "paperless" means of communication and, except to the extent expressly provided by the Model Law, the Model Law is not intended to alter traditional rules on paper-based communications.

25. Moreover, it was felt that the Model Law should contain an indication that its focus was on the types of situations encountered in the commercial area and that it had been prepared against the background of trade relationships. For that reason, article 1 refers to "commercial activities" and provides, in footnote ****, indications as to what is meant thereby. Such indications, which may be particularly useful for those countries where there does not exist a discrete body of commercial law, are modeled, for reasons of consistency, on the footnote to article 1 of the UNCITRAL Model Law on International Commercial Arbitration. In certain countries, the use of footnotes in a statutory text would not be regarded as acceptable legislative practice. National authorities enacting the Model Law might thus consider the possible inclusion of the text of footnotes in the body of the Law itself.

26. The Model Law applies to all kinds of data messages that might be generated, stored, or communicated, and nothing in the Model Law should prevent an enacting State from extending the scope of the Model Law to cover uses of electronic commerce outside the commercial sphere. For example, while the focus of the Model Law is not on the relationships between users of electronic commerce and public authorities, the Model Law is not intended to be inapplicable to such relationships. Footnote *** provides for alternative wordings, for possible use by enacting states, that would consider it appropriate to extend the scope of the Model Law beyond the commercial sphere.

27. Some countries have special consumer protection laws that may govern certain aspects of the use of information systems. With respect to such consumer legislation, as was the case with previous UNCITRAL instruments (e.g., the UNCITRAL Model Law on International Credit Transfers), it was felt that an indication should be given that the Model Law had been drafted without special attention being given to issues that might arise in the context of consumer protection. At the same time, it was felt that there was no reason why situations involving consumers should be excluded from the scope of the Model Law by way of a general provision, particularly since the provisions of the Model Law might be found appropriate for consumer protection, depending on legislation in each enacting State. Footnote ** thus recognizes

that any such consumer protection law may take precedence over the provisions in the Model Law. Legislators may wish to consider whether the piece of legislation enacting the Model Law should apply to consumers. The question of which individuals or corporate bodies would be regarded as "consumers" is left to applicable law outside the Model Law.

28. Another possible limitation of the scope of the Model Law is contained in the first footnote. In principle, the Model Law applies to both international and domestic uses of data messages. Footnote * is intended for use by enacting states that might wish to limit the applicability of the Model Law to international cases. It indicates a possible test of internationality for use by those states as a possible criterion for distinguishing international cases from domestic ones. It should be noted, however, that in some jurisdictions, particularly in federal states, considerable difficulties might arise in distinguishing international trade from domestic trade. The Model Law should not be interpreted as encouraging enacting states to limit its applicability to international cases.

29. It is recommended that application of the Model Law be made as wide as possible. Particular caution should be used in excluding the application of the Model Law by way of a limitation of its scope to international uses of data messages, since such a limitation may be seen as not fully achieving the objectives of the Model Law. Furthermore, the variety of procedures available under the Model Law (particularly articles 6–8) to limit the use of data messages if necessary (e.g., for purposes of public policy) may make it less necessary to limit the scope of the Model Law. As the Model Law contains a number of articles (articles 6, 7, 8, 11, 12 , 15, and 17) that allow a degree of flexibility to enacting states to limit the scope of application of specific aspects of the Model Law, a narrowing of the scope of application of the text to international trade should not be necessary. Moreover, dividing communications in international trade into purely domestic and international parts might be difficult in practice. The legal certainty to be provided by the Model Law is necessary for both domestic and international trade, and a duality of regimes governing the use of electronic means of recording and communication of data might create a serious obstacle to the use of such means.

References[6]

A/50/17, paragraphs 213–219;

---

6   Reference materials listed by symbols in this Guide belong to the following three categories of documents: (1) A/50/17 and A/51/17 are the reports of UNCITRAL to the General Assembly on the work of its twenty-eighth and twenty-ninth sessions, held in 1995 and 1996, respectively; (2) A/CN.9/. . . documents are reports and notes discussed by UNCITRAL in the context of its annual session, including reports presented by the Working Group to the Commission; (3) A/CN.9/WG.IV/. . . documents are working papers considered by the UNCITRAL Working Group on Electronic Commerce (formerly known as the UNCITRAL Working Group on Electronic Data Interchange) in the preparation of the Model Law.

A/CN.9/407, paragraphs 37–40;

A/CN.9/406, paragraphs 80–85; A/CN.9/WG.IV/WP.62, article 1;

A/CN.9/390, paragraphs 21–43; A/CN.9/WG.IV/WP.60, article 1;

A/CN.9/387, paragraphs 15–28; A/CN.9/WG.IV/WP.57, article 1;

A/CN.9/373, paragraphs 21–25 and 29-33; A/CN.9/WG.IV/WP.55, paragraphs 15–20.

Article 2. Definitions

"Data message"

30. The notion of "data message" is not limited to communication but also is intended to encompass computer-generated records that are not intended for communication. Thus, the notion of "message" includes the notion of "record". However, a definition of "record" in line with the characteristic elements of "writing" in article 6 may be added in jurisdictions where that would appear to be necessary.

31. The reference to "similar means" is intended to reflect the fact that the Model Law was not intended only for application in the context of existing communication techniques but also to accommodate foreseeable technical developments. The aim of the definition of "data message" is to encompass all types of messages that are generated, stored, or communicated in essentially paperless form. For that purpose, all means of communication and storage of information that might be used to perform functions parallel to the functions performed by the means listed in the definition are intended to be covered by the reference to "similar means", although, for example, "electronic" and "optical" means of communication might not be, strictly speaking, similar. For the purposes of the Model Law, the word "similar" connotes "functionally equivalent".

32. The definition of "data message" also is intended to cover the case of revocation or amendment. A data message is presumed to have a fixed information content, but it may be revoked or amended by another data message.

"Electronic Data Interchange (EDI)"

33. The definition of EDI is drawn from the definition adopted by the Working Party on Facilitation of International Trade Procedures (WP.4) of the Economic Commission for Europe, which is the United Nations body responsible for the development of UN/EDIFACT technical standards.

34. The Model Law does not settle the question of whether the definition of EDI necessarily implies that EDI messages are communicated electronically from computer to computer, or whether that definition, while primarily covering situations where data messages are communicated through a telecommunications

system, also would cover exceptional or incidental types of situation where data structured in the form of an EDI message would be communicated by means that do not involve telecommunications systems, for example, the case where magnetic disks containing EDI messages would be delivered to the addressee by courier. However, irrespective of whether digital data transferred manually is covered by the definition of "EDI", it should be regarded as covered by the definition of "data message" under the Model Law.

"Originator" and "Addressee"

35. In most legal systems, the notion of "person" is used to designate the subjects of rights and obligations and should be interpreted as covering both natural persons and corporate bodies or other legal entities. Data messages that are generated automatically by computers without direct human intervention are intended to be covered by subparagraph (c). However, the Model Law should not be misinterpreted as allowing for a computer to be made the subject of rights and obligations. Data messages that are generated automatically by computers without direct human intervention should be regarded as "originating" from the legal entity on behalf of which the computer is operated. Questions relevant to agency that might arise in that context are to be settled under rules outside the Model Law.

36. The "addressee" under the Model Law is the person with whom the originator intends to communicate by transmitting the data message, as opposed to any person who might receive, forward, or copy the data message in the course of transmission. The "originator" is the person who generated the data message even if that message was transmitted by another person. The definition of "addressee" contrasts with the definition of "originator", which is not focused on intent. It should be noted that, under the definitions of "originator" and "addressee" in the Model Law, the originator and the addressee of a given data message could be the same person, for example, in the case where the data message was intended for storage by its author. However, the addressee who stores a message transmitted by an originator is not itself intended to be covered by the definition of "originator".

37. The definition of "originator" should cover not only the situation where information is generated and communicated, but also the situation where such information is generated and stored without being communicated. However, the definition of "originator" is intended to eliminate the possibility that a recipient who merely stores a data message might be regarded as an originator.

"Intermediary"

38. The focus of the Model Law is on the relationship between the originator and the addressee, and not on the relationship between either the originator or the addressee and any intermediary. However, the Model Law does not ignore the paramount importance of intermediaries in the field of electronic

communications. In addition, the notion of "intermediary" is needed in the Model Law to establish the necessary distinction between originators or addressees and third parties.

39. The definition of "intermediary" is intended to cover both professional and non-professional intermediaries, i.e., any person (other than the originator and the addressee) who performs any of the functions of an intermediary. The main functions of an intermediary are listed in subparagraph (e), namely, receiving, transmitting, or storing data messages on behalf of another person. Additional "value-added services" may be performed by network operators and other intermediaries, such as formatting, translating, recording, authenticating, certifying and preserving data messages and providing security services for electronic transactions. "Intermediary" under the Model Law is defined not as a generic category but with respect to each data message, thus recognizing that the same person could be the originator or addressee of one data message and an intermediary with respect to another data message. The Model Law, which is focused on the relationships between originators and addressees, does not, in general, deal with the rights and obligations of intermediaries.

"Information system"

40. The definition of "information system" is intended to cover the entire range of technical means used for transmitting, receiving, and storing information. For example, depending on the factual situation, the notion of "information system" could be indicating a communications network, and in other instances could include an electronic mailbox or even a telecopier. The Model Law does not address the question of whether the information system is located on the premises of the addressee or on other premises, since location of information systems is not an operative criterion under the Model Law.

References

A/51/17, paragraphs 116–138;

A/CN.9/407, paragraphs 41–52;

A/CN.9/406, paragraphs 132–156; A/CN.9/WG.IV/WP.62, article 2;

A/CN.9/390, paragraphs 44–65; A/CN.9/WG.IV/WP.60, article 2;

A/CN.9/387, paragraphs 29–52; A/CN.9/WG.IV/WP.57, article 2;

A/CN.9/373, paragraphs 11–20, 26–28, and 35–36; A/CN.9/WG.IV/WP.55, paragraphs 23–26;

A/CN.9/360, paragraphs 29–31; A/CN.9/WG.IV/WP.53, paragraphs 25–33.

Article 3. Interpretation

41. Article 3 is inspired by article 7 of the United Nations Convention on Contracts for the International Sale of Goods. It is intended to provide guidance for interpretation of the Model Law by courts and other national or local authorities. The expected effect of article 3 is to limit the extent to which a uniform text, once incorporated in local legislation, would be interpreted only by reference to the concepts of local law.

42. The purpose of paragraph (1) is to draw the attention of courts and other national authorities to the fact that the provisions of the Model Law (or the provisions of the instrument implementing the Model Law), while enacted as part of domestic legislation and therefore domestic in character, should be interpreted with reference to its international origin in order to ensure uniformity in the interpretation of the Model Law in various countries.

43. As to the general principles on which the Model Law is based, the following non-exhaustive list may be considered: (1) to facilitate electronic commerce among and within nations; (2) to validate transactions entered into by means of new information technologies; (3) to promote and encourage the implementation of new information technologies; (4) to promote the uniformity of law; and (5) to support commercial practice. While the general purpose of the Model Law is to facilitate the use of electronic means of communication, it should not be construed in any way as imposing their use.

References

A/50/17, paragraphs 220–224;

A/CN.9/407, paragraphs 53–54;

A/CN.9/406, paragraphs 86–87; A/CN.9/WG.IV/WP.62, article 3;

A/CN.9/390, paragraphs 66–73; A/CN.9/WG.IV/WP.60, article 3;

A/CN.9/387, paragraphs 53–58; A/CN.9/WG.IV/WP.57, article 3;

A/CN.9/373, paragraphs 38–42; A/CN.9/WG.IV/WP.55, paragraphs 30–31.

Article 4. Variation by agreement

44. The decision to undertake the preparation of the Model Law was based on the recognition that, in practice, solutions to the legal difficulties raised by the use of modern means of communication are mostly sought within contracts. The Model Law is thus intended to support the principle of party autonomy. However, that principle is embodied only with respect to the provisions of the Model Law contained in chapter III of part 1. The reason for such a limitation is that the provisions contained in chapter II of part 1 may, to some extent, be regarded as a collection of exceptions to well-established rules regarding the form of legal transactions. Such well-established rules are normally of a

mandatory nature since they generally reflect decisions of public policy. An unqualified statement regarding the freedom of parties to derogate from the Model Law might thus be misinterpreted as allowing parties, through a derogation to the Model Law, to derogate from mandatory rules adopted for reasons of public policy. The provisions contained in chapter II of part 1 should be regarded as stating the minimum acceptable form requirement and are, for that reason, to be regarded as mandatory, unless expressly stated otherwise. The indication that such form requirements are to be regarded as the "minimum acceptable" should not, however, be construed as inviting states to establish requirements stricter than those contained in the Model Law.

45. Article 4 is intended to apply not only in the context of relationships between originators and addressees of data messages but also in the context of relationships involving intermediaries. Thus, the provisions of chapter III of part 1 could be varied either by bilateral or multilateral agreements between the parties, or by system rules agreed to by the parties. However, the text expressly limits party autonomy to rights and obligations arising as between parties so as not to suggest any implication as to the rights and obligations of third parties.

References

A/51/17, paragraphs 68, 90–93, 110, 137, 188, and 207 (article 10);

A/50/17, paragraphs 271–274 (article 10);

A/CN.9/407, paragraph 85;

A/CN.9/406, paragraphs 88–89; A/CN.9/WG.IV/WP.62, article 5;

A/CN.9/390, paragraph 74; A/CN.9/WG.IV/WP.60, article 5;

A/CN.9/387, paragraphs 62–65; A/CN.9/WG.IV/WP.57, article 5;

A/CN.9/373, paragraph 37; A/CN.9/WG.IV/WP.55, paragraphs 27–29.

Chapter II. Application of legal requirements to data messages

Article 5. Legal recognition of data messages

46. Article 5 embodies the fundamental principle that data messages should not be discriminated against, i.e., that there should be no disparity of treatment between data messages and paper documents. It is intended to apply notwithstanding any statutory requirements for a "writing" or an original. That fundamental principle is intended to find general application, and its scope should not be limited to evidence or other matters covered in chapter II. It should be noted, however, that such a principle is not intended to override any of the requirements contained in articles 6 to 10. By stating that "information shall not be denied legal effectiveness, validity or enforceability solely on the grounds that it is in the form of a data message", article 5 merely

indicates that the form in which certain information is presented or retained cannot be used as the only reason for which that information would be denied legal effectiveness, validity, or enforceability. However, article 5 should not be misinterpreted as establishing the legal validity of any given data message or of any information contained therein.

References

A/51/17, paragraphs 92 and 97 (article 4);

A/50/17, paragraphs 225–227 (article 4);

A/CN.9/407, paragraph 55;

A/CN.9/406, paragraphs 91–94; A/CN.9/WG.IV/WP. 62, article 5 *bis*;

A/CN.9/390, paragraphs 79–87;

A/CN.9/WG.IV/WP. 60, article 5 *bis*;

A/CN.9/387, paragraphs 93–95.

Article 5 bis. Incorporation by reference

46-1. Article 5 *bis* was adopted by the Commission at its thirty-first session, in June 1998. It is intended to provide guidance as to how legislation aimed at facilitating the use of electronic commerce might deal with the situation where certain terms and conditions, although not stated in full but merely referred to in a data message, might need to be recognized as having the same degree of legal effectiveness as if they had been fully stated in the text of that data message. Such recognition is acceptable under the laws of many states with respect to conventional paper communications, usually with some rules of law providing safeguards, for example, rules on consumer protection. The expression "incorporation by reference" is often used as a concise means of describing situations where a document refers generically to provisions which are detailed elsewhere, rather than reproducing them in full.

46-2. In an electronic environment, incorporation by reference is often regarded as essential to widespread use of electronic data interchange (EDI), electronic mail, digital certificates, and other forms of electronic commerce. For example, electronic communications are typically structured in such a way that large numbers of messages are exchanged, with each message containing brief information, and relying much more frequently than paper documents on reference to information accessible elsewhere. In electronic communications, practitioners should not have imposed upon them an obligation to overload their data messages with quantities of free text when they can take advantage of extrinsic sources of information, such as databases, code lists, or glossaries, by making use of abbreviations, codes, and other references to such information.

46-3. Standards for incorporating data messages by reference into other data messages also may be essential to the use of public-key certificates, because these certificates are generally brief records with rigidly prescribed contents that are finite in size. The trusted third party which issues the certificate, however, is likely to require the inclusion of relevant contractual terms limiting its liability. The scope, purpose, and effect of a certificate in commercial practice, therefore, would be ambiguous and uncertain without external terms being incorporated by reference. This is the case especially in the context of international communications involving diverse parties who follow varied trade practices and customs.

46-4. The establishment of standards for incorporating data messages by reference into other data messages is critical to the growth of a computer-based trade infrastructure. Without the legal certainty fostered by such standards, there might be a significant risk that the application of traditional tests for determining the enforceability of terms that seek to be incorporated by reference might be ineffective when applied to corresponding electronic commerce terms because of the differences between traditional and electronic commerce mechanisms.

46-5. While electronic commerce relies heavily on the mechanism of incorporation by reference, the accessibility of the full text of the information being referred to may be considerably improved by the use of electronic communications. For example, a message may have embedded in it uniform resource locators (URLs), which direct the reader to the referenced document. Such URLs can provide "hypertext links" allowing the reader to use a pointing device (such as a mouse) to select a key word associated with a URL. The referenced text would then be displayed. In assessing the accessibility of the referenced text, factors to be considered may include: availability (hours of operation of the repository and ease of access); cost of access; integrity (verification of content, authentication of sender, and mechanism for communication error correction); and the extent to which that term is subject to later amendment (notice of updates; notice of policy of amendment).

46-6. One aim of article 5 *bis* is to facilitate incorporation by reference in an electronic context by removing the uncertainty prevailing in many jurisdictions as to whether the provisions dealing with traditional incorporation by reference are applicable to incorporation by reference in an electronic environment. However, in enacting article 5 *bis*, attention should be given to avoid introducing more restrictive requirements with respect to incorporation by reference in electronic commerce than might already apply in paper-based trade.

46-7. Another aim of the provision is to recognize that consumer-protection or other national or international law of a mandatory nature (e.g., rules protecting weaker parties in the context of contracts of adhesion) should not be interfered with. That result could also be achieved by validating incorporation by reference in an electronic environment "to the extent permitted by law", or by listing the rules of law that remain unaffected by article 5*bis*. Article 5*bis* is not to be interpreted as creating a specific legal regime for incorporation by reference in an electronic environment. Rather, by establishing a principle of non-discrimination, it is to be construed as making the domestic rules applicable to incorporation by reference in a paper-based environment equally applicable to incorporation by reference for the purposes of electronic commerce. For example, in a number of jurisdictions, existing rules of mandatory law only validate incorporation by reference provided that the following three conditions are met: (a) the reference clause should be inserted in the data message; (b) the document being referred to, e.g., general terms and conditions, should actually be known to the party against whom the reference document might be relied upon; and (c) the reference document should be accepted, in addition to being known, by that party.

References

A/53/17, paragraphs 212–221;

A/CN.9/450;

A/CN.9/446, paragraphs 14–24;

A/CN.9/WG.IV/WP.74;

A/52/17, paragraphs 248–250;

A/CN.9/437, paragraphs 151–155;

A/CN.9/WG.IV/WP. 71, paragraphs 77–93;

A/51/17, paragraphs 222–223;

A/CN.9/421, paragraphs 109 and 114;

A/CN.9/WG.IV/WP.69, paragraphs 30, 53, 59–60 and 91;

A/CN.9/407, paragraphs 100–105 and 117;

A/CN.9/WG.IV/WP.66;

A/CN.9/WG.IV/WP.65;

A/CN.9/406, paragraphs 90 and 178–179;

A/CN.9/WG.IV/WP.55, paragraph 109–113;

A/CN.9/360, paragraphs 90–95;

A/CN.9/WG.IV/WP.53, paragraphs 77–78;

A/CN.9/350, paragraphs 95–96;

A/CN.9/333, paragraphs 66–68.

Article 6. Writing

47. Article 6 is intended to define the basic standard to be met by a data message in order to be considered as meeting a requirement (which may result from statute, regulation, or judge-made law) that information be retained or presented "in writing" (or that the information be contained in a "document" or other paper-based instrument). It may be noted that article 6 is part of a set of three articles (articles 6, 7, and 8), which share the same structure and should be read together.

48. In the preparation of the Model Law, particular attention was paid to the functions traditionally performed by various kinds of "writings" in a paper-based environment. For example, the following non-exhaustive list indicates reasons why national laws require the use of "writings": (1) to ensure that there would be tangible evidence of the existence and nature of the intent of the parties to bind themselves; (2) to help the parties be aware of the consequences of their entering into a contract; (3) to provide that a document would be legible by all; (4) to provide that a document would remain unaltered over time and provide a permanent record of a transaction; (5) to allow for the reproduction of a document so that each party would hold a copy of the same data; (6) to allow for the authentication of data by means of a signature; (7) to provide that a document would be in a form acceptable to public authorities and courts; (8) to finalize the intent of the author of the "writing" and provide a record of that intent; (9) to allow for the easy storage of data in a tangible form; (10) to facilitate control and sub-sequent audit for accounting, tax, or regulatory purposes; and (11) to bring legal rights and obligations into existence in those cases where a "writing" was required for validity purposes.

49. However, in the preparation of the Model Law, it was found that it would be inappropriate to adopt an overly comprehensive notion of the functions performed by writing. Existing requirements that data be presented in written form often combine the requirement of a "writing" with concepts distinct from writing, such as signature and original. Thus, when adopting a functional approach, attention should be given to the fact that the requirement of a "writing" should be considered as the lowest layer in a hierarchy of form requirements, which provide distinct levels of reliability, traceability, and unalterability with respect to paper documents. The requirement that data be presented in written form (which can be described as a "threshold requirement") should thus not be confused with more stringent requirements such as "signed writing", "signed original", or "authenticated legal act". For example, under certain national laws, a written document that is neither dated nor signed, and the author of which either is not identified in the written document or is identified by a mere letterhead, would be regarded as a "writing" although it might be of little evidential weight in the absence of

other evidence (e.g., testimony) regarding the authorship of the document. In addition, the notion of unalterability should not be considered as built into the concept of writing as an absolute requirement since a "writing" in pencil might still be considered a "writing" under certain existing legal definitions. Taking into account the way in which such issues as integrity of the data and protection against fraud are dealt with in a paper-based environment, a fraudulent document would nonetheless be regarded as a "writing". In general, notions such as "evidence" and "intent of the parties to bind themselves" are to be tied to the more general issues of reliability and authentication of the data and should not be included in the definition of a "writing".

50. The purpose of article 6 is not to establish a requirement that, in all instances, data messages should fulfill all conceivable functions of a writing. Rather than focusing upon specific functions of a "writing", for example, its evidentiary function in the context of tax law or its warning function in the context of civil law, article 6 focuses upon the basic notion of the information being reproduced and read. That notion is expressed in article 6 in terms that were found to provide an objective criterion, namely, that the information in a data message must be accessible so as to be usable for subsequent reference. The use of the word "accessible" is meant to imply that information in the form of computer data should be readable and interpretable, and that the software that might be necessary to render such information readable should be retained. The word "usable" is not intended to cover only human use but also computer processing. As to the notion of "subsequent reference", it was preferred to such notions as "durability" or "non-alterability", which would have established too harsh standards, and to such notions as "readability" or "intelligibility", which might constitute too subjective criteria.

51. The principle embodied in paragraph (3) of articles 6 and 7, and in paragraph (4) of article 8, is that an enacting State may exclude from the application of those articles certain situations to be specified in the legislation enacting the Model Law. An enacting State may wish to exclude specifically certain types of situations, depending in particular on the purpose of the formal requirement in question. One such type of situation may be the case of writing requirements intended to provide notice or warning of specific factual or legal risks, for example, requirements for warnings to be placed on certain types of products. Another specific exclusion might be considered, for example, in the context of formalities required pursuant to international treaty obligations of the enacting State (e.g., the requirement that a check be in writing pursuant to the Convention providing a Uniform Law for Checks, Geneva, 1931) and other kinds of situations and areas of law that are beyond the power of the enacting State to change by means of a statute.

52. Paragraph (3) was included with a view to enhancing the acceptability of the Model Law. It recognizes that the matter of specifying exclusions should be left to enacting states, an approach that would take better account of differences in national circumstances. However, it should be noted that the objectives of the Model Law would not be achieved if paragraph (3) were used to establish blanket exceptions, and the opportunity provided by paragraph (3) in that respect should be avoided. Numerous exclusions from the scope of articles 6 to 8 would raise needless obstacles to the development of modern communication techniques, since what the Model Law contains are very fundamental principles and approaches that are expected to find general application.

References

A/51/17, paragraphs 180–181 and 185–187 (article 5);

A/50/17, paragraphs 228–241 (article 5);

A/CN.9/407, paragraphs 56–63;

A/CN.9/406, paragraphs 95–101; A/CN.9/WG.IV/WP.62, article 6;

A/CN.9/390, paragraphs 88–96; A/CN.9/WG.IV/WP.60, article 6;

A/CN.9/387, paragraphs 66–80; A/CN.9/WG.IV/WP.57, article 6; A/CN.9/WG.IV/WP.58, annex;

A/CN.9/373, paragraphs 45–62; A/CN.9/WG.IV/WP.55, paragraphs 36–49;

A/CN.9/360, paragraphs 32–43; A/CN.9/WG.IV/WP.53, paragraphs 37–45;

A/CN.9/350, paragraphs 68–78;

A/CN.9/333, paragraphs 20–28;

A/CN.9/265, paragraphs 59–72.

Article 7. Signature

53. Article 7 is based on the recognition of the functions of a signature in a paper-based environment. In the preparation of the Model Law, the following functions of a signature were considered: to identify a person; to provide certainty as to the personal involvement of that person in the act of signing; and to associate that person with the content of a document. It was noted that, in addition, a signature could perform a variety of functions, depending on the nature of the document that was signed. For example, a signature might attest to the intent of a party to be bound by the content of a signed contract; the intent of a person to endorse authorship of a text; the intent of a person to associate itself with the content of a document written by someone else; and the fact that, and the time when, a person had been at a given place.

54. It may be noted that, alongside the traditional handwritten signature, there exist various types of procedures (e.g., stamping, and perforation), sometimes also referred to as "signatures", which provide various levels of certainty. For example, in some countries, there exists a general requirement that contracts for the sale of goods above a certain amount should be "signed" in order to be enforceable. However, the concept of a signature adopted in that context is such that a stamp, perforation, or even a typewritten signature or a printed letterhead might be regarded as sufficient to fulfill the signature requirement. At the other end of the spectrum, there exist requirements that combine the traditional handwritten signature with additional security procedures, such as the confirmation of the signature by witnesses.

55. It might be desirable to develop functional equivalents for the various types and levels of signature requirements in existence. Such an approach would increase the level of certainty as to the degree of legal recognition that could be expected from the use of the various means of authentication used in electronic commerce practice as substitutes for "signatures". However, the notion of signature is intimately linked to the use of paper. Furthermore, any attempt to develop rules on standards and procedures to be used as substitutes for specific instances of "signatures" might create the risk of tying the legal framework provided by the Model Law to a given state of technical development.

56. With a view to ensuring that a message that was required to be authenticated should not be denied legal value for the sole reason that it was not authenticated in a manner peculiar to paper documents, article 7 adopts a comprehensive approach. It establishes the general conditions under which data messages would be regarded as authenticated with sufficient credibility and would be enforceable in the face of signature requirements which currently present barriers to electronic commerce. Article 7 focuses on the two basic functions of a signature, namely, to identify the author of a document and to confirm that the author approved the content of that document. Paragraph (1)(a) establishes the principle that, in an electronic environment, the basic legal functions of a signature are performed by way of a method that identifies the originator of a data message and confirms that the originator approved the content of that data message.

57. Paragraph (1)(b) establishes a flexible approach to the level of security to be achieved by the method of identification used under paragraph (1)(a). The method used under paragraph (1)(a) should be as reliable as is appropriate for the purpose for which the data message is generated or communicated, in the light of all the circumstances, including any agreement between the originator and the addressee of the data message.

58. In determining whether the method used under paragraph (1) is appropriate, legal, technical, and commercial factors that may be taken into account

include the following: (1) the sophistication of the equipment used by each of the parties; (2) the nature of their trade activity; (3) the frequency at which commercial transactions take place between the parties; (4) the kind and size of the transaction; (5) the function of signature requirements in a given statutory and regulatory environment; (6) the capability of communication systems; (7) compliance with authentication procedures set forth by intermediaries; (8) the range of authentication procedures made available by any intermediary; (9) compliance with trade customs and practice; (10) the existence of insurance coverage mechanisms against unauthorized messages; (11) the importance and the value of the information contained in the data message; (12) the availability of alternative methods of identification and the cost of implementation; (13) the degree of acceptance or non-acceptance of the method of identification in the relevant industry or field both at the time the method was agreed upon and the time when the data message was communicated; and (14) any other relevant factor.

59. Article 7 does not introduce a distinction between the situation in which users of electronic commerce are linked by a communication agreement and the situation in which parties had no prior contractual relationship regarding the use of electronic commerce. Thus, article 7 may be regarded as establishing a basic standard of authentication for data messages that might be exchanged in the absence of a prior contractual relationship and, at the same time, to provide guidance as to what might constitute an appropriate substitute for a signature if the parties used electronic communications in the context of a communication agreement. The Model Law is thus intended to provide useful guidance both in a context where national laws would leave the question of authentication of data messages entirely to the discretion of the parties and in a context where requirements for signature, which were usually set by mandatory provisions of national law, should not be made subject to alteration by agreement of the parties.

60. The notion of an "agreement between the originator and the addressee of a data message" is to be interpreted as covering not only bilateral or multilateral agreements concluded between parties exchanging directly data messages (e.g., "trading partners agreements", "communication agreements", or " interchange agreements") but also agreements involving intermediaries such as networks (e.g., "third-party service agreements"). Agreements concluded between users of electronic commerce and networks may incorporate "system rules", i.e., administrative and technical rules and procedures to be applied when communicating data messages. However, a possible agreement between originators and addressees of data messages as to the use of a method of authentication is not conclusive evidence of whether that method is reliable or not.

61. It should be noted that, under the Model Law, the mere signing of a data message by means of a functional equivalent of a handwritten signature is

not intended, in and of itself, to confer legal validity on the data message. Whether a data message that fulfilled the requirement of a signature has legal validity is to be settled under the law applicable outside the Model Law.

References

A/51/17, paragraphs 180–181 and 185–187 (article 6);

A/50/17, paragraphs 242–248 (article 6);

A/CN.9/407, paragraphs 64–70;

A/CN.9/406, paragraphs 102–105; A/CN.9/WG.IV/WP.62, article 7;

A/CN.9/390, paragraphs 97–109; A/CN.9/WG.IV/WP.60, article 7;

A/CN.9/387, paragraphs 81–90; A/CN.9/WG.IV/WP.57, article 7; A/CN.9/WG.IV/WP.58, annex;

A/CN.9/373, paragraphs 63–76; A/CN.9/WG.IV/WP.55, paragraphs 50–63;

A/CN.9/360, paragraphs 71–75; A/CN.9/WG.IV/WP.53, paragraphs 61–66;

A/CN.9/350, paragraphs 86–89;

A/CN.9/333, paragraphs 50–59;

A/CN.9/265, paragraphs 49–58 and 79–80.

Article 8. Original

62. If "original" were defined as a medium on which information was fixed for the first time, it would be impossible to speak of "original" data messages, since the addressee of a data message would always receive a copy thereof. However, article 8 should be put in a different context. The notion of "original" in article 8 is useful since in practice many disputes relate to the question of originality of documents, and in electronic commerce the requirement for presentation of originals constitutes one of the main obstacles that the Model Law attempts to remove. Although in some jurisdictions the concepts of "writing", "original", and "signature" may overlap, the Model Law approaches them as three separate and distinct concepts. Article 8 also is useful in clarifying the notions of "writing" and "original", in particular in view of their importance for purposes of evidence.

63. Article 8 is pertinent to documents of title and negotiable instruments, in which the notion of uniqueness of an original is particularly relevant. However, attention is drawn to the fact that the Model Law is not intended only to apply to documents of title and negotiable instruments, or to such areas of law where special requirements exist with respect to registration or notarization of "writings", e.g., family matters or the sale of real estate. Examples of

documents that might require an "original" are trade documents such as weight certificates, agricultural certificates, quality or quantity certificates, inspection reports, insurance certificates, etc. While such documents are not negotiable or used to transfer rights or title, it is essential that they be transmitted unchanged, that is, in their "original" form, so that other parties in international commerce may have confidence in their contents. In a paper-based environment, these types of document are usually only accepted if they are "original" to lessen the chance that they be altered, which would be difficult to detect in copies. Various technical means are available to certify the contents of a data message to confirm its "originality". Without this functional equivalent of originality, the sale of goods using electronic commerce would be hampered since the issuers of such documents would be required to retransmit their data message each and every time the goods are sold, or the parties would be forced to use paper documents to supplement the electronic commerce transaction.

64. Article 8 should be regarded as stating the minimum acceptable form requirement to be met by a data message for it to be regarded as the functional equivalent of an original. The provisions of article 8 should be regarded as mandatory, to the same extent that existing provisions regarding the use of paper-based original documents would be regarded as mandatory. The indication that the form requirements stated in article 8 are to be regarded as the "minimum acceptable" should not, however, be construed as inviting states to establish requirements stricter than those contained in the Model Law.

65. Article 8 emphasizes the importance of the integrity of the information for its originality and sets out criteria to be taken into account when assessing integrity by reference to systematic recording of the information, assurance that the information was recorded without lacunae, and protection of the data against alteration. It links the concept of originality to a method of authentication and puts the focus on the method of authentication to be followed in order to meet the requirement. It is based on the following elements: a simple criterion as to "integrity" of the data; a description of the elements to be taken into account in assessing the integrity; and an element of flexibility, i.e., a reference to circumstances.

66. As regards the words "the time when it was first generated in its final form" in paragraph (1)(a), it should be noted that the provision is intended to encompass the situation where information was first composed as a paper document and subsequently transferred on to a computer. In such a situation, paragraph (1)(a) is to be interpreted as requiring assurances that the information has remained complete and unaltered from the time when it was composed as a paper document onwards, and not only as from the time when it was translated into electronic form. However, where several drafts were

created and stored before the final message was composed, paragraph (1)(a) should not be misinterpreted as requiring assurance as to the integrity of the drafts.

67. Paragraph (3)(a) sets forth the criteria for assessing integrity, taking care to except necessary additions to the first (or "original") data message, such as endorsements, certifications, notarizations, etc. from other alterations. As long as the contents of a data message remain complete and unaltered, necessary additions to that data message would not affect its "originality". Thus when an electronic certificate is added to the end of an "original" data message to attest to the "originality" of that data message, or when data is automatically added by computer systems at the start and the finish of a data message in order to transmit it, such additions would be considered as if they were a supplemental piece of paper with an "original" piece of paper, or the envelope and stamp used to send that "original" piece of paper.

68. As in other articles of chapter II of part 1, the words "the law" in the opening phrase of article 8 are to be understood as encompassing not only statutory or regulatory law but also judicially created law and other procedural law. In certain common law countries, where the words "the law" would normally be interpreted as referring to common law rules, as opposed to statutory requirements, it should be noted that, in the context of the Model Law, the words "the law" are intended to encompass those various sources of law. However, "the law", as used in the Model Law, is not meant to include areas of law that have not become part of the law of a State and are sometimes, somewhat imprecisely, referred to by expressions such as *lex mercatoria* or "law merchant".

69. Paragraph (4), as was the case with similar provisions in articles 6 and 7, was included with a view to enhancing the acceptability of the Model Law. It recognizes that the matter of specifying exclusions should be left to enacting states, an approach that would take better account of differences in national circumstances. However, it should be noted that the objectives of the Model Law would not be achieved if paragraph (4) were used to establish blanket exceptions. Numerous exclusions from the scope of articles 6 to 8 would raise needless obstacles to the development of modern communication techniques, since what the Model Law contains are very fundamental principles and approaches that are expected to find general application.

References

A/51/17, paragraphs 180–181 and 185–187 (article 7);

A/50/17, paragraphs 249–255 (article 7);

A/CN.9/407, paragraphs 71–79;

A/CN.9/406, paragraphs 106–110; A/CN.9/WG.IV/WP.62, article 8;

A/CN.9/390, paragraphs 110–133; A/CN.9/WG.IV/WP.60, article 8;

A/CN.9/387, paragraphs 91–97; A/CN.9/WG.IV/WP.57, article 8; A/CN.9/WG.IV/WP.58, annex;

A/CN.9/373, paragraphs 77–96;

A/CN.9/WG.IV/WP.55, paragraphs 64–70;

A/CN.9/360, paragraphs 60–70; A/CN.9/WG.IV/WP.53, paragraphs 56–60;

A/CN.9/350, paragraphs 84–85;

A/CN.9/265, paragraphs 43–48.

Article 9. Admissibility and evidential weight of data messages

70. The purpose of article 9 is to establish both the admissibility of data messages as evidence in legal proceedings and their evidential value. With respect to admissibility, paragraph (1), establishing that data messages should not be denied admissibility as evidence in legal proceedings on the sole ground that they are in electronic form, puts emphasis on the general principle stated in article 4 and is needed to make it expressly applicable to admissibility of evidence, an area in which particularly complex issues might arise in certain jurisdictions. The term "best evidence" is a term understood in, and necessary for, certain common law jurisdictions. However, the notion of "best evidence" could raise a great deal of uncertainty in legal systems in which such a rule is unknown. states in which the term would be regarded as meaningless and potentially misleading may wish to enact the Model Law without the reference to the "best evidence" rule contained in paragraph (1).

71. As regards the assessment of the evidential weight of a data message, paragraph (2) provides useful guidance as to how the evidential value of data messages should be assessed (e.g., depending on whether they were generated, stored or communicated in a reliable manner).

References

A/50/17, paragraphs 256–263 (article 8);

A/CN.9/407, paragraphs 80–81;

A/CN.9/406, paragraphs 111–113; A/CN.9/WG.IV/WP.62, article 9;

A/CN.9/390, paragraphs 139–143; A/CN.9/WG.IV/WP.60, article 9;

A/CN.9/387, paragraphs 98–109; A/CN.9/WG.IV/WP.57, article 9; A/CN.9/WG.IV/WP.58, annex;

A/CN.9/373, paragraphs 97–108; A/CN.9/WG.IV/WP.55, paragraphs 71–81;

A/CN.9/360, paragraphs 44–59; A/CN.9/WG.IV/WP.53, paragraphs 46–55;

A/CN.9/350, paragraphs 79–83 and 90–91;

A/CN.9/333, paragraphs 29–41;

A/CN.9/265, paragraphs 27–48.

Article 10. Retention of data messages

72. Article 10 establishes a set of alternative rules for existing requirements regarding the storage of information (e.g., for accounting or tax purposes) that may constitute obstacles to the development of modern trade.

73. Paragraph (1) is intended to set out the conditions under which the obligation to store data messages that might exist under the applicable law would be met. Subparagraph (a) reproduces the conditions established under article 6 for a data message to satisfy a rule which prescribes the presentation of a "writing". Subparagraph (b) emphasizes that the message does not need to be retained unaltered as long as the information stored accurately reflects the data message as it was sent. It would not be appropriate to require that information should be stored unaltered, since usually messages are decoded, compressed or converted in order to be stored.

74. Subparagraph (c) is intended to cover all the information that may need to be stored, which includes, apart from the message itself, certain transmittal information that may be necessary for the identification of the message. Subparagraph (c), by imposing the retention of the transmittal information associated with the data message, is creating a standard that is higher than most standards existing under national laws as to the storage of paper-based communications. However, it should not be understood as imposing an obligation to retain transmittal information additional to the information contained in the data message when it was generated, stored, or transmitted, or information contained in a separate data message, such as an acknowledgement of receipt. Moreover, while some transmittal information is important and has to be stored, other transmittal information can be exempted without the integrity of the data message being compromised. That is the reason why subparagraph (c) establishes a distinction between those elements of transmittal information that are important for the identification of the message and the very few elements of transmittal information covered in paragraph (2) (e.g., communication protocols), which are of no value with regard to the data message and which, typically, would automatically be stripped out of an incoming data message by the receiving computer before the data message actually entered the information system of the addressee.

75. In practice, storage of information, and especially storage of transmittal information, may often be carried out by someone other than the originator or the addressee, such as an intermediary. Nevertheless, it is intended that the person obligated to retain certain transmittal information cannot escape meeting

that obligation simply because, for example, the communications system operated by that other person does not retain the required information. This is intended to discourage bad practice or willful misconduct. Paragraph (3) provides that in meeting its obligations under paragraph (1), an addressee or originator may use the services of any third party, not just an intermediary.

References

A/51/17, paragraphs 185–187 (article 9);

A/50/17, paragraphs 264–270 (article 9);

A/CN.9/407, paragraphs 82–84;

A/CN.9/406, paragraphs 59–72; A/CN.9/WG.IV/WP.60, article 14;

A/CN.9/387, paragraphs 164–168;

A/CN.9/WG.IV/WP.57, article 14;

A/CN.9/373, paragraphs 123–125; A/CN.9/WG.IV/WP.55, paragraph 94.

Chapter III. Communication of data messages

Article 11. Formation and validity of contracts

76. Article 11 is not intended to interfere with the law on formation of contracts but rather to promote international trade by providing increased legal certainty as to the conclusion of contracts by electronic means. It deals not only with the issue of contract formation but also with the form in which an offer and an acceptance may be expressed. In certain countries, a provision along the lines of paragraph (1) might be regarded as merely stating the obvious, namely, that an offer and an acceptance, as any other expression of will, can be communicated by any means, including data messages. However, the provision is needed in view of the remaining uncertainties in a considerable number of countries as to whether contracts can validly be concluded by electronic means. Such uncertainties may stem from the fact that, in certain cases, the data messages expressing offer and acceptance are generated by computers without immediate human intervention, thus raising doubts as to the expression of intent by the parties. Another reason for such uncertainties is inherent in the mode of communication and results from the absence of a paper document.

77. It also may be noted that paragraph (1) reinforces, in the context of contract formation, a principle already embodied in other articles of the Model Law, such as articles 5, 9, and 13, all of which establish the legal effectiveness of data messages. However, paragraph (1) is needed since the fact that electronic messages may have legal value as evidence and produce a number of effects, including those provided in articles 9 and 13, does not necessarily mean that they can be used for the purpose of concluding valid contracts.

78. Paragraph (1) covers not merely the cases in which both the offer and the acceptance are communicated by electronic means but also cases in which only the offer or only the acceptance is communicated electronically. As to the time and place of formation of contracts in cases where an offer or the acceptance of an offer is expressed by means of a data message, no specific rule has been included in the Model Law in order not to interfere with national law applicable to contract formation. It was felt that such a provision might exceed the aim of the Model Law, which should be limited to providing that electronic communications would achieve the same degree of legal certainty as paper-based communications. The combination of existing rules on the formation of contracts with the provisions contained in article 15 is designed to dispel uncertainty as to the time and place of formation of contracts in cases where the offer or the acceptance are exchanged electronically.

79. The words "unless otherwise stated by the parties", which merely restate, in the context of contract formation, the recognition of party autonomy expressed in article 4, are intended to make it clear that the purpose of the Model Law is not to impose the use of electronic means of communication on parties who rely on the use of paper-based communication to conclude contracts. Thus, article 11 should not be interpreted as restricting in any way party autonomy with respect to parties not involved in the use of electronic communication.

80. During the preparation of paragraph (1), it was felt that the provision might have the harmful effect of overruling otherwise applicable provisions of national law, which might prescribe specific formalities for the formation of certain contracts. Such forms include notarization and other requirements for "writings", and might respond to considerations of public policy, such as the need to protect certain parties or to warn them against specific risks. For that reason, paragraph (2) provides that an enacting State can exclude the application of paragraph (1) in certain instances to be specified in the legislation enacting the Model Law.

References

A/51/17, paragraphs 89–94 (article 13);

A/CN.9/407, paragraph 93;

A/CN.9/406, paragraphs 34–41; A/CN.9/WG.IV/WP.60, article 12;

A/CN.9/387, paragraphs 145–151; A/CN.9/WG.IV/WP.57, article 12;

A/CN.9/373, paragraphs 126–133; A/CN.9/WG.IV/WP.55, paragraphs 95–102;

A/CN.9/360, paragraphs 76–86; A/CN.9/WG.IV/WP.53, paragraphs 67–73;

A/CN.9/350, paragraphs 93–96;

A/CN.9/333, paragraphs 60–68.

Article 12. Recognition by parties of data messages

81. Article 12 was added at a late stage in the preparation of the Model Law, in recognition of the fact that article 11 was limited to dealing with data messages that were geared to the conclusion of a contract, but that the draft Model Law did not contain specific provisions on data messages that related not to the conclusion of contracts but to the performance of contractual obligations (e.g., notice of defective goods, an offer to pay, notice of place where a contract would be performed, and recognition of debt). Since modern means of communication are used in a context of legal uncertainty, in the absence of specific legislation in most countries, it was felt appropriate for the Model Law not only to establish the general principle that the use of electronic communication should not be discriminated against, as expressed in article 5, but also to include specific illustrations of that principle. Contract formation is but one of the areas where such an illustration is useful, and the legal validity of unilateral expressions of will, as well as other notices or statements that may be issued in the form of data messages, also needs to be mentioned.

82. As is the case with article 11, article 12 is not to impose the use of electronic means of communication but to validate such use, subject to contrary agreement by the parties. Thus, article 12 should not be used as a basis to impose on the addressee the legal consequences of a message, if the use of a non-paper-based method for its transmission comes as a surprise to the addressee.

References

A/51/17, paragraphs 95–99 (new article 13 bis).

Article 13. Attribution of data messages

83. Article 13 has its origin in article 5 of the UNCITRAL Model Law on International Credit Transfers, which defines the obligations of the sender of a payment order. Article 13 is intended to apply where there is a question as to whether a data message was really sent by the person who is indicated as being the originator. In the case of a paper-based communication, the problem would arise as the result of an alleged forged signature of the purported originator. In an electronic environment, an unauthorized person may have sent the message, but the authentication by code, encryption, or the like would be accurate. The purpose of article 13 is not to assign responsibility. It deals rather with attribution of data messages by establishing a presumption that, under certain circumstances, a data message would be considered as a

message of the originator, and goes on to qualify that presumption in case the addressee knew or ought to have known that the data message was not that of the originator.

84. Paragraph (1) recalls the principle that an originator is bound by a data message if it has effectively sent that message. Paragraph (2) refers to the situation where the message was sent by a person other than the originator who had the authority to act on behalf of the originator. Paragraph (2) is not intended to displace the domestic law of agency, and the question as to whether the other person did in fact and in law have the authority to act on behalf of the originator is left to the appropriate legal rules outside the Model Law.

85. Paragraph (3) deals with two kinds of situations, in which the addressee could rely on a data message as being that of the originator: firstly, situations in which the addressee properly applied an authentication procedure previously agreed to by the originator; and secondly, situations in which the data message resulted from the actions of a person who, by virtue of its relationship with the originator, had access to the originator's authentication procedures. By stating that the addressee "is entitled to regard a data as being that of the originator", paragraph (3) read in conjunction with paragraph (4)(a) is intended to indicate that the addressee could act on the assumption that the data message is that of the originator up to the point in time it received notice from the originator that the data message was not that of the originator, or up to the point in time when it knew or should have known that the data message was not that of the originator.

86. Under paragraph (3)(a), if the addressee applies any authentication procedures previously agreed to by the originator and such application results in the proper verification of the originator as the source of the message, the message is presumed to be that of the originator. That covers not only the situation where an authentication procedure has been agreed upon by the originator and the addressee, but also situations where an originator, unilaterally or as a result of an agreement with an intermediary, identified a procedure and agreed to be bound by a data message that met the requirements corresponding to that procedure. Thus, agreements that became effective not through direct agreement between the originator and the addressee but through the participation of third-party service providers are intended to be covered by paragraph (3)(a). However, it should be noted that paragraph (3)(a) applies only when the communication between the originator and the addressee is based on a previous agreement, but it does not apply in an open environment.

87. The effect of paragraph (3)(b), read in conjunction with paragraph (4)(b), is that the originator or the addressee, as the case may be, is responsible for any unauthorized data message that can be shown to have been sent as a result of negligence of that party.

88. Paragraph (4)(a) should not be misinterpreted as relieving the originator from the consequences of sending a data message, with retroactive effect, irrespective of whether the addressee had acted on the assumption that the data message was that of the originator. Paragraph (4) is not intended to provide that receipt of a notice under subparagraph (a) would nullify the original message retroactively. Under subparagraph (a), the originator is released from the binding effect of the message after the time notice is received and not before that time. Moreover, paragraph (4) should not be read as allowing the originator to avoid being bound by the data message by sending notice to the addressee under subparagraph (a), in a case where the message had, in fact, been sent by the originator and the addressee properly applied agreed or reasonable authentication procedures. If the addressee can prove that the message is that of the originator, paragraph (1) would apply and not paragraph (4)(a). As to the meaning of "reasonable time", the notice should be such as to give the addressee sufficient time to react. For example, in the case of just-in-time supply, the addressee should be given time to adjust its production chain.

89. With respect to paragraph (4)(b), it should be noted that the Model Law could lead to the result that the addressee would be entitled to rely on a data message under paragraph (3)(a) if it had properly applied the agreed authentication procedures, even if it knew that the data message was not that of the originator. It was generally felt when preparing the Model Law that the risk that such a situation could arise should be accepted, in view of the need for preserving the reliability of agreed authentication procedures.

90. Paragraph (5) is intended to preclude the originator from disavowing the message once it was sent, unless the addressee knew, or should have known, that the data message was not that of the originator. In addition, paragraph (5) is intended to deal with errors in the content of the message arising from errors in transmission.

91. Paragraph (6) deals with the issue of erroneous duplication of data messages, an issue of considerable practical importance. It establishes the standard of care to be applied by the addressee to distinguish an erroneous duplicate of a data message from a separate data message.

92. Early drafts of article 13 contained an additional paragraph, expressing the principle that the attribution of authorship of a data message to the originator should not interfere with the legal consequences of that message, which should be determined by other applicable rules of national law. It was later felt that it was not necessary to express that principle in the Model Law but that it should be mentioned in this Guide.

References

A/51/17, paragraphs 189–194 (article 11);

A/50/17, paragraphs 275–303 (article 11);

A/CN.9/407, paragraphs 86–89;

A/CN.9/406, paragraphs 114–131; A/CN.9/WG.IV/WP.62, article 10;

A/CN.9/390, paragraphs 144–153; A/CN.9/WG.IV/WP.60, article 10;

A/CN.9/387, paragraphs 110–132; A/CN.9/WG.IV/WP.57, article 10;

A/CN.9/373, paragraphs 109–115; A/CN.9/WG.IV/WP.55, paragraphs 82–86.

Article 14. Acknowledgement of receipt

93. The use of functional acknowledgements is a business decision to be made by users of electronic commerce; the Model Law does not intend to impose the use of any such procedure. However, taking into account the commercial value of a system of acknowledgement of receipt and the widespread use of such systems in the context of electronic commerce, it was felt that the Model Law should address a number of legal issues arising from the use of acknowledgement procedures. It should be noted that the notion of "acknowledgement" is sometimes used to cover a variety of procedures, ranging from a mere acknowledgement of receipt of an unspecified message to an expression of agreement with the content of a specific data message. In many instances, the procedure of "acknowledgement" would parallel the system known as "return receipt requested" in postal systems. Acknowledgements of receipt may be required in a variety of instruments, e.g., in the data message itself, in bilateral or multilateral communication agreements, or in "system rules". It should be borne in mind that variety among acknowledgement procedures implies variety of the related costs. The provisions of article 14 are based on the assumption that acknowledgement procedures are to be used at the discretion of the originator. Article 14 is not intended to deal with the legal consequences that may flow from sending an acknowledgement of receipt, apart from establishing receipt of the data message. For example, where an originator sends an offer in a data message and requests acknowledgement of receipt, the acknowledgement of receipt simply evidences that the offer has been received. Whether or not sending that acknowledgement amounted to accepting the offer is not dealt with by the Model Law but by contract law outside the Model Law.

94. The purpose of paragraph (2) is to validate acknowledgement by any communication or conduct of the addressee (e.g., the shipment of the goods as an acknowledgement of receipt of a purchase order) where the originator has not agreed with the addressee that the acknowledgement should be in a particular form. The situation where an acknowledgement has been unilaterally requested by the originator to be given in a specific form is not expressly addressed by article 14, which may entail as a possible consequence that a unilateral requirement by the originator as to the form of acknowledgements would not affect the right of the addressee to acknowledge receipt by any

communication or conduct sufficient to indicate to the originator that the message had been received. Such a possible interpretation of paragraph (2) makes it particularly necessary to emphasize in the Model Law the distinction to be drawn between the effects of an acknowledgement of receipt of a

data message and any communication in response to the content of that data message, a reason why paragraph (7) is needed.

95. Paragraph (3), which deals with the situation where the originator has stated that the data message is conditional on receipt of an acknowledgement, applies whether or not the originator has specified that the acknowledgement should be received by a certain time.

96. The purpose of paragraph (4) is to deal with the more common situation where an acknowledgement is requested, without any statement being made by the originator that the data message is of no effect until an acknowledgement has been received. Such a provision is needed to establish the point in time when the originator of a data message who has requested an acknowledgement of receipt is relieved from any legal implication of sending that data message if the requested acknowledgement has not been received. An example of a factual situation where a provision along the lines of paragraph (4) would be particularly useful would be that the originator of an offer to contract who has not received the requested acknowledgement from the addressee of the offer may need to know the point in time after which it is free to transfer the offer to another party. It may be noted that the provision does not create any obligation binding on the originator, but merely establishes means by which the originator, if it so wishes, can clarify its status in cases where it has not received the requested acknowledgement. It also may be noted that the provision does not create any obligation binding on the addressee of the data message, who would, in most circumstances, be free to rely or not to rely on any given data message, provided that it would bear the risk of the data message being unreliable for lack of an acknowledgement of receipt. The addressee, however, is protected since the originator who does not receive a requested acknowledgement may not automatically treat the data message as though it had never been transmitted, without giving further notice to the addressee. The procedure described under paragraph (4) is purely at the discretion of the originator. For example, where the originator sent a data message which under the agreement between the parties had to be received by a certain time, and the originator requested an acknowledgement of receipt, the addressee could not deny the legal effectiveness of the message simply by withholding the requested acknowledgement.

97. The rebuttable presumption established in paragraph (5) is needed to create certainty and would be particularly useful in the context of electronic communication between parties that are not linked by a trading-partners agreement. The second sentence of paragraph (5) should be read in

conjunction with paragraph (5) of article 13, which establishes the conditions under which, in case of an inconsistency between the text of the data message as sent and the text as received, the text as received prevails.

98. Paragraph (6) corresponds to a certain type of acknowledgement, for example, an EDIFACT message establishing that the data message received is syntactically correct, i.e., that it can be processed by the receiving computer. The reference to technical requirements, which is to be construed primarily as a reference to "data syntax" in the context of EDI communications, may be less relevant in the context of the use of other means of communication, such as telegram or telex. In addition to mere consistency with the rules of "data syntax", technical requirements set forth in applicable standards may include, for example, the use of procedures verifying the integrity of the contents of data messages.

99. Paragraph (7) is intended to dispel uncertainties that might exist as to the legal effect of an acknowledgement of receipt. For example, paragraph (7) indicates that an acknowledgement of receipt should not be confused with any communication related to the contents of the acknowledged message.

References

A/51/17, paragraphs 63–88 (article 12);

A/CN.9/407, paragraphs 90–92;

A/CN.9/406, paragraphs 15–33; A/CN.9/WG.IV/WP.60, article 11;

A/CN.9/387, paragraphs 133–144; A/CN.9/WG.IV/WP.57, article 11;

A/CN.9/373, paragraphs 116–122; A/CN.9/WG.IV/WP.55, paragraphs 87–93;

A/CN.9/360, paragraph 125; A/CN.9/WG.IV/WP.53, paragraphs 80–81;

A/CN.9/350, paragraph 92;

A/CN.9/333, paragraphs 48–49.

Article 15. Time and place of dispatch and receipt of data messages

100. Article 15 results from the recognition that, for the operation of many existing rules of law, it is important to ascertain the time and place of receipt of information. The use of electronic communication techniques makes those difficult to ascertain. It is not uncommon for users of electronic commerce to communicate from one State to another without knowing the location of information systems through which communication is operated. In addition, the location of certain communication systems may change without either of the parties being aware of the change. The Model Law is thus intended to reflect the fact that the location of information systems is irrelevant and sets

forth a more objective criterion, namely, the place of business of the parties. In that connection, it should be noted that article 15 is not intended to establish a conflict-of-laws rule.

101. Paragraph (1) defines the time of dispatch of a data message as the time when the data message enters an information system outside the control of the originator, which may be the information system of an intermediary or an information system of the addressee. The concept of "dispatch" refers to the commencement of the electronic transmission of the data message. Where "dispatch" already has an established meaning, article 15 is intended to supplement national rules on dispatch and not to displace them. If dispatch occurs when the data message reaches an information system of the addressee, dispatch under paragraph (1) and receipt under paragraph (2) are simultaneous, except where the data message is sent to an information system of the addressee that is not the information system designated by the addressee under paragraph (2)(a).

102. Paragraph (2), the purpose of which is to define the time of receipt of a data message, addresses the situation where the addressee unilaterally designates a specific information system for the receipt of a message (in which case the designated system may or may not be an information system of the addressee), and the data message reaches an information system of the addressee that is not the designated system. In such a situation, receipt is deemed to occur when the data message is retrieved by the addressee. By "designated information system", the Model Law is intended to cover a system that has been specifically designated by a party, for instance, in the case where an offer expressly specifies the address to which acceptance should be sent. The mere indication of an electronic mail or telecopy address on a letterhead or other document should not be regarded as express designation of one or more information systems.

103. Attention is drawn to the notion of "entry" into an information system, which is used for both the definition of dispatch and that of receipt of a data message. A data message enters an information system at the time when it becomes available for processing within that information system. Whether a data message which enters an information system is intelligible or usable by the addressee is outside the purview of the Model Law. The Model Law does not intend to overrule provisions of national law under which receipt of a message may occur at the time when the message enters the sphere of the addressee, irrespective of whether the message is intelligible or usable by the addressee. Nor is the Model Law intended to run counter to trade usages, under which certain encoded messages are deemed to be received even before they are usable by, or intelligible for, the addressee. It was felt that the Model Law should not create a more stringent requirement than currently exists in a paper-based environment, where a message can be considered to be received

even if it is not intelligible for the addressee or not intended to be intelligible to the addressee (e.g., where encrypted data is transmitted to a depository for the sole purpose of retention in the context of intellectual property rights protection).

104. A data message should not be considered to be dispatched if it merely reached the information system of the addressee but failed to enter it. It may be noted that the Model Law does not expressly address the question of possible malfunctioning of information systems as a basis for liability. In particular, where the information system of the addressee does not function at all or functions improperly or, while functioning properly, cannot be entered into by the data message (e.g., in the case of a telecopier that is constantly occupied), dispatch under the Model Law does not occur. It was felt during the preparation of the Model Law that the addressee should not be placed under the burdensome obligation to maintain its information system functioning at all times by way of a general provision.

105. The purpose of paragraph (4) is to deal with the place of receipt of a data message. The principal reason for including a rule on the place of receipt of a data message is to address a circumstance characteristic of electronic commerce that might not be treated adequately under existing law, namely, that very often the information system of the addressee where the data message is received, or from which the data message is retrieved, is located in a jurisdiction other than that in which the addressee itself is located. Thus, the rationale behind the provision is to ensure that the location of an information system is not the determinant element, and that there is some reasonable connection between the addressee and what is deemed to be the place of receipt, and that that place can be readily ascertained by the originator. The Model Law does not contain specific provisions as to how the designation of an information system should be made, or whether a change could be made after such a designation by the addressee.

106. Paragraph (4), which contains a reference to the "underlying transaction", is intended to refer to both actual and contemplated underlying transactions. References to "place of business", "principal place of business", and "place of habitual residence" were adopted to bring the text in line with article 10 of the United Nations Convention on Contracts for the International Sale of Goods.

107. The effect of paragraph (4) is to introduce a distinction between the deemed place of receipt and the place actually reached by a data message at the time of its receipt under paragraph (2). That distinction is not to be interpreted as apportioning risks between the originator and the addressee in case of damage or loss of a data message between the time of its receipt under paragraph (2) and the time when it reached its place of receipt under paragraph (4). Paragraph (4) merely establishes an irrebuttable presumption

regarding a legal fact, to be used where another body of law (e.g., on formation of contracts or conflict of laws) requires determination of the place of receipt of a data message. However, it was felt during the preparation of the Model Law that introducing a deemed place of receipt, as distinct from the place actually reached by that data message at the time of its receipt, would be inappropriate outside the context of computerized transmissions (e.g., in the context of telegram or telex). The provision was thus limited in scope to cover only computerized transmissions of data messages. A further limitation is contained in paragraph (5), which reproduces a provision already included in articles 6, 7, 8, 11, and 12 (see above, paragraph 69).

References

A/51/17, paragraphs 100–115 (article 14);

A/CN.9/407, paragraphs 94–99;

A/CN.9/406, paragraphs 42–58; A/CN.9/WG.IV/WP.60, article 13;

A/CN.9/387, paragraphs 152–163; A/CN.9/WG.IV/WP.57, article 13;

A/CN.9/373, paragraphs 134–146; A/CN.9/WG.IV/WP.55, paragraphs 103–108;

A/CN.9/360, paragraphs 87–89; A/CN.9/WG.IV/WP.53, paragraphs 74–76;

A/CN.9/350, paragraphs 97–100;

A/CN.9/333, paragraphs 69–75.

Part 2: Electronic commerce in specific areas

108. As distinct from the basic rules applicable to electronic commerce in general, which appear as part 1 of the Model Law, part 2 contains rules of a more specific nature. In preparing the Model Law, the Commission agreed that such rules dealing with specific uses of electronic commerce should appear in the Model Law in a way that reflected both the specific nature of the provisions and their legal status, which should be the same as that of the general provisions contained in part 1 of the Model Law. While the Commission, when adopting the Model Law, only considered such specific provisions in the context of transport documents, it was agreed that such provisions should appear as chapter I of part 2 of the Model Law. It was felt that adopting such an open-ended structure would make it easier to add further specific provisions to the Model Law, as the need might arise, in the form of additional chapters in part 2.

109. The adoption of a specific set of rules dealing with specific uses of electronic commerce, such as the use of EDI messages as substitutes for transport documents, does not imply that the other provisions of the Model Law are not applicable to such documents. In particular, the provisions of part 2, such

as articles 16 and 17 concerning transfer of rights in goods, presuppose that the guarantees of reliability and authenticity contained in articles 6 to 8 of the Model Law are also applicable to electronic equivalents to transport documents. Part two of the Model Law does not in any way limit or restrict the field of application of the general provisions of the Model Law.

Chapter I. Carriage of goods

110. In preparing the Model Law, the Commission noted that the carriage of goods was the context in which electronic communications were most likely to be used and in which a legal framework facilitating the use of such communications was most urgently needed. Articles 16 and 17 contain provisions that apply equally to non-negotiable transport documents and to transfer of rights in goods by way of transferable bills of lading. The principles embodied in articles 16 and 17 are applicable not only to maritime transport but also to transport of goods by other means, such as road, railroad, and air transport.

Article 16. Actions related to contracts of carriage of goods

111. Article 16, which establishes the scope of chapter I of part two of the Model Law, is broadly drafted. It would encompass a wide variety of documents used in the context of the carriage of goods, including, for example, charter-parties. In the preparation of the Model Law, the Commission found that, by dealing comprehensively with contracts of carriage of goods, article 16 was consistent with the need to cover all transport documents, whether negotiable or non-negotiable, without excluding any specific document such as charter-parties. It was pointed out that, if an enacting State did not wish chapter I of part 2 to apply to a particular kind of document or contract, for example, if the inclusion of such documents as charter-parties in the scope of that chapter was regarded as inappropriate under the legislation of an enacting State, that State could make use of the exclusion clause contained in paragraph (7) of article 17.

112. Article 16 is of an illustrative nature and, although the actions mentioned therein are more common in maritime trade, they are not exclusive to such type of trade and could be performed in connection with air transport or multimodal carriage of goods.

References

A/51/17, paragraphs 139–172 and 198–204 (draft article x);

A/CN.9/421, paragraphs 53–103; A/CN.9/WG.IV/WP.69, paragraphs 82–95;

A/50/17, paragraphs 307–309;

A/CN.9/407, paragraphs 106–118; A/CN.9/WG.IV/WP.67, annex; A/CN.9/WG.IV/WP.66, annex II;

A/49/17, paragraphs 198, 199, and 201;

A/CN.9/390, paragraphs 155–158.

Article 17. Transport documents

113. Paragraphs (1) and (2) are derived from article 6. In the context of transport documents, it is necessary to establish not only functional equivalents of written information about the actions referred to in article 16, but also functional equivalents of the performance of such actions through the use of paper documents. Functional equivalents are particularly needed for the transfer of rights and obligations by transfer of written documents. For example, paragraphs (1) and (2) are intended to replace both the requirement for a written contract of carriage and the requirements for endorsement and transfer of possession of a bill of lading. It was felt in the preparation of the Model Law that the focus of the provision on the actions referred to in article 16 should be expressed clearly, particularly in view of the difficulties that might exist, in certain countries, for recognizing the transmission of a data message as functionally equivalent to the physical transfer of goods, or to the transfer of a document of title representing the goods.

114. The reference to "one or more data messages" in paragraphs (1), (3), and (6) is not intended to be interpreted differently from the reference to "a data message" in the other provisions of the Model Law, which should also be understood as covering equally the situation where only one data message is generated and the situation where more than one data message is generated as support of a given piece of information. A more detailed wording was adopted in article 17 merely to reflect the fact that, in the context of transfer of rights through data messages, some of the functions traditionally performed through the single transmission of a paper bill of lading would necessarily imply the transmission of more than one data message and that such a fact, in itself, should entail no negative consequence as to the acceptability of electronic commerce in that area.

115. Paragraph (3), in combination with paragraph (4), is intended to ensure that a right can be conveyed to one person only, and that it would not be possible for more than one person at any point in time to lay claim to it. The effect of the two paragraphs is to introduce a requirement which may be referred to as the "guarantee of singularity". If procedures are made available to enable a right or obligation to be conveyed by electronic methods instead of by using a paper document, it is necessary that the guarantee of singularity be one of the essential features of such procedures. Technical security devices providing such a guarantee of singularity would almost necessarily be

built into any communication system offered to the trading communities and would need to demonstrate their reliability. However, there also is a need to overcome requirements of law that the guarantee of singularity be demonstrated, for example, in the case where paper documents such as bills of lading are traditionally used. A provision along the lines of paragraph (3) is thus necessary to permit the use of electronic communication instead of paper documents.

116. The words "one person and no other person" should not be interpreted as excluding situations where more than one person might jointly hold title to the goods. For example, the reference to "one person" is not intended to exclude joint ownership of rights in the goods or other rights embodied in a bill of lading.

117. The notion that a data message should be "unique" may need to be further clarified, since it may lend itself to misinterpretation. On the one hand, all data messages are necessarily unique, even if they duplicate an earlier data message, since each data message is sent at a different time from any earlier data message sent to the same person. If a data message is sent to a different person, it is even more obviously unique, even though it might be transferring the same right or obligation. Yet, all but the first transfer might be fraudulent. On the other hand, if "unique" is interpreted as referring to a data message of a unique kind, or a transfer of a unique kind, then in that sense no data message is unique, and no transfer by means of a data message is unique. Having considered the risk of such misinterpretation, the Commission decided to retain the reference to the concepts of uniqueness of the data message and uniqueness of the transfer for the purposes of article 17, in view of the fact that the notions of "uniqueness" or "singularity" of transport documents were not unknown to practitioners of transport law and users of transport documents. It was decided, however, that this Guide should clarify that the words "a reliable method is used to render such data message or messages unique" should be interpreted as referring to the use of a reliable method to secure that data messages purporting to convey any right or obligation of a person might not be used by, or on behalf of, that person inconsistently with any other data messages by which the right or obligation was conveyed by or on behalf of that person.

118. Paragraph (5) is a necessary complement to the guarantee of singularity contained in paragraph (3). The need for security is an overriding consideration, and it is essential to ensure not only that a method is used that gives reasonable assurance that the same data message is not multiplied, but also that no two media can be simultaneously used for the same purpose. Paragraph (5) addresses the fundamental need to avoid the risk of duplicate transport documents. The use of multiple forms of communication for different purposes, e.g., paper-based communications for ancillary messages and

electronic communications for bills of lading, does not pose a problem. However, it is essential for the operation of any system relying on electronic equivalents of bills of lading to avoid the possibility that the same rights could at any given time be embodied both in data messages and in a paper document. Paragraph (5) also envisages the situation where a party having initially agreed to engage in electronic communications has to switch to paper communications where it later becomes unable to sustain electronic communications.

119. The reference to "terminating" the use of data messages is open to interpretation. In particular, the Model Law does not provide information as to who would effect the termination. Should an enacting State decide to provide additional information in that respect, it might wish to indicate, for example, that, since electronic commerce is usually based on the agreement of the parties, a decision to "drop down" to paper communications should also be subject to the agreement of all interested parties. Otherwise, the originator would be given the power to choose unilaterally the means of communication. Alternatively, an enacting State might wish to provide that, since paragraph (5) would have to be applied by the bearer of a bill of lading, it should be up to the bearer to decide whether it preferred to exercise its rights on the basis of a paper bill of lading or on the basis of the electronic equivalent of such a document, and to bear the costs for its decision.

120. Paragraph (5), while expressly dealing with the situation where the use of data messages is replaced by the use of a paper document, is not intended to exclude the reverse situation. The switch from data messages to a paper document should not affect any right that might exist to surrender the paper document to the issuer and again start using data messages.

121. The purpose of paragraph (6) is to deal directly with the application of certain laws to contracts for the carriage of goods by sea. For example, under the Hague and Hague-Visby Rules, a contract of carriage means a contract that is covered by a bill of lading. Use of a bill of lading or similar document of title results in the Hague and Hague-Visby Rules applying compulsorily to a contract of carriage. Those rules would not automatically apply to contracts effected by one or more data message. Thus, a provision such as paragraph (6) is needed to ensure that the application of those rules is not excluded by the mere fact that data messages are used instead of a bill of lading in paper form. While paragraph (1) ensures that data messages are effective means for carrying out any of the actions listed in article 16, that provision does not deal with the substantive rules of law that might apply to a contract contained in, or evidenced by, data messages.

122. As to the meaning of the phrase "that rule shall not be inapplicable" in paragraph (6), a simpler way of expressing the same idea might have been to provide that rules applicable to contracts of carriage evidenced by paper

documents should also apply to contracts of carriage evidenced by data messages. However, given the broad scope of application of article 17, which covers not only bills of lading but also a variety of other transport documents, such a simplified provision might have had the undesirable effect of extending the applicability of rules such as the Hamburg Rules and the Hague-Visby Rules to contracts to which such rules were never intended to apply. The Commission felt that the adopted wording was more suited to overcome the obstacle resulting from the fact that the Hague-Visby Rules and other rules compulsorily applicable to bills of lading would not automatically apply to contracts of carriage evidenced by data messages, without inadvertently extending the application of such rules to other types of contracts.

References

A/51/17, paragraphs 139–172 and 198–204 (draft article x);

A/CN.9/421, paragraphs 53–103; A/CN.9/WG.IV/WP.69, paragraphs 82–95;

A/50/17, paragraphs 307–309

A/CN.9/407, paragraphs 106–118, A/CN.9/WG.IV/WP.67, annex; A/CN.9/WG.IV/WP.66, annex II;

A/49/17, paragraphs 198, 199, and 201;

A/CN.9/390, paragraphs 155–158.

III. History and Background of the Model Law

123. The UNCITRAL Model Law on Electronic Commerce was adopted by the United Nations Commission on International Trade Law (UNCITRAL) in 1996 in furtherance of its mandate to promote the harmonization and unification of international trade law, so as to remove unnecessary obstacles to international trade caused by inadequacies and divergences in the law affecting trade. Over the past quarter of a century, UNCITRAL, whose membership consists of states from all regions and of all levels of economic development, has implemented its mandate by formulating international conventions (the United Nations Conventions on Contracts for the International Sale of Goods, on the Limitation Period in the International Sale of Goods, on the Carriage of Goods by Sea, 1978 ("Hamburg Rules"), on the Liability of Operators of Transport Terminals in International Trade, on International Bills of Exchange and International Promissory Notes, and on Independent Guarantees and Stand-by Letters of Credit), model laws (the UNCITRAL Model Laws on International Commercial Arbitration, on International Credit Transfers and on Procurement of Goods, Construction and Services), the UNCITRAL Arbitration Rules, the UNCITRAL

Conciliation Rules, and legal guides (on construction contracts, counter-trade transactions and electronic funds transfers).

124. The Model Law was prepared in response to a major change in the means by which communications are made between parties using computerized or other modern techniques in doing business (sometimes referred to as "trading partners"). The Model Law is intended to serve as a model to countries for the evaluation and modernization of certain aspects of their laws and practices in the field of commercial relationships involving the use of computerized or other modern communication techniques, and for the establishment of relevant legislation where none presently exists. The text of the Model Law, as reproduced above, is set forth in annex I to the report of UNCITRAL on the work of its twenty-ninth session.[7]

125. The Commission, at its seventeenth session (1984), considered a report of the Secretary-General entitled "Legal aspects of automatic data processing" (A/CN.9/254), which identified several legal issues relating to the legal value of computer records, the requirement of a "writing", authentication, general conditions, liability, and bills of lading. The Commission took note of a report of the Working Party on Facilitation of International Trade Proce dures (WP.4), which is jointly sponsored by the Economic Commission for Europe and the United Nations Conference on Trade and Development, and is responsible for the development of UN/EDIFACT standard messages. That report suggested that, since the legal problems arising in this field were essentially those of international trade law, the Commission, as the core legal body in the field of international trade law, appeared to be the appropriate central forum to undertake and coordinate the necessary action.[8] The Commission decided to place the subject of the legal implications of automatic data processing to the flow of international trade on its program of work as a priority item.[9]

126. At its eighteenth session (1985), the Commission had before it a report by the Secretariat entitled "Legal value of computer records" (A/CN.9/265). That report came to the conclusion that, on a global level, there were fewer problems in the use of data stored in computers as evidence in litigation than might have been expected. It noted that a more serious legal obstacle to the use of computers and computer-to-computer telecommunications in international trade arose out of requirements that documents had to be signed or be

---

7 *Official Records of the General Assembly*, Fifty-first Session, Supplement Number 17 (A/51/17), Annex I.

8 "Legal aspects of automatic trade data interchange" (TRADE/WP.4/R.185/Rev.1). The report submitted to the Working Party is reproduced in A/CN.9/238, Annex.

9 *Official Records of the General Assembly*, Thirty-ninth Session, Supplement Number 17 (A/39/17), paragraph 136.

in paper form. After discussion of the report, the Commission adopted the following recommendation, which expresses some of the principles on which the Model Law is based:

"The United Nations Commission on International Trade Law,

"Noting that the use of automatic data processing (ADP) is about to become firmly established throughout the world in many phases of domestic and international trade as well as in administrative services,

"Noting also that legal rules based upon pre-ADP paper-based means of documenting international trade may create an obstacle to such use of ADP in that they lead to legal insecurity or impede the efficient use of ADP where its use is otherwise justified,

"Noting further with appreciation the efforts of the Council of Europe, the Customs Co-operation Council and the United Nations Economic Commission for Europe to overcome obstacles to the use of ADP in international trade arising out of these legal rules,

"Considering at the same time that there is no need for a unification of the rules of evidence regarding the use of computer records in international trade, in view of the experience showing that substantial differences in the rules of evidence as they apply to the paper-based system of documentation have caused so far no noticeable harm to the development of international trade,

"Considering also that the developments in the use of ADP are creating a desirability in a number of legal systems for an adaptation of existing legal rules to these developments, having due regard, however, to the need to encourage the employment of such ADP means that would provide the same or greater reliability as paper-based documentation,

"1. Recommends to governments:

"(a) to review the legal rules affecting the use of computer records as evidence in litigation in order to eliminate unnecessary obstacles to their admission, to be assured that the rules are consistent with developments in technology, and to provide appropriate means for a court to evaluate the credibility of the data contained in those records;

"(b) to review legal requirements that certain trade transactions or trade related documents be in writing, whether the written form is a condition to the enforceability or to the validity of the transaction or document, with a view to permitting, where appropriate, the transaction or document to be recorded and transmitted in computer-readable form;

"(c) to review legal requirements of a handwritten signature or other paper-based method of authentication on trade related documents with a view to permitting, where appropriate, the use of electronic means of authentication;

"(d) to review legal requirements that documents for submission to governments be in writing and manually signed with a view to permitting, where appropriate, such documents to be submitted in computer-readable form to those administrative services which have acquired the necessary equipment and established the necessary procedures;

"2. Recommends to international organizations elaborating legal texts related to trade to take account of the present Recommendation in adopting such texts and, where appropriate, to consider modifying existing legal texts in line with the present Recommendation."[10]

127. That recommendation (hereinafter referred to as the "1985 UNCITRAL Recommendation") was endorsed by the General Assembly in resolution 40/71, paragraph 5(b), of 11 December 1985 as follows:

"The General Assembly,

". . . Calls upon governments and international organizations to take action, where appropriate, in conformity with the Commission's recommendation so as to ensure legal security in the context of the widest possible use of automated data processing in international trade . . .".[11]

128. As was pointed out in several documents and meetings involving the international electronic commerce community, e.g. in meetings of WP. 4, there was a general feeling that, in spite of the efforts made through the 1985 UNCITRAL Recommendation, little progress had been made to achieve the removal of the mandatory requirements in national legislation regarding the use of paper and handwritten signatures. It has been suggested by the Norwegian Committee on Trade Procedures (NORPRO) in a letter to the Secretariat that "one reason for this could be that the 1985 UNCITRAL Recommendation advises on the need for legal update, but does not give any indication of how it could be done". In this vein, the Commission considered what follow-up action to the 1985 UNCITRAL Recommendation could usefully be taken so as to enhance the needed modernization of legislation. The decision by UNCITRAL to formulate model legislation on legal issues of electronic data interchange and related means of communication may be regarded as a consequence of the process that led to the adoption by the Commission of the 1985 UNCITRAL Recommendation.

---

10 *Official Records of the General Assembly,* Fortieth Session, Supplement Number 17 (A/40/17), paragraph 360.

11 Resolution 40/71 was reproduced in *United Nations Commission on International Trade Law Yearbook,* 1985, vol. XVI, Part 1, D. (United Nations publication, Sales Number E.87.V.4).

129. At its twenty-first session (1988), the Commission considered a proposal to examine the need to provide for the legal principles that would apply to the formation of international commercial contracts by electronic means. It was noted that there existed no refined legal structure for the important and rapidly growing field of formation of contracts by electronic means and that future work in that area could help to fill a legal vacuum and to reduce uncertainties and difficulties encountered in practice. The Commission requested the Secretariat to prepare a preliminary study on the topic.[12]

130. At its twenty-third session (1990), the Commission had before it a report entitled "Preliminary study of legal issues related to the formation of contracts by electronic means" (A/CN.9/333). The report summarized work that had been undertaken in the European Communities and in the United States of America on the requirement of a "writing" as well as other issues that had been identified as arising in the formation of contracts by electronic means. The efforts to overcome some of those problems by the use of model communication agreements were also discussed.[13]

131. At its twenty-fourth session (1991), the Commission had before it a report entitled "Electronic Data Interchange" (A/CN.9/350). The report described the current activities in the various organizations involved in the legal issues of electronic data interchange (EDI) and analyzed the contents of a number of standard interchange agreements already developed or then being developed. It pointed out that such documents varied considerably according to the various needs of the different categories of users they were intended to serve and that the variety of contractual arrangements had sometimes been described as hindering the development of a satisfactory legal framework for the business use of electronic commerce. It suggested that there was a need for a general framework that would identify the issues and provide a set of legal principles and basic legal rules governing communication through electronic commerce. It concluded that such a basic framework could, to a certain extent, be created by contractual arrangements between parties to an electronic commerce relationship and that the existing contractual frameworks that were proposed to the community of users of electronic commerce were often incomplete, mutually incompatible, and inappropriate for international use since they relied to a large extent upon the structures of local law.

132. With a view to achieving the harmonization of basic rules for the promotion of electronic commerce in international trade, the report suggested

---

12 *Official Records of the General Assembly*, Forty-third Session, Supplement Number 17 (A/43/17), paragraphs 46 and 47, and *ibid.*, Forty-fourth Session, Supplement Number 17 (A/44/17), paragraph 289.

13 *Official Records of the General Assembly*, Forty-fifth Session, Supplement Number 17 (A/45/17), paragraphs 38–40.

that the Commission might wish to consider the desirability of preparing a standard communication agreement for use in international trade. It pointed out that work by the Commission in this field would be of particular importance since it would involve participation of all legal systems, including those of developing countries that were already or would soon be confronted with the issues of electronic commerce.

133. The Commission was agreed that the legal issues of electronic commerce would become increasingly important as the use of electronic commerce developed and that it should undertake work in that field. There was wide support for the suggestion that the Commission should undertake the preparation of a set of legal principles and basic legal rules governing communication through electronic commerce.[14] The Commission came to the conclusion that it would be premature to engage immediately in the preparation of a standard communication agreement and that it might be preferable to monitor developments in other organizations, particularly the Commission of the European Communities and the Economic Commission for Europe. It was pointed out that high-speed electronic commerce required a new examination of basic contract issues, such as offer and acceptance, and that consideration should be given to legal implications of the role of central data managers in international commercial law.

134. After deliberation, the Commission decided that a session of the Working Group on International Payments would be devoted to identifying the legal issues involved and to considering possible statutory provisions, and that the Working Group would report to the Commission on the desirability and feasibility of undertaking further work, such as the preparation of a standard communication agreement.[15]

135. The Working Group on International Payments, at its twenty-fourth session, recommended that the Commission should undertake work towards establishing uniform legal rules on electronic commerce. It was agreed that the goals of such work should be to facilitate the increased use of electronic commerce and to meet the need for statutory provisions to be developed in the field of electronic commerce, particularly with respect to such issues as formation of contracts; risk and liability of commercial partners and third-party service providers involved in electronic commerce relationships; extended definitions of "writing" and "original" to be used in an electronic commerce environment; and issues of negotiability and documents of title (A/CN.9/360).

---

14   It may be noted that the Model Law is not intended to provide a comprehensive set of rules governing all aspects of electronic commerce. The main purpose of the Model Law is to adapt existing statutory requirements so that they would no longer constitute obstacles to the use of paperless means of communication and storage of information.

15   *Official Records of the General Assembly,* Forty-sixth Session, Supplement Number 17 (A/46/17), paragraphs 311–317.

136. While it was generally felt that it was desirable to seek the high degree of legal certainty and harmonization provided by the detailed provisions of a uniform law, it was also felt that care should be taken to preserve a flexible approach to some issues where legislative action might be premature or inappropriate. As an example of such an issue, it was stated that it might be fruitless to attempt to provide legislative unification of the rules on evidence that may apply to electronic commerce massaging (*ibid.*, paragraph 130). It was agreed that no decision should be taken at that early stage as to the final form or the final content of the legal rules to be prepared. In line with the flexible approach to be taken, it was noted that situations might arise where the preparation of model contractual clauses would be regarded as an appropriate way of addressing specific issues (*ibid.*, paragraph 132).

137. The Commission, at its twenty-fifth session (1992), endorsed the recommendation contained in the report of the Working Group (*ibid.*, paragraphs 129–133) and entrusted the preparation of legal rules on electronic commerce (which was then referred to as "electronic data interchange" or "EDI") to the Working Group on International Payments, which it renamed the Working Group on Electronic Data Interchange.[16]

138. The Working Group devoted its twenty-fifth to twenty-eighth sessions to the preparation of legal rules applicable to "electronic data interchange (EDI) and other modern means of communication" (reports of those sessions are found in documents A/CN.9/373, 387, 390, and 406).[17]

139. The Working Group carried out its task on the basis of background working papers prepared by the Secretariat on possible issues to be included in the Model Law. Those background papers included A/CN.9/WG.IV/WP.53 (Possible issues to be included in the program of future work on the legal aspects of EDI) and A/CN.9/WG.IV/WP.55 (Outline of possible uniform rules on the legal aspects of electronic data interchange). The draft articles of the Model Law were submitted by the Secretariat in documents A/CN.9/WG.IV/WP.57, 60, and 62. The Working Group also had before it a proposal by the United

---

16 *Official Records of the General Assembly*, Forty-seventh Session, Supplement Number 17 (A/47/17), paragraphs 141-148.

17 The notion of "EDI and related means of communication" as used by the Working Group is not to be construed as a reference to narrowly defined EDI under article 2(b) of the Model Law but to a variety of trade-related uses of modern communication techniques that was later referred to broadly under the rubric of "electronic commerce". The Model Law is not intended only for application in the context of existing communication techniques but rather as a set of flexible rules that should accommodate foreseeable technical developments. It should also be emphasized that the purpose of the Model Law is not only to establish rules for the movement of information communicated by means of data messages but equally to deal with the storage of information in data messages that are not intended for communication.

Kingdom of Great Britain and Northern Ireland relating to the possible contents of the draft Model Law (A/CN.9/WG.IV/WP.58).

140. The Working Group noted that, while practical solutions to the legal difficulties raised by the use of electronic commerce were often sought within contracts (A/CN.9/WG.IV/WP.53, paragraphs 35 and 36), the contractual approach to electronic commerce was developed not only because of its intrinsic advantages such as its flexibility, but also for lack of specific provisions of statutory or case law. The contractual approach was found to be limited in that it could not overcome any of the legal obstacles to the use of electronic commerce that might result from mandatory provisions of applicable statutory or case law. In that respect, one difficulty inherent in the use of communication agreements resulted from uncertainty as to the weight that would be carried by some contractual stipulations in case of litigation. Another limitation to the contractual approach resulted from the fact that parties to a contract could not effectively regulate the rights and obligations of third parties. At least for those parties not participating in the contractual arrangement, statutory law based on a model law or an international convention seemed to be needed (see A/CN.9/350, paragraph 107).

141. The Working Group considered preparing uniform rules with the aim of eliminating the legal obstacles to, and uncertainties in, the use of modern communication techniques, where effective removal of such obstacles and uncertainties could only be achieved by statutory provisions. One purpose of the uniform rules was to enable potential electronic commerce users to establish a legally secure electronic commerce relationship by way of a communication agreement within a closed network. The second purpose of the uniform rules was to support the use of electronic commerce outside such a closed network, i.e., in an open environment. However, the aim of the uniform rules was to enable, and not to impose, the use of EDI and related means of communication. Moreover, the aim of the uniform rules was not to deal with electronic commerce relationships from a technical perspective but rather to create a legal environment that would be as secure as possible, so as to facilitate the use of electronic commerce between communicating parties.

142. As to the form of the uniform rules, the Working Group was agreed that it should proceed with its work on the assumption that the uniform rules should be prepared in the form of statutory provisions. While it was agreed that the form of the text should be that of a "model law", it was felt, at first, that, owing to the special nature of the legal text being prepared, a more flexible term than "model law" needed to be found. It was observed that the title should reflect that the text contained a variety of provisions relating to existing rules scattered throughout various parts of the national laws in an enacting State. It was thus a possibility that enacting states would not incorporate the text as a whole and that the provisions of such a "model law"

might not appear together in any one particular place in the national law. The text could be described, in the parlance of one legal system, as a "miscellaneous statute amendment act". The Working Group agreed that this special nature of the text would be better reflected by the use of the term "model statutory provisions". The view was also expressed that the nature and purpose of the "model statutory provisions" could be explained in an introduction or guidelines accompanying the text.

143. At its twenty-eighth session, however, the Working Group reviewed its earlier decision to formulate a legal text in the form of "model statutory provisions" (A/CN.9/390, paragraph 16). It was widely felt that the use of the term "model statutory provisions" might raise uncertainties as to the legal nature of the instrument. While some support was expressed for the retention of the term "model statutory provisions", the widely prevailing view was that the term "model law" should be preferred. It was widely felt that, as a result of the course taken by the Working Group as its work progressed towards the completion of the text, the model statutory provisions could be regarded as a balanced and discrete set of rules, which could also be implemented as a whole in a single instrument (A/CN.9/406, paragraph 75). Depending on the situation in each enacting State, however, the Model Law could be implemented in various ways, either as a single statute or in various pieces of legislation.

144. The text of the draft Model Law as approved by the Working Group at its twenty-eighth session was sent to all governments and to interested international organizations for comment. The comments received were reproduced in document A/CN.9/409 and Add.1-4. The text of the draft articles of the Model Law as presented to the Commission by the Working Group was contained in the annex to document A/CN.9/406.

145. At its twenty-eighth session (1995), the Commission adopted the text of articles 1 and 3 to 11 of the draft Model Law and, for lack of sufficient time, did not complete its review of the draft Model Law, which was placed on the agenda of the twenty-ninth session of the Commission.[18]

146. The Commission, at its twenty-eighth session,[19] recalled that, at its twenty-seventh session (1994), general support had been expressed in favor of a recommendation made by the Working Group that preliminary work should be undertaken on the issue of negotiability and transferability of rights in goods in a computer-based environment as soon as the preparation

---

18   *Official Records of the General Assembly*, Fiftieth Session, Supplement Number 17 (A/50/17), paragraph 306.
19   *Official Records of the General Assembly*, Supplement Number 17 (A/50/17), paragraph 307.

of the Model Law had been completed.[20] It was noted that, on that basis, a preliminary debate with respect to future work to be undertaken in the field of electronic data interchange had been held in the context of the twenty-ninth session of the Working Group (for the report on that debate, see A/CN.9/407, paragraphs 106–118). At that session, the Working Group also considered proposals by the International Chamber of Commerce (A/CN.9/WG.IV/WP.65) and the United Kingdom of Great Britain and Northern Ireland (A/CN.9/WG.IV/WP.66) relating to the possible inclusion in the draft Model Law of additional provisions to the effect of ensuring that certain terms and conditions that might be incorporated in a data message by means of a mere reference would be recognized as having the same degree of legal effectiveness as if they had been fully stated in the text of the data message (for the report on the discussion, see A/CN.9/407, paragraphs 100–105). It was agreed that the issue of incorporation by reference might need to be considered in the context of future work on negotiability and transferability of rights in goods (A/CN.9/407, paragraph 103). The Commission endorsed the recommendation made by the Working Group that the Secretariat should be entrusted with the preparation of a background study on negotiability and transferability of EDI transport documents, with particular emphasis on EDI maritime transport documents, taking into account the views expressed and the suggestions made at the twenty-ninth session of the Working Group.[21]

147. On the basis of the study prepared by the Secretariat (A/CN.9/WG.IV/WP.69), the Working Group, at its thirtieth session, discussed the issues of transferability of rights in the context of transport documents and approved the text of draft statutory provisions dealing with the specific issues of contracts of carriage of goods involving the use of data messages (for the report on that session, see A/CN.9/421). The text of those draft provisions as presented to the Commission by the Working Group for final review and possible addition as part II of the Model Law was contained in the annex to document A/CN.9/421.

148. In preparing the Model Law, the Working Group noted that it would be useful to provide in a commentary additional information concerning the Model Law. In particular, at the twenty-eighth session of the Working Group, during which the text of the draft Model Law was finalized for submission to the Commission, there was general support for a suggestion that the draft Model Law should be accompanied by a guide to assist states in enacting and applying the draft Model Law. The guide, much of which could be drawn from the *travaux prparatoires* of the draft Model Law, also would be helpful

---

20   *Official Records of the General Assembly*, Forty-ninth Session, Supplement Number 17 (A/49/17), paragraph 201.

21   *Official Records of the General Assembly*, Fiftieth Session, Supplement Number 17 (A/50/17), paragraph 309.

to users of electronic means of communication as well as to scholars in that area. The Working Group noted that, during its deliberations at that session, it had proceeded on the assumption that the draft Model Law would be accompanied by a guide. For example, the Working Group had decided in respect of a number of issues not to settle them in the draft Model Law but to address them in the guide so as to provide guidance to states enacting the draft Model Law. The Secretariat was requested to prepare a draft and submit it to the Working Group for consideration at its twenty-ninth session (A/CN.9/406, paragraph 177).

149. At its twenty-ninth session, the Working Group discussed the draft Guide to Enactment of the Model Law (hereinafter referred to as "the draft Guide") as set forth in a note prepared by the Secretariat (A/CN.9/WG.IV/WP.64). The Secretariat was requested to prepare a revised version of the draft Guide reflecting the decisions made by the Working Group and taking into account the various views, suggestions, and concerns that had been expressed at that session. At its twenty-eighth session, the Commission placed the draft Guide to Enactment of the Model Law on the agenda of its twenty-ninth session.[22]

150. At its twenty-ninth session (1996), the Commission, after consideration of the text of the draft Model Law as revised by the drafting group, adopted the following decision at its 605th meeting, on 12 June 1996:

"The United Nations Commission on International Trade Law,

"Recalling its mandate under General Assembly resolution 2205 (XXI) of 17 December 1966 to further the progressive harmonization and unification of the law of international trade, and in that respect to bear in mind the interests of all peoples, and in particular those of developing countries, in the extensive development of international trade,

"Noting that an increasing number of transactions in international trade are carried out by means of electronic data interchange and other means of communication commonly referred to as 'electronic commerce', which involve the use of alternatives to paper-based forms of communication and storage of information,

"Recalling the recommendation on the legal value of computer records adopted by the Commission at its eighteenth session, in 1985, and paragraph 5(b) of General Assembly resolution 40/71 of 11 December 1985 calling upon governments and international organizations to take action, where appropriate, in conformity with the recommendation of the

---

22 Official Records of the General Assembly, Fiftieth Session, Supplement Number 17 (A/50/17), paragraph 306.

Commission[23] so as to ensure legal security in the context of the widest possible use of automated data processing in international trade,

"Being of the opinion that the establishment of a model law facilitating the use of electronic commerce, and acceptable to states with different legal, social and economic systems, contributes to the development of harmonious international economic relations,

"Being convinced that the UNCITRAL Model Law on Electronic Commerce will significantly assist all states in enhancing their legislation governing the use of alternatives to paper-based forms of communication and storage of information, and in formulating such legislation where none currently exists,

"1. Adopts the UNCITRAL Model Law on Electronic Commerce as it appears in annex I to the report on the current session;

"2. Requests the Secretary-General to transmit the text of the UNCITRAL Model Law on Electronic Commerce, together with the Guide to Enactment of the Model Law prepared by the Secretariat, to governments and other interested bodies;

"3. Recommends that all states give favorable consideration to the UNCITRAL Model Law on Electronic Commerce when they enact or revise their laws, in view of the need for uniformity of the law applicable to alternatives to paper-based forms of communication and storage of information."[24]

---

23 *Official Records of the General Assembly*, Fortieth Session, Supplement Number 17 (A/40/17), paragraphs 354–360.

24 *Official Records of the General Assembly*, Fifty-first Session, Supplement Number 17 (A/51/17), paragraph 209.

Appendix IV

UNCITRAL Model Law on Electronic Signatures of 2001

RESOLUTION ADOPTED BY THE GENERAL ASSEMBLY

Resolution adopted by the General Assembly [on the report of the Sixth Committee (A/56/588)]

56/80 Model Law on Electronic Signatures adopted by the United Nations Commission on International Trade Law

The General Assembly,

Recalling its resolution 2205 (XXI) of 17 December 1966, by which it established the United Nations Commission on International Trade Law, with a mandate to further the progressive harmonization and unification of the law of international trade and in that respect to bear in mind the interests of all peoples, and particularly those of developing countries, in the extensive development of international trade,

Noting that an increasing number of transactions in international trade are carried out by means of communication commonly referred to as electronic commerce, which involves the use of alternatives to paper-based forms of communication, storage, and authentication of information,

Recalling the recommendation on the legal value of computer records adopted by the Commission at its eighteenth session, in 1985, and paragraph 5(b) of General Assembly resolution 40/71 of 11 December 1985, in which the Assembly called upon governments and international organizations to take action, where appropriate, in conformity with the recommendation of the Commission,[1] so as to ensure legal security in the context of the widest possible use of automated data processing in international trade,

Recalling also the Model Law on Electronic Commerce adopted by the Commission at its twenty-ninth session, in 1996,[2] complemented by an additional article 5 *bis* adopted by the Commission at its thirty-first session, in 1998,[3] and paragraph 2 of General Assembly resolution 51/162 of 16 December 1996, in which the Assembly recommended that all states should give favorable consideration to the Model Law when enacting or revising their laws, in view of the need for uniformity of the law applicable to alternatives to paper-based methods of communication and storage of information,

Convinced that the Model Law on Electronic Commerce is of significant assistance to states in enabling or facilitating the use of electronic commerce, as demonstrated by the enactment of that Model Law in a number of countries and its universal recognition as an essential reference in the field of electronic commerce legislation,

---

1   *Official Records of the General Assembly*, Fortieth Session, Supplement Number 17 (A/40/17), chapter VI, section B.

2   *Ibid.*, Fifty-first Session, Supplement Number 17 (A/51/17), paragraph 209.

3   *Ibid.*, Fifty-third Session, Supplement Number 17 (A/53/17), chapter III, B.

Mindful of the great utility of new technologies used for personal identification in electronic commerce and commonly referred to as electronic signatures,

Desiring to build on the fundamental principles underlying article 7 of the Model Law on Electronic Commerce[4] with respect to the fulfillment of the signature function in an electronic environment, with a view to promoting reliance on electronic signatures for producing legal effect where such electronic signatures are functionally equivalent to handwritten signatures,

Convinced that legal certainty in electronic commerce will be enhanced by the harmonization of certain rules on the legal recognition of electronic signatures on a technologically neutral basis and by the establishment of a method to assess in a technologically neutral manner the practical reliability and the commercial adequacy of electronic signature techniques,

Believing that the Model Law on Electronic Signatures will constitute a useful addition to the Model Law on Electronic Commerce and significantly assist states in enhancing their legislation governing the use of modern authentication techniques and in formulating such legislation where none currently exists,

Being of the opinion that the establishment of model legislation to facilitate the use of electronic signatures in a manner acceptable to states with different legal, social, and economic systems could contribute to the development of harmonious international economic relations,

1. Expresses its appreciation to the United Nations Commission on International Trade Law for completing and adopting the Model Law on Electronic Signatures contained in the annex to the present resolution, and for preparing the Guide to Enactment of the Model Law;

2. Recommends that all states give favorable consideration to the Model Law on Electronic Signatures, together with the Model Law on Electronic Commerce adopted in 1996 and complemented in 1998, when they enact or revise their laws, in view of the need for uniformity of the law applicable to alternatives to paper-based forms of communication, storage, and authentication of information;

3. Recommends also that all efforts be made to ensure that the Model Law on Electronic Commerce and the Model Law on Electronic Signatures, together with their respective Guides to Enactment, become generally known and available.

85th plenary meeting, 12 December 2001

---

4   General Assembly resolution 51/162, annex.

Article 1. Sphere of application

This Law applies where electronic signatures are used in the context[5] of commercial[6] activities. It does not override any rule of law intended for the protection of consumers.

Article 2. Definitions for the purposes of this Law:

(a) "Electronic signature" means data in electronic form in, affixed to, or logically associated with, a data message, which may be used to identify the signatory in relation to the data message and to indicate the signatory's approval of the information contained in the data message;

(b) "Certificate" means a data message or other record confirming the link between a signatory and signature creation data;

(c) "Data message" means information generated, sent, received, or stored by electronic, optical, or similar means including, but not limited to, electronic data interchange (EDI), electronic mail, telegram, telex, or telecopy; and acts either on its own behalf or on behalf of the person it represents;

(d) "Signatory" means a person that holds signature creation data and acts either on its own behalf or on behalf of the person it represents;

(e) "Certification service provider" means a person that issues certificates and may provide other services related to electronic signatures;

(f) "Relying party" means a person that may act on the basis of a certificate or an electronic signature.

Article 3. Equal treatment of signature technologies

Nothing in this Law, except article 5, shall be applied so as to exclude, restrict, or deprive of legal effect any method of creating an electronic signature that satisfies the requirements referred to in article 6, paragraph 1, or otherwise meets the requirements of applicable law.

---

5 The Commission suggests the following text for states that might wish to extend the applicability of this Law: "This Law applies where electronic signatures are used, except in the following situations: [. . .]".

6 The term "commercial" should be given a wide interpretation so as to cover matters arising from all relationships of a commercial nature, whether contractual or not. Relationships of a commercial nature include, but are not limited to, the following transactions: any trade transaction for the supply or exchange of goods or services; distribution agreement; commercial representation or agency; factoring; leasing; construction of works; consulting; engineering; licensing; investment; financing; banking; insurance; exploitation agreement or concession; joint venture and other forms of industrial or business cooperation; and carriage of goods or passengers by air, sea, rail, or road.

Article 4. Interpretation

1. In the interpretation of this Law, regard is to be had to its international origin and to the need to promote uniformity in its application and the observance of good faith.

2. Questions concerning matters governed by this Law which are not expressly settled in it are to be settled in conformity with the general principles on which this Law is based.

Article 5. Variation by agreement

The provisions of this Law may be derogated from or their effect may be varied by agreement, unless that agreement would not be valid or effective under applicable law.

Article 6. Compliance with a requirement for a signature

1. Where the law requires a signature of a person, that requirement is met in relation to a data message if an electronic signature is used that is as reliable as was appropriate for the purpose for which the data message was generated or communicated, in the light of all the circumstances, including any relevant agreement.

2. Paragraph 1 applies whether the requirement referred to therein is in the form of an obligation or whether the law simply provides consequences for the absence of a signature.

3. An electronic signature is considered to be reliable for the purpose of satisfying the requirement referred to in paragraph 1 if:

   (a)   The signature creation data are, within the context in which they are used, linked to the signatory and to no other person;

Part 1: UNCITRAL Model Law on Electronic Signatures 2001

   (b)   The signature creation data were, at the time of signing, under the control of the signatory and of no other person;

   (c)   Any alteration to the electronic signature, made after the time of signing, is detectable; and

   (d)   Where a purpose of the legal requirement for a signature is to provide assurance as to the integrity of the information to which it relates, any alteration made to that information after the time of signing is detectable.

4. Paragraph 3 does not limit the ability of any person:

(a) To establish in any other way, for the purpose of satisfying the requirement referred to in paragraph 1, the reliability of an electronic signature; or

(b) To adduce evidence of the non-reliability of an electronic signature.

5. The provisions of this article do not apply to the following: [. . .]

Article 7. Satisfaction of article 6

1. [Any person, organ, or authority, whether public or private, specified by the enacting state as competent] may determine which electronic signatures satisfy the provisions of article 6 of this Law.

2. Any determination made under paragraph 1 shall be consistent with recognized international standards.

3. Nothing in this article affects the operation of the rules of private international law.

Article 8. Conduct of the signatory

1. Where signature creation data can be used to create a signature that has legal effect, each signatory shall:

(a) Exercise reasonable care to avoid unauthorized use of its signature creation data;

(b) Without undue delay, utilize means made available by the certification service provider pursuant to article 9 of this Law, or otherwise use reasonable efforts, to notify any person that may reasonably be expected by the signatory to rely on or to provide services in support of the electronic signature if:

  (i) The signatory knows that the signature creation data have been compromised; or

  (ii) The circumstances known to the signatory give rise to a substantial risk that the signature creation data may have been compromised;

(c) Where a certificate is used to support the electronic signature, exercise reasonable care to ensure the accuracy and completeness of all material representations made by the signatory that are relevant to the certificate throughout its life cycle or that are to be included in the certificate.

2. A signatory shall bear the legal consequences of its failure to satisfy the requirements of paragraph 1.

Article 9. Conduct of the certification service provider

1. Where a certification service provider provides services to support an electronic signature that may be used for legal effect as a signature, that certification service provider shall:

  (a) Act in accordance with representations made by it with respect to its policies and practices;

  (b) Exercise reasonable care to ensure the accuracy and completeness of all material representations made by it that are relevant to the certificate throughout its life cycle or that are included in the certificate;

  (c) Provide reasonably accessible means that enable a relying party to ascertain from the certificate:

    (i) The identity of the certification service provider;

    (ii) That the signatory that is identified in the certificate had control of the signature creation data at the time when the certificate was issued;

    (iii) That signature creation data were valid at or before the time when the certificate was issued;

  (d) Provide reasonably accessible means that enable a relying party to ascertain, where relevant, from the certificate or otherwise:

    (i) The method used to identify the signatory;

    (ii) Any limitation on the purpose or value for which the signature creation data or the certificate may be used;

    (iii) That the signature creation data are valid and have not been compromised;

    (iv) Any limitation on the scope or extent of liability stipulated by the certification service provider;

    (v) Whether means exist for the signatory to give notice pursuant to article 8, paragraph 1(b), of this Law;

    (vi) Whether a timely revocation service is offered;

  (e) Where services under subparagraph (d)(v) are offered, provide a means for a signatory to give notice pursuant to article 8, paragraph 1(b), of this Law and, where services under subparagraph (d)(vi) are offered, ensure the availability of a timely revocation service;

  (f) Utilize trustworthy systems, procedures, and human resources in performing its services.

2. A certification service provider shall bear the legal consequences of its failure to satisfy the requirements of paragraph 1.

Article 10. Trustworthiness

For the purposes of article 9, paragraph 1(f), of this Law in determining whether, or to what extent, any systems, procedures, and human resources utilized by a certification service provider are trustworthy, regard may be had to the following factors:

(a) Financial and human resources, including existence of assets;

(b) Quality of hardware and software systems;

(c) Procedures for processing of certificates and applications for certificates and retention of records;

(d) Availability of information to signatories identified in certificates and to potential relying parties;

(e) Regularity and extent of audit by an independent body;

(f) The existence of a declaration by the state, an accreditation body, or the certification service provider regarding compliance with or existence of the foregoing; or

(g) Any other relevant factor.

Article 11. Conduct of the relying party

A relying party shall bear the legal consequences of its failure:

(a) To take reasonable steps to verify the reliability of an electronic signature; or

(b) Where an electronic signature is supported by a certificate, to take reasonable steps:

(i) To verify the validity, suspension, or revocation of the certificate; and

(ii) To observe any limitation with respect to the certificate.

Article 12. Recognition of foreign certificates and electronic signatures

1. In determining whether, or to what extent, a certificate or an electronic signature is legally effective, no regard shall be had:

(a) To the geographic location where the certificate is issued or the electronic signature created or used; or

(b) To the geographic location of the place of business of the issuer or signatory.

2. A certificate issued outside [the enacting state] shall have the same legal effect in [the enacting state] as a certificate issued in [the enacting state] if it offers a substantially equivalent level of reliability.

3. An electronic signature created or used outside [the enacting state] shall have the same legal effect in [the enacting state] as an electronic signature created or used in [the enacting state] if it offers a substantially equivalent level of reliability.

4. In determining whether a certificate or an electronic signature offers a substantially equivalent level of reliability for the purposes of paragraph 2 or 3, regard shall be had to recognized international standards and to any other relevant factors.

5. Where, notwithstanding paragraphs 2, 3, and 4, parties agree, as between themselves, to the use of certain types of electronic signatures or certificates, that agreement shall be recognized as sufficient for the purposes of cross-border recognition, unless that agreement would not be valid or effective under applicable law.

Part 2: Guide to Enactment of the UNCITRAL Model Law on Electronic Signatures of 2001

Purpose of this Guide

1. In preparing and adopting the UNCITRAL Model Law on Electronic Signatures (also referred to in this publication as "the Model Law" or "the new Model Law"), the United Nations Commission on International Trade Law (UNCITRAL) was mindful that the Model Law would be a more effective tool for states modernizing their legislation if background and explanatory information were provided to executive branches of governments and legislators to assist them in using the Model Law. The Commission also was aware of the likelihood that the Model Law would be used in a number of states with limited familiarity with the type of communication techniques considered in the Model Law. This Guide, much of which is drawn from the *travaux preparatoires* of the Model Law, also is intended to be helpful to other users of the text, such as judges, arbitrators, practitioners, and academics. Such information might also assist states in considering which, if any, of the provisions should be varied in order to be adapted to any particular national circumstances necessitating such variation. In the preparation of the Model Law, it was assumed that the Model Law would be accompanied by such a guide. For example, it was decided in respect of a number of issues not to settle them in the Model Law but to address them in the Guide so as to provide guidance to states enacting the Model Law. The information presented in this Guide is intended to explain why the provisions in the Model Law have been included as essential basic features of a statutory device designed to achieve the objectives of the Model Law.

2. The present Guide to Enactment has been prepared by the Secretariat pursuant to the request of UNCITRAL made at the close of its thirty-fourth session, in 2001. It is based on the deliberations and decisions of the Commission at that session,[7] when the Model Law was adopted, as well as on considerations of the Working Group on Electronic Commerce, which conducted the preparatory work.

Chapter I. Introduction to the Model Law

I. Purpose and origin of the Model Law

A. Purpose

[. . .]

3. The increased use of electronic authentication techniques as substitutes for handwritten signatures and other traditional authentication procedures has suggested the need for a specific legal framework to reduce uncertainty as to the legal effect that may result from the use of such modern techniques (which may be referred to generally as "electronic signatures"). The risk that diverging legislative approaches be taken in various countries with respect to electronic signatures calls for uniform legislative provisions to establish the basic rules of what is inherently an international phenomenon, where legal harmony as well as technical interoperability is a desirable objective.

4. Building on the fundamental principles underlying article 7 of the UNCITRAL Model Law on Electronic Commerce (always referred to in this publication under its full title to avoid confusion) with respect to the fulfillment of the signature function in an electronic environment, this new Model Law is designed to assist states in establishing a modern, harmonized, and fair legislative framework to address more effectively the issues of electronic signatures. In a modest but significant addition to the UNCITRAL Model Law on Electronic Commerce, the new Model Law offers practical standards against which the technical reliability of electronic signatures may be measured. In addition, the Model Law provides a linkage between such technical reliability and the legal effectiveness that may be expected from a given electronic signature. The Model Law adds substantially to the UNCITRAL Model Law on Electronic Commerce by adopting an approach under which the legal effectiveness of a given electronic signature technique may be predetermined (or assessed prior to being actually used). The Model Law is thus intended to foster the understanding of electronic signatures and the confidence that certain electronic signature techniques can be relied upon in

---

7   *Official Records of the General Assembly*, Fifty-sixth session, Supplement Number 17
      (A/56/17), paragraphs 201–284.

legally significant transactions. Moreover, by establishing with appropriate flexibility a set of basic rules of conduct for the various parties that may become involved in the use of electronic signatures (i.e., signatories, relying parties, and third-party certification service providers) the Model Law may assist in shaping more harmonious commercial practices in cyberspace.

5. The objectives of the Model Law, which include enabling or facilitating the use of electronic signatures and providing equal treatment to users of paper-based documentation and users of computer-based information, are essential for fostering economy and efficiency in international trade. By incorporating the procedures prescribed in the Model Law (and also the provisions of the UNCITRAL Model Law on Electronic Commerce) in its national legislation for those situations where parties opt to use electronic means of communication, an enacting state would appropriately create a media-neutral environment. The media-neutral approach also used in the UNCITRAL Model Law on Electronic Commerce is intended to provide in principle for the coverage of all factual situations where information is generated, stored, or communicated, irrespective of the medium on which such information may be affixed (see the Guide to Enactment of the UNCITRAL Model Law on Electronic Commerce, paragraph 24). The words "a media-neutral environment", as used in the UNCITRAL Model Law on Electronic Commerce, reflect the principle of non-discrimination between information supported by a paper medium and information communicated or stored electronically. The new Model Law equally reflects the principle that no discrimination should be made among the various techniques that may be used to communicate or store information electronically, a principle that is often referred to as "technology neutrality" (A/CN.9/484, paragraph 23).

B. Background

6. The Model Law constitutes a new step in a series of international instruments adopted by UNCITRAL, which are either specifically focused on the needs of electronic commerce or were prepared bearing in mind the needs of modern means of communication. In the first category, specific instruments geared to electronic commerce comprise the Legal Guide on Electronic Funds Transfers (1987), the UNCITRAL Model Law on International Credit Transfers (1992), and the UNCITRAL Model Law on Electronic Commerce (1996 and 1998). The second category consists of all international conventions and other legislative instruments adopted by UNCITRAL since 1978, all of which promote reduced formalism and contain definitions of "writing" that are meant to encompass dematerialized communications.

7. The best known UNCITRAL instrument in the field of electronic commerce is the UNCITRAL Model Law on Electronic Commerce. Its preparation in the early 1990s resulted from the increased use of modern means of

communication, such as electronic mail and electronic data interchange (EDI), for the conduct of international trade transactions. It was realized that new technologies had been developing rapidly and would develop further as technical supports such as information highways and the Internet, became more widely accessible. However, the communication of legally significant information in the form of paperless messages was hindered by legal obstacles to the use of such messages, or by uncertainty as to their legal effect or validity. With a view to facilitating the increased use of modern means of communication, UNCITRAL has prepared the UNCITRAL Model Law on Electronic Commerce. The purpose of the UNCITRAL Model Law on Electronic Commerce is to offer national legislators a set of internationally acceptable rules as to how a number of such legal obstacles may be removed and how a more secure legal environment may be created for what has become known as "electronic commerce".

8. The decision by UNCITRAL to formulate model legislation on electronic commerce was taken in response to the fact that, in a number of countries, the existing legislation governing communication and storage of information was inadequate or outdated because it did not contemplate the use of electronic commerce. In certain cases, existing legislation still imposes or implies restrictions on the use of modern means of communication, for example by prescribing the use of "written", "signed", or "original" documents. With respect to the notions of "written", "signed" and "original" documents, the UNCITRAL Model Law on Electronic Commerce adopted an approach based on functional equivalence. The "functional equivalent approach" is based on an analysis of the purposes and functions of the traditional paper-based requirement with a view to determining how those purposes or functions can be fulfilled through electronic-commerce techniques (see the Guide to Enactment of the UNCITRAL Model Law on Electronic Commerce, paragraphs 15–18).

9. At the time when the UNCITRAL Model Law on Electronic Commerce was being prepared, a few countries had adopted specific provisions to deal with certain aspects of electronic commerce. However, there existed no legislation dealing with electronic commerce as a whole. This could result in uncertainty as to the legal nature and validity of information presented in a form other than a traditional paper document. Moreover, while sound laws and practices were necessary in all countries where the use of EDI and electronic mail was becoming widespread, this need also was felt in many countries with respect to such communication techniques as telecopy and telex. Under article 2(b) of the UNCITRAL Model Law on Electronic Commerce, EDI is defined as "the electronic transfer from computer to computer of information using an agreed standard to structure the information".

10. The UNCITRAL Model Law on Electronic Commerce also helped to remedy disadvantages that stemmed from the fact that inadequate legislation at the national level created obstacles to international trade, a significant amount of which is linked to the use of modern communication techniques. To a large extent, disparities among, and uncertainty about, national legal regimes governing the use of such communication techniques may still contribute to limiting the extent to which businesses may access international markets.

11. Furthermore, at an international level, the UNCITRAL Model Law on Electronic Commerce may be useful in certain cases as a tool for interpreting existing international conventions and other international instruments that create legal obstacles to the use of electronic commerce, for example, by prescribing that certain documents or contractual clauses be made in written form. As between those states parties to such international instruments, the adoption of the UNCITRAL Model Law on Electronic Commerce as a rule of interpretation might provide the means to recognize the use of electronic commerce and obviate the need to negotiate a protocol to the international instrument involved.

C. History

12. After adopting the UNCITRAL Model Law on Electronic Commerce, the Commission, at its twenty-ninth session, in 1996, decided to place the issues of digital signatures and certification authorities on its agenda. The Working Group on Electronic Commerce was requested to examine the desirability and feasibility of preparing uniform rules on those topics. It was agreed that the uniform rules to be prepared should deal with such issues as the legal basis supporting certification processes, including emerging digital authentication and certification technology; the applicability of the certification process; the allocation of risk and liabilities of users, providers and third parties in the context of the use of certification techniques; the specific issues of certification through the use of registries; and incorporation by reference.[8]

13. At its thirtieth session, in 1997, the Commission had before it the report of the Working Group on the work of its thirty-first session (A/CN.9/437), conducted on the basis of a note prepared by the Secretariat (A/CN.9/WG.IV/WP.71). The Working Group indicated to the Commission that it had reached consensus as to the importance of, and the need for, working towards harmonization of legislation in that area. While no firm decision as to the form and content of such work had been reached, the Working Group had come to the preliminary conclusion that it was feasible to undertake the preparation

---

8   Official Records of the General Assembly, Fifty-first Session, Supplement Number 17 (A/51/17), paragraphs 223 and 224.

of draft uniform rules at least on issues of digital signatures and certification authorities, and possibly on related matters. The Working Group recalled that, alongside digital signatures and certification authorities, future work in the area of electronic commerce might also need to address: issues of technical alternatives to public-key cryptography; general issues of functions performed by third-party service providers; and electronic contracting (A/CN.9/437, paragraphs 156 and 157). The Commission endorsed the conclusions reached by the Working Group and entrusted it with the preparation of uniform rules on the legal issues of digital signatures and certification authorities.

14. With respect to the exact scope and form of the uniform rules, the Commission generally agreed that no decision could be made at that early stage of the process. It was felt that, while the Working Group might appropriately focus its attention on the issues of digital signatures in view of the apparently predominant role played by public-key cryptography in the emerging electronic-commerce practice, the uniform rules should be consistent with the media-neutral approach taken in the UNCITRAL Model Law on Electronic Commerce. Thus, the uniform rules should not discourage the use of other authentication techniques. Moreover, in dealing with public key cryptography, the uniform rules might need to accommodate various levels of security and to recognize the various legal effects and levels of liability corresponding to the various types of services being provided in the context of digital signatures. With respect to certification authorities, while the value of market driven standards was recognized by the Commission, it was widely felt that the Working Group might appropriately envisage the establishment of a minimum set of standards to be met by certification authorities, in particular where cross-border certification was sought.[9]

15. The Working Group began the preparation of the uniform rules (to be adopted later as the Model Law) at its thirty-second session on the basis of a note prepared by the Secretariat (A/CN.9/WG.IV/WP.73).

16. At its thirty-first session, in 1998, the Commission had before it the report of the Working Group on the work of its thirty-second session (A/CN.9/446). It was noted that the Working Group, throughout its thirty-first and thirty-second sessions, had experienced manifest difficulties in reaching a common understanding of the new legal issues that arose from the increased use of digital and other electronic signatures. It also was noted that a consensus was still to be found as to how those issues might be addressed in an internationally acceptable legal framework. However, it was generally felt by the Commission that the progress realized so far indicated

---

9   *Official Records of the General Assembly*, Fifty-second Session, Supplement Number 17 (A/52/17), paragraphs 249–251.

that the uniform rules were progressively being shaped into a workable structure. The Commission reaffirmed the decision made at its thirtieth session as to the feasibility of preparing such uniform rules and expressed its confidence that more progress could be accomplished by the Working Group at its thirty-third session on the basis of the revised draft prepared by the Secretariat (A/CN.9/WG.IV/WP.76). In the context of that discussion, the Commission noted with satisfaction that the Working Group had become generally recognized as a particularly important international forum for the exchange of views regarding the legal issues of electronic commerce and for the preparation of solutions to those issues.[10]

17. The Working Group continued revision of the uniform rules at its thirty-third session, in 1998, and thirty-fourth session, in 1999, on the basis of notes prepared by the Secretariat (A/CN.9/WG.IV/WP.76, A/CN.9/WG.IV/WP.79, and A/CN.9/WG.IV/WP.80). The reports of the sessions are contained in documents A/CN.9/454 and A/CN.9/457.

18. At its thirty-second session, in 1999, the Commission had before it the report of the Working Group on those two sessions (A/CN.9/454 and A/CN.9/457). The Commission expressed its appreciation for the efforts accomplished by the Working Group in its preparation of the uniform rules. While it was generally agreed that significant progress had been made at those sessions in the understanding of the legal issues of electronic signatures, it also was felt that the Working Group had been faced with difficulties in the building of a consensus as to the legislative policy on which the uniform rules should be based.

19. The view was expressed that the approach currently taken by the Working Group did not sufficiently reflect the business need for flexibility in the use of electronic signatures and other authentication techniques. As currently envisaged by the Working Group, the uniform rules placed excessive emphasis on digital signature techniques and, within the sphere of digital signatures, on a specific application involving third-party certification. Accordingly, it was suggested that work on electronic signatures by the Working Group should either be limited to the legal issues of crossborder certification or be postponed altogether until market practices were better established. A related view expressed was that, for the purposes of international trade, most of the legal issues arising from the use of electronic signatures had already been solved in the UNCITRAL Model Law on Electronic Commerce (see below, paragraph 28). While regulation dealing with certain uses of electronic signatures might be needed outside the scope of commercial law, the Working Group should not become involved in any such regulatory activity.

---

10 *Official Records of the General Assembly,* Fifty-third Session, Supplement Number 17 (A/53/17), paragraphs 207–211.

20. The widely prevailing view was that the Working Group should pursue its task on the basis of its original mandate. With respect to the need for uniform rules on electronic signatures, it was explained that, in many countries, guidance from UNCITRAL was expected by governmental and legislative authorities that were in the process of preparing legislation on electronic signature issues, including the establishment of public-key infrastructures (PKI) or other projects on closely related matters (see A/CN.9/ 457, paragraph 16). As to the decision made by the Working Group to focus on PKI issues and PKI terminology, it was recalled that the interplay of relationships between three distinct types of parties (i.e., signatories, certification authorities, and relying parties) corresponded to one possible PKI model, but that other models were conceivable, for example, where no independent certification service provider was involved. One of the main benefits to be drawn from focusing on PKI issues was to facilitate the structuring of the uniform rules by reference to three functions (or roles) with respect to key pairs, namely, the key issuer (or subscriber) function, the certification function, and the relying function. It was generally agreed that those three functions were common to all PKI models. It also was agreed that those three functions should be dealt with irrespective of whether they were in fact served by three separate entities or whether two of those functions were served by the same person (e.g., where the certification service provider also was a relying party). In addition, it was widely felt that focusing on the functions typical of PKI and not on any specific model might make it easier to develop a fully media-neutral rule at a later stage (see A/CN.9/457, paragraph 68).

21. After discussion, the Commission reaffirmed its earlier decisions as to the feasibility of preparing such uniform rules and expressed its confidence that more progress could be accomplished by the Working Group at its forthcoming sessions.[11]

22. The Working Group continued its work at its thirty-fifth session, in September 1999, and its thirty-sixth session, in February 2000, on the basis of notes prepared by the Secretariat (A/CN.9/WG.IV/WP.82 and A/CN.9/WG.IV/WP.84). At its thirty-third session, in 2000, the Commission had before it the report of the Working Group on the work of those two sessions (A/CN.9/465 and A/CN.9/467). It was noted that the Working Group, at its thirty-sixth session, had adopted the text of draft articles 1 and 3–12 of the uniform rules. It was stated that some issues remained to be clarified as a result of the decision by the Working Group to delete the notion of enhanced electronic signature from the uniform rules. Concern was expressed that, depending on the decisions to be made by the Working Group with respect to

---

11   *Official Records of the General Assembly,* Fifty-fourth Session, Supplement Number 17 (A/54/17), paragraphs 308–314.

draft articles 2 and 13, the remainder of the draft provisions might need to be revisited to avoid creating a situation where the standard set forth by the uniform rules would apply equally to electronic signatures that ensured a high level of security and to low-value certificates that might be used in the context of electronic communications that were not intended to carry significant legal effect.

23. At its thirty-third session, in 2000, the Commission expressed its appreciation for the efforts extended by the Working Group and the progress achieved in the preparation of the uniform rules. The Working Group was urged to complete its work with respect to the uniform rules at its thirty-seventh session.[12] In preparing the Model Law, the Working Group noted that it would be useful to provide in a commentary additional information concerning the Model Law. Following the approach taken in the preparation of the UNCITRAL Model Law on Electronic Commerce, there was general support for a suggestion that the new Model Law should be accompanied by a guide to assist states in enacting and applying that Model Law. The guide, much of which could be drawn from the *travaux preparatoires* of the Model Law, would also be helpful to other users of the Model Law. The Commission requested the Working Group to review the draft guide to enactment to be prepared by the Secretariat.

24. The Working Group completed the preparation of the uniform rules at its thirty-seventh session, in September 2000. The report of that session is contained in document A/CN.9/483. In the context of its thirty-seventh and thirty-eighth sessions, the Working Group also discussed the guide to enactment on the basis of a draft prepared by the Secretariat (A/CN.9/ WG.IV/WP.88). The report of the thirty-eighth session of the Working Group is contained in document A/CN.9/484. The Secretariat was requested to prepare a revised version of the draft guide reflecting the decisions made by the Working Group, based on the various views, suggestions, and concerns that had been expressed. The Working Group noted that the uniform rules (in the form of a draft UNCITRAL Model Law on Electronic Signatures), together with the draft guide to enactment, would be submitted to the Commission for review and adoption at its thirty-fourth session, in 2001.

25. In preparation for the thirty-fourth session of the Commission, the text of the draft Model Law as approved by the Working Group was circulated to all governments and to interested international organizations for comment. At that session, the Commission had before it the reports of the Working Group on the work of its thirty-seventh and thirty-eighth sessions, the comments received from governments and international organizations (A/CN.9/492

---

12 *Official Records of the General Assembly,* Fifty-fifth Session, Supplement Number 17 (A/55/17), paragraphs 380–383.

and Add.1-3), as well as the revised draft guide to enactment prepared by the Secretariat (A/CN.9/493). At the outset of the discussion, the Commission considered the comments received from governments and international organizations (A/CN.9/492 and Add. 1–3). Having completed its consideration of the proposals that were raised by delegations on the basis of the comments submitted by governments and interested international organizations, the Commission proceeded with a systematic review of the draft articles and a review of the draft guide to enactment prepared by the Secretariat (A/CN.9/493). Subject to any amendment that might be necessary to reflect the deliberations and decisions of the Commission with respect to both the text of the Model Law and the draft guide itself and subject to any editorial changes that might be necessary to ensure consistency in terminology, the Commission found that the text of the draft guide adequately implemented the Commission's intent to assist states in enacting and applying the Model Law and to provide guidance to other users of the Model Law. The Secretariat was requested to prepare the definitive version of the Guide and to publish it together with the text of the Model Law. After consideration of the text of the draft Model Law as revised by the drafting group and the draft guide to enactment prepared by the Secretariat (A/CN.9/493), the Commission adopted the following decision at its 727th meeting, on 5 July 2001:

> "The United Nations Commission on International Trade Law,
>
> "Recalling its mandate under General Assembly resolution 2205 (XXI) of 17 December 1966 to further the progressive harmonization and unification of the law of international trade and in that respect to bear in mind the interests of all peoples, and particularly those of developing countries, in the extensive development of international trade,
>
> "Noting that an increasing number of transactions in international trade are carried out by means of communication commonly referred to as 'electronic commerce', which involve the use of alternatives to paper-based forms of communication, storage and authentication of information,
>
> "Recalling the recommendation on the legal value of computer records adopted by the Commission at its eighteenth session, in 1985, and paragraph 5(b) of General Assembly resolution 40/71 of 11 December 1985, in which the Assembly called upon governments and international organizations to take action, where appropriate, in conformity with the recommendation of the Commission so as to ensure legal security in the context of the widest possible use of automated data processing in international trade,
>
> "Recalling also the UNCITRAL Model Law on Electronic Commerce adopted by the Commission at its twenty-ninth session, in 1996, and

complemented by an additional article 5 *bis* adopted by the Commission at its thirty-first session, in 1998,

"Convinced that the UNCITRAL Model Law on Electronic Commerce is of significant assistance to states in enabling or facilitating the use of electronic commerce through the enhancement of their legislation governing the use of alternatives to paper-based forms of communication and storage of information and through the formulation of such legislation where none currently exists,

"Mindful of the great utility of new technologies used for personal identification in electronic commerce and commonly referred to as 'electronic signatures',

"Desirous of building on the fundamental principles underlying article 7 of the UNCITRAL Model Law on Electronic Commerce with respect to the fulfillment of the signature function in an electronic environment,

"Convinced that legal certainty in electronic commerce will be enhanced by the harmonization of certain rules on the legal recognition of electronic signatures on a technologically neutral basis,

"Believing that the UNCITRAL Model Law on Electronic Signatures will significantly assist states in enhancing their legislation governing the use of modern authentication techniques and in formulating such legislation where none currently exists,

"Being of the opinion that the establishment of model legislation to facilitate the use of electronic signatures in a manner acceptable to states with different legal, social and economic systems could contribute to the development of harmonious international economic relations,

"1. Adopts the UNCITRAL Model Law on Electronic Signatures as it appears in annex II to the report of the United Nations Commission on International Trade Law on its thirty-fourth session,[13] together with the Guide to Enactment of the Model Law;

"2. Requests the Secretary-General to transmit the text of the UNCITRAL Model Law on Electronic Signatures, together with the Guide to Enactment of the Model Law, to governments and other interested bodies;

"3. Recommends that all states give favorable consideration to the newly adopted UNCITRAL Model Law on Electronic Signatures, together with the UNCITRAL Model Law on Electronic Commerce adopted in 1996 and complemented in 1998, when they enact or revise their laws, in view of the

---

13   *Official Records of the General Assembly*, Fifty-sixth Session, Supplement Number 17 (A/56/17), paragraphs 204, 238, 274, and 283.

need for uniformity of the law applicable to alternatives to paper-based forms of communication, storage and authentication of information."[14]

II. The Model Law as a tool for harmonizing laws

26. As the UNCITRAL Model Law on Electronic Commerce, the new Model Law is in the form of a legislative text that is recommended to states for incorporation into their national law. The Model Law is not intended to interfere with the normal operation of the rules of private international law (see below, paragraph 136). Unlike an international convention, model legislation does not require the state enacting it to notify the United Nations or other states that may have also enacted it. However, states are strongly encouraged to inform the UNCITRAL Secretariat of any enactment of the new Model Law (or any other model law resulting from the work of UNCITRAL).

27. In incorporating the text of the model legislation into its legal system, a state may modify or leave out some of its provisions. In the case of a convention, the possibility of changes being made to the uniform text by the states parties (normally referred to as "reservations") is much more restricted, trade law conventions in particular usually either totally prohibit reservations or allow only very few, specified ones. The flexibility inherent in model legislation is particularly desirable in those cases where it is likely that the state would wish to make various modifications to the uniform text before it would be ready to enact it as national law. Some modifications may be expected, in particular when the uniform text is closely related to the national court and procedural system. This, however, also means that the degree of, and certainty about, harmonization achieved through model legislation is likely to be lower than in the case of a convention. However, this relative disadvantage of model legislation may be balanced by the fact that the number of states enacting model legislation is likely to be higher than the number of states adhering to a convention. In order to achieve a satisfactory degree of harmonization and certainty, it is recommended that states make as few changes as possible in incorporating the new Model Law into their legal systems and that they take due regard of its basic principles, including technology neutrality, nondiscrimination between domestic and foreign electronic signatures, party autonomy and the international origin of the Model Law. In general, in enacting the new Model Law (or the UNCITRAL Model Law on Electronic Commerce), it is advisable to adhere as much as possible to the uniform text in order to make the national law as transparent and familiar as possible for foreign users of the national law.

---

14   *Official Records of the General Assembly,* Fifty-sixth Session, Supplement Number 17 (A/56/17), paragraph 284.

28. It should be noted that some countries consider that the legal issues related to the use of electronic signatures have already been solved by the UNCITRAL Model Law on Electronic Commerce and do not plan to adopt further rules on electronic signatures until market practices in that new area are better established. However, states enacting the new Model Law alongside the UNCITRAL Model Law on Electronic Commerce may expect additional benefits. For those countries where governmental and legislative authorities are in the process of preparing legislation on electronic signature issues, including the establishment of PKI, certain provisions of the Model Law offer the guidance of an international instrument that was prepared with PKI issues and PKI terminology in mind. For all countries, the Model Law offers a set of basic rules that can be applied beyond the PKI model, since they envisage the interplay of two distinct functions that are involved in any type of electronic signature (i.e., creating and relying on an electronic signature), and a third function involved in certain types of electronic signatures (i.e., certifying an electronic signature). Those three functions should be dealt with irrespective of whether they are in fact served by three or more separate entities (e.g., where various aspects of the certification function are shared between different entities) or whether two of those functions are served by the same person (e.g., where the certification function is served by a relying party). The Model Law thus provides common grounds for PKI systems relying on independent certification authorities and electronic signature systems where no such independent third party is involved in the electronic signature process. In all cases, the new Model Law provides added certainty regarding the legal effectiveness of electronic signatures, without limiting the availability of the flexible criterion embodied in article 7 of the UNCITRAL Model Law on Electronic Commerce (see below, paragraphs 67 and 70–75).

III. General remarks on electronic signatures[15]

A. Functions of signatures

29. Article 7 of the UNCITRAL Model Law on Electronic Commerce is based on the recognition of the functions of a signature in a paper-based environment. In the preparation of the UNCITRAL Model Law on Electronic Commerce, the Working Group discussed the following functions traditionally performed by handwritten signatures: to identify a person; to provide certainty as to the personal involvement of that person in the act of signing; and to associate that person with the content of a document. It was noted that, in addition, a signature could perform a variety of functions, depending on the nature of the document that was signed. For example, a signature might attest to: the intent of a party to be bound by the content of

---

15   This section is drawn from document A/CN.9/WG.IV/WP.71, part I.

a signed contract; the intent of a person to endorse authorship of a text (thus displaying awareness of the fact that legal consequences might possibly flow from the act of signing); the intent of a person to associate itself with the content of a document written by someone else; and the fact that, and the time when, a person had been at a given place. The relationship of the new Model Law with article 7 of the UNCITRAL Model Law on Electronic Commerce is further discussed below, in paragraphs 65, 67, and 70–75 of this Guide.

30. In an electronic environment, the original of a message is indistinguishable from a copy, bears no handwritten signature, and is not on paper. The potential for fraud is considerable, due to the ease of intercepting and altering information in electronic form without detection, and the speed of processing multiple transactions. The purpose of various techniques currently available on the market or still under development is to offer the technical means by which some or all of the functions identified as characteristic of handwritten signatures can be performed in an electronic environment. Such techniques may be referred to broadly as "electronic signatures".

B. Digital signatures and other electronic signatures

31. In discussing the desirability and feasibility of preparing the new Model Law and in defining the scope of uniform rules on electronic signatures, UNCITRAL has examined various electronic signature techniques currently being used or still under development. The common purpose of those techniques is to provide functional equivalents to (a) handwritten signatures; and (b) other kinds of authentication mechanisms used in a paper-based environment (e.g., seals or stamps). The same techniques may perform additional functions in the sphere of electronic commerce, which are derived from the functions of a signature but correspond to no strict equivalent in a paper-based environment.

32. As indicated above (see paragraphs 21 and 28), guidance from UNCITRAL is expected in many countries, by governmental and legislative authorities that are in the process of preparing legislation on electronic signature issues, including the establishment of PKI or other projects on closely related matters (see A/CN.9/457, paragraph 16). As to the decision made by UNCITRAL to focus on PKI issues and PKI terminology, it should be noted that the interplay of relationships between three distinct types of parties (i.e., signatories, suppliers of certification services, and relying parties) corresponds to one possible PKI model, but other models are already commonly used in the marketplace (e.g., where no independent certification service provider is involved). One of the main benefits to be drawn from focusing on PKI issues was to facilitate the structuring of the Model Law by reference to three functions (or roles) with respect to electronic signatures, namely, the

signatory function, the certification function, and the relying function. Two of those functions are common to all PKI models (i.e., creating and relying on an electronic signature). The third function is involved in many PKI models (i.e., certifying an electronic signature). Those three functions should be dealt with irrespective of whether they are in fact served by three or more separate entities (e.g., where various aspects of the certification function are shared between different entities), or whether two of those functions are served by the same person (e.g., where the certification service provider also is a relying party). Focusing on the functions performed in a PKI environment and not on any specific model also makes it easier to develop a fully media-neutral rule to the extent that similar functions are served in non-PKI electronic signature technology.

1. Electronic signatures relying on techniques other than public-key cryptography

33. Alongside "digital signatures" based on public-key cryptography, there exist various other devices, also covered in the broader notion of "electronic signature" mechanisms, which may currently be used, or considered for future use, with a view to fulfilling one or more of the abovementioned functions of handwritten signatures. For example, certain techniques would rely on authentication through a biometric device based on handwritten signatures. In such a device, the signatory would sign manually, using a special pen, either on a computer screen or on a digital pad. The handwritten signature would then be analyzed by the computer and stored as a set of numerical values, which could be appended to a data message and displayed by the relying party for authentication purposes. Such an authentication system would presuppose that samples of the handwritten signature have been previously analyzed and stored by the biometric device. Other techniques would involve the use of personal identification numbers (PINs), digitized versions of handwritten signatures, and other methods, such as clicking an "OK-box".

34. UNCITRAL has intended to develop uniform legislation that can facilitate the use of both digital signatures and other forms of electronic signatures. To that effect, UNCITRAL has attempted to deal with the legal issues of electronic signatures at a level that is intermediate between the high generality of the UNCITRAL Model Law on Electronic Commerce and the specificity that might be required when dealing with a given signature technique. In any event, consistent with media neutrality in the UNCITRAL Model Law on Electronic Commerce, the new Model Law is not to be interpreted as discouraging the use of any method of electronic signature, whether already existing or to be implemented in the future.

2. Digital signatures relying on public-key cryptography[16]

35. In view of the increasing use of digital signature techniques in a number of countries, the following introduction may be of assistance.

(a) Technical notions and terminology

(i) Cryptography

36. Digital signatures are created and verified by using cryptography, the branch of applied mathematics that concerns itself with transforming messages into seemingly unintelligible form and back into the original form. Digital signatures use what is known as "public-key cryptography", which is often based on the use of algorithmic functions to generate two different but mathematically related "keys" (i.e., large numbers produced using a series of mathematical formulae applied to prime numbers). One such key is used for creating a digital signature or transforming data into a seemingly unintelligible form, and the other one for verifying a digital signature or returning the message to its original form. Computer equipment and software utilizing two such keys are often collectively referred to as "cryptosystems" or, more specifically, "asymmetric cryptosystems" where they rely on the use of asymmetric algorithms.

37. While the use of cryptography is one of the main features of digital signatures, the mere fact that a digital signature is used to authenticate a message containing information in digital form should not be confused with a more general use of cryptography for purposes of confidentiality. Confidentiality encryption is a method used for encoding an electronic communication so that only the originator and the addressee of the message will be able to read it. In a number of countries, the use of cryptography for confidentiality purposes is limited by law for reasons of public policy that may involve considerations of national defense. However, the use of cryptography for authentication purposes by producing a digital signature does not necessarily imply the use of cryptography to make any information confidential in the communication process, since the encrypted digital signature may be merely appended to a non-encrypted message.

(ii) Public and private keys

38. The complementary keys used for digital signatures are named the "private key", which is used only by the signatory to create the digital signature, and the "public key", which is ordinarily more widely known and is used by a relying party to verify the digital signature. The user of a private key is

---

16 Numerous elements of the description of the functioning of a digital signature system in this section are based on the ABA Digital Signature Guidelines, at pp. 8–17.

expected to keep the private key secret. It should be noted that the individual user does not need to know the private key. Such a private key is likely to be kept on a smart card, or to be accessible through a personal identification number or through a biometric identification device, for example, through thumb print recognition. If many people need to verify the signatory's digital signatures, the public key must be available or distributed to all of them, for example, by publication in an online repository or any other form of public directory where it is easily accessible. Although the keys of the pair are mathematically related, if an asymmetric cryptosystem has been designed and implemented securely, it is virtually impossible to derive the private key from knowledge of the public key. The most common algorithms for encryption through the use of public and private keys are based on an important feature of large prime numbers: once they are multiplied together to produce a new number, it is particularly difficult and time-consuming to determine which two prime numbers created that new, larger number.[17]

39. It should be noted, however, that the concept of public-key cryptography does not necessarily imply the use of the above-mentioned algorithms based on prime numbers. Other mathematical techniques are currently used or under development, such as cryptosystems relying on elliptic curves, which are often described as offering a high degree of security through the use of significantly reduced key-lengths.

(iii) Hash function

40. In addition to the generation of key pairs, another fundamental process, generally referred to as a "hash function", is used in both creating and verifying a digital signature. A hash function is a mathematical process, based on an algorithm which creates a digital representation, or compressed form of the message, often referred to as a "message digest", or "fingerprint" of the message, in the form of a "hash value" or "hash result" of a standard length that is usually much smaller than the message but nevertheless substantially unique to it. Any change to the message invariably produces a different hash result when the same hash function is used. In the case of a secure hash f

---

17   Certain existing standards, such as the ABA Digital Signature Guidelines, refer to the notion of "computational unfeasibility" to describe the expected irreversibility of the process, that is, the hope that it will be impossible to derive a user's secret private key from that user's public key. "Computationally unfeasible' is a relative concept based on the value of the data protected, the computing overhead required to protect it, the length of time it needs to be protected, and the cost and time required to attack the data, with such factors assessed both currently and in the light of future technological advance" (ABA Digital Signature Guidelines, at p. 9, note 23). Thus, although many people may know the public key of a given signatory and use it to verify that signatory's signatures, they cannot discover that signatory's private key and use it to forge digital signatures.

h function, sometimes called a "one-way hash function", it is virtually impossible to derive the original message from knowledge of its hash value. Hash functions therefore enable the software for creating digital signatures to operate on smaller and predictable amounts of data, while still providing robust evidentiary correlation to the original message content, thereby efficiently providing assurance that there has been no modification of the message since it was digitally signed.

(iv) Digital signature

41. To sign a document or any other item of information, the signatory first delimits precisely the borders of what is to be signed. Then a hash function in the signatory's software computes a hash result unique (for all practical purposes) to the information to be signed. The signatory's software then transforms the hash result into a digital signature using the signatory's private key. The resulting digital signature is thus unique to both the information being signed and the private key used to create the digital signature.

42. Typically, a digital signature (a digitally signed hash result of the message) is attached to the message and stored or transmitted with that message. However, it also may be sent or stored as a separate data element, as long as it maintains a reliable association with the corresponding message. Since a digital signature is unique to its message, it is inoperable if permanently disassociated from the message.

(v) Verification of digital signature

43. Digital signature verification is the process of checking the digital signature by reference to the original message and a given public key, thereby determining whether the digital signature was created for that same message using the private key that corresponds to the referenced public key. Verification of a digital signature is accomplished by computing a new hash result of the original message by means of the same hash function used to create the digital signature. Then, using the public key and the new hash result, the verifier checks whether the digital signature was created using the corresponding private key, and whether the newly computed hash result matches the original hash result that was transformed into the digital signature during the signing process.

44. The verification software will confirm the digital signature as "verified" if: (a) the signatory's private key was used to sign digitally the message, which is known to be the case if the signatory's public key was used to verify the signature because the signatory's public key will verify only a digital signature created with the signatory's private key; and (b) the message was unaltered, which is known to be the case if the hash result computed by the verifier is identical to the hash result extracted from the digital signature during the verification process.

(b) Public-key infrastructure and suppliers of certification services

45. To verify a digital signature, the verifier must have access to the signatory's public key and have assurance that it corresponds to the signatory's private key. However, a public- and private-key pair has no intrinsic association with any person; it is simply a pair of numbers. An additional mechanism is necessary to associate reliably a particular person or entity to the key pair. If public-key cryptography is to serve its intended purposes, it needs to provide a way to make keys available to a wide variety of persons, many of whom are not known to the signatory, where no relationship of trust has developed between the parties. To that effect, the parties involved must have a degree of confidence in the public and private keys being issued.

46. The requested level of confidence may exist between parties who trust each other, who have dealt with each other over a period of time, who communicate on closed systems, who operate within a closed group, or who are able to govern their dealings contractually, for example, in a trading partner agreement. In a transaction involving only two parties, each party can simply communicate (by a relatively secure channel, such as a courier or telephone, with its inherent feature of voice recognition) the public key of the key pair each party will use. However, the same level of confidence may not be present when the parties deal infrequently with each other, communicate over open systems (e.g., the World Wide Web on the Internet), are not in a closed group or do not have trading partner agreements or other laws governing their relationships.

47. In addition, because public-key cryptography is a highly mathematical technology, all users must have confidence in the skill, knowledge, and security arrangements of the parties issuing the public and private keys.[18]

48. A prospective signatory might issue a public statement indicating that signatures verifiable by a given public key should be treated as originating from that signatory. The form and the legal effectiveness of such a statement would be governed by the law of the enacting state. For example, a presumption of attribution of electronic signatures to a particular signatory could be established through publication of the statement in an *official bulletin* or in a document recognized as "authentic" by public authorities (see A/CN.9/484, paragraph 36). However, other parties might be unwilling to accept the statement, especially where there is no prior contract establishing the legal effect of that published statement with certainty. A party relying upon such an unsupported published statement in an open system would run a great risk of inadvertently trusting an impostor or of having to disprove a false denial of a digital signature (an issue often referred to in the

---

18   In situations where public and private cryptographic keys would be issued by the users themselves, such confidence might need to be provided by the certifiers of public keys.

context of "non-repudiation" of digital signatures) if a transaction should turn out to prove disadvantageous for the purported signatory.

49. One type of solution to some of these problems is the use of one or more third parties to associate an identified signatory or the signatory's name with a specific public key. That third party is generally referred to as a "certification authority", "certification service provider", or "supplier of certification services" in most technical standards and guidelines (in the Model Law, the term "certification service provider" has been chosen). In a number of countries, such certification authorities are being organized hierarchically into what is often referred to as a "public-key infrastructure" (PKI). Other solutions may include, for example, certificates issued by relying parties.

(i) Public-key infrastructure

50. Setting up a PKI is a way to provide confidence that: (a) a user's public key has not been tampered with and in fact corresponds to that user's private key; and (b) the cryptographic techniques being used are sound. To provide the confidence described above, a PKI may offer a number of services, including the following: (a) managing cryptographic keys used for digital signatures; (b) certifying that a public key corresponds to a private key; (c) providing keys to end users; (d) publishing a secure directory of public keys or certificates; (e) managing personal tokens (e.g., smart cards) that can identify the user with unique personal identification information or can generate and store an individual's private keys; (f) checking the identification of end users, and providing them with services; (g) providing time-stamping services; and (h) managing cryptographic keys used for confidentiality encryption where the use of such a technique is authorized.

51. A PKI is often based on various hierarchical levels of authority. For example, models considered in certain countries for the establishment of possible PKIs include references to the following levels: (a) a unique "root authority", which would certify the technology and practices of all parties authorized to issue cryptographic key pairs or certificates in connection with the use of such key pairs and would register subordinate certification authorities;[19] (b) various certification authorities, placed below the "root" authority, which would certify that a user's public key actually corresponds to that user's private key (i.e., has not been tampered with); and (c) various local registration authorities, placed below the certification authorities, and receiving requests from users for cryptographic key pairs or for certificates in connection with the use of such key pairs, requiring proof of identification and checking

---

19   The question as to whether a government should have the technical ability to retain or recreate private confidentiality keys may be dealt with at the level of the root authority.

identities of potential users. In certain countries, it is envisaged that notaries public might act as, or support, local registration authorities.

52. The issues of PKI may not lend themselves easily to international harmonization. The organization of a PKI may involve various technical issues, as well as issues of public policy that may better be left to each individual state at the current stage.[20] In that connection, decisions may need to be made by each state considering the establishment of a PKI, for example as to: (a) the form and number of levels of authority that should be comprised in a PKI; (b) whether only certain authorities belonging to the PKI should be allowed to issue cryptographic key pairs or whether such key pairs might be issued by the users themselves; (c) whether the certification authorities certifying the validity of cryptographic key pairs should be public entities or whether private entities might act as certification authorities; (d) whether the process of allowing a given entity to act as a certification service provider should take the form of an express authorization, or "licensing", by the state, or whether other methods should be used to control the quality of certification authorities if they were allowed to operate in the absence of a specific authorization; (e) the extent to which the use of cryptography should be authorized for confidentiality purposes; and (f) whether government authorities should have the right to gain access to encrypted information, through a mechanism of "key escrow" or otherwise. The Model Law does not deal with those issues.

(ii) Certification service provider

53. To associate a key pair with a prospective signatory, a certification service provider (or certification authority) issues a certificate, an electronic record that lists a public key together with the name of the certificate subscriber as the "subject" of the certificate, and may confirm that the prospective signatory identified in the certificate holds the corresponding private key. The principal function of a certificate is to bind a public key with a particular signatory. A "recipient" of the certificate desiring to rely upon a digital signature created by the signatory named in the certificate can use the public key listed in the certificate to verify that the digital signature was created with the corresponding private key. If such verification is successful, a level of assurance is provided technically that the digital signature was created by the signatory and that the portion of the message used in the hash function (and, consequently, the corresponding data message) has not been modified since it was digitally signed.

---

20   However, the context of cross-certification, the need for global interoperability requires that PKIs established in various countries should be capable of communicating with each other.

54. To assure the authenticity of the certificate with respect to both its contents and its source, the certification service provider digitally signs it. The issuing certification service provider's digital signature on the certificate can be verified by using the public key of the certification service provider listed in another certificate by another certification service provider (which may but need not be on a higher level in a hierarchy), and that other certificate can in turn be authenticated by the public key listed in yet another certificate, and so on, until the person relying on the digital signature is adequately assured of its genuineness. Among other possible ways of verifying the digital signature of the certification service provider is that the digital signature also can be recorded in a certificate issued by that certification service provider itself, sometimes referred to as a "root certificate".[21] In each case, the issuing certification service provider must digitally sign its own certificate during the operational period of the other certificate used to verify the certification service provider's digital signature. Under the laws of some states, a way of building trust in the digital signature of the certification service provider might be to publish the public key of the certification service provider (see A/CN.9/484, paragraph 41) or certain data pertaining to the root certificate (such as a "digital fingerprint") in an official bulletin.

55. A digital signature corresponding to a message, whether created by the signatory to authenticate a message or by a certification service provider to authenticate its certificate, should generally be reliably time-stamped to allow the verifier to determine reliably whether the digital signature was created during the "operational period" stated in the certificate, which is a condition of the verifiability of a digital signature.

56. To make a public key and its correspondence to a specific signatory readily available for verification, the certificate may be published in a repository or made available by other means. Typically, repositories are online databases of certificates and other information available for retrieval and use in verifying digital signatures.

57. Once issued, a certificate may prove to be unreliable, for example, in situations where the signatory misrepresents its identity to the certification service provider. In other circumstances, a certificate may be reliable enough when issued, but it may become unreliable sometime thereafter. If the private key is "compromised", for example, through loss of control of the private key by the signatory, the certificate may lose its trustworthiness or become unreliable, and the certification service provider (at the signatory's request or even without the signatory's consent, depending on the circumstances) may suspend (temporarily interrupt the operational period) or revoke (

---

21 *Official Records of the General Assembly*, Fifty-sixth Session, Supplement Number 17 (A/56/17), paragraph 279.

permanently invalidate) the certificate. Immediately upon suspending or revoking a certificate, the certification service provider may be expected to publish notice of the revocation or suspension or notify persons who enquire or who are known to have received a digital signature verifiable by reference to the unreliable certificate.

58. Certification authorities could be operated by government authorities or by private sector service providers. In a number of countries, it is envisaged that, for public policy reasons, only government entities should be authorized to operate as certification authorities. In other countries, it is considered that certification services should be open to competition from the private sector. Irrespective of whether certification authorities are operated by public entities or by private sector service providers and of whether certification authorities would need to obtain a license to operate, there is typically more than one certification service provider operating within the PKI. Of particular concern is the relationship between the various certification authorities. Certification authorities within a PKI can be established in a hierarchical structure, where some certification authorities only certify other certification authorities, which provide services directly to users. In such a structure, certification authorities are subordinate to other certification authorities. In other conceivable structures, all certification authorities may operate on an equal footing. In any large PKI, there would likely be both subordinate and superior certification authorities. In any event, in the absence of an international PKI, a number of concerns may arise with respect to the recognition of certificates by certification authorities in foreign countries. The recognition of foreign certificates is often achieved by a method called "cross-certification". In such a case, it is necessary that substantially equivalent certification authorities (or certification authorities willing to assume certain risks with regard to the certificates issued by other certification authorities) recognize the services provided by each other, so their respective users can communicate with each other more efficiently and with greater confidence in the trustworthiness of the certificates being issued.

59. Legal issues may arise with regard to cross-certifying or chaining of certificates when there are multiple security policies involved. Examples of such issues may include determining whose misconduct caused a loss and upon whose representations the user relied. It should be noted that legal rules considered for adoption in certain countries provide that, where the levels of security and policies are made known to the users and there is no negligence on the part of certification authorities, there should be no liability.

60. It may be incumbent upon the certification service provider or the root authority to ensure that its policy requirements are met on an ongoing basis. While the selection of certification authorities may be based on a number of factors, including the strength of the public key being used and the identity of

the user, the trustworthiness of any certification service provider also may depend on its enforcement of certificate-issuing standards and the reliability of its evaluation of data received from users who request certificates. Of particular importance is the liability regime applying to any certification service provider with respect to its compliance with the policy and security requirements of the root authority or superior certification service provider, or with any other applicable requirement, on an ongoing basis. Of equal importance is the obligation of the certification service provider to act in accordance with the representations made by it with respect to its policies and practices, as envisaged in article 9, paragraph 1 (a), of the new Model Law (see A/CN.9/484, paragraph 43).

61. In the preparation of the Model Law, the following elements were considered as possible factors to be taken into account when assessing the trustworthiness of a certification service provider: (a) independence (i.e., absence of financial or other interest in underlying transactions); (b) financial resources and financial ability to bear the risk of being held liable for loss; (c) expertise in public-key technology and familiarity with proper security procedures; (d) longevity (certification authorities may be required to produce evidence of certification or decryption keys many years after the underlying transaction has been completed, in the context of a lawsuit or property claim); (e) approval of hardware and software; (f) maintenance of an audit trail and audit by an independent entity; (g) existence of a contingency plan (e.g., "disaster recovery" software or key escrow); (h) personnel selection and management; (i) protection arrangements for the certification service provider's own private key; (j) internal security; (k) arrangements for termination of operations, including notice to users; (l) warranties and representations (given or excluded); (m) limitation of liability; (n) insurance; (o) interoperability with other certification authorities; and (p) revocation procedures (in cases where cryptographic keys might be lost or compromised).

(c) Summary of the digital signature process

62. The use of digital signatures usually involves the following processes, performed either by the signatory or by the receiver of the digitally signed message:

(a) The user generates or is given a unique cryptographic key pair;

(b) The signatory prepares a message (for example, in the form of an electronic mail message) on a computer;

(c) The signatory prepares a "message digest", using a secure hash algorithm. Digital signature creation uses a hash result derived from and unique to the signed message;

(d) The signatory encrypts the message digest with the private key. The private key is applied to the message digest text using a mathematical algorithm. The digital signature consists of the encrypted message digest;

(e) The signatory typically attaches or appends its digital signature to the message;

(f) The signatory sends the digital signature and the (unencrypted or encrypted) message to the relying party electronically;

(g) The relying party uses the signatory's public key to verify the signatory's digital signature. Verification using the signatory's public key provides a level of technical assurance that the message came exclusively from the signatory;

(h) The relying party also creates a "message digest" of the message, using the same secure hash algorithm;

(i) The relying party compares the two message digests. If they are the same, then the relying party knows that the message has not been altered after it was signed. Even if one bit in the message has been altered after the message has been digitally signed, the message digest created by the relying party will be different from the message digest created by the signatory;

(j) Where the certification process is resorted to, the relying party obtains a certificate from the certification service provider (including through the signatory or otherwise), which confirms the digital signature on the signatory's message (see A/CN.9/484, paragraph 44). The certificate contains the public key and name of the signatory (and possibly additional information), digitally signed by the certification service provider.

IV. Main features of the Model Law A. Legislative nature of the Model Law

63. The new Model Law was prepared on the assumption that it should be directly derived from article 7 of the UNCITRAL Model Law on Electronic Commerce and should be considered as a way to provide detailed information as to the concept of a reliable "method used to identify" a person and "to indicate that person's approval" of the information contained in a data message (see A/CN.9/WG.IV/WP.71, paragraph 49).

64. The question of what form the instrument might take was raised and the importance of considering the relationship of the form to the content was noted. Different approaches were suggested as to what the form might be, which included contractual rules, legislative provisions, or guidelines for

states considering enacting legislation on electronic signatures. It was agreed as a working assumption that the text should be prepared as a set of legislative rules with commentary, and not merely as guidelines (see A/CN.9/437, paragraph 27; A/CN.9/446, paragraph 25; and A/CN.9/457, paragraphs 51 and 72). The text was finally adopted as a Model Law (A/CN.9/483, paragraphs 137 and 138).

B. Relationship with the UNCITRAL Model Law on Electronic Commerce

1. New Model Law as a separate legal instrument

65. The new provisions could have been incorporated in an extended version of the UNCITRAL Model Law on Electronic Commerce, for example, to form a new part III of the UNCITRAL Model Law on Electronic Commerce. With a view to indicating clearly that the new Model Law could be enacted either independently or in combination with the UNCITRAL Model Law on Electronic Commerce, it was eventually decided that the new Model Law should be prepared as a separate legal instrument (see A/CN.9/465, paragraph 37). That decision results mainly from the fact that, at the time the new Model Law was being finalized, the UNCITRAL Model Law on Electronic Commerce had already been successfully implemented in a number of countries and was being considered for adoption in many other countries. The preparation of an extended version of the UNCITRAL Model Law on Electronic Commerce might have compromised the success of the original version by suggesting a need to improve on that text by way of an update. In addition, preparing a new version of the UNCITRAL Model Law on Electronic Commerce might have introduced confusion in those countries which had recently adopted the UNCITRAL Model Law on Electronic Commerce.

2. New Model Law fully consistent with the UNCITRAL Model Law on Electronic Commerce

66. In drafting the new Model Law, every effort was made to ensure consistency with both the substance and the terminology of the UNCITRAL Model Law on Electronic Commerce (A/CN.9/465, paragraph 37). The general provisions of the UNCITRAL Model Law on Electronic Commerce have been reproduced in the new instrument. These are articles 1 (Sphere of application), 2 (a), (c), and (d) (Definitions of "data message", "originator", and "addressee"), 3 (Interpretation), 4 (Variation by agreement), and 7 (Signature) of the UNCITRAL Model Law on Electronic Commerce.

67. Based on the UNCITRAL Model Law on Electronic Commerce, the new Model Law is intended to reflect in particular: the principle of media-neutrality; an approach under which functional equivalents of traditional paper-based concepts and practices should not be discriminated against; and extensive reliance on party autonomy (A/CN.9/WG.IV/WP.84, paragraph 16). It is

intended for use both as minimum standards in an "open" environment (i.e., where parties communicate electronically without prior agreement) and, where appropriate, as model contractual provisions or default rules in a "closed" environment (i.e., where parties are bound by pre-existing contractual rules and procedures to be followed in communicating by electronic means).

3. Relationship with article 7 of the UNCITRAL Model Law on Electronic Commerce

68. In the preparation of the new Model Law, the view was expressed that the reference to article 7 of the UNCITRAL Model Law on Electronic Commerce in the text of article 6 of the new Model Law was to be interpreted as limiting the scope of the new Model Law to situations where an electronic signature was used to meet a mandatory requirement of law that certain documents had to be signed for purposes of validity. Under that view, since the law of most nations contained very few such requirements with respect to documents used for commercial transactions, the scope of the new Model Law was very narrow. It was generally agreed, in response, that such interpretation of article 6 (and of article 7 of the UNCITRAL Model Law on Electronic Commerce) was inconsistent with the interpretation of the words "the law" adopted by the Commission in paragraph 68 of the Guide to Enactment of the UNCITRAL Model Law on Electronic Commerce, under which "the words 'the law' are to be understood as encompassing not only statutory or regulatory law but also judicially-created law and other procedural law". In fact, the scope of both article 7 of the UNCITRAL Model Law on Electronic Commerce and article 6 of the new Model Law is particularly broad, since most documents used in the context of commercial transactions are likely to be faced, in practice, with the requirements of the law of evidence regarding proof in writing (A/CN.9/ 465, paragraph 67).

C. "Framework" rules to be supplemented by technical regulations and contract

69. As a supplement to the UNCITRAL Model Law on Electronic Commerce, the new Model Law is intended to provide essential principles for facilitating the use of electronic signatures. However, as a "framework", the Model Law itself does not set forth all the rules and regulations that may be necessary (in addition to contractual arrangements between users) to implement those techniques in an enacting state. Moreover, as indicated in this Guide, the Model Law is not intended to cover every aspect of the use of electronic signatures. Accordingly, an enacting state may wish to issue regulations to fill in the procedural details for procedures authorized by the Model Law and to take account of the specific, possibly changing, circumstances at play in the enacting state, without compromising the objectives of

the Model Law. It is recommended that, should it decide to issue such regulation, an enacting state should give particular attention to the need to preserve flexibility in the operation of electronic signature systems by their users. Commercial practice has a long-standing reliance on the voluntary technical standards process. Such technical standards form the bases of product specifications, of engineering and design criteria and of consensus for research and development of future products. To assure the flexibility such commercial practice relies on, to promote open standards with a view to facilitating interoperability, and to support the objective of cross-border recognition (as described in article 12), states may wish to give due regard to the relationship between any specifications incorporated in or authorized by national regulations, and the voluntary technical standards process (see A/CN.9/484, paragraph 46).

70. It should be noted that the electronic signature techniques considered in the Model Law, beyond raising matters of procedure that may need to be addressed in implementing technical regulations, may raise certain legal questions, the answers to which will not necessarily be found in the Model Law, but rather in other bodies of law. Such other bodies of law may include, for example, the applicable administrative, contract, tort, criminal, and judicial-procedure law, which the Model Law is not intended to deal with.

D. Added certainty as to the legal effects of electronic signatures

71. One of the main features of the new Model Law is to add certainty to the operation of the flexible criterion set forth in article 7 of the UNCITRAL Model Law on Electronic Commerce for the recognition of an electronic signature as functionally equivalent to a handwritten signature.

Article 7 of the UNCITRAL Model Law on Electronic Commerce reads as follows:

> "(1) Where the law requires a signature of a person, that requirement is met in relation to a data message if:

> "(a) a method is used to identify that person and to indicate that person's approval of the information contained in the data message; and

> "(b) that method is as reliable as was appropriate for the purpose for which the data message was generated or communicated, in the light of all the circumstances, including any relevant agreement.

> "(2) Paragraph (1) applies whether the requirement therein is in the form of an obligation or whether the law simply provides consequences for the absence of a signature.

> "(3) The provisions of this article do not apply to the following: [. . .]."

72. Article 7 is based on the recognition of the functions of a signature in a paper-based environment, as described in paragraph 29 above.

73. With a view to ensuring that a message that was required to be authenticated should not be denied legal value for the sole reason that it was not authenticated in a manner peculiar to paper documents, article 7 adopts a comprehensive approach. It establishes the general conditions under which data messages would be regarded as authenticated with sufficient credibility and would be enforceable in the face of signature requirements that currently present barriers to electronic commerce. Article 7 focuses on the two basic functions of a signature, namely, to identify the author of a document and to confirm that the author approved the content of that document. Paragraph 1(a) establishes the principle that, in an electronic environment, the basic legal functions of a signature are performed by way of a method that identifies the originator of a data message and confirms that the originator approved the content of that data message.

74. Paragraph 1 b) establishes a flexible approach to the level of security to be achieved by the method of identification used under paragraph 1(a). The method used under paragraph 1(a) should be as reliable as is appropriate for the purpose for which the data message is generated or communicated, in the light of all the circumstances, including any agreement between the originator and the addressee of the data message.

75. In determining whether the method used under paragraph 1 is appropriate, legal, technical, and commercial factors that may be taken into account include the following: (a) the sophistication of the equipment used by each of the parties; (b) the nature of their trade activity; (c) the frequency at which commercial transactions take place between the parties; (d) the kind and size of the transaction; (e) the function of signature requirements in a given statutory and regulatory environment; (f) the capability of communication systems; (g) compliance with authentication procedures set forth by intermediaries; (h) the range of authentication procedures made available by any intermediary; (i) compliance with trade customs and practice; (j) the existence of insurance coverage mechanisms against unauthorized messages; (k) the importance and the value of the information contained in the data message; (l) the availability of alternative methods of identification and the cost of implementation; (m) the degree of acceptance or non-acceptance of the method of identification in the relevant industry or field both at the time the method was agreed upon and the time when the data message was communicated; and (n) any other relevant factor (Guide to Enactment of the UNCITRAL Model Law on Electronic Commerce, paragraphs 53 and 56–58).

76. Building on the flexible criterion expressed in article 7, paragraph 1(b), of the UNCITRAL Model Law on Electronic Commerce, articles 6 and 7 of the

new Model Law establish a mechanism through which electronic signatures that meet objective criteria of technical reliability can be made to benefit from early determination as to their legal effectiveness. Depending on the time at which certainty is achieved as to the recognition of an electronic signature as functionally equivalent to a handwritten signature, the Model Law establishes two distinct regimes. The first and broader regime is that described in article 7 of the UNCITRAL Model Law on Electronic Commerce. It recognizes any "method" that may be used to fulfill a legal requirement for a handwritten signature. The legal effectiveness of such a "method" as an equivalent of a handwritten signature depends upon demonstration of its "reliability" to a trier of fact. The second and narrower regime is that created by the new Model Law. It contemplates methods of electronic signature that may be recognized by a state authority, a private accredited entity, or the parties themselves, as meeting the criteria of technical reliability set forth in the Model Law (see A/CN.9/484, paragraph 49). The advantage of such recognition is that it brings certainty to the users of such electronic signature techniques before they actually use the electronic signature technique.

E. Basic rules of conduct for the parties involved

77. The Model Law does not deal in any detail with the issues of liability that may affect the various parties involved in the operation of electronic signature systems. Those issues are left to applicable law outside the Model Law. However, the Model Law sets out criteria against which to assess the conduct of those parties, that is, the signatory, the relying party and the certification service provider.

78. As to the signatory, the Model Law elaborates on the basic principle that the signatory should apply reasonable care with respect to its electronic signature creation data. The signatory is expected to exercise reasonable care to avoid unauthorized use of that signature creation data. The digital signature in itself does not guarantee that the person who has in fact signed is the signatory. At best, the digital signature provides assurance that it is attributable to the signatory (see A/CN.9/484, paragraph 50). Where the signatory knows or should have known that the signature creation data has been compromised, the signatory should give notice without undue delay to any person who may reasonably be expected to rely on, or to provide services in support of, the electronic signature. Where a certificate is used to support the electronic signature, the signatory is expected to exercise reasonable care to ensure the accuracy and completeness of all material representations made by the signatory in connection with the certificate.

79. A relying party is expected to take reasonable steps to verify the reliability of an electronic signature. Where the electronic signature is supported by a

certificate, the relying party should take reasonable steps to verify the validity, suspension, or revocation of the certificate and to observe any limitation with respect to the certificate.

80. The general duty of a certification service provider is to utilize trustworthy systems, procedures, and human resources and to act in accordance with representations that the supplier makes with respect to its policies and practices. In addition, the certification service provider is expected to exercise reasonable care to ensure the accuracy and completeness of all material representations it makes in connection with a certificate. In the certificate, the supplier should provide essential information allowing the relying party to identify the supplier. It also should represent that: (a) the signatory that is identified in the certificate had control of the signature creation data at the time when the certificate was issued; and (b) the signature creation data was operational on or before the date when the certificate was issued. For the benefit of the relying party, the certification service provider should provide additional information as to: (a) the method used to identify the signatory; (b) any limitation on the purpose or value for which the signature creation data or the certificate may be used; (c) the operational condition of the signature creation data; (d) any limitation on the scope or extent of liability of the certification service provider; (e) whether means exist for the signatory to give notice that a signature creation data has been compromised; and (f) whether a timely revocation service is offered.

81. For the assessment of the trustworthiness of the systems, procedures, and human resources utilized by the certification service provider, the Model Law provides an open-ended list of indicative factors.

F. A technology-neutral framework

82. Given the pace of technological innovation, the Model Law provides criteria for the legal recognition of electronic signatures irrespective of the technology used (e.g., digital signatures relying on asymmetric cryptography; biometric devices (enabling the identification of individuals by their physical characteristics, whether by hand or face geometry, fingerprint reading, voice recognition or retina scan, etc.); symmetric cryptography, the use of PINs; the use of "tokens" as a way of authenticating data messages through a smart card or other device held by the signatory; digitized versions of handwritten signatures; signature dynamics; and other methods, such as clicking an "OK-box"). The various techniques listed could be used in combination to reduce systemic risk (see A/CN.9/484, paragraph 52).

G. Non-discrimination of foreign electronic signatures

83. The Model Law establishes as a basic principle that the place of origin, in and of itself, should in no way be a factor determining whether and to what

extent foreign certificates or electronic signatures should be recognized as capable of being legally effective in an enacting state (see A/CN.9/484, paragraph 53). Determination of whether, or the extent to which, a certificate or an electronic signature is capable of being legally effective should not depend on the place where the certificate or the electronic signature was issued (see A/CN.9/483, paragraph 27), but on its technical reliability. That basic principle is elaborated upon in article 12 (see below, paragraphs 152–160).

V. Assistance from the UNCITRAL secretariat

A. Assistance in drafting legislation

84. In the context of its training and assistance activities, the UNCITRAL secretariat assists states with technical consultations for the preparation of legislation based on the UNCITRAL Model Law on Electronic Signatures. The same assistance is brought to governments considering legislation based on other UNCITRAL model laws (i.e., the UNCITRAL Model Law on International Commercial Arbitration, the UNCITRAL Model Law on International Credit Transfers, the UNCITRAL Model Law on Procurement of Goods, Construction and Services, the UNCITRAL Model Law on Electronic Commerce, and the UNCITRAL Model Law on Cross-Border Insolvency) or considering adhesion to one of the international trade law conventions prepared by UNCITRAL.

85. Further information concerning the Model Law and other model laws and conventions developed by UNCITRAL may be obtained from the secretariat at the address below:

International Trade Law Branch, Office of Legal Affairs United Nations Vienna International Centre, P.O. Box 500, A-1400 Vienna, Austria, Telephone: (+43-1) 26060-4060 or 4061, Telecopy: (+43-1) 26060-5813, Electronic mail: uncitral@uncitral.org Internet home page: http://www.uncitral.org

B. Information on the interpretation of legislation based on the Model Law

86. The secretariat welcomes comments concerning the Model Law and the Guide, as well as information concerning enactment of legislation based on the Model Law. Once enacted, the Model Law will be included in the CLOUT information system, which is used for collecting and disseminating information on case law relating to the conventions and model laws that have emanated from the work of UNCITRAL. The purpose of the system is to promote international awareness of the legislative texts formulated by UNCITRAL and to facilitate their uniform interpretation and application. The secretariat publishes, in the six official languages of the United Nations, abstracts of decisions and makes available, against reimbursement of copying expenses, the decisions on the basis of which the abstracts were prepared. The system is explained in a user's guide

that is available from the secretariat in hard copy (A/CN.9/SER.C/GUIDE/1) and on the above-mentioned Internet home page of UNCITRAL.

Chapter II. Article-by-article remarks Title

"Model Law"

87. Throughout its preparation, the instrument has been conceived of as an addition to the UNCITRAL Model Law on Electronic Commerce, which should be dealt with on an equal footing and share the legal nature of its forerunner.

Article 1. Sphere of application

This Law applies where electronic signatures are used in the context[22] of commercial[23] activities. It does not override any rule of law intended for the protection of consumers.

General remarks

88. The purpose of article 1 is to delineate the scope of application of the Model Law. The approach used in the Model Law is to provide in principle for the coverage of all factual situations where electronic signatures are used, irrespective of the specific electronic signature or authentication technique being applied. It was felt during the preparation of the Model Law that exclusion of any form or medium by way of a limitation in the scope of the Model Law might result in practical difficulties and would run counter to the purpose of providing truly "media-neutral" as well as "technology-neutral" rules. In the preparation of the Model Law, the principle of technology neutrality was observed by the UNCITRAL Working Group on Electronic Commerce, although it was aware that "digital signatures", that is, those electronic signatures obtained through the application of dual-key cryptography, were a particularly widespread technology (see A/CN.9/484, paragraph 54).[24]

---

22   The Commission suggests the following text for states that might wish to extend the applicability of this Law: "This Law applies where electronic signatures are used, except in the following situations: [. . .]".

23   The term "commercial" should be given a wide interpretation so as to cover matters arising from all relationships of a commercial nature, whether contractual or not. Relationships of a commercial nature include, but are not limited to, the following transactions: any trade transaction for the supply or exchange of goods or services; distribution agreement; commercial representation or agency; factoring; leasing; construction of works; consulting; engineering; licensing; investment; financing; banking; insurance; exploitation agreement or concession; joint venture and other forms of industrial or business cooperation; and carriage of goods or passengers by air, sea, rail or road.

24   The Commission suggests the following text for states that might wish to extend the applicability of this Law: "This Law applies where electronic signatures are used, except in the following situations: [. . .]".

89. The Model Law applies to all kinds of data messages to which a legally significant electronic signature is attached, and nothing in the Model Law should prevent an enacting state from extending the scope of the Model Law to cover uses of electronic signatures outside the commercial sphere. For example, while the focus of the Model Law is not on the relationships between users of electronic signatures and public authorities, the Model Law is not intended to be inapplicable to such relationships. Footnote * provides for alternative wordings, for possible use by enacting states that would consider it appropriate to extend the scope of the Model Law beyond the commercial sphere.

90. It was felt that the Model Law should contain an indication that its focus was on the types of situations encountered in the commercial area and that it had been prepared against the background of relationships in trade and finance. For that reason, article 1 refers to "commercial activities" and provides, in footnote **, indications as to what is meant thereby. Such indications, which may be particularly useful for those countries where there does not exist a discrete body of commercial law, are modeled, for reasons of consistency, on the footnote to article 1 of the UNCITRAL Model Law on International Commercial Arbitration (also reproduced as footnote **** to article 1 of the UNCITRAL Model Law on Electronic Commerce). In certain countries, the use of footnotes in a statutory text would not be regarded as acceptable legislative practice. National authorities enacting the Model Law might thus consider the possible inclusion of the text of footnotes in the body of the text itself.

Consumer protection

91. Some countries have special consumer protection laws that may govern certain aspects of the use of information systems. With respect to such consumer legislation, as was the case with previous UNCITRAL instruments (e.g., the UNCITRAL Model Law on International Credit Transfers and the UNCITRAL Model Law on Electronic Commerce), it was felt that an indication should be given that the Model Law had been drafted without special attention being given to issues that might arise in the context of consumer protection. At the same time, it was felt that there was no reason why situations involving consumers should be excluded from the scope of the Model Law by way of a general provision, particularly since the provisions of the Model Law might be found very beneficial for consumer protection, depending on legislation in each enacting state. Article 1 thus recognizes that any such consumer protection law may take precedence over the provisions in the Model Law. Should legislators come to different conclusions as to the beneficial effect of the Model Law on consumer transactions in a given country, they might consider excluding consumers from the sphere of application of the piece of legislation enacting the Model Law. The question of which

individuals or corporate bodies would be regarded as "consumers" is left to applicable law outside the Model Law.

Use of electronic signatures in international and domestic transactions

92. It is recommended that application of the Model Law be made as wide as possible. Particular caution should be used in excluding the application of the Model Law by way of a limitation of its scope to international uses of electronic signatures, since such a limitation may be seen as not fully achieving the objectives of the Model Law. Furthermore, the variety of procedures available under the Model Law to limit the use of electronic signatures if necessary (e.g., for purposes of public policy) may make it less necessary to limit the scope of the Model Law. The legal certainty to be provided by the Model Law is necessary for both domestic and international trade. Discrimination between electronic signatures used domestically and electronic signatures used in the context of international trade transactions might result in a duality of regimes governing the use of electronic signatures, thus creating a serious obstacle to the use of such techniques (see A/CN.9/484, paragraph 55).

References to UNCITRAL documents

Official Records of the General Assembly, Fifty-sixth Session,

Supplement Number 17 (A/56/17), paragraphs 241, 242, and 284; A/CN.9/493, annex, paragraphs 88–92; A/CN.9/484, paragraphs 54 and 55;

A/CN.9/WG.IV/WP.88, annex, paragraphs 87–91; A/CN.9/467, paragraphs 22–24;

A/CN.9/WG.IV/WP.84, paragraph 22; A/CN.9/465, paragraphs 36–42;

A/CN.9/WG.IV/WP.82, paragraph 21; A/CN.9/457, paragraphs 53–64.

Article 2. Definitions for the purposes of this Law

(a) "Electronic signature" means data in electronic form in, affixed to, or logically associated with, a data message, which may be used to identify the signatory in relation to the data message and to indicate the signatory's approval of the information contained in the data message;

(b) "Certificate" means a data message or other record confirming the link between a signatory and signature creation data;

(c) "Data message" means information generated, sent, received, or stored by electronic, optical, or similar means including, but not limited to, electronic data interchange (EDI), electronic mail, telegram, telex, or telecopy;

(d) "Signatory" means a person that holds signature creation data and acts either on its own behalf or on behalf of the person it represents;

(e) "Certification service provider" means a person that issues certificates and may provide other services related to electronic signatures;

(f) "Relying party" means a person that may act on the basis of a certificate or an electronic signature.

Definition of "electronic signature"

Electronic signature as functional equivalent of handwritten signature

93. The notion of "electronic signature" is intended to cover all traditional uses of a handwritten signature for legal effect, such uses to identify a person and to associate that person with the content of a document being no more than the smallest common denominator to the various approaches to "signature" found in the various legal systems (see below, paragraphs 117 and 120). Those functions of a handwritten signature were already discussed in the context of the preparation of article 7 of the UNCITRAL Model Law on Electronic Commerce. Thus, defining an electronic signature as capable of indicating approval of information amounts primarily to establishing a technical prerequisite for the recognition of a given technology as capable of creating an equivalent to a handwritten signature. The definition does not disregard the fact that technologies commonly referred to as "electronic signatures" could be used for purposes other than creating a legally significant signature. The definition simply illustrates the focus of the Model Law on the use of electronic signatures as functional equivalents of handwritten signatures (see A/CN.9/483, paragraph 62). In order not to introduce or suggest any technical limitation regarding the method that could be used by a signatory to perform the functional equivalent of a handwritten signature, flexible wording referring to "data" that "may be used" has been preferred to any reference to the means used by the signatory being "technically capable" of performing such functions.[25]

Possible other uses of an electronic signature

94. A distinction should be drawn between the legal notion of "signature" and the technical notion of "electronic signature", a term of art that covers practices that do not necessarily involve the production of legally significant signatures. In the preparation of the Model Law, it was felt that the attention of users should be brought to the risk of confusion that might result from the use of the same technical tool for the production of a legally meaningful signature and for other authentication or identification functions (see A/CN.9/483, paragraph 62). Such a risk of confusion might arise regarding the intent of the signatory, in particular, if the same "electronic signature" technique was used to express the signatory's approval of the information being "signed" and

---

25   *Official Records of the General Assembly,* Fifty-sixth Session, Supplement Number 17 (A/56/17), paragraph 244.

could be used also to perform identification functions that would merely associate the signatory's name with the transmission of the message, without indicating approval of its contents (see below, paragraph 120). To the extent an electronic signature is used for the purposes expressly covered in the Model Law (i.e., to express the signatory's approval of the information being signed), it might happen in practice that the creation of such an electronic signature occurs prior to its actual use. In such a case, the signatory's approval should be gauged at the time when the electronic signature is affixed to the message rather than at the time when the signature was created.[26]

Definition of "certificate", Need for a definition

95. The term "certificate", as used in the context of certain types of electronic signatures and as defined in the Model Law, differs little from its general meaning of a document by which a person would confirm certain facts. The only difference is that the certificate is in electronic rather than paper form (see A/CN.9/484, paragraph 56). However, since the general notion of "certificate" does not exist in all legal systems or indeed in all languages, it was felt useful to include a definition in the context of the Model Law (see A/CN.9/483, paragraph 65).

Purpose of a certificate

96. The purpose of the certificate is to recognize, show, or confirm a link between signature creation data and the signatory. That link is created when the signature creation data is generated (A/CN.9/483, paragraph 67).

"Signature creation data"

97. In the context of electronic signatures which are not digital signatures, the term "signature creation data" is intended to designate those secret keys, codes, or other elements which, in the process of creating an electronic signature, are used to provide a secure link between the resulting electronic signature and the person of the signatory (see A/CN.9/484, paragraph 57). For example, in the context of electronic signatures based on biometric devices, the essential element would be the biometric indicator, such as a fingerprint or retina-scan data. The description covers only those core elements which should be kept confidential to ensure the quality of the signature process, to the exclusion of any other element that, although it might contribute to the signature process, could be disclosed without jeopardizing the reliability of the resulting electronic signature. On the other hand, in the context of digital signatures relying on asymmetric cryptography, the core operative element that could be described as "linked to the signatory" is the cryptographic key pair. In the case of digital signatures, both the public and the private key

---

26   *Official Records of the General Assembly*, Fifty-sixth Session, Supplement Number 17 (A/56/17), paragraph 245.

are linked to the person of the signatory. Since the prime purpose of a certificate, in the context of digital signatures, is to confirm the link between the public key and the signatory (see paragraphs 53–56 and 62 (j) above), it also is necessary that the public key be certified as belonging to the signatory. While only the private key is covered by this description of "signature creation data", it is important to state, for the avoidance of doubt, that in the context of digital signatures the definition of "certificate" in article 2, subparagraph (b), should be taken to include the confirming of the link between the signatory and the signatory's public key. Also among the elements not to be covered by this description is the text being electronically signed, although it also plays an important role in the signature-creation process (through a hash function or otherwise). Article 6 expresses the idea that the signature creation data should be linked to the signatory and to no other person (A/CN.9/483, paragraph 75).

Definition of "data message"

98. The definition of "data message" is taken from article 2 of the UNCITRAL Model Law on Electronic Commerce as a broad notion encompassing all messages generated in the context of electronic commerce, including Web-based commerce (A/CN.9/483, paragraph 69). The notion of "data message" is not limited to communication but also is intended to encompass computer-generated records that are not intended for communication. Thus, the notion of "message" includes the notion of "record".

99. The reference to "similar means" is intended to reflect the fact that the Model Law was not intended only for application in the context of existing communication techniques but also to accommodate foreseeable technical developments. The aim of the definition of "data message" is to encompass all types of messages that are generated, stored, or communicated in essentially paperless form. For that purpose, all means of communication and storage of information that might be used to perform functions parallel to the functions performed by the means listed in the definition are intended to be covered by the reference to "similar means", although, for example, "electronic" and "optical" means of communication might not be, strictly speaking, similar. For the purposes of the Model Law, the word "similar" connotes "functionally equivalent".

100. The definition of "data message" also is intended to apply in case of revocation or amendment. A data message is presumed to have a fixed information content, but it may be revoked or amended by another data message (see the Guide to Enactment of the UNCITRAL Model Law on Electronic Commerce, paragraphs 30–32).

Definition of "signatory", "Person"

101. Consistent with the approach taken in the UNCITRAL Model Law on Electronic Commerce, any reference in the new Model Law to a "person"

should be understood as covering all types of persons or entities, whether physical, corporate or other legal persons (A/CN.9/483, paragraph 86).

"On behalf of the person it represents"

102. The analogy to handwritten signatures may not always be suitable for taking advantage of the possibilities offered by modern technology. In a paper-based environment, for instance, legal entities cannot strictly speaking be signatories of documents drawn up on their behalf, because only natural persons can produce authentic handwritten signatures. Electronic signatures, however, can be conceived so as to be attributable to companies or other legal entities (including governmental and other public authorities), and there may be situations where the identity of the person who actually generates the signature, where human action is required, is not relevant for the purposes for which the signature was created (A/CN.9/483, paragraph 85).

103. Nevertheless, under the Model Law, the notion of "signatory" cannot be severed from the person or entity that actually generated the electronic signature, since a number of specific obligations of the signatory under the Model Law are logically linked to actual control over the signature creation data. However, in order to cover situations where the signatory would be acting in representation of another person, the phrase "or on behalf of the person it represents" has been retained in the definition of "signatory". The extent to which a person would be bound by an electronic signature generated "on its behalf" is a matter to be settled in accordance with the law governing, as appropriate, the legal relationship between the signatory and the person on whose behalf the electronic signature is generated, on the one hand, and the relying party, on the other hand. That matter, as well as other matters pertaining to the underlying transaction, including issues of agency and other questions as to who bears the ultimate liability for failure by the signatory to comply with its obligations under article 8 (whether the signatory or the person represented by the signatory) are outside the scope of the Model Law (A/CN.9/483, paragraphs 86 and 87).

Definition of "certification service provider"

104. As a minimum, the certification service provider as defined for the purposes of the Model Law would have to provide certification services, possibly together with other services (A/CN.9/483, paragraph 100).

105. No distinction has been drawn in the Model Law between situations where a certification service provider engages in the provision of certification services as its main activity or as an ancillary business, on a habitual or an occasional basis, directly or through a subcontractor. The definition covers all entities that provide certification services within the scope of the Model Law, that is, "in the context of commercial activities". However, in view of

that limitation in the scope of application of the Model Law, entities that issued certificates for internal purposes and not for commercial purposes would not fall under the category "certification service providers" as defined in article 2 (A/CN.9/483, paragraphs 94–99).

Definition of "relying party"

106. The definition of "relying party" is intended to ensure symmetry in the definition of the various parties involved in the operation of electronic signature schemes under the Model Law (A/CN.9/483, paragraph 107). For the purposes of that definition, "act" should be interpreted broadly to cover not only a positive action but also an omission (A/CN.9/483, paragraph 108).

References to UNCITRAL documents

Official Records of the General Assembly, Fifty-sixth Session, Supplement Number 17 (A/56/17), paragraphs 205–207, 243–251, and 284; A/CN.9/493, annex, paragraphs 93–106; A/CN.9/484, paragraphs 56 and 57;

A/CN.9/WG.IV/WP.88, annex, paragraphs 92–105; A/CN.9/483, paragraphs 59–109;

A/CN.9/WG.IV/WP.84, paragraphs 23–36; A/CN.9/465, paragraph 12;

A/CN.9/WG.IV/WP.82, paragraphs 22–33; A/CN.9/457, paragraphs 22–47, 66, 67, 89, and 109;

A/CN.9/WG.IV/WP.80, paragraphs 7–10;

A/CN.9/WG.IV/WP.79, paragraph 21; A/CN.9/454, paragraph 20;

A/CN.9/WG.IV/WP.76, paragraphs 16–20;

A/CN.9/446, paragraphs 27–46 (draft article 1), 62–70 (draft article 4), 113–131 (draft article 8) and 132 and 133 (draft article 9);

A/CN.9/WG.IV/WP.73, paragraphs 16–27, 37, 38, 50–57, and 58–60; A/CN.9/437, paragraphs 29–50 and 90–113 (draft articles A, B, and C); and

A/CN.9/WG.IV/WP.71, paragraphs 52–60.

Article 3. Equal treatment of signature technologies

Nothing in this Law, except article 5, shall be applied so as to exclude, restrict, or deprive of legal effect any method of creating an electronic signature that satisfies the requirements referred to in article 6, paragraph 1, or otherwise meets the requirements of applicable law.

Neutrality as to technology

107. Article 3 embodies the fundamental principle that no method of electronic signature should be discriminated against, that is, that all technologies would be given the same opportunity to satisfy the requirements of article 6.

As a result, there should be no disparity of treatment between electronically signed messages and paper documents bearing handwritten signatures or between various types of electronically signed messages, provided that they meet the basic requirements set forth in article 6, paragraph 1, of the Model Law or any other requirement set forth in applicable law. Such requirements might, for example, prescribe the use of a specifically designated signature technique in certain identified situations or might otherwise set a standard that might be higher or lower than that set forth in article 7 of the UNCITRAL Model Law on Electronic Commerce (and article 6 of the Model Law). The fundamental principle of non-discrimination is intended to find general application. It should be noted, however, that such a principle is not intended to affect the freedom of contract recognized under article 5. As between themselves and to the extent permitted by law, the parties should thus remain free to exclude by agreement the use of certain electronic signature techniques. By stating that "nothing in this Law shall be applied so as to exclude, restrict or deprive of legal effect any method of creating an electronic signature", article 3 merely indicates that the form in which a certain electronic signature is applied cannot be used as the only reason for which that signature would be denied legal effectiveness. However, article 3 should not be misinterpreted as establishing the legal validity of any given signature technique or of any electronically signed information.

References to UNCITRAL documents

Official Records of the General Assembly, Fifty-sixth Session,

Supplement Number 17 (A/56/17), paragraphs 252, 253, and 284; A/CN.9/493, annex, paragraph 107;

A/CN.9/WG.IV/WP.88, annex, paragraph 106; A/CN.9/467, paragraphs 25–32;

A/CN.9/WG.IV/WP.84, paragraph 37; A/CN.9/465, paragraphs 43–48;

A/CN.9/WG.IV/WP.82, paragraph 34; A/CN.9/457, paragraphs 53–64.

Article 4. Interpretation

1. In the interpretation of this Law, regard is to be had to its international origin and to the need to promote uniformity in its application and the observance of good faith.

2. Questions concerning matters governed by this Law which are not expressly settled in it are to be settled in conformity with the general principles on which this Law is based.

Source

108. Article 4 is inspired by article 7 of the United Nations Convention on Contracts for the International Sale of Goods and reproduced from article 3

of the UNCITRAL Model Law on Electronic Commerce. It is intended to provide guidance for interpretation of the Model Law by arbitral tribunals, courts, and national or local administrative authorities. The expected effect of article 4 is to limit the extent to which a uniform text, once incorporated in local legislation, would be interpreted only by reference to the concepts of local law.

Paragraph 1

109. The purpose of paragraph 1 is to draw the attention of any person that might be called upon to apply the Model Law to the fact that the provisions of the Model Law (or the provisions of the instrument implementing the Model Law), while enacted as part of domestic legislation and therefore domestic in character, should be interpreted with reference to its international origin in order to ensure uniformity in the interpretation of the Model Law in all enacting countries.

Paragraph 2

110. Among the general principles on which the Model Law is based, the following non-exhaustive list may be found applicable: (a) to facilitate electronic commerce among and within nations; (b) to validate transactions entered into by means of new information technologies; (c) to promote and encourage in a technology-neutral way the implementation of new information technologies in general and electronic signatures in particular; (d) to promote the uniformity of law; and (e) to support commercial practice. While the general purpose of the Model Law is to facilitate the use of electronic signatures, it should not be construed in any way as imposing their use.

References to UNCITRAL documents

Official Records of the General Assembly, Fifty-sixth Session, Supplement Number 17 (A/56/17), paragraphs 254, 255, and 284; A/CN.9/493, annex, paragraphs 108–110;

A/CN.9/WG.IV/WP.88, annex, paragraphs 107–109; A/CN.9/467, paragraphs 33–35;

A/CN.9/WG.IV/WP.84, paragraph 38; A/CN.9/465, paragraphs 49 and 50;

A/CN.9/WG.IV/WP.82, paragraph 35.

Article 5. Variation by agreement

The provisions of this Law may be derogated from or their effect may be varied by agreement, unless that agreement would not be valid or effective under applicable law.

Deference to applicable law

111. The decision to undertake the preparation of the Model Law was based on the recognition that, in practice, solutions to the legal difficulties raised by the use of modern means of communication are sought mostly within contracts. The Model Law is thus intended to support the principle of party autonomy. However, applicable law may set limits to the application of that principle. Article 5 should not be misinterpreted as allowing the parties to derogate from mandatory rules, for example, rules adopted for reasons of public policy. Neither should article 5 be misinterpreted as encouraging states to establish mandatory legislation limiting the effect of party autonomy with respect to electronic signatures or otherwise inviting states to restrict the freedom of parties to agree as between themselves on issues of form requirements governing their communications.

112. The principle of party autonomy applies broadly with respect to the provisions of the Model Law, since the Model Law does not contain any mandatory provision. That principle also applies in the context of article 12, paragraph 1. Therefore, although the courts of the enacting state or authorities responsible for the application of the Model Law should not deny or nullify the legal effects of a foreign certificate only on the basis of the place where the certificate is issued, paragraph 1 of article 12 does not limit the freedom of the parties to a commercial transaction to agree on the use of certificates that originate from a particular place (A/CN.9/483, paragraph 112).

Expressed or implied agreement

113. As to the way in which the principle of party autonomy is expressed in article 5, it was generally admitted in the preparation of the Model Law that variation by agreement might be expressed or implied. The wording of article 5 has been kept in line with article 6 of the United Nations Convention on Contracts for the International Sale of Goods (A/CN.9/467, paragraph 38).

Bilateral or multilateral agreement

114. Article 5 is intended to apply not only in the context of relationships between originators and addressees of data messages but also in the context of relationships involving intermediaries. Thus, the provisions of the Model Law could be varied either by bilateral or multilateral agreements between the parties, or by system rules agreed to by the parties. Typically, applicable law would limit party autonomy to rights and obligations arising as between parties so as to avoid any implication as to the rights and obligations of third parties.

References to UNCITRAL documents

Official Records of the General Assembly, Fifty-sixth Session,

Supplement Number 17 (A/56/17), paragraphs 208, 209, 256, 257, and 284;

A/CN.9/493, annex, paragraphs 111–114;

A/CN.9/WG.IV/WP.88, annex, paragraphs 110–113; A/CN.9/467, paragraphs 36–43;

A/CN.9/WG.IV/WP.84, paragraphs 39 and 40; A/CN.9/465, paragraphs 51–61;

A/CN.9/WG.IV/WP.82, paragraphs 36–40; A/CN.9/457, paragraphs 53–64.

Article 6. Compliance with a requirement for a signature

1. Where the law requires a signature of a person, that requirement is met in relation to a data message if an electronic signature is used that is as reliable as was appropriate for the purpose for which the data message was generated or communicated, in the light of all the circumstances, including any relevant agreement.

2. Paragraph 1 applies whether the requirement referred to therein is in the form of an obligation or whether the law simply provides consequences for the absence of a signature.

3. An electronic signature is considered to be reliable for the purpose of satisfying the requirement referred to in paragraph 1 if:

(a) The signature creation data are, within the context in which they are used, linked to the signatory and to no other person;

(b) The signature creation data were, at the time of signing, under the control of the signatory and of no other person;

(c) Any alteration to the electronic signature, made after the time of signing, is detectable; and

(d) Where a purpose of the legal requirement for a signature is to provide assurance as to the integrity of the information to which it relates, any alteration made to that information after the time of signing is detectable.

4. Paragraph 3 does not limit the ability of any person:

(a) To establish in any other way, for the purpose of satisfying the requirement referred to in paragraph 1, the reliability of an electronic signature; or

(b) To adduce evidence of the non-reliability of an electronic signature.

5. The provisions of this article do not apply to the following: [. . .]. Importance of article 6.

115. Article 6 is one of the core provisions of the Model Law. Article 6 is intended to build upon article 7 of the UNCITRAL Model Law on Electronic Commerce and to provide guidance as to how the test of reliability in paragraph 1 (b) of article 7 can be satisfied. In interpreting article 6, it should be borne in mind that the purpose of the provision is to ensure that, where any legal consequence would have flowed from the use of a handwritten signature, the same consequence should flow from the use of a reliable electronic signature.

Paragraphs 1, 2, and 5

116. Paragraphs 1, 2, and 5 of article 6 introduce provisions drawn from article 7, paragraphs (1)(b), (2), and (3) of the UNCITRAL Model Law on Electronic Commerce, respectively. Wording inspired by article 7, paragraph 1(a), of the UNCITRAL Model Law on Electronic Commerce is already included in the definition of "electronic signature" under article 2, subparagraph (a).

Notions of "identity" and "identification"

117. The Working Group agreed that, for the purpose of defining "electronic signature" under the Model Law, the term "identification" could be broader than mere identification of the signatory by name. The concept of identity or identification includes distinguishing him or her, by name or otherwise, from any other person, and may refer to other significant characteristics, such as position or authority, either in combination with a name or without reference to the name. On that basis, it is not necessary to distinguish between identity and other significant characteristics, nor to limit the Model Law to those situations in which only identity certificates that name the signatory are used (A/CN.9/467, paragraphs 56–58).

Effect of the Model Law varying with level of technical reliability

118. In the preparation of the Model Law, the view was expressed that (either through a reference to the notion of "enhanced electronic signature" or through a direct mention of criteria for establishing the technical reliability of a given signature technique) a dual purpose of article 6 should be to establish: (a) that legal effects would result from the application of those electronic signature techniques that were recognized as reliable; and (b), conversely, that no such legal effects would flow from the use of techniques of a lesser reliability. It was generally felt, however, that a more subtle distinction might need to be drawn between the various possible electronic signature techniques, since the Model Law should avoid discriminating against any form of electronic signature, unsophisticated and insecure though it might appear in given circumstances. Therefore, any electronic signature technique applied for the purpose of signing a data message under article 7, paragraph 1 (a), of the UNCITRAL Model Law on Electronic Commerce would be likely to produce legal effects, provided that it was sufficiently reliable in the light of all

the circumstances, including any agreement between the parties. However, under article 7 of the UNCITRAL Model Law on Electronic Commerce, the determination of what constitutes a reliable method of signature, in the light of the circumstances, can be made only by a court or other trier of fact intervening *ex post*, possibly long after the electronic signature has been used. In contrast, the new Model Law is expected to create a benefit in favor of certain techniques, which are recognized as particularly reliable, irrespective of the circumstances in which they are used. That is the purpose of paragraph 3, which is expected to create certainty (through either a presumption or a substantive rule), at or before the time any such technique of electronic signature is used (*ex ante*), that using a recognized technique will result in legal effects equivalent to those of a handwritten signature. Thus, paragraph 3 is an essential provision if the new Model Law is to meet its goal of providing more certainty than readily offered by the UNCITRAL Model Law on Electronic Commerce as to the legal effect to be expected from the use of particularly reliable types of electronic signatures (see A/CN.9/465, paragraph 64).

Presumption or substantive rule

119. In order to provide certainty as to the legal effect resulting from the use of an electronic signature as defined under article 2, paragraph 3 expressly establishes the legal effects that would result from the conjunction of certain technical characteristics of an electronic signature (see A/CN.9/484, paragraph 58). As to how those legal effects would be established, enacting states, depending on their law of civil and commercial procedure, should be free to adopt a presumption or to proceed by way of a direct assertion of the linkage between certain technical characteristics and the legal effect of a signature (see A/CN.9/467, paragraphs 61 and 62).

Intent of signatory

120. A question remains as to whether any legal effect should result from the use of electronic signature techniques that may be made with no clear intent by the signatory of becoming legally bound by approval of the information being electronically signed. In any such circumstance, the second function described in article 7, paragraph (1)(a), of the UNCITRAL Model Law on Electronic Commerce is not fulfilled since there is no "intent of indicating any approval of the information contained in the data message". The approach taken in the Model Law is that the legal consequences of the use of a handwritten signature should be replicated in an electronic environment. Thus, by appending a signature (whether handwritten or electronic) to certain information, the signatory should be presumed to have approved the linking of its identity with that information. Whether such a linking should produce legal effects (contractual or other) would result from the nature of the information being signed, and from any other circumstances, to be assessed according to the law applicable outside the Model Law. In that

context, the Model Law is not intended to interfere with the general law of contracts or obligations (see A/CN.9/465, paragraph 65).

Criteria of technical reliability

121. Subparagraphs (a)–(d) of paragraph 3 are intended to express objective criteria of technical reliability of electronic signatures. Subparagraph (a) focuses on the objective characteristics of the signature creation data, which must be "linked to the signatory and to no other person". From a technical point of view, the signature creation data could be uniquely "linked" to the signatory, without being "unique" in itself. The linkage between the data used for creation of the signature and the signatory is the essential element (A/CN.9/467, paragraph 63). While certain electronic signature creation data may be shared by a variety of users, for example, where several employees would share the use of a corporate signature creation data, that data must be capable of identifying one user unambiguously in the context of each electronic signature.

Sole control of signature creation data by the signatory

122. Subparagraph (b) deals with the circumstances in which the signature creation data are used. At the time they are used, the signature creation data must be under the sole control of the signatory. In relation to the notion of sole control by the signatory, a question is whether the signatory would retain its ability to authorize another person to use the signature creation data on its behalf. Such a situation might arise where the signature creation data are used in the corporate context where the corporate entity would be the signatory but would require a number of persons to be able to sign on its behalf (A/CN.9/467, paragraph 66). Another example may be found in business applications, such as the one where signature creation data exist on a network and are capable of being used by a number of people. In that situation, the network would presumably relate to a particular entity which would be the signatory and maintain control over the signature creation data. If that was not the case, and the signature creation data were widely available, they should not be covered by the Model Law (A/CN.9/467, paragraph 67). Where a single key is operated by more than one person in the context of a "split-key" or other "shared-secret" scheme, reference to "the signatory" means a reference to those persons jointly (A/CN.9/483, paragraph 152).

Agency

123. Subparagraphs (a) and (b) converge to ensure that the signature creation data are capable of being used by only one person at any given time, principally the time of signing, and not by some other person as well (see above, paragraph 103). The question of agency or authorized use of the signature creation data is addressed in the definition of "signatory" (A/CN.9/467, paragraph 68).

Integrity

124. Subparagraphs (c) and (d) deal with the issues of integrity of the electronic signature and integrity of the information being signed electronically. It would have been possible to combine the two provisions to emphasize the notion that, where a signature is attached to a document, the integrity of the document and the integrity of the signature are so closely related that it is difficult to conceive of one without the other. However, it was decided that the Model Law should follow the distinction drawn in the UNCITRAL Model Law on Electronic Commerce between articles 7 and 8. Although some technologies provide both authentication (article 7 of the UNCITRAL Model Law on Electronic Commerce) and integrity (article 8 of the UNCITRAL Model Law on Electronic Commerce), those concepts can be seen as distinct legal concepts and treated as such. Since a handwritten signature provides neither a guarantee of the integrity of the document to which it is attached nor a guarantee that any change made to the document would be detectable, the functional equivalence approach requires that those concepts should not be dealt with in a single provision. The purpose of paragraph 3 (c) is to set forth the criterion to be met in order to demonstrate that a particular method of electronic signature is reliable enough to satisfy a requirement of law for a signature. That requirement of law could be met without having to demonstrate the integrity of the entire document (see A/CN.9/467, paragraphs 72–80).

125. Subparagraph (d) is intended primarily for use in those countries where existing legal rules governing the use of handwritten signatures could not accommodate a distinction between integrity of the signature and integrity of the information being signed. In other countries, subparagraph (d) might create a signature that would be more reliable than a handwritten signature and thus go beyond the concept of functional equivalent to a signature. In certain jurisdictions, the effect of subparagraph (d) may be to create a functional equivalent to an original document (see A/CN.9/484, paragraph 62).

Electronic signature of portion of a message

126. In subparagraph (d), the necessary linkage between the signature and the information being signed is expressed so as to avoid the implication that the electronic signature could apply only to the full contents of a data message. In fact, the information being signed, in many instances, will be only a portion of the information contained in the data message. For example, an electronic signature may relate only to information appended to the message for transmission purposes.

Variation by agreement

127. Paragraph 3 is not intended to limit the application of article 5 and of any applicable law recognizing the freedom of the parties to stipulate in any

relevant agreement that a given signature technique would be treated among themselves as a reliable equivalent of a handwritten signature.

128. Paragraph 4(a) is intended to provide a legal basis for the commercial practice under which many commercial parties would regulate by contract their relationships regarding the use of electronic signatures (see A/CN.9/484, paragraph 63).

Possibility to adduce evidence of the non-reliability of an electronic signature

129. Paragraph 4(b) is intended to make it clear that the Model Law does not limit any possibility that may exist to rebut the presumption contemplated in paragraph 3 (see A/CN.9/484, paragraph 63).

Exclusions from the scope of article 6

130. The principle embodied in paragraph 5 is that an enacting state may exclude from the application of article 6 certain situations to be specified in the legislation enacting the Model Law. An enacting state may wish to exclude specifically certain types of situations, depending in particular on the purpose for which a formal requirement for a handwritten signature has been established. A specific exclusion might be considered, for example, in the context of formalities required pursuant to international treaty obligations of the enacting state and other kinds of situations and areas of law that are beyond the power of the enacting state to change by means of a statute.

131. Paragraph 5 was included with a view to enhancing the acceptability of the Model Law. It recognizes that the matter of specifying exclusions should be left to enacting states, an approach that would take better account of differences in national circumstances. However, it should be noted that the objectives of the Model Law would not be achieved if paragraph 5 were used to establish blanket exceptions, and the opportunity provided by paragraph 5 in that respect should be avoided. Numerous exclusions from the scope of article 6 would raise needless obstacles to the development of electronic signatures, since what the Model Law contains are very fundamental principles and approaches that are expected to find general application (see A/CN.9/484, paragraph 63).

References to UNCITRAL documents

Official Records of the General Assembly, Fifty-sixth Session,

Supplement Number 17 (A/56/17), paragraphs 258, 259, and 284; A/CN.9/493, annex, paragraphs 115–131; A/CN.9/484, paragraphs 58–63;

A/CN.9/WG.IV/WP.88, annex, paragraphs 114–126; A/CN.9/467, paragraphs 44–87;

A/CN.9/WG.IV/WP.84, paragraphs 41–47; A/CN.9/465, paragraphs 62–82;

A/CN.9/WG.IV/WP.82, paragraphs 42–44; A/CN.9/457, paragraphs 48–52;

A/CN.9/WG.IV/WP.80, paragraphs 11 and 12.

Article 7. Satisfaction of article 6

1. [Any person, organ, or authority, whether public or private, specified by the enacting state as competent] may determine which electronic signatures satisfy the provisions of article 6 of this Law.

2. Any determination made under paragraph 1 shall be consistent with recognized international standards.

3. Nothing in this article affects the operation of the rules of private international law.

Predetermination of status of electronic signature

132. Article 7 describes the role played by the enacting state in establishing or recognizing any entity that might validate the use of electronic signatures or otherwise certify their quality. Like article 6, article 7 is based on the idea that what is required to facilitate the development of electronic commerce is certainty and predictability at the time when commercial parties make use of electronic signature techniques, not at the time when there is a dispute before a court. Where a particular signature technique can satisfy requirements for a high degree of reliability and security, there should be a means for assessing the technical aspects of reliability and security and for according the signature technique some form of recognition.

Purpose of article 7

133. The purpose of article 7 is to make it clear that an enacting state may designate an organ or authority that will have the power to make determinations as to what specific technologies may benefit from the rule established under article 6. Article 7 is not an enabling provision that could, or would, necessarily be enacted by states in its present form. However, it is intended to convey a clear message that certainty and predictability can be achieved by determining which electronic signature techniques satisfy the reliability criteria of article 6, provided that such determination is made in accordance with international standards. Article 7 should not be interpreted in a manner that would either prescribe mandatory legal effects for the use of certain types of signature techniques, or would restrict the use of technology to those techniques determined to satisfy the reliability requirements of article 6. Parties should be free, for example, to use techniques that had not been determined to satisfy article 6, if that was what they had agreed to do. They also should be free to show, before a court or arbitral tribunal, that the method of signature they had chosen to use did satisfy the requirements of article 6, even though not the subject of a prior determination to that effect.

Paragraph 1

134. Paragraph 1 makes it clear that any entity that might validate the use of electronic signatures or otherwise certify their quality would not have to be established as a state authority. Paragraph 1 should not be read as making a recommendation to states as to the only means of achieving recognition of signature technologies, but rather as indicating the limitations that should apply if states wished to adopt such an approach.

Paragraph 2

135. With respect to paragraph 2, the notion of "standard" should not be limited to standards developed, for example, by the International Organization for Standardization (ISO) and the Internet Engineering Task Force (IETF), or to other technical standards. The word "standards" should be interpreted in a broad sense, which would include industry practices and trade usages, "voluntary standards" (as described in paragraph 69, above), texts emanating from such international organizations as the International Chamber of Commerce, the regional accreditation bodies operating under the aegis of ISO (see A/CN.9/484, paragraph 66), the World Wide Web Consortium (W3C), regional standardization bodies,[27] as well as the work of UNCITRAL itself (including this Model Law and the UNCITRAL Model Law on Electronic Commerce). The possible lack of relevant standards should not prevent the competent persons or authorities from making the determination referred to in paragraph 1. As to the reference to "recognized" standards, a question might be raised as to what constitutes "recognition" and of whom such recognition is required (see A/CN.9/465, paragraph 94). That question is discussed under article 12 (see below, paragraph 159).

Paragraph 3

136. Paragraph 3 is intended to make it abundantly clear that the purpose of article 7 is not to interfere with the normal operation of the rules of private international law (see A/CN.9/467, paragraph 94). In the absence of such a provision, article 7 might be misinterpreted as encouraging enacting states to discriminate against foreign electronic signatures on the basis of non-compliance with the rules set forth by the relevant person or authority under paragraph 1.

References to UNCITRAL documents

Official Records of the General Assembly, Fifty-sixth Session,

Supplement Number 17 (A/56/17), paragraphs 210, 211, 260, 261, and 284;

---

27 *Official Records of the General Assembly*, Fifty-sixth Session, Supplement Number 17 (A/56/17), paragraphs 275–277.

A/CN.9/493, annex, paragraphs 132–136; A/CN.9/484, paragraphs 64–66;

A/CN.9/WG.IV/WP.88, paragraphs 127–131; A/CN.9/467, paragraphs 90–95;

A/CN.9/WG.IV/WP.84, paragraphs 49–51; A/CN.9/465, paragraphs 90–98;

A/CN.9/WG.IV/WP.82, paragraph 46; A/CN.9/457, paragraphs 48–52;

A/CN.9/WG.IV/WP.80, paragraph 15.

Article 8. Conduct of the signatory

1. Where signature creation data can be used to create a signature that has legal effect, each signatory shall:

(a) Exercise reasonable care to avoid unauthorized use of its signature creation data;

(b) Without undue delay, utilize means made available by the certification service provider pursuant to article 9 of this Law, or otherwise use reasonable efforts, to notify any person that may reasonably be expected by the signatory to rely on or to provide services in support of the electronic signature if:

    (i) The signatory knows that the signature creation data have been compromised; or

    (ii) The circumstances known to the signatory give rise to a substantial risk that the signature creation data may have been compromised;

(c) Where a certificate is used to support the electronic signature, exercise reasonable care to ensure the accuracy and completeness of all material representations made by the signatory that are relevant to the certificate throughout its life cycle or that are to be included in the certificate.

2. A signatory shall bear the legal consequences of its failure to satisfy the requirements of paragraph 1.

Title

137. Article 8 (and articles 9 and 11) had been initially planned to contain rules regarding the obligations and liabilities of the various parties involved (the signatory, the relying party, and any certification services provider). However, the rapid changes affecting the technical and commercial aspects of electronic commerce, together with the role currently played by self-regulation in the field of electronic commerce in certain countries, made it difficult to achieve consensus as to the contents of such rules. The articles have been drafted so as to embody a minimal "code of conduct" of the various parties. As   indicated in the context of article 9 with respect to

certification service providers (see below, paragraph 144), the Model Law does not require from a signatory a degree of diligence or trustworthiness that bears no reasonable relationship to the purposes for which the electronic signature or certificate is used (see A/CN.9/484, paragraph 67). The Model Law thus favors a solution that links the obligations set forth in both articles 8 and 9 to the production of legally significant electronic signatures (A/CN.9/483, paragraph 117). The principle of the signatory's liability for failure to comply with paragraph 1 is set forth in paragraph 2; the extent of such liability for failure to abide by that code of conduct is left to the law applicable outside the Model Law (see below, paragraph 141).

Paragraph 1

138. Subparagraphs (a) and (b) apply generally to all electronic signatures, while subparagraph (c) applies only to those electronic signatures that are supported by a certificate. The obligation in paragraph 1(a), in particular, to exercise reasonable care to prevent unauthorized use of signature creation data, constitutes a basic obligation that is, for example, generally contained in agreements concerning the use of credit cards. Under the policy adopted in paragraph 1, such an obligation also should apply to any electronic signature creation data that could be used for the purpose of expressing legally significant intent. However, the provision for variation by agreement in article 5 allows the standards set in article 8 to be varied in areas where they would be thought to be inappropriate, or to lead to unintended consequences. When interpreting the notion of "reasonable care", relevant practices, if any, need to be taken into account. "Reasonable care" under the Model Law also should be interpreted with due regard being given to its international origin, as indicated in article 4.[28]

139. Paragraph 1(b) establishes a flexible requirement to use "reasonable efforts" to notify any person that might be expected to rely on the electronic signature in cases where the electronic signature appeared to have been compromised. In view of the fact that it might be impossible for the signatory to track down every person that might rely on the electronic signature, it would be excessively burdensome to charge the signatory with the obligation to achieve the result of actually notifying every person that might conceivably rely on the signature. The notion of "reasonable efforts" should be interpreted in the light of the general principle of good faith expressed in article 4, paragraph 1.[29] The reference to the "means made available by the certification service provider" reflects certain practical instances where means are

---

28 *Official Records of the General Assembly*, Fifty-sixth Session, Supplement Number 17 (A/56/17), paragraph 214.

29 *Official Records of the General Assembly*, Fifty-sixth Session, Supplement Number 17 (A/56/17), paragraph 216.

placed at the disposal of a signatory by a certification service provider, for example, in the context of procedures to be applied where it appears that the electronic signature has been compromised. Such procedures can generally not be varied by the signatory. The effect of such a reference is to provide the signatory with a "safe harbor" provision that enables a signatory to demonstrate that it has been sufficiently diligent in attempting to notify potentially relying parties if the signatory has used the means placed at its disposal.[30] With respect to such potentially relying parties, paragraph 1 (b) refers to the notion of "person who may reasonably be expected by the signatory to rely on or to provide services in support of the electronic signature". Depending on the technology being used, such a "relying party" may be not only a person that might seek to rely on the signature, but also a person such as a certification service provider, a certificate revocation service provider, and any other interested party.

140. Paragraph 1(c) applies where a certificate is used to support the signature creation data. The "life cycle" of the certificate is intended to be interpreted broadly as covering the period starting with the application for the certificate or the creation of the certificate and ending with the expiry or revocation of the certificate.

Paragraph 2

141. With respect to the consequences that might flow from failure by the signatory to comply with the requirements set forth in paragraph 1, paragraph 2 does not specify either the consequences or the limits of any liability, both of which are left to national law. However, even though it leaves the liability or other consequences up to national law, paragraph 2 serves to give a clear signal to enacting states that consequences should attach to a failure to satisfy the obligations set forth in paragraph 1. Paragraph 2 is based on the conclusion reached during the preparation of the Model Law that it might be difficult to achieve consensus in the form of a uniform rule as to what consequences might flow from the liability of the signatory. Depending on the context in which the electronic signature is used, such consequences might range, under existing law, from the signatory being bound by the contents of the message to liability for damages. Other possible consequences would not necessarily involve liability but might include, for example, the faulty party being stopped from denying the binding effect of the electronic signature. To encompass such additional consequences, and also to avoid creating the mistaken impression that the Model Law was intended to establish a principle of strict liability, the notion of liability has not been expressly mentioned in paragraph 2. Paragraph 2 merely establishes the principle that the signatory

---

30   *Official Records of the General Assembly,* Fifty-sixth Session, Supplement Number 17
      (A/56/17), paragraph 217.

should bear the legal consequences of its failure to comply with the requirements of paragraph 1, and leaves the entire issue of the legal consequences to be drawn from such failure to the law applicable outside the Model Law in each enacting state.[31]

References to UNCITRAL documents

Official Records of the General Assembly, Fifty-sixth Session, Supplement Number 17 (A/56/17), paragraphs 212, 222, 262, 263, and 284; A/CN.9/493, annex, paragraphs 137–141; A/CN.9/484, paragraphs 67–69;

A/CN.9/WG.IV/WP.88, annex, paragraphs 132–136; A/CN.9/467, paragraphs 96–104;

A/CN.9/WG.IV/WP.84, paragraphs 52 and 53; A/CN.9/465, paragraphs 99–108;

A/CN.9/WG.IV/WP.82, paragraphs 50–55; A/CN.9/457, paragraphs 65–98;

A/CN.9/WG.IV/WP.80, paragraphs 18 and 19.

Article 9. Conduct of the certification service provider

1. Where a certification service provider provides services to support an electronic signature that may be used for legal effect as a signature, that certification service provider shall:

(a) Act in accordance with representations made by it with respect to its policies and practices;

(b) Exercise reasonable care to ensure the accuracy and completeness of all material representations made by it that are relevant to the certificate throughout its life cycle or that are included in the certificate;

(c) Provide reasonably accessible means that enable a relying party to ascertain from the certificate:

   (i) The identity of the certification service provider;

   (ii) That the signatory that is identified in the certificate had control of the signature creation data at the time when the certificate was issued;

   (iii) That signature creation data were valid at or before the time when the certificate was issued;

(d) Provide reasonably accessible means that enable a relying party to ascertain, where relevant, from the certificate or otherwise:

---

31 *Official Records of the General Assembly*, Fifty-sixth Session, Supplement Number 17 (A/56/17), paragraphs 219–221.

(i) The method used to identify the signatory;

(ii) Any limitation on the purpose or value for which the signature creation data or the certificate may be used;

(iii) That the signature creation data are valid and have not been compromised;

(iv) Any limitation on the scope or extent of liability stipulated by the certification service provider;

(v) Whether means exist for the signatory to give notice pursuant to article 8, paragraph 1(b), of this Law;

(vi) Whether a timely revocation service is offered;

(e) Where services under subparagraph (d)(v) are offered, provide a means for a signatory to give notice pursuant to article 8, paragraph 1(b), of this Law and, where services under subparagraph (d)(vi) are offered, ensure the availability of a timely revocation service;

(f) Utilize trustworthy systems, procedures, and human resources in performing its services.

2. A certification service provider shall bear the legal consequences of its failure to satisfy the requirements of paragraph 1.

Paragraph 1

142. Subparagraph (a) expresses the basic rule that a certification service provider should adhere to the representations and commitments made by that supplier, for example, in a certification practices statement or in any other type of policy statement.

143. Subparagraph (c) defines the essential contents and the core effect of any certificate under the Model Law. It is important to note that, in the case of digital signatures, it must also be possible to ascertain the association of the signatory with the public key, as well as with the private key (A/CN.9/484, paragraph 71). Subparagraph (d) lists additional elements to be included in the certificate or otherwise made available or accessible to the relying party, where they would be relevant to a particular certificate. Subparagraph (e) is not intended to apply to certificates such as transactional certificates, which are one-time certificates, or low-cost certificates for low-risk applications, both of which might not be subject to revocation.

144. It may be thought that the duties and obligations provided in article 9 can reasonably be expected to be complied with by any certification service provider and not only those who issue "high value" certificates. However, the Model Law does not require from a signatory or a certification service provider a degree of diligence or trustworthiness that bears no reasonable relationship to the purposes for which the electronic signature or certificate is

used (see above, paragraph 137). The Model Law thus favors a solution that links the obligations set forth in both articles 8 and 9 to the production of legally significant electronic signatures (A/CN.9/483, paragraph 117). By limiting the scope of article 9 to the broad range of situations where certification services are provided to support an electronic signature that may be used for legal effect as a signature, the Model Law does not intend to create new types of legal effects for signatures (A/CN.9/483, paragraph 119).

Paragraph 2

145. Parallel to paragraph 2 of article 8, paragraph 2 leaves it up to applicable national law to determine the legal consequences of failure to comply with the requirements set forth in paragraph 1 (see above, paragraph 141, and A/56/17, paragraph 230). Subject to applicable rules of national law, paragraph 2 is not intended by its authors to be interpreted as a rule of absolute or strict liability. It was not foreseen that the effect of paragraph 2 would be to exclude the possibility for the certification service provider to prove, for example, the absence of fault or contributory fault.

146. Early drafts of article 9 contained an additional paragraph, which addressed the consequences of liability as set forth in paragraph 2. In the preparation of the Model Law, it was observed that the question of the liability of certification service providers would not be sufficiently addressed by adopting a single provision along the lines of paragraph 2. While paragraph 2 may state an appropriate principle for application to signatories, it may not be sufficient for addressing the professional and commercial activities covered by article 9. One possible way of compensating such insufficiency would have been to list in the text of the Model Law the factors to be taken into account in assessing any loss resulting from failure by the certification service provider to satisfy the requirements of paragraph 1. It was finally decided that a non-exhaustive list of indicative factors should be contained in this Guide. In assessing the liability of the certification service provider, the following factors should be taken into account, *inter alia*: (a) the cost of obtaining the certificate; (b) the nature of the information being certified; (c) the existence and extent of any limitation on the purpose for which the certificate may be used; (d) the existence of any statement limiting the scope or extent of the liability of the certification service provider; and (e) any contributory conduct by the relying party. In the preparation of the Model Law, it was generally agreed that, in determining the recoverable loss in the enacting state, weight should be given to the rules governing limitation of liability in the state where the certification service provider was established or in any other state whose law would be applicable under the relevant conflict-of-laws rule (A/CN.9/484, paragraph 74).

References to UNCITRAL documents

Official Records of the General Assembly, Fifty-sixth Session, Supplement Number 17 (A/56/17), paragraphs 223–230, 264, 265, and 284;

A/CN.9/493, annex, paragraphs 142–146;

A/CN.9/484, paragraphs 70–74;

A/CN.9/WG.IV/WP.88, annex, paragraphs 137–141; A/CN.9/483, paragraphs 114–127;

A/CN.9/467, paragraphs 105–129;

A/CN.9/WG.IV/WP.84, paragraphs 54–60; A/CN.9/465, paragraphs 123–142 (draft article 12);

A/CN.9/WG.IV/WP.82, paragraphs 59–68 (draft article 12); A/CN.9/457, paragraphs 108–119;

A/CN.9/WG.IV/WP.80, paragraphs 22–24.

Article 10. Trustworthiness

For the purposes of article 9, paragraph 1(f), of this Law in determining whether, or to what extent, any systems, procedures, and human resources utilized by a certification service provider are trustworthy, regard may be had to the following factors:

(a) Financial and human resources, including existence of assets;

(b) Quality of hardware and software systems;

(c) Procedures for processing of certificates and applications for certificates and retention of records;

(d) Availability of information to signatories identified in certificates and to potential relying parties;

(e) Regularity and extent of audit by an independent body;

(f) The existence of a declaration by the state, an accreditation body, or the certification service provider regarding compliance with or existence of the foregoing; or

(g) Any other relevant factor.

Flexibility of the notion of "trustworthiness"

147. Article 10 was initially drafted as part of article 9. Although that part later became a separate article, it is mainly intended to assist with the interpretation of the notion of "trustworthy systems, procedures and human resources" in article 9, paragraph 1(f). Article 10 is set forth as a non-exhaustive list of factors to be taken into account in determining trustworthiness. That list is intended to provide a flexible notion of trustworthiness, which could vary in content depending upon what is expected of the certificate in the context in which it is created.

References to UNCITRAL documents

Official Records of the General Assembly, Fifty-sixth Session, Supplement Number 17 (A/56/17), paragraphs 231–234, 266, 267, and 284;

A/CN.9/493, annex, paragraph 147;

A/CN.9/WG.IV/WP.88, annex, paragraph 142; A/CN.9/483, paragraphs 128–133; A/CN.9/467, paragraphs 114–119.

Article 11. Conduct of the relying party

A relying party shall bear the legal consequences of its failure:

 (a) To take reasonable steps to verify the reliability of an electronic signature; or

 (b) Where an electronic signature is supported by a certificate, to take reasonable steps:

   (i) To verify the validity, suspension, or revocation of the certificate; and

   (ii) To observe any limitation with respect to the certificate.

Reasonableness of reliance

148. Article 11 reflects the idea that a party that intends to rely on an electronic signature should bear in mind the question whether and to what extent such reliance is reasonable in the light of the circumstances. It is not intended to deal with the issue of the validity of an electronic signature, which is addressed under article 6 and should not depend upon the conduct of the relying party. The issue of the validity of an electronic signature should be kept separate from the issue of whether it is reasonable for a relying party to rely on a signature that does not meet the standard set forth in article 6.

Consumer issues

149. While article 11 might place a burden on relying parties, in particular where such parties are consumers, it may be recalled that the Model Law is not intended to overrule any rule governing the protection of consumers. However, the Model Law might play a useful role in educating all the parties involved, including relying parties, as to the standard of reasonable conduct to be met with respect to electronic signatures. In addition, establishing a standard of conduct under which the relying party should verify the reliability of the signature through readily accessible means may be seen as essential to the development of any public-key infrastructure system.

Notion of "relying party"

150. Consistent with its definition, the notion of "relying party" is intended to cover any party that might rely on an electronic signature. Depending on the circumstances, a "relying party" might thus be any person having or not a

contractual relationship with the signatory or the certification services provider. It is even conceivable that the certification services provider or the signatory might itself become a "relying party". However, that broad notion of "relying party" should not result in the subscriber of a certificate being placed under an obligation to verify the validity of the certificate it purchases from the certification services provider.

Failure to comply with requirements of article 11

151. As to the possible impact of establishing as a general obligation that the relying party should verify the validity of the electronic signature or certificate, a question arises where the relying party fails to comply with the requirements of article 11. Should it fail to comply with those requirements, the relying party should not be precluded from availing itself of the signature or certificate if reasonable verification would not have revealed that the signature or certificate was invalid. The requirements of article 11 are not intended to require the observation of limitations, or verification of information, not readily accessible to the relying party. Such a situation may need to be dealt with by the law applicable outside the Model Law. More generally, the consequences of failure by the relying party to comply with the requirements of article 11 are governed by the law applicable outside the Model Law (see A/CN.9/484, paragraph 75). In that respect, parallel wordings have been adopted in article 11 and in paragraph 2 of articles 8 and 9. During the preparation of the Model Law, it was suggested that a distinction should be made between the legal regime applicable to the signatory and the certification service provider, on the one hand (both of whom should be faced with obligations regarding their conduct in the context of the electronic signature process), and the regime applicable to the relying party, on the other hand (for whom the Model Law might appropriately establish rules of conduct but which should not be faced with the same level of obligations as the other two parties). However, the prevailing view was that the question of establishing such a distinction should be left to the law applicable outside the Model Law.[32]

References to UNCITRAL documents

Official Records of the General Assembly, Fifty-sixth Session, Supplement Number 17 (A/56/17), paragraphs 235, 236, 268, 269, and 284; A/CN.9/493, annex, paragraphs 148–151;

A/CN.9/484, paragraph 75;

A/CN.9/WG.IV/WP.88, annex, paragraphs 143–146; A/CN.9/467, paragraphs 130–143;

---

32   Official Records of the General Assembly, Fifty-sixth Session, Supplement Number 17 (A/56/17), paragraphs 220 and 221.

A/CN.9/WG.IV/WP.84, paragraphs 61–63; A/CN.9/465, paragraphs 109–122 (draft articles 10 and 11);

A/CN.9/WG.IV/WP.82, paragraphs 56–58 (draft articles 10 and 11); A/CN.9/457, paragraphs 99–107;

A/CN.9/WG.IV/WP.80, paragraphs 20 and 21.

Article 12. Recognition of foreign certificates and electronic signatures

1. In determining whether, or to what extent, a certificate or an electronic signature is legally effective, no regard shall be had:

   (a) To the geographic location where the certificate is issued or the electronic signature created or used; or

   (b) To the geographic location of the place of business of the issuer or signatory.

2. A certificate issued outside [the enacting state] shall have the same legal effect in [the enacting state] as a certificate issued in [the enacting state] if it offers a substantially equivalent level of reliability.

3. An electronic signature created or used outside [the enacting state] shall have the same legal effect in [the enacting state] as an electronic signature created or used in [the enacting state] if it offers a substantially equivalent level of reliability.

4. In determining whether a certificate or an electronic signature offers a substantially equivalent level of reliability for the purposes of paragraph 2 or 3, regard shall be had to recognized international standards and to any other relevant factors.

5. Where, notwithstanding paragraphs 2, 3, and 4, parties agree, as between themselves, to the use of certain types of electronic signatures or certificates, that agreement shall be recognized as sufficient for the purposes of cross-border recognition, unless that agreement would not be valid or effective under applicable law.

General rule of non-discrimination

152. Paragraph 1 is intended to reflect the basic principle that the place of origin, in and of itself, should in no way be a factor determining whether and to what extent foreign certificates or electronic signatures should be recognized as capable of being legally effective. Determination of whether, or the extent to which, a certificate or an electronic signature is capable of being legally effective should not depend on the place where the certificate or the electronic signature was issued (see A/CN.9/483, paragraph 27), but on its technical reliability.

"Substantially equivalent level of reliability"

153. The purpose of paragraph 2 is to provide the general criterion for the cross-border recognition of certificates without which suppliers of certification services might face the unreasonable burden of having to obtain licenses in multiple jurisdictions. However, paragraph 2 is not intended to place foreign suppliers of certification services in a better position than domestic ones.[33] For that purpose, paragraph 2 establishes a threshold for technical equivalence of foreign certificates based on testing their reliability against the reliability requirements established by the enacting state pursuant to the Model Law (see A/CN.9/483, paragraph 31). That criterion is to apply regardless of the nature of the certification scheme obtaining in the jurisdiction from which the certificate or signature emanated (A/CN.9/483, paragraph 29).

Level of reliability varying with the jurisdiction

154. Through a reference to the central notion of a "substantially equivalent level of reliability", paragraph 2 acknowledges that there might be significant variance between the requirements of individual jurisdictions. The requirement of equivalence, as used in paragraph 2, does not mean that the level of reliability of a foreign certificate should be exactly identical with that of a domestic certificate (A/CN.9/483, paragraph 32).

Level of reliability varying within a jurisdiction

155. In addition, it should be noted that, in practice, suppliers of certification services issue certificates with various levels of reliability, according to the purposes for which the certificates are intended to be used by their customers. Depending on their respective level of reliability, certificates and electronic signatures may produce varying legal effects, both domestically and abroad. For example, in certain countries, even certificates that are sometimes referred to as "low-level" or "low-value" certificates might, in certain circumstances (e.g., where parties have agreed contractually to use such instruments), produce legal effect (see A/CN.9/ 484, paragraph 77). Therefore, in applying the notion of equivalence as used in paragraph 2, it should be borne in mind that the equivalence to be established is between functionally comparable certificates. However, no attempt has been made in the Model Law to establish a correspondence between certificates of different types issued by different suppliers of certification services in different jurisdictions. The Model Law has been drafted so as to contemplate a possible hierarchy of different types of certificate. In practice, a court or arbitral tribunal called upon to decide on the legal effect of a foreign certificate would

---

33   *Official Records of the General Assembly,* Fifty-sixth Session, Supplement Number 17 (A/56/17), paragraph 282.

normally consider each certificate on its own merit and try to equate it with the closest corresponding level in the enacting state (A/CN.9/483, paragraph 33).

Equal treatment of certificates and other types of electronic signatures

156. Paragraph 3 expresses with respect to electronic signatures the same rule as set forth in paragraph 2 regarding certificates (A/CN.9/483, paragraph 41).

Recognizing some legal effect to compliance with the laws of a foreign country

157. Paragraphs 2 and 3 deal exclusively with the cross-border reliability test to be applied when assessing the reliability of a foreign certificate or electronic signature. However, in the preparation of the Model Law, it was borne in mind that enacting states might wish to obviate the need for a reliability test in respect of specific signatures or certificates, when the enacting state was satisfied that the law of the jurisdiction from which the signature or the certificate originated provided an adequate standard of reliability. As to the legal techniques through which advance recognition of the reliability of certificates and signatures complying with the law of a foreign country might be made by an enacting state (e.g., a unilateral declaration or a treaty), the Model Law contains no specific suggestion (A/CN.9/483, paragraphs 39 and 42).

Factors to be considered when assessing the substantial equivalence of foreign certificates and signatures

158. In the preparation of the Model Law, paragraph 4 was initially formulated as a catalogue of factors to be taken into account when determining whether a certificate or an electronic signature offers a substantially equivalent level of reliability for the purposes of paragraph 2 or 3. It was later found that most of these factors were already listed under articles 6, 9, and 10. Restating those factors in the context of article 12 would have been superfluous. Alternatively, cross-referencing, in paragraph 4, the appropriate provisions in the Model Law where the relevant criteria were mentioned, possibly with the addition of other criteria particularly important for crossborder recognition, was found to result in an overly complex formulation (see, in particular, A/CN.9/483, paragraphs 43–49). Paragraph 4 was eventually turned into an unspecific reference to "any relevant factor", among which the factors listed under articles 6, 9, and 10 for the assessment of domestic certificates and electronic signatures are particularly important. In addition, paragraph 4 draws the consequences from the fact that assessing the equivalence of foreign certificates is somewhat different from assessing the trustworthiness of a certification service provider under articles 9 and 10. To that effect, a reference has been added in paragraph 4 to "recognized international standards".

Recognized international standards

159. The notion of "recognized international standard" should be interpreted broadly to cover both international technical and commercial standards (i.e., market-driven standards), standards and norms adopted by governmental or

intergovernmental bodies (A/CN.9/483, paragraph 49), and "voluntary standards" (as described in paragraph 69 above).[34] "Recognized international standard" may be statements of accepted technical, legal or commercial practices, whether developed by the public or private sector (or both), of a normative or interpretative nature, which are generally accepted as applicable internationally. Such standards may be in the form of requirements, recommendations, guidelines, codes of conduct, or statements of either best practices or norms (A/CN.9/483, paragraphs 101–104).

Recognition of agreements between interested parties

160. Paragraph 5 provides for the recognition of agreements between interested parties regarding the use of certain types of electronic signatures or certificates as sufficient grounds for cross-border recognition (as between those parties) of such agreed signatures or certificates (A/CN.9/483, paragraph 54). It should be noted that, consistent with article 5, paragraph 5 is not intended to displace any mandatory law, in particular any mandatory requirement for handwritten signatures that enacting states might wish to maintain in applicable law (A/CN.9/483, paragraph 113). Paragraph 5 is needed to give effect to contractual stipulations under which parties may agree, as between themselves, to recognize the use of certain electronic signatures or certificates (that might be regarded as foreign in some or all of the states where the parties might seek legal recognition of those signatures or certificates), without those signatures or certificates being subject to the substantial-equivalence test set forth in paragraphs 2, 3, and 4. Paragraph 5 does not affect the legal position of third parties (A/CN.9/483, paragraph 56).

References to UNCITRAL documents

Official Records of the General Assembly, Fifty-sixth Session, Supplement Number 17 (A/56/17), paragraphs 237, 270–273 and 284; A/CN.9/493, annex, paragraphs 152–160; A/CN.9/484, paragraphs 76–78;

A/CN.9/WG.IV/WP.88, annex, paragraphs 147–155; A/CN.9/483, paragraphs 25–58 (article 12);

A/CN.9/WG.IV/WP.84, paragraphs 61–68 (draft article 13); A/CN.9/465, paragraphs 21–35;

A/CN.9/WG.IV/WP.82, paragraphs 69–71; A/CN.9/454, paragraph 173;

A/CN.9/446, paragraphs 196–207 (draft article 19);

A/CN.9/WG.IV/WP.73, paragraph 75;

A/CN.9/WG.IV/WP.71, paragraphs 73–75.

---

34 *Official Records of the General Assembly*, Fifty-sixth Session, Supplement Number 17 (A/56/17), paragraph 278.

APPENDIX V

REPORT OF THE UNCITRAL WORKING GROUP ON ELECTRONIC COMMERCE ON THE WORK OF ITS 44TH SESSION (VIENNA, 11– 22 OCTOBER 2004)

ANNEX

DRAFT CONVENTION ON THE USE OF ELECTRONIC COMMUNICATIONS IN INTERNATIONAL CONTRACTS

Chapter I. Sphere of Application

Article 1. Scope of Application

1.   This Convention applies to the use of electronic communications in connection with the formation or performance of a contract between parties whose places of business are in different States.

2.   The fact that the parties have their places of business in different States is to be disregarded whenever this fact does not appear either from the contract or from any dealings between the parties or from information disclosed by the parties at any time before or at the conclusion of the contract.

3.   Neither the nationality of the parties nor the civil or commercial character of the parties or of the contract is to be taken into consideration in determining the application of this Convention.

Article 2. Exclusions

1.   This Convention does not apply to electronic communications relating to any of the following:

 (a) Contracts concluded for personal, family, or household purposes;

 (b) (i) Transactions on a regulated exchange; (ii) foreign exchange transactions; (iii) inter-bank payment systems, inter-bank payment agreements, or clearance and settlement systems relating to securities or other financial assets or instruments; (iv) the transfer of security rights in, sale, loan, or holding of or agreement to repurchase securities or other financial assets or instruments held with an intermediary.

2.   This Convention does not apply to bills of exchange, promissory notes, consignment notes, bills of lading, warehouse receipts or any transferable document or instrument that entitles the bearer or beneficiary to claim the delivery of goods or the payment of a sum of money.

Article 3. Party Autonomy

The parties may exclude the application of this Convention or derogate from or vary the effect of any of its provisions.

Chapter II. General Provisions

Article 4. Definitions

For the purposes of this Convention:

(a)   "Communication" means any statement, declaration, demand, notice, or request, including an offer and the acceptance of an offer, that the parties are required to make or choose to make in connection with the formation or performance of a contract;

(b)   "Electronic communication" means any communication that the parties make by means of data messages;

(c)   "Data message" means information generated, sent, received, or stored by electronic, magnetic, optical, or similar means including, but not limited to, electronic data interchange (EDI), electronic mail, telegram, telex, or telecopy;

(d)   "Originator" of an electronic communication means a party by whom, or on whose behalf, the electronic communication has been sent or generated prior to storage, if any, but it does not include a party acting as an intermediary with respect to that electronic communication;

(e)   "Addressee" of an electronic communication means a party who is intended by the originator to receive the electronic communication, but does not include a party acting as an intermediary with respect to that electronic communication;

(f)   "Information system" means a system for generating, sending, receiving, storing, or otherwise processing data messages;

(g)   "Automated message system" means a computer program or an electronic or other automated means used to initiate an action or respond to data messages or performances in whole or in part, without review or intervention by a person each time an action is initiated or a response is generated by the system;

(h)   Place of business" means any place where a party maintains a non-transitory establishment to pursue an economic activity other than the temporary provision of goods or services out of a specific location.

Article 5. Interpretation

1.   In the interpretation of this Convention, regard is to be had to its international character and to the need to promote uniformity in its application and the observance of good faith in international trade.

2.   Questions concerning matters governed by this Convention which are not expressly settled in it are to be settled in conformity with the general principles on which it is based or, in the absence of such principles, in conformity with the law applicable by virtue of the rules of private international law.

Article 6. Location of the Parties

1.   For the purposes of this Convention, a party's place of business is presumed to be the location indicated by that party, unless another party demonstrates that the party making the indication does not have a place of business at that location.

2.   If a party has not indicated a place of business and has more than one place of business, then, subject to paragraph 1 of this article, the place of business for the purposes of this Convention is that which has the closest relationship to the relevant contract, having regard to the circumstances known to or contemplated by the parties at any time before or at the conclusion of the contract.

3.   If a natural person does not have a place of business, reference is to be made to the person's habitual residence.

4.   A location is not a place of business merely because that is: (a) where equipment and technology supporting an information system used by a party in connection with the formation of a contract are located; or (b) where the information system may be accessed by other parties.

5.   The sole fact that a party makes use of a domain name or electronic mail address connected to a specific country does not create a presumption that its place of business is located in that country.

Article 7. Information Requirements

Nothing in this Convention affects the application of any rule of law that may require the parties to disclose their identities, places of business or other information, or relieves a party from the legal consequences of making inaccurate or false statements in that regard.

Chapter III. Use of Electronic Communications in International Contracts

Article 8. Legal Recognition of Electronic Communications

1.   A communication or a contract shall not be denied validity or enforceability on the sole ground that it is in the form of an electronic communication.

2.   Nothing in this Convention requires a party to use or to accept electronic communications, but a party's agreement to do so may be inferred from the party's conduct.

Article 9. Form Requirements

1.   Nothing in this Convention requires a communication or a contract to be made or evidenced in any particular form.

2.   Where the law requires that a communication or a contract should be in writing, or provides consequences for the absence of a writing, that requirement is met by an electronic communication if the information contained therein is accessible so as to be usable for subsequent reference.

3.   Where the law requires that a communication or a contract should be signed by a party, or provides consequences for the absence of a signature, that requirement is met in relation to an electronic communication if:

  (a) A method is used to identify the party and to indicate that party's approval of the information contained in the electronic communication; and

  (b) That method is as reliable as appropriate to the purpose for which the electronic communication was generated or communicated, in the light of all the circumstances, including any relevant agreement.

4.   Where the law requires that a communication or a contract should be presented or retained in its original form, or provides consequences for the absence of an original, that requirement is met in relation to an electronic communication if:

  (a) There exists a reliable assurance as to the integrity of the information it contains from the time when it was first generated in its final form, as an electronic communication or otherwise; and

  (b) Where it is required that the information it contains be presented, that information is capable of being displayed to the person to whom it is to be presented.

5.   For the purposes of paragraph 4(a):

  (a) The criteria for assessing integrity shall be whether the information has remained complete and unaltered, apart from the addition of any endorsement and any change which arises in the normal course of communication, storage, and display; and

(b) The standard of reliability required shall be assessed in the light of the purpose for which the information was generated and in the light of all the relevant circumstances.

[6. Paragraphs 4 and 5 do not apply where a rule of law or the agreement between the parties requires a party to present certain original documents for the purpose of claiming payment under a letter of credit, a bank guarantee, or a similar instrument.]

Article 10. Time and Place of Dispatch and Receipt of Electronic Communications

1. The time of dispatch of an electronic communication is the time when it leaves an information system under the control of the originator or of the party who sent it on behalf of the originator or, if the electronic communication has not left an information system under the control of the originator or of the party who sent it on behalf of the originator, the time when the electronic communication is received.

2. The time of receipt of an electronic communication is the time when it becomes capable of being retrieved by the addressee at an electronic address designated by the addressee. The time of receipt of an electronic communication at another electronic address of the addressee is the time when it becomes capable of being retrieved by the addressee at that address and the addressee becomes aware that the electronic communication has been sent to that address. An electronic communication is presumed to be capable of being retrieved by the addressee when it reaches the addressee's electronic address.

3. An electronic communication is deemed to be dispatched at the place where the originator has its place of business and is deemed to be received at the place where the addressee has its place of business, as determined in accordance with article 6.

4. Paragraph 2 of this article applies notwithstanding that the place where the information system supporting an electronic address is located may be different from the place where the electronic communication is deemed to be received under paragraph 3 of this article.

Article 11. Invitations to Make Offers

A proposal to conclude a contract made through one or more electronic communications which is not addressed to one or more specific parties, but is generally accessible to parties making use of information systems, including proposals that make use of interactive applications for the placement of orders through such information systems, is to be considered as an invitation to make offers, unless it clearly indicates the intention of the party making the proposal to be bound in case of acceptance.

Article 12. Use of Automated Message Systems for Contract Formation

A contract formed by the interaction of an automated message system and a natural person, or by the interaction of automated message systems, shall not be denied validity or enforceability on the sole ground that no natural person reviewed each of the individual actions carried out by the systems or the resulting contract.

Article 13. Availability of Contract Terms

Nothing in this Convention affects the application of any rule of law that may require a party that negotiates some or all of the terms of a contract through the exchange of electronic communications to make available to the other contracting party those electronic communications that contain the contractual terms in a particular manner, or relieves a party from the legal consequences of its failure to do so.

Article 14. Error in Electronic Communications

1.   Where a natural person makes an input error in an electronic communication exchanged with the automated message system of another party and the automated message system does not provide the person with an opportunity to correct the error, that person, or the party on whose behalf that person was acting, has the right to withdraw the electronic communication in which the input error was made if:

(a) The person, or the party on whose behalf that person was acting, notifies the other party of the error as soon as possible after having learned of the error and indicates that he or she made an error in the electronic communication;

(b) The person, or the party on whose behalf that person was acting, takes reasonable steps, including steps that conform to the other party's instructions, to return the goods or services received, if any, as a result of the error or, if instructed to do so, to destroy the goods or services; and

(c) The person, or the party on whose behalf that person was acting, has not used or received any material benefit or value from the goods or services, if any, received from the other party.

2.   Nothing in this article affects the application of any rule of law that may govern the consequences of any errors made during the formation or performance of the type of contract in question other than an input error that occurs in the circumstances referred to in paragraph 1.

Chapter IV. Final Provisions

Article 18. Declarations on the Scope of Application

1.   Any State may declare, in accordance with article 20, that it will apply this Convention only:

 (a) When the States referred to in article 1, paragraph 1 are Contracting States to this Convention;

 (b) When the rules of private international law lead to the application of the law of a Contracting State; or

 (c) When the parties have agreed that it applies.

2.   Any State may exclude from the scope of application of this Convention the matters it specifies in a declaration made in accordance with article 20.

Article 19. Communications Exchanged under other International Conventions

1.   The provisions of this Convention apply to the use of electronic communications in connection with the formation or performance of a contract or agreement to which any of the following international conventions, to which a Contracting State to this Convention is or may become a Contracting State, apply:

Convention on the Recognition and Enforcement of Foreign Arbitral Awards (New York, 10 June 1958);

Convention on the Limitation Period in the International Sale of Goods (New York, 14 June 1974) and Protocol thereto (Vienna, 11 April 1980);

United Nations Convention on Contracts for the International Sale of Goods (Vienna, 11 April 1980);

United Nations Convention on the Liability of Operators of Transport Terminals in International Trade (Vienna, 19 April 1991);

United Nations Convention on Independent Guarantees and Stand-by Letters of Credit (New York, 11 December 1995);

United Nations Convention on the Assignment of Receivables in International Trade (New York, 12 December 2001).

2.   The provisions of this Convention apply further to electronic communications in connection with the formation or performance of a contract or agreement to which another international convention, treaty, or agreement not specifically referred to in paragraph 1 of this article, and to which a Contracting State to this Convention is or may become a Contracting State, applies, unless the State has declared, in accordance with article 20, that it will not be bound by this paragraph.

3.   A State that makes a declaration pursuant to paragraph 2 of this article may also declare that it will nevertheless apply the provisions of this Convention to the use of electronic communications in connection with the formation or performance of any contract or agreement to which a specified international convention, treaty or agreement applies to which the State is or may become a Contracting State.

4.   Any State may declare that it will not apply provisions of this Convention to the use of electronic communications in connection with the formation or performance of a contract or agreement to which any international convention, treaty or agreement specified in that State's declaration, to which the State is or may become a Contracting State, applies, including any of the conventions referred to in paragraph 1 of this article, even if such State has not excluded the application of paragraph 2 of this article by a declaration made in accordance with article 20.

INDEX